P9-EEI-332

THE MIDDLE EAST

THE
MIDDLE EAST

A PHYSICAL, SOCIAL, AND

REGIONAL GEOGRAPHY

BY

W. B. FISHER

B.A., DR. DE L'UNIV.

Professor of Geography in the
University of Durham

LONDON: METHUEN & CO LTD
NEW YORK: E. P. DUTTON & CO INC

First published September 28, 1950
Second edition 1952
Third edition 1956
Reprinted with minor corrections 1957
Fourth edition, revised and reset, 1961
Fifth edition 1963
© 1963 by W. B. Fisher
Printed in Great Britain by
Butler & Tanner Ltd, Frome and London
and bound by James Burn, Esher
Catalogue No. (Methuen) 2/4252/10
5.1

Preface

In a foreword to his *History of the Habsburg Monarchy*, Mr A. J. P. Taylor quotes the saying that in order to be able to write a history of Austria, one must speak seventeen languages, and live ten times as long as mortal man. This phrase has frequently come to mind in the writing of the present volume on the geography of the Middle East: an area larger in extent than Austro-Hungary, more varied in its peoples, and with the longest continuous history of any region in the world.

My attempt, however indifferent, to present a reasoned account of human life in the Middle East and its environmental background owes something to the accident of war. During 1942–5 I had the opportunity of gaining first-hand knowledge of conditions in south-west Asia, and in southern Europe; and was able to profit in some small degree from the large number of investigations and research projects that were carried out as a contributing element in the military campaigns of the period. In particular, new aspects of climate and weather in the Middle East were investigated, and upon some of these studies I have based my interpretation of the climatic mechanism in the eastern Mediterranean basin. I am conscious that the approach is in many respects unusual, if not unorthodox; but, remembering the words of Professor Wooldridge that new views would receive sympathetic consideration, I am encouraged to put my own forward as a contribution to the closer understanding of prevailing conditions.

No better model could be found for an exposition of Middle Eastern geography than the remarkable studies of the late Professor Weulersse, in whose writings there is propounded the thesis that only by a close integration of geography and history can full understanding of human society be achieved. Because of the length of human occupation in the Middle East, the extent of interaction between man and his environment has proceeded further than in most other places on the globe, and an unusual stage of development has been reached: 'le fellah est tout le contraire d'un primitif; ce serait plutôt un hypercivilisé . . . écrasé sous le poids des siècles'. For this reason, I have endeavoured to give some weight to historical considerations, sometimes possibly at the cost of discursiveness, and a certain scrappiness and repetition; but

v

I am strongly of the opinion that the method followed in this book is justified by the character of the material studied. As in many parts of the Middle East the Archaean basement rocks occasionally obtrude at the surface to form important elements in the modern landscape, so also we find a parallel in that contemporary social life is markedly coloured by past events, with an unaltered persistence of some practices throughout many thousands of years.

The technique of intermingling history and geography has been extensively developed by French writers, but is still rather unusual in Britain where it is too often the custom to regard the subjects as separate, even opposed, disciplines. Such an attitude is unfortunately particularly prominent in the northern half of our island, where in school curricula a choice must normally be made between the two subjects. However, after surveying the achievements of French geography, one may be tempted to believe that 'they order these things better in France'.

With limitation of space, it has been inevitable that certain aspects of the geography of the Middle East have had to be treated summarily, or omitted. The problem of Palestine is an outstanding instance; but the literature of Arab and Zionist viewpoints is so voluminous that it would be impossible to do justice to the claims of either side even in an entire volume. Another difficulty arises from the inadequacy of information for some regions. Despite this, it has been my aim to present a general exposition, with some mention of all areas. It is often tempting under such circumstances to devote exclusive attention to 'sample' districts; but although I have given relatively greater emphasis to the Levant than its size or population would warrant, I hope to avoid the criticism that my pages are merely arbitrary selections from the geography of the area, and do not fully live up to their title.

A word may be necessary to explain the usage of certain terms. I have taken the expression 'Levant' as indicating the coastal areas of the eastern Mediterranean lying between the Sinai and the Amanus range of Turkey – i.e. Israel, the Lebanon, and western Syria and Transjordan, together with the island of Cyprus. Since over the past few years official practice of the government has changed, I have used 'Iran' and 'Persia' interchangeably. I have also preferred the modern Turkish spelling of place-names, e.g. Izmir and Eregli, instead of the older Smyrna and Heraclea.

The writing of this book could not have been accomplished, even in the present inadequate way, without the help generously given from many quarters. In the first place, I should like to pay tribute to Emeritus-Professor H. J. Fleure, F.R.S., under whose guidance I began work as a student. Though there are few textual references to Professor Fleure's publications, it is upon his teaching and example that much of this book is based, and, were it possible, I should be proud to think that the following pages could convey even the slightest echo of the lofty thought, brilliance in interpretation, and warm humanism that are characteristic of Professor Fleure's approach to geography. To the inspiration of the late Professor Demangeon, of the University of Paris, one of the greatest of a unique group of geographers, I owe an abiding interest in human geography, and recall with gratitude and a sense of privilege the time spent working under his direction. I am also considerably indebted to Mr A. C. O'Dell, Head of the Department of Geography, Aberdeen University, for encouragement, valuable criticism, and timely suggestions that have improved the text, and greatly eased the task of writing.

For several years, it was my good fortune to be associated with a profound and indefatigable investigator whose knowledge of parts of the Middle East is unrivalled: Dr L. Dubertret, Head of the Geological Survey of Syria, who made available many of his own researches, and through whose good offices I was able to undertake certain field investigations in the Levant. My sincerest thanks are also due to Dr G. M. Lees, F.R.S., of the Anglo-Iranian Oil Company, for helpful comment, and material on the structure and oil resources of the Middle East; to Dr W. T. H. Williamson, Head of the Soil Science Department, Aberdeen University, who has revised the chapter on soils; to Professor E. E. Evans-Pritchard, of All Souls College, Oxford, who has kindly allowed me to use the results of surveys carried out by him in Cyrenaica; to Dr E. C. Willatts, of the Ministry of Town and Country Planning, whose work on Palestine has been extensively quoted; to Dr Bayard Dodge, formerly President of the American University of Beirut, for facilities and advice afforded to me during 1942–6; and to Professor H. A. R. Gibb, of St John's College, Oxford, to whom I am indebted for an interpretation of present-day cultural trends in the Middle East.

In conclusion, I wish to record my grateful obligations to Miss K. M. Holmes, B.A., of University College, London, who has read much of the manuscript; to Mr J. Morland Craig, of the Department of Geography, Aberdeen, who has prepared a number of the illustrations, and to Mr R. MacNay, B.Sc., Mr U. A. Wannop, and

Mr A. M. North, of Aberdeen Grammar School, who have also given valuable assistance in preparing maps and diagrams; and finally to the American Geographical Society of New York, for kind permission to reproduce material from two articles of mine that have appeared in the *Geographical Review*; and to the Royal Geographical Society, London, which has been good enough to allow me to reproduce one illustration from the *Geographical Journal*.

W. B. F.

DARWEN, LANCASHIRE
December 1948

Preface to Fifth Edition

With no abatement – rather, an acceleration – in the process of internal economic and social change, and a continuing strategic and political importance, the Middle East consequently remains a focus of world attention. The appearance of a further edition of this book allows revision and re-appraisal that can be increasingly based on detailed field-studies by a growing number of students of Middle Eastern conditions.

There is also the pleasant duty and opportunity of recognising generous assistance and helpful comment from many friends and well-wishers in various parts of the world: and especially to Dr J. I. Clarke and Mr J. C. Dewdney of my own Department for, respectively, Figures 39 and 40, and 63; to the Petroleum Information Board, London, for statistics; and to the Rockefeller Trustees, whose second generous grant in aid of Middle Eastern research has been both timely and an adumbration of a policy that now commends itself to the British Government as a line of development within British Universities.

W. B. F.

Durham 1963

Contents

I. INTRODUCTORY *page* 1

PART I
PHYSICAL GEOGRAPHY OF
THE MIDDLE EAST

II. LAND FORMS AND STRUCTURE 11

III. CLIMATE 35

IV. SOILS AND NATURAL VEGETATION 66

PART II
SOCIAL GEOGRAPHY OF
THE MIDDLE EAST

V. PEOPLES 87

VI. HUMAN SOCIETY IN THE MIDDLE EAST 122

VII. ASPECTS OF THE HISTORICAL GEOGRAPHY OF THE MIDDLE EAST – (I) THE RISE OF EMPIRES IN RELATION TO THEIR GEOGRAPHICAL SETTING 135

VIII. ASPECTS OF THE HISTORICAL GEOGRAPHY OF THE MIDDLE EAST – (II) THE POLITICAL BACK-GROUND. A.D. 1800 TO THE PRESENT DAY 155

IX. GENERAL ECONOMIC LIFE (1) 191

X. GENERAL ECONOMIC LIFE (2) 213

XI. OIL RESOURCES OF THE MIDDLE EAST 230

XII. DEMOGRAPHIC TRENDS IN THE MIDDLE EAST 263

PART III
REGIONAL GEOGRAPHY OF
THE MIDDLE EAST

XIII. PERSIA *page* 277

XIV. ASIA MINOR 315

XV. THE TIGRIS–EUPHRATES LOWLANDS 361

XVI. THE COASTLANDS OF THE LEVANT 396

XVII. THE COASTLANDS OF THE LEVANT (*continued*) 444

XVIII. THE ARABIAN PENINSULA 456

XIX. THE LOWER NILE VALLEY 481

XX. LIBYA 512

APPENDIX I 536

APPENDIX II 543

APPENDIX III 548

APPENDIX IV 550

APPENDIX V 552

BIBLIOGRAPHY 553

INDEX 561

Maps and Diagrams

FOLDER I.   The Countries of the Middle East   *at end*
FOLDER II. Middle East, Annual Rainfall   *at end*

FIG.

1. Sketch of Gondwanaland and the Sea of the Tethys   *page* 13
2. Structural Units of the Middle East   15
3. Types of Drainage   27
4. Profile of a Wadi Bed   28
5. Typical River Regimes   29
6. Diagram of a Foggara   32
7. Pressure Distribution in Summer   36
8. Pressure Situations in Winter   38
9. Tracks and Regions of Origin of Mediterranean Depressions   40
10. Shlouq Conditions in Syria   45
11. Variation in Air Mass, with Characteristic Alignment of Fronts   50
12. Mean Daily Minima of Temperature (January) and Mean Daily
      Maxima (July)   52
13. Daily Rainfall at the Cedars   58
14. Soil Profiles under Humid and Arid Climatic Conditions   67
15. Former and Latter Rains   77
16. Types of Vegetation   79
17. Regions of Relatively Easy Movement   89
18. Racial Stocks in the Middle East   97
19. Language Distribution in the Middle East   103
20. Nomadism   123
21. Division of the Empire of Alexander the Great   140
22. The Roman Limes in Syria   142
23. Islamic Conquests   145
24. Crusader States in the Levant   148
25. The Ottoman Empire   150
26. Railway Concessions in the Ottoman Empire   156
27. The Maronite Homeland   163
28. Proposals for Partitioning the Ottoman Empire   164
29. Russian Expansion, and Spheres of Influence in Persia   173
30. Kurdish Nationalist Claims   182

FIG.

31. Fragmentation and Dispersal of Land Holdings *page* 195
32. Cultivated Areas in the Middle East 199
33. The Incidence of Malaria in one District of the Levant 211
34. The Inland Fishing Grounds of Egypt 228
35. Geological Conditions for the Occurrence of Oil 232
36. The Oilfields of Iran and Iraq, 1948 235
37. Structure of Arabian and Iranian Oil Domes 238
38. The Oilfields of the Middle East, 1962 240
39. Oil Development in Libya, 1962 246
40. Oil Concessions in Libya, 1962 254
41. Oil Concessions in 1954 255
42. Oil Production, World and the Middle East 259
43. Oil Production and Consumption 261
44. Sketch of Population Distribution in the Middle East 264
45. Natural Regions of Persia 277
46. North-west Persia 279
47. South and East Persia, and the Helmand Basin 286
48. Sketch of Population Distribution in Persia 305
49. Persia, Railways 308
50. Teheran City 310
51. The Port of Abadan 312
52. Natural Regions of Asia Minor 315
53. Structure of the Black Sea Coast 316
54. The Straits and Aegean Coastlands 320
55. South and Central Anatolia 322
56. Eastern Anatolia 326
57. Distribution of Crops in Asia Minor 334
58. The Coal Basin of Eregli-Zonguldak 344
59. Mineral Distribution in Asia Minor 347
60. Railway Construction in Asia Minor 352
61. The Sites of Istanbul and Izmir 354
62. The Sites of Ankara and Adana 357
63. Turkey: Population 359
64. Natural Physical Units 361
65. The Regimes of the Tigris and Euphrates 364
66. Stages in the Recession of the Persian Gulf 366
67. Lower Mesopotamia 368
68. The Upper Valley Region 371
69. Rainfall and Settlement in Iraq 374

FIG.

70. Cereal Crops *page* 377
71. Irrigation in Iraq 382
72. The Sites of Baghdad and Basra 393
73. The Geographical Sub-regions of the Levant 397
74. Sections, Ansarieh, Lebanon, Anti-Lebanon, and Judaean Ranges 401
75. Profile of the Jordan Depression 408
76. Rainfall in the Levant 411
77. Fruit Crops 418
78. Commercial Crops 420
79. The Oasis of Damascus 423
80. Mountain Roads in the Levant 427
81. Jewish Settlement; and Proposals for the Partition of Palestine 431
82. Jewish Colonisation in Palestine, 1944 435
83. The Sites of Aleppo, Latakia, Tripoli, and Beirut 439
84. The Growth of Beirut City 441
85. The Sites of Haifa, Jaffa–Tel Aviv, and Jerusalem 442
86. Cyprus: The Orography and Structure 444
87. Cyprus: Rainfall 446
88. Towns and Roads in Cyprus 454
89. Natural Regions of Arabia 458
90. The West and South of Arabia 464
91. Oman and Eastern Arabia 470
92. Kuwait: Natural Regions 473
93. The Interior of Arabia 476
94. Natural Regions of Egypt 482
95. Sinai and the Eastern Highlands of Egypt 484
96. The Oases and Depressions of the Western Desert 485
97. Irrigation Works on the Nile 494
98. Egypt: Railways 507
99. The Site of Cairo 509
100. The Site of Alexandria 510
101. Libya 513
102. Libya: Structural 514
103. The Jefara of Tripolitania 516
104. Cyrenaica: Physical 519
105. Vegetation Zones in Cyrenaica 524
106. The Oasis of Jalo 526
107. Land Use in Northern Tripolitania 529
108. The Site of Tripoli City 532
109. The Sites of Benghazi and Tobruk 533

CHAPTER 1

Introductory

The first task in an account of the geography of the region under consideration must be one of definition. The term 'Middle East' cannot unfortunately be said to command universal acceptance in a single strict sense, and it is therefore essential to delimit the region to which the name is held to refer, and to indicate how 'Middle East' gained acceptance in its present meaning.

Up to 1939, there prevailed a somewhat vague and loose division of southern Asia into Near, Middle, and Far East. The Far East was generally taken as connoting China, Japan, and, less frequently, Indo-China and Indonesia. The Middle East included Iran and Arabia, usually also the lower basin of the Euphrates-Tigris, and occasionally Afghanistan and India; while the Near East began in the Balkans and included most of the countries adjacent to the basin of the eastern Mediterranean. No precise definition could, however, be said to be in general use, and for an indication of the inadequacy of the terms employed, and the looseness with which they were applied, we need only refer to current geographical literature of the past few years. Sir Percy Loraine, speaking before the Royal Geographical Society of Britain, defined the Near East as the Balkan states, Egypt, and the coastal areas on the eastern shores of the Mediterranean and of the Black Sea. An American geographer, Col. L. Martin, would qualify this definition to read 'and sometimes Egypt'. On the other hand, Sir P. Loraine described the Middle East 'roughly as being Iran, Iraq, Afghanistan, and the Arabian peninsula'; but E. Jurkat, another American writer on S.W. Asia, shows the Near East as extending from Afghanistan to Crete, both inclusive, but exclusive of Egypt, whilst C. S. Coon on the other hand includes Morocco in the Middle East. The inadequacy of 'Near East' is also apparent from the titles *The Nearer East* of Hogarth, and *Nationalism and Imperialism in the Hither East* of Kohn.

The war of 1939 at one stroke removed the question of territorial definition in western Asia from the academic groves to which it had hitherto been mainly confined. There came the *fait accompli* by which a military province stretching from Iran to Tripolitania was created and named 'Middle East'. Establishment in this region of large military supply bases brought the necessity to reorganise both the political and economic life of the countries concerned, in order to meet the changed conditions of war. A resident Minister of State was appointed to deal with political matters, and an economic organisation, the Middle East Supply Centre, orginally British, but later Anglo-American, was set up to handle economic questions. It was inevitable that the territorial designation already adopted by the military authorities should continue in the new sphere; hence 'Middle East' took on full official sanction, and became the standard term of reference, exclusively used in the numerous governmental publications summarising political events, territorial surveys, and schemes of economic development.

Following the practice of their respective governments, a number of learned societies in both countries have adopted the new term. Equally significantly, the name has been adopted in the countries to which it is held to refer. The former Jewish Agency in Jerusalem employed it in their publications,[1] and the Arab Offices in London and Washington showed no reluctance to follow the same usage.

There were those, however, who did not look altogether favourably on the new and extended use of 'Middle East'; and in 1946 a deputation from the Royal Geographical Society placed this view before the Prime Minister of Great Britain. No change in policy took place, so that it is still the official practice of the British government to refer to Egypt, Israel, Jordan, and Syria as forming part of the 'Middle East'.

Under these circumstances, it would seem difficult to challenge the validity of 'Middle East', particularly as the general public in Britain and America has become accustomed to the usage – in some cases as the result of first-hand acquaintance with the region during military service. It is true that there is little logicality in applying the term 'Middle East' to countries of the eastern Mediterranean littoral; yet, as shown above, 'Near East' – the only possible replacement – has an equally vague connotation; and to some, moreover, takes on a historical flavour associated with nineteenth-century events in Balkan Europe. Thus despite the considerable geographical illogicality of 'Middle East' there is one compensation: in its wider meaning this term can be held to denote a single geographical region with certain elements of marked physical and social unity. This consideration has led to its use in the present volume.

[1] e.g. in *Statistical Handbook of Middle Eastern Countries*, published 1943.

TERRITORIAL LIMITS

The next step is to arrive at a precise definition of the territories which it is proposed to group under the description 'Middle East'. In its official publications, the British government has included up to twenty-one regions – Malta, Tripolitania, Cyrenaica, Egypt, Cyprus, the Lebanon, Syria, Israel, Jordan, Iraq, Iran, the sheikhdoms of the Persian Gulf, Saudi Arabia, the Yemen, Aden and the protectorate, Eritrea, Ethiopia, British, French, and Italian Somaliland, and the Anglo-Egyptian Sudan. The inclusion of some of these countries was, however, the result of fortuitous administrative grouping by military authorities. It would seem greatly preferable to omit from this list the Sudan, Eritrea, Ethiopia, and the three Somalilands, which are all more properly considered as parts of intertropical Africa, and to replace them by Turkey, which, intimately linked to its southern and eastern neighbours by ties of geography, was not included in the governmental publications because of a purely temporary and political separation from the rest of the Middle East.

The position of Malta is open to doubt. European in political out-look and tradition, there are however certain features arising from geographical position that link it to Africa and south-west Asia: 80 per cent. of the natural vegetation forms are African by origin, and the Maltese language is Semitic. Malta is nevertheless overwhelmingly an extension of Europe, to which it is much more closely tied by life and outlook.

Libya, on the other hand, would seem to have strongest links with its eastern neighbour, Egypt. The culture of Cyrenaica has been described by Evans-Pritchard as 'more Arab than that of any other region except peninsular Arabia'; and whilst Hamitic and Berber elements are present in Tripolitania there is much more affinity, geographical and cultural, with Egypt rather than with Tunisia and Algeria. The western desert of Egypt continues without real break into eastern Libya, whilst there is a marked topographical change between Libya and Tunis. Economically and culturally, Libya can be said to look much more to the east than to the west.

The position of Persia, as easternmost member of the Middle East region, is less open to doubt. Despite the barrier of encircling mountain ranges, and the abrupt separation from the Tigris lowlands, connexion with the west is the outstanding feature. The bulk of the Iranian popula-tion lies close to the western frontier, and Iranian interests are closely bound up with those of Iraq, Turkey, and Russia, rather than with India.[1] Between Persia and its eastern neighbours lies a desolate belt of mountain ranges, salt steppe, and irregular *playa*, all of which are for the most part uninhabited or very sparsely peopled. This belt acts as an effective zone of separation, and can hence be taken as the eastern boundary of our Middle East region.

With these changes, it would appear possible to postulate on geographical grounds the existence of a natural region to which the name Middle East can be applied. It is true that the division proposed is open to certain criticism; but the course of history, including war-time experiences during 1939–45, has shown that within this region are common elements of natural environment and social organisation. Herein, as it is hoped that this study will make reasonably clear, lies the justification for treating the Middle East as a single unit. It may be permitted to indicate that this unity stems basically from the distinctive and highly unusual regime of climate, which in turn controls types of agriculture, ways of life, and hence perhaps, ideas, thought, and general culture.

GENERAL CONSIDERATIONS

In a previous volume of this series, Professor Griffith Taylor contrasted the simplicity of geographical features in Australia with the complexity of conditions in Europe. A similar relationship – in ascending order – might be worked out between Europe and the Middle East, for within a physical environment that is at least as varied as that of Europe, one finds a pattern of human response that is infinitely more involved. Europe has its representatives of three races, but in the Middle East there are four, if not five, major racial elements; Europe is at least predominantly Christian, but the Middle East is the home of three contrasting religious systems, and with a gradation from almost unrelieved paganism to the most advanced forms of Judaism, Christianity, and Islam. Ways of life, too, show a greater variation than those of Europe: communities of hunters are still to be found in parts of Arabia, and nomadism is predominant in many areas, whilst on the other hand, in certain favoured spots, standards of life approximate to

[1] Cf. (a) The religious link – Iraq and Persia are the only states in which the Shi'a form of Islam predominates, (b) commercial relations – almost all of which are with the north and west, and (c) the movement of nomadic tribes, many of which pass part of the year in Persia, and part in Iraq and Turkey.

the highest of Europe and America. Moreover, no visitor to the Middle East can fail to be conscious of the wide gap in living conditions and mental outlook which separates the townsfolk from the peasants, or the leaders of society from the common man. Within one single geographical region can be found traders and merchants in touch with international markets – in oil, textiles, fruit, and grain – and political or religious leaders fully conscious of their part as members of world-wide organisations; and yet alongside such highly developed groups occur large communities of farmers and herdsmen living at the extreme level of subsistence, whose total annual income is less than £10 or £25, and whose experience is limited to the immediate district in which they live.

The complexity of geographical conditions within the Middle East has for long been a considerable barrier to study. The country itself, largely mountain or desert, offers considerable physical obstacles to movement; and its relatively large size, and the poverty and emptiness of many regions have been further restrictive factors. Besides the so-called Empty Quarter of Arabia, which has been traversed by Europeans only within the last four decades, parts of central and southern Anatolia are unsurveyed – it cannot yet be stated with finality how many component ranges make up the Anti-Taurus system – and wide stretches of marshland in southern Iraq, and of salt desert in central Persia, are still unknown.

To these natural obstacles must be added the reluctance of native communities in some areas to admit outsiders, and the mutual jealousies of outside powers, each anxious to preserve for itself the exploitation of spheres of influence. For example, because of rivalry over the control of oil resources, even topographical and geological surveys have taken on a strong political implication. Moreover, to many Middle Easterners, any form of census or economic survey can arouse misgiving and sometimes active opposition. Under such conditions, it may be difficult to obtain a picture of reality, and any study of the Middle East must still rely to some extent on estimates, outline surveys, and the reports of travellers.

Importance in World Affairs. Conditions are, however, in process of altering considerably because of the changed position of the Middle East in world affairs. Until the middle of the nineteenth century, S.W. Asia was a backwater, isolated from the main currents of political and economic activity, and neglected even by its nominal rulers, the Ottoman Sultans. This situation, as an outlying and unvalued portion

of the domains of the 'Sick Man of Europe', began to alter after the
Suez Canal was cut, following which the eastern Mediterranean and
Red Seas became a principal artery of communication between Europe
and Asia.

Developments in air transport have enormously increased the
importance of the Middle East. The prevalence of steppe and desert,
not normally a favourable factor, has shown itself to have some
advantages – in the matter of weather conditions, which are usually
very favourable for flying, and in providing abundant stretches of open,
level country where airfields can easily be constructed. Egypt has
become a nodal centre of air-routes, with more flights from Britain than
to any other part of the world outside western Europe; Beirut had one
of the very first jet airports in existence, and the general situation of the
Middle East has inevitably given considerable impetus to the development of transport by air. The effects of nodality are seen in the enhanced political and economic status of the region as a whole: hence the
Middle East, that less than a century ago occupied a remotely marginal
position, has now become a cross-roads and point of junction. With the
rise of Russia, developments in further Asia and in Africa, and the
closer relations of Europe with Australasia, the significance of the
Middle East is naturally far greater.

This enhanced importance is indicated by the intense interest of outside powers in Middle East affairs, and their attempts to obtain strategic
and economic advantages by the possession of bases or concessions. As
a further indication of the changed role of the Middle East, it may be
useful to recall that during the war of 1914–18 the campaigns of Allenby
were regarded as a 'side-show'; whilst in 1942 the victory of Alamein
was a turning-point in the war.

Another outstandingly important – probably the principal – factor
in the rise of the Middle East to a position of world importance, is the
presence of oil deposits, reserves of which are now known to exceed
those of the whole of the remaining parts of the world. In certain
respects the Middle East is a region of great poverty, but development
of oil resources has already begun to bring about far-reaching changes
through development schemes that are increasingly financed from oil
royalties. Moreover the world's largest single oil-refining plant is
located in Persia – not, as might be expected, in North America; and
an Arab state, Kuwait, is currently the largest individual oil-exporting
country in the world.

Another topic might be opened up at this juncture, were it not too great in scope for an introductory chapter. This relates to the political situation in the Middle East, which has now come to exert an influence far beyond the borders of the countries directly concerned. Even thirty years ago, it could hardly have been foreseen that Arab-Jewish relations could become a domestic political issue within the U.S.A., that the Arab policies pursued by Britain and France could become a source of discord not merely among themselves but also in the U.S.A. and much of the rest of the world, or that the mantle of Disraeli as champion of the Turks against Russia, should descend on the Presidents of America.

Poverty in Resources. Throughout the pages of this volume, one theme will recur. This is the poverty and depressed level of existence that prevail over the whole of the Middle East. Despite enhanced strategic and nodal importance, and despite the richness of oil deposits – the benefits from the exploitation of which, however, do not always reach the indigenous population – natural resources are in general very small as compared with those of other regions, and the sparse natural wealth that does exist is only too often inefficiently or incompletely utilised.

A mere 5 per cent. of the total area is regarded as cultivable, while mineral resources, with the single exception of oil, are scanty. Thus the economic potentialities of the Middle East are not large, and it is regrettable that within the last few years there should have appeared a number of inflated estimates of possible future development in the Middle East. Such views must be set in relation to the factual information available, from which a much more modest and sober picture has to be drawn. With a rapidly rising population in many parts, existing standards of living, low though these may be, are in danger of further decline, so that for some communities it is a case of running hard, like Lewis Carroll's Red Queen, in order to keep in the same place. This is the view of a former Director of Food in the Middle East Supply Centre,[1] and one that is difficult to challenge.

Present Society in the Middle East. In conclusion, a word may be said concerning the rapid break-up and alteration of existing ways of life. Forms of society that have endured since the Middle Ages or earlier are now in rapid decay, bringing the urgent problem of creating a new social order. Religious feeling, once the mainspring of most forms of cultural and political activity, is now largely in eclipse or subject to fanaticism or distortion. Frequently, a spirit of materialist nationalism is taking its place, with widespread rejection of tradition and democratic political methods, and a growing cynicism or easy acceptance of

---

[1] K. A. H. Murray, *Some Regional Economic Problems of the Middle East.*

autarchic rule. A new, but increasingly significant element in this situation is the fact that recently won independence has brought its own problems, among them the necessity of relying on one's own efforts: it is now no longer possible to ascribe difficulties and backwardness as due wholly to foreign dominance and imperialism. In the economic sphere, ancient methods of agriculture, stock-raising, and commerce are proving inadequate to modern conditions – hence, quoting from Drs Keen and Worthington, although 'husbandry may be kept going by the resources of modern science, they are only palliatives. . . . Clearly there is some fundamental difficulty.' As a result, 'the whole area with a few local exceptions must be classed with the worst nourished parts of the world'.[1]

Faced with disintegration within, and foreign pressure from without, Middle Eastern peoples are being driven to adopt new ideas and new techniques, but this process, neither easy nor harmonious, is responsible for much of the unrest which is characteristic of contemporary affairs. At the present time, we are witnessing a rapid and fundamental re-organisation of society. Vociferous nationalism is exerting an increasing appeal, often based on extreme xenophobia and dislike of 'western' models; whilst at the same time there is a powerful feeling that existing political units are becoming obstacles to development, and that organisation on a wider pattern may produce improved standards of life and enhanced international prestige. As well, the appeal of Communism, now dominant over half of Asia, is strong and gaining ground. For those Westerners who are genuinely and deeply concerned for the well-being of the Middle East, the best course would appear to lie in the provision of enlightened and disinterested aid, both technical and financial, allowing the application of modern scientific principles to the utilisation of resources. One lesson afforded by Middle Eastern history may well be that when well organised in relatively large units, prosperity is more easily attainable.

[1] B. A. Keen, *Agricultural Development of the Middle East*; E. B. Worthington, *Middle East Science*.

PART I

Physical Geography

CHAPTER II

Land Forms and Structure

Geological Exploration. In discussing the structure of the Middle East, reference must first be made to the lack of detailed geological information in many areas. Interest in the potentialities of mineral deposits has led to detailed investigation of a few favoured regions, but elsewhere knowledge is in a much less advanced state, and may in certain instances consist merely of incidental surveys carried out by travellers. The complex structure of the Middle East is itself an important obstacle to investigation. Recent phases of vulcanicity, particularly in Turkey, Armenia, and Iran, have covered a few districts under masses of lava; and metamorphism has been a further hindrance to identification of rock structures both in the lava areas and in the folded zones. The floors of a large number of inland basins are covered by thick deposits of salt, or of saline, semi-liquid mud; and elsewhere whole river valleys are filled with detritus, alluvium, or marsh. Thus entire geological structures may be masked by later deposits which offer little aid to the interpretation of underlying series. On the other hand, it should also be stated that arid country can often show excellent outcrops of rock strata, and thus the geology of some districts may be much better known than that of many regions covered by forest or alluvial plains.

Some of the earliest geological work took place in Iran, with interest first in the folded zone of the south-west. Prospection for petroleum and other deposits has now continued for three-quarters of a century, and gradually knowledge has been extended – the salt basins and sand deserts of the centre and south however proving a considerable obstacle. Now, a detailed geological map has recently appeared; although there is still discussion over details, and regarding the tectonic history of the region.

Geological exploration in Turkey, and its former dependencies Syria and Palestine, owed much in the early stages to the work of Germans. Apart from a certain political influence in pre-1914 days which tended to make Turkey increasingly a German preserve, investigation was directed towards the exploitation of Turkey's scattered mineral resources. The difficulties of terrain alluded to above, particularly as regards eastern Turkey, tended for long to restrict investigation to local and regional problems; and it was not until 1946 that the first complete geological map of Turkey was published by the Ministry of the Interior.

In Syria and Palestine preliminary work by Germans was carried a stage further by French and British geologists. In these regions structure and stratigraphy offer much less difficulty to the investigator, and maps of the whole area have been available for some years. A similar state of affairs exists in Iraq, where considerable interest has centred on the oil-bearing series of the Zagros foreland.

For long, little could be said regarding the geology of the Arabian plateau beyond the fact that the fundamental feature was the presence of an underlying platform of Archaean rocks. It is now apparent that there is an extensive and continuous cover of permeable sedimentaries, since rainfall from the west would seem to percolate as far eastward as the shores of the Persian Gulf. Intensive interest in oil prospection over the past twenty years (especially by American companies) has transformed the situation, though for commercial reasons many details of local geology have not so far been published.

Studies by British, French, and German geologists have advanced our knowledge of Egypt, and a detailed geological map was published in Cairo as early as 1910. As in modern Turkey, the constitution of a governmental Survey Department has greatly aided progress, and oil prospecting in the Tertiary series of the north has been a further favourable factor.

The situation as described above for Arabia also holds true in Libya. Here also the main element in structure is the occurrence of an ancient granitic basement complex, overlain by later sedimentaries, and penetrated by intrusive basaltic series. Again, intensive prospection is in progress, with only a fraction of the results so far available to the general reader.

Structural Units. Though detailed information for some areas may be lacking, it is nevertheless possible to outline the broad features of structure in the Middle East. Most of the south and west of the region consists of a series of plateaus or tablelands formed by the deposition of later, less resistant sediments upon or contiguous to a basement of ancient crystalline rocks. This basement once formed an integral part (or extension according to Picard) of the enormous continental block known as Gondwanaland, which included much of the African continent, and portions of Australia, the Deccan, and South America. The Gondwanaland block proved resistant to mountain building movements which in other parts of the world gave rise at various ages to folded ranges, such as the mountains of Central Europe, Alps and Himalaya; and hence fold structures are either absent or poorly developed in most southern parts of the Middle East.

Though folding was not an important feature, the Gondwana block did not prove entirely resistant to crustal movements, and where these disturbances were on a sufficiently large scale, fracturing and faulting

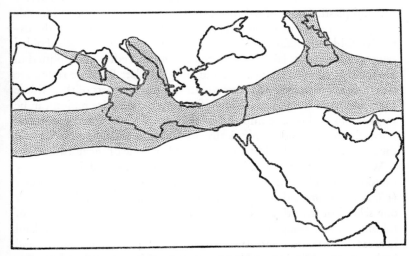

Fig. 1. Sketch of Gondwanaland and the Sea of the Tethys in early Permian times (after Schuchert). Sea stippled

occurred, so that marginal portions of the Gondwana continent have become detached as distinct fragments. This was the case in Arabia, which became separated from the main mass of Africa by the development of a series of parallel rifts in the area of the Red Sea. Smaller fragments of ancient structures would also seem to occur among the fold structures of Asia Minor and Iran: and Klemme has suggested that such fragments may have greatly influenced the character and disposition of later structures, in that they gained accretions of other rocks, sedimentary, igneous and metamorphic, and thus grew in size as it were outward from their earlier restricted extent (for a discussion of this view, see pp. 541–2).

To the north of Gondwanaland lay a sea area of fluctuating extent, but often considerable depth, in which sedimentary material accumulated in great quantity. As the waters were rich in marine life, a large proportion of the sediments laid down on its floor derived from the hard calcareous parts of the bodies of marine organisms, and thus limestone and chalk were formed on an extensive scale; though non-calcareous rocks such as sandstones and shales were also produced. The sea area, which formed a portion of a larger geosynclinal trough to which the name Tethys has been applied, had a basement of less resistant rock; hence when earth movements occurred, the relatively soft and plastic layers of sedimentary material underwent considerable compression and distortion, giving rise to the development of the extensive fold mountains, with an adjacent geosynclinal trough. Folded ranges of sediments laid down in the sea of the Tethys and uplifted in phases beginning in Cretaceous, and ending in late Pliocene times, are therefore characteristic of the northern and eastern parts of the Middle East; and from the point of view of structure the entire region can be regarded in outline as composed of two sharply contrasted provinces: a sourthern Foreland, geologically ancient and relatively stable; and the more recent and highly disturbed Folded Zone of the north.

Within recent years there have been attempts to expand this summary division. The ideas of Argand on superficial and deep-seated folding (*plis de couverture* and *de fond*) have been applied to the Middle East by one school of investigators, who see in the relatively slight degree of folding evident along the coastlands of the Mediterranean, and inland in areas of Syria, Iraq, and Arabia, examples of 'plis de couverture'; and in the massifs of Turkey and Persia instances of deep-seated folding. But in the Lebanon, where mountain ranges reach 10,000 feet above sea level, are the folds to be classed as deep-seated, or merely as superficial? One other view, put forward by Birot and Dresch, is that the Middle East shows the presence of three differing tectonic systems: (i) the African, characterised by slight deformation northward and westward, (ii) an extensive perialpine pattern marked by tectonics in the form of arcs and garlands (as shown in Iraq, Syria, Cyprus, Crete, and Malta), and (iii) an Alpine-Tauric system mainly trending east–west, and characterised by very deep-seated movements often resulting in a southward overthrust. In the Levant, geographically at the centre of the Middle East, all three tectonic patterns meet and merge, producing structural forms which, whilst of apparent simplicity, offer considerable difficulties to interpretation, and have provoked varying and some-

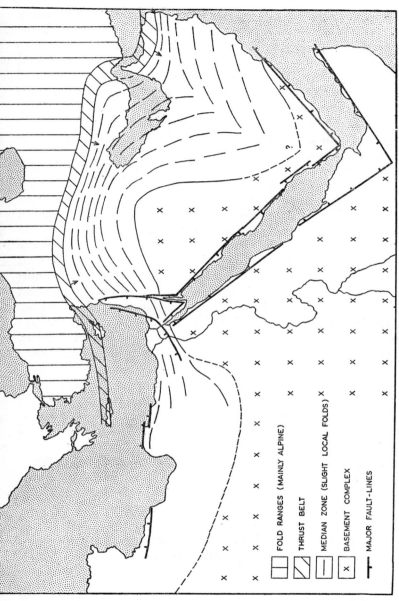

Fig. 2. Structural Units of the Middle East. Minor folds of Median Zone shown

FOLD RANGES (MAINLY ALPINE)

THRUST BELT

MEDIAN ZONE (SLIGHT LOCAL FOLDS) ×

BASEMENT COMPLEX ×

MAJOR FAULT-LINES

times even diametrically opposed views.[1] Although folding, fracturing and vertical displacement all occur in the Levant on a large scale, the preponderant influence would appear to have been vertical movement – this is most widespread in extent, and the earliest in geological time; hence it tended to control the pattern of later evolution in land forms, in that it regulated the disposition of areas of marine transgression and of the accumulation of continentally formed deposits. Folding and fracturing seem to have occurred at a later period (Oligocene or lower Miocene), and to have been extensively influenced by the pre-existing structures.

The Foreland. This zone includes Arabia and most of Egypt and Libya, with the basement of Archaean series as a fundamental feature. Towards the north of this zone, the basement is usually overlain by younger sedimentaries, offering varied resistance to erosion, and disposed in horizontal layers, or in very shallow domes and troughs. Further south in the Sahara and Arabian areas, more of the basement is exposed, and differences of rock-type can give rise to varied land forms. In some districts of southern Arabia, isolated massifs of granite stand at a higher level than surrounding schists; steep conical hills of pegmatite occur in the Hadhramaut; and in the Sinai and Sahara, especially resistant quartzites outcrop as imposing ridges. Although the concordance between land forms and rock type can hence be close, it is not complete; and it is important to note that the Archaean basement itself, where exposed, is far from being merely a featureless surface.

The series overlying this primitive nucleus consist of sandstones and limestones of varying composition, thickness, and extent. Jurassic, Cretaceous, and Eocene limestones are well represented, and a formation of particular interest is Nubian Sandstone, a concretion of sand grains laid down by aeolian deposition at differing geological periods – e.g. in parts of Libya this series is ascribed to the Carboniferous; but in most other areas to the Permian-Cretaceous. Individual sand grains are aligned along well-defined axes, and recent geophysical research has suggested that the trend of these axes, where pronounced, may have been produced by prevailing winds. Hence these series may give an indication of planetary winds, pressure zones, and the position of the geographical poles and equator at earlier geological periods. Marine transgressions have mainly affected the northern margins, which there-

[1] e.g. L. Dubertret considers the Bekaa valley of the Lebanon as a rift, with *down*throw in places of 8,000 feet, whilst E. de Vaumas regards the same valley to be a syncline that has been *up*warped.

fore show a greater variety and thickness of later sedimentary deposits as compared with the interior.

As we have seen, despite the absence of major fold-structures, variety in land forms may occur. The dominating element is usually a plateau or lowland plain with a sharp delimiting scarp produced by erosive action. Under the particularly arid climatic regime of the south, sandstones are much more readily eroded than are limestones, hence it is frequently the case that valleys and depressions tend to develop on sandstone outcrops, with limestones as residual areas of more vigorous relief. On the Foreland there is typically an extensive development of *hamad* – a level plain sometimes covered in exfoliated material (stones of various size, flint, etc.), or sometimes an expanse of hardened calcareous series. *Cuestas* resulting from differential erosion are also frequent: Egypt and Libya provide examples on a small scale, whilst in central Arabia the same structural pattern gives rise to major relief features.

Faulting is also present to a highly significant degree. Most impressive are the enormous fault-scarps delimiting the Red Sea trough, with extensions northward into the Jordan valley and Gulf of Suez. Besides these, however, relatively minor cross-faults aligned generally on east–west lines have broken up the basement into rectilinear masses that exhibit what is sometimes termed 'chess-board relief'. This is especially the case in S.W. Arabia, Asir, the Yemen, and part of the Hadhramaut. Faulting of east–west trend also defines the northern edges of the interior plateaus in Libya. Finally, faulting of more irregular pattern has produced a number of rift-valleys in the interior of Arabia and north-east Africa. These, partly enlarged by water action at an earlier period, and subsequently by aeolian erosion, and now partially covered by loose sand, serve in some instances as routes giving access to the interior.

Whilst many fault-lines give an impression of comparatively recent origin owing to the steepness and unbroken nature of their slopes, it is clear that others have been extensively eroded back and now exist as primary or even secondary fault-line scarps.

A further feature is the tendency for a fault-line to be highly complicated in nature. Besides the various sorts of faulting (normal, reversed, etc.) the zone of dislocation itself may exist as a single major plane or sometimes as a complex of smaller parallel faults.

In frequent association with the fault zones of the south occur extensive areas of vulcanicity. The most extensive of these areas lies at the southern end of the Red Sea, and on either side of the Gulf of Aden.

Basaltic 'trap' rocks have spread by fissure eruption over an area including much of the Yemen, Hadhramaut, and Somali shores of the Red Sea and Gulf of Aden, as well as a considerable area further inland in Arabia. The basalts, of Eocene age, are closely comparable with the 'trap' rocks of the Indian Deccan, and occur in layers of between 1,000–3,000 feet in thickness.

Vulcanicity of another type and later period (Miocene-Quaternary) is a feature in the same regions, producing well-defined cones and craters which, often superimposed above the basaltic layer and uptilted plateau edges, produce striking effects on relief. The site of Aden town is formed of twin volcanic craters, and close by in the Strait of Bab el Mandeb there are a number of volcanic islands still showing eruptive activity. Similar conditions, with slight eruptivity and the occurrence of solfataras and mofettes, are characteristic of the Yemen and Hadhramaut.

To the north, lava flows were of a quieter type, though more extensive: many of the highlands of Asir and the Hedjaz owe at least part of their height to superimposed basaltic sheets – harras, which are barren lava-fields showing various forms of eruption. Further north still, near the Gulf of Akaba and the Sinai, lava areas are less prominent, though present, and here it is noteworthy that the fissures from which flows have occurred lie to the east of the main fault-lines.

On the borders of Syria and Jordan vulcanicity again becomes extremely widespread, with the Hauran, Jebel Druse and upper Jordan valley as the principal zones. Here there have been many flows at successive geological periods, resulting in an extremely complicated topography. The Jebel Druse region exhibits many types of cone: ash, scoriae, and acidic (Hawaiian type) together with convoluted sheet eruption. Maximum activity here would seem to have been during the Pliocene, but there has been much emission in Quaternary and even recent times. Flows across the Jordan valley have impounded the Sea of Galilee and the former Lake Huleh; and there are hot springs and solfataras around and beneath the Sea of Galilee (e.g. at Tiberias). Lava flows are also a feature of south-western Syria in the region of Homs, Hama, and Aleppo.

Another major area of vulcanicity is the Libyan plateau area south of Tripoli. Here, land forms somewhat reminiscent of Arabia and Syria occur – extensive harra areas, with lines of volcanic peaks – e.g. the Jebel es Soda (Black Mountains) – rising above the plateau level.

The extreme north of the Foreland shows somewhat distinctive characteristics as the region of junction of foreland and geosyncline. Here, in an intermediate broad zone extending from Cyrenaica through Cyprus, Syria, the Lebanon, parts of Jordan, Israel, and Iraq as far as Oman, sediments greatly overlap the Archaean basement, which has had the effect of restricting geosynclinal disturbances. In the extreme north, the basement disappears, and sediments become increasingly thicker and more disturbed. Krenkel has delimited a considerable area which he terms the Syrian arc, extending through Cyprus and Crete as far as Cyrenaica and even Tunisia. The greater part of this intermediate zone is characterised by thinly bedded rock measures, and by folding and fracturing on a restricted scale.

The highlands of this intermediate zone are all anticlinal in structure, with, in some cases, further modification by later faulting. The upfold of Judaea is perhaps the simplest structure, but is nevertheless very characteristic of most of the other highland masses of the area. Folding has been relatively gentle, and overthrusting almost absent. A similar anticline of larger dimensions forms the Lebanon Mountains – the highest in the median zone – and further to the east a system of smaller but more numerous folds extends north-eastwards like the fingers of an open hand. The westernmost member, the Anti-Lebanon Mountains, is aligned parallel to the Lebanon, but the others diverge towards the north-east, with the minor knot of Mount Hermon forming the 'palm' in the south-west (see Fig. 73, p. 397).

The folds of western Syria can be traced in a huge arc around the northern tip of the Arabian foreland, although structures are progressively smaller and even more open than in the west. The Jebel Sinjar and Jebel Makhal, on the borders of Iraq and Syria, are the principal members of the eastern fold system. The northward sweep of the arc would appear to indicate that the Archaean basement underlies much of the interior of Syria and Iraq, although no certain confirmation of this is as yet available.

The contrast between east and west in the median zone is very striking. For the most part, the rock series of Iraq lie almost horizontally, and edges of the various strata, outcropping one above the other, often provide the chief topographical features. In many parts of Iraq, this succession of rock measures has been worked upon by erosion, and appears as a cliff, which forms a western boundary for the valley of Mesopotamia. From this, according to some, the name Iraq (Arabic *cliff*) is derived.

The Folded Zone. Evidence suggests that much of the folded zone of

B

the Middle East came into existence following pressure outwards from the interior of Asia; that is to say, movement was from the north, and the deposits of the Tethys were folded towards the south. The north-eastern portions of the Gondwana continent tended to function as passive agents against which earth movements acted. Only in a few restricted areas, and for special reasons, such as the presence of pre-existing structures, was this trend of folding altered. In southern Europe, on the other hand, movement is thought to have been from the south towards the north.

The Middle East came more directly under Asiatic influences, and hence the direction of folding is predominantly towards the south; but in the west, another different component appears to have been super-imposed upon the major thrust. This would seem to have produced a certain lateral deformation in the arcs of folding, which, instead of lying in parallel lines, have tended to assume a sinuous trend. In Asia Minor, shearing of the folds is also a feature.

Distinction can as a result be made between the east, where folding, although more intense, tended to be from a single origin; and the west of the Middle Eastern region, where the basic pattern was complicated by other movements originating further in the south and west. Hence in the east, closely packed symmetrical folds with a single dominant trend are characteristic; but in the north and west closely disposed asymmetrical arcs and garlands, reminiscent on a small scale of eastern Asia, are more frequent. The Persian Zagros consists in its best developed portions of a series of enormous 'hog's back' structures, with marked regularity of strike and continuity of folding. Overthrusting, with extensive nappe formation, is however also a feature. The southern coast of Asia Minor on the other hand consists of a series of irregular folds, many crescent-shaped, others straight, terminated by well-developed cross-faults and downthrow basins. At Andifli the main western Taurus range plunges abruptly below sea level; and the Amanus Mountains show lithological affinities to the twin hill-ranges of Cyprus, indicating that the island and also possibly Crete are, so to speak, a double garland of arcs related to the main mass of Asia Minor.

A further matter of importance is the presence of older resistant blocks actually within the fold structures of Asia Minor. These blocks vary both in size – from a few square miles in extent to what amount to sub-continental fragments; and also in age – some are pre-Cambrian, but others suggest formation at periods no earlier than the Hercynian.

This juxtaposition of resistant masses and pliable series is most characteristic of Asia Minor; in Iran folding seems to have been on a larger scale with a fuller development of fold structures much less interrupted by older fragments. In Turkey relatively narrow zones of sediments were compressed against numerous small and irregular blocks, with the result that folds are small in extent, few in number and irregular in disposition. In Iran a more developed and extensive geosynclinal trough was squeezed between larger masses, sub-continental in size, and perhaps of more regular shape.

Considerable difficulty exists in ascertaining the origin of the central plateau block of Persia which separates the Elburz from the Zagros, and its role in influencing the folding of the regions round it. The position in Turkey is relatively clear: that of central Persia is at the present time the subject of some controversy. A recent study by Furon suggests that the Ural Mountains of Russia may continue far to the south, by way of central Persia, into the southern Indian Ocean. Unfortunately, however, the plateau area shows a large number of fold movements of differing geological phases, without any simple pattern or uniform direction of strike. Thus although signs of folding of Hercynian (i.e. Ural) age, and of north–south trend, can be found in central Persia, these are of such restricted extent that other authorities cannot believe that the Ural arc ever reached Persia.

A second problem of the Persian plateau is the extent of its influence on later folding. The greatly restricted degree of sedimentation during Palaeozoic, Mesozoic, and Tertiary periods indicates a certain stability of the plateau; and the extent to which it would seem to have transmitted pressure to the Zagros on the south, either from its own movement, or from that of Angaraland, make it appear that central Iran could be regarded as an ancient stable mass comparable, on a smaller scale, with the major continents of Gondwanaland and Angaraland.

Recent studies have, however, drawn attention to the extensive fold structures of the region, and to the considerable thickness of Tertiary deposits in a few small areas. These are evidence of a considerably lesser degree of stability than was at first supposed; and the previous conception of the Persian plateau would accordingly seem to require modification. Further information on the geology of the region will be required before the question can be resolved, but it can, however, be stated in general terms that there is a fundamental similarity of structure between Persia and Turkey. Both areas are basically zones of folding with embedded resistant fragments. Much differential movement has occurred, producing local horsts and downthrow basins, and in many of the latter thick Tertiary sediments have been deposited. In close association with these fault-structures occurs sharp folding, especially at the periphery of the entire mass.

Land Forms. The vigour and freshness of relief forms in the Middle East is in overwhelming part due to structural origin; but this is by no means the entire story. Evidence is present suggesting extensive cycles of erosion and peneplanation – mainly the unusual pattern of drainage, which in many instances is far from being in direct and simple relation to structure or to topography. Surveys by Hassan Awad and others have shown that an extensive erosion surface developed on the basement rock layers in lower Palaeozoic times. This planation of the surface would also seem to have been accompanied by a certain amount of oscillation, which produced local transgressions by the Tethys, and hence ultimate variations in surface level. The region round the head of the Red Sea (Sinai, N.W. Hedjaz, eastern Egypt) shows one very extensive erosion surface at a low level, with another of probable later date (late Mesozoic) at a higher level. Concordance between these surfaces is however incomplete, due partly to insufficient observation.

Further north, in the Levant, oscillation of the surface was more marked than in the main Foreland zone; and here, numerous erosion surfaces have been distinguished: of Eocene age in the Lebanon, Anti-Lebanon, Jebel Ansarieh, and East Jordan; and Miocene in the Negeb and adjacent regions on the north. Many individual surfaces of an extremely complex pattern have recently been postulated; and it is not easy to reconcile in detail the various ideas put forward for differing regions. Support for the general conception of significant periods of erosion is nevertheless to be found in the drainage pattern of the region. The curious courses of the Litani, Barada, and Orontes rivers in relation to present-day relief suggest partial superimposition and antecedent directions of flow, controlled by pre-existing land forms: the remarkable elbow of the Litani river, which breaks through mountainous country to reach the Mediterranean instead of Lake Tiberias, as would have seemed more natural; the former swamp area of the middle Orontes again succeeded by a sharp westward bend to the Mediterranean; and the way in which the Barada has cut through anticline and syncline in order to follow an obsequent trend towards central Syria.

In addition to the major planifications, there are clear signs of minor oscillation in level, indicated by suites of terraces both on the western shores and around many of the larger lakes, and basins of inland drainage. McBurney and Hey have drawn attention to the terraces of the Cyrenaican coast; and Wetzel, Haller, and de Vaumas have distinguished fairly continuous series along most of the Libano-Syrian coast between Mount Carmel and the Turkish frontier, at intervals of 5, 17, 45, 100, 150, 170–250, 300–380, and 400–500 feet above present sea level. As will be noted from these figures, the lower terraces tend to be sharper and more clearly defined, the upper ones more broken and irregular in pattern.

South of Mount Carmel as far as Sinai, the present coastline corresponds fairly closely with fault-lines parallel to the Jordan rift; and a further important feature has been extensive sedimentation by drift from the Nile delta. Hence marine terraces do not exist along the coasts of Israel and eastern Egypt, but buried levels of earlier periods (Pliocene to early Pleistocene) would seem to occur below the present-day coastal deposits.

The major river valleys of the Middle East also contain a number of well-developed terraces. The Nile shows many low- and high-level sequences, and there has been inconclusive discussion as to whether these are of fluvial or marine origin – both are known to occur, indicating extensive transgression by the Mediterranean. In its upper part the valley of the Euphrates is deeply incised into the present land surface, and three terrace-levels at 50, 100, and 200 feet can be observed in numerous localities. Because, however, of the more complex structure of the region traversed by the Tigris river in its upper portion (a transverse crossing of folds instead of incision into horizontally bedded layers) the effects of any possible oscillation and terrace formation are much more difficult to trace.

Strand lines around water surfaces such as Lake Urmia, the Red Sea, and the Caspian are extremely numerous and well formed. Three major terraces are visible in the lower Jordan valley, with smaller and restricted levels of erosion and deposition that indicate minor changes in topography and climate. Eustatic movement and changes in volume of water both seem to have been involved.

Besides their significance as indicating more precise stages in the origin of the land forms, and allowing some broad reconstruction of the pattern of landscape at earlier periods, the terraces and erosion surfaces are of great interest in that they provide facts about earlier phases of climate. Their position, altitude, character, and distribution indicate phases of low and high sea levels, varied river flow, extent of deposited and transported material, and hence the direction and flow of both water and ice. From these items comes further evidence regarding pluvial, arid, cold, and warm phases. As well, many of the earliest human settlements developed upon the flatter terraces, which provided a convenient and often more productive terrain. Consequently much recent archaeological investigation has centred upon terrace cultures, especially in Palestine and the Nile valley.

Rock Types. It would not be appropriate in the present study to undertake a detailed description of rock series; but interest attaches to certain strata which are of importance in the economic and social life of the region. Accordingly, without referring to age, or precise form of deposition, we may note the occurrence of a number of rock measures that have a special relationship to human activity.

It is first useful to note the abundance of *calcareous strata* in the Middle East. The Zagros is overwhelmingly calcareous in character, and many other series are markedly lime-rich. Parts of Turkey also show outcrops of calcareous sediments laid down in the Tethys; and older limestones occur towards the north.

All the mountain ranges of the western Levant have a core of Jurassic or Cretaceous limestone, with calcareous beds of later age forming a cap in many places. Other limestone formations extend eastwards into the Arabian and Syrian deserts, as far as Iraq. Finally, many of the shallow bedded sediments on the southern foreland consist of calcareous series of mainly Jurassic, Cretaceous, Eocene, and Miocene age. The Jebel Akhdar of Cyrenaica is a massive arch of Eocene limestone, whilst much of the northern Jebel of Tripolitania is composed of Jurassic and Cretaceous series, with in places a Miocene cap.

The strata termed calcareous include series ranging from limestone to chalk and marl. Thus in the Lebanon and north-west Syria massive Jurassic limestone, pale blue in colour, and of great chemical purity, is characteristic. Elsewhere, fine-grained yellowish or grey limestones occur, some of very variable composition; and oolitic beds formed of minute concretions often provide a useful building stone. An intermixture of calcium and magnesium carbonates gives rise to dolomite, a type of limestone with a grained texture that is more resistant to erosion than pure limestone.

A large number of marls occur in the Middle East. In Iraq and Iran brown, red, yellow, grey, or white marls alternate with limestone beds; and the Judaean wilderness is composed of a mass of chalky marl, grey-white in colour. Water can easily penetrate certain marl series, either downwards by seepage, or upwards, in response to capillary attraction due to heating of the surface. The latter movement may in time result in the formation of a hard 'pan' or crust (also termed calcrete). Differences between rock series can produce corresponding and very striking variations in topography: marls and gypsum can produce 'badlands', and limestones may give rise to bare pavements or Karst. Such variation is especially characteristic of Iran.

The occurrence over wide areas of strata which are permeable to a varying degree has considerable effects on drainage and water supply, and therefore on human activity. The relationship between rock formations and drainage will be discussed in a later section of this chapter; at this stage we may, however, note that because of a deficiency of surface water supplies, the distribution of human settlement is in many areas sharply controlled by the occurrence of springs. Closely grouped habitations, rather than dispersed settlements, are hence highly characteristic in calcareous areas of the Middle East.

It may also be noted that the rock series described as permeable show considerable variations. In the case of coarser limestones, actual fissures may allow water to percolate rapidly downwards, even though the rock itself may not be especially porous. Other types of limestone may have a slower seepage, due either to more restricted fissuring, or to percolation within a porous structure.

With the limestones must be considered certain *basalts* which, although quite impermeable, are so highly fissured that water can penetrate to considerable depths. The plateau basalts of the Hauran and Jordan include series of this kind, which give rise to springs where they are underlain by other types of non-permeable rock, or where fissuring ceases. Many settlements have grown up on sites determined by the apparently paradoxical phenomenon of springs issuing from basalt series.

The *igneous intrusions* of the north form a second group. Main interest lies in the fact that metallic ores occur in association with the igneous veins. Hence the greater part of the metallic mineral wealth of the Middle East occurs in those regions that have undergone disturbance and where fracturing has allowed the rise of magma from below. Turkey is the most favoured region in this respect, since the more plastic series of the Zagros have tended to restrict fracturing.

A wide variety of minerals occur in Turkey, but owing to extreme irregularity in disposition, the ore bodies themselves are generally small in amount and difficult to exploit. The gold fields in the Sardis district of western Turkey, once part of the domain of King Croesus, were among the earliest to be worked; but modern attention is now focused on such metals as chromium and manganese.

The Archaean basement rocks also contain small amounts of precious ores, and these have also been irregularly exploited since earliest times. The wide extent of the Archaean table has made gold one of the traditional products of Arabia, though individual production is very small.

Precious and semi-precious stones, the product of metamorphism, also have a wide distribution in both the folded and pre-Cambrian series, but individual deposits are not rich, and cannot compare with such areas as the Rand. Nevertheless, metals and precious stones have formed part of the basis of commercial exchange in the Middle East since the dawn of history.

The mineral wealth of the sedimentary measures consists of oil, mineral salts, coal, and gypsum. Consideration of the oil resources of the Middle East is deferred to a later chapter, and there is little to say of the other three. Salt beds of many ages are known and an extensive Cambrian series in the central and southern Zagros had had a modifying action on the later topographical features, and itself forms mountains in southern Iran. As a product of arid climatic regimes, surface salt deposits are frequent throughout the Middle East, and the inhabitants are often more concerned with the removal of unwanted salt from agricultural land, than with the commercial possibilities of its extraction. In a few areas, notably the Dead Sea, potassium and bromine are extracted from saline deposits, but with the exception of the Dead Sea area, exploitation is nowhere on a large scale.

Within the last few years, important deposits of phosphate rock have been discovered in Jordan, in the Israeli Negeb, and in Egypt. Exploitation in Jordan and Egypt is advanced, that in the Negeb has been slower because of political and other difficulties. Another mineral resource long known to exist but only recently developed is an iron-ore bed near Aswan. This is thought by some to be extremely rich and to offer considerable prospects for the future.

The coal measures of the Middle East are extremely scanty. Deposits of Carboniferous age are preserved in a small district of Turkey between Eregli (Heraclea) and Zonguldak. This coal is of high quality but is greatly limited in quantity, and cannot supply even the modest needs of Turkey. Nevertheless, the Turkish field is the most important in the Middle East. Other deposits of later age are believed to occur in Armenia – but are little exploited – also in northern Iran where coal

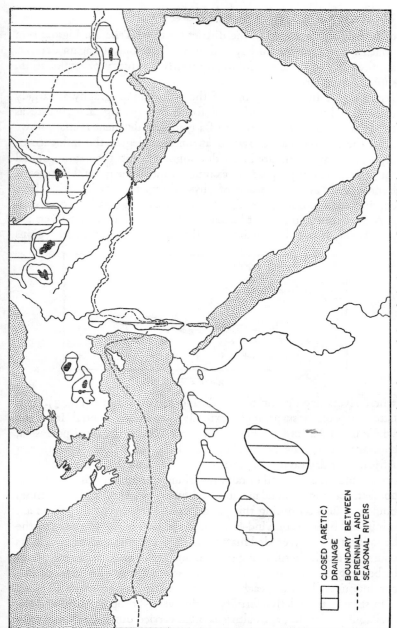

Fig. 3. Types of Drainage. The boundaries between drainage basins in eastern Iran and Turkestan are only approximate

CLOSED (ARETIC) DRAINAGE

BOUNDARY BETWEEN PERENNIAL AND SEASONAL RIVERS

of Jurassic age is mined in the district north of Teheran. Lignite of a poor quality exists in Turkey and in the Lebanon, but again deposits are few. In the Lebanon, following nearly a century of exploitation, supplies seem largely exhausted.

Hydrography. In most regions of the world hydrography is largely controlled by rainfall, with land forms and geological structure as subsidiary factors. As the result of a generally deficient rainfall, how-ever, the Middle East shows to an unusual degree the influence of topography and structure in the development of its river systems; and for this reason it is proposed to examine some of the general features of hydrography as an extension of physical structure, rather than defer consideration, as is more usual, until climatic factors have been discussed.

A demarcation must first be made between regions where rivers are permanent, with a flow maintained throughout the year, and regions

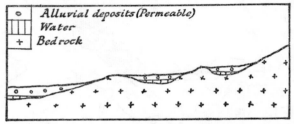

Fig. 4. Profile of a Wadi Bed

where rivers dry up completely during certain seasons (Fig. 3). This latter division is surprisingly extensive, including central Iran, the whole of Arabia and the plateau of central Syria, the Sinai peninsula, and, apart from the Nile valley and delta, the whole of north-east Africa. Here dry ravines or water-courses fill for a short time, and with great rapidity, after a fall of rain. A rushing torrent may rise 10 or even 20 feet, carrying abundant fine sediment, pebbles, and sometimes boulders. Erosion during this period can be rapid, but the effects are minimised by drifts of wind-borne material later in the year, and by the deposition of much eroded material at only a slightly lower level in its course by a quickly subsiding stream. Such river valleys, or *wadis*, tend to be irregular in outline, with the floor consisting of a series of dis-continuous rock basins, each filled with alluvium or pebbles (Fig. 4).

In spite of the relative fertility of the water-borne deposits, and the availability of water, agriculture is often carried out in the wadis only with difficulty. Many streams change their course as the result of rapid erosion, or equally rapid deposition in their bed, so that floods are by no means uncommon, incredible though this might appear in regions termed desert. If dams or irrigation channels are constructed, these are very liable to become filled with sediment brought down in flood periods; and, at the present time, several Roman irrigation works on the borders of the Syrian desert can be seen completely buried in alluvial deposits.[1]

As many as ten to fifteen 'floods' (*seil*) may occur in a particular valley, especially where this latter is deeply incised and is formed largely of impermeable strata. Such is the case in S.W. Arabia, where rainfall can be moderately heavy for a short time, and where often either volcanic or Archaean rocks are exposed. Elsewhere, floods are somewhat less violent, but still equally erratic, and even normally dry areas

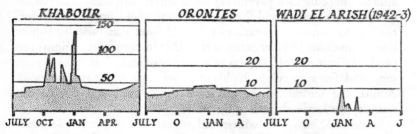

Fig. 5. Typical River Regimes (in part, after Dubertret and Weulersse). Flow in m.³/sec.

like the Sinai or Libya can experience raging torrential flows for a few days in most years.

The area of perennial rivers corresponds, in the main, with the regions of heavier rainfall. Geological structure, however, plays a considerable part, since permeable strata may retain water in large quantities, and such water emerges as springs to feed rivers throughout the dry season. Extensive limestone outcrops to the south of the Anti-Taurus Range, along the Turco-Syrian frontier, give rise to numerous springs, from which rise the rivers Balikh, Khabour, and Jagh-Jagh to make their way across the Syrian desert to join the Euphrates.

Thus the effects of a limited rainfall, which might in regions of different geological structure be dissipated as torrents of a few days' duration, are spread throughout the year. Similar instances can be found in many areas of Asia Minor; in the Zagros, where a large

[1] The barrage at Çubuk in Turkey built in 1936 is now one-third filled by alluvial deposits.

number of important tributaries flow south-westwards to join the Tigris; and in the western borders of Syria and the Lebanon. The river Orontes, which rises from a spring in the Lebanon Mountains, is an excellent example of the effects of six months' rainfall spread throughout the whole year by slow percolation through porous rock; the Khabour of north-east Syria shows the further superposition of direct run-off in the rainy season upon regular flow from springs; and the flow in the Wadi el Arish (Sinai) is an extreme case of intermittent flooding (Fig. 5).

There have been a number of attempts to distinguish the proportion of rainfall that is directly evaporated from the surface, or absorbed into the subsoil, or given out from springs, or which runs off directly on the surface. Because of the open nature of the surface in some areas (i.e. approaching bare rock pavement), the occurrence of maximum rainfall at the coldest season, and the intensity of rainfall – both latter factors tending to reduce evaporation – it would seem that rainfall of quite limited amounts (smaller actually than that in temperate regions) can produce direct run-off. Figures of a quarter of an inch only have been suggested for impervious highland zones such as the mountains of Arabia, the central Sahara and even the Levant, and double this quantity for lowlands such as Egypt.

In general, however, widespread occurrence of permeable strata (ranging from sandstones, limestones, and even some basalts to sand and gravel) result in the greater proportion of rainfall being absorbed by the ground. This fraction has been estimated as 60 per cent. of total precipitation in the wetter parts of the Levant, 75–80 per cent. in Jordan, and over 90 per cent. in much of the southern Foreland region. Of the remainder, Ionides has calculated that in the Jordan basin about 13 per cent. of precipitation flows as surface streams; 7 per cent. as direct run-off, and the remaining 6 per cent. as water fed by springs.

A second feature of the hydrography of the Middle East is the frequency of aretic (i.e. closed or inland) drainage. One factor is, of course, the intermittent erosive action of many streams; but topography has again an important role. Interior basins shut off from the sea by encircling fold ranges; recent lava flows across existing valleys; warping of plateau-blocks; and the development of troughs along tectonic lines; all these, together with rapid evaporation and deficient rainfall, present too great an opposition to the relatively feeble erosive power of the rivers.

Practically all the closed basins are strongly saline; some exceptions do, however, occur when a stream is swallowed by porous rock measures. The greatest extent of inland drainage occurs in Iran, where almost all of the interior plateau is divided among salt basins. Only in the extreme north-west are the streams sufficiently developed to break through the surrounding fold mountains and find their way either to the Caspian Sea or to the Persian Gulf, this despite the presence of cross-faulted valleys.

Similar topography on a smaller scale exists in Asia Minor. In this region heavier rainfall on the coastal margins has led to a greater development of rivers, which have in many instances cut back through the coastal ranges into the plateau basins of the interior. The Kizil Irmak and Yezil Irmak Rivers, flowing to the Black Sea, have greatly reduced the areas of inland drainage in Anatolia, which now lie mainly in the south-central portion of the plateau, with an eastward extension through Lake Van to the Urmia basin of Iran.

An extensive zone of inland drainage lies at some distance inland from the coast of the Levant. The tectonic trough of the Jordan contains probably the best-known salt basin of the Middle East – the Dead Sea; but further to the north, in Syria-Lebanon, the trough has been broken through by the rivers Litani, Nahr el Kebir, and Orontes, all of which reach the sea. A region of inland drainage lies to the east of the trough, on the margins of the Syrian desert. It is noteworthy that the two great cities of Aleppo and Damascus (and also to a certain extent Jerusalem) stand on streams which ultimately terminate in salt basins – but in the upper reaches where the water is still sweet and fresh, and not, as is more usual, in the lower, wider parts.

The normal course of river development, as defined by geographers for better watered regions, is only rarely achieved in the Middle East. In the absence of regular and permanent flow, with an increase of volume towards the mouth from the entry of tributaries, there exist certain anomalies and unusual phenomena in the rivers of the Middle East which from the earliest times have excited the wonder and curiosity of all who observed them. The majestic Euphrates and Tigris, changing their relative level as they flow together in a single valley, the underground Lethe of Cyrenaica, the sacred Adonis River of Phoenicia, clear in summer and red in spring, the holy Jordan and Abana, and the Nile, greatest riddle of all, in that it floods at the hottest and driest time of the year, are probably without parallel elsewhere in the world.

An approach to the development of a uniform thalweg in the shape of a parabola, typical of mature streams, is realised only by a few great rivers which have maintained a course antecedent in certain parts to the topography of their valleys. Of the remainder, the majority consist of short streams making a rapid way down steep and rugged mountain flanks. The Anatolian plateau is ringed by a number of such rivers that are broken by cascades and waterfalls, and frequently hidden in the depths of huge gorges. Only in a few instances, as for example that of the Büyük Menderes (Meander), is the profile sufficiently developed to reach a mature stage. The western Zagros shows an even greater elaboration of short, immature streams plunging through spectacular rifts and gorges to reach the plains of Iraq. The Karun, a large and extremely swift river, carries down annually to the head of the Persian Gulf an immense mass of silt eroded from the central Zagros.

In areas where perennial streams are lacking, human existence, in the absence of water storage facilities, must depend upon wells and springs.

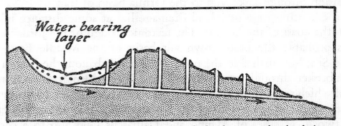

Fig. 6. Diagram of a Foggara. If because of a level topography the drainage tunnel cannot emerge at the surface, the last vertical shaft is used as a well

Water can, of course, be found where a permeable rock measure, underlain by impermeable strata, retains a proportion of the rainfall. The quantity of water may in certain instances be sufficient to give rise to surface springs, or to maintain a level of water in a well sunk into the permeable rock; but this is a feature only of favoured areas. In drier regions more elaborate methods must be used to obtain water, the principle of these methods being the construction of a *foggara*. This consists of a very gently sloping tunnel driven into a water-bearing layer from a lower level, so that the water held in the permeable rock is drained off. As the work of construction proceeds, numerous vertical shafts are driven from the tunnel to the surface, in order to provide air for the tunneller, and to furnish a means of disposing of the rubble. A foggara may extend for several miles across country, and is always marked by a line of cones of debris, giving the impression of a number of miniature volcanoes spaced at regular intervals. The course of the tunnel is to some extent independent of surface features; and foggaras of Roman construction are still important sources of water in several areas of the Levant. In Iran the name *qanat* is applied to similar tunnels (which are very widespread in some parts) and certain tribes and clansmen (especially those from around Yazd) have the reputation of being specially skilled in their construction. A third term, *karez*, is used in Iraq, and *feledj* in Oman. Some foggaras may have a flow of several gallons of water per second, from which wide areas are irrigated (Fig. 6).

Water can also be found in the subsoil of dry river valleys in certain arid regions, provided that the underlying rock formation is impermeable. Although the greater proportion of the scanty rainfall soon runs away as a surface stream, a small amount sinks through the permeable alluvium or gravel of the wadi bed, and may be retained by the basin-like structure of the underlying rock. Such water-bearing strata, although small in extent, are of considerable value to the desert nomads of Arabia, Syria, and Libya. Temporary wells sunk in dry river beds may also support caravan traffic, and permit the establishment of trade routes across regions that are almost devoid of surface drainage. (See Fig. 4.)

The hydrographic system of the Middle East gives two impressions: firstly, as we have seen, of the interrupted and unusual nature of the courses produced by the dominance of land forms and structure, which have been less eroded than in many other parts of the world. Secondly, the observer cannot fail to be aware of something of a discrepancy as between the immature and feeble drainage system described above, which prevails over large areas of the Middle East, and the actual land forms of the region, which show many large and well developed valleys. The physical map reveals a considerable number of structures that in better watered areas would be described as deeply dissected land forms: Arabia in particular, though devoid of permanent rivers, is deeply eroded by valley formations running inland from the Red Sea, Indian Ocean, and Persian Gulf.

This mature landscape is even more apparent to the traveller by air. Broad wadis several hundred miles in length, and occupied by torrents only for several months, or even days, in the year; extensive alluvial basins never entirely covered by a river, even at its maximum flood; cols etched by water action in high mountain ranges – these phenomena, highly developed in Arabia and Iran, are also to be found along the Libyan coast. Moreover, in the region of perennial streams round the north-eastern Mediterranean, small rivers of inconsiderable volume lie in crevasses and canyons several thousand feet deep; and the greater part of Syrian desert is diversified by dry, but well marked river beds trending towards the Euphrates. None of the present streams, which trickle among the pebbles for a few days in each year, could have carved out the rock basins marking their course, or have deposited the masses of sediment and scree that cover their beds.

The existing hydrographic system of the Middle East is thus obviously to a large extent a misfit, with attenuated rivers occupying channels that were developed at an earlier and wetter period. The precise age at which more abundant rainfall occurred, whether in historic time, or more remotely, is best considered as an aspect of climatology; and discussion of climatic changes in the Middle East is therefore relegated to the succeeding chapter.

CHAPTER III

Climate

It is becoming increasingly difficult to separate climatology, which has been for the greater part the domain of the geographer, from meteorology, which in some respects is properly the concern of the physicist. Modern tendency is to make more and more use of the detailed mechanism of everyday weather to explain the larger features of climate; and this new approach, known as 'synoptic climatology', is proving valuable in amplifying certain aspects of climate that up to the present have been dealt with rather inadequately. The geographer cannot be expected to follow in detail all the physical phenomena occurring in the atmosphere; but in discussing climatic factors, an outline knowledge of the main physical features involved, with their broader effects, avoids the danger of loose generalisation. For instance, the development of the 'Mediterranean' type of climate is usually ascribed to the northward migration of the Doldrum belt of high pressure. As we shall see later, this is only partly true for the Mediterranean itself. Similarly, it is not easy, except by reference to meteorology, to understand why rainfall in some parts of the world is sharply controlled by topography, whilst in others, this control is much less – why, for example, in the Black Sea region, Sebastopol should have less than 20 inches of rain annually and Batum over 90 inches, yet in France, at approximately the same latitude, Bordeaux has 31 inches, and Clermont-Ferrand 25 inches.

The Middle East lends itself admirably to the exposition of climate on the synoptic basis. The extreme variability of conditions both seasonally and as between sub-regions is best understood if reference is made to the air masses of very different character that displace each other over the area. Our plan will be first to establish the scheme of pressure distribution, from which prevailing winds can be deduced. Following this, the origin and character of the air masses that reach the Middle East can then be discussed. Finally, a survey of actual conditions of temperature, humidity, and rainfall will provide the basis for a climatic division on general lines. Local climatic distribution will be considered in more detail in the last section of this volume, under the appropriate regional study.

PRESSURE

Summer. Intensive heating of the southern part of Asia gives rise to the well-known monsoonal low-pressure area of India.[1] This low-pressure zone, centred over the north-western provinces and the Gulf of Oman,

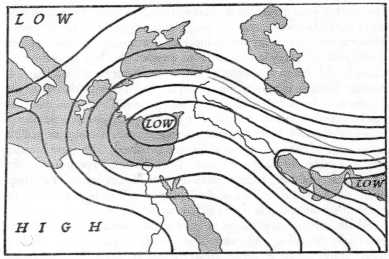

Fig. 7. Pressure Distribution in Summer

is a permanent feature of the summer months, and the strongly developed wind system to which it gives rise affects not only India but, in addition, almost all of the Middle East (Fig. 7).

The centre of the low is prolonged over the Persian Gulf towards Iran, and a minor centre of low pressure also develops over or near the island of Cyprus. This minor low is persistent, and has a marked effect on pressure and wind distribution in the Middle East. The Cyprus low develops primarily as the result of unequal heating of sea and land, and

[1] The atmosphere responds to changes of temperature by changes in volume and density. Increase in temperature leads to expansion, with a consequent fall in density; and, conversely, reduced temperature is followed by reduced volume and a higher density. Pressure is in direct relation to density, and hence atmospheric heating leads to a fall in pressure, because of the reduction in density; atmospheric cooling to higher pressure.

in all probability the basin-like structure of the island has a slight further effect. Any modifying influence from the sea is reduced by a ring of mountains that lies close to much of the coast, and in the interior heating is intensified by bare ridges that shut in the central plain. Abnormally high temperatures prevailing in the interior of Cyprus during summer justify a description of the island as a *plaque chauffante*.

The summer low of Cyprus maintains a separate existence, being divided from the main monsoonal low by a shallow isobaric col situated over N.W. Syria. Air currents originating over the Indian Ocean are thus drawn into the monsoonal circulation, and, except near the centres of low pressure, follow a somewhat involved path anti-clockwise round the entire low-pressure system.[1] Starting over the Deccan, winds turn northwards and westwards, parallel to the Himalaya, and then over the Zagros ranges into western Iran. Continuing northwards into Armenia, the wind track turns to the west in Asia Minor, then southwards over the Aegean, south-eastwards in the eastern Mediterranean, in response to the pull of the Cyprus low, eastwards over the Levant; and south-eastwards over Arabia.

Conditions over Arabia are less easy to define, but it is apparent that further deviation to the south-west then takes place, owing to the development of a third low-pressure zone in the region of Abyssinia and the Upper Nile valley. This third area probably has the effect of drawing in the returning Middle East current from the north-east, together with a supply of very damp air either from the Indian Ocean to the south-east, or from the Gulf of Guinea in the Atlantic Ocean. From the latter is thought to come the well-known summer rainfall of Abyssinia and the Upper Nile that produces the Nile floods.[2] A second pressure col must lie over S.E. Arabia, separating the African centre from the main monsoonal low of N.W. India.

[1] A small proportion of the air in the monsoonal circulation describes a short, simple path round the centres of low pressure. In both instances passage over the sea takes place, and the air becomes sufficiently damp to give rain on reaching the land. This rainfall is more marked in India, where the low is more developed, but the Cyprus low would also seem to produce a slight summer rainfall in the south-east coastlands of Turkey, and in the Hatay.

[2] This distribution of winds would at first sight seem to be highly peculiar. Controversy has occurred as to whether the damp summer winds of Abyssinia and the Yemen do in fact come all the way from the Atlantic, or whether they are drawn in more directly from the Indian Ocean. At present, the more accepted view is that air currents originate far to the west, over the Gulf of Guinea; and important evidence in support of this theory is the entire lack of summer rainfall on the coastlands of southern Arabia – a steady monsoonal inflow from the Indian Ocean would presumably give a regime at Aden comparable with that prevailing at Bombay. This is definitely not the case, since only the uplands of south-west Arabia receive any rainfall during summer.

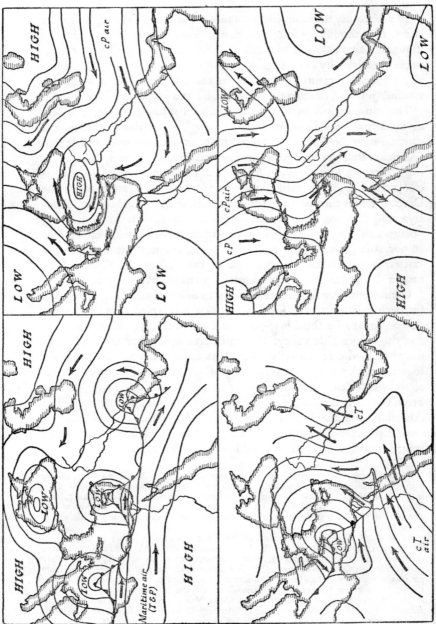

Fig. 8. Pressure Situations in Winter

Further complication arises from the meeting of tropical and equatorial air at a zone now termed the Inter-Tropical Front. This tends to occur in the Middle East over southern Arabia and occasionally south and east Libya. The significance of this zone is on the whole distinctly less than that of the frontal zones of higher (temperate) latitudes, but nevertheless it has importance in the weather regime of the Red Sea area at certain seasons of the year.

This composite pressure system is a permanent feature from late May or June until September. Minor variations of pressure occur from time to time, with a slight deepening or filling up of the three centres, but the general disposition of isobars remains unchanged, and remarkable regularity in wind direction is a feature.

Winter. High pressure covers the interior of Asia, and extends as far south as Iran. Owing to the elevation of the Anatolian plateau very low temperatures occur; and a second, smaller anticyclone develops over the region. This is a minor feature, hardly comparable with the Siberian anticyclone, since it disappears completely from time to time, as depressions advance eastwards across the Mediterranean or Black Seas. Over the entire Middle East, pressure conditions are very variable (Fig. 8). Outlying portions of the Siberian anticyclone may extend westwards for a short period, and cover much of the Middle East; but a disturbed cyclonic development associated with generally low-pressure conditions is more characteristic at this season.

Atlantic depressions arrive via N.W. Europe, Spain, or N.W. Africa, and, rejuvenated by contact with the sea, often continue via the Mediterranean as far as Armenia or Iran. More frequently, however, low-pressure systems develop within the Mediterranean area itself, which, with its contrasts of sea and land, warm plain and cold mountain, and damp coastline and arid interior, favours the growth of atmospheric disturbances. Overspilling into the Mediterranean basin of air from another region provides the first impetus to development, and, once formed, these depressions are liable to further intensification as they pass eastwards.

Certain regions stand out as especially favourable for the development or intensification of low-pressure systems. Chief of these is in northern Italy, from which a considerable number of disturbances originate and move south-eastwards into the eastern Mediterranean. Since 1942 it has also been established that depressions can form south of the Atlas Mountains, and move into the central Mediterranean. Both the Italian and Atlas lows may form particularly as 'lee' effects –

i.e. when there is a strong and well-established current blowing over a major mountain mass, eddies and changes of pressure can develop in the lee of the crests. Another, most recent view is that because of the considerable temperature differences between the ice-covered Alps and the intensely hot Sahara there is a strong thermal gradient over the central Mediterranean area, which can give rise to local 'jet streams' of considerable intensity. The effect of these streams on pressure conditions within the area may be important. In the east, the Gulf of Sirte has a marked influence on the weather of Cyrenaica and Lower Egypt; and Cyprus is particularly noteworthy as an area in which depressions

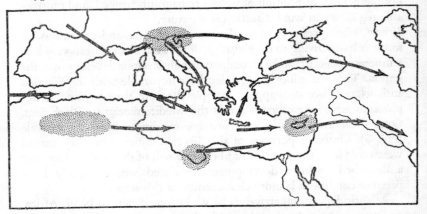

Fig. 9. Tracks and Regions of Origin of Mediterranean Depressions

develop. 'Cyprus lows', small, rapidly moving disturbances, are a prominent feature of autumn, winter, and spring (Fig. 9).

It cannot be too strongly urged that the Mediterranean must not be regarded as a simple eastward extension of the Atlantic Ocean, and therefore as a channel by which Atlantic depressions reach southern Europe and S.W. Asia. Although it is true that a certain number of Mediterranean depressions develop far to the west, the majority are autochthonous in origin, and the weather to which they give rise is essentially different from that of 'Polar' depressions of the Atlantic. Warm sectors in depressions of cool temperate latitudes are associated with extensive cloud masses, and high humidities; in the Mediterranean, warm sectors may be almost cloudless and quite dry: or again, the north winds of winter often give clear, brilliant weather in the south, but very different conditions in northern Europe.

A further point of difference arises in the relative shallowness and small extent of Mediterranean depressions. Whereas Atlantic depressions may cover half the entire ocean, with a minimum pressure approaching 960 millibars, disturbances in the Mediterranean are usually much smaller, and pressure rarely falls below 990 millibars. This does not mean that the depression is less intense; but the duration of bad weather is definitely shorter, and greater variety in conditions is experienced.

It is not considered necessary to follow the tracks of Mediterranean depressions in much detail. Carefully defined routes tend to be somewhat misleading, since a feature of any depression is its irregularity of movement. Broadly speaking, however, depressions tend to follow a sea track. From northern Italy, they frequently pass down the Adriatic into the Ionian Sea. Here the track divides, under the influence of the land mass of Asia Minor. Many depressions continue eastwards into the Levant and Iraq, whilst others move northwards into the Aegean and Black Seas, ultimately reaching the Caspian. A second route lies in the south of the Mediterranean basin. In this case an uninterrupted sea track brings rain to the Levant coastlands, and depressions often reach the Persian Gulf, or even the interior of Iran.

In summer and early autumn, cyclonic disturbances rarely affect the Middle East. A more northerly track takes them across the northern Balkans to the Black Sea, where they bring rainfall to the eastern coastlands. (Cf. conditions at Batum.)

Of recent years, interesting effects have been observed in the upper atmosphere. Because of the very great contrasts in temperature – e.g. as between the snowcapped mountains of Europe, Asia Minor, and Iran, and the warm seas and hot deserts immediately south, high-velocity jet streams develop at heights of 30,000–50,000 feet over the central and eastern Mediterranean basins, and also further east. According to some writers one such jet stream is located over Iran; and its location shifts seasonally north and south.

RAINFALL AT BATUM (inches)

J	F	M	A	M	J	J	A	S	O	N	D	Total
10·2	6·0	6·2	5·0	2·8	5·9	6·0	8·2	11·9	8·8	12·2	10·0	93·3

AIR MASS CLIMATOLOGY IN THE MIDDLE EAST

Air masses are conservative with respect to changes of temperature and humidity; that is, they tend to gain or lose heat and moisture relatively slowly. This has important effects for climatology, since if two air masses of differing temperatures are brought into contact, transfer of heat by diffusion from the warmer to the colder mass does not readily occur. In place of a rapid equalisation of temperature throughout both masses, original characteristics persist, with the two air masses in juxtaposition retaining a separate identity, rather than mingling to form a single larger mass of intermediate qualities. A sharp boundary develops between the warm and the cold air, and it is in this zone that relatively slow transfer of heat and moisture takes place.

From this change of heat and moisture in a narrow zone arise many of the phenomena of weather; and Bjerknes has developed his well-known Polar Frontal Theory from consideration of the behaviour of air masses and their boundary zones, or 'fronts'.

Bjerknes' conception of weather as due to the juxtaposition of air masses of differing qualities is now recognised as of fundamental importance in the study of meteorology and climatology. First elaborated for the meteorology of temperate latitudes, frontal analysis can be applied to most areas of the world, although in doing so, it is necessary to introduce certain modifications. As regards the Middle East, the Polar Frontal Theory is valuable as a basis, but the principles elaborated for higher latitudes do not always apply in detail.[1] This reservation concerns not only the mode or origin of fronts, but also the weather conditions prevailing in frontal zones.

The observer should therefore be ready to recognise that frontal analysis, although an extremely valuable approach, does not offer a complete explanation of the weather phenomena encountered in tropical and sub-tropical latitudes. Moreover, at the present stage of development of the science of meteorology, certain fundamental questions (particularly those concerning the reason for the development of high- and low-pressure areas) await a fuller answer.

The special situation of the Middle East with respect to temperature zones must first be noted. A link between Africa and Asia, the Middle East lies close to two of the hottest regions of the world, the Sahara, and N.W. India: yet at the same time it forms a part of the continent of Asia, which in winter develops the lowest temperatures occurring on the globe. Intermediate between these regions of extremes, the Middle East can easily fall for a short time under the influence of one or the

[1] One of these concerns conditions at a warm front, i.e. the boundary between cold air and an advancing warm mass. In high latitudes this is regarded essentially as a stable area, but in the tropics marked instability, leading to thunderstorms, is frequently observed.

other; and the relative closeness of such reservoirs of heat and cold means that little modification can take place as air currents make their way outwards from their regions of origin. Here is the first contrast with cool temperate latitudes: air arriving in N.W. Europe, for example, whether polar or tropical in origin, is nearly always considerably modified during its long journey north or south, and best described as relatively cold (polar) or warm (tropical); but in the Middle East little doubt as to area of origin is possible. By reason of its scorching heat and dust-laden appearance, African air can be felt and seen to be a 'breath of the desert'; whilst at other times cold spells of Siberian intensity may freeze rivers in the north and east.

It is customary to divide air masses according to their area of origin, either polar or tropical. Further division is then made on the basis of humidity – continental air is generally drier than that originating over oceans. This gives four main types of air masses: polar maritime and polar continental; and tropical maritime and tropical continental. Division on these lines is, however, not entirely satisfactory for the Middle East, since maritime influences are less important, and continental origins cannot always be simply defined as tropical or polar.

For the purposes of this study, the following classification of air masses is adopted:

(1) Monsoon air, originating over the Indian Ocean and therefore tropical maritime, but considerably modified by the time of arrival in the Middle East.
(2) Maritime air from the Atlantic, reaching the Middle East via the Mediterranean. This can be either tropical or polar in origin.
(3) Tropical continental air.
(4) Polar continental air.

Monsoon Air. A feature of the summer months only, and brought into the Middle East by the development of summer low pressure. This air originates over the Indian Ocean, and is drawn into the interior of India from the month of June onwards. Initially very moist, the monsoon current becomes progressively drier during its passage of the Deccan and Ganges valley; and on arrival in Iran, it is almost completely devoid of moisture. An occasional shower may occur on final uplift over the Makran and eastern Zagros ranges, but for the rest of its course no rain clouds develop. During its passage over Iran, Armenia, and Asia Minor, the air is relatively stale, and stability is increased by slight adiabatic warming on descent from the Anatolian plateau to the Mediterranean (Fig. 7).

A short sea passage in the west is insufficient to restore its former high humidity, and the air arrives in Egypt and the Levant largely unaffected, except in the lowest layer. The Mediterranean has, however, some slight influence in that the lowest 2,000 feet of the air mass become highly charged with moisture. This is insufficient to give rise to rainfall, but a marked cloud effect is seen on the coast of the Mediterranean, and onshore winds are extremely humid. Dry conditions, however, persist above 2,000 feet, and the whole mass becomes dried out at a short distance inland.

For the rest of its course, the monsoonal current remains dry; and over most of the interior of S.W. Asia clear skies are common, with days and sometimes weeks of entire absence of cloud – an indication of the extent to which the original monsoon air has been modified.

Inflow of unmodified (i.e. humid) monsoon air from Africa occurs on a small scale in southern Arabia, and gives rise to the summer maximum of rainfall in the Yemen and Dhofar, comparable in regime, though not in amount, with that of India. (See footnote 2, p. 37.)

From the beginning of June till mid-September, no other air mass penetrates into the Middle East, so strongly developed is the monsoonal circulation. Later in September, however, bursts of maritime air from the Mediterranean increasingly disturb the monsoonal flow, and finally displace it towards the end of autumn. Some cooler and more unstable air from Russia and the Black Sea may also reach the Middle East at this time.

Maritime Air. Dampness is the chief characteristic, but a generally lower temperature is also found. This air usually originates over the Atlantic, passing into the Mediterranean either by way of N.W. Europe, Spain, or N.W. Africa. There may thus be considerable differences in the air mass itself, some parts being polar and others tropical in origin. Temperature characteristics are, however, modified during the long passage over land and sea, so that often on arrival in the eastern Mediterranean no special features can be discerned. Humidity is, on the other hand, largely unaltered, as the track of the air has lain over sea areas. On uplift, or on inter-mixture with other masses, considerable condensation takes place, with consequent heavy rainfall.

Maritime air currents blowing generally from a westerly direction penetrate the entire Middle East region between October and May.

Differences set up by slight changes within the air mass itself, or by

interaction with other masses of more widely divergent type, give rise
to disturbances which produce a kind of weather similar to that of the
cyclonic belt of cool temperate latitudes. Strings of small depressions
are a feature of the maritime regime, and the intensity of these latter
depends upon the degree of contrast in temperature and humidity of
the varied air masses that form them (Fig. 8, top left).

Maritime air exerts its greatest influence on the western margins of
the Middle East, but we have seen that depressions can penetrate as far
east as Iran. Like the monsoon current in India, the westerlies of the
Middle East become progressively drier as they advance into the continental interior, and the weather disturbances to which they give rise
become increasingly feeble.

The inflow of maritime air, although predominant throughout much
of the year between October and May, is interrupted from time to

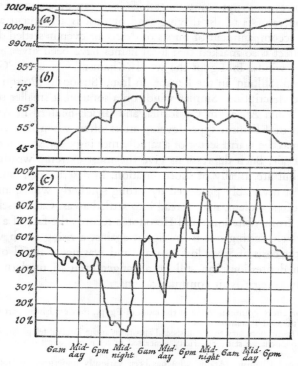

Fig. 10. Shlouq Conditions in Syria, March 10th to 12th, 1928
(after Dubertret and Weulersse). (a) pressure; (b) temperature;
(c) relative humidity

time by outbursts of air of two largely differing types, that are yet to be considered.

Tropical Continental Air. A feature of the Middle East is the proximity of wide expanses of desert, from which intensely hot and dry air may be drawn by the passage of depressions. If a southerly gradient of pressure develops, air from North Africa and Arabia floods northwards on a large scale, producing highly special weather conditions (Fig. 8, bottom left, and Fig. 10).

A portion of the great quantity of heat energy is transferred to the pressure field, giving rise to strong winds, which frequently reach gale force. Temperatures rise – sometimes by 30° or 40° F. in a few hours; and relative humidity falls to figures of less than 10 per cent. Crops may be withered in a day, a rise in the death rate is often noticed in large cities[1] and nervous tension and irritability affect most people. Electrical disturbances interrupt communications, and can be a danger to telephone operators,[2] whilst driving sand or dust is a frequent and unpleasant accompaniment of bursts of desert air even in settled districts.

The effect is so marked that local names have been given to these southerly winds. In Egypt the word 'Khamsin'[3] is used, 'Gibli' in Libya, and 'Shlouq' in the Levant. In Iran, 'Simoom' (Poison Wind) is a good description. Similar winds on a somewhat smaller scale are termed 'Santa Annas' in California, and 'Brick-fielders' in Australia.

Winds of Khamsin type develop most often when tropical air is drawn in as the warm sector of a rapidly moving depression formed in maritime air. Such depressions give the most extreme weather conditions, but are usually of short duration. In desert areas, sandstorms are almost invariably produced by strong southerly winds, and these storms, often violent, may spread into settled areas. Cairo itself is not immune from visitations; and Herodotus records the fate of a Persian army which, setting out from Egypt against a rising south wind to subdue the oasis of Siwa, lost its way, and was never heard of again. Khamsin depressions can still be a danger even to modern armies, especially as regards air communications.

---

[1] Such an effect, common today in the cities of Egypt, may explain in part the Tenth Plague of the Old Testament.

[2] It was found necessary to install special apparatus at the Tobruk telephone exchange, in order to discharge static electricity generated in telephone wires during periods of low humidity.

[3] The word Khamsin (Arabic *fifty*) has been variously understood to refer to the average duration of the hot wind (50 hours), to its annual frequency (50 times) and to its season of maximum onset, the fifty days including and after the Coptic Easter. The third explanation seems to us closest to the truth.

Autumn and spring, particularly the latter, are the chief seasons at which hot winds occur. In spring, the southern deserts heat up rapidly whilst the rest of the Middle East is still cold, and favourable conditions are thus established for mixture of differing air streams. Owing to the extreme dryness of the desert air, rainfall, which normally results from mixing of two air masses, is very scanty or entirely absent.

The frequency of hot spells during the season when new crops are beginning to grow is particularly unfortunate (chiefly spring, but also autumn, as both winter and summer crops are grown). Much damage can be done to young plants.

Polar Continental Air. In winter and spring, waves of cold air flow southward and westward from the intensely cold interior of Eurasia. Two widely differing types of air can be distinguished. The first, originating in south-central Asia, overflows into Iran, and may for a short time reach the Mediterranean. The air is cold, but very stable, deriving from the Siberian anticyclone, and days are fine and clear. Over the Iranian and Anatolian plateaus very low temperatures occur but sunshine during the day mitigates the worst effects, particularly as humidity is low (Fig. 8, top right).

Further to the west, the air undergoes slight adiabatic heating as it descends the edges of the Zagros, and the plateaus of Anatolia and Syria. Fine weather prevails, with low temperatures inland, but moderately warm conditions on the coastlands. Fog, the frequent accompaniment of winter high pressure in western Europe, is absent, as the air is very dry.[1] Anticyclonic waves are frequent in the Middle East during autumn and the early part of winter; but later in the year continental air of a very different type makes its way in from the north-west (Fig. 8, bottom right).

Anticyclonic conditions frequently develop in central and eastern Europe during January, February, and March. A reservoir of cold air builds up, and this, unlike the air outflowing from the dry heart of Asia, is damp, since it is merely chilled and modified maritime air originating from the Atlantic. From time to time, currents of this European air are drawn into the rear of a cycle of depressions moving east along the Mediterranean; and on reaching the Middle East, the lower layers of this quasi-continental air have been subjected to contact heating during the southward passage over the warm sea. Considerable quantities of moisture have also been absorbed.

---

[1] Fog occurs for the most part in the Middle East only during inflow of maritime air from the west.

Unlike the adiabatic heating of the Asiatic continental air, which affects all layers, differential heating of only the lowest layers in the European current produces much instability; and this, together with high humidity, gives rise to heavy rainfall of a showery type.[1] Practically all the snowfall, and much of the rainfall of the Middle East, develop in outbursts of cold damp air from central and eastern Europe. Late winter and early spring are unpleasant seasons, liable to prolonged periods of raw, cold conditions, with frequent and heavy precipitation. If these conditions persist for any length of time, they may become intensified as much colder Arctic air ultimately becomes drawn across central Europe from the north. This can give periods of thoroughly unsettled and unseasonable weather for a few days even as far south as the Sahara and central Egypt.

FRONTAL DEVELOPMENT

The 'classic' theory of Polar Depressions postulates the existence in most atmospheric depressions of the 'warm sector', bounded on the side towards which the depression is advancing, by a warm front; and on the rear, by a cold front. As the depression matures, the entire warm sector becomes occluded in the mass of cold air, that is, it is lifted away from the surface; and the two fronts coalesce to form an occluded front, in which the characteristics of both warm and cold fronts are to some extent combined.

As regards depressions affecting the Middle East, several qualifications must be made to this general theory. In the first place, many depressions form air masses that are homogeneous – that is, without discontinuities of temperature and pressure. Frontal conditions are therefore absent, and weather is fine. The summer low of Cyprus is an outstanding example, and we have the curious position that although pressure is on average distinctly lower in summer than in winter over most of the Middle East (because of the persistence of monsoonal lows), weather is almost uniformly good. Similar, but more transitory nonfrontal depressions also occur in winter.

We have noted that in cases where warm air is drawn northwards to form the warm sector of a normal frontal depression, dryness of the warm air, or the generally high temperature of the entire region, may

[1] Heating applied equally to an entire air mass raises the temperature absolutely, but does not alter the temperature *difference* between highest and lowest layers and has therefore no effect on the stability of the air mass. Heating applied only to the lowest layer increases this difference, and hence tends to produce instability.

prevent the development of weather conditions usually present at a warm front. In higher latitudes air forming a warm sector has almost always travelled over oceanic areas, and is extremely damp; hence it gives rise to a dense mass of cloud extending for several hundred miles in advance of the warm front. Moderate, but prolonged and steady, rainfall is highly characteristic of such frontal developments. In the Middle East, however, warm air originates in continental areas, and, initially very dry, has no prolonged sea track during which it could absorb moisture. Warm fronts are thus very infrequent and poorly developed – some occurring almost entirely without cloud. As a factor affecting rainfall, their influence is slight.

Rainfall in the Middle East is almost entirely from cold fronts, which show an especially marked development. Cold fronts are always regions of instability, and this phenomenon tends to be greatly increased over regions of high relief. Cold fronts meeting mountain ranges or plateau edges are therefore much intensified; but rapid weakening also occurs on the leeward side of the high ground. In this way, wide variation in climatic conditions may occur, since local topography assumes great importance in the development of weather. Rainfall is heavy on the windward side of mountain ranges, but much reduced on the leeward side. This helps to explain why the edge of the Syrian desert approaches so closely to the shores of the Mediterranean, although prevailing winds are onshore throughout most of the year.

Depressions of N.W. Europe develop fronts that are in active motion, and aligned in a characteristic pattern *across* the isobars. Exceptions occur in the Middle East when a boundary develops between two air masses, and frontal conditions are set up along a line *parallel* to the isobars (Fig. 11). The phenomenon of air mass boundaries, using the term as implying something different from the 'front' of Bjerknes, is of importance in the Middle East, where air masses of different qualities may flow side by side without giving rise to the rapid formation of an atmospheric depression such as would occur in higher latitudes. Asia Minor and Libya are most liable to develop boundary fronts of this type, which are often more persistent than normal fronts. The practical importance of such boundary fronts is greatest for the meteorologist: to the student of climate, chief interest lies in the indication that air mass climatology developed for higher latitudes may not always apply in similarly precise detail to warmer regions.

TEMPERATURE AND HUMIDITY

Chief features are the high temperatures of summer, and a wide range, both annual and diurnal. Clear skies are the main factor in developing intense heating; and it is useful to note the contrast with regions nearer the equator, where a summer rainfall restricts direct insolation, owing to the prevalence of cloud.

Minor influences are the mountainous coastline of much of the Middle East, which limits the tempering influence of the sea to a

AVERAGE TEMPERATURE IN JULY

	° F.		° F.
Cairo	83	Colon	80
Beirut	82	Freetown	78
Basra	97	Bombay	80
Teheran	85	Delhi	86

narrow strip; and the absence of soil and vegetation, which favours intense heating of the arid surface.

In view of the wide range of temperatures, both daily and seasonal,

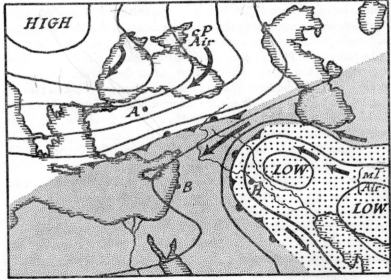

Fig. 11. Variation in Air Mass, with characteristic alignment of Fronts, during period 24–26/3/45. A – Ankara, temp. 36° F.; B – Beirut, 61° F.; H – Habbaniya, 72° F.; Large dots – unmodified tropical air; Stipple – modified continental air

averages such as those quoted above give a somewhat misleading impression of actual conditions, and it is preferable to refer to average maxima and minima of temperature. For instance, in the table above, it would seem that temperatures in Cairo and Beirut are very similar: in fact, Cairo often tops 100° F. during the day, but has a cool night; Beirut rarely rises above 90° F., but there is only 11° difference between day and night temperatures. The figures below will bring out more clearly the extent to which conditions actually experienced differ from statistical means.

A marked simplicity of rhythm prevails throughout the Middle East. With a few exceptions, July is the hottest month inland, but on the coast, the maximum is delayed until August, because of the slower absorption of heat by the sea. Egypt shows a good example of this tendency, with a July maximum in the Nile valley, and an August maximum on the Mediterranean and Red Sea coasts. Towards the extreme south, in Upper Egypt and Arabia, the maximum tends to occur in June, under the influence of the more direct solar heating at the solstice.

January is everywhere the coldest month, but any considerable rise in temperature is often delayed until the end of February or early March. Once begun, however, this is rapid. Considerable differences are apparent in winter between the north-eastern part of the Middle

AVERAGE MEAN MAXIMA AND MINIMA, AND RANGE OF TEMPERATURE (° F.)

	Monthly Av.		Mean Daily Max.		Mean Daily Min.		Diurnal Range		Annual Range
	Jan.	July	Jan.	July	Jan.	July	Jan.	July	
Istanbul	41	74	46	82	38	67	8	25	33
Ankara	28	73	39	86	17	54	22	32	45
Aleppo	42	83	50	97	34	69	16	28	41
Beirut	56	82	62	87	50	76	12	11	26
Mosul	41	95	50	110	32	80	18	30	54
Basra	52	97	62	111	42	81	20	30	45
Jerusalem	47	75	54	87	41	63	11	24	28
Teheran	35	85	44	99	26	71	18	28	50
Cairo	54	84	63	96	45	72	9	24	30
Alexandria	59	80	66	86	51	73	15	13	22*
Tobruk	56	79	62	84	51	73	11	11	13*
Aden	79	88	85	94	73	82	12	12	9

* Taken between January and August (hottest months).

C

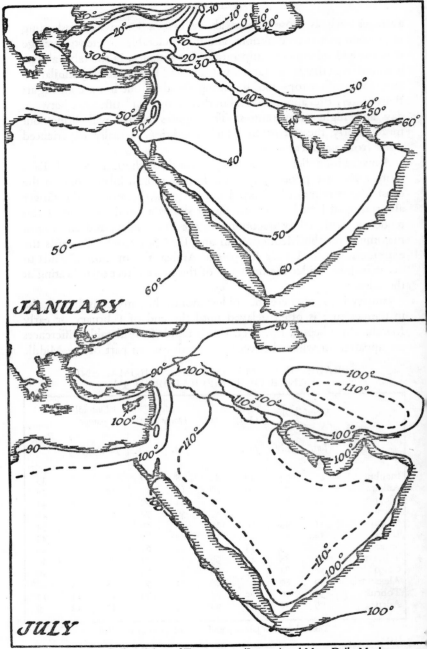

Fig. 12. Mean Daily Minima of Temperature (January) and Mean Daily Maxima (July). Broken isotherms based on scanty data

East, and the centre and south. Continental influences are marked in the former area, and these are heightened by the effects of topography. Extremely low temperatures occur in Asia Minor, Armenia, and much of Iran. Meteorological observations are scanty, but one small permanent glacier is known to exist in the Zagros, and conditions at Erzerum indicate the intensity of winter cold. (January mean 12° F., average day max. 34°, average night min. – 17°, absolute min. – 40° F.)

The Bosphorus and Black Sea sometimes become jammed by pack-ice; and inland, snowstorms isolate many districts, even as far south as Syria, where the Beirut–Damascus railway runs for a few miles in permanent snowsheds. Small quantities of snow may fall in regions of lower elevation, and except for southern Arabia, no part of the Middle East can be said to be entirely free from snowfall. Even the plateau of Cyrenaica, the lower Nile valley, and the highlands of Yemen experience slight falls, when cold air makes its way south from Europe. In Libya, the edge of the Tripolitanian Jebel may have several feet of snow, and Garian in this area which records one of the highest temperatures in the Middle East, may also experience 2–4 feet of winter snow.

Diurnal variation of temperature is important at all seasons, but most developed in summer. In coastal areas, maritime influences restrict the temperature range; but at a short distance inland, great heat during the day gives place at night to a most refreshing coolness. In Egypt, and the Red Sea coastlands, night cooling may even bring the air below its dew-point, so that early morning fog is a feature of the late spring and early summer in parts of the Red Sea coast, the Lower Nile valley, and even the Mediterranean coast of the Libyan desert. Topography is a controlling factor – regions of high altitude have a reduced night temperature, although by day little difference is apparent. (Cf. the July minima for Istanbul and Ankara, or Basra and Teheran.) The Lebanon derives much wealth from numerous mountain resorts which by day have a temperature of over 80° F., whilst at night temperature falls by 20° or 30°, as compared with 10° on the coast.

Humidity. The Middle East shows considerable local variation in humidity – perhaps the widest of any region in the world. An average estimate for the area as a whole would show 50 to 70 per cent. relative humidity – a figure much below the average for Europe. On the coast, however, some unusually high humidities can occur. Wherever a narrow coastal plain is backed by a mountain barrier, well-developed sea breezes bring in much moisture, which remains concentrated in the coastal zone, instead of spreading into the interior. High humidity, together with high temperatures, makes living conditions extremely unpleasant during the summer season, when inland transfer of moisture from the sea is greatest. Certain parts of the Middle East have an unenviable reputation in this respect: the Persian Gulf coast is most notorious but the shores of the Red Sea and Mediterranean are also unpleasantly affected.

'Jidda', de Gaury writes, 'is hot and damp almost beyond belief for some three hundred days of the year. . . . Newspapers flop into rag, matches refuse to strike, and keys rust in the pocket.'

In some places (e.g. Beirut and Oman), humidity is actually at its highest for the year during the summer months, in spite of a complete absence of rainfall, and dew can occur on 200–250 days per annum, producing up to a quarter of the total recorded precipitation. Heavy dew on the Red Sea coastlands is an important aid to agriculture in the Yemen, and in this respect, one will recall the similarity with western California.

NUMBER OF DAYS WITH DEW AT HAIFA (1938)

J	F	M	A	M	J	J	A	S	O	N	D	Total
o	3	1	11	17	25	18	19	22	19	o	o	135

In the interior, humidity is generally low, but a marked increase often occurs in winter, when maritime air replaces the dried-out monsoonal streams of summer. Winter mist and fog are by no means uncommon; and although these occur generally in riverine valleys, they are also met with in arid areas. The salt marshes and deserts of Iran experience winter fogs which are at times dangerous to travellers.

Tolerance. The effects of high humidity in bringing down for humans the limit of tolerability of high temperatures are very marked. Hence the high temperatures of the dry interior are often more easily borne than the muggy heat of the coastlands, and Beirut, with a summer maximum of 89° F. (70 per cent. R. Hum.), feels quite as hot and exhausting as Damascus (97° F., 30 to 40 per cent. R. Hum.).

It is also interesting to note one physiological effect of very low humidity. After a short time the nervous system is unduly stimulated, and irritability and nervous strain develop. In the Sahara, where low humidity is frequent, the name *cafard* has been given by Foreign Legionaires to the peculiar state of mind resulting, at least in part, from continued exposure to dry heat.

Something has been said of the deleterious effects of certain features of Middle East climate; but a more important aspect remains. Average conditions approach closely to the optimum for human and plant life. The extremes of prolonged growth-retarding cold, and overwhelming heat, are limited to certain regions only, and the influence of climate on the rise of civilisation in the Middle East would seem to have been profound. Primitive man, unable greatly to change his material environment, found best help in the region of 'summer's shine and winter's rain'.

RAINFALL

Except in two small regions, one in the extreme north, and the other in the extreme south, the whole of the Middle East has a strongly marked Mediterranean rhythm of summer drought and winter rain. The underlying cause is inflow of maritime air from the west, due to the southward migration of certain pressure zones during the winter, which brings the disturbed zone of westerlies over the Mediterranean. During summer, higher pressures in the western Mediterranean act as a buffer between the low pressures of the north Atlantic and the monsoonal lows of the Middle East, shutting out oceanic influences from the west. For the western Mediterranean then, these highs can thus be regarded as directly influencing the development of dry conditions. It is, however, hardly correct to regard the summer drought of the Middle East as directly due to the elaboration of a single zone of high pressure covering the whole of the Mediterranean, since we have seen that in the Middle East region, pressures are actually lower in summer than in winter.

ATMOSPHERIC PRESSURE
(monthly average in millibars)

	Benghazi Sea Level	Istanbul Sea Level	Limassol Sea Level	Basra Sea Level	Muscat Sea Level
Jan.	1010	1019	1017	1019	1019
July	1005	1012	1007	997	998

Rainfall occurs in early autumn, when dry air of the monsoonal circulation is shouldered out by damper and more vigorous currents from the west. A few short showers only occur during September, but towards the end of October, heavier and more prolonged falls, often with spectacular thunderstorms, announce the end of summer. These usually clear up after a few days; and a relatively fine period ensues until December. The real rainy season does not begin until about Christmas, and may even be delayed until the New Year. Over the western half of the Middle East, January is the rainiest month but a slight tendency to a December maximum is noticeable in a few areas. Towards the east, the maximum is increasingly delayed. Syria shows a January maximum in the extreme west, and a February maximum in the remainder of the country. In eastern Iraq and in Iran, March is often the wettest month; and on the shores of the Caspian, a double rhythm with a minor maximum in spring and a main maximum in autumn shows the influence of a different climatic regime.

Such influences are also apparent in Asia Minor, where the Black Sea coastlands as far west as Sinop have a pronounced autumnal maximum. In the Aegean area, November or December are the wettest months, but on the Mediterranean coast, more normal Middle East conditions once again prevail, and the maximum occurs in January or February. Inland, much local variation occurs, with traces of a double maxima in spring and autumn. Konya, with a maximum of 1·9 inches both in May and December, is probably typical of many parts of the western plateau; and Diyarbekir, with a single maximum in March, shows the approach to Mesopotamian conditions further to the east.

By the middle of June, rain has ceased over most of the Middle East, and south of a line from the Elburz range to Iskanderun and Crete, no rain falls for a period of ten to fifteen weeks. North of this line, a certain rainfall persists, though rather irregular, and except on the eastern Black Sea coast, very small in amount.

The distribution of rainfall in the Middle East is largely controlled by two factors: topography and the disposition of land and sea in relation to rain-bearing winds. It must be remembered that the Middle East is predominantly a continental area, influenced only in certain regions by proximity of relatively small areas of sea. Hence air masses reaching the Middle East from the west, even though of oceanic origin, have lost some of their moisture; and it is only where a sea track has allowed partial rejuvenation that considerable rainfall can develop.

It might therefore be said that in most regions, rainfall tends to occur in proportion to the length of coastline – or even in proportion to the length of westward-facing coastline. Regional contrasts are striking: the westward-facing shore of the Gulf of Sirte has a marked effect on the rainfall of Cyrenaica; and the absence of such configuration in Egypt condemns the country to a scanty rainfall. At Benghazi, at the western end of the Cyrenaican Jebel, annual rainfall amounts to over 11 inches, with 15-20 inches over the hills to the east, as compared with 3 inches at Port Said. The narrowness of the Red Sea is reflected in the lower rainfall of Arabia: whilst, on the other hand, the influence of the broader Mediterranean is clearly shown in Asia Minor and Levant. It is also believed that the proximity of the Persian Gulf has a favourable effect on the rainfall in the Zagros.

With such a delicate balance between dampness and aridity, it is inevitable that altitude should exercise a control equally as important, if not more so, than that of physical configuration. It has already been stated that the greater part of the Middle East rainfall develops under conditions of instability, to which the uplift of air currents as they are forced to rise over mountain ranges, is a very powerful contributing factor. Warm frontal rainfall develops over a vertical distance of as much as 25,000 feet; and a few thousand feet of dynamical uplift in the lowest layers has no undue effect, as ascent of air has begun independently of conditions near the ground, and precipitation continues after high land is past. On the other hand, a cold front may not develop any precipitation whatever until the 'trigger action' of sudden uplift over high ground is first applied. Attention has been drawn to the marked predominance of cold frontal conditions in the Middle East.

Control by topography is so great that isohyets tend to follow contour lines, with westward-facing mountain ranges or plateau edges experiencing heavier rainfall at the expense of eastward-facing slopes and lowlands. The swing of the isohyets in response to the south-eastwards curve of the Turkish highlands towards the Zagros system gives rise to the beautifully developed 'fertile crescent' of steppe land linking the east and west of the Old World. Control by topography has resulted in the elaboration of striking regional contrasts – a short journey brought the Israelites from the rain-shadow areas of Sinai and eastern Jordan into the milk and honey of the damper uplands of Judaea; and Palmyra, a caravan city of the Syrian desert, could pasture its beasts of burden on the grassy spurs of the Anti-Lebanon ranges a few miles away.

In view of its occurrence under conditions of instability, rainfall in the Middle East is often extremely heavy, but short in duration, and very capricious. The coastlands of the Levant, with an annual fall of over 30 inches, receive more rain than parts of the British Isles, but this is crowded into little more than six months; and even so, the wettest month has only fourteen to seventeen rainy days. Conditions at the

Cedars, a mountain resort 6,000 feet above sea level, and one of the wettest places in the Middle East, are illustrative (Fig. 13).

A great deal of rain may thus fall in a short time. One inch per hour is by no means unusual; and in 1945 Damascus, with an annual average of less than 10 inches, received 4 inches in a single morning. 'Cloud-bursts' are a feature of most years, but their effects are often extremely local, so that one side of a street may be quite dry, whilst the other is streaming with rain. Jarvis described a small valley of the Sinai region that had produced a record grain crop, yet two miles away, there had been insufficient rain to germinate the seed.

Rainfall is exceedingly variable in amount from year to year. There

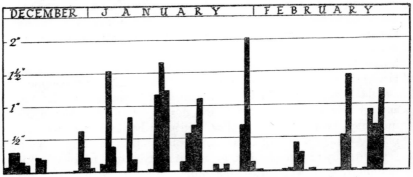

Fig. 13. Daily Rainfall at the Cedars, 1943–4. (Data by D. Buchanan)

is little to parallel the regular onset of monsoonal rains in India; and the failure of rain in a particular season is a source of considerable and frequent anxiety to the cultivator. Averages are again misleading; few regions outside the highlands can count on a regular rainfall, and whole areas in Egypt and Arabia may go years without a fall of any kind. A heavy fall once in several years appears in climatic statistics averaged out as a fictitious annual figure. Some, but not all, of the summer rain in Turkey and Persia is of this type. In successive years, Jerusalem once had 41 inches of rainfall, then 12; and Baghdad 17 and 2 inches; whilst drought is the rule in Libya about two years in ten.

ANNUAL RAINFALL AT KSARA (CENTRAL LEBANON)
(inches)

1920	1921	1922	1923	1924	1925	1926	1927	1928	1929	1930	1931	1932
15	24	27	24	28	15	37	23	24	34	19	25	13

Some distinction must now be made in the case of two regions lying outside the area of true Mediterranean climate. In the extreme north, the summer track of westerly winds lies across central Europe into southern Russia. Reference has already been made to the fact that this air stream is kept out of the central and western Mediterranean by a 'cushion' of high pressure; but in the north-east, intermingling with monsoonal air takes place, and a perceptible summer rainfall occurs. We have seen that over much of Asia Minor, the summer is not entirely arid; and in the eastern Black Sea, a tendency to develop atmospheric disturbances is accentuated by the westward-facing coast, backed by the Caucasus Mountains. The eastern Black Sea coastal region of Turkey has a pronounced summer rainfall, and so falls outside the Mediterranean climatic zone. Small, and of restricted importance, this region belongs, climatically speaking, to the Caucasus provinces of Russia. Conditions at Rize are typical, and contrast with those of Istanbul, which has a dry, but not entirely arid summer.

RAINFALL (inches)

	J	F	M	A	M	J	J	A	S	O	N	D	Total
Rize	9·2	8·3	6·6	5·8	2·9	6·6	8·9	6·8	12·4	11·8	13·3	12·3	105·3
Istanbul	3·2	2·7	2·5	1·6	1·2	1·3	1·2	1·7	2·0	2·7	3·6	4·8	28·8

Some reference has also been made to a degenerate form of monsoonal conditions prevailing in south-west Arabia. Information is lacking, but there would appear to be heavy summer rains over the highlands of the Sudan, Abyssinia, and the Yemen. As much as 25 inches may fall in the region of Sa'ana while, on the coast, Aden averages only 2 inches per annum, with a spring maximum that shows an affinity to Mediterranean conditions.

An interesting point which follows from what has so far been stated concerning rainfall, is that so far there would seem to be little in Middle Eastern rainfall to parallel the 'cycles' of Bruckner and Penck – one difficulty, however, being the lack of statistics covering a long period.

Cloudiness. Study of clouds is more the concern of the meteorologist, but it is useful for the climatologist to note a few general tendencies in cloud development as indicative of climatic features. Conditions in Syria–Lebanon provide an accurate summary of the Middle East as a whole. Damascus typifies the open, arid interior; and Beirut, where a range of mountains rises to 9,000 feet behind the city, the damper coastlands.

MEAN CLOUD AMOUNT
(tenths of sky covered)

	J	F	M	A	M	J	J	A	S	O	N	D
Damascus	5	5	3	3	3	1	0	0	1	3	4	5
Beirut	6	6	5	5	4	2	2	3	2	3	5	6

The small amount of cloud prevailing at all seasons is very remarkable. Even Beirut, with 35 inches of rain annually, has no more than six-tenths of cloud during its wettest month. This is because most of the cloud is of the cumuliform type, rapid in development, but equally rapid in clearance. In summer, fair-weather cumulus develops regularly each morning, and disperses at dusk, so that nights are always quite clear; and even in winter, the same tendency to nocturnal clearance is present. Days of thick layer cloud, with prolonged rain, are very uncommon; and usually, even the rainiest day of mid-winter clears for some time to allow a glimpse of the sun.

VARIATION OF CLIMATE WITHIN HISTORIC TIME

One cannot proceed very far in any study of environment in the Middle East without encountering the problem of a possible variation in climatic conditions. Much of the geomorphology of the area points overwhelmingly to some major changes in climate: periglacial and torrential deposits that are frequent even in such relatively small upland areas as the Lebanon and Anti-Lebanon piedmonts; the extensive occurrence of fluviatile deposits in now arid areas; strand lines, both marine and continental, as already referred to; and finally, the misfit and attenuated river systems of the present day in relation to land forms. Moreover, it is difficult to relate contemporary conditions of frequently hostile climatic environment to the brilliant historical past of many Middle Eastern countries.

At a first examination conditions would appear strongly to suggest marked climatic change at a relatively recent period, with progressive desiccation as the main feature. It is in fact indisputable that in comparatively recent geological time, a wetter climate prevailed. Many of the rock series of late Tertiary and Quaternary Age were deposited locally in the Middle East under conditions of greater precipitation; and other evidence suggests that in Quaternary times cycles of colder wetter weather, comparable to those of Europe, produced ice-cap conditions in the plateaus of Turkey and Persia. Further evidence comes from archaeological sources, indicating that early human settlement was considerable north and south of the mountain zone, but sparse or entirely lacking in the highlands themselves. Some results of investigation suggest that present-day land forms in the Sinai, and central and eastern Lebanon, are at least in part the work of ice; though these views are not undisputed, it is obvious that much of the erosion and deposition could not occur under a semi-arid climatic regime.

It is more certain that the erosive power of the Nile was in certain regions much greater than now, and the existence of extremely deeply incised wadis on the land-surfaces around the head of the Red Sea suggest a phase of much wetter climate. Other evidence comes from the existence of 'fossil soils' in regions now too dry to produce comparable developments; and a further important feature is the occurrence of surface depressions, or closed basins, especially in Libya, Egypt, and the Arabian deserts, which show some signs of original erosion by water – though this is by no means the whole story. Finally, there is recent evidence (from pollen analysis) that as late as 3000 B.C. a fully 'Mediterranean' flora extended as far south as the Tibesti Highlands – i.e. some 1,000–2,000 miles further south than now.

With these points in mind, it would seem reasonable to infer that minor climatic changes have continued into modern times, and that during the historic period (i.e. from about 4000 B.C. onwards) rainfall has tended to decrease. Again, there is much in the historic period that can be interpreted as evidence of desiccation. Many irrigation works now stand ruined or neglected in completely arid areas. Buried dams, empty channels, and dry wells or cisterns, often located in places where there is no obvious water supply, would seem to show that surface water has become scarcer. In some instances, modern efforts have been made to repair ancient irrigation works, with varying results. Certain wells were cleared in Jordan, with the hope of finding water, but most of these remained dry. Further to the south, however, near the Gulf of Akaba, a number of Roman channels were repaired, and a new flow of water occurred, corresponding exactly in amount with that for which the channels were originally designed.

On the human side, the great wealth and power in ancient times of countries of the Middle East can be taken as an indication of a larger population and a higher level of economic development. For most regions of the Middle East, it is easy to point to at least one former period of outstanding prosperity; and for the area as a whole, it is fair to say that population was more numerous in Roman and early

Islamic times even than at the present day. Numerous ruins, particularly on the desert margins, indicate both a richness of culture and an intensity of economic exploitation that is often far in advance of modern conditions. In north-west Syria whole towns lie abandoned – Devlin and Gillingham counted over a hundred settlements of Byzantine age within fifty miles of Aleppo – and in Persia many caravan routes are bordered by now deserted villages. Roman Palmyra was a commercial metropolis with continent-wide relations; the modern village, less in extent than the burial grounds of the ancient city, is largely dependent for its existence upon a military garrison.

To these physical and human considerations must be added certain biological factors. Ancient Egyptian and Mesopotamian art frequently depicted crocodiles or such animals as the lion and the gazelle – all of which are at home in a damper environment. Recent investigation has shown that a species of snail, which is restricted to regions with more than 20 inches of rainfall, once existed in the Libyan desert. In this case, however, it is probable that the snails are evidence only of wetter conditions at a period immediately subsequent to the Ice Age, and that they died out in Neolithic times.

On the basis of such evidence, Ellsworth Huntington postulated his well-known theories of gradual desiccation during historic time in south-west Asia. Unfortunately, however, later opinion inclines to the view that much of the evidence put forward by Huntington can be interpreted in more than one way; and that, on balance, facts are definitely against any major significant change in climate within the last five or six thousand years. A summary of present views suggests that between the sixth and the third millennia B.C. rainfall and humidity were distinctly greater than now. Shortly before 2000 B.C. a considerable change of climate supervened, producing conditions that were possibly even more arid than those of today. Ultimately, however, towards the end of the last millennium B.C. (i.e. some few centuries before the birth of Christ), there was some slight oscillation towards cooler and damper conditions, giving rise to the present climatic regime. From time to time, shorter temporary and local variations have also occurred – e.g. archaeological evidence suggests, without affording incontrovertible proof, that in a coastal zone some 30–50 miles deep extending from Tripolitania to the Nile Delta there has been slight desiccation over the last two thousand years.

Many ancient irrigation works were abandoned solely because of unsettled political conditions. Misrule and exaction, but most of all devastation due to war and barbarian invasion, have greatly reduced irrigation in the Middle East; and in a survey of the economic potentialities of Iraq in 1911, Sir W. Willcocks stated that the problem was in large measure that of restoring the ancient irrigation system, rather than that of developing entirely new canals. At the same time, it is undoubtedly true that in some instances the water table in the soil has fallen. This can, however, be ascribed either to a lowering of the base line of drainage, due to continued erosion of the bed of the river;[1] or to a loss of sub-surface water because of soil erosion following destruction of the surface vegetation, including deforestation. The latter is a pronounced feature of many parts of the Middle East. Reckless cutting of trees, for timber and fuel, unrestricted grazing by herds of animals, and unintelligent methods of agriculture in a land occupied continuously since the dawn of history, have greatly contributed to extensive soil erosion, with consequent decrease in water resources.

Moreover, archaeological research has shown that many of the deserted settlements were not contemporaneous – that is, they were not all inhabited at one particular time. Many factors – security, economic resources, or even, as commonly in the Middle East, a growing problem of sanitation, may have caused the abandonment of one site in favour of another; so that a survey of settlement cannot, of itself, be taken as a reliable indication of population density. Even now, it is unwise to regard the size of a modern Oriental city as strictly indicative of the number of its inhabitants, because although some parts are heavily overcrowded, others may be completely derelict and abandoned.

The long continuity of life in the Middle East suggests that little change has taken place in environmental conditions. Desert herders – 'plain men living in tents' – are as characteristic of modern times as of the age of Jacob; and agricultural technique, portrayed in ancient literature and art, still survives in many places with little alteration at the present day. Moreover, the weather conditions described in early literature bear close resemblance to actual conditions now – we have seen something of this earlier in the chapter from the writings of Herodotus – and many of the relics of Ancient Egypt would hardly have survived had the climate of the country been damper.

Another important point is the permanence of overland trade routes across arid regions. Caravans have followed tracks through certain

---

[1] The river Nile is known to have lowered its bed by 23 feet at one point since 1900 B.C., and though this is an extreme case, other instances could be cited.

oases for many centuries, and any deviations that occurred were largely due to unsettled political conditions – routes now drier than those at present in use do not seem ever to have been followed. It is difficult to see why such cities as Damascus and Aleppo should have maintained their function as points of departure for desert traffic over several thousand years if we assume that the cities did not at one time lie on the border between steppe and desert. The existence of the series of ancient caravan centres – Medina, Petra, Jerash, Bosra, Damascus, Palmyra, Aleppo, and Dura-Europus – can be related to present conditions of rainfall; if we move the desert boundary further inland, these towns lose their *raison d'être*. Similarly, many other ancient settlements of the Middle East show careful siting in relation to water supplies. This fact, together with the presence of numerous irrigation works, may be taken as showing that rainfall was no more plentiful then than now.

Another very important matter is the existence of very large sand dunes in the deserts of North Africa and Arabia. Observed rates of accumulation of desert sand taken in relation to present-day size of dunes, which can be of the order of several hundred feet in height and 20–30 miles in length, strongly suggest that extremely arid conditions must have prevailed over many thousands of years.

In short, it would appear that wetter climatic conditions prevailed in the Middle East only in late Tertiary and Quaternary times. During this period, the comparatively recent land forms described in a previous chapter came into existence as the result of fluvial and sub-aerial erosion and also deposition. During Neolithic times, a period of desiccation accompanied the final retreat of the ice-cap in Eurasia; but by the opening of the historic era this increase in aridity had come to an end. Environmental changes which have supervened during the last five or six thousand years can be traced to one or more of the following causes: (a) lowering of the bed of the streams as the result of normal erosion. This has also lowered the water table in the soil itself, and left many irrigation canal intakes above the new water level; (b) soil erosion, due to wasteful agricultural methods, or to destruction of existing types of vegetation; and (c) misrule, war, and invasion. In this connexion it is interesting to note that experiments in French North Africa have shown that when the slope of land brought under cultivation exceeds 3–5 per cent., continuous cultivation using normal methods of ploughing will lead to almost complete soil erosion within ten years, to the point that the terrain is no longer usable.

By these means, a deeper layer of soil, and thicker vegetation cover, both relics of earlier wetter periods, were gradually removed. This natural patrimony might have been preserved by careful utilisation, but once soil and vegetation had disappeared, natural conditions were against a renewal. Thus it is man, and not natural causes, who is chiefly responsible for the gradual deterioration of conditions in the Middle East; and human occupation, not climatic variation, appears as the main factor in alteration of environment. This fact gives some hope for the future, because whereas man can do little to influence the operation of natural forces leading to climatic change, he can do much to repair damage that he himself has caused. If soil and vegetation could be restored, the prosperity of ancient days might return; and accordingly, emphasis is now being placed on soil conservation, re-afforestation, and intelligent exploitation of the land as essential elements in the future development of economic life in the Middle East.

CHAPTER IV

Soils and Natural Vegetation

I. SOILS OF THE MIDDLE EAST

Of recent years, considerable attention has been given to the question of soil character and development, and though many aspects still remain to be elucidated, knowledge of the soils of the Middle East has greatly advanced within the last few years, to the point that a number of generalised statements are now possible.

The soils of the Middle East are slow in forming, therefore often in thin or scanty layers, with a poorly defined structure and mineral constituents that show relatively little alteration. Organic material is scanty in amount, of considerable chemical complexity, and either spread relatively evenly through an entire soil layer or almost entirely absent except in the upper portions. Complexes of colloidal clays are often strongly developed; and a prominent feature is the occurrence of soluble compounds at the surface, or else at lower layers, either in the form of 'crusts' or of hard nodules. The predominance of calcium compounds is also highly characteristic; and in many parts strong concentrations of gypsum or other mineral salts are a feature.

Soil formation is still imperfectly understood in detail, but several elements contribute to the process. In the case of recently formed soils, the relationship between soil and parent rock is often close, and classification on a geological basis is sometimes undertaken. For more mature soils, however, climatic conditions exert an increasing, and most probably a predominant control – it has, for example, been shown by Reifenberg that in northern Israel limestone and basalt have weathered to give soils of almost identical chemical composition. Topography, and geomorphology – slope, relation to drainage, and mode of origin – also enter in; whilst a fourth important factor is the distribution and character of vegetation and animal life. Thus soil formation is an extremely complex process, controlled by several main agencies, with climate playing a highly significant part. Consequently, many modern investigators have attempted a classification of soils which is directly related in the main to climatic factors: although it is clear that even with such a scheme, other elements enter in.

It is useful here to refer to a general theory of soil development, which distinguishes an *eluvial* horizon (or layer), *from* which soluble compounds are washed by rainfall; and an *illuvial* horizon, into which these compounds are later carried by water action, and later redeposited. In humid climates, the greater transfer of soil water is downwards, and the top layers of soil therefore tend to form the eluvial horizon, with the illuvial layer below. In arid climates, scanty rainfall may penetrate the soil, but as the result of capillary attraction due to strong surface heating, it is soon drawn back to the surface, so that the final transfer of water may be upward, with an accumulation of mineral salts near the surface.

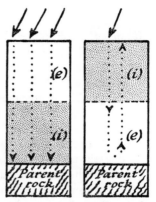

Fig. 14. Soil Profiles under Humid and Arid Climatic Conditions. Illuvial layer stippled

As the result of low rainfall in many parts of the Middle East, soils can thus often be of the second type, i.e. with the illuvial layer uppermost. Slightly greater rainfall or rapid mechanical percolation may, however, result also in an even distribution of some soluble elements throughout the soil layer – i.e. an obliteration of horizons. Finally, in a few favoured areas, substantial rainfall may produce the third condition of the eluvial layer above. Thus a fairly wide range of soil type characterises the Middle East as a whole, with conditions varying from the often heavily saline (alkaline) deposits of arid regions to the leached, almost podsolised (acidic) soils of the higher mountain zones. The following summarises the views of several investigators into soil types and conditions in the Middle East:

I. DESERTIC SOILS (annual rainfall of 4 inches or less)

Because of the considerable extremes of temperature and strength of the wind, many of the soils of the desert are in fact largely various kinds of rock debris, produced by mechanical abrasion, exfoliation, or aeolian action. Chemical alteration and breakdown of mineral structure are not strongly developed – hence it could be argued that much of the deposits of the desert are hardly true 'soil' at all, but really degraded rock structures. Such desertic formations may be of several kinds:

(*a*) a mass of pebbles, coarse sand and even sometimes angular fragments, often with a certain degree of wind abrasion visible on these last rock masses. The surface of the individual fragments may be covered with a hard, lustrous coating of chemicals somewhat resembling enamel – the so-called 'desert lac', formed, under conditions of varying heat and cold, by interaction of compounds of iron;

(b) material transported by wind: mainly sands of fairly fine consistency. These are often characteristically deposited in dunes, which range enormously in size, from small crescents in the lee of plants, boulders, etc., to massive accumulations many miles in extent. The Arabic names *nebkha*, *barkan*, and *erg* are respectively applied to the tiny dunes, shifting dunes of moderate size, and large massive dunes;

(c) soils formed by deposition due to water or slope action – i.e. deposits in the beds of torrents, or at the foot of land slopes. The size of the material may be surprisingly large, and also variable;

(d) efflorescences of gypsum or other mineral substances. These occur as outwashes from lower layers following a period of rainfall.

Finally, parent rock can have a very considerable influence in that some types of rock are hard and impermeable (e.g. granite, certain sandstones), whilst others are porous and more easily reduced. In the latter instance there can be alteration to mineral content, due to absorption of soluble material and material in suspension; and also from the spread of plant roots. In this case a soil layer of differing character can develop.

II. SOILS OF ARID AREAS (annual rainfall 4–10 inches)

Some development is found beyond the stage characteristic of the fully desertic zones; but true soil formation may be restricted to several months of the year only. The role of physical factors is still predominant in producing these soils, though chemical interaction and the biological factor now have an enhanced importance. Soils of this second group can often be much thicker in depth; and humus content, although still distinctly limited, is appreciably higher. A distinction is sometimes made on a basis of humus content:

(a) grey or red desertic soils. These are markedly sandy in texture, and show a slight differentiation into horizons: an upper layer very near the surface with a slight fraction of organic material. The difference in colour is thought to be due to climatic oscillation, the reddish soils of this group having been affected by an earlier slightly wetter phase of climate;

(b) a group somewhat richer in humus, having in consequence a colour nearer to brown; and also showing a better developed profile. There is also a pronounced calcium content to this sub-group of soils, which are termed *sierozems* by Russian writers.

In both sub-types of soil, a high degree of salinity may occur, but whilst in the *sierozems* maximum concentration is at some depth rather than at the surface, with the desertic soils this can be at or near the surface. Pale grey, red, or even almost white, these soils are sometimes described as 'white alkali' or *solonchak* soils. In certain parts, white salt crust may cover the surface, entirely preventing vegetative growth; where salt concentration is less, a scanty covering of salt-resistant plants may occur. With irrigation, agriculture may be possible, provided that the soil can first be washed clear of any salts, and that steps can be taken to guard against a recrudescence of salinity after cultivation has begun.

Deposits of loess are a feature in certain arid areas, particularly in the Sinai and central Persia. Formed by erosion and transport of surface material by the strong winds of the regions, loess differs from true arid zone sandy soils both in physical character and chemical composition. Besides fine quartz grains are a variety of other materials, chief of which are calcareous particles derived from the numerous limestone outcrops of the Middle East, together with some water-formed silt and clay. Whereas the true desertic sands are typically composed of 90–95 per cent. quartz grains (sand) and 5–10 per cent. soluble chemical compounds, loess as analysed for the Sinai–Gaza areas composed: sand 61 per cent., silt 25 per cent., clay 14 per cent. It will thus be apparent that with irrigation loess soils offer many more possibilities for agriculture. Given a non-saline water supply, good crops can be raised; and there is not the same necessity to guard against gradually increasing salinity of the soil itself, following saturation by irrigation water, which is sometimes a feature of desert marls when these latter are brought under cultivation. By reason of its origin, loess can form comparatively rapidly, and certain parts of the desert zone and its margins are being gradually buried under loess deposits. Archaeological evidence shows that near Gaza, approximately 10 feet of loess has accumulated within the last 4,000 years.

III. SOILS OF SEMI-ARID AREAS (10–15 inches annual rainfall)

Main features are: an organic content of 2–3 per cent.; lower concentration of calcium in the upper layers and a concentration at some depth (about half-way in the profile); often a marked concentration of gypsum and soluble salts in the lowest level; and a distinctly brown colour. Most characteristic of this zone are the 'brown steppe' soils, but other types may also occur – skeletal soils (rock debris and sands), and solonchaks of various kinds.

(a) *Brown Steppe Soils.* Bordering the loess regions, in areas where rainfall is heavier, are brownish loamy soils, formed by intermixture with loess of material eroded by water action. Owing to the damper climate, a lower concentration of mineral salts occurs, with a due balance between the small quantities necessary for successful agriculture, and the sterility of overcharged desert soils. Such steppe loams are among the most valuable in the Middle East; and when irrigated, heavy crops can be raised. The limiting factor is obviously water supply, and throughout later historic time, these regions have been extremely productive when developed by strong governments able to organise an efficient system of irrigation. During periods of weakness or anarchy, water supplies have failed, and the steppes have tended to return to desert conditions.

(b) *Dune Sands.* Rainfall is still often insufficient to hold down lighter material against the force of the wind; and shifting dunes can sometimes occur. Although predominantly sandy, dunes of semi-arid regions can contain a small quantity of clay and silt, and their high degree of porosity generally prevents the formation of saline deposits at the surface; since water percolates rapidly through the sand before capillary action can draw it back to the surface.

Dune sands thus offer some potentialities for agriculture and citrus fruit plantations have been established on them on some parts, chiefly S.W. Israel. Like loess, dune sands are mobile, and can overwhelm stretches of more productive land, hence efforts must sometimes be made to 'fix' the dunes by planting species of grass and tamarisk: this has been done in Libya and in Israel.

(c) *Solonchak Soils.* Because of the more abundant precipitation mineral efflorescences can be very highly developed. Various kinds of these are distinguished: white saline zones produced mainly by concentrations of chlorides and sulphates of sodium, magnesium, and calcium; black saline areas due to a rise of coloured organic material that is dissolved out from lower layers chiefly by sodium carbonate; and soils of a high humidity, produced by a concentration of hygroscopic calcium chloride.

One very characteristic feature of semi-arid zone soils is the formation of a 'hard pan' (crust) or calcrete, composed either of gypsum or compounds of calcium. At times two distinct layers can be observed; and the pan appears as a hard mass resembling concrete, sometimes massive and uniform, sometimes in rounded nodular formations. Different processes would seem to be responsible for the formation of these 'pans' or 'crusts', which, being impermeable, can often seal off the lower soil from the surface. Some have apparently been produced by the evaporation of water surfaces, and are thus associated with closed, aretic drainage basins. Others are due to outwash from highly calcareous soils, whilst Aubert suggests that in some instances a dual process has taken place: leaching of steppe soils and re-precipitation (higher annual rainfall followed immediately by an intensely hot, dry summer is a significant factor) together with slow underground percolation of highly charged soil-water. The action of algae may also be involved in some areas. Dubertret draws attention to the Saida area of the Lebanon, where a 'pan' some 13 feet thick has developed in chalky soils; whilst Reifenberg describes a rather similar, though thinner, layer in Israel, termed *Nazzaz*.

The distribution of these crusts may reflect a delicate balance in annual rainfall, temperature conditions, chemical content of the soil, and biological conditions. Most though not all seem to be associated with brown steppe soils: on the borders of the Jebel Akhdar of Cyrenaica, towards the Libyan Desert, as far as Tobruk, a discontinuous and poorly developed crust is found, whilst more extensive deposits occur on the somewhat better-watered flanks of the Judaean and Syrian mountains, and towards the foothills of the Zagros and uplands of Asia Minor. Some authorities believe that all crusts were formed at earlier, wetter, phases, and that they are therefore a kind of fossil relic: others dispute this.

Normally, hard pan occurs at some distance below the surface; and in certain areas, its appearance actually at the surface raises the interesting question of a possible erosion of the former upper layer of the soil during a temporary and damper climatic phase at an earlier period. Some regions now too dry for crust formation show a well-formed layer; and further investigation of crustal distribution, hardly as yet attempted, may increase our knowledge of earlier climatic cycles in the Middle East.

The presence of a hard pan has, on occasion, considerable social and economic effects. Only relatively shallow-rooted plants such as cereals can grow unless a hole is first driven by man through the hard layer.

Orchards and groves of trees may thus represent much effort on the part of the cultivator, each tree having required an individual break-through to the subsoil. Once established, fruit trees are not easily replanted elsewhere – a factor in the extreme traditionalism of agricultural methods.

Areas of extensive crustal development have as a result a very characteristic appearance – wide, open landscapes, often highly cultivated with cereals, but entirely devoid of natural bush and woodland, and planted with a few fruit trees only in the vicinity of settlements. The absence of any kind of timber prevents the use of beams and rafters in building construction; and the normal flat-roofed houses of the peasants are not found. Instead, a domed roof of hardened mud is characteristic, giving the impression of a cluster of large beehives; and around Aleppo and in Iran, many villages of this sort occur. Moreover, the presence of hard pan at a shallow depth demands a special technique of ploughing. The light wooden *araire* which can follow varying depths of soil, is better adapted to conditions in hard pan areas than the modern steel plough; and efforts to replace this ancient implement, used for centuries in Mediterranean lands, have often been unsuccessful.

In arid zones there is often a close relationship between soil type and geomorphology: because of the limited effects of water erosion, slope and aspect play a heightened role in soil formation. Thus it has been observed that saline soils tend to occur much more frequently on the lower river terraces as compared with higher terraces; and striking correlations between salinity and altitude have been observed not only as regards quantities of soluble salts, but also in regard to kind. In the lowest levels of arid basins, calcium, magnesium, and sodium chlorides predominate: at medium levels sulphates are of these more important elements; whilst at highest levels calcium and cabonates tend to be dominant. This 'ring effect' is particularly noticeable in Iran, and to a somewhat less extent in Asia Minor.

IV. SOILS OF HUMID CLIMATES

In view of the pronounced summer drought of the Middle East, the term 'humid climate' can have only a somewhat restricted meaning, though as compared with the regions already dealt with, rainfall is definitely more abundant. Nevertheless, from the point of view of soil formation in general, one cannot rank the parts of the Middle East designated as 'humid' with other regions of the world (e.g. the tropical forest zones) in which abundant rainfall is well distributed throughout the year. Instead, a special type of soil has developed under the influence of the unusual climatic regime of abundant winter rain followed by summer drought; and to this soil the name 'Terra Rossa' is given. As defined by Reifenberg, Terra Rossa

> develops on limestone under the conditions of Mediterranean climate. In comparison with its parent material, the limestone, it has been greatly enriched in sesquioxides of iron and in silica. In comparison with the soils of humid climates, it contains large quantities of salts of the alkalis. . . . The high iron content together with the low humus content, are responsible for the red colour, which is often brilliant.

Emphasis is placed on climate as the principal factor in the development of Terra Rossa; and it was stated earlier that non-calcareous rocks such as basalt or serpentine could give rise to soils showing great similarity to true Terra Rossa, although slight differences of chemical composition may result in a duller red, or chestnut-brown colour. Thus Terra Rossa and its associated soils are a widespread feature not merely in the Middle East, but throughout the Mediterranean basin as a whole.

Cereals do well on this soil; and where the layer is at all thick, fruit trees can be grown. One disadvantage, however, is a marked liability to erosion, necessitating terracing in regions of varied relief. With an increase in rainfall, the red colour tends to disappear, so that in the most mountainous parts of the Middle East, a yellowish soil of Terra Rossa type is found on those rocks which are more easily eroded. Where the parent rock is resistant, as for example in the southern ranges of the Taurus, which consist of igneous and metamorphosed series, the soil cover is very thin or even entirely absent, and large expanses of bare rock pavement are a feature.

V. ALLUVIAL SOILS

Large areas of the Middle East consist of alluvial basins or troughs with a soil which is the product of fluvial erosion, and quite unconnected with any climatic regime. In sharp contrast to the generally light soils formed by surface weathering, the alluvial soils of the Middle East are heavy, with a high clay content. Because of close association with water, amounting in many instances to periodic flooding, certain alluvial soils contain a proportion of humus derived from the lush aquatic vegetation of the river banks; and such soils are hence comparable with the well-known Chernozems or black earths of Russia. There is little need to comment either on the distribution of alluvial soils, or on their great suitability for agriculture. It may, however, be noted that the cultivation of heavy soils demands a technique different from that necessary in drier areas; and also that trees do not grow by any means as well as shallower rooted plants.

Attention has been drawn to the generally low humus content of most Middle Eastern soils. This arises as the result of high temperature during the summer, when most organic material is in effect burnt out of the soil by extremely rapid oxidation. In this connexion it is interesting to note that the burning of animal dung for fuel by natives of the Middle East, long condemned by more progressive Westerners as one of the root causes of agricultural backwardness, may be better adapted to geographical conditions than its detractors first realised. If animal manure were to be applied directly to the fields, much of it would be lost to the soil by rapid oxidation and the formation of gaseous products, as the result of high soil temperatures (up to 160° F.). Because of the small residue left after direct application, much the same results accrue when dung is first burnt and the ashes used as fertiliser; and, in fact, there would seem little to choose between western and indigenous practice, except that the latter provides, in addition, a much needed domestic fuel. The problem of using organic and chemical fertilisers in such a way as to avoid loss during the summer is one of fundamental importance to the Middle East agriculture, and still remains to be solved.

IRRIGATION

From the foregoing, it will be apparent that in the Middle East irrigation is not merely the supplying of water to arid areas, but in addition, the intelligent use of water in relation to soil deficiencies or to climatic conditions. Certain types of soil such as desert marl, or even river alluvium, at first productive under irrigation, can become saline and sterile, because the presence of water may induce chemical reactions that could not otherwise take place. Moreover, much water obtained from artesian borings and wells in arid areas is brackish and often unfit for use; and even originally sweet water may become contaminated by contact with mineral salts.[1] Irrigation canals, wells, and *qanats* must therefore be made with great care, to avoid contact with saline layers. Many projects over the last 20 years (in Khuzistan, Konya, Cyprus, and Israel) have shown that irrigation schemes can fail, unless soil problems

[1] Cf. C. S. Jarvis, 'An analysis of Sinai water is a most alarming thing to read, and one marvels at the ingenuity of the chemist at detecting so many weird constituents – until one has tasted it oneself, when one comes to the conclusion that less than justice has been done to it.'

are carefully studied in relation to water supply. Moreover, originally sweet water may itself become salinated if used for irrigation in successive regions. This is a problem on the Nile, Tigris, and Euphrates, especially the last two, where the salt content doubles during the rivers' passage through Iraq. Here no less than 70–80 per cent. of all irrigated land is to some extent saline, and instances are known (e.g. near Baghdad) of land unused for centuries that could only produce one crop under modern irrigation before becoming too salty. This explains why the Iraqi government is at present spending some £100 million on land drainage and salt-leaching schemes. Two main methods of control are feasible: the provision of an extensive network of drainage ditches, which carry away soil water before it can evaporate, and by pumping groundwater out of the soil from specially made wells, thus inducing a rapid underground flow. The former method has several drawbacks: much valuable land is occupied by the channels, weeds and mosquitoes thrive, and communications are hindered. The second method is however by no means universally practicable, and is also expensive to maintain.

Besides the question of salinity, irrigation may disturb a delicate ecological balance involving insect pests. At the Middle East Agricultural Conference of 1944, it was stated that in one area of Egypt, the effects of increasing supplies of irrigation water had raised the incidence of bilharziasis and malaria from 5 to 45 or even 75 per cent. of the total population of the region. 'In Iraq, the increased use of pumps, and the construction of permanent canals for irrigation has led to a very serious increase of malaria in the area between Basra and Baghdad during the last twenty-five years.' [1] Such unfortunate consequences do not necessarily follow in all extensions of irrigation systems; but sufficient has been said for it to be apparent that irrigation involves much more than problems of structural engineering.

II. NATURAL VEGETATION

Control by climate is very clearly apparent in both the character and the distribution of vegetation within the Middle East. Most outstanding

[1] E. B. Worthington, *Middle East Science*. Another aspect of the malaria problem is the effect of irrigation schemes in attracting new settlers, many of whom are from non-malarial areas. 'Reclamation of land has meant moving in an entirely new population, which is quite often unaccustomed and not immunised to the effect of the fever. It has been found, particularly in India, that many reclamation schemes have failed, due to the fact that people unused to malarial conditions are moved into an area where there is not adequate protection against fever.' Report of the Middle East Supply Conference, 1944.

are, of course, the effects of widespread aridity and high summer
temperatures; and we must first discuss the influence of these upon the
plant life of the region. There are two ways in which vegetation can
survive a prolonged period of heat and drought; the first is by completing the cycle of growth during the cooler, rainy season; and the
second is by special structural adaptation to resist deleterious conditions.

Plants of the first group usually germinate in late autumn, with the
first onset of heavy rains, and grow rapidly throughout the winter,
reaching maturity in late spring or early summer. As summer draws on,
the plant itself is shrivelled and dies; but the seeds survive, to repeat the
annual cycle during the next season. To this group belong grasses and
cereals – wheat, barley, and millet, some of which are indigenous to the
Middle East, and have later spread into other lands.

Structural adaptation to counter lack of rainfall may take the form of
very deep or extensive roots – as for example in the vine. In some
instances roots spread out just below the surface, and are hence able to
absorb quantities of night dew which, as we have seen, is a feature of
summer in coastal regions. Other plants lie dormant during the dry
season, losing much or all of their portion above ground, and maintaining a stock of nutriment in bulbs, tubers, or rhizomes. To this group
belong the anemone, asphodel, iris and lily, tulip and narcissus – plants
characteristic of the Mediterranean – which flower in spring, and die
down with the onset of summer.

Another group of plants remains in more or less active growth
during the hot season, but shows special structural adaptation with the
object of reducing water-loss. Certain species develop a thick outer
layer; on the stem or trunk as in the case of the cork oak; or on the
leaves, as in the case of evergreens (laurel, evergreen oak, and box).
In other instances, leaf surface and size are reduced – the olive being of
this type – and the process may be carried further by the shrinkage of
leaves to scales or spines, e.g. in tamarisk and thorn bushes. Leaves may
even be dropped at the onset of summer, the stem then performing the
normal function of leaves; and this occurs amongst certain species of
broom and asparagus. Finally, a thick hairy coating may develop, by
which the inner fleshy parts are protected from the heat. An example
of this latter development is found in the hyssop.

Because of this adaptation to climatic conditions, involving in many
instances a resting season during the summer, agricultural practice in
the Middle East differs considerably in certain respects from that of
cooler regions. Sowing can take place in early autumn; and although

outside a narrow coastal zone frost may retard growth for some weeks, the rapid change to warmer conditions in March allows harvesting during April, May, or June. Some plants, notably the orange and lemon, bear during the winter, and cropping begins in November, lasting until February or March.

The rainfall regime has a special significance. Heavy showers in the latter part of October mark the end of summer, and the beginning of the annual cycle of growth. These showers are the 'former rains' of the Bible – the reviving influence that quickens new plant life. Then in the mid-spring there is usually a final onset of rain: a week or ten days of intermittent showers following on an increasingly dry spell. This is the real end of the rainy reason; and the 'latter rains', as the Bible terms them, though not of necessity particularly heavy, are of great importance in the agricultural life of the Middle East (Fig. 15).

Where abundant water supplies are available, as in the great river valleys, a short cycle of growth allows several crops in one year. By careful husbandry, involving the maintenance of soil fertility, as many as three or even four crops per year are sometimes obtained in the Nile valley; and with judicious use of cereals, vines, fruit trees and vegetables, together with such cash crops as cotton, a type of mixed farming with an almost continuous yield is possible. Certain districts of the Middle East are capable of considerable further development, providing that the two limiting factors of low soil fertility and deficient water supply can be overcome.

Aridity is, however, by no means characteristic of all parts of the Middle East; and towards the north, more abundant rainfall gives rise to extensive forests. It has been shown how

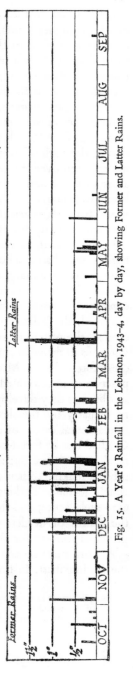

Fig. 15. A Year's Rainfall in the Lebanon, 1943-4, day by day, showing Former and Latter Rains.

closely rainfall in the Middle East is related to topography, and the generally higher rainfall of mountainous areas, together with lower temperatures, favours the growth of a vegetation type very different from that of the warm dry lowlands. In certain parts of the high plateaus of Asia Minor and north-west Iran, conditions even approximate to those of the fold mountains of central Europe, with a characteristic alpine vegetation of pasture and dwarf plants.

Reference must be made to a second controlling factor in the vegetation type of the Middle East – that of adaptation by man. Long occupation of the region has meant that much of the original natural growth has been removed: the most striking change is the replacement in many areas of forest and woodland by scrub and heath. Deforestation has been particularly widespread in the Levant, reaching a peak in the years 1914–18, when much timber was recklessly cut by the Turkish authorities partly for use as fuel.[1]

In the Levant, as well as in southern Asia Minor and the Zagros region, woodland, when once destroyed, is not easily renewed, since it is now really a marginal growth, with natural conditions only barely suitable for its continued existence. In one sense, forests can even be considered as expendable legacies from an earlier, wetter past. Once removed, the balance turns against renewed growth: soil is quickly eroded, the water table may fall, and tree seedlings are not sufficiently vigorous to thrive in competition with scrub vegetation that springs up on deforested sites. More harmful than any of these, however, is the practice of unrestrained grazing, chiefly by goats, which destroys the seedlings as they develop. In the opinion of some, unrestricted grazing, particularly by 'the sharp poisoned tooth of the goat', is one of the fundamental causes of agricultural backwardness in the Middle East. Gradual loss of forest cover leads to uncontrolled water run-off, with resultant soil erosion; and this in turn lowers the water table in the subsoil, making difficult the supply of water for cultivation. In Cyprus, Israel, Jordan, Turkey, the Lebanon, and Syria, the problem is extremely acute; and the difficulties of holding a just balance between the claims of herders and the rights of agriculturalists has been a principal concern for all five governments.

A word must be said regarding the extreme richness of plant life in the Middle East. In the desert and on its margins alone, over 2,000

---

[1] Further factors in the disappearance of the forests of the Levant have been the accessibility of the wooded areas, and the absence of trees in the neighbouring regions of Arabia, Mesopotamia and Egypt.

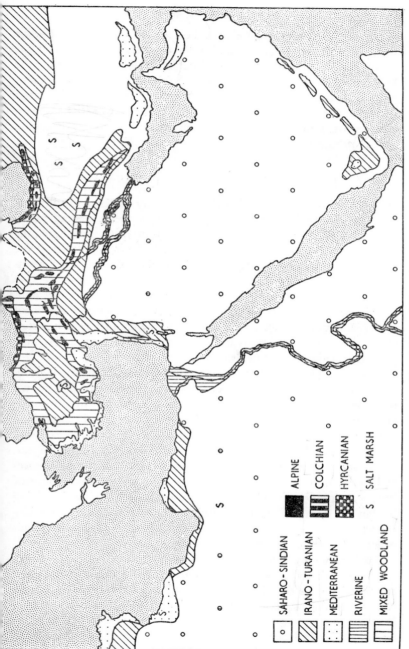

SAHARO-SINDIAN

IRANO-TURANIAN

MEDITERRANEAN

RIVERINE

MIXED WOODLAND

ALPINE

COLCHIAN

HYRCANIAN

S   SALT MARSH

Fig. 16. Types of Vegetation

species of plants occur, and many of these are indigenous to the Middle East. Once again we are reminded of the corridor function of the region, for in addition to a type of flora associated specifically with the Mediterranean, there are plants belonging to two other botano-geographic provinces, one predominantly Asiatic, and the other African. Moreover, the regions of the Black Sea and the southern Caspian coasts each possess a special and distinctive type of vegetation that is without parallel elsewhere in the world (Fig. 16).

III. VEGETATION TYPES

(1) *Mediterranean Vegetation*. This has a relatively restricted distribution, being mainly confined to the wetter parts of the Mediterranean coastal area – that is to say, to the narrow coastal plains of Cyprus, Israel, the Lebanon, Syria, and Turkey, together with the lower flanks of the mountain ranges immediately inland. In addition to the 'classic' plants of the Mediterranean regime – vines, wheat, olive and fruit trees – a large number of shrubs and herbs, many evergreen, flourish in regions of thinner soil. During the spring numerous bulbs make a brilliant show. Walnut and poplar trees flourish in the damper places: cactus, although native to a drier environment, grows luxuriantly, and is often planted as hedges round fields.

Besides the plants mentioned above, the Mediterranean flora includes several highly characteristic plant complexes or groupings. Best known is the *maquis* or *macchia*, which, most fully developed in Corsica, is fairly widespread throughout the Mediterranean basin, in association with siliceous soils. Densely set evergreen oaks, myrtles, and broom, with a thick undergrowth of thorn bushes and shrubs, form a vegetative covering that is sufficiently extensive to afford shelter to refugees and outlaws. Because of this connexion, the term maquis, once of botanical significance only, has taken on a wider meaning involving human and even political relationships. Maquis is not especially widespread in the Middle East; instead, two degenerate types of maquis vegetation, *garrigue* and *phrygana*, are more characteristic.

Garrigue is associated with the thinner soils of calcareous outcrops. Evergreen oaks, which are tolerant of greater aridity, persist – although at wider intervals than in true maquis – but tall shrubs are much less common, and a low scrub of dwarf bushes and thorns takes their place. Because of the more open nature of this vegetation, which rarely exceeds 5 feet in height, perennial plants can develop, and for some weeks after the spring rains, a carpet of flowers and herbs makes a striking display. Garrigue is often discontinuous, with bare patches of soil or rock interspersed with plants; and if maquis is cleared, it is frequently found that garrigue takes its place, especially if animal grazing prevents the re-growth of taller trees and shrubs. For this reason, garrigue is more characteristic of the Mediterranean zone of the Middle East than is true maquis, and much of the vegetation of Cyprus and the western Levant states is of the former type.

Phrygana, a term employed by the ancient Greeks, denotes a special type of thorn scrub, which is restricted to western Asia Minor and the Aegean region. Unlike garrigue, which includes many differing types of plant, phrygana consists principally of thorn bushes, of only moderate growth, but very spiny and closely set. Bands of thorn scrub, occupying the deeper valley bottoms, can be a considerable obstacle to movement in districts where they occur.

(2) *Steppe Vegetation.* A special type of vegetation has evolved under the influence of steppe climate, of which the chief features are wide seasonal variation of temperature, and generally lower rainfall. A botanical province has been recognised, corresponding to the geographical distribution of steppe conditions; and to this province the name Irano-Turanian is given. As the name implies, Irano-Turanian vegetation is best developed in central Asia, but a westward extension has occurred through Asia Minor and Iraq into central Syria.

On the lower slopes of the mountains flanking the steppe, a park-like vegetation is found, with scattered carob, juniper and terebinth trees, and bushes of Christ thorn, wild plum, or thorn and wormwood, separated by expanses of smaller shrubs (sage, thyme, and thorn cushions) or creepers. In regions of true steppe, trees are absent, and various species of grass appear, although these have sharply restricted seasonal growth. Many grasses show adaptation to semi-arid conditions: one species has a hygroscopic seed casing with a stiff pointed top, by means of which the seed, after being driven into the hard ground, is supplied with water; and another has developed a system of propagation by means of small swellings on parts of the leaves that remain underground.

More than half of the plants of the steppe region disappear in summer. There is hence a considerable difference in aspect between late winter and early spring, when numerous species of flowers and grass are in rapid growth, and the rest of the year, when most plants are shrivelled up or have not yet germinated. For a few weeks each year the steppe presents an amazing picture of luxuriant, almost lush, vegetation; but with the approach of summer, only hardier bushes and thorns remain above the ground, and vast expanses of bare earth appear, upon which are strewn the withered remains of earlier plant growth.

The steppes are the home of pastoral nomadism, and it will easily be seen how narrow is the margin of existence in these regions – an extra week of rain (i.e. prolonged latter rains) will mean a more than corresponding lengthening of the spring pasture season, with great increase of flocks and herds during the ensuing year; and early cessation of rainfall means a long summer, with much hardship until the next spring. Under such conditions even a small climatic fluctuation can have a disproportionately large effect upon human activity, and a few seasons of deficient rainfall may lead to widespread movements within the steppes, culminating in the invasion of adjoining lands, with vast consequences for human societies as a whole. Such great events as the Indo-Aryan invasions of Europe and the Middle East during the second millennium B.C., the Israelitish occupation of Palestine, and the rise of Islam in the seventh century A.D. can all be traced to slight changes in environmental conditions within the steppe lands of Eurasia (Chapter VII).

(3) *Desert Vegetation.* To a third major botanical grouping, characteristic of arid conditions, the name Saharo-Sindian has been given. Many plants of this grouping show an extreme degree of adaptation to dry or saline conditions; and of these, thorns (chiefly tamarisk) are the most important.

Camel thorn, a shrub of the pea family, and also certain kinds of tamarisk, exude a brown, sweetish sap, which, when hardened on contact with the atmosphere, forms the Biblical manna. Other desert plants complete their growing cycle within a few weeks after the end of the winter rains; and throughout late spring, one sees an extraordinary variety and abundance of flowering grasses. Such vegetation may, however, last only for a matter of days.

(4) *Mountain Vegetation.* Four distinctive types of vegetation occur on the higher mountains of the Middle East. Of these, three are forest growths, and the fourth, alpine pasture or heath.

The first type of woodland is of mixed evergreen, coniferous, and deciduous trees. Evergreen oaks generally grow on the lower hill slopes, up to about 3,000 feet, and associated with these are the carob, and a species of pine that is native to the Mediterranean basin. At higher levels are found cedars, maple, juniper, firs, and two other species of oak and pine—the valonia oak, which yields an extract valuable for tanning leather, and the Aleppo pine, which like the Mediterranean variety, is smaller and more bushy in appearance than the conifers of northern latitudes. The famous cedars of Lebanon, large but extremely slow-growing trees, now exist only in scattered clumps as the result of centuries of exploitation. The largest of these clumps, numbering some 400 trees, occurs at a height of over 6,000 feet between Tripoli and Baalbek; and, like many isolated groves in the Middle East, has acquired a semi-sacred character that may help towards its future preservation. By far the greatest extent of forest land exists in Asia Minor (with limited extensions southwards along the crests of the Zagros) and in western Syria and the Lebanon. About one-eighth of the state of Turkey is classified as forest land.

Above 5,000 to 6,000 feet, or exceptionally, 7,000 to 8,000 feet in the Elburz Mountains of Persia, forests die out, and are replaced by scrub or dwarf specimens of true forest trees. In eastern Anatolia and Azerbaijan, temperatures are lower than elsewhere in the Middle East, and a kind of Alpine vegetation appears. In the wetter parts, small areas of grassland reminiscent of Swiss pastures may occur; but more often, conditions are too dry, and vegetation is limited to bushes, creepers and 'cushion' plants.

The second type of forest is found on the northern slopes of the Elburz Mountains, towards the Caspian Sea. Oak, hazel, alder, maple, hornbeam, hawthorn, wild plum, and wild pear are the characteristic trees, and these are festooned by a dense growth of brambles, ivy, and other creepers. Here and there are openings occupied by box, thorn-bushes, pomegranate, and medlar trees. To this luxuriant growth, peculiar to the region, and developing under conditions of abundant rainfall throughout the year with high or moderate temperatures, the name Hyrcanian forest is sometimes given. One interesting feature is the absence of conifers.

A third type of woodland – the Colchian or Pontic forest – has developed in response to the warm humid climate of the southern Caucasus and eastern Black Sea.[1] An indigenous species of beech, with oak, hazel, walnut, maple, and hornbeam, form the chief trees, and a dense undergrowth of climbing plants is again found, with widespread occurrence of the rhododendron. Best developed near the southern

---

[1] One element in the unusually high winter temperatures of the south-eastern Black Sea coastal margins is the frequent occurrence of Föhn winds which descend from the high inland plateaus of eastern Anatolia.

D

Caucasus, the Colchian forest extends westwards in an increasingly attenuated form along the north-eastern edge of the Anatolian plateau as far west as Sinop. It has been suggested that, like the Hyrcanian forest further to the east, the Colchian forest is the remnant of a flora that was characteristic of much larger areas of the Middle East during Tertiary and early Quaternary times.

(5) *Riverine Vegetation.* The extensive alluvial lowlands of the great rivers have a special type of vegetation. Aquatic grasses, papyrus, lotus, and reeds that sometimes attain a height of 25 feet, make up a thick undergrowth in deltaic regions, and in the lower courses of the Tigris and Euphrates. Scattered willow, poplar, and alder trees occur, particularly in Mesopotamia; but the outstanding tree is the date palm, which is extremely tolerant of excessive water, provided that the temperature remains high. Cultivated palms are therefore a feature of riverine lowlands in Egypt and lower Mesopotamia. Another wild plant of economic importance is the liquorice, a bush that is fairly widely distributed along the banks of the middle and upper Euphrates and Tigris. Juice is extracted from the underground stem, and this forms an important item of trade in the districts of Aleppo and Mosul.

PART II

Social Geography

CHAPTER V

Peoples

Few regions in the world can surpass the Middle East in heterogeneity of population. From earliest times, the region has attracted waves of immigrants from various parts of the Old World, and fusion of diverse elements has sometimes tended to be slow, or even incomplete. Frequent reference in the literatures of various peoples of the Middle East indicate an acute awareness of racial and cultural distinction; and insistence by these groups on their separate identity can be taken as an indication of the close juxtaposition of many types of racial stock, cultural patterns, and social organisation.

The pictorial art of ancient Egypt was always concerned to depict the Egyptians themselves, by means of a special coloration, as a separate and distinctive group: and there is little need to comment on the theme of fierce tribal exclusiveness that permeates much of the Old Testament. The Greeks too had a marked appreciation of racial differences, not merely as between themselves and their neighbours, but also in a wider sense, as, for example, when Herodotus notes that Egyptian skulls could be distinguished from Persian, owing to the greater fragility of the latter. Distinctions between Jew and Christian, Believer and Infidel, Turk or Arab, Semite and Hamite, or between mountaineer and plainsman, and Badawin (herders) and Hadhar (cultivators) have long coloured the geography of the Middle East, and are still at the present day factors of prime importance in the human relations of the region.

It has proved difficult to establish criteria by which the peoples of the world may be classified. Physique, language, religion, and nationality have all been invoked as a basis of definition, but none is completely acceptable. For the Middle East, the insufficiency of any one of these criteria is easy to demonstrate. We speak of an 'Arab' people; but, as will be seen later, physical type amongst this group shows very wide variation: or we may adopt language as a basis of division, in which case we find that an Arabic-speaking group would include some inhabitants of Persia, but would exclude important Armenian, Circassian, and Greek-speaking minorities in Egypt, Syria, and Jordan. With religious beliefs as a criterion, we find firstly that a number of undoubted 'Arabs' are Christians; secondly, that Islam itself is much divided, with sectarian divisions almost as extensive as those of Christendom; and thirdly, that religious life within the Middle East shows an infinite gradation from almost complete paganism to the fullest development of Christianity, Islam, and Judaism. Finally, nationalism offers little guide to effective classification. For some Middle Eastern communities, nationalism has no meaning, and sectarian feeling takes its place – when asked their nationality, some individuals would reply 'I am a Christian'. In other communities national consciousness exists, but various practical difficulties such as smallness of numbers, intermingling with other groups, or external political obstacles interfere with its effective realisation. Moreover, one can hardly say that existing national frontiers in the Middle East allow complete political expression to all nationally conscious peoples of the region.

Hence, in an attempt to throw further light on the complicated question of cultural, political, and social organisation, the population of the Middle East will be considered in turn from the standpoint of the five criteria of race, language, religion, social organisation, and national consciousness. This examination will, however, of necessity be limited in detail, since in some instances, our knowledge of facts and events is only in the earliest stages.

Before commencing such an examination it is, however, first useful to note the influence on the peoples of the Middle East of certain geographical factors. The region has a dual aspect – that of a broad corridor linking several major parts of the globe, whilst at the same time a number of smaller component areas show an isolation and remoteness that is at complete variance with the character of the Middle East as a whole. Viewed generally, the Middle East has served as a routeway for the migration of peoples ever since early man began to disperse throughout the world. Here and there, however, as it were in quiet backwaters, local environment has favoured the preservation of racial and social strains as remnants of wider movements that in more open areas have been submerged by later arrivals.

A discontinuous belt of relatively fertile land runs along the southern slopes of the Elburz Mountains of Iran, and is followed by an ancient route that in the opinion of some anthropologists was one avenue by which certain types of early man spread into western Eurasia. Further to the west, the route divides, one branch turning south-west into south-west Persia and Iraq; and the other continuing through Azerbai-jan to Asia Minor. A zone of steppe-land in inner Anatolia completes the link between central Asia and Europe.

More strongly marked is the steppe area of the Fertile Crescent which links western Persia, Iraq, south-east Anatolia, and the Levant. By this route numerous invaders from the east and north have gained the shores of the Mediterranean and the Nile valley; and as a return movement Egyptian culture has also spread into Asia. The Medi-terranean itself has facilitated rather than impeded intercourse between the peoples near its shores. The island-studded Aegean was a nursery

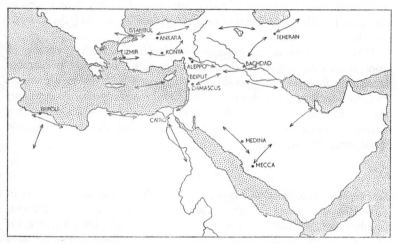

Fig. 17. Regions of relatively Easy Movement

for man's first sea adventures; and it is not surprising that some of the earliest cultural developments occurred in Cyprus, which is visible both from Asia Minor and the mainland of the Levant. In the south, close physical connexion between Arabia and North Africa is paralleled by similar cultural contact. The Sinai has formed a major route for move-ment of peoples, and some authorities stress the importance of the Bab el Mandeb region as a gateway between Arabia and Sudan. A certain degree of racial contact has developed across the Sahara desert. Central African peoples were brought chiefly as slaves via the oases of the central Sahara and East Africa to the Mediterranean coast, Arabia, and the Persian Gulf; and this has left an influence on the population especially of present-day Libya.

Alongside the *durchgangsland* of the Middle East, there occur regions in which difficulty of access or hostile natural conditions have restricted penetration. Largest of these is the desert of Arabia, the Jezirat al Arab (Island of the Arabs), where, in the words of Hitti, 'ethnic purity is a reward . . . of ungrateful and isolated environment'. Other such regions may be seen in the highland plateaus of the Mediterranean seaboard, and here Samaritans, Druses, Maronites, Metwalis, Alawites, and various sects of Asia Minor such as the Bakhtahis and Takhtajis, have preserved a certain cultural autonomy, if not always a pure racial type. Further east, the Kurds of the Anatolian and Zagros mountain belts have maintained a separate identity; and smaller units can be traced in the Yezidis of the Jebel Sinjar of north Iraq, the Circassians (Cherkesses), and the Turcomans.

This alternation of intermixture and seclusion is the keynote of population distribution in the Middle East. In the easily penetrable lands assimilation of successive ethnic influences has produced a mixed race, in which original elements are difficult to recognise. Away from the corridor regions the palimpsest of communities gives place to a simpler structure of isolated groups preserving their characteristic racial stock or culture.

RACE[1]

A scheme of classification based on certain physical qualities that are in the main susceptible of actual measurement recognises head form, bodily build, and hair character as principal distinguishing features. Of head form, the cephalic index, or breadth of head expressed as a percentage of maximum length; and, to a less degree, nasal character, are generally considered the more important elements.[2]

[1] Before discussing racial theories in detail, it is first necessary to make a general qualifying comment. At one time, much importance was attached to racial characters, and it was thought that by developing a comprehensive scheme of classification, it might be possible to arrive ultimately at a complete understanding of the origins of all peoples. This hope has not been entirely fulfilled: instead, recent evidence has revealed a number of inconsistencies in earlier views, and diverging opinions have arisen. On the one hand, there is difficulty in deciding how far mental qualities can justifiably be related to physical characters, and on the other, the more serious problem of evaluating the influence due to environment as opposed to that exerted by heredity, and of relating both factors to accepted biological theories of evolution and inheritance. Again, by carrying race theories to absurd lengths, the Nazis of Hitlerite Germany have also served to cast a certain discredit on the subject. Nevertheless, there is still considerable value in race-study, particularly as an indication of the movements of peoples, and their cultural connexions.

[2] Blood grouping is now increasingly recognised as an important distinguishing feature between races. Little information is however as yet available for the populations of the Middle East.

For a discussion of ethnology and anthropology in general terms, the reader is referred to studies such as Haddon's *Races of Man* and Buxton's *Peoples of Asia*. In the present instance, it is proposed merely to sketch the outstanding racial elements of south-west Asia and to indicate their distribution, as an aspect of the social geography of the region. Once again, detailed information is scanty; and anthropologists are not entirely agreed, even on matters of nomenclature – hence it is difficult to arrive at a simplified, yet adequate, picture of racial distribution.

As a preliminary, we shall describe in outline the racial strains which are to be found in the Middle East, and afterwards proceed, region by region, to a discussion of the actual population itself. Racial strains are: (1) *Mediterranean Race*. The majority of peoples living around the Mediterranean have been recognised as forming a special racial group termed by some anthropologists the Mediterranean, and by others the Brown, race. This group, one of five principal divisions of mankind, is characterised by long-headedness – cephalic index ranging from 67 to 75 per cent. – by marked brunetness, by wavy hair, and by relatively small stature and slight or moderate build. The Mediterranean race has a wide distribution in the Old World, not merely around the sea basin itself, but also in India, where the Dravidian population is recognised as part of the same race, and on the Atlantic coast of north-west Europe, where Irish, Welsh, Cornish, and Breton peoples show some racial affinity to the Mediterranean.

It is believed that at one time, peoples of Mediterranean type formed the bulk of the populations of the Middle East. Later arrivals, in all probability from central Asia, displaced or intermingled with the older established race, so that at the present time, relatively pure Mediterranean stocks are found only in the south and west of the Middle East areas.

(2) *Armenoid Race*. – A second major race of mankind is associated with the highland belt that runs from east to west across southern Eurasia. The chief distinguishing features are roundness of head, and moderate height, together with stocky or somewhat heavy build. Several sub-types of this highland or Alpine race are recognised, of which the Armenoid or west Asiatic race is one. This latter race, or better, sub-race, has certain outstanding characteristics. Head form is markedly round, with a cephalic index that averages 86, but occasionally exceeds 100; whilst dark hair and eyes, thick lips and a strong jaw, 'frizzy' hair, and a strongly curved nose make up the physiognomy that

is often, although sometimes falsely, caricatured as typical of the Jewish people. Another characteristic of the Armenoids is a flattened 'wall-like' back of the head, with little or no occiput.

This people would appear to be closely related to the central Asiatic groups of Turkic stock; and it is more than likely that they spread westward from central Asia into various parts of the Middle East. Such movement must have started at a very early date; and Buxton suggests that the Armenoid race may even have formed the aboriginal stock of the north-eastern parts of the Middle East, since they may have been associated with two of the oldest civilisations of the area – those of Akkad and Sumer. The appearance of Armenoids in the Mediterranean basin at a very early date is confirmed by the fact that they had reached Malta within Bronze Age times.

(3) *Iranian (Scythian) Race.* More difficulty attaches to discussion of this third group, since opinion is divided both as to nomenclature and as to affinity, and there is even some doubt as to whether the Iranians can justifiably be distinguished as a separate sub-race. On the whole, it would seem that this group should be regarded as a branch of the great Alpine race, because head form is round (cephalic index, 78 to 79 per cent.) although much less so than among the Armenoids. Stature, too, is more variable, and the almost universal brown hair and eyes of the Armenoids is rather less frequent. Lighter colouring and less strongly marked facial characteristics have led some anthropologists to link the Iranian race with the Nordic peoples, who may well have developed on the plains of Turkestan. Such connexion is more doubtful, although later intermixture with Nordic strains is possible.

As would be expected, the Iranian race is best represented in Persia, where it forms a large part of the population of the plateau, and a less important sub-stratum elsewhere. Waves of this people also appear to have spread westward across the Middle East from time to time, and their influence can be traced as far as the shores of the Levant.

(4) *Proto-Nordic (Indo-Aryan) Race.* Observers have recorded the presence of a long-headed, tall and often surprisingly fair element in the population of the Middle East and northern India; and most are agreed that this element is in some way related to the Nordic strain of Europe. Cephalic index averages 69 to 70 per cent. and various names have been used to describe the people. Haddon's 'Proto-Nordic' is probably best: the nearest alternative of 'Indo-Aryan' being properly a linguistic term, and totally inapplicable to a single racial group, since

Indo-Aryan languages are often spoken by non-Nordic or mixed racial communities.

The Proto-Nordic race became differentiated in the plains of west-central Asia; and at a comparatively late date various groups moved south into India and Mesopotamia, and west into Asia Minor and Europe. The social and historical implications of these invasions by Nordic peoples, with the possibility of Nordics forming an aristocracy of higher culture and initiative amongst population of different racial character has given rise to much discussion. In view of the fact that early civilisation first developed in those regions of the Middle East where intermingling of diverse racial strains has been a pronounced feature, it would, however, seem preferable to attach greater importance to inter-mixture of stocks as a factor in human progress, rather than to ascribe the greatest proportion of ability and initiative to one particular group such as the Nordics. Hybridisation as between a number of varied racial strains, not strict selection involving only one people, would appear to have had the greatest favourable influence on man's cultural development.

(5) *Turki (Turanian) Race.* In Asia Minor and Persia certain elements of the populations show affinities to the Mongoloid races of central and eastern Asia. Again, opinions are somewhat at variance: Deniker uses the term 'Mongoloid' in a general way, to describe a large number of peoples living in central and eastern Asia; whilst others prefer to distinguish a Finno-Ugrian or western branch of the Mongoloid race, in which racial characters best developed in eastern Asia appear some-what modified by contact with non-Mongoloid groups. At all events, it will be sufficient for our present purpose to note the existence within the Middle East of certain groups of people, relatively small in number, that derive racially from the north and east of Asia. To these the collective name of Turki or Turanian has been applied; and a number of small communities have migrated south-westwards from the steppes of inner Asia. Most prominent of such groups were the Mongol 'hordes' of Gengis Khan and Tamerlane; and the Osmanli or Ottoman Turks, who entered Asia Minor during the eleventh century A.D.

Round-headedness, small stature, and a yellowish skin are the more outstanding features of Mongoloid peoples. In addition, hair is almost always straight and black; and two well-known characteristics, high cheek bones and the 'almond eye', are frequent but not universal. It is easy to recognise this physical appearance as the one colloquially termed 'Asiatic'; but in the Middle East, by no means all these characters are present in the Turki population. Almond eyes, for example, occur in only 25 to 50 per cent. of the Turki people living on or near the Siberian plains, and in Iran and Asia Minor the proportion of Mongolian features is much less. The slightness of the distinction between Mongoloid and non-Mongoloid becomes apparent in western Asia Minor, where the Turki race approximates closely to the Armenoids. Buxton has even suggested that the peoples of central Asia, of which the Turki form a part, represent a specialised development from a basic Armenoid stock.

(6) *Negrito Race.* Little need be said about this race. Although many negroid elements can be traced in south-east Asia, it is very doubtful whether there are any indigenous negrito populations of long standing in the Middle East. On the other hand, a certain negroid element of recent arrival can definitely be found in the descendants of African slaves brought into the Middle East from the south-west. Here and there, particularly in Arabia, north-east Africa, and south Persia, darker skin, heavier features and thickening of the lips suggest African influences, just as in the Levant occasional blond Arabs with Arabicised family names of European origin recall Crusader invasion.

It is hardly possible to follow in detail the processes of intermingling by which the present populations of the Middle East have come into existence. Nevertheless, it can be seen that in the main, there has been a drift of peoples south-westwards from Iran and central Asia into the Middle East. This trend of movement has predominated, although a slight return movement north-eastwards from Egypt had some influence on the pre-1948 populations of Palestine, Jordan, and south Syria.

Four large-scale migrations of peoples can be traced within historic time.[1] The first, occurring at about 4000 B.C., brought a round-headed race from the mountain zone of the north into the riverine lands of Mesopotamia. This so-called Akkadian migration was followed at some time before 2500 B.C. by a second wave of peoples from the north-east, less markedly round-headed, and possibly of the Iranian sub-race. These latter established themselves on the shores of the Mediterranean, where they formed the well-known Phoenician and Canaanite peoples. In about 1350 B.C. the Aramaeans, of similar origin and ethnic character, pushed into Syria and north Palestine by way of Damascus. Finally, the Islamic migration outwards from central Arabia during the seventh century A.D. was anthropologically speaking of much less importance,

[1] For a possible reason for these migrations see page 82.

the actual numbers involved being small. Cultural changes as the result of this invasion were, however, enormous, and most countries between Spain and Java were affected, some to such an extent as to alter completely the course of their history.

DISTRIBUTION OF RACIAL STOCKS IN THE MIDDLE EAST

Most outstanding in the population of *Asia Minor* is the Armenoid element, which appears in its purest form in the mountainous districts of the interior, and in various swampy and marshy regions. Armenia itself is, as would be expected, a stronghold of this racial type; but complete racial homogeneity amongst all Armenians does not seem to occur, since some authorities see a slight strain of long-headedness in this people.

Intermixture of Armenoid and Mediterranean stocks is found on a much larger scale in western Anatolia, where the majority of the population shows an even balance between long- and round-headedness. This mixed population occurs on the coast, and in the towns; and is due, in all probability, to later immigration of Armenoids into a region at one time predominantly Mediterranean in ethnic type.

Further complication arises in the extreme west from a possible invasion by Nordic elements in early historic time. Whether or not this view of the existence of the Proto-Nordic (Indo-Aryan) groups in western Turkey is held, the basic facts of population composition in Asia Minor are beyond dispute: in the difficult mountainous terrain of the east, racial purity is best developed, with Armenoids as practically the only type. Further west, intermixture increases, until near the shores of the Aegean extreme heterogeneity prevails. Invasion after A.D. 1000 by various Mongoloid groups had only a small effect on the population. In particular, the Ottoman Turks added little to the ethnic character of Asia Minor, since the number of people involved was small. The Ottomans settled down for the greater part as a landed aristocracy, in a way somewhat similar to that of the Normans in England.

Cyprus, structurally an outpost of Asia Minor, shows a similar affinity in racial distribution. The population of the island, partly long- and partly round-headed, closely resembles that of maritime Anatolia, and appears to have varied little since Neolithic times.

Important off-shoots of Armenoid peoples occur in the *Levant* and in *Iraq*. The southward continuation of Turkish mountain chains into south-west Syria, the Lebanon, and north Palestine has an ethnic parallel in that the populations of these areas are racially akin to those of the mountains of Asia Minor. The Alawites of the Jebel Ansarieh, the Metwali of the Orontes valley, the Lebanese, and the Druses of south Lebanon, the Jebel Druse and northern Israel stand apart, by reason of rounder head form and heavier build, from the slighter Syrian population immediately to the east. Further south, the Armenoid strain dies out at the Plain of Esdraelon in Israel, leaving the northern indigenous Jews somewhat distinct from their kinsmen of the plateaus of Samaria and Judaea.

On the east, Armenoid affinities are easily discerned in the peoples of northern and central Iraq. A religious sect known as the Chaldeans, fairly widespread in the Fertile Crescent, and strongest in northern Iraq, shows this strain to a considerable degree; but Armenoid influence is also dominant in most of the Iraqi population north of the latitude of Baghdad. South of Baghdad round-headedness decreases but is still present. In Mesopotamia we therefore have once again a Mediterranean population overlain by an Armenoid element that becomes progressively weaker away from the highland zone.

The two southward extending tongues of Armenoid peoples partially enclose a large area in which occur populations of two contrasting types. We have seen in the case of the Armenians that hostile environment tends to favour the preservation of a single unmixed racial stock; similarly, the Badawin of the deserts of *Syria* and *North* and *Central Arabia* show a high degree of ethnic purity, as a branch of the Mediterranean race. Cephalic index is amongst the lowest of any population of the Middle East; and slimness of build often differentiates the desert dweller from Arabs of the towns.

Between the Badawin and the round-heads of the northern Levant occur a group of peoples about whom little has so far been said. Mention was earlier made of the Canaanite-Phoenician and Aramaean invasion of Palestine and south-west Syria, for which the Damascus region seems to have been the gateway; and the name Iranian was tentatively given to the racial stock from which these invaders may derive. The Canaanite-Phoenician-Aramaean type stands out as neither markedly long- nor round-headed; and in this connexion, it is useful to note the difference in cephalic index between a mixed population of long- and round-heads, such as that of western Anatolia, in which the arithmetical average of two measured maxima peaks (at 73 and 83) falls at 78; and a homogeneous population like the Aramaean stock, with a

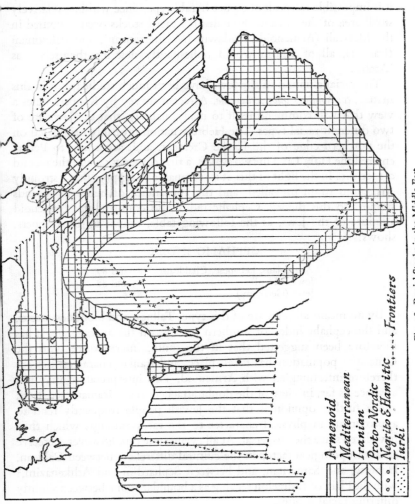

Fig. 18. Racial Stocks in the Middle East

Armenoid
Mediterranean
Iranian
Proto~Nordic
Negrito & Hamitic
Turki
·-·+·+· Frontiers

single measured peak at 78.[1] Most of the Palestinian Arabs are of Aramaean stock; and we therefore have the important point that racially it is impossible to speak of a pure 'Arab' type, since within a relatively small area of the Levant, three distinct racial stocks occur, typified in the Metwali (Armenoid), Badawin (Mediterranean), and Palestinian (Iranian), all of whom would unhesitantly describe themselves as 'Arabs'.

The racial affinities of the Jews have been much studied, but in this matter, *tot homines quot sententiae*. A recent survey by Kappers states a view that will commend itself to many, namely, that the Jews are of two different racial types. The Hebrew nation probably originated on the northern edge of the Fertile Crescent, and, according to Petrie, entered the Holy Land in two waves, a first *c.* 1900 B.C., and the second *c.* 1200 B.C. In the light of this, it is reasonable to suppose that a strongly Armenoid strain prevailed; and the appearance of many Jews lends support to this theory. Cephalic index also confirms the Armenoid affinities of the Jews, as the following table, drawn up by Kappers, shows:

CEPHALIC INDEX

Armenians, Lebanese, Chaldeans	83 and 87
Jews (Mosul)	83 and 88
Jews (Germany)	83.5

By no means all Jews are of this type. Tallness and blondness occur, and the cephalic index of southern Jews is, on the average, 77. It has therefore been suggested that in the south, intermixture with the Canaanite population has taken place, and Iranian characteristics are therefore intermingled with Armenoid. This interpretation may not advance us far, in view of the doubt attached to the Iranian race itself; and a further opinion is that the Jewish people frequently tend to approximate in physical character to the races amongst which they have lived since the Dispersal. At all events, one can, however, perceive an anthropological factor in the cultural differences between Galilean, Hebrew, and Samaritan, and between Sephardim and Ashkenazim,[2] with the Plain of Esdraelon serving as a boundary zone between slightly differing racial groups.

For *Southern Arabia*, data is scanty, but Buxton believes that there has

---

[1] i.e. the first is in a sense artificial, and fictitious; the second does in fact correspond to actual conditions amongst the population.

[2] Names used to distinguish Jews who have lived in southern and northern Europe since the Dispersal (p. 110). For a statement on the post-1948 racial composition of Israel see Appendix IV.

been a considerable influx of round-headed people from Mesopotamia by way of south-east Arabia. The aboriginal long-heads, still characteristic of north and central Arabia, have been absorbed into the composite stock, in which round-headedness may even predominate. With its mixture of peoples, southern Arabia to some extent resembles Asia Minor; but in the absence of detailed information, no answer can be given to the interesting geographical problem of how such a region of extreme difficulty came to acquire a mixed population.

Although the population of *Egypt* is in the main of Mediterranean stock, important round-headed elements are found, showing considerable entry from the north. Worrell also draws attention to various cultural and ethnic features which seem to have been derived from the negro populations to the south. Neither of these tendencies is surprising, in view of the topography and space relations of Egypt: a corridor *par excellence* between tropical Africa and Eurasia. Outside the Nile valley intermixture is much less a feature, and a predominantly Mediterranean racial type is found similar to that of northern Arabia. The persistence of this type both in the Nile valley, and on the margins, including *Cyrenaica*, since very early times, is perhaps the most important single feature in the ethnology of Egypt.

Iran remains to be discussed, but little can be said with finality, since extensive intermingling of peoples and inadequacy of information have given rise to many conflicting theories, particularly in relation to the Nordic or Indo-Aryan element of the population. The Iranian race forms a sub-stratum of most of the population, with strongest representation in the northern plateau regions. To this basic element have been added groups of Armenoids, most important of whom are the Bakhtiari tribes of the central Zagros. This people, which has greatly influenced the history of Iran, exhibits a very high cephalic index; and, according to Hitti, is related to the Druses of south-west Syria. In this connexion, it is interesting to note that the Bakhtiari themselves have a tradition that they originated in Damascus. The Qashqai tribes, also of the central Zagros, seem, on the other hand, to be descended from Mongoloid invaders of the Asiatic steppe.

In central Iran a long-headed strain occurring amongst the Zoroastrian sect suggests connexion with the Proto-Nordic race; and an even more markedly long-headed group settled around the southern shores of the Caspian may be direct descendants of a wave of Indo-Aryans that migrated from the steppe-lands of central Asia in approximately 2000 B.C.

Much anthropological contact seems to have taken place between lower Mesopotamia and southern Persia. The districts of Shiraz, Kirman, and Bushire have a very mixed population, in which racial strains from many areas are represented. To what might be called the indigenous peoples of the Middle East are added African slave elements, and, towards the coast, a slight Indian admixture. Negroid characteristics are so apparent in certain populations living at the head of the Persian Gulf as to have given rise to speculation whether or not an indigenous negrito population did not at one time exist there.

Besides the peoples described above, numerous small, but racially and socially distinct groups also exist in the Middle East, often as political minorities in a larger national state. Many of these groups are best characterised as the heterodox religious sects, but certain racial differences sometimes appear, since a marked clan feeling has resulted in a strong tendency to marry within the group, with a consequent preservation of original racial stock. Von Luschan saw in these minority groups remnants of ancient peoples that elsewhere were submerged by later immigrants; but it is more likely that some minorities were themselves the last comers, and remained unabsorbed by the indigenous population of the regions into which they came.

Chief of such minorities are the Kurds, a people living in the debatable hill country between Turkey, Russia, Persia, Iraq, and Syria. Physically, the Kurds are of large stature, and vary considerably in colouring. An average cephalic index of 78 may indicate affinities to the Iranian race, or may equally well indicate an intermixture of Armenoid and Mediterranean types, since variation from this average is wide. A further suggestion has been made that there is a Nordic strain in the Kurds. Colonies of this people are found away from the main group of the mountains, in Iraq and Damascus. It has also been suggested that the Yezidi, a small group of people living on the Jebel Sinjar of Iraq, and notable as a semi-pagan community, may be Kurdish in origin. As, however, the Yezidi seem to show more strongly marked Armenoid characteristics, this connexion appears doubtful, although a certain intermixture with the Kurds may have occurred.

To the east of Kurdistan, the peoples of Azerbaijan are considered to show intermixture of Iranian and Armenoid stocks. Wide variation in physical type makes it difficult to discover any marked racial affinities; and it is likely that traces of Turki blood have been added at a comparatively recent date. Turki strains also occur further to the south-east, along the Zagros, and in Persia, where, as we have seen, certain tribes, e.g. the Qashqai of the central Zagros, stand apart in physical type from their neighbours. Finally, some reference must be made to the Circassians, numerically a very small group, but of a certain renown in the former Ottoman Empire, and now existing in scattered groups in Turkey, Iraq, and the Levant. The Circassian homeland was originally in the north-western Caucasus, from which active migration took place to various parts of the Ottoman Empire. This migration was not always voluntary, particularly during the nineteenth century, when Russian expansion southward drove many Circassians to seek refuge in a Moslem state. Before this too, for many years previously, the beauty of the Circassian women had made them eagerly sought after as occupants for Moslem harems. One such colony of Circassians settled in the 1870's and re-created the village that has grown into Amman city.

In Libya there occur a few vestiges of Berber admixture. The Berbers, dominant today only in parts of Algeria and Morocco, are racially distinct from the Arabs, and their language is also markedly different. It would appear that within Libya Arab immigrants have ousted an earlier Berber population, which is now represented only by a few Berber-speaking settlements: e.g. Aujila and Zuara, and parts of the Tripolitanian hills.

Summing up, we may say that from the point of view of the anthropologist, it is impossible to speak with any accuracy either of an Arab or of a Semitic people. Both terms connote a mixed population varying widely in physical character and in racial origin, and are best used purely as cultural and linguistic terms respectively. Similarly, present national frontiers are often far from coinciding with ethnic boundaries, although it must be added that intermingling of races is so pronounced a feature that no system of delimitation could possibly be devised on a strictly ethnic basis. Racial minorities are therefore likely to remain a feature of the human geography of the Middle East and in many instances the claims of one community to achieve political and national unity appear to have succeeded only at the expense of denying the same privileges to smaller ethnic groups with which the first group is in close contact.

LANGUAGE DISTRIBUTION

As regards language, the position in the Middle East is much clearer. Although it is possible that at one time each racial group had its own language, intercourse soon breaks down linguistic differences, and one language may quickly establish a dominance, to the complete exclusion of others. Whereas physical characters can persist through many generations as a result of biological inheritance, a cultural feature such as language often becomes modified within a short time, and may even die out, particularly if the language itself possesses no literature.

Our present purpose is merely to note the distribution of existing languages within the Middle East, with incidental references to earlier periods only as they affect modern conditions. In the north, Turkish, as the language of Osmanli conquerors, became dominant in Asia Minor. Spoken only by Asiatic nomads, Turkish at first possessed no alphabet, and Arabic characters were borrowed; but as these letters are not particularly well adapted to expressing the sounds of Turkish, Roman letters replaced Arabic script in 1923, by decree of the Turkish Republic.

At the present time, Turkish is by no means universally spoken in Asia Minor. Towards the east, Armenian, a more ancient language with its own characters and literature, still persists; and further to the south, Kurdish has a wide extension. In the difficult and inaccessible hill districts near the Russian frontier many remnants of Caucasian languages occur – Circassian, Lazi, and Mingrelian being among the chief. Some of these represent ancient cultural or racial groups submerged by later arrivals, but others are Finno-Ugrian dialects brought in at comparatively recent dates by invaders from the east.

At one time Greek was spoken by a considerable minority in western Anatolia; and until the forcible deportations of 1922, Izmir (Smyrna) was at least as much Greek as Turkish. At the present time, Greek is still spoken in the islands of the Aegean, and is the native tongue of three-quarters of the inhabitants of Cyprus – the remainder speaking Turkish. Greek cultural influence is of great importance in the life of the island, and recent political developments have given emphasis to the question of a possible union of Greek-speaking peoples.

From the interior of Arabia have come two great groups of languages, North Semitic and South Semitic. To the first group belong the Aramaean and the Canaanitish dialects – Aramaic proper, Hebrew, Phoenician, and Palmyrene (the now extinct language of the inhabitants of Palmyra): to the second group, Arabic. In the first and second millennia B.C., extensive folk migrations spread North Semitic languages into Mesopotamia, Syria, and the Levant. Aramaic, the language of a people living on the western edge of the Syrian desert, became current over a wide area in the Middle East, most probably because of

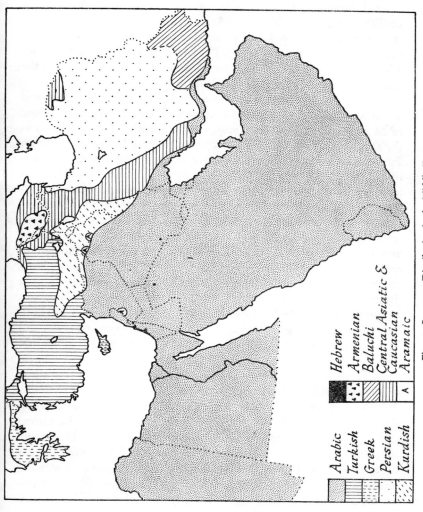

Fig. 19. Language Distribution in the Middle East

Arabic
Turkish
Greek
Persian
Kurdish

Hebrew
Armenian
Baluchi
Central Asiatic &
Caucasian
Aramaic

the extensive commercial relations developed by the Aramaean states. Aramaic dialect was the vernacular of Palestine during the time of Christ; and at least one of the Gospels can be considered as pure Aramaic literature, with several words even surviving unaltered in the English translation of the Bible.[1] Aramaic also had a considerable effect on certain languages spoken in Persia, and traces are still apparent in the north-west of the country today. The language is not completely dead; it lingers still in a few villages near Damascus and Mosul, and is the sacred language of a number of Christian sects in both countries.

Arabic, originally spoken by a small group of traders, townsfolk, and desert nomads in the district of Medina and Mecca, was the language of Muhammad and his early followers, and with the rise of Islam in the seventh century A.D. quickly replaced existing languages in Libya, Egypt, the Levant, and Iraq. As the language of the Koran, Arabic is one of the great unifying influences of the Muhammadan world, since although local deviation in vocabulary and pronunciation occur, a standard form of classical Arabic is understood by most literate Moslems.[2]

It should be noted that the dominance of Arabic in the Middle East is by no means complete: penetration of the mountain zone of the east and north did not occur. In Asia Minor, as we have seen, Arabic script only was adopted, and the numerous non-Semitic languages of the region remained in current use. Similarly, Persia retained its own distinctive speech, which can best be described as an ancient indigenous language (termed Pahlevi) much modified by extraneous influences. Extensive interchange of vocabulary and ideas between Persian and Arabic shows that the cultural influences of Arabic have been strong, yet not sufficient to drive out the native form of speech. Again reminiscent of Asia Minor, Persia has a number of minority languages, chiefly spoken by tribes living in the Zagros regions.

Broadly speaking, the Middle East can thus be divided into (a) an Arabic area, in which a single language predominates to the virtual exclusion of all others; and (b) a composite region, in which many languages, recent and ancient, remain current. It may be significant that the boundary of these two areas coincides for the greater part with the southern edge of the geological folded zone; and the effect of topography in restricting the spread of language would seem to be marked.

[1] e.g. The Last Words of Christ (Mark xv, 34).
[2] North African, Egyptian, Palestinian, Syrian, and Iraqi 'dialects' of Arabic occur. Some of these differ only in pronunciation (e.g. as between spoken English in London, Lancashire, or Scotland), but in other instances the colloquial forms may be as wide apart as, say, French, Spanish, or Italian.

SPECIMENS OF SCRIPTS IN CURRENT USE IN THE MIDDLE EAST

(I) Read from right to left:

Arabic, في البدي كان الكلمة

Aramaic (Syriac), ܚܲܝ̈ܠܐ ܐܣܝܘܣܘ ܝܘܐ ܐܠܗܐ

Hebrew, בראשית היה הדבר

(II) Read from left to right:

Armenian, Սկզբումն էր Բանն

Greek, 'Εν ἀρχῇ ἦν ὁ λόγος.

Cyrillic (Russian),[1] Въ началъ было Слово.

The examples given are all translations of John 1, i, 'In the beginning was the Word'.

RELIGIOUS DIFFERENCES

Religion, which may be defined as the awareness by man of existence of forces which are outside his own control, has been a feature of the human race at all stages of development. In the view of Dr Marett, religion is an effort to face a crisis – whenever man feels that he is likely to suffer, or to incur danger, he tries to control and influence outside forces, in the attempt to achieve a result favourable to himself. From this it is therefore possible to argue that the practice of religion by a group of people can be regarded as an endeavour, by indirect means, to serve the collective ends of the community involved.

In the view of some ethnologists, though the point is open to argument, religious belief shows stages of evolution paralleling the grades of social development in human societies. Amongst communities at a low level of civilisation, religion has a correspondingly simple form: as culture develops, spiritual beliefs assume an increasingly complex and mature pattern. Among the most primitive peoples, religion is probably most frequently concerned with efforts to ensure a plentiful supply of animals for prey. The Australian aborigines hold ceremonies in which the kangaroo and witchetty grub 'spirits' are conciliated and cajoled, in order that both of these creatures may be abundant in the path of the

[1] Used by a very few Slav-speaking groups formerly living in the Balkans and Russia.

hunter; and similarly, the Eskimo practise a form of placation of the spirits of the walrus that they are obliged to kill.

In this way, there develops in the mind of the savage a certain connexion between animals and a number of unseen but powerful forces, of which the animals tend to be regarded as a living embodiment. Such ideas, involving the association of living creatures with the forces of nature, are termed *animistic*, and would seem to be a widespread feature in human societies at an early stage of development. By a process of extension, not merely animals, but also trees, rocks, and other natural features may come to be regarded as in some way linked to the unseen powers of the world, i.e. sacred, and hence to be conciliated or invoked in order to further man's personal desires.

In societies at a higher level of development, agriculture may replace hunting as a means of livelihood; and religious practices show a corresponding evolution. Man is still concerned to invoke the forces of nature in order to increase his food supply, but abundance of animals for prey is now made much less desirable – instead, importance centres on the 'annual miracle' of plant fertility, by which regular crops are assured to the community. Favourable wind and temperature conditions, and rainfall at the due season, are essential to agriculture, and are hence matters over which man might attempt to exercise control, however indirect and remote, by means of entreaty (prayer), and bribery (sacrifice). Most of all, however, the mystery of annually recurring fertility, by which the cycle of seasonal growth is perpetuated, comes to be the fundamental element in religion; and a number of deities have personified the revival of Nature after a period of death and absence from the earth.[1] Worship of fertility can be traced in various forms in most parts of the world, and is at the present day highly characteristic of India and central Africa.

It is also interesting to note that whereas primitive man tended to ascribe to his deities an animal form, amongst agricultural peoples divinities took on human attributes. This evolution is well seen in the religion of ancient Egypt, which, at first purely animistic, with gods in the form of animals, developed at a later stage into a system in which the gods were partly human and partly animal in form, but entirely human in mental attributes. Another feature was the growth of moral and ethical ideas. Animistic religion is in effect wholly self-seeking; at a later stage, general standards of conduct appear, to which all men must conform – that is to say, altruism begins to exist alongside self-

[1] Cf. the legends of Adonis, of Persephone, and of Balder.

interest; and the practice of religion involves a wider conception of man's obligations as a member of a community. If, therefore, man has a duty to his neighbour, some sort of compulsion becomes necessary at times to make him understand this. We thus arrive at the idea of a judgment of souls after death, by which 'good' is rewarded and 'evil' is punished. In this way, altruism is strengthened at the expense of self-interest. Such a development in ethical ideas occurred in Egyptian religion as early as 3000 B.C.

Vegetational growth is influenced by many factors, a large proportion of which are purely local in origin. Moreover, agricultural communities tend to live in small, scattered groups rather than in large agglomerations, because of the necessity of being in close contact with the fields. A further factor – that of local variation in terrain – also enters in; and this, as we have seen, is highly characteristic of geographical conditions in the Middle East. The deities of agricultural communities therefore tend to be numerous, as reflecting the varied natural forces that affect the growing of crops; and because of small local differences in environment, the relative importance of each natural force, and therefore of each deity, varies from one place to another, with different names for individual deities. Rain, sunshine, and wind gods – sometimes one god for each wind – river deities in places where rainfall might be deficient; and even spirits, dryads, or nymphs associated with particular topographical features, all come to be regarded as having special attributes and powers as members of a vast divine community or pantheon that exerts control over man's activities on earth. Very frequently, there also appears the idea that the most important member of the pantheon is a mother-goddess, the source of fertility, by whose beneficent power life is maintained. Such a belief can be traced amongst many agricultural communities, from the ancient Egyptians and Greeks to modern Hindus, and would seem to be particularly characteristic of the agricultural civilisations of the Mediterranean basin.

Among pastoral communities, fertility is much less of a mystery since herders control it for their own purposes in the breeding of their animals. The nomadic way of life, involving extensive journeys from one region to another, also involved a certain acquaintance with many types of environment and many ways of life; so that unlike the settled cultivators, whose activities were influenced by local factors and whose view of life was often sharply circumscribed, the nomads tended to develop a broader outlook, and a wider conception of the world. This difference is clearly shown in the religious practices of many pastoral communities. By their wanderings, which brought them into contact with numerous local gods worshipped by settled peoples, the nomads had a better opportunity of realising that the spiritual forces that influence men's lives are fewer, but of greater magnitude – the sun has the same beneficent effect throughout the world, even though it might be worshipped, by different rites, as Apollo in Greece, as Baal in Phoenicia, and as Ra in Egypt; or, at a higher plane, ethical principles often have the same validity in human society whatever the deities with which they may be associated.

Hence the elaborate pantheon of agricultural communities, with its emphasis on fertility, was rejected amongst nomads in favour of a simpler code that was based on the relationship between individual man and the powers of morality and personal behaviour – 'What does God require of thee?' – and so self-interest, the original impulse in primitive religion, gave way in more evolved societies to a doctrine of right for right's sake. This growth of ethical content in religion can be traced in agricultural communities; but it was frequently overlain by other, often sensual, elements; and its highest elaboration would seem to occur amongst pastoral peoples.

The idea of close individual relationship to God has another implication. It is significant that from nomadic peoples, or from peoples closely in contact with nomadic ways of life, has come the belief in personal revelation of the deity. The prophets of the Old Testament, Zoroaster (Zarathustra), Jesus Christ, and Muhammad, all proclaimed the doctrine of divine revelation through man himself.

Finally, there would seem to be some connexion between the religious beliefs of pastoral peoples, and the idea of a single god. The influences tending to reduce the number of gods in nomadic societies have already been touched on; and although the link between environment and religion is tenuous and may easily be over-emphasised, there remains the historical fact that practically all of the great monotheistic religions of the world seem to have arisen on the margins of the great deserts of Eurasia, where pastoral peoples came into contact with the polytheism of settled areas. Zoroastrianism, Judaism, Buddhism, Christianity, and Islam, at once the highest developed of all religious systems of the world, share one common feature – the fact of origin under closely similar geographical environment.

The development of religious thought has been treated at some length, because in the Middle East older beliefs and practices have not entirely died out, and their influence remains to colour the observances of the newer religions – often to a surprising degree. The Greek Orthodox Church has recognised as saints and martyrs a number of what would seem to be local deities of an older, pagan, pantheon; whilst in the Lebanon a group of trees near the mouth of the Nahr Ibrahim, once hung with votive rags by the worshippers of Adonis, are still decked with strips of cloth at Eastertime by a Christian population.

Perhaps more striking still, the Ka'aba or Black Stone at Mecca, now a holy relic of Islam, had originally no connexion in any way with Muhammad, but was worshipped long before his time as a tribal fetish. Other influences deriving from more primitive forms of religion will be discussed at a later stage: it now remains to sketch the origin and features of the chief religious groupings in the Middle East, as an important element of the social life of the region.

Zoroastrianism and Judaism. These were the first of the monotheistic religions. Zoroaster, or Zarathustra, a native of Persia, lived during the period 700–550 B.C., and his teaching that human life is a battleground for opposing forces, good and evil, was adapted as the official creed of the Persian Empire under Cyrus and his successors (p. 138). The religion of Zoroaster, by its insistence on moral and ethical standards, represented a great advance on the older pagan and polytheistic creeds, which had frequently appealed to the baser human instincts of self-interest and sensuality. The older gods were, however, not entirely abandoned, but retained as subsidiary in influence to a single Lord of Goodness and Light, or sometimes as demons. Association of the Lord of Goodness[1] with light led in time to the use of fire as an important element in Zoroastrian worship; and with the spread of religion amongst peoples who found difficulty in appreciating the abstract conceptions of Zoroaster, some earlier ideas were abandoned in favour of a simpler form of belief that was greatly influenced by pre-existing pagan creeds. Fire also came to be used as the principal element of ritual. Thus Zoroastrianism became associated with fire-worship, and remained the distinctive religion of Persia until the rise of Islam. Moslem persecution over a long period has reduced the fire-worshippers to a small remnant, who now exist as a minority in the Kirman and Yezd districts of Persia. Large numbers emigrated to India, where they form the Parsee community.

The Jewish people entered Palestine during the second millennium B.C. and successfully established a small state in the highlands of Judaea.

[1] Ahura-Mazda, or Ormuzd. Cf. a modern commercial use of the name.

It was subsequent to this entry into Palestine that the religion of the Jewish people, at first worship of a purely tribal deity, and strongly influenced by a pastoral way of life,[1] developed the lofty conceptions which now characterise it. Following conquest by the Assyrian king in 722 B.C. the first dispersal of the Jewish people took place, when numbers of Jews were forcibly settled in Mesopotamia. Later, however, these immigrants were allowed to return, and the Jewish state revived. In A.D. 71, as the result of a revolt against Roman overlords, a second and more permanent Dispersal (Diaspora) took place. Jews became established in many parts of Europe and Asia, where they absorbed much of the culture and even some of the racial traits of the peoples amongst whom they settled. Yemenite, Persian, Turcoman, Georgian, and even Abyssinian Jews are distinguishable at the present day; and by reason of their oriental culture and outlook, these groups are in sharp contrast to the Jews of Europe. Numbers of Oriental Jews settled in Palestine during the Ottoman period, and for a time in the twentieth century showed some disinclination to identify themselves with Zionism. (See also Appendix IV.)

Of the European Jews, a minority settled in the Iberian peninsula and adopted much of the Spanish–Arab culture of the region. These Jews, spoken of as Sephardim, have been considered by some to be the *élite* of the Jewish people. The remainder, settled chiefly in Poland and adjacent countries, are known as Ashkenazim; and it is from this latter group that the majority of modern immigrants to Palestine have come. *Christianity.* In A.D. 313 Christianity was adopted as the official religion of the Roman Empire.[2] This adoption led to many changes in Christianity itself, which, from being the fiercely held creed of an active, but disliked and mistrusted minority, became an accepted and integral part of the Roman state. In undergoing this development, Christianity was subjected to two influences. The first, an attempt at defining a single body of dogma and ritual in order to preserve unity within the Church, is of little concern to the geographer; but the second,

---

[1] Of all the books in the Old Testament, only one, that of Ruth, shows the predominating influence of an agricultural tradition.

[2] There were many reasons for this change, some of which were mainly political in character. The Roman Emperor Constantine saw in Christianity a strong, positive social bond, by which the increasing disunity of a declining empire might be counteracted. The older Roman state, vigorous and secure, could afford to ignore the cohesive power of religion, and therefore tolerated many religious beliefs within its frontiers. At a later date, in face of disintegration within, and barbarian pressure without the empire, tolerance was abandoned in favour of a single positive religious system from which the state could derive support, and which in turn could benefit from official recognition.

the creation of administrative provinces on a territorial basis, has much geographical interest.

With the Roman world, four cities could claim a certain material and intellectual pre-eminence. Rome itself, for long the centre of the empire, began to decline in influence with the increasing economic and political importance of the lands of the eastern Mediterranean during the later Roman period; and a symptom of this shift of balance was the corresponding rise of Constantinople, which supplanted Rome as the capital of the Roman Empire in A.D. 330.

Further to the east, Alexandria and Antioch, both extremely wealthy commercial centres, had each developed a distinctive tradition based on special regional interests. Accordingly, the early Christian Church was organised into four provinces, based on the four cities, with each province headed by a patriarch. Within a relatively short time, however, instead of the unity that had been hoped for, strong regional particularism came to be manifest.

The province of Constantinople was in closest touch with the seat of government, and therefore came to be identified with imperial authority. Moreover, by reason of its location, the Church in Constantinople was greatly influenced by Classical Greek rationalist thought, and, like the older pagan religions of the country, tended to employ much painting, sculpture, and music in its ritual.

In the west, the patriarch of Rome inherited much of the ancient authoritarian tradition of the former capital city, and in spite of the newer supremacy of Constantinople, was able to exert a dominating influence on the Christians of the west. Far less affected by Greek thought, the Church in Rome developed a separate tradition of its own, more particularly as a western European church.

Christianity in Alexandria and Antioch was influenced to a varying extent by Oriental mysticism and speculation. Traces of the religion of ancient Egypt were manifest in the dogma and ritual adopted by the province of Alexandria; and other differences became apparent in Antioch. How far we can ascribe these variations in observance to historical accident, and how far to the slow operation of geographical factors is a matter beyond our present scope: the main result is, however, of immediate importance, since within a relatively short space of time increasing divergence in doctrine and ritual led to a complete separation of the four provinces. From Constantinople arose the Greek Orthodox Church; from Rome the Roman Catholic or Latin Church; from Alexandria the Coptic Church; and from Antioch the

Syrian or Jacobite Church; all of which soon came to possess complete independence in organisation.

Further division, reflecting other regional diversity, rapidly occurred. By the fourth century, an independent Armenian (Gregorian) Church had come into existence; and the teachings of Nestorius, denounced as heresy in the west, were adopted by many in Iraq, Iran, and countries further east. At a somewhat later period the sect of Maronites, followers of St John Maroun, came into existence in north-west Syria.

Later political developments in Europe and western Asia had great influence on the various religious communities of the Middle Eastern region. The supremacy of Constantinople passed away, and effective leadership amongst Christian peoples was taken over by the Church of Rome. The impact of Moslem conquest fell chiefly on the Christians of the east, so that groups like the Copts, Jacobites, Maronites, and Nestorians (or Chaldeans) dwindled to tiny communities, whilst the Churches of Rome and Constantinople continued to flourish. At a later date, further expansion of Moslem power reduced the importance of the Greek Orthodox community, but later still this decline was partly offset by the rise of Russia, which adopted the Greek faith in preference to that of Rome.

During periods of Moslem persecution, the autonomous Christian sects of the east obtained support from the Church of Rome, but often at the price of obedience to Rome. Agreements were made whereby in return for recognition of the Pope as head of the community, local usages in doctrine and ritual were permitted to continue. Hence a number of eastern Christians broke away from sects such as the Jacobites or Nestorians, and formed what are known as the Uniate Churches – i.e. communities with practices that differ widely from those of the main Roman Church,[1] but which nevertheless accept the supremacy of the Pope. There have thus come into existence the Armenian Catholic, the Greek Catholic, the Syrian Catholic, the Coptic Catholic, and the Chaldean (Nestorian) Catholic Churches. The entire Maronite Church entered into communion with Rome in the twelfth century. Formation of the Uniate Churches did not extinguish the older sects, some of which preferred a precarious independence; hence at the present time representatives of both groups, Uniate and non-Uniate, are to be found in the Middle East.

The Lebanon, and western Syria, where a mountainous topography

---

[1] Chief of these are the use of Aramaic or Arabic instead of Latin in the liturgy, and a dispensation allowing lower orders of priests to marry.

has afforded shelter to refugees, yet has also offered some reward to exploitation, now hold the greatest number of religious sects; and it is noteworthy that even as late as 1939, when the region of Alexandretta (Iskanderun) was ceded to Turkey, a number of Armenian Christians preferred to emigrate to Syria rather than remain to become Turkish citizens.

CHRISTIAN SECTS OF THE MIDDLE EAST

Ecclesiastical Provinces of the Later Roman Empire	Churches which derive from Roman Provinces (Independent)	Uniate Churches (in communion with Church of Rome)
Constantinople	→ Orthodox (Greek)	Greek Catholic
Rome	→ Latin (Roman Catholic)	
Alexandria	→ Coptic (Egyptian)	Coptic Catholic
Antioch	→ Jacobite (Syrian)	Syrian Catholic

	Later Churches (also Independent)	
	Armenian Orthodox	Armenian Catholic
	Nestorian (Chaldean or Assyrian)	Chaldean Catholic
	Maronite (until twelfth century)	Maronite (after twelfth century)
	Protestants (small in number. Due to missionary activity in nineteenth century from Europe and America)	

Political Effects. The origin and character of certain religious communities has been described at some length, because many features of social and political life in the modern Middle East derive from religious matters. Following conquest of much of the region by the Osmanli Turks after 1229, the *Millet* system was adopted as the basis of civil administration in the Turkish Empire.

A *millet* was a separate religious community, with a leader who was recognised by the Ottoman Sultan as having important religious and civil functions.[1] This arose from the fact that, owing to the view that Islam was both a religious creed and a form of civil government, the status of non-Moslems was dubious, and had to be regulated in a special manner. Each head of a *millet* was a member of the local provincial administrative body, with right of direct access to the Sultan; and was

[1] Many, but not all, of the Christian sects enumerated above were recognised as *millets*. Most important was the Greek Orthodox *millet*.

in addition permitted to maintain a kind of law-court of his own, which supervised such matters as marriage, dowries, and even the inheritance of property among his co-religionists. A most important feature was the fact that non-Moslem communities were in some cases allowed to operate their own code of law, even when this differed from the official law of the Ottoman Empire.

Hence, in addition to his ecclesiastical function, the head of a *millet* had a considerable legal and civil power; and he could also call upon Turkish civil officials to give effect to his decisions. Moreover, considerable economic power sometimes lay in the hands of the head of a *millet* by reason of the Moslem system of land tenure, which gave him some responsibility for the division of holdings amongst a number of tenant farmers (see p. 193).

The result of such organisation was ultimately to create a number of 'states within a state'; and as time elapsed, the heads of certain *millets* grew sufficiently powerful to obtain substantial privileges from the Sultan.

Another feature of the *millet* system was the opening given to interference by outside powers. France, as 'eldest daughter of the Church', assumed the role of champion of the Roman Catholic and Uniate communities; and, after the eighteenth century, Russia, a Greek Orthodox state, increasingly intervened in favour of the Greek Christians. One of the many issues of the Crimean War concerned the rivalry of Uniate and Orthodox communities in Jerusalem, and their position in relation to the Ottoman government.

In the nineteenth century, American, British, and German Protestant missionary activity gave rise to a number of educational and cultural establishments in various parts of the Middle East. These enterprises were unofficial, and, generally speaking, the various national governments concerned made little attempt to use them as grounds for intervention in the politics of the Middle East.[1] The intellectual influence of these institutions has, however, been great, particularly in the case of certain American schools and universities, so that at the present time there is something of a cultural link between the United States and the Middle East.[2]

---

[1] There were no Protestant *millets* in the Ottoman Empire. The cynic might also argue that Britain and Germany had no need to concern themselves deeply with religious matters, since much more fertile pretexts for intervention in Ottoman affairs could be found in economic and external political spheres.

[2] It is probable that during the French occupation of Syria and the Lebanon the Mandatory power did not always view the American educational establishments of Beirut,

A further feature deriving from the *millet* system has been the emphasis given to religion as a basis of political grouping. Although *millets* ended with the fall of the Ottoman Empire in 1918, the habit of associating politics with religion still persists in the Middle East. Insistence on sectarian differences as a basis of political grouping has tended to produce an atmosphere of strife and conflict, and the restlessness, faction, and extreme individualism that characterise many present-day political affairs hinder co-operation, and hence retard the development of a stable form of government.

At the present time, party politics in a number of states are still organised on a religious basis. The Lebanon, where parliamentary seats are allocated on a pro-rata basis of so many per religious group, and where the Maronites, as the largest single party, have the tacit right of nominating the President of the Republic, is an extreme example; but other instances occur, notably in Iraq, Jordan, and even Israel. This leads to a degree of clerical influence in politics that has been unknown in Britain and America since the eighteenth century.

Islam. Shortly after A.D. 600 Muhammad,[1] an obscure member of the Arabian tribe of the Qureish, began to preach a doctrine that had come to him by divine revelation. His message was first received with amusement and indifference, later with hostility; so that in A.D. 622 he decided to leave his native city of Mecca, and establish himself at Medina. This flight, or *Hegira*, from Mecca to Medina is taken as the beginning of the Muhammadan era, though it was not until some time after that Muhammad's doctrines were accepted by the Meccans. Much of Muhammad's teaching was his own; part was derived from Christian and Jewish beliefs, with which he had a slight acquaintance; all was strongly influenced by the circumstances of his life as a semi-nomad. A disdain of agriculture,[2] a 'snobisme du désert', the inferior status of women,[3] simplicity of organisation both in political and economic matters, and insistence on almsgiving and hospitality, are still as characteristic of the desert people as they were in the seventh century A.D.

Muhammad preached submission (*Islam*) to the will of one god, Allah, of whom Muhammad was the chosen prophet. The chief duties

---

Tripoli, and Aleppo with whole-hearted approval, because of the non-French outlook of these institutions.

[1] This form of the name is somewhat closer to the Arabic sound than the more usual Mohammed.

[2] Cf. Koran, 'A plough is never taken into a house without baseness going in also'.

[3] How far St Paul, himself closely in touch with desert life, held a similar view, will be a matter of discussion.

E

enjoined on Moslems were (a) prayer, five times daily, (b) the giving of alms, (c) abstention from alcohol, tobacco, and the flesh of the pig,[1] (d) fasting during the month of Ramadan, and (e) pilgrimage to Mecca. Islam was a brotherhood of men, with no social distinctions, and with no consecrated priesthood. Any man, even a youth or a slave, might act as leader in prayer; and the mosque was regarded merely as a convenient meeting place for prayer.

One important feature of Islam has been the close connexion between religion and civil government. To Muhammadans, Islam *is* the state, so that whilst acts of civil government have had religious sanction, religious leaders have also been able to exercise important influence on policy.[2] The political head of the state held important religious functions which were recognised in the title Defender or Leader of the Faith (Caliph).

Within a very few years, from being an obscure doctrine held by a small group of townsfolk and nomads in the arid interior of Arabia, Islam had spread into Palestine, Syria, Egypt, Iraq, and Iran. The surprising political success of the new religion in establishing itself alongside the Byzantine and Iranian Empires, which at that time divided the Middle East, is startling when one considers how poor were the followers of Muhammad in numbers and material resources. In order to explain how a group of shepherds, merchants, and camel drivers came to wrest the greater part of the Middle East, within a few decades, from the successors of Imperial Rome, a number of factors must be considered.

Politically and militarily, both the Byzantine Empire to the west and the Sassanid Empire of Iran were exhausted. Long continued warfare between the two powers, with Armenia, Syria, Iraq, and Palestine as a battleground, had achieved no definite result, since both belligerents were too large and too remote to be entirely over-run by the other. Border raids and skirmishes had, however, devastated much of the central part of the Middle East,[3] and high taxation and misery that resulted had made local populations very ready to acquiesce in a change

---

[1] The geographer may note with some interest the possible operation of a climatic factor. Pigs in the Middle East are much less healthy than in cooler latitudes, being often infested with parasites that can be transferred to humans. It would also seem that in a warmer climate, the intoxicating effect of alcohol is heightened.

[2] Cf. the institution of Waqf (p. 193). At the present day, capital sentences in the Law Courts of Egypt are confirmed by a religious body, the Ulema.

[3] Jerusalem was burnt by the Sassanids in 615; and a retaliatory expedition shortly afterwards devastated the centre of Iranian fire-worship at Urmia, the birthplace of Zoroaster.

of masters. Rigid social divisions, and indifference to the lot of the peasant did not serve to popularise either Byzantine or Sassanid rule.

Spiritually too the common people of the Middle East had become weary. Unending theological debates in the Christian world, with intricate discussions of forms of belief and doctrine, were frequently beyond understanding by the average Anatolian or Syrian peasant; but the charges of schism and heresy that resulted led to much general persecution and oppression, first by one sect, then by another. This in contrast was not without direct effect on the native population. In Iran, the finer ideas of Zoroaster had become overlain by a number of gross practices borrowed from earlier religions, or else were too abstract in conception for the mass of the people. In either instance the appeal of a new religion, direct and simple to understand, with a clear relationship to matters of everyday life, and which offered a brotherhood of man in place of the formalities of Zoroastrianism or the strict class distinctions of Byzantine society, had an immediate appeal. Sectarian differences among Christians were in fact so acute that on some occasions, persecuted minorities opened the gates of Byzantine cities to Moslem attackers.

Later Developments. In 632 Muhammad died, leaving no sons, and the question of a successor as Caliph immediately arose. The majority of Moslems took the view that succession should be made elective – that is, the Caliphate should not be hereditary, but could pass from one family to another. A smaller group maintained that succession ought to remain as a hereditary office within the family of Muhammad; and a nephew of the Prophet named Ali, who also married Muhammad's only surviving daughter, was recognised by them as rightful Caliph. Ali was murdered by the majority party, who became known as Sunni;[1] and a division was perpetuated between the Sunni and the followers of Ali, who took the name of Shi'a (partisans). This divergence was at first purely political, but very soon differences of doctrine and outlook also entered in.

The stronghold of the Shi'a party came to be Persia and Iraq, where a cultural life somewhat separate and distinct from that of the rest of the Middle East appears to have developed. In this one can see the operation of certain geographical factors. Iraq, and more particularly Persia, are to some extent isolated from the rest of the Middle East by vast deserts, swamps, and mountain ranges. Civilisation had to 'overcome the obstacles Nature had placed in the way of bare existence'

[1] Sunni means 'majority' or 'orthodox'.

(Haas) rather than profit from the opportunities that were more freely offered in the Mediterranean lands. In the second place, because of the widely dispersed character of Iranian settlements, with scattered towns dominating a relatively empty countryside, Hellenic influence spread by Alexander the Great took deeper root in Persia than in more closely settled agricultural regions of the Levant and Egypt (see p. 140). Some authorities see in the differences between Sunni and Shi'a a reflexion of the separate cultural evolution of the Iranian world.

Iranian contributions to the development of Islam were numerous, particularly during the period A.D. 750–1258 when, following a century of rule from Damascus under the Omeyyad dynasty, the Caliphate moved to Baghdad. It is, however, interesting to note that whilst Arabian religion penetrated into Iran, even though in a slightly altered form, the Arabic language made little headway.

Moslem Sects. As time went on, divisions within Islam increased. A number of Shi'a Moslems held that divine succession in the family of Ali came to an end when the twelfth 'Imam' or leader, a young boy, disappeared at Samarra, in Iraq, in the year A.D. 878.[1] These Moslems are known as 'Twelvers'; and one group with the local name of Metwali form a compact community in the southern and eastern Lebanon.

A son of the sixth Imam, named Ismail, was disinherited by his father for unworthy conduct, and is hence not regarded by some Shi'a adherents as a true Imam. Others, however, regard him both as divinely inspired, and the last of the Imams, seven being a mystic and complete number. From the 'Seveners' have developed numerous sects:

(a) The Qarmatians, who flourished in Persia and Iraq during the Middle Ages, and had pronounced views of a revolutionary and communistic nature. Following persecution, the sect has now almost died out.

(b) The Druses. These people combine Shi'a rites with a certain degree of animism, and a belief in the transmigration of souls. Fairly widespread in the southern Lebanon, many Druses migrated to the volcanic plateau of the Hauran as the result of Sunni persecution, and a few settled in northern Palestine. Small groups also occur in Iraq, and in western Iran.

(c) The Ismaili or Assassins developed as an extremist political group

---

[1] It is, however, believed that one day this Imam will return to the earth as the Mahdi (divinely guided one) and will conquer the world for Islam.

about the twelfth century A.D.[1] By daring attacks on their enemies they terrorised large parts of the Middle East and held much power until they were suppressed in 1250. Ismailis still live in north-west Syria, and other communities are scattered throughout Iran, Oman, Zanzibar, and India. The head of the Ismaili Moslems is the Agha Khan, who is a descendant of the last Sheikh el Jebel, himself a descendant of the seventh Imam.

(*d*) The Alawi (Ansarieh or Nusayris). Ostensibly Shi'a Moslems, the Alawi have adopted some practices, i.e. the recognition of Christmas, from Christianity. Other features, such as fertility ceremonies, have a pagan origin. The Alawi, numbering about 300,000, live in the Jebel Ansarieh of north-west Syria, and also further to the north, in the mountains of Cilicia.

(*e*) More recent Shi'a offshoots. These include the Zaidis, who are the predominant group in the Yemen; the Ali Ilahis, a sect recognising Ali as the deity, and who occur in Persia and Turkestan; and a number of Turkish communities – the Bakhtahis, who live in Albania and Anatolia, the Qizil Bashis (red-heads) of east Anatolia, and the Takhtajis (woodcutters) of west Anatolia.

Shi'a Moslems, including the communities named above, number some 25 million, that is, approximately 10 per cent. of the Moslem world.

Sectarian divisions on a less important scale have also occurred within the Sunni group. A tendency to mysticism, with the worship of saints, has given rise to a number of various orders of dervishes, who by their demonstration of 'wonders' like the handling of snakes and scorpions, or self-wounding without pain, recall the fakirs of India. Another group comprises the Sanussi of Cyrenaica. This community, with centres at the oases of Kufra and Jarabub, has played an important part in the history of the region, particularly by reason of its hostility to Italian penetration during the twentieth century. Traces of shamanism brought in from the steppes of Asia by Turki invaders appear in the Sunni Muhammadanism of parts of Anatolia and western Iran; but these influences are of restricted importance.

[1] According to contemporary accounts, the Ismailis were organised under a Grand Master known as the Sheikh el Jebel (Old Man of the Mountains). From his strongholds in the Elburz and Syrian mountains, the Sheikh dispatched retainers to carry out spectacular assassinations of leading statesmen, both Christian and Moslem; and the retainers, young men stupefied by hashish (hence *hashishin* = *assassin*), showed complete indifference to their subsequent fate – a feature that added terror to their attacks.

Some reference must next be made to the Wahhabi movement of Arabia. In the eighteenth century, a desire arose for the purification of Islam, with a shedding of all the accretions that had obscured the primitive simplicity of the faith as preached by Muhammad. It was felt that there had been much backsliding; many of the precepts of Islam, especially those relating to self-indulgence,[1] were ignored; and, in addition, much superstition and unnecessary elaboration had crept into religious observance. The Wahhabi preached a return to austerity and simplicity, and may thus be called the Puritans of Islam. After some three centuries of existence as a small and uninfluential desert group, the Wahhabi came into great prominence under the leadership of the late King Ibn Saud (d. 1954); and by their conquest of the Holy cities of Mecca and Medina, the rest of the Moslem world has been forced to give attention to Wahhabi doctrines. The newly created state of Saudi Arabia, which in one or two respects recalls the early Moslem Empire of the time of Muhammad, has under the strong and skilful rule of Ibn Saud become an important factor in Middle Eastern affairs.

Finally, the Senussi movement is of interest. This arose in North Africa during the nineteenth century, based on *zawiyas* (or lodges) for contemplation, instruction, and missionary activity. Leadership was by an Algerian who became known as the Grand Senussi. The movement affected Algeria, Egypt, and Arabia, but took deepest root in Libya, where after the withdrawal of Ottoman Turkish rulers in 1912–18 the Senussi played a leading part in the Arab struggle against Italian penetration. Following the Second World War, the (by then) exiled Senussi leader, the Emir Idris, was recognised as head of the Libyan people; and in 1951 with the attainment of independence, became king of the Libyan federation.

Paganism. Something may be said concerning the survival of pagan customs in a few districts of the Middle East. Reference has already been made to traces of Adonis worship that still persist near the Nahr Ibrahim of the Lebanon; further inland, less innocent practices are said still to occur in one or two localities. Fertility rites and cults tend to occur in many rural areas alongside more orthodox religious observances. Two distinct communities practise religious observances in which both Christian and Zoroastrian borrowings can be discerned – curiously enough, little seems to have come from Moslem sources. The Yezidi of the Jebel Sinjar region, on the borders of Turkey, Iraq,

---

[1] i.e. the prohibition of smoking, and drinking of alcohol.

and Syria, are usually spoken of as worshippers of Satan, but it would be more exact to describe their religion as propitiation of the power of evil, which, possibly not without some justification, they regard as the chief influence in the world. Numbering between 40,000 and 50,000, the Yezidi owe their survival as a separate religious community to the difficult nature and isolation of the terrain they inhabit.

The Mandeans or Sabians, much smaller in number, live in Lower Mesopotamia, in close proximity to the rivers. About one-fifth of the community lives in the Iranian districts of Ahwaz and Khurramshahr, the rest in Iraq.

Religion and Modern Life. The present age is one of sharp religious transition and re-appraisal. In some states, notably Turkey, Egypt, Syria, and to some extent Iran, nationalism is tending to replace religion as the principal socially cohesive force. In certain other countries, e.g. the Yemen, Saudi Arabia, and Libya, religious feeling is still the mainspring of rule, and the sovereign derives much authority from his acceptance as a religious leader. Jordan and the Lebanon occupy something of a middle place; but for Iraq it should be noted that whilst many of the rulers are Sunni, the majority of the people are Shi'a; and in the Lebanon relations between various sects are a fundamental issue. In Israel, too, differences between traditionalist and modernist interpretations of Judaism are important matters, and have on occasion since 1948 resulted in a change of Cabinet.

For Muhammadans there are at present certain acute issues: whether to revive Islam in its older and therefore more primitive forms – i.e. a 'return to Muhammad'; whether to abandon the Faith and substitute materialist nationalism – the ultimate logical expression of which might be a form of Communism – or whether to attempt a middle way. In Turkey, after a somewhat violent phase of attempting to reduce the links between the state and Islam (1923–50) the Democratic party quietly allowed a partial return to Islam, which is now for example taught in state schools. The differing views regarding the role of religion in a modern state are clearly obstacles (possibly minor ones) in the way of Arab unity, and further complication arises because of the personal rivalries of various rulers. The king of Jordan has inherited a feud with the Wahhabi monarchs of Arabia, who ousted his family as rulers of Mecca in 1923; and modern demagogic leaders sometimes show impatience with monarchs whose authority rests partly on a religious basis.

CHAPTER VI

Human Society in the Middle East

Writing in the thirteenth century A.D. the Arab geographer Ibn Battuta was greatly impressed by the contrasts in ways of life and social organisation shown by various communities of the Middle East. In particular, he devoted special attention to the differences between nomadic peoples, known collectively by the Arabic term of Badawin (singular: *Badawi*), and settled cultivators, or *Hadhar*. Such contrasts are still as characteristic of the peoples of the Middle East now at the present day as they were in the time of Ibn Battuta, and in examining the problems of human relationships in the region, it is useful at the outset to outline some of the chief features of social organisation. Attention will first be given to two relatively small groups – nomads and townspeople: conditions amongst the Hadhar, who form the majority of the population of the Middle East, will be dealt with at more length in succeeding chapters.

The Badawin. The main feature of this group is of course regular movement in search of pasture for animals. For the greater part, this movement is from one district to another – i.e. true nomadism; but in mountain regions different levels in the same district are occupied successively, and this is termed transhumance.[1] The Badawin of Arabia may be cited as true nomads whilst the Kurds of Anatolia and the western Zagros tend rather to practise transhumance.

With rainfall, and therefore pasture, both scanty in amount and liable to much variation from one year to another, the nomads have found that experience provides the best means of survival. Thus to the oldest members of the group is given the task of making decisions which guide the activities of the entire community – accent is, so to speak, on age, not youth. Frequently too, in the face of sudden crisis – failure of wells, or attack by outsiders – rapid decision is called for, and one man alone rather than a group, is looked to as supreme leader – in warfare particularly more confidence is felt in a single man than in a

---

[1] True nomadism is, in effect, horizontal movement, transhumance is more a change in altitude.

committee. This type of social organisation, termed patriarchal, places the life of a community under the control of a chosen man, and is highly characteristic of nomadic pastoralists. The chief (sheikh) of the community has considerable personal power, which is tempered only by precedent (the collective experience of the group as a whole) and by the opinion of older members of the tribe. There is little place for individuality, or for innovation, and patriarchal communities have kept their ways of life largely unaltered through many centuries. It has been said that if Abraham were to return, he would find little change in the habits of the present inhabitants of the Syrian and Arabian

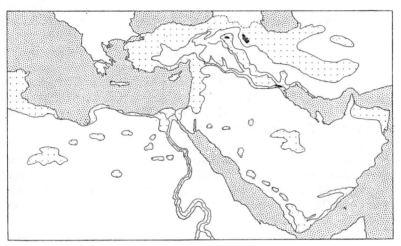

Fig. 20. Nomadism. Areas of nomadism unshaded. Settled and semi-settled occupation shown lightly dotted

deserts; and, apart from effects following the introduction first of iron in the second millennium B.C., and later of firearms, life among the Kurds seems scarcely to have varied since their present homeland was first occupied in *c.* 2400 B.C.

A sharp limit to the size of social groupings amongst nomads is set by natural resources, which in a given district can support only a relatively small number of people. Thus the unit amongst Badawin is the tribe – a group large enough to profit by advantage of numbers, yet small enough to exist under desert conditions. Family relationship is strong, and perpetuated by emphasis on intermarriage within the group. Yet although tribal solidarity and discipline are conspicuous features, it has been the weakness of Badawin society throughout the ages that political combinations larger than the tribe have been achieved merely for a very short time. An outstanding leader has brought together a number of tribes into one larger unit, but union has proved temporary; and more often than not on the death of the leader, his organisation has dissolved again into smaller groups. Large-scale political organisation is therefore not a feature of Badawin society, and resulting intertribal feuds, inveterate warfare, political instability and inconstancy have had an effect not merely on desert and steppe life, but also on that of the settled lands of the arid borders. It is also possible to see why, in the absence of strong internal political organisation, so much of the Middle East has in the past fallen under the control of outside powers.

To each tribe belong certain rights of pasture and occupation. The limits of each tribal territory are carefully defined, and generally comprise a summer and a winter camping ground. Exact size of territory usually has a certain relation to the physical force and prestige commanded by each tribe, and limits therefore vary from one period to another. Weaker tribes seek 'protection' from a larger.

Environmental conditions within desert areas vary considerably, with resulting variation in influence on the precise way of life of the inhabitants. For example, the northern part of the Arabian desert is a vast open tableland, dissected into occasional shallow valleys or closed basins; whilst further south, topography varies from a succession of jagged uplands, *poljes*, lava-fields, highly eroded basins and valleys, passing eastward into distinctly more subdued relief. Climate, especially rainfall, also shows significant variation: in western Arabia there can be sufficient for sporadic cultivation, with or without irrigation.

Human response to these conditions is extremely varied in character. Near the Euphrates, relatively short-distance movement with sheep- and goat-rearing is the rule, with an approach to transhumance rather than full nomadism in the extreme north on the edge of the mountain rim of Turkey–Kurdistan. Further south, in the open zones between Damascus, Baghdad, and Jordan, more extensive migration based on the use of the camel is characteristic; whilst in Arabia proper there are all stages from extensive movement involving camels as the basis of the economy, to partial nomadism only, with an approach to cultivation and semi-settlement. A similar state of affairs exists in the deserts of Libya. On the Jebel Akhdar of Cyrenaica, nomads have a complicated annual routine involving a double seasonal movement to and from the uplands; with an approach to cultivation. Further south, movement is around wells within the more arid zones, whilst the presence of oases allows the existence of completely settled agricultural communities.

It is hence possible to draw a summary distinction between camel-nomads, who usually cover great distances; shepherds, whose territory may be more confined; and semi-nomadic or transhumant groups who practise some degree of cultivation. This pattern is in constant fluctuation, partly as the result of climatic vagaries, and also with slower changes in numbers and influence. Moreover, with the increased political control of desert areas by local governments there has been a strong tendency for nomads to become more settled. Where tribal territories cross international frontiers, special problems arise, and whilst agreements give to nomads temporary nationality of the country in which they find themselves, this arrangement is not wholly agreeable to the governments involved.

Because of the necessity for constant movement, the material culture of the Badawin is poor. Chief possession of the tribesman, after his animals, is a tent, usually black, and woven of camel or goat hair. When in good repair, these tents are quite waterproof – sufficient to withstand the infrequent, but severe downpours which occur – and the size of the tent, shown by the number of tent poles used, is an indication of the affluence and social standing of the owner. The interior is divided, on the right for men, and on the left for women. One side away from the wind is usually left open, with a coffee hearth in front. The coffee hearth is the social centre of the household; and the head of the family, although leaving the entire preparation of food to his womenfolk, will himself undertake the preparation and serving of coffee. True Badawi coffee is strong, devoid of milk or sugar, but flavoured with herbs; and its consumption is the occasion of much social activity – the rounding off of the day, and an opportunity for discussion, and the reception of guests. For the Badawin, if not for city dwellers, coffee is truly the 'wine of Islam', and the equipment of all Badawin households includes at least one carpet, which is spread before the hearth, a mortar, and coffee pots and cups. A few cooking pots, and one or two large trays and bowls for communal eating make up the remainder of the culinary equipment.

Clothing of the Badawin is simple. A long robe of thick material is the principal, sometimes in fact the only, garment. In winter a waterproof cloak of woven camel hair is worn. A voluminous headcloth, held in place by a rope or band, is wound round the head so as to give protection to the face and neck, and rawhide, heelless sandals are worn on the feet.

Water is usually too precious for much washing[1] – indeed, the Koran permits the ceremonial use of sand in the daily ablutions which are enjoined on all Moslems – and animal urine is frequently used as a substitute. Badawin food is monotonous and scanty. Most important are milk products: curds, buttermilk, various kinds of cheese – of which *labné*, a kind of cream cheese, is the most widespread – and *samné*, or butter. In addition, wheat, barley, and occasionally a little rice are obtained by barter, blackmail, or brigandage from agriculturalists, or else grown very sporadically by the nomads themselves.[2] Small amounts of dried fruit, usually dates, are also eaten. Meat is provided only as a great luxury, since animals themselves are in effect a kind of fixed capital – owners must live from the yield, not upon the animal itself. Apart, then, from occasions of high festival, when special slaughtering takes place, only those animals that die naturally are eaten.

Meals are served first to the older men of the tent, each man using his dagger as a knife, and fingers as a fork,[3] after which, when they are satisfied, it is the turn of the younger men and boys. Later still come the women and finally the girls – the sexes never intermingling during meals. On occasion when supplies are plentiful, the Badawin eat copiously, because the time and scale of the next meal may be uncertain. In general, the standard of nutrition of the Badawin is low – in the opinion of some, below the level necessary in other regions to sustain life. As a result, the Badawin are small, even stunted, and lightly built, though their physical powers and endurance are great. Life is, however, very hard; and by forty, particularly in the case of women, old age has begun. Fifty years is a long life for a nomad.

One means of supplementing the deficiencies in arid areas is by raiding. Amongst the Badawin the *ghazu* (*rhazw, razzia,* or *rezzou*) is a recognised activity amounting almost to sport, but it also fulfils a definite economic function. The effects of a bad season are mitigated, as when rains have failed in the desert the Badawi has a choice of taking what he requires by force from other people, or of starving. The word

---

[1] It has been said of a certain present-day Wahhabi tribe of Arabia that all adult members have at least once in their lifetime been forced to exist on water taken from the hump of a camel.

[2] Patches of ground are roughly sown with grain, and later in the year tribesmen return to harvest the crop.

[3] As far as possible, use of the left hand is avoided in polite Arab society – this hand is employed for menial and unpleasant tasks.

'sport' has been used, because although fundamentally a serious matter, Badawin raids are conducted under certain conventions – almost, one might say, rules.[1] Rapid, unlooked-for coups, using cunning and guile, are most favoured: bloodshed is as far as possible avoided, though goods, womenfolk, and children become the property of the victors under a kind of slavery. Successful leadership in tribal raids is the means by which personal reputation and power is built up: King Ibn Saud, originally a dispossessed desert nomad, gained absolute power in Arabia through successful tribal encounters on an increasingly large scale. Badawin raids may be directed against other tribes, but frequently, toll is levied on agricultural settlements on the fringe of the desert. Less able to resist, and with more at stake than the nomad, settled cultivators sometimes remain under permanent tribute to Badawin tribes, and supply a quantity of needed foodstuffs to their overlords. The name *khaoua* (tribute of friendship) is applied to such transactions. Raiding is now declining, because of increasing control by local governments, but in addition to the political problem presented in controlling outbreaks, there is the economic factor of providing alternative occupation to ensure a livelihood.[2] Though declining, the practice is still not extinct. For as recently as 1946, J. C. Crowfoot could write, 'Arabs are now raiding each other in Fords and Chevrolets.'

Strict discipline, necessary both in everyday routine and because of liability to attack, has left its mark on Badawin ways of thought. In religion, there is little room for compromise or doubt – a strong, vivid, and intolerant faith is held. Similarly, there is a strict code of behaviour. Hospitality, in an environment without fixed routes or settlements, is a highly regarded virtue, and ordinary social intercourse has been developed into an elaborate code of manners and conduct. In view of the vagaries of human existence amongst the Badawin, it is hardly surprising that superstition and fatalism are also strongly marked. The operation of the 'evil eye' and malevolent spirits is seen in everyday life – nothing is praised directly without attributing its excellence as due to God – and men and animals wear charms.[3]

Possibly as a result of reduced physical strength, and their enforced preoccupation with household tasks, the status of women is low. Although not veiled, like the women of the settled areas, Badawin

[1] There are only three sources of amusement or distraction in Badawin life: conversation round a coffee hearth, family life, and raiding.
[2] Cf. the decline in population of the Barbary coastlands since the suppression of piracy in the Mediterranean. There, precisely the same economic factor was involved.
[3] Even Arab taxis in the cities carry a charm on the radiator.

women are regarded as in all things the inferiors of men. It may be significant that among pastoral communities, religious deities are regarded as masculine in attribute. Only in the religious systems of non-pastoral peoples do we find female deities – mother-goddesses of wide influence – with a corresponding rise in importance of women above the level of mere drudges and bearers of children.

Though Badawin life is hard and unrewarding, those who follow it value it highly. A true Badawi looks down with disdain on other ways of life, particularly that of cultivators in better watered districts, for whom he often has a profound contempt as effete and subservient. Despite their own strict social organisation, the Badawin can contrast the dull routine of agricultural practice, and the looseness and self-indulgence of city life with their own courage, independence of thought, abstemiousness, and mobility.

Nomadism is a special response to environment, by which the frontier of human occupation is pushed further within a region of increasing difficulty. In the past, nomadism has often been regarded as an unsatisfactory alternative to agriculture; it was believed that primitive man passed from a life of hunting and collecting first into a stage of pastoralism, and later, in places where conditions were favourable, to the fullest development of a life based on cultivation. In the opinion of H. J. Fleure and others this view must be modified – pastoralism may, in some instances, represent a special, later development *from* agriculture – a dynamic response to environmental conditions, and not a degeneration, or a mere half-stage towards something better.

In certain cases, nomadism represents the only possible utilisation of limited geographical opportunities. This observation may seem trite, but it would not seem to be fully appreciated even by some governments of states in which pastoral nomadism exists. A number of Middle Eastern rulers have tended to regard their nomadic peoples as an inferior community to be 'civilised' as quickly as possible by the imposition of a different way of life, usually agriculture. In the recent past, forcible measures have been taken to settle nomadic tribesmen (e.g. in Persia and Turkey), but it was often found that mental qualities declined, and poverty and disease increased to such an extent as to bring about virtual extinction of some communities. Now, with the development of oil pipelines across arid areas, there is scope for new employment; and in Arabia especially oil revenues have enabled the rulers to enforce partial sedentarisation; or to achieve this through the higher living standards that follow employment by an oil company. The sharp conflict of views regarding nomads is clear from a report ('Problems of the Arid Zone') made by U.N.E.S.C.O. One writer, an Arab, speaks of the 'urgent duty [of working out] a policy for dealing with nomadic groups, usually aiming at complete or partial settlement' and 'It seems desirable that economic integration through sedentarisation should be followed by social integration with the rest of the population'. Barth (a Norwegian) however writes in the same volume, 'the possibilities of modification and adaptation of nomadic forms to present conditions have not been sufficiently considered'. This is also the view of the present writer: despite considerable changes, nomadism has a continuing, though greatly reduced significance in Middle East economy and social life. Few reliable estimates of numbers exist, but a figure of 5–7 per cent. of the total population of the Middle East would be a reasonable approximation. Most nomads live in Turkey, Persia, and Arabia, with 1–2 million nomads in each country; Syria has 10 per cent. – about 400,000; Iraq 8 per cent. – 384,000; Egypt 50,000, Israel 18,000, with perhaps 200,000 in Libya.

Commerce and the Growth of Towns. Situated at the junction of three continents, and fringed by areas of sea or desert, both of which may be considered as open to navigation of a certain kind, the Middle East region has developed extensive trading relations, not only within itself, but more important, with China, India, Europe, and to a less extent, Africa. From earliest times commerce has played a conspicuous part in Middle Eastern affairs, and the existence of a merchant community, with special outlook and interests, has had considerable repercussion on cultural development.

Commerce as carried on under Middle Eastern conditions can be said to represent a kind of integration of several ways of life. Besides the merchant body, directly engaged in exchange of products, the organisation of long-distance transport involves a supply of foodstuffs and other agricultural products, and hence the Hadhar of the countryside have some part to play. Caravan activity across desert and steppe also necessitates the employment of Badawin as guides and drivers – and sometimes subsidies are paid to tribesmen to secure safe passage of caravans. The list could be extended to include woodmen and foresters, useful as producers of timber for shipbuilding, and of charcoal, the only fuel (until the modern use of petroleum) that was available for local industry. To an unusual degree, therefore, activities related to commerce permeate the life of the Middle East; and though the benefits from trading fall very unequally as between merchants and others, yet a slight influence can be traced amongst almost all communities.

By its need of fixed points and a measure of security in which exchange can take place, commerce can be regarded as the main contributing factor to the rise and growth of towns; and because of the unusual extent of commercial relations in the Middle East, town life also shows exceptional development – so great, in fact, as to give rise to disharmony between urban and rural areas. The countryside, given over to agriculture or nomadism, is on the whole poor in resources, and the general standard of life is low; but in cities, continent-wide trading relations have led to considerable accretion of wealth. Trading involves acquaintance with many different communities and ways of life – hence open-mindedness, adaptability and receptiveness for new ideas tend to be characteristic of commercial peoples, and in towns, material progress has often been accompanied by cultural development.

In addition to commerce, there are other factors which have contributed to the extraordinary development of town life in the Middle East. We may first note the purely geographical control of a restricted water supply – because of salinity or deficiency of water, people have been forced to congregate in a few favoured spots where supplies were available. Secondly, the course of Middle Eastern history reveals that time and time again, a vigorous yet small community has asserted political domination over a large area, but because of numerical inferiority, has been unable to undertake extensive colonisation: instead, a hold has been maintained on towns, from which an alien countryside has been ruled. The ancient Persians, Greeks, Romans, early Arabs, and the Turks have all followed this plan, so that a tradition of rule and dominance has come to be characteristic of the towns.

Thirdly, there is the religious aspect. As we have now seen, the great religions of the Middle East spread from small beginnings, and this spread has been easiest and most marked among urban populations, who by their receptiveness for outside ideas, formed a favourable ground for the propagation of new creeds. Amongst a conservative and backward peasantry, propagation was slower: even now Christianity and Islam as practised in remote rural areas are often very different from the same religions in the towns.

To a great extent, therefore, religious life has come to be associated chiefly with towns and cities – we need only think of Jerusalem and Mecca in this connexion, though the list could be extended to include the holy cities of Iran and Iraq. The growth of religious traditions has in turn further stimulated commercial activity, especially through pilgrimage.

It is interesting to observe that, with a basis of trading activity, administrative control, and religious association, the cities of the region have been able to maintain an uninterrupted tradition over several thousand years. Political groupings come to an end, but the importance of towns continues: in the Middle East cities outlast empires.

By contrast to China, where towns are of relatively minor import-ance, and social life derives most closely from the countryside, urban life in the Middle East stands out sharply against a background of rural poverty and backwardness. The town-dweller has by far the larger share of available amenities in buildings, communications, public health, education, and entertainment – very few professional men of any kind practise outside the towns.[1] Hence the wealthy landowner, unlike his European counterpart, avoids living on his estates, and passes his time in the city, away from the archaic, disease-ridden, under-privileged, and despised countryside. In the words of Dubertret and Weulersse, 'there is an extraordinary inequality between town and country. The former gathers to itself power and wealth, whilst rural communities remain singularly disinherited.' This process has even tended to develop faster during the present century, with a consequent widening of the gulf between city and countryside, and concentration of political and economic power in fewer hands.

As a further element in the disharmony between town and country, Weulersse also points out that great racial and cultural differences are sometimes apparent between towns and their immediate hinterlands. As examples, he cites the towns of north-west Syria and the Hatay: Latakia, the 'Capital of the Alawi region', without any Alawi popula-tion, but inhabited by Christians and Sunni Moslems; Hama, an Arab town in a Badawin and Alawi countryside; and Antakya, a Turkish settlement in an Alawi and Arab rural area.

A further point of interest is the character and morphology of a Middle Eastern town. The main features are (1) the grouping of population often by sect, rather than social class – as is usual in European towns, (2) the tendency for trades to gather in the same street or location, and (3) the lack of development in civic consciousness. Grouping by religion gives rise to the idea of 'quarters' – i.e. Armenian districts are common in many cities, and there are some, or all, of

[1] e.g. about one-half of all Iraqi doctors live in Baghdad city.

'Shi'a', 'Coptic', 'Greek', or 'Frangi' (= Frank, west European) districts in such cities as Beirut, Damascus, Jerusalem, Baghdad, and Cairo. This derives in large part from the '*Millet*' days, and the need of a minority for solidarity and protection.

A similar community feeling among merchants, tradesmen, and artisans in the face of arbitrary exaction by rulers and officials has led to grouping by trades, so that one finds a whole street of vendors or producers of the same article – oil seeds, cloth, or ironmongery. Merchants with valuable commodities find it convenient to live in streets that can be closed off entirely all night: and from this has developed the *suq* or trading centre, which is a prominent feature of nearly all Middle Eastern towns. One of the finest is the Aleppo suq, which is a bewildering labyrinth of tunnels lined by alcoves where goods are displayed. Above these, and reached by winding awkward stairs (to discourage assault), are workrooms and living quarters, some of which are real treasure-houses. Old Jerusalem is almost all of this pattern, with only two streets usable for any length by wheeled vehicles, and the covered labyrinths are so confusing to visitors that many are glad after mounting bewilderment to pay to be led out – since there are only four gateways.

With strong sectional rivalries, and often unsympathetic, arbitrary rule, it is hardly surprising that civic feeling and municipal government is not always strong. Drainage or even the supply of drinking water may be entirely by surface runnels – and civic government is relatively undeveloped compared with the mediaeval town of western Europe, where a vigorous middle class took over town rule from feudal lords. The Middle Eastern town offers more scope to the individualist, and retains more than a trace of feudal control. It is only within the last few decades that there have arisen municipal councils with elected representatives and general powers over town development.

The Middle Eastern town shows many contrasts with its European counterpart. Because of general insecurity[1] and sectional feeling, houses of any size tend to present few openings to the outside, with solid bare walls devoid of ornament, heavy doors and window shutters. Life centres on an interior courtyard. With the grouping by religion or occupation, rather than wealth, there can be juxtaposition of large and mean houses; though modern suburbs in the European style are now increasingly common. Most shops in towns carry a heavy iron roller

[1] Over £40 million of damage was done by rioters in Cairo in 1951; and an even greater amount in Istanbul in 1956 and in Beirut in 1957.

shutter that can cover the entire front: this is a precaution against the disturbances that are all too frequent.

Increasingly, modern governments are giving attention to replacement of old, squalid city-centres by new departmental stores, offices, and wider roads. This is conceived on the style of Haussmann – besides the principal aims of improving amenities, appearance, and communications, straight streets rather than crooked alleys also tend to reduce risings and riots; they are far more easily controlled by police and the military.

In closing this outline of social grouping, it may be of interest to suggest a relationship of physical environment to human activity: there may be a limited connexion between type of terrain and the features of social grouping discussed in the present chapter.

The Foreland stands out as the home of pastoral nomadism at its fullest development. Here, as we have seen, has arisen a special culture and way of life – hard, patriarchal, and intensely spiritual and occupied with the things of the mind, often particularist, narrow, and unprogressive, yet spreading outward from time to time with immense impact on neighbouring regions.

The mountaineers of the north stand somewhat apart. Practising a transhumance from summer to winter pastures that rivals in extent the migration of desert herders, their social organisation has many points of similarity with that of the Badawin Arabs, but because of a land connexion with inner Asia, marked racial differences have entered in. It is difficult – and dangerous – to discuss mental qualities in relation to the racial origin, but there are grounds for distinguishing certain special qualities amongst these mountain peoples. Less given to speculation and inquiry, the mountaineers have displayed a more solid talent for administration and military virtues – qualities that are more mundane and pedestrian, yet demand longer sustained activity. If Muhammad and Moses can be said to typify southern nomad, then Saladin, Cyrus, or Kemal Atatürk (and even Joseph Stalin) might equally represent the northern warrior-governor.

There remains a third group, that living in the zone of transition between Foreland and Mountain zone. Here a concern with material objects, and due appreciation of the benefits of intercourse and trade, have contributed to a broadness, or even suppleness of mind that has often earned the scorn of more primitive and ingenuous nomads and mountaineers. In this area of wider opportunity and richer culture based on commerce and agriculture, contributions first made by outsiders have frequently been developed into intellectual or political forces large enough to affect world history. It is also fair to state that many other cultural developments of importance have spent themselves in a morass of sectarian rivalry, regional jealousy, or enervating luxury. The laws of Moses, promulgated in the wilderness, gave way to worship of the Golden Calf; but the polity elaborated by an orphan brought up amongst camel-drivers preserved much of the learning of the Ancient World at a time when the Dark Ages of Europe threatened its extinction.

CHAPTER VII

Aspects of the Historical Geography of the Middle East

I. THE RISE OF EMPIRES IN RELATION TO THEIR GEOGRAPHICAL SETTING

It is the opinion of most archaeologists that civilisation first developed in the Middle East, where, of all regions of the world, natural conditions offered the greatest assistance to man in his change-over from a life of nomadic wandering as a hunter to settled occupation of the soil. The regular rise of the three larger rivers, Nile, Euphrates, and Tigris; annual renewal of soil fertility by the deposition of a layer of silt; and the generally warm climate, favourable both to the growth of a rich plant-life, and to the activities of man himself, were all special inducements to the adoption of a way of life based on agriculture.

Until recently, many archaeologists took the view that civilised communities first arose in Egypt, though only a very short time before a similar development in Mesopotamia: a more recent opinion is now that the earliest advances may have taken place in Mesopotamia. Whichever view is followed, it is necessary to bear in mind that geographical conditions in both regions were not identical, and it can in fact be stated that in Mesopotamia environmental factors were not as wholly favourable as in the valley of the Nile. The Nile is a single stream, without tributaries in its lower course; but the Tigris and Euphrates are both braided streams, and the former receives important affluents which bring down immense masses of silt that block the lower courses of both rivers, giving rise to swamps, lagoons, shifting banks, and coastlines. Moreover, the floods of Mesopotamia are more variable, since they depend on rainfall that occurs within the Middle East area, and this, as we have seen, tends to be capricious and unreliable. Further, because of their direct relationship to winter rainfall (either from run-off, or the later melting of snow), Mesopotamian floods occur in spring; not, as in Egypt, during the late summer. Flooding by the Tigris and Euphrates, which can be sudden and variable in character, follows hard upon the rainy season, giving a long dry period throughout more than half the year: in Egypt, floods as it were complement the rainy season by splitting the year into four shorter seasons – one of slight rainfall, one of flood, and two of drought. Of the two regions, Egyptian conditions might be considered as more 'manageable', and would seem to demand less experience and resource.

At all events, whichever view obtains, it is clear that by about 4000–3500 B.C., both Egypt and Mesopotamia had a highly evolved social life, with organised civil and religious bodies. Copper and bronze were used, although on a limited scale; and trading contacts with other regions had begun. Many of these contacts were with Syria, which, lying between Egypt and Mesopotamia, and easy of access from the south and east, participated at an early date in the general advance of material and cultural development. Syria was endowed with a number of products that were lacking elsewhere: neither Egypt nor Mesopotamia could grow trees of any size, hence the abundant forests of the Syrian coastal fringe were exploited for timber, and for the oils prized by the Egyptians for use in embalming. Much trade was developed by sea; Byblos, which served as an outlet for the timber of the Lebanon Hills, can with reason claim to be one of the oldest ports of the Mediterranean, if not the oldest continuously inhabited site in the world.[1]

Cultural development in the three regions, Egypt, Mesopotamia, and Syria, followed somewhat different courses. In Egypt a clearly marked unity was most characteristic; and this seems to have owed much to physical factors: the strongly developed rhythm of the seasons, an unfailing annual flood, and most of all, the nature of the river valley itself, which, sharply defined as a single trench, was isolated on three sides by desert, and on the fourth by the sea. Within this physical framework there grew up a stable and extremely traditional civilisation of consistently high level.

In Mesopotamia the unity deriving from a single river valley was not present, and, though potentially a rich area on a scale larger than in Egypt, physical changes within the region itself – alteration in river course, and the possible recession of the head of the Persian Gulf towards the south-east – had a disturbing effect. The space-relationships of the country, which was more open to outside influence from east, north, and west, had at times a further disruptive influence on cultural development, so that although civilisation in Mesopotamia reached a

---

[1] Another product of the Byblos region was papyrus, from which developed a commerce in manuscripts and 'books'. Hence the name Bible, the 'Great Books'.

high level, at best fully comparable with, and possibly superior to that of Egypt, there were on the other hand periods of regression and anarchy, with a certain discontinuity that stands in contrast to conditions in the Nile valley. It is significant that during earlier historic times, Syria, which by virtue of its position might have been expected to lie within the Mesopotamian orbit, was more closely under the influence of Egypt.

The richness of Syria attracted the attention of outsiders; but here natural conditions were against the development of a politically unified community. The coastal plain is narrow and broken, with the Lebanon and Ansarieh ranges as a real barrier to movement inland; in the hilly country, settlement is restricted to valley floors, or to the very small extent of level plateau; whilst further inland still, because of lower rainfall, favourable sites occur only in close proximity to springs, rivers, and lakes. Hence city-states came to be more characteristic of Syria. These were of small size, often dependent on intercourse and trade, and markedly jealous of their immediate neighbours, from whom they were usually separated by a slight topographical barrier. Such a collection of small-scale units could easily fall prey to piecemeal absorption by aggressive outsiders; hence one can see why Syria, though naturally rich, has so rarely existed as an independent political unit.

The early part of the second millennium B.C. was marked by a number of incursions by pastoral peoples from the north. The Hyksos or Shepherd Kings invaded Egypt from eastern Syria, whilst the Kassites entered lower Mesopotamia. Two other peoples, the Mitanni and the Hittites, became settled respectively in north-east Syria between the Tigris and the Euphrates, and in Anatolia. These pastoral communities, though originally of lower cultural development than the agriculturalists they had conquered, quickly absorbed existing ideas, and also made important new contributions to the life of the Middle East. To them are due the introduction of the horse and the chariot; and to the Hittites in particular, the invention of iron, which was first developed as a curiosity in about 1300 B.C., and later replaced bronze as the chief metal of everyday use.[1]

During the same epoch further incursions brought the Aramaean peoples from the deserts of Arabia to the better watered regions of the Levant, and numerous small communities established themselves in various parts of Syria and Palestine, amongst them the Canaanites,

---

[1] For further details of this period, the student is referred to *Corridors of Time*, Vol. X, 'The Horse and the Sword', by H. J. E. Peake and H. J. Fleure.

Israelites, Philistines, and Phoenicians. The power of the ancient king-doms of Egypt and Mesopotamia declined – many petty states developed in the region of the Fertile Crescent, and the rise of Phoenician settlements is a feature at this period.

As the result of the extensive commercial relations developed by the Phoenicians,[1] Aramaic languages now began to spread over much of the Middle East, reaching as far as Persia. One factor in the spread was the Phoenician invention of the alphabet, which represented a consider-able advance on the cumbrous hieroglyphics of Egypt and the cunei-form characters of Mesopotamia, which were best adapted to writing on clay tablets.

In 1200–1000 B.C. there came the rise of Assyria. Based on the fertile plains of the upper Tigris, the Assyrian state combined a measure of trade with a well-developed agricultural system that relied on rainfall rather than on irrigation – a new feature which illustrates the progress of agricultural technique. Copper and iron from Anatolia and the Zagros were exchanged for agricultural and animal produce of the adjacent riverine and steppe regions; and an important transit trade linked Assyria with Syria and Persia. Because of their close relations with areas of production, the Assyrians were able to make much use of iron in military weapons, which by reason of a greater size and power were superior to those of their enemies.

In 539 B.C. the Mesopotamian lowland was conquered by Cyrus of Persia; and within a short time a considerable empire extending from the Hindu Kush to the Aegean, and including Egypt, had been created. This organisation of the Middle East as a single unit, occurring for the first time, brought many changes in outlook and material development. Until the rise of Persia, little had taken place to modify the regional political units which had developed within the framework imposed by natural conditions. The ancient communities of Egypt and Meso-potamia had evolved an economic life based primarily on cultivation by irrigation, supplemented by some sheep rearing, and by a restricted amount of outside trade and commerce. Elsewhere in the Middle East, development had been largely on the Syrian pattern of city-states.

Following the Persian conquest, successful attempts were made to develop the Middle East as a single unit. Roads were constructed with a system of posts and resthouses, to link various parts of the Empire; a

---

[1] The chief Phoenician cities were Tyre, Sidon, and Arad (Ruad). Further inland Aram (Damascus) had a considerable trans-desert trade, but did not form part of the Phoenician confederation.

centralised administration, with efficient civil servants, came into being; and attention was paid to expanding economic life. One factor in the success of Persian rule was the widespread use of Aramaic, which became the official language of the Empire; and another was the adoption of a metal coinage, first used a short time before by the Midas dynasty of Lydia (Asia Minor), the last monarch of which (Croesus) was defeated by the Persians in 546 B.C.

The change of space-relationships following the breakdown of older regional groupings had important consequences in Mesopotamia, which, formerly on the edge of the civilised world, now profited from a central position. Although sea communications were not developed in the Persian Gulf, a considerable number of land routes from Egypt, Syria, Anatolia, Arabia, and Persia converged in the valley of the Euphrates–Tigris; and Mesopotamia became a centre of exchange for the whole Empire. With settled political conditions, and the stimulus of efficient organisation, trade developed on a more extensive scale – as intercourse between districts increased, products from various parts of the Empire were more quickly and easily exchanged. A tax assessment of the period (see *Cambridge Ancient History*) gives some indication of the economic importance of Mesopotamia under Persian rule.

ANNUAL ASSESSMENT FOR TAX

		Talents
Satrapy of Assyria and Babylonia		1,000
„ „ Egypt		700
„ „ Cilicia		360
„ „ Syria (including Palestine and Cyprus)		350

Further changes resulting from the Persian conquests were the incorporation of Asia Minor and Persia in the main stream of Middle Eastern culture. Development in Asia Minor was uneven: the advanced communities of the western plateau, and especially of the coastlands (e.g. Lydia), made important contributions to the general life of the Empire; but towards the north and east, more backward peoples remained in isolation as nomads and barbarians. In Persia, a considerable Indo-Aryan racial element had developed special features of culture which were markedly different from those of the Semitic civilisations of Egypt, Mesopotamia, and Syria. Juxtaposition and later fusion of the two cultures – Indo-Aryan and Semitic – produced important advances; from the process of intermixture, recurring at intervals over many centuries, can be traced a number of outstanding developments, chief of which may be counted the rise of the Parthian Empire in opposition to the Romans; and some centuries later, the development of Shi'a heresies within the Moslem world.

Classical Period. In 331 B.C. Alexander (the Great) of Macedon defeated the Persian monarch Darius at Arbela (Erbil), and annexed the entire Persian Empire, to which he added his own conquests in Europe, Turkestan, and India. Although Alexander himself died very shortly afterwards, Hellenic influence in the Middle East was maintained by a number of his generals, who established themselves as successors of Alexander in various parts of the region. To one such general, named

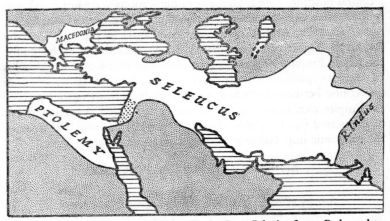

Fig. 21. Division of the Empire of Alexander the Great. Palestine first to Ptolemy, later to descendants of Seleucus

Ptolemy, fell control of Egypt, with, at first, Syria and Palestine; and the Ptolemaic dynasty, to which belonged Cleopatra, ruled Egypt until the Roman conquest of the country in 30 B.C. Another general, Seleucus, established a dynasty in Persia, Mesopotamia, and, at a later date, in Syria. Themselves of partly Indo-Iranian origin, the Macedonians found much in common with the defeated Persian aristocracy, with whom they intermarried and formed a Perso-Macedonian ruling class. A strong military tradition, with extensive use of the horse; a talent for organisation; and a bent for speculation and intellectual inquiry seem to have been characteristic of both peoples.

A further bond was the emphasis given by both Macedonians and Persians to town life. The Macedonians especially, as a small minority group, found that Hellenic influence could be extended far more easily amongst the townspeople than amongst large and scattered bodies of cultivators. Accordingly, emphasis was placed on the development of towns and cities: old centres were renamed and expanded, and new sites were carefully chosen.[1] In this way a very small racial minority was able to maintain a political supremacy, and to make a disproportionately large contribution to the cultural life of the Middle East. Within the towns, Hellenism was often dominant; in the countryside, older Semitic traditions persisted.[2]

Greek influence in the Middle East gradually declined as the original invaders became assimilated into the native populations. A gradual breakdown of the Ptolemaic and Seleucid kingdoms was accompanied by the rise of militant Judaism in Palestine under the Maccabees, and by the rise of native kingdoms in Armenia, and in Persia, where a Parthian dynasty established its rule in the second century B.C., finally defeating the Seleucids in 83 B.C. Another factor in the extinction of the successors of Alexander was the rise of Rome, which, following an entry into Asia Minor in 189 B.C., eventually absorbed by slow degrees during the next two centuries both the Ptolemaic kingdom and the remnant of Seleucid territory left outside the Parthian sphere.

The Romans were unable to make headway against the newly created Parthian state; so that whereas the western portion of the Middle East fell under Roman influence, the east remained separate, as part of a native Persian (Parthian) kingdom. Thus there came into existence a frontier region: in the south, the empty deserts of Arabia were a sufficient barrier; in the extreme north, the difficult hill country of Armenia, much of it over 7,000 feet in height, and gashed by immense canyons, fulfilled a similar function. Between the two, in the more open areas of the Syrian steppe, a military 'defence in depth' was created by the Romans. Based to the north on the highland massifs near Nisibin, the defence line ran via the Jebel Sinjar across the desert to the uplands of the Hauran and Jebel Druse, being marked along its whole length by forts, signalling stations, and fortified towns. During the Roman period, these latter fulfilled the dual role of military bases in time of disturbance, and of trading centres in time of peace (Fig. 22).

Despite the power of Rome, the centres of the Parthian Empire,

---

[1] e.g. in Syria the already existing Haleb (Aleppo) and Carchemish were re-named Beroea and Doura; whilst new towns were created: Alexandretta, Laodicea (Latakia), from the name of a sister of Seleucus, Antiochia, and Heliopolis (Baalbek).

[2] Cf. Pontius Pilate's inscription on the Cross of Christ: in Latin, the language of the conquerors, in Greek, the language of the native townsmen and officials, and in Aramaic, the Semitic language of the peasantry.

doubly screened by the Syrian desert and by the rampart of the Zagros Mountains, were too remote to be attacked in strength; conversely, the Parthians could never conquer the western provinces of Syria, which were sustained by a powerful Roman fleet.

Under Roman rule, western Anatolia, Syria, Palestine, and Egypt entered upon a period of prosperity which has probably never since been equalled. Away from the *Limes* tranquillity of conditions led to a

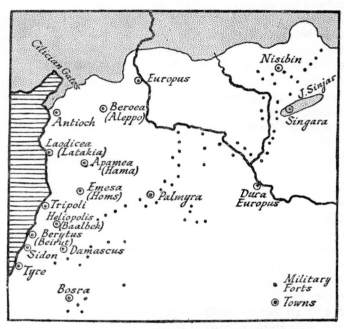

Fig. 22. The Roman *Limes* in Syria (after Rostovtzeff and Stein). Highland in north stippled

great expansion in agriculture and trade. Irrigation was practised on a scale much greater than that prevailing today; and, in addition to supplying a numerous local population, the rich cornlands of Egypt and Syria had a constantly increasing market in Italy itself. As Italian agriculture declined in the later Roman period, the greater became the demand for Middle Eastern wheat. Increase in material prosperity stimulated a demand for manufactured goods. A textile industry, first woollen and linen, then silk, had the advantage of abundant raw materials and natural dyes – saffron, umber, and purple from the murex shells of Tyre. Glass-blowing and metal-working also reached a high level; and at a number of centres on the coast, easily accessible woodlands provided material for shipbuilding.

The Middle East as a whole derived much profit from an expansion in world relations which took place under the Romans. Besides the two empires of Rome and Parthia, there were now equally highly developed civilisations in India and China; and trade contacts between Rome and the east began to assume importance. Silk was for long a Chinese monopoly, but an extensive demand by wealthy Romans led to a considerable transit traffic through Parthia and the Middle East. Other eastern products were jewels, spices, drugs, and sandalwood. Pliny estimated the value of annual importations from the east into the Roman Empire at 100 million sesterces; and, in view of the fact that this traffic was not balanced by a flow of Roman goods eastwards, modern authorities consider that between one-quarter and one-half of the precious metals of the Roman Empire ultimately drained to Asia in payment for Oriental luxuries.

Land and sea routes were both used, but land transport, although more costly, was preferred as safer. A northern route passed via the central Asian oases of Khokand, Bokhara, and Merv to Hamadan in Iran, where it was joined by another route from India via southern Iran. From Hamadan the route continued to Babylon, which was still a focus of communications, and then turned northwards by way of the middle Euphrates, whence a choice of routes skirting the Syrian desert led to Palmyra, Aleppo and Antioch, and Damascus. Access was then gained to the numerous Syrian ports. A more southerly route utilised the Indian Ocean and Red Sea as far as the Gulfs of Suez and Aqaba. From the latter point transhipment then took place by way of Petra to the south Syrian ports; from Suez, a route also led overland through Egypt to Alexandria, which rivalled Tyre and Sidon as an entrepôt. The amazing prosperity of the Roman Middle East, with its dense population and high level of culture, is attested by the numerous remains which are still to be seen. Of these, the temple at Heliopolis is one of the most impressive. Situated at an altitude of 3,000 feet, on the low watershed between the Orontes and Leontes (Litani) rivers, the temple was erected in A.D. 200–400, partly from stone quarried in Egypt, and rests on a foundation course that consists of hewn stone blocks each weighing 450 tons. Antioch, the metropolis of Roman Syria, is estimated to have had a population of three-quarters of a million, a number in excess of the combined populations of early twentieth-century

Aleppo, Beirut, and Damascus; even so, the greater number of Syrians lived in the country rather than in the towns.

Further to the east, the Parthians also derived much advantage from trade routes. It is customary in the west to regard the Roman Empire as surrounded by barbarians: as concerns Parthia, this was by no means the case, since both states dealt politically on equal terms, and both appreciated the usefulness of commercial activities. The Parthians maintained active trading relations with China, India, Arabia, and Siberia,[1] in addition to those with Rome; but they were particularly anxious to keep a monopoly of trade in their own region – foreign merchants were not welcomed in Parthia itself, and all dealings were strictly supervised. The Romans have left an extensive literature, but the Parthians have left almost no written records, and much of our impression of them is thus derived from extraneous and not always impartial contemporary sources. Nevertheless, it is clear that the Parthians had a relatively high level of cultural development, in which, however, the Hellenic influence of Seleucid times gradually gave way to an increasingly native and Oriental outlook.

In A.D. 224 a dynasty known as the Sassanids gained power in Parthia, and though most of the existing Parthian way of life continued, the later Iranian Empire showed itself increasingly Oriental in its internal life, and in external affairs more aggressive in the west, against the slowly weakening power of Rome. A long period of intermittent fighting between Rome and Parthia, with border skirmishes and occasional major expeditions, continued until the downfall of both Empires in the seventh century A.D. The Roman Empire had at some time previously fallen into an eastern and a western portion, and of these, the former, now spoken of as the Byzantine Empire,[2] took up the Iranian challenge. The Middle East from the Black Sea to the deserts of Arabia became a battleground, and the inconclusive results of this warfare, prolonged over many years, led to the ultimate exhaustion of both sides. The resulting material devastation, and crippling taxation of the native population of the Middle East, were important contributing factors in the rise of Islam during the seventh century A.D.

Arab Period. The Arab conquest of the Middle East between A.D. 630 and 640 brought an active, virile, but rough and uncultured desert community into contact with the rich and highly evolved civilisations of Rome and Iran. The early followers of Muhammad were largely

---

[1] Siberian gold is known to have reached Parthia by way of Samarkhand.
[2] The effective date of the creation of the Byzantine Empire is usually taken as A.D. 373.

desert Badawin – 'plain men living in tents', and without any tradition except that of a hard, patriarchal society existing as pastoralists or caravan traders.

The rapidity with which these semi-nomads were absorbed into existing life in the Middle East, and the extraordinary cultural development that resulted from the fusion of the two groups must be considered one of the outstanding events in the development of human society. Politically the Islamic state at first enjoyed unbroken success. With the capture of Mecca in A.D. 630 as a beginning, there followed in 636 the seizure of Syria, of Egypt in 640, and of Libya in 642. Within a century, the whole of North Africa and most of Spain had

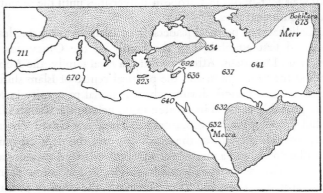

Fig. 23. Islamic Conquests, with dates of capture

become Moslem, and France and Italy were threatened. In the east, Islam had reached the oases of Turkestan, and was stretching towards India and China. Only in the north was expansion arrested, and that only temporarily, by the reduced but revivified Byzantine Empire.

Materially, the impressive level of achievement of the Roman era was maintained. Egypt and Syria retained a high agricultural productivity; taxation was lighter than in Byzantine times; and a degree of religious toleration allowed collaboration between various sects, with a fruitful interchange of ideas.[1] In Mesopotamia, the development of irrigation reached its highest point with the construction of numerous canals, many of them navigable, linking the Euphrates and Tigris. We may recall the statement in an earlier chapter (p. 63) that the modern irrigation problems of Iraq would be largely solved by the reconstruction of the early Arab system of canals.

[1] A number of high officials of the early Arab state were Christians.

An important number of manufactures – metal-work, leather, and textiles[1] – gave additional prosperity, and ancient trade-routes between Europe and the Far East continued in full use. Intellectually, at a period when learning was practically extinguished in Europe, the Arabs took over and expanded classical philosophy, particularly in the fields of medicine and science, adding a considerable body of new thought, partly developed by themselves, and partly derived from Persian and even Hindu sources.[2] It may therefore be said that almost until the Renaissance, the main stream of traditional classical culture deriving from the Ancient World was to be found in Arab lands rather than in Europe; and Arab commentaries and expositions on ancient authors were used as text-books in European universities until the seventeenth and eighteenth centuries.

The Caliphate, or political leadership of Islam, was on the death of Muhammad first established in the family of the Omeyyads, who reigned from Damascus. After a century, a rival family, the Abbasids, supplanted the Omeyyads; and the political centre of Islam shifted to Baghdad. To this period, during which material prosperity in Mesopotamia probably reached its greatest peak, belong the Caliph Haroun al Rashid (786–809) and the Barmekids, hereditary Grand Viziers.

Later, towards the end of the ninth century, the political unity of Islam broke down, and a number of adventurers seized various parts of the Middle East as independent kingdoms. A succession of native dynasties arose in Persia; and thence onwards, the country pursued an increasingly independent political life, interrupted only by a temporary conquest which united Iran to Mesopotamia between the years 1055 and 1220. The remainder of the Middle East was partitioned between the Fatimids, an Egyptian dynasty, and the Hamdanids of Syria, with central and southern Arabia as virtually independent tribal areas. In addition to political anarchy, the growth of Moslem sects had introduced a further element of discord and disunity – the great cleavage between Sunni and Shi'a had begun, and Christian and Jewish minori-

[1] The names damask, muslin (Mosul), and tabby (Arabic attabi, originally cloth with stripes in various colours), indicate the extent of Arab textile production.

[2] Our debt to the Arabs is indicated by the words alchemy (from which chemistry), algebra, alcohol, alkali, admiral, julep, and soda. A number of chemical substances such as borax, sal ammoniac, nitre, and sulphuric acid were brought into use by the Arabs, who also introduced paper from China, where it was first invented (Arabic rizma, a bundle, hence ream). Two other contributions were the present system of numerals, a great advance on the cumbrous Roman figures, and the use of the zero sign.

In view of the extent of Arab dominions, and the necessity for pilgrimage, great attention centred on geographical studies, and to the Arabs must be ascribed the regional concept in geography.

ties were looked on with increasing disfavour. Ever since the original rise of Islam the Byzantines had succeeded in holding Asia Minor; and the existence of this advanced base of Christianity greatly favoured the operations of the first European Crusaders, who in A.D. 1097 landed in Asia Minor, and proceeded to an invasion of Syria.

Crusader Period. Within a short time, the coastal area of the Levant, from Cilicia to central Palestine, had fallen under Crusader domination. Feudal principalities were established on the European model, and Jerusalem was held from 1099 until its recapture by Saladin in 1187. The Crusaders did not, however, penetrate far inland. Except for somewhat more extensive, but short-lived kingdoms in Cilicia (kingdom of Armenia) and Judaea (kingdom of Jerusalem), their influence ceased at the crest of the mountain ranges backing the coast, and the important cities of Aleppo, Hama, and Damascus remained in Moslem hands. There is a curious similarity between Crusader occupation and the Phoenician kingdoms of the second millennium B.C.: both were small enclaves, often at odds amongst themselves, and both suffered the same fate of gradual absorption by outside powers.[1]

The Crusaders were not wholly inspired by religious motives. Trading activities had a certain attraction, especially to the Genoese and Venetians, who supplied sea transport for Crusading armies in return for substantial commercial concessions. Throughout most of the hundred years of occupation by the Crusaders, a considerable volume of trade in precious stones, spices, silks, and other luxuries was carried on with the Moslem states, part being a transit traffic from China and India. It is also interesting to note that, on balance, the East had more to offer than the West in the way of material and cultural amenities. The Crusaders learned much from Islam – an indication of the advances made in the Middle East during the period of the Dark Ages in Europe.

During the thirteenth century Arab power revived, and the Crusaders were gradually driven from Syria. By 1299 Acre, the last Christian stronghold, had been taken. A remnant of Crusader refugees fled from the mainland of the Levant, and established themselves in the island of Cyprus, where European control, first under a Crusader dynasty named Lusignan, and later under the rule of the Republic of Venice, lasted until 1571. The Lusignan period was one of great brilliance in the history of Cyprus, for the island became an entrepôt between Europe

---

[1] Had the Crusaders been able to hold the cities of the desert border, they might have been able to repeat the Roman strategy of using the desert as an outer protection.

F

and the East. Trading posts on the mainland of Asia, first developed under the Crusaders, continued to function after the Moslem re-conquest; and European traders, chiefly Italian and French, had depôts at Latakia, Tripoli, Beirut, and Alexandria. Much commerce passed through Cyprus, which, secure from attack because of the lack of a seafaring tradition amongst the earlier Moslems – a situation that altered at a later date – took its place as a natural centre of the eastern Mediterranean. The wealth of individual merchants of Famagusta, Limassol, and Nicosia is said to have exceeded that of many European monarchs; and the extensive Gothic buildings still existing in Cyprus somewhat incongruously among classical Greek and later Islamic architecture testify to the prosperous condition of the island under the Lusignans. It was not until the sixteenth century when a new power, the Ottoman Turks, had been sufficiently long in contact with the sea to have developed a maritime tradition, that invasion was attempted, and the island passed to Muhammadan control.

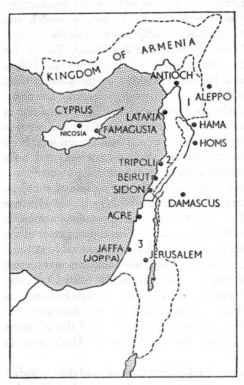

Fig. 24. Crusader States in the Levant
1. Principality of Antioch.   2. County of Tripoli.
3. Kingdom of Jerusalem

From the Crusader period onwards, repeated incursions of Mongols from the steppes of central Asia caused much destruction and devastation from which certain regions of the Middle East have never really recovered. The brunt of Mongol attacks fell on Persia, where between 1220 and 1227 the 'hordes' of Jengiz Khan sacked and almost completely destroyed most of the cities, massacring the inhabitants.

Many of the irrigation works maintained for centuries now fell into disrepair, and vast stretches returned to steppe or desert. By 1258 the terror had reached Mesopotamia. Baghdad was destroyed and the Abbasid Caliphate extinguished.

A century later, fresh Mongol invasions occurred. The armies of Timurlane reached Syria, where Aleppo, Homs, and Damascus were burned and looted; whilst in Persia, the Nestorian Christian community which had played a great part in the intellectual life of the country was reduced to a tiny minority. Mongol invasions were, however, arrested in Asia Minor, where a new power, the Ottoman Turks, had risen to importance.

Ottoman Period 1517–1923. In the thirteenth century A.D. a small group of Mongols known as the Ottoman or Osmanli Turks invaded Asia Minor, and received a grant of territory in north-west Anatolia from a somewhat uneasy Sultan.[1] By 1400, the Ottomans had extended their domains to include central and many parts of western Anatolia, together with a considerable area of Balkan Europe. In 1453, after a number of previous attempts, the great city of Constantinople was taken, and the Byzantine Empire, of which it had been the capital, finally destroyed. Thence ônwards, the expansion of the Ottoman state was rapid. By 1566 the entire north coast of Africa as far as Algiers had been occupied, together with Egypt, Syria, Palestine, Anatolia, and Iraq. In addition, the whole of south-east Europe between Croatia and the lower Don fell into Ottoman hands, and Austria found herself menaced. A number of campaigns had led to a stalemate in the east, where a 'debatable ground' in the region of eastern Armenia, the Caucasus and Zagros Mountains separated the Ottoman state from Iran, which was able to retain its independence.

The early expansion of Ottoman power was accompanied by a process of administrative reorganisation, as the result of which there came into existence a form of government that lasted without serious change from the fifteenth to the twentieth centuries. Certain features of Turkish rule are extremely interesting as showing to a marked degree the influence of the social background of the early Ottoman tribesmen, who became the ruling class of the new Empire.

The Ottomans had entered Anatolia as pastoral nomads from the steppes of Asia; and it has been said of them that they brought to the task of administering their Empire much of the technique that had

---

[1] One may recall grants of land, under somewhat similar circumstances, to the followers of the Saxons Hengist and Horsa, and also to Rollo, first Duke of Normandy.

served them in the handling of animals.[1] In the first place, as a herdsman keeps separate his sheep and goats, the Ottomans made no attempt to develop a single, unified state, but were rather content to allow existing differences of race, religion, and outlook to continue unchecked. At first, this tolerance of division amongst peoples of the Ottoman Empire was probably mere indifference; but at a later period, it became an important basis of policy: 'divide and rule' was the principle by which the weaker Ottoman Sultans were able to maintain their rule over a restive but heterogeneous population. Moslem was turned against

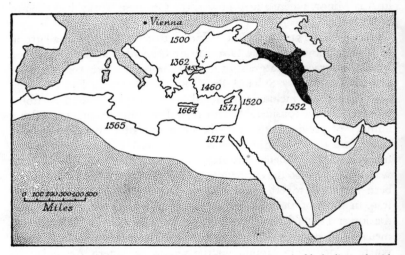

Fig. 25. The Ottoman Empire, with dates of conquest. Area in black disputed with Persia

Christian, Shi'a against Sunni, Kurd against Armenian, and Orthodox Greek against Roman Catholic. Sectarian feeling was provoked and increased by the creation of the *Millet* system (p. 113); and after the seventeenth century, the grant of Capitulations to various non-Turkish nationals (p. 155) was a further recognition of the separate status of certain communities within the Empire. Provided that the subjects of the Sultan showed themselves amenable to rule, and willing to pay the taxes demanded, the state showed little further concern with the well-being of its peoples.

A shepherd employs dogs to control his flocks: similarly the Ottomans created a special corps of picked subjects to police the Empire.

[1] J. L. Myres, *Mediterranean Civilisation*; and A. J. Toynbee, *A Study of History*, Vol. III.

These men, known as Janissaries, were brought up from earliest youth in military barracks, under the strictest discipline. Bought as slaves from neighbouring states, or obtained as tribute – usually from Christian families – within the Empire, the Janissaries were separated from their parents, whom they never knew, and hence grew up without family ties or local sympathies. Obedient and ruthless, and fanatically Moslem by reason of their early training, the Janissaries were the instrument by which the Turkish government maintained a hold upon its mixed population. Those among the young Janissaries who displayed bookish rather than military abilities were trained as administrators, and often provided the Ottoman state with civil officials.

As a purely pastoral tribe, the Ottomans had had no tradition of industry and commerce, and in their Empire, both were despised or ignored, and left to Armenians, Greeks, Jews, or foreigners. Trade activities were tolerated, but no positive encouragement was afforded by the government; and from time to time, rapacious and arbitrary exactions were levied on commercial communities. Much business was therefore carried on half secretly, as far as possible without attracting attention, in the face of indifference, discouragement, or worse, from official quarters. Even the houses of many merchants were miniature fortresses, capable of withstanding attack. This long tradition of secrecy and dissimulation in business has had a most harmful effect. Even in some modern Middle Eastern states, methods inherited from the not-too-remote past still persist. Accounting systems are rare, banks are often mistrusted, and tend to be inefficient, 'presents' are frequent accompaniments to commercial transactions, and fixed prices, even in retail shops, are by no means universal.[1] Under such conditions, business probity is not at times a conspicuous feature; and a problem of many modern governments is to apply taxation to traders, often the wealthier section of the community, but also the more adept at concealing their resources.[2]

Another feature of the Ottomans deriving from their origin as nomads has been a lack of material amenities in everyday life. It has been said of a Turkish household that as regards furnishings and material

[1] Haggling over the price of goods in retail shops is still accepted as customary, and the shopkeeper often tends to despise anyone who pays the first price asked. Unless the sign *Prix Fixe* is displayed prominently in a shop, the customer can assume that bargaining is called for.

[2] In 1945, the merchants of the Lebanese state compounded with the government for a fixed sum of money to be paid by the general merchant body in lieu of all direct taxation of individual traders – an indication of the inability of the government to impose direct taxation.

comforts, there is frequently the impression that the owner has only recently arrived, and intends to move off the next day – furniture is scanty and utilitarian, and the house itself incompletely adapted for habitation. The palace of the Sultan in Constantinople impressed one observer merely as a 'warren of undistinguished apartments'.

Finally, it may be noted that the Ottomans achieved power after a long series of wars mainly against Christians. Unlike the original followers of Muhammad, who practised some toleration of Christians and Jews, the Turks were fanatical Moslems, and destruction of Infidels became a highly meritorious action. Intolerance and fanaticism led to a narrowing of outlook among Moslems themselves: Christian and ancient Greek philosophy which had been drawn on by early Arab thinkers, were rejected; and Islam became a closed and rigid system which ceased to develop further. How far the present weakness of Islam vis-à-vis the West can be traced to a narrowing of outlook as the result of increasing intolerance is a matter of some interest.

The discovery in 1498 by the Portuguese of the Cape route to India had a profound effect in the Middle East. A transit traffic between Europe and Asia, which from time immemorial had enriched the countries of the Middle East, was now diverted to the sea; and despite efforts by the Ottoman Sultan to intervene against Portuguese traders in the Indian Ocean, the flow of goods through Iran, Syria, and Egypt entirely ceased. Establishment in 1514 of a Portuguese fort at Ormuz at the head of the Persian Gulf excluded the Ottomans from any possibility of interference with Portuguese communications with India; as a result, the Middle East entered upon a period of decline. It was not until the cutting of the Suez Canal in 1869, and the development of motor and air transport later still that the region recovered some of its ancient importance. Between the sixteenth and late nineteenth centuries the Middle East was increasingly a backwater, remote from the main commercial currents of the world.

In the political sphere, the Ottoman Empire reached its maximum of power during the seventeenth century, when Austria was threatened and Vienna besieged. From this high-water mark, with a turning-point at the repulse of the Ottomans outside Vienna in 1683, the Empire entered on a period of slow decline. One reason for the decline was pressure by newly developing states such as Russia and Austro-Hungary, but the principal factor was unrest amongst non-Turkish subjects of the Empire, especially amongst Christian communities. A symptom of the growing weakness of the Ottomans was the rise of autonomy in outlying provinces, where the governors, at one time mere officials appointed by the Sultan from Constantinople, tended to follow an increasingly independent policy, and ultimately became hereditary rulers. The Sultan could do no more than issue a formal confirmation on the succession of a new provincial ruler. Such a development occurred in Algiers, Tunis, Egypt, and the centre and south of Arabia, all of which by the nineteenth century had evolved into more or less independent states.[1]

Commercial decline in the Asiatic and African provinces of the Empire, together with the rise of political autonomy in certain regions, caused the Ottoman rulers to devote greatest attention and interest to the European part of their dominions. By the later nineteenth century, however, the rise of national feeling amongst Balkan peoples and the aggressive action of outside powers was rapidly reducing Ottoman territory in Europe; and the Sultan felt it necessary to revise the system that had been followed in non-European districts. Accordingly, a 'forward' policy, designed to re-assert Turkish supremacy, was undertaken in the Middle Eastern provinces. Its exponent, Sultan Abdul Hamid II, was aided by the recent construction of the Suez Canal, which allowed the easier movements of troops from Turkey southwards. Garrisons of Ottoman soldiers were established in the Hedjaz (1869), the Yemen (1872), and Hasa (1871).

Further steps in the strengthening of Turkish control in the Middle East were taken by the construction of railway routes that were designed to bring outlying provinces into closer contact with Constantinople. Lines were built with the aid of foreign capital (chiefly German) from Anatolia south-eastwards to Baghdad via Aleppo, and southwards from Aleppo through Damascus and Ma'an as far as Medina. The latter railway, said to have been built well away from the coast in order to be out of range of the British fleet, proved more of a liability than an asset during the war of 1914.

The efforts of Abdul Hamid delayed but did not prevent the break-up of Ottoman power. Nationalist feeling continued to develop, and although at first restricted to the Christian peoples of the Balkans, this later became a disruptive factor amongst the Islamic populations of the Ottoman state. Arab as distinct from Turkish national feeling was fostered by the rise of semi-independent tribal leaders in Arabia, and by the organisation of secret political societies of anti-Turkish complexion,

[1] Egypt, although in effect completely independent during most of the nineteenth century, remained technically a part of the Ottoman Empire until 1914.

chiefly in Syria. By the twentieth century, nationalism had begun to affect the Turkish people themselves. In 1908 a revolution occurred, as the result of which Abdul Hamid was deposed, and a more strongly nationalist impulse given to the policy of the Empire. Six years later Turkey entered the First Great War on the side of Germany; and following her defeat in 1918, the complete extinction of Turkish power seemed at hand. An unlooked-for revival under Mustapha Kemal and his Nationalist party altered the situation, however; and a new, purely Turkish state came into being. For a short time the Ottoman Sultanate continued, although without effective power; but in 1923 Turkey was declared a Republic. A year later the religious title of Caliph, which had been borne by the Sultan, was also extinguished, and since that date Turkey has functioned as a nationalist, secular state.

CHAPTER VIII

Aspects of the Historical Geography of the Middle East

II. THE POLITICAL BACKGROUND
A.D. 1800 TO THE PRESENT DAY

Western Imperialism. One element in the long-continued decline of Ottoman power was the control gained by foreigners over much of the economic life of the Turkish state. As the result of Ottoman indifference to commercial development, the way had been largely left clear for activities by outsiders. Even in the sixteenth century, when Turkish power was at its height, commercial treaties were negotiated with France, by which French merchants enjoyed special privileges within Turkish dominions. During subsequent years, other European nations followed the French lead, with the result that by the end of the nineteenth century a considerable body of rights, concessions and privileges, known collectively as Capitulations, had been granted to foreign traders. Capitulations gave to nationals of Austro-Hungary, France, Germany, Great Britain, Italy, and Russia virtual exemption from most of the internal taxation of the Turkish state, together with immunity from police search of foreign-owned premises. Foreigners were also immune from trial in a Turkish court of law, special tribunals being appointed for each nationality.

As originally granted, Capitulations were designed to secure outside commercial assistance on terms favourable both to the Ottomans and to the foreigners concerned; but in their later phase Capitulations led to much corruption within Turkey, and, equally seriously, to undisguised commercial penetration by outsiders. Concessionaires gained control of resources which were then exploited without regard to the interests of the country; and by lending money at usurious rates foreigners gained a stranglehold on much of the economic life of the whole Ottoman Empire – e.g. most gas, electricity, and water companies, where these existed, together with the greater part of the railway system, were foreign owned; and the fact that all mineral resources of the Empire were regarded as the personal property of the Sultan, to be disposed of as he wished, led to a form of exploitation that benefited only a few foreign commercial interests.[1] Profits from economic activity were drained away from the country, and, at the same time, the Turkish state was confronted with numerous non-Turkish communities over which it had no legal jurisdiction. In effect,

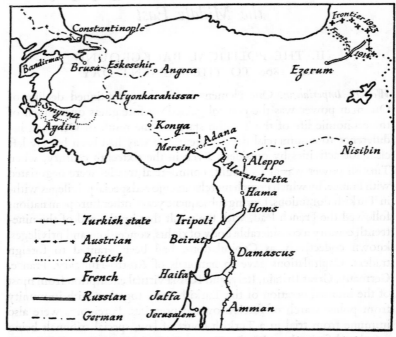

Fig. 26. Railway Concessions in the Ottoman Empire. Names of towns as before 1923

further 'states within a state' had been created, and thus Capitulations were a kind of economic *Millet*.

Further emphasising the economic dominance of foreign powers, the Ottoman government had been forced to agree that its national debt, amounting to some £150 million ($750,000,000), should be administered by an international committee, the 'Council of Administration

[1] Always chronically in debt, Sultan Abdul Hamid raised money for immediate needs by the sale of mineral concessions. Once sold, however, the concessions brought no further profit to the Turkish state; and by the opening of the twentieth century the availability of new concessions was running short, and Turkey had in effect almost ceased to derive advantage from the existence of mineral wealth within her boundaries.

of the Ottoman Public Debt', which, presided over alternately by a Frenchman and an Englishman, was composed of nationals from Austro-Hungary, Germany, Holland, Italy, and Turkey, together with a representative of the Imperial Ottoman Bank which was itself largely foreign owned. The Council repaid interest and capital from the ordinary revenues of the Turkish state, and hence had a certain control of taxation within Ottoman dominions.[1]

Although foreign ownership was widespread in most fields of economic activity, it was particularly prominent in railway development. We have noted some of the internal political circumstances that impelled Sultan Abdul Hamid to press on with railway construction, and the great nations of Europe saw in the extension of a rail network a means of expanding their own economic and political influence in the Middle East. Best known was the Berlin–Baghdad scheme, sponsored by Germany as an important element in the *Drang nach Osten* policy of the Imperial government; but French interests were active in Syria, and a British line between Baghdad and Basra was constructed in the early twentieth century.

Economic penetration of the Ottoman Empire was accompanied by equally active political pressure. The remark of the Czar in 1844 'We have a sick man on our hands. It would be a grave misfortune if we were not to provide beforehand for the contingency of his death' could be taken as a summary of the attitude of most of the powers of Europe; but actual break-up of Turkish domains was delayed because of mutual jealousies among these interested powers: at times various European states were prepared to acquiesce in a continuance of Turkish power and postpone their own designs, rather than see a rival gain advantages. So in 1854 Britain and France went to war to thwart Russian schemes of expansion at Turkey's expense in the Black Sea and eastern Anatolia, and the former again threatened war in 1878 – a policy that was reversed in 1914; whilst the role of protector of Turkish interests, undertaken first by the British and later by Germany, could not be called an entirely disinterested one.[2]

In Ottoman affairs, the nineteenth century was a period of accelerated decline as the result both of internal weakness and of outside pressure.

---

[1] Chief creditors were: France (60 per cent. of the total debt), Germany (20 per cent.), Britain (15 per cent.). Staff of the Council of Administration numbered in 1912 approximately 9,000 persons.

[2] Witness the cession of Cyprus to Britain in 1878 'as a base for the defence of the Ottoman Empire', and the grant of concessions for the 'Berlin–Baghdad' railway to Germany.

The more outlying provinces of the Empire, those of north-west Africa, achieved virtual independence, only to fall later under French, Spanish, and Italian dominance; and by the opening of the nineteenth century even the position of Egypt as an Ottoman province had become increasingly doubtful.

EGYPT

During this period an Albanian adventurer named Mohammed Ali rose to power in Egypt, and succeeded in maintaining his position despite efforts by the Ottomans to dislodge him. At one time it seemed as though Mohammed Ali might successfully overturn the Ottomans in Syria and Crete, and establish an Egyptian Empire; but European intervention, with Austria and Britain supporting the Turks, and France supporting Mohammed Ali, led to the defeat of Mohammed Ali's wider aspirations, although he remained as ruler of Egypt, where his dynasty reigned until 1953.

The rise of Egypt under Mohammed Ali owed something to French influence and support. The Egyptian campaigns of Napoleon in 1798 had stimulated European, and particularly French interest in the country – it is not always remembered that Napoleon included a number of archaeologists and scientists in his invading army, or that the deciphering of ancient Egyptian hieroglyphics may be said to date from the discovery of the Rosetta Stone during French occupation – in effect, four centuries of isolation as a remote backwater were coming to an end. Mohammed Ali, an exact contemporary of Napoleon (both were born in 1769), had great admiration for the conqueror of Europe, and imitated his methods, often with success. Traces of French influence came therefore to be a feature in the state of Mohammed Ali and his successors; and it is significant that at the present day, French language and culture still persist among the educated classes of Egypt. The government employs French in preference to English when a language other than Arabic is desired (e.g. in decrees, and in time-tables of the Egyptian State Railway); and the publication of several daily newspapers in the French language is an indication of the strong Francophil tendencies of certain groups of the population.

A further link between Egypt and France was the construction by de Lesseps in 1869 of the Suez Canal, a project that had been actively opposed by Britain. It seemed as though Egypt was slowly moving within the French orbit, but in the words of H. A. L. Fisher, 'it was England that stumbled into the inheritance which France had marked

for her own'. In 1874 a successor of Mohammed Ali, the Khedive
Ismail, who had been allotted a large number of foundation shares in
the Suez Canal Company, found himself in difficult financial straits,
and decided to sell his holding in the Canal Company. At the instigation of Disraeli, then Prime Minister, the British government quickly
came forward as a buyer, and by the purchase of the Khedive's shares
for £4,000,000, found itself the majority shareholder in the Suez
Canal Company, and the possessor of an important stake in Egyptian
affairs. This sale by the Khedive did little to ameliorate his financial
position, and within a very few years, as the result of continued
extravagance, Ismail was once more heavily in debt, chiefly to British
and French bond-holders.

The British government ultimately determined to take action in
order to secure repayment of its nationals who had lent money in
Egypt, and France, encouraged by Bismarck, who was anxious that
France should find colonial commitments,[1] joined with Britain in
securing the deposition of Ismail, and the reorganisation of Egyptian
finances. The latter proved to be a longer and more difficult task than
had been anticipated, and France subsequently withdrew. As a result,
control of Egyptian affairs fell entirely to Great Britain. This task was
unwillingly undertaken in 1881 by the Gladstone administration, which,
at first genuinely anxious to be rid of Imperialist commitments, found
itself obliged first to undertake control of financial matters within
Egypt, and later to intervene in the question of the Sudan.[2]

Before 1800, the Sudan had stood in relation to Egypt somewhat
in the same position as Arabia in relation to Turkey – i.e. a vague
suzerainty existed, though in fact various tribal chiefs were more or less
completely independent. The position had, however, been altered by
Mohammed Ali, who undertook a re-conquest of the Sudan, and was
later able to use Sudanese troops in his campaigns against the Ottomans.
Garrisons of Egyptian troops were maintained in the Sudan both by

[1] As a distraction from a possible war of revenge over Alsace-Lorraine.
[2] An excellent example of what is often called abroad British duplicity and hypocrisy.
There is no doubt that in their own minds the Gladstonian Liberals would have been
pleased to withdraw from Egypt, but having taken the first step, Britain was drawn
further and further into Egyptian affairs, and despite its inner convictions, the Liberal
cabinet found itself committed to an active policy in Egypt and the Sudan. In this way
the followers of Gladstone, having defeated Disraeli at the polls on the issue of colonial
expansion, found themselves driven to adopt the policy of imperialism which they themselves had denounced. Foreign observers, unable to follow this intricate evolution in
political affairs, generally preferred to explain events in Egypt as premeditated imperialism
cloaked in its early stages by specious protestations of disinterestedness – a further contribution to the legend of perfidious Albion.

Mohammed Ali and his descendant Ismail, so that when British inter-vention in Egyptian affairs began, these garrisons, precariously main-tained by a now weakened government among a hostile population, had become a special preoccupation.

In 1881 an outbreak of religious fanaticism occurred in the Sudan, where an obscure Muhammadan from Dongola proclaimed himself the Mahdi (p. 118) and announced as his object the conquest of the world. A body of Egyptian troops commanded by an Englishman was destroyed, and in order to avoid further entanglement in Sudanese affairs, the British government determined to evacuate the region.

General Gordon was accordingly sent to the Sudan with explicit in-structions to withdraw all Egyptian garrison troops, but the military forces necessary to cover this withdrawal were not supplied, and more-over, Gordon did not make the fullest use of the time at his disposal. Within a few months the situation had deteriorated further, and Gordon was murdered by followers of the Mahdi. A wave of popular feeling swept Britain, where Gordon came to be regarded as a victim of governmental fumbling and ineptitude, and the Liberal cabinet of Gladstone fell. Thence onwards, British policy was firmly directed towards complete re-occupation and pacification of the Sudan. After thirteen years of oppressive tribal rule, the power of the native Sudanese dervishes was finally broken at Omdurman (1898), by com-bined British and Egyptian forces under Kitchener and joint rule by Britain and Egypt (a Condominium) established.[1]

Rule by condominium in effect gave the larger share of influence in the Sudan to Britain, but it is necessary to note that Egypt's special position as legal co-ruler was recognised until the final attainment of Sudan independence in 1956. This gave rise to much difficulty, since to most Egyptians the Sudan was and perhaps should still be an integral part of national territory. Besides the political supremacy established before British occupation of Egypt, there has been the highly important economic factor of Nile river control: with the present situation of almost complete utilisation of Nile water within Egypt, the key to future expansion of irrigation development lies within the Sudan – as is underlined by the latest Aswan scheme of 1959. Many Egyptian statesmen hoped that the Sudan would opt to join with Egypt; and although the Sudanese have so far preferred complete independence,

---

[1] Though in fact the re-conquest had been carried out by British troops, it will be remembered that the Sudan was technically an Egyptian province, and that Britain was merely acting legally on behalf of Egypt in intervening in Sudanese affairs.

there is no doubt that union with the Sudan remains one of the highly desired aims of United Arab Republic policy.

In 1914, on the declaration of war by Turkey, Egypt, which had remained nominally under Ottoman suzerainty, was declared independent, though in fact internal control remained largely in British hands, and British forces were stationed in the country.[1] At the end of the war, Egyptian agitation developed, with the aim of securing effective independence, and in 1924 a treaty was signed by which Britain handed over control of the bulk of her affairs to Egypt herself, retaining the right to maintain garrisons of British troops in Egypt for the defence of the Suez Canal. Changes in the political situation during the next decade led to a further treaty in 1936. By this time, the tide of nationalist feeling in Egypt was running more strongly, and some revulsion against overseas commitments was apparent in Britain. But the rise of Germany and Italy – the latter with an active policy in the Mediterranean and north-east Africa – gave some pause to ardent nationalists in Egypt, so that the 1936 treaty, though conceding many points to the latter country (e.g. the abolition of Mixed Courts, in which law cases concerning non-Egyptian nationals were tried), also confirmed the continued presence of British garrisons. Later changes in the political situation – the eclipse of Italy, the enhanced wealth of Egypt following the war of 1939, together with a decline in British influence following the Second World War, led to more and more insistent demands for complete independence. By slow stages British garrisons were withdrawn and bases evacuated; until, following the 1956 Suez episode, the last remaining groups – civilian technicians in Canal Zone bases – were withdrawn. Egypt then found herself entirely in control of all her territories, and the leader of Arab nationalism in the Middle East.

ASIA MINOR AND THE LEVANT

Throughout the nineteenth century Asia Minor and the Levant – 'heartland' of the Ottoman Empire – remained outside foreign political control. As we have seen, attempts at political domination were largely thwarted by international rivalries, and by the adroitness with which the Sultans played off one predatory foreign power against another. Penetration of these regions was limited to the economic and cultural spheres, and in the latter instance sectarian differences provided the

[1] Cyprus, also technically Ottoman territory, passed at the same time under direct British rule as a Crown Colony.

main opening for intervention: Russia remained in close contact with Orthodox Christian minorities, France championed the Uniates, and Britain supported Muhammadanism, sometimes orthodox, sometimes heretical, as in the case of the Druses during the 1840's. Jerusalem came naturally to be a focus of religious rivalry.[1]

In 1860 events took a sharper turn with the massacre of a number of Lebanese Christians by the Druses, under conditions of apathy or actual encouragement by the Turkish authorities. These Lebanese Christians, chiefly Maronites, inhabited the mountainous district immediately to the north-east of Beirut, whilst the Druses also lived alongside the Maronites in the mountains a little to the south of Beirut.

The massacres reached a scale sufficient to attract general attention in Europe, and to provoke the joint intervention of a number of European powers. A naval demonstration by the combined fleets of Austria, Britain, and France was followed by the landing of French troops at Beirut. At this, the Sultan took alarm; action was begun to end the disorders, and to punish supine or partisan Ottoman officials in the Lebanon. As a gesture to the concert of European powers the Sultan was forced to agree to a special statute by which the Christians of the Mount Lebanon were accorded a degree of autonomy from Ottoman rule, and exempted from conscription into the Turkish army. The 'Organic State of Mount Lebanon' was to be ruled by a Christian Governor nominated by the great powers of Europe, and confirmed in office by the Sultan. The governor also had the right of direct access to the Imperial authorities in Constantinople, and was hence outside the control of the governor (Vali) of Syria.

Here was a further declension of Ottoman power, since a committee of European nations now had the right of intervening in the internal affairs of a portion of the Turkish Empire. It should also be noted, however, that the territory of Mount Lebanon, being limited to the higher parts of the northern Lebanon range, was cut off from the sea, and contained no important towns. Baabda, a village on the outskirts of Beirut, served as a winter capital, and Beit-ed-Dine, a mountain settlement, seat of the former Emirs of the Lebanon, fulfilled a similar function in summer.

Reference has previously been made to the growth of Arab as dis-

---

[1] The authors of *1066 And All That* have epitomised the situation in the words 'The French thought that the Holy Places ought to be guarded by Latin monks, while the Turks thought that they ought to be guarded by Greek monks. England quite rightly declared war on Russia, who immediately occupied Rumania. The war was consequently fought near Persia.'

tinct from Turkish nationalism during the last century; and by 1914 a number of secret societies designed to advance Arab nationalist aims were in existence, chiefly in Damascus and Beirut. When war broke out between Turkey and the Western Powers, these societies attracted the attention of Britain, and encouragement of Arab nationalism both in Syria (i.e. Syria in 1914, which included Palestine and Transjordan) and Arabia proper came to be appreciated as a useful political weapon in the struggle against Turkey. A small group within the Allied armies in the Middle East was allotted the task of fostering Arab revolt against Ottoman overlords by means of monetary subsidies and small-scale military assistance, and best known of this group was T. E. Lawrence, whose outstanding qualities largely contributed to the success of the Arab rising.

It was, however, quite apparent that the development of Arab nationalism was far from being the sole Allied war aim in the Middle East.

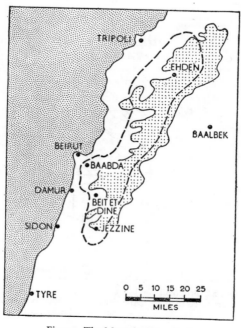

Fig. 27. The Maronite Homeland.
Highland over 5,000 ft. stippled

With Britain, France, and Russia now finally committed to attempting a complete break-up of Ottoman power after decades of hesitation, suspicion, and mutual jealousy, it became essential to make political provision for the future of the Middle East. A further complicating factor was the position of Italy, who although party to a treaty (the Triple Alliance) that ranged her on the side of Germany and Austria, showed no enthusiasm for the cause of her allies. It therefore became an object of Franco-British policy to detach Italy from the Triple Alliance. For some time previously, Italy had joined in the struggle for overseas colonial territory. Repulsed during the 1880's in Tunis, and in 1896 in Abyssinia, she was more successful in Libya, where, during Turkish preoccupations in the Balkan wars of 1910-12, a hold was gained on the northern coastlands of Tripolitania and Cyrenaica. Moreover, Italy had also at the same time seized the Dodecanese Islands of the Aegean, and came to possess important economic

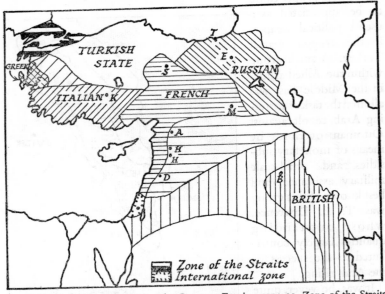

Fig. 28. Proposals for Partitioning the Ottoman Empire, 1914-20. Zone of the Straits as proposed in 1920. Close shading – absolute control by country named. Open shading – sphere of influence for country named

advantages in Asia Minor, notably a concession for railways in the Adana region, and a large interest in the coal basin of Eregli-Zonguldak.

Both the Allied and Central Powers made efforts to win Italy to their side by the promise of territory in Europe and Asia; and as in the long run the former group could offer most,[1] Italy finally entered the war in 1915 as an ally of Britain and France. Part of the price were substantial concessions in Asia Minor and the Levant; and a number of secret agreements were drawn up to delimit the spheres of influence of Allied powers. As the war proceeded, it later became

[1] Germany was in the unfortunate position that her two principal allies, Austria and Turkey, were precisely those countries from which Italy was most interested in obtaining territory. Hence German bargaining powers were sharply limited.

important to secure Greek adhesion to the Allied cause – accordingly, Greece was offered an interest in the Smyrna district of Asia Minor, which held a large Greek-speaking population. The Dodecanese islands, also Greek-speaking, and strongly Hellenic in culture, remained outside this offer, and Italian control remained until the peace treaty of 1947.

In 1916, an agreement (the Sykes-Picot Treaty) was drawn up between Britain, France, and Russia, by which each country was to receive various territories either in full possession, or as spheres of influence in a reduced Turkish state. Under this treaty, Britain at last brought herself to acquiesce in Russian expansion into eastern Asia Minor, and in the Russian control of the Bosphorus and Dardanelles; France was to fulfil an ancient ambition by acquiring Syria and a large region of southern Anatolia; whilst Britain obtained control of Mesopotamia and part of Palestine. The Sykes-Picot agreement remained a dead letter, however, since Czarist Russia collapsed in the following year, before Turkey was defeated, and the treaty is interesting only as reflecting the balance of power as it existed in 1914–16 between the three countries.

With the defeat of the Ottomans in 1918, it seemed as though the end of Turkey as a state was at hand. Despite Russian preoccupations, which prevented her claiming her allotted share in the division of the country, British, French, Italian, and Greek influence was paramount, and the Treaty of Sèvres, proposed as a political re-settlement of Asia Minor in 1920, would have resulted in a virtual extinction of Turkish power. In effect, the position of Britain, France, Italy, and Greece as previously defined in 1914–16 was to continue unaltered; new elements were that the zone of the Straits, formerly allocated to Russia, were to pass under international control, and American interest in Armenian problems led to a proposal that an independent state of Armenia, with boundaries defined by President Wilson, should be created in the former Russian zone of eastern Anatolia. The Treaty of Sèvres can be regarded as the high-water mark of European intervention in the Middle East – had it been implemented, practically the whole of the Middle East region, except for Persia and inner Arabia, would have fallen under foreign domination or influence.[1]

Faced with the possibility of near extinction as a political unit,

[1] Some exception to this generalisation might have been made had an independent state of Armenia come into existence, but it is doubtful whether in the end even an Armenian state could have escaped falling under the influence of a larger nation such as Russia, Britain, France, or even the U.S.A.

the Turks rallied, and, owing partly to division between the Allies (especially as affecting Britain and France), partly to general war-weariness, and partly to their own courage, sustained by desperation, an unlooked-for revival of Turkish power occurred under the leadership of Mustapha Kemal Pasha. After some months of fighting, the French withdrew claims to the part of Anatolia allotted to them under the Treaty of Sèvres, though certain commercial privileges giving France a leading position in these provinces were retained. A year later the Greek-held city of Smyrna was taken by storm, and a large Greek population, numbering over half a million, fled to Greece or was forcibly expelled – many being literally driven into the sea, or massacred. The total of Greek deaths is estimated at one million. In this manner a great measure of ethnic and political unity was achieved in western Asia Minor, though at a heavy price both in human suffering and in economic disruption. The former Greek population was highly skilled, and formed the greater part of the artisan and trading classes in Turkey – communities that the new state, deeply involved in reconstruction problems, could ill afford to lose.

In the east, the Armenian question had been to some extent resolved by massacre of large numbers of Armenians by the Kurds; and outside military support from one of the great nations would have been necessary in order to erect a separate Armenian state. This support was not forthcoming; and to date the nearest solution of Armenian problems – though hardly one which is satisfactory to all Armenians – has been the creation of an Armenian Soviet Republic within the Soviet Union. Hence, untouched on the east and victorious in the west, the new Turkish state was able to negotiate a more advantageous peace settlement, the Treaty of Lausanne (1923), by which control of Asia Minor and the adjacent area of European Turkey remained firmly in Turkish hands. Since that time Turkey has developed further in internal strength, as the result of fundamental social and economic reforms undertaken by Kemal Pasha (Ataturk). Now, in terms of area, population, and economic potential, Turkey regards herself as the leading Middle Eastern state, and rivalry with Egypt over this issue has been a feature of the last few years. The growth of Russian power, always dreaded in Turkey, has driven the country, unlike most others of the Middle East, actively to seek alliances in the West; and at her own pressing request, Turkey joined NATO in 1952. America has provided considerable amounts of military, financial, and technical assistance,[1]

[1] Since 1948 over $500 million has been voted by Congress for military aid alone.

and an economic link of longer standing with Western Germany has also greatly revived since 1945.

The Levant. In enlisting Arab help (as an 'irregular right wing' on the flank of the Turkish army) against the Ottomans during 1914–18, the promise was made by the British that Arabs should achieve independence and sovereignty in Arab lands captured from the Turks. A reservation was, however, made in the case of Palestine, concerning which promises had also been made to the Jews. Following the entry of the Arabs into Damascus in 1918, the Arab leader Feisul took over, with British acquiescence, control of government in Syria. France had long entertained the ambition to rule in Damascus and Aleppo, and, not being a party to the negotiations between Britain and the Arab leaders, considered herself free to follow another policy in Syria.

During the peace conference of 1919, there was much discussion, at times acrimonious, concerning the final division of responsibility in the Levant.[1] Britain had binding engagements towards both Arabs and Jews, and was herself interested in Mesopotamia and the oilfields of the vilayet of Mosul. France was at the same time passionately determined to 'fulfil her destiny' in Syria, and, in 1920, after some months of uneasy joint occupation of the Levant by British and French troops, during which time France became increasingly mistrustful of the presence of Feisul's government in Damascus, the French determined to bring Syria more effectively under French control. Following the proclamation by Arab nationalists of Feisul as king of an independent Syria, the French undertook a military campaign to expel him, and with the defeat of his army outside Damascus, Feisul was forced to leave the country. Thence onwards, Syria was administered under Mandate, as a federation of territorial units. This scheme, by which six theoretically autonomous political units were created, proved unworkable after a few years, and was later modified.

The ruling of Syria proved an onerous task, and relations between France and the local population were rarely harmonious. One major rebellion took place in 1925, when French hold over Syria was severely shaken for some months. During the next fifteen years Syrian exasperation mounted as first Egypt and then Iraq shook off British tutelage, the former by the treaty of 1924, the latter by the ending of the British Mandate in 1932. A treaty reducing French influence in Syrian

[1] It is significant to note that a Peace Conference Commission, composed solely of American members because of the non-participation of the French and the withdrawal of British delegates, reported that local feeling in Palestine and Syria was for the grouping of both regions as a single political unit.

affairs had, however, been negotiated during 1938; but this was rejected by the French Chamber of Deputies in Paris, and the war of 1939 began with Syria firmly held as a part of French overseas possessions. In 1941, with the occupation of metropolitan France, Syria came to be used as a German base for operations in the Middle East. When this trend became apparent, British and Free French forces invaded Syria, and after some months of fighting occupied the country. It was stated at the time of entry of British and Free French troops that Syrian and Lebanese independence would be recognised,[1] but for some time, partly because of the exigencies of war, no action was taken to make this independence effective. In 1944, when the tide of war had receded from the Middle East, differences between Free French and Syrians once more became acute; and in the following year open military clashes occurred. The French undertook a bombardment of Damascus, in order to reduce the main centre of Syrian nationalism; at the same time French garrisons in some other towns of Syria were made prisoner by the Arabs. A large-scale rising, involving the whole of Syria and the Lebanon, seemed imminent; and in view of the import-ance of Syria as a part of the corridor linking Europe to the war areas of the Far East, the British government decided to intervene.

British forces in Syria were increased, and energetic steps taken to end the military clashes in Damascus and elsewhere. Within a year, both French and British forces had been withdrawn from Syria, and complete independence was at last attained, with a formal ending of the Mandate and the creation of sovereign republics of Syria and the Lebanon. For some years the two countries maintained an economic union; but in 1950 this was dissolved. Between 1958 and 1962 Syria joined with Egypt to form the United Arab Republic.

Palestine. At the same time that France received a Mandate for Syria, Britain was also allotted a similar Mandate for Palestine and the region lying east of the Jordan river. In the former area Britain was com-mitted to what has since proved the impossible task of creating a 'National Home for the Jews', without prejudicing the rights of Arabs living there; in the latter, a purely Arab area, the Emir Abdullah, an elder brother of the Emir Feisul, was proclaimed ruler of a state of Transjordan, under British Mandate. Though small and poor, the country of Transjordan proved to be a stable political unit, and after

---

[1] Declaration by General Catroux, commander of the Free French forces, at Damascus, September 1941. It should be noted that on occupying Syria, the Free French authorities assumed full control of the country, as the legal rulers recognised by Britain.

some twenty-five years as Mandated territory, during which a slow but consistent development has taken place, the full independence of Transjordan was recognised in 1946.[1]

In Palestine, on the contrary, unrest and disturbance were often conspicuous features. Large-scale immigrations of Jews gave some apprehension amongst the Arab majority that Palestine would eventually become a predominantly Jewish area; and ground was later given for this apprehension as the earlier Jewish call for 'refuge' and 'a home' in Palestine turned after 1940 into more insistent demands for a sovereign Jewish state. Although during the first decade of the Mandate conditions were relatively quiet, and considerable economic development took place, Arab mistrust later culminated in widespread riots with the object of securing a reduction of Jewish immigration, which, following the persecution of Hitler, had shown a marked increase after 1933.

This disorder and rioting achieved a certain success in that a limit (75,000 persons within five years) was placed on Jewish immigration, but the lesson that the Mandatory power was amenable to influence by rebellion and armed revolt was not lost on the minority group in Palestine.[2] During the war of 1939 arms and ammunition were accumulated by both Arabs and Jews, and with the end of warfare in 1945 the extremist section of the Zionists opened a campaign of terrorism and intimidation to effect a return to unrestricted Jewish immigration, as the first step to the final objective of a Jewish Palestine.[3]

In 1947 the question of settlement in Palestine was referred to the United Nations Organisation, and a Commission – the nineteenth in twenty-five years – once more surveyed conditions in the country. The report of the Commission was in favour of partitioning the country between Arabs and Jews, with Jerusalem under international control. But mounting terrorist action, chiefly by Zionists, prevented implementation of the report, and in May 1948 British Mandatory rule was

[1] Close political relations with Britain are maintained, under a Treaty of Friendship negotiated in 1946. Since 1949 the country has been known as the Hashemite Kingdom of Jordan.

[2] 'The Jews in Palestine are convinced that Arab violence paid.' Report of the Anglo-American Committee of Inquiry, 1946.

[3] This movement in favour of unrestricted immigration from Europe into Palestine had a certain amount of support from France, Russia, and the U.S.A. In all three countries motives were mixed – there was a humanitarian desire to help the distressed Jews of central Europe, freed from persecution in Hitlerite Germany; but there was also some tinge of political animus against Great Britain, as the result of which none of the three countries was wholly averse to witnessing an increase in Britain's difficulties. France, in particular, had reason to recall the events of 1945 in Syria, and the part Britain had played in bringing about the end of the French Mandate.

officially declared at an end. Three months later the last British forces were withdrawn, and fighting immediately broke out between Zionists and the states of the Arab League. Some 700,000 to 1 million Arabs fled from Palestine into nearby Arab countries, where most still remain as destitute refugees. Eventually an armistice was declared, with existing battle-positions stabilised to form a frontier. A small strip near Gaza occupied by the Egyptian army was incorporated into Egypt, and portions of the Judaean highlands and Jordan valley held by the forces of King Abdullah formed an enlarged state of Transjordan, then re-named Jordan. The remainder of Palestine (including the New City of Jerusalem but not the Old City) became the Jewish state of Israel. Officially there is still only an armistice between Israel and the Arab League; hence a state of war persists, and at the time of writing (1962) no diplomatic or commercial relations exist between Israel and her Arab neighbours.

Iraq. Though strictly speaking the region cannot be considered as part of the Levant, it is convenient at this stage to discuss the political evolution of Iraq, since, like the Levant states, the present political unit came into existence after the Versailles settlement of 1919. It was to a great extent inevitable that control of the lower valleys of the Tigris and Euphrates should fall to Britain. River navigation and rail communications had for long been in British hands; the development of oil in Iran had enhanced the value of the river ports of the Shatt el Arab; and British influence was paramount in the Persian Gulf.

Britain was first allotted a Class A Mandate for Iraq south of latitude 35° N.,[1] and shortly afterwards, the Emir Feisul was elected king by almost unanimous plebiscite. Thus Britain could claim that promises made to Arab nationalists were to a great extent fulfilled – states ruled by the leaders of the revolt, Feisul and Abdullah, had come into existence, though subordinate for a limited term of years to a Mandatory power.

Some difficulty was experienced in regard to frontiers. In the south-west, the population is almost entirely nomadic, so that tribes spend part of the year in territory claimed by Iraq, and the other part in territory claimed by Ibn Saud, ruler of Arabia. Eventually, a number of agreements were arrived at regulating boundaries in Iraq, Transjordan, Palestine, and Saudi Arabia, by which certain tribes were allocated to

---

[1] A Class A Mandate – under which Syria and the Lebanon, Palestine, Transjordan and Iraq were all held – envisaged a limited term of rule by the Mandatory, following which independence would be granted.

each country, and the passing of caravans and merchants controlled. An interesting feature, related to the seasonal movement of tribes, was the creation of a lozenge-shaped neutral zone on the borders of Iraq and Saudi Arabia. On the north, a frontier was not fully defined until 1926, when the Mosul vilayet was finally awarded to Iraq.

Though the British Mandate ended in 1932, and a treaty negotiated by which Iraq took over full powers of government,[1] the political evolution of the country can hardly be said to have been of the happiest. For some 25 years after 1933 Iraqi politics were controlled by a Sunni clique of landowners, officials, and townsmen governing a Shi'a rural population for whom they had little sympathy or conscious bond. In 1958 a revolution led by General Kassem overthrew the Hashemite dynasty and since then Iraq has pursued a policy aligned more closely towards friendship with Russia. At the same time, internal strains arising from near-dictatorship seem to have impelled an aggressive foreign policy – e.g. against Iran (over the Shatt el Arab), Kuwait, Jordan, and even at times the United Arab Republic.

PERSIA

Events in Persia have been influenced by the internal decline of the country from the position of great strength in the eighteenth century, when northern India was held as a Persian dependency; and by the accompanying rise of Russia as an imperial power. By the end of the eighteenth century a Russian advance south-eastwards had absorbed the Tartar tribes of the lower Volga region, and had begun to extend along the western shores of the Caspian Sea, directly threatening Persia. In the first years of the nineteenth century Persian-owned territory was reached with the occupation of Georgia, and further Russian gains at the expense of Persia seemed likely.

During this time, however, the Emperor Napoleon had developed a number of schemes of conquest in the Middle East and India; and as Russia was at this period hostile to France (1804–7) a treaty was negotiated with the Shah of Persia by which a French military mission undertook the training and re-equipping of the Persian army (Treaty of Finkenstein, 1807). This reorganisation under French direction did little to save Persia, however, since in two wars with Russia during 1804–13 and 1825–8 the Persians suffered a series of disastrous defeats which marked the end of effective Persian military power in Asia. French interest in Persian affairs provoked counter-measures from

[1] Britain retained the right to maintain certain airfields in Iraq.

Britain, and when in 1807, after the Treaty of Tilsit, French policy veered round to friendship with Russia, French influence in Persia declined. In 1814 a defensive alliance was concluded between Britain and Persia, by which Persia was to assist at need in the defence of Afghanistan, in return for a money subsidy.[1]

Despite this alliance, Persia lost much territory between 1804 and 1828. As we have seen, the ruler of Georgia, formerly a client of the Shah, was forced to accept Russian suzerainty in 1800, and Persian attempts to recover Georgia led to the loss of further territory. By the Treaty of Turcomanchai, which closed the war in 1828, Persia was forced to agree not only to the loss of Georgia, but also of the districts of Erivan and Lenkoran; to the payment of an indemnity to Russia; and to the grant of capitulatory rights within Persia to Russian citizens.[2] It was this treaty that brought into existence the present Russo-Persian frontier between the Black Sea and the Caspian; and thence onwards, Persia was never again able to face Russia on politically equal terms.

Thus reduced in influence, and unable to resist either Russian or British inroads on her sovereignty, Persian diplomacy has aimed at playing off one country against the other. Unable, since the Treaty of Turcomanchai, to counter either power directly, the most that Persians have hoped to achieve is a stalemate between the two. This situation has been the fundamental feature in Persian affairs down to the present day, and although one side has at times gained a temporary advantage, the balance has in the main been preserved, and still continues its uneasy existence.[3] At the time of writing a dispute has developed between Iraq and Persia regarding rights on the Shatt el Arab.

With the western shores of the Caspian occupied, the Russians were free to turn their attention to the east; and, after 1840, a series of aggressive expeditions brought Turcoman and Uzbeg tribesmen living in the Aral region under Russian rule. In 1864 Tashkent was taken, in 1868 Samarkhand, in 1873 Khiva, and in 1876 Khokhand. The final state was reached between 1880 and 1893, when the northern slopes of the Kopet Dagh ranges were occupied, and Merv, loosely held by Persia, passed to Russian control. A series of boundary commissions fixed the final Russo-Persian frontier east of the Caspian Sea, as the result

[1] It should be noted that this treaty was directed against France, who had recently threatened India. Nothing was stipulated regarding Russia, with which Britain was at the time an ally, in the war against Napoleon.

[2] Capitulations had previously been granted to British nationals during the seventeenth century.

[3] A recent feature is the participation of the U.S.A. in Persian politics as an opponent of Russia.

of which the fertile lower slopes of the Kopet Dagh were allotted as part of the Russian Empire, to the disadvantage of Persia.

During the same period, the Persian frontier with Afghanistan was demarcated by a number of British officials; but Persia remained dissatisfied, and the question was finally settled by a Turkish arbitrator

Fig. 29. Russian Expansion and Spheres of Influence in Persia (1907)

during 1934–35. On the west, the ancient indefinite frontier zone between the Ottoman and Persian states was precisely delimited by an Anglo-Russian commission, following which a small area now developed as the Naft Khaneh oilfield passed under Turkish (later Iraqi) ownership. A curious feature was the allocation of the entire Shatt el Arab to Turkey (Iraq), with the frontier on the eastern bank, to the detriment of Persia, and not down the centre of the waterway, as is more usual. Persia is thus without control of port facilities in the river delta region of Iraq, and has been forced to develop her own terminals on the shores of the Persian Gulf.

With Iran closely enveloped on the north, attention subsequently shifted to the Persian Gulf, where at first Persia found herself strong enough to maintain or even extend her hold over a number of islands (Qishm, Hormuz, Larak and Henjam). Here in the south, though, the influence of sea-power based on India gave to Britain a specially advantageous position; and on the southern shores of the Gulf a number of Arab sheikhdoms (Bahrein, Kuwait, Muscat), were induced to accept British protection. One reason for British interest in the Gulf was the prevalence of slave-trading, with victims seized from East Africa and Baluchistan. Other prominent activities were gun-running and piracy; and it was largely owing to British efforts that all three practices were more or less suppressed.

In the last few years of the nineteenth century, Russian eyes were turned towards the Persian Gulf as a possible site for a warm-water port. This provoked strong reaction from Britain, and Russia was directly warned that attempts to establish her influence in the Gulf would be forcibly resisted (Curzon Declaration of 1902).

Within Persia itself, however, the situation was very different, being by far the more favourable for Russia, which directly enveloped Persia on three sides. It therefore seemed credible to assume at the beginning of the twentieth century that the whole country would ultimately fall under Russian influence – Russian traders were most numerous in the region, the rich Caspian provinces, with valuable sturgeon fisheries, were tending to become economic dependencies of Russia, and, as a symptom of the control exercised by Russia, we may note the fact that Russian opposition successfully prevented Baron de Reuter from obtaining a mining concession in Persia (p. 248). The long-continued expansion of Russian power was, however, checked by the Russo-Japanese War of 1904, which revealed unsuspected Russian weakness; and in 1907 a compromise was arrived at over Persia by which the country was partitioned into three zones, one Russian, one British, and one neutral[1] (Fig. 29). Russia held exclusive rights concerning economic matters within her own zone, as did the British in the south, and both nations were free to seek concessions and influence in the neutral centre zone.

As at first drawn up, the Treaty of 1907 seemed to give by far the

[1] Another reason for the conclusion of the 1907 Treaty was the rise of an aggressive Germany – a potential enemy both of Russia and of Great Britain.

greater advantage to Russia, since the Russian zone included most of the towns and the fertile land of Persia. But the subsequent discovery of oilfields in the neutral zone, and their development by British capital with the British government as a large shareholder, made the entire neutral area in effect a British preserve, thus restoring the balance. Once again, Britain and Russia were able to confront each other in Persia on equal terms.

With the outbreak of war in 1914, Persia, though ostensibly neutral, found herself immediately involved, as both warring sides fought across her territory. A Russian attack on north-eastern Turkey, partly over Persian soil, provoked a counter-attack by the Turks in the district of Lake Urmia; whilst further south, Turkish armies attempted to penetrate from Mesopotamia through the Zagros Mountains by way of Kermanshah. From the start British forces had occupied the head of the Persian Gulf in order to protect the oilfields of south-west Persia; and Turkish and German agents attempted to embarrass the British by fomenting guerilla warfare and attacks on the oilfields by nomadic tribes living in the Zagros. These attempts were on a considerable scale[1] and gave anxiety on many occasions.

British intervention in Persia increased after the Russian collapse in 1917, and a British force was sent to north-west Persia to resist German and Turkish pressure in the Caucasus district. This force, under General Dunsterville,[2] was supported at first by scattered White Russian units, so that the British became increasingly at odds with the newly-formed Bolshevik armies, and events finally reached the stage of active warfare between Britain and Soviet Russia.

This friction gave favourable conditions for a revival of Persian strength, and from 1919 onwards a marked improvement began. The revival, like that in Turkey, was fostered by an ex-army officer, Riza Khan, who by means of a *coup d'état* in 1921 marched on Teheran and seized power from the hands of a feeble and bankrupt Shah. A treaty, remarkably favourable to Persia, was negotiated with the Russians, who relinquished all their commercial and economic rights in Persia, with the exception of control of the Caspian fisheries. Strengthened in this way, Riza Khan was able first to undertake a reduction of British influence, and later, a pacification of the tribal areas, which had for long been almost independent of Teheran. Kurds, Lurs, Qashqai, Bakhtiari,

---

[1] It is interesting to note that whereas in 1914–18 German agents took on the guise of 'archaeologists', in 1939–42 they were 'tourists' – a possible sidelight on social changes in Europe during the intervening years.   [2] Kipling's *Stalky*.

and Khuzistan tribesmen were in turn subdued by military force; and thus, master of Persia, Riza Khan was able to secure the deposition of the reigning Shah, and to assume the title himself (1925).[1] One will note the close similarity between events in Persia and the policy of Kemal Pasha, whose activities in Turkey were an example and stimulus to his fellow-autocrat in Persia.

After 1925, Riza Shah embarked on a policy of extensive modernisation. Besides enforcing the wearing of European dress, and the emancipation of women, attention was paid to expanding economic life by the development of modern industry. Perhaps most important of all, since the greatest number of people were involved, numerous nomadic tribesmen were forcibly settled and compelled to adopt cultivation as a livelihood. There was in this an underlying political motive – as a sedentary population, the tribesmen would be less independent and troublesome.

At the outset of his reign, Riza Shah achieved many beneficial results: stagnant life in Persia revived, and a certain amount of prosperity returned. It seemed that the country might successfully follow the example of Turkey in surviving the upheavals of the early twentieth century, and in adapting herself to modern conditions. But Riza Shah became increasingly tyrannical, and his heavy financial exactions were less and less devoted to benefiting the affairs of state – instead, an increasing share of the national wealth was diverted to his private usage. By the outbreak of war in 1939, he had lost much of his early hold on the Persian people, and when in 1941 he refused to expel German agents at the request of Britain and Russia, he overestimated the strength of his own position. Under stress of events in Europe, Anglo-Russian differences were temporarily forgotten, and for Persia it was no longer possible to follow the traditional plan of playing off the two rivals one against the other. A joint Anglo-Russian invasion followed, and the Shah was deposed, to be succeeded as ruler by his son.

During the war years, 1941–5, Persia became an important supply base for the Middle East, particularly as regards the transference of materials to Russia. Roads and railways were built on a relatively lavish scale to link the Persian Gulf and Russia; but this economic advantage was offset by a considerable volume of inflation, as the result of which prices rose by 1,000 or 1,500 per cent. With the end of the war, Persia found herself once again subjected to pressure from outside. In addition

---

[1] Riza Khan took the title of Riza Shah Pahlevi – an emphasis on the purely native origin of the new ruler. (Pahlevi means Persian.)

to the long-standing rivalry of Russia and Britain, intensified if any-thing as the result of a temporary lull during 1941–5, America began to display a growing and major interest in the Middle East, both strategically, as a counter to Communist influence, and also in relation to oil concessions (Chapter XI). Since 1945 sporadic and repeated out-bursts in various parts of Persia (especially Persian Azerbaijan, which feels itself as a 'deprived' area), coupled with demands for regional autonomy, and the creation of a vigorous and vocal political party, the Tudeh, with pronounced communistic views, have had the sympathy, if not a certain measure of active support, of the Soviety Union. By supporting dissident elements within the Persian state, Russia is in a strong position for economic and political bargaining, and it was against a background of unrest within Persia that Russia was able to negotiate a comprehensive oil concession covering the northern part of the country.[1]

The situation is not improved by the decline in internal strength which has followed the abdication of Riza Shah. Governmental power is weak, internal economic conditions have deteriorated because of inflation during the war years, and with the strong hand of Riza Shah removed, there has been a recrudescence of tribal independence. A slight, but significant feature is that some Persian women have resumed the veil when appearing in public. How far, in the face of internal weakness, Persia will be able to maintain political independence, sub-ject as she still is to competing imperialisms, time alone will show.

ARABIA

The peninsula of Arabia long remained, as the result of isolation and poverty in natural resources, for the greater part outside the main sphere of imperialist influence. It was only on the coast that European occupation occurred – Britain, anxious to secure bases for her sea routes to India, obtained control of the Aden district in 1839. Further British expansion in Arabia followed, with the double aim of ending slave-raiding and also as a counterpoise to Russian designs in Persia. With the southern shores of the Persian Gulf in British hands, Russian influence in the north could be checked, and the route to India safeguarded. Hence a number of treaties were negotiated with the Sheikhs of coastal territories in Arabia, by which British protection was accepted, but internal affairs were left to the jurisdiction of native rulers. This was a

[1] Though negotiated, the Persian Prime Minister was able first to delay and then abrogate operation of the concession by a series of subterfuges and politic delays.

policy *par excellence* of 'marginal control', and the precise degree to which British influence extended inland was never fully defined.

In the interior, Turkish hold on the tribes was shadowy and precarious even after the Ottoman revival under Abdul Hamid II. Away from the garrison towns of Mecca, Medina, and Sa'ana tribal government and intertribal rivalry and warfare persisted. Most important of the non-Turkish rulers in Arabia at the beginning of the twentieth century was King Hussein, Sherif of Mecca, Hereditary Guardian of the Holy Places of Islam, and direct descendant of the Prophet Muhammad. In 1914, Hussein was persuaded to take up the cause of Arab nationalism, and though Hussein himself had no active share in the fighting, his son Feisul assumed command of the Arab army that conducted irregular operations against the Turks in Arabia and Syria; and it was to this army that T. E. Lawrence was attached during the campaigns of 1914–18.

The early years of the twentieth century also saw the rise of a second Arab leader in Arabia. This was Abdul-Aziz ibn Saud, formerly an indigent and dispossessed chieftain of the uninfluential Wahhabi sect, who were regarded with suspicion and some derision as ultra-reactionary upholders of a primitive form of Islam. The energy and skill of Ibn Saud brought him and his followers, as time went on, to a commanding position in Arabian affairs; and, after the war of 1914, the Wahhabi were able to dispute with the Sherif Hussein the leadership of Arabia. In 1925, Ibn Saud defeated the Sherif, who retired to Cyprus; and for the first time in many centuries the interior of Arabia was united under a single ruler. It is noteworthy that the association of King Ibn Saud with the British was less close than in the case of the Sherif Hussein. Although Ibn Saud accepted British subsidies during 1914–18 to fight againt the Ottomans, he at times forcibly opposed British policy in Arabia; and in the Sherifian-Wahhabi war of 1925 he overthrew a ruler who had strong claims on British support. Generally speaking, King Ibn Saud pursued a more strictly Arab policy, and the British, as the foreign power most deeply interested in Arabian affairs, have at times been regarded with some suspicion.[1]

Apart from Aden and other British protectorates in the coastlands of southern and eastern Arabia, and the Saudi kingdom with its capital at Riadh, the only other separate political unit in the Arabian peninsula

[1] How far Ibn Saud was impelled by these considerations to grant oil concessions during the 1930's to American rather than to British interests is a matter of some doubt. It has been said that Ibn Saud may have opted for the country situated furthest away from Arabia; but on the other hand, it may also seem that the British had an opportunity which they declined to take (Twitchell).

is the Imamate of the Yemen. Difficulty of access – the greater part of the country is well over 5,000 feet in height – and scantiness of resources have aided the Yemen in maintaining an aloofness from the currents of foreign penetration that have been so active elsewhere in the Middle East. During the decade before the war of 1939, an attempt was made by Italy to develop interests in the country in opposition to British influence in Aden and the Red Sea; and for a time, it seemed possible that following on the occupation of Abyssinia and Eritrea, the next stage in Italian expansion might lie in the Yemen. In 1943, however, Italian influence in Arabia came to an end.

The most recent phase in political manoeuvring concerns demarcation of land frontiers round the Persian Gulf, previously left vague because of the fewness of inhabitants. Iran claims part of the southern shores of the Gulf as national territory; Iraq claims Kuwait; and there is a dispute over the position of the frontier between Saudi Arabia and the Trucial Sheikdoms, especially in relation to Buraimi oasis – in this Saudi Arabia is supported by the U.S.A., and the Sheikh by Great Britain. All these claims arise, of course, because of the oil potentialities.

LIBYA

At the opening of the present century, Libya was under Ottoman rule, with Turkish officials and military garrisons. Economically, the region was extremely retarded: two mainstays had been piracy,[1] and a small but regular slave-trade across the Sahara. The former had ended in the early nineteenth century; the latter ceased in the 1930's (the last slave was publicly sold in 1934), and the trans-Saharan caravan trade dwindled to tiny proportions. In 1911–12 during Turkish preoccupations in a Balkan war, Italy occupied Tripoli, and at the start of the First World War was in process of extending its hold on the country. Main opposition to Italian penetration came from the Senussi under their leader the Grand Senussi, who was seconded at first by a number of notable Turkish officers, among them Kemal and Enver Pasha. The presence of a Senussi-Turkish army was for some time a threat to the British position in Egypt; but after 1918 Italian forces gradually subdued the coast, and later the interior. Pacification was however not complete until about 1934. Under Mussolini Libya was divided into four provinces: Tripolitania, Misurata, Benghazi and Derna; and about

---

[1] One of the earliest exploits of the American Corps of Marines (commemorated in the National Anthem) was a punitive expedition against Libyan corsairs.

G

250,000 settlers from Italy were established as artisans, shopkeepers, farmers, and officials.

During the Second World War, the British entered into an agreement with the Grand Senussi of the time (who was living in exile in Egypt) and recognised him first as the ruler of Cyrenaica, where Senussi adherents are most numerous, and later as king of a united Libya. Full independence was gained in 1951 (after Russia had put forward a request for a Mandate); and Libya is now a federal state composed of three sovereign territories – Tripolitania, Cyrenaica, and the Fezzan. At first, the chief town of each territory was annually and successively the Federal capital; but space-relationships involved in regarding a remote oasis as temporary capital led to a restriction – Tripoli and Benghazi now alternate as chief Federal centre.

PRESENT POLITICAL GROUPING

It has largely been inevitable that the present national frontiers, drawn in lands where sectarian and social divisions are strong, and where political consciousness is merely in the first stage of development, should in some instances give incomplete realisation to the political needs and aspirations of Middle Eastern peoples. Although it is probably impossible to devise frontiers which would be even moderately satisfactory in this respect, present boundaries offer a number of outstanding difficulties. Palestine/Israel was and still remains a problem on its own; but three other communities – the Kurds, the Armenians, and the Assyrian Christians – find themselves without a political future, and present special problems to the national governments of the various states in which they live.

The Kurds are a semi-nomadic pastoral people, living in the highlands of eastern Anatolia and the north-western Zagros. Transhumance between summer pastures on the higher mountain slopes, and winter quarters in the valleys and lowlands (sometimes involving movement between widely separated districts), has brought the Kurds into conflict with the four national governments, because their homeland is now divided among Turkey, Syria, Persia, and Iraq. It has been said of this people that they have claims to racial purity and to continuity of culture that are stronger than those of any European nation, since the Kurds have been settled in their present home since about 2400 B.C.; but the term 'culture' must be taken in a limited sense, for the Kurds are renowned as a fierce and predatory people, and their social organisation has progressed little beyond the level of tribal grouping. Their occupation of eastern Anatolia and the northern Zagros has given them command of a number of important trade-routes, from which they have derived considerable revenue by means of heavy exactions on trading caravans. The Kurds have the reputation of being pre-eminently a people that it is unsafe to trifle with, and their tendency to shoot on sight at moving objects has kept outside interference to a minimum.[1] Even the Ottoman Turks could do little to subjugate them, and they remained free from Turkish taxation and military conscription.

For obvious reasons, detailed figures as to the number of the Kurds are not available,[2] but estimates, some of them much out of date, give a total of some 5 millions, distributed as follows:

Turkey	2,250,000
Iraq	500,000
Persia	1,500,000
Syria	250,000
Transcaucasian Russia	250,000
Afghanistan	50,000
Baluchistan	350,000

The Kurds have rarely been able to combine for long in a stable large-scale political organisation. Individualism and local tribal feeling have been the chief characteristics, and their predilection tends to be strongly against any other group that has tried to rule them, rather than definitely pro-Kurdish. Since 1923 there have been ten or possibly eleven serious revolts against various national governments: two against Turkey, four in Persia, and five in Iraq. Such revolts lend themselves to intervention by outside powers, a fact of which Russia has not been slow to take advantage.

Since 1927 a Kurdish independence movement, the 'Khoibun', has been in existence, but its activities for long had little success owing to jealousy, factiousness, and lack of co-operation of the Kurds themselves. Of recent years, however, Kurdish students and others educated abroad have shown keen and growing nationalist sentiment; and in 1945 a Congress was held to advance Kurdish separatist aims. Fig. 30 shows in an extreme form the territory claimed as Kurdish. The idea of Pakistan is said by some to have germinated among politically minded Muslim students in Cambridge: possibly one should therefore not entirely discount a somewhat similar development among the nationally conscious Kurdish students of the present day.

[1] This is the verdict of a succession of travellers in the region, from Alexander the Great and Xenophon to Marco Polo and the Peace Treaty Commission of 1919.
[2] In modern Turkish statistics the Kurds are described as 'Mountain Turks'.

The Armenians formed a majority in certain parts of eastern Asia Minor, where, in sharp contrast to the Kurds, they lived as settled peasant cultivators, exploiting the occasional patches of richer land on valley floors. A markedly high birth-rate, coupled with lack of opportunity in their homeland, led to much emigration, so that Armenians are also found in other parts of the Middle East, and to some extent in Europe and America. Again, unlike the Kurds, the Armenians

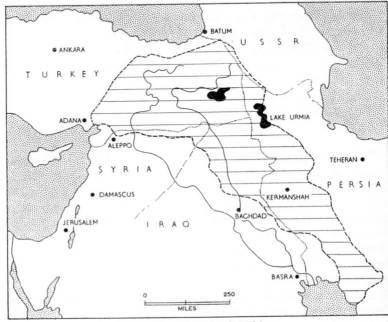

Fig. 30. Kurdish Nationalist Claims

outside Armenia have settled as townspeople, and their frequently high level of intelligence has made it possible for them to enter commerce and the skilled professions. A relatively large proportion of the trade of the Middle East is carried on by Armenians, and many Armenian musicians, teachers, lawyers, doctors, and dentists are to be found.[1] In some respects, therefore, and particularly by reason of their interest in commerce, and their mental and artistic ability, the Armenians can be compared with the Jewish people.

[1] Most Armenians can be readily distinguished by the act that the majority of their surnames end in 'ian', e.g. Khatchaturian, Mikoyan.

During the war of 1914–18 the Armenians, as Christians, gave support to the Czarist armies against the Turks, their overlords; and, following the retreat of the Russians in 1915–16, the Armenians were exposed to Turkish vengeance. About half a million of the former were massacred by the Kurds, at the instigation of the Turks, and a larger number saved themselves only by flight – either into Russia, or into Iraq and Syria. There are now about 3 million Armenians in the U.S.S.R., including nearly 2 million (1960) in the Soviet Socialist Republic of Armenia, which centres on the city of Erivan.

In other adjacent regions, especially Iraq and Syria, the Armenian refugees were not particularly welcome, as imposing an extra burden on scanty local resources, and also as swelling a Christian minority in Moslem states, thereby provoking a change in the balance of political power. A recent estimate gives the numbers of Armenian refugees as follows:

In Syria	120,000
European Turkey and Greece	50,000
Bulgaria	45,000
Egypt	25,000
France	55,000

The Soviet authorities have made strong efforts to secure Armenian loyalty by furthering economic development in the Soviet Republic of Armenia. Outside observers have also agreed that a high degree of autonomy is allowed, and that no anti-religious policy is imposed. As a result, some 16,000 refugees entered Soviet Armenia from the Middle East between 1926 and 1936, and others after 1945. The claims of Russia to have secured the continued survival of the Armenian people are therefore strong.

Like the Kurds, the Armenians have a desire for a politically independent national state, but here the comparison ends, because the latter people are scattered over the world, and as traders and intellectuals have means of forwarding their cause that are denied to the illiterate, semi-civilised mountaineers of Kurdistan.[1] American interest in the Armenian problem was shown by the action of President Wilson in 1919, when he went so far as to draw up boundaries for a projected Armenian state – a proposal that, as we have seen, never reached realisation: and latterly, the question of Armenian aspirations has become directly related to Russian affairs. The problem is in one sense simple: Armenians

[1] The parallel will be noted in this respect between Armenian nationalism and political Zionism.

have now the possibility of settling in an Armenian state, but at the price of accepting Russian tutelage – a condition that some Armenians, strongly religious, or living by commerce under capitalist conditions, do not care to accept. Once again there is the further question of Russian influence in the Middle East. With a majority of Armenians now resident in the Soviet Union, and as protector of the Armenian Republic, Russia has grounds for interesting herself in the districts of Turkish Cilicia and Lake Van, until thirty years ago the ancient homelands of the Armenian people, and now possibly a future component, with the Soviet Armenia as a nucleus, of a wider Armenian state. On this issue, and as a summary of the whole problem, it is useful to cite the opinion of Professor Westermann: that during 1914–19 American, British, and French political sympathy with Armenian aims, together with highly-financed American interest, achieved no practical benefit – rather indeed did it lead to misery and death for many of the unfortunate Armenians. Therefore, as a practical issue, the Soviet solution would seem to have something to commend it.

The Assyrians.[1] This people, very much smaller in number than either Kurds or Armenians, was settled in the Mosul district of the upper Tigris, and was recognised by the Ottomans as a separate *Millet.* The Assyrians were prosperous until the Mongol devastations of the Middle Ages, but by the nineteenth century they were no more than a small group of abjectly poor peasant cultivators. As a Christian community, they attracted some interest in Europe, and in 1881 the Archbishop of Canterbury sent an Anglican mission as a means of reviving the Assyrian link with Christianity. During 1914–18 the Assyrians, like the Armenians, threw in their lot with the British and Russian armies, and on the withdrawal of these forces, suffered the same fate as the Armenians. In the region of Lake Urmia about half of the Assyrian population, including the head of the sect, the Mar Shimun, was murdered by the Kurds. The remainder fled to Iraq, where camps were set up by the British to receive them.

In 1933, shortly after the granting of full independence to Iraq, 600 Assyrians were massacred by Iraqis, and a body of 8,000 Assyrians fled to Syria, where they were hardly *personae gratae* either to the French authorities, or to the Syrian Moslems. Proposals, and no more, have since been made to settle them in Tanganyika, Kenya, Argentina,

[1] This name has no racial or cultural meaning, and has no connexion with the ancient Assyrians. The modern community is an autonomous Christian sect, closest in form of worship to the Nestorian churches, and at the present time the name Assyrian has no more than a sectarian, and therefore a political, connotation.

Matto Grosso, and British Guiana. The Assyrians number only some 40,000, of which 8,500 are in Syria in the region between the Euphrates and the Tigris rivers, 25,000 in Iraq, and a few hundreds in Russia and Greece. With such a small number involved a separate state is out of the question, even by Middle Eastern standards (cf. the Lebanon, Israel, and Jordan, all with less than 2 million inhabitants), yet under existing circumstances this people faces complete extinction. From certain viewpoints, the problem of the Assyrians epitomises many political difficulties throughout the Middle East: as a Christian community, it is difficult to fit them into any Moslem state because of sectarian rivalry, and in those countries where sectarian feeling is less pronounced, as in Turkey and Iran, the Assyrians are suspect as former British, and possibly future Russian, protégés – in either instance the 'Trojan Horse' of interference by outside powers.

The survey given above serves to indicate the complexity and wide range of Middle Eastern problems. Existing national states, having achieved a hardly-won independence, are little disposed to tolerate any shift of internal power to minorities, even when this means denying to smaller groups the same rights that they claim for themselves. Any infraction of present unity – any 'boat-rocking' by dissident sects or parties – may lead to a break-up of existing autonomy, and extreme methods, even direct repression and persecution, appear justified, so long as outward unity in political grouping is maintained. The position is complicated too by the existence of nomadic or minority groups, partly inside, and partly outside various national states. Iran and Turkey went to war during the nineteenth century because both countries claimed the Kurds as their own nationals – a somewhat barren quarrel since the Kurds were little disposed to admit the effective suzerainty of either state.

Then there is a wider problem involving outside powers. French support of Uniate Christians, British interest in Druses and Assyrians, and American activities on behalf of Armenians and Zionists have served to transform questions that were at first purely local into inter-national issues involving major states and even 'blocks' of states. Turkish claims to possession of the Mosul region in 1926 immediately brought into discussion the position of the Kurds, Armenians, and Assyrians; and Britain, as a Christian power, found herself in opposition not only to Turkey, but also to France, who was not anxious to see a further extension of British influence in the Middle East. Turkish claims also received support from American organisations interested in the exploitation of oilfields. Similarly, and more recently, we have seen how Palestine and Syria have embittered Anglo-French and Anglo-American relations, and how Palestine could become a domestic political issue in America.

Finally, there is the question of Russia. As the one major power that directly adjoins Middle Eastern territory, Russia has a special interest, and special advantages. No other country can influence Middle Eastern affairs so easily and quickly, either by direct action, or by using the aspirations and mutual jealousies of minorities within various national states. During the last thirty years, Russia has made use of Kurdish separatism once to thwart British influence in Iran (1918), and three times to exert pressure on the native government of Iran (1921, 1942, 1946), and by creating an Armenian Republic within Soviet territory, she has obtained a weapon for use against Turkey. One reason for the reluctance in some quarters to support Kurdish and Armenian nationalist aims has been the thought that these would weaken both Iran and Turkey *vis-à-vis* Russia.

It is easily possible to see in the present political situation of the Middle East a recapitulation on a vaster and more complex scale of the Balkan position of 1914. Local sectarian and communal feeling is slowly and painfully transforming itself into political organisation, but the process is often crude and incomplete, with manifest deficiencies. These defects give possibility of interference for their own purposes by non-Middle Eastern powers; and as Austria and Russia opposed each other before 1914 over Serbia, so American, British, French, and Russian interests now clash in the Middle East. Moreover, there are richer prizes at stake: unlike the Balkans, the Middle East is no isolated peninsula, but, as, has been emphasised, a corridor of unique strategic importance between an awakened Asia and the West; and far more valuable than anything in the Balkans, are the oilfields of the Middle East, potentially the most important in the world.

A further problem arises from the archaic social structure of many Middle Eastern countries. In general, contact by western nations has been with an *élite* – a ruling class based on hereditary position or wealth – since social grouping in the Middle East, often tribal or communal, has tended to concentration of effective power in the hands of a few leaders of great influence. Today, the basis of that order is being increasingly questioned, and with the examples of Russia and China not far off, social revolution has already begun on a limited scale, with the chance of it going further. By past tradition, America, Britain and France are committed to dealing with the present ruling class of territorial landlords, tribal leaders, capitalist traders, and religious heads. So also is Russia,[1] but Russia can in addition follow a different line. Willing on occasion to negotiate with the present rulers in the Middle East, she can also appeal over their heads to a proletariat, as in Persia, when workers in British oilfields were incited to strike in 1947, or when Communist separatism was encouraged in Azerbaijan (1946), and in Iraq (1958). Social revolution, extinguishing the present ruling class in the Middle East, would probably be little to the taste of America or Britain; but the same can hardly be said as regards Russia, and there is hence a considerable possibility of a sudden rise of militant Communism in S.W. Asia similar to that already experienced in China, Korea, and S.E. Asia.

THE ARAB LEAGUE

The 'secret' treaties made by Britain, France, and Russia during 1914–20 can be taken as marking the maximum of outside designs on Middle Eastern territory; and from that time onwards, there appears to have been a decline in foreign influence. An increasing number of Arab states shook off outside domination and achieved independence, and the process reached a further stage during 1945–8 with the ending of the Mandates for Syria and Palestine.

The emergence of Italy as a 'Mediterranean power' during the 1930's, and the steps taken by Mussolini to extend Italian overseas possessions came, however, as a rude awakening to a number of Middle Eastern states. It was borne home by the lesson of Abyssinia that imperialist penetration was to be regarded as by no means at an end, and though the further expansion of British and French power seemed unlikely, the prevailing tendency towards Arab independence might easily be reversed, with other aggressive outsiders seeking to obtain colonial territories in the Middle East. One result of Middle Eastern apprehensions was the Treaty of Saadabad between Iran, Iraq, Turkey, and Afghanistan (1936) by which ancient grudges over frontiers were forgotten, and a defensive alliance between the four countries arranged.

Though this treaty had little positive result, the way had been pointed for further collaboration; and when four years later the Middle

---

[1] e.g. the appeals of Arab League notables – the majority of them men of hereditary wealth – for Russian support over Palestine during the United Nations Organisation discussions of 1947.

East had been drawn into the Second World War, and for the second time in twenty-five years opposing armies from Europe were fighting across Arab soil, the idea of political co-operation returned. On this occasion Egypt took the lead, and invitations were issued to a number of Arab states in order to discuss the possibility of advancing Arab interests by joint collaboration in measures to reduce foreign intervention. As a result, the Arab League was formed in 1945[1] with the states of Egypt, Iraq, the Lebanon, Saudi Arabia, Syria, and Transjordan as members. The Arab community of Palestine was also represented; and Libya applied for admission in 1952.

The League is designed to oppose foreign domination by collective action on the part of all members. Thus in one sense it is a negative movement – a reaction against outside influence; it is unfortunate that so far there has been little genuine positive co-operation between member states either in the political or economic spheres. The various collaborating states are very unequal in wealth and prestige, and therefore have differing interests and aims; and in addition to the personal rivalry between heads of states – e.g. as between the rulers of Egypt, Saudi Arabia, Jordan, and Iraq, there are traditional differences in culture, religion, and outlook. A number of Arab states, for example Egypt and Syria, feel that foreign influence should be entirely excluded, whilst others desire a limited connexion with outside capital as a means of developing internal economic life, e.g. by oil exploitation, revenues from which play a very important part in the state budgets of Iran, Saudi Arabia, and Iraq; and also as a backing for local currency. Despite strong Syrian disapproval, the Lebanese pound still remains linked to the French franc, even though the French Mandate has ended.

There was, however, at the start a substantial basis for agreement and co-operation – all members of the Arab League were at one in desiring to limit Jewish claims in Palestine. This led to a certain amount of joint action, e.g. a boycott on Jewish goods, the establishment of a propaganda bureau, and ultimately a joint declaration of war in 1948 against the Zionists.

Thus far, the Arab League has had only limited objectives – resistance to Zionism and support of Zionism by Western powers; but attempts have been made of recent years to expand collaboration into technical and cultural fields. These attempts have had only very limited results – there is a certain amount of cultural exchange, but even here national

---

[1] The first discussions between various interested states took place in 1944, but formal adhesion to the League did not occur until the following year.

rivalries remain: and schemes for economic development tend to break down on the hard facts (*a*) that few states will agree to genuine collaboration, and (*b*) the richer states are not very willing to spread their riches to others. Ideas for an Arab Development Bank have been put forward, and from time to time there are plans for a more egalitarian use of oil royalties as between 'have' and 'have-not' countries – but enthusiasm for these tends to be one-sided. In short, the Arab League can claim only partial success, at best.

A second major difficulty in the Middle East, and one that is closely linked to the future of the Arab League, is the spiritual and ideological crisis referred to in Chapter I, which is bringing into question the entire basis of Arab society. Recent experience of domination by outsiders has exposed the weakness of the Islamic world alongside the West; and this had led to much self-questioning and self-criticism by Moslems themselves. The first problem in the minds of many is whether the Islamic way of life has failed. Does the future lie in complete abandonment of the former way of life, with rapid and unquestioning acceptance of all the beliefs, spiritual values, and methods of Europe and America? Is it possible to pursue a middle course between both Western and Islamic traditions? Or is it a failure to live fully up to the true Islamic code that lies at the root of present difficulties, and should there hence be a return to a more simple and primitive Islamic life? These questions are in the minds of many of the more enlightened people of the Middle East at the present day, and as a powerful influencing factor, there is the example of Europe and America, where nationalism and materialism have been accepted as the basis of national life, apparently with great success.

Refugees. A living demonstration of the harshness and severity of political problems is the existence of a refugee group, numbering about 800,000. These are former Palestinian Arabs, who, according to Arab leaders, fled from their homes in 1947 under threat of imminent massacre by Jewish soldiers. According to the Israeli government they fled of their own accord, or were deliberately moved away by Arab leaders. These people are now miserably housed and fed in refugee camps mainly located in Jordan, but also in the Lebanon, Syria, Iraq, and Egypt. The Israeli government will not have them back: their lands are now occupied by Jewish immigrants, and they would moreover become a troublesome and dangerous minority element. The various Arab states are so far vehemently unwilling to attempt to absorb the refugees, on the grounds (*a*) that to do so would be tantamount to acquiescing in the permanent loss of Palestine, (*b*) that there would be enormous social and economic difficulties in absorption – Jordan especially has changed radically in social composition even as it is; and (*c*) so long as the refugees remain as they are, there is still the hope that they might one day return or even receive some reparation (as did ultimately the Jewish refugees from Germany). In the meantime, the refugees remain in enforced squalor and idleness, fed at subsistence level by United Nations; their principal occupation that of maintaining a very high birth-rate.

CHAPTER IX

General Economic Life (1)

In this and the succeeding chapters it is proposed to describe in general terms a number of features of economic life that are common to many regions of the Middle East. This discussion should be viewed as a background to the detailed survey of economic activities given under the appropriate regional heading.

I. AGRICULTURE

Agriculture is by far the most important economic activity in the Middle East, since between 70 per cent. and 80 per cent. of the total working population is directly engaged in cultivation, and a further proportion is dependent upon the products of agriculture either as a supplement to the main livelihood of pastoral nomadism, or as a source of raw materials for industrial occupations.

Although agriculture plays such a large part in the life of the region, by no means all the Middle East is cultivated or even cultivable. The following table brings out striking regional differences in land utilisation, and indicates where potentialities for future development lie. Some further reduction must be made to the figures, because on average one-third to one-half of the land stated as under cultivation actually lies fallow each year. In irrigated areas, the proportion of fallow is much less, because annual flooding renews soil fertility; but in regions dependent on rainfall, fields are sometimes cultivated only once in two, three, or even five years.

Land Holding and Tenancy. At the present time, some confusion attaches to land holding in the Middle East. A number of titles to land have no other backing than that of tradition – a difficult matter in a region where nomadism and shifting cultivation persist – and in other cases where ownership was legally registered, records have been lost. Moreover, although the Ottoman rule has ended, the Ottoman land code still remains effective throughout many parts of the Middle East; and re-distribution of land, though being undertaken in many countries, is

	Total area (sq. miles)	Proportion Cultivable (per cent.)	Proportion Actually Cultivated (per cent.)
Cyprus	3,500	65	55
Iran	626,000	10	3
Iraq	175,000	20	3
Israel	8,000	35	22
Jordan	35,000	9	5
Lebanon	4,000	60	44
Libya	270,000	1	0·5
Saudi Arabia	930,000	4	2
Syria	66,000	20	10
Turkey	299,000	30	21
U.A.R. (Egypt)	386,000	5	4

See also Figure 31

still far from complete – laws stipulating maximum permissible holdings may be only partially applied. One of the principal tasks of the last thirty years has been the completion of a full cadastral survey for the registration and stabilisation of land holdings, but some of these surveys still remain unfinished.

Methods of land holding and tenancy have been greatly influenced by social and environmental conditions, and are hence studied in some detail. Five main types of land holding are recognised:

(1) *Mulk.* This is land held in full ownership. The holder is thus able to develop it as he wishes; and, since any improvements remain as his own property, initiative and foresight are encouraged. Unfortunately, however, mulk land is not widespread in the Middle East.

(2) *Miri* (= from the emir) represents land originally held by the state, and transferred, often to feudal landlords, in return for services to the Sultan. In some cases, full ownership was transferred, except for the right to dedicate the land to *waqf* (see (5) below), and the land was therefore in effect equivalent to *mulk*; but in other instances, transfer was made only for a fixed term of years, and sometimes for payment, like a European leasehold. About one-half of the land of Iraq is held in this second category of miri; and, where tenancies are short, there is an incentive to aim at rapid exploitation of the soil, without thought of long-term improvements.

(3) *Matrukhi* denotes in Iraq land used for public benefit, i.e. for government buildings, schools, or threshing floors; and is thus very small in amount. Elsewhere, matrukhi land is regarded as

the property of an entire community, and may be allocated in shares to each individual member, or even developed in such a way as to produce an income which is then divided amongst all participants. More frequently, however, matrukhi land is kept as grazing grounds for the community as a whole. Matrukhi of this latter class is widespread in mountainous areas, and appears as a frequent feature of tribal organisation, particularly amongst pastoral nomads. Kurdistan, western Persia, and Arabia are the chief regions of its occurrence.

(4) *Masha* (*mushaa*) is in some respects similar to matrukhi, since there is again communal ownership by a single group. Allocation is made on a basis of one share per male member of the family, including children. With such a scheme, by which a family of boys will receive a far greater holding than a family of girls, the social inferiority of women is emphasised. In this can be seen the influence of a strongly patriarchal social organisation which, although most characteristic of pastoral and nomadic peoples, has also spread into cultivated regions on the desert margins. Eastern Syria, Jordan, and parts of Libya are the areas in which *masha* holdings are most numerous.

Masha and *matrukhi* holdings may often be legally registered in the names of a few notables of the group; and under the *millet* system, the head of the *millet* frequently held land in trust for his community. From this derived some of the civil and financial power of religious leaders, whose influence on the everyday life of their followers had thus both a spiritual and an economic basis. It is in the light of such organisation that the present close association of political and religious feeling in the Middle East must be viewed.

(5) *Waqf* (Turkish *vaquf*) represents a kind of religious or charitable trust by which the revenues of dedicated land are applied under the supervision of special Government Departments in each state to religious objects, and to the charitable maintenance of persons or institutions. Once dedicated, waqf comes under state control, and is subject to a considerable number of restrictions. Rights in waqf can be inherited; hence as waqf continues unaltered after the death of the original owner, holdings often become minutely subdivided between an increasing number of heirs. Because of the many restrictions that apply to waqf holdings, and the generally small size of the plots of land, attempts at improvement

by tenants are largely discouraged, and short-term exploitation without a thought of the future is aimed at.[1] Waqf is therefore regarded by many as an obstacle to agricultural development in the Middle East; but because of its religious associations and wide extent waqf presents an extremely difficult problem. Even now, waqf in Egypt covers an area approximating to one-tenth of the total cultivated area of the country.

In the past, because of lower taxes on waqf,[2] many dedications were made by collusion, whereby religious foundations or even pseudo-charities received the title, but returned most of the revenue to the original owner. At one time, more than half of the entire area of Turkey was supposed to be held as waqf, but it has been the policy of modern governments, particularly in Turkey and Persia, to resume state ownership. The student of economic history will note a similarity between waqf and mortmain, which presented an analogous fiscal problem to the monarchs of mediaeval Europe.

The three types of land holdings, matrukhi, masha, and waqf, have the general disadvantage of discouraging improvements and long-term development. Cultivators are unwilling to grow anything but crops that offer the quickest return; rotation to conserve soil fertility is rarely practised; and fruit trees, that need many years to mature, are never planted on holdings that will be re-allocated to a neighbour at the end of a few months. Besides all this, waqf in particular leads to absenteeism – an owner may not find it possible, even with the best intentions, to visit a plot several hundred miles away which has come to him as an inheritance; yet such a holding of scattered plots may not be grouped together, or sold.

A second evil of Middle Eastern land holdings is excessive sub-division, which often arises because of the large size of Middle Eastern families. Weulersse quotes the instance of Bar Elias, a Lebanese village where 5,285 acres came to be divided into 32,643 plots; and Fig. 31 gives a similar example from Palestine. Recent experience has shown that when communal lands held as matrukhi or masha are stabilised (i.e. re-allocation is stopped) in order to avoid the evils of shifting cultivation, the opposite extreme of subdivision is liable to develop, so that the limit of viability is passed, and conditions become worse than

---

[1] Because it cannot be transferred, except by inheritance, waqf cannot be used as security for loans or mortgages, since the lender cannot foreclose in the event of default.

[2] As a charity explicitly enjoined in the Koran, waqf was liable to no tax beyond the Koranic 10 per cent. levied on the revenue. The land itself was not taxed.

before. Before the re-allocation and limitation of size of holdings in Egypt, which began after the end of the monarchy, 94 per cent. of all owners held only 37 per cent. of the total cultivated area of Egypt; and of these 2⅓ million held less than 2 feddans – this last figure being also

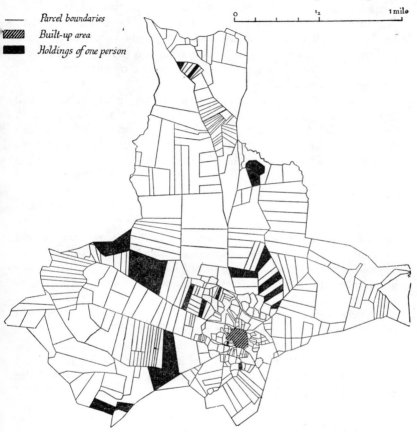

Fig. 31. Fragmentation and Dispersal of Land Holdings in an Arab Village of Palestine (1945). Data by permission of the Palestine Government, and reproduced by the courtesy of Dr E. C. Willatts and the Royal Geographical Society

regarded by authorities on Egyptian economy as the minimum area on which an average peasant family could live. A contrast from one point of view exists in Iraq, where 70 per cent. of the cultivated area is held in units of over 500 acres.

Tenancy. The most widespread form of tenancy is share-cropping

(métayage). Under this scheme the landlord provides seed, and sometimes implements, and receives a proportion, usually at least one-half,
of the yield after taxes are paid. At best, share-cropping is intended to
protect both landlord and tenant against the vagaries of Nature in a
frequently difficult environment – the loss is equally borne if crop fails –
but in practice, share-cropping has led to short-term, exhaustive
methods of cultivation, with the tenant frequently in debt to landlords
and usurers. Initiative is again discouraged, and as it is easiest for the
landlord to give out a portion of last year's crop for next season's
sowing, rotation is little practised.

Cash rents are rarely paid. Two exceptions may, however, be noticed:
in rich market gardening areas near the cities, profits are relatively high,
and tenants have sufficient capital to avoid dependence on the landlord
for seed. On the margins of the desert, cash rents are also a feature but
for a very different reason – the landlord wishes to avoid the total loss
resulting from a Badawin raid, and is the stronger party as compared
with his tenant.

In many areas, agricultural labourers are paid in the form of shares
in the crop, that is, by a kind of métayage; but the proportion received
is lower than in the case of settled tenant farmers. Overseers (sarkals)
are employed to supervise numbers of labourers, and this form of
exploitation is particularly widespread in Iraq. Landlords themselves
are comparatively rarely resident on their estates, most preferring to
live in the towns, and visiting their estates only at harvest time – sometimes even with an armed guard. The high proportion of city dwellers
of this kind is one of the social features of the Middle East, and stands
in contrast to conditions in Europe. One factor in the situation is the
limited extent of openings for capital investment. Banks are few and
mistrusted; there have been several devaluations of currency and also
considerable inflation;[1] and there is still only restricted possibility of
investment in industry. Hence the profits of commerce are most
frequently invested in landed estates, as a fixed asset which cannot easily
be stolen, or depreciate in value.[2]

Some mention must be made of the schemes of redistribution of land
for the benefit of landless peasants. Such schemes have been a feature in
Persia, Syria, Iraq, and Egypt. But even though laws have been enacted,

---

[1] Cf. the French franc, worth 10d. in 1914 and now 13·74 to the £ sterling; the Israeli
£, at par with sterling in 1948 and now worth 2s. 3d.; and the £ itself which has lost 75 per
cent. of its purchasing power.
[2] Losses by theft are extremely common in all parts of the Middle East, and every
house, whether large or a mere hut, has built-in bars on every ground-floor window.

these have become in some instances dead-letters or only partially enforced; and sometimes there has been collusion over disguised sale, or by which a wealthy owner has managed to hand over part of his forfeited land to children or relatives. Moreover, redistribution of large holdings to peasants, though well publicised, may affect only a relatively small number of people – e.g. the redistribution laws of Egypt enacted in 1952 affected only 10·6 per cent. of the cultivable area, and could only benefit 150,000 peasant farmers (with an average family of five, a total of 800,000 people in all) out of a total estimated farming population of 13 million. Nevertheless the schemes have had some useful results – possibly economic, and certainly political, social, and psychological.

Life of the Cultivators. Throughout the Middle East, the vast majority of cultivators exist at extremely low standards of living. Communications are often poor, so that all the produce of one district tends to find its way to a single local market, where in times of plenty the price falls because of a glut, and high prices occur only when crops have failed. Under such conditions, 'cornering' by middlemen can easily take place; and as an example we need only go back to 1942–3 when something approaching military force had to be used to feed the cities of Syria from wheat produced in the immediate neighbourhood.[1]

Rents and taxes may absorb as much as five-sixths of the total produce of a holding, and the tenant cultivator must frequently have recourse to moneylenders. Usury is specifically forbidden by Moslem Law, but the threat of severe penalties has merely made the trade dangerous, and not suppressed it. Interest rates of 50 per cent. to 200 per cent. are therefore demanded; so that the cultivator rarely escapes from the moneylenders once he has made their acquaintance.

A summary of conditions in southern Iraq (due to D. Warriner) gives a typical apportionment of the income from land as follows:

Per cent.

To Government (taxes)	10
Landowner	40
Sub-tenant (sheikh)	7½
Sarkal (overseer)	2½
Fellah (occupier)	40

From his 40 per cent., the Fellah must also pay a rent for the upkeep of irrigation canals, amounting to one-fifth or one-half of his income.

It must also be stated that legislation has recently been introduced in

[1] In 1914–18, when similar methods were not used, actual starvation occurred on a large scale.

some countries to alter this situation (e.g. in Egypt, leases are restricted to three-year periods, and rates of interest and repayment controlled so as to amount to no more than 50 per cent. of the gross income of a holding).

It is fair to say that the greater number of peasants live on the extreme margin of subsistence. A windowless hut of dried mud, of palm leaves, or of flattened petrol cans, is often shared by humans and animals alike; and rags for a bed, a few communal cooking and eating utensils, and clay bins for grain form the entire household possessions of the family. Water is often too scarce for washing, and may have to be brought several miles; whilst dried animal dung provides the only fuel in many parts outside Asia Minor. No margin is left for medical attention, for the simplest anti-malarial precautions, or for amusements: the peasant if ill must find his own cure; and it is significant that the greater proportion of children born in rural areas are likely to die before reaching the age of ten.[1]

Crops. Much of the Middle Eastern agriculture is still in a stage of development comparable with that of mediaeval Europe; i.e. subsistence is the over-riding consideration, with the aim of feeding the local population upon local produce. Under such a system, foodstuffs tend to be the main crop, regardless of whether they are suited to geographical conditions in the area, and specialisation in a few products that might succeed better is generally avoided. Only in a few favoured regions is specialisation possible; elsewhere there is a remarkably uniform pattern of mixed cereal cultivation, with a number of extras such as fruit, vegetables, tobacco, and cotton on a small scale. Conditions in the Middle East thus appear in sharp contrast to those of Australia, or the United States, for there are no corn, cotton, or wheat 'belts': instead, small enclaves of minor crops – cotton or tobacco – tend to appear in areas given over to cereals, and one plant is often grown alongside another of a very different kind.

(*a*) *Cereals.* Overwhelming importance attaches to cereal cultivation, since apart from the value of the crops themselves, the relatively slow development of fruit trees and conditions of land tenure combine to put a premium on crops that develop in as short a time as possible. Wheat and barley, grown as winter crops (i.e. sown in autumn and harvested in late spring or early summer), are by far the most important, with wheat predominating in all areas except Egypt, Libya, and Iraq. The chief summer crops are maize, a recent introduction from the New

[1] In 1942–5, investigation showed that in one region of the Lebanon the average expectation of life at birth was five years only. This situation has improved in many areas, but not everywhere.

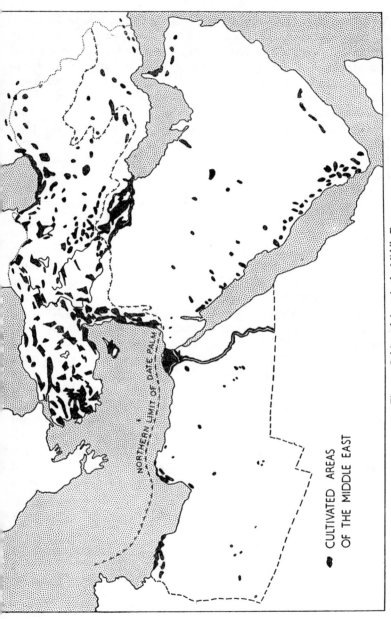

NORTHERN LIMIT OF DATE PALM

● CULTIVATED AREAS
OF THE MIDDLE EAST

Fig. 32. Cultivated Areas in the Middle East

World which is likely to play an increasing role in Middle East agriculture; varieties of millet; and rice. Summer crops are usually sown in spring and harvested in summer or early autumn. Maize has now become the most important cereal crop of Egypt, and ranks third to wheat and barley in Israel and Jordan. Rice, originally from south-east Asia, is important in the alluvial lowlands of the great rivers; and oats are grown in the cooler mountainous regions of the north.

Wheat and barley are native of the Middle East. As a wild plant barley has a wide distribution, ranging from Tunisia through Tripolitania, Cyrenaica, and the Sinai to the Levant and Asia Minor, with extensions to the north-east as far as Transcaucasia, Turkestan, and Afghanistan. The fact that in Mesopotamia measures of barley were taken as standards of value at least as early as 2000 B.C. indicated the importance and antiquity of the plant, which is still the chief crop of Iraq.[1]

The origin and distribution of wheat is a more complicated matter. In the first place, the bread wheat now in common use as a food would appear to be a hybrid, developed by cultivation from other strains, and not a domesticated wild species, as is the case with the remaining cereals. Ruggles Gates has suggested that bread wheat has arisen from the crossing of two inferior wheat strains; (a) einkorn (alternative name dinkel and spelt) which is a small plant that grows wild in Greece and the northern part of the Middle East, and (b) emmer, a much more productive species, which is still widely cultivated in regions of warm dry summers. Most of the hard wheats used in the making of food pastes – macaroni, etc. – are of the emmer group. Wild emmer has a more restricted distribution; the only area where its occurrence seems definite is a narrow strip immediately to the east of the Jordan depression, between Syria and the Nejd. Another possible area is the northern Caucasus. A theory has been put forward to the effect that bread wheat formed by the crossing of einkorn and emmer must therefore have been first grown in the region where both species grow wild – that is to say, in south-west Syria or Transcaucasia.[2] A second theory due to Vavilov

[1] The question has arisen as to which of the two grains barley and wheat was the first to be cultivated by early civilised man. From the botanical and archaeological evidence available, H. J. E. Peake concludes that in all probability, the cultivation of wheat preceded that of barley, although no final answer can be given.

[2] Further light on the origin of bread comes from certain features of cell structure. The cells of einkorn (Triticum monococcum) show a chromosome grouping of seven; those of emmer (typical varieties T. dicoccum and T. durum) a grouping of fourteen; and those of bread wheat (T. vulgare) a grouping of twenty-one – strong evidence in favour of crossing between the first two species.

places the origin of bread wheat in eastern Afghanistan, Iran, or Transcaucasia. This theory is less generally accepted, since it conflicts in some measure with archaeological evidence.

Except in Asia Minor, where it is still an important crop, einkorn is now little grown; but emmer, because of its tolerance of high altitudes and a cooler climate, is widely grown, particularly in mountainous or semi-mountainous regions. With bread wheat, emmer is the staple food grain of most agricultural areas of the Middle East, barley now being used increasingly for animal fodder, and for export as malting barley.[1]

(b) *Fruit and Vegetables.* Because of a deficiency of pasture, fruit and vegetables form an essential part of the diet of most natives of the Middle East. Not only the peasant, but the industrial worker and casual labourer of the towns make a usual midday meal of bread, olives, and onions, with rarer additions such as dates, figs, or apricots. Orchards and gardens are hence an important complement to ploughed land, and, whenever possible, the peasant tries to have a proportion of both. As we shall see later, it is sometimes possible to sow orchards with cereals; more usually, orchards and gardens are planted round houses, since shifting cultivation prevents the establishment of fruit trees on ploughed land.

Thanks to a climate which combines certain of the features of both tropical and temperate regimes, the already abundant natural vegetation of the Middle East has been enriched by the successful introduction of numerous other species from north to south. To the indigenous olive, vine, apricot, fig, pomegranate, cherry, peach, and carob, have been added the banana, orange, and sugar cane, natives of the tropical south; and from the north, the apple, strawberry, and potato.

It is estimated that the olive occupies one-quarter to one-half of the total area planted in fruit trees throughout the Middle East – an indication of the importance of the olive as a source of food. The better fraction of the oil is used in cooking, giving a characteristic style of food preparation; and the olive itself, easily stored and carried, is often eaten raw. A general lack of animal fat in Middle Eastern diet is largely made up from olive oil; and the preparation termed *kubbeh*, spoken of as the national dish of the Lebanese peasant, and consisting of chopped vegetables mixed with olive oil, is a typical sample of Middle Eastern food. In addition, the poorer oil is used as an illuminant, and as the

---

[1] By reason of its pale golden colour, barley from some regions of the Middle East, notably Cyprus, Cyrenaica, Israel, and Jordan, commands a higher price as an ingredient in the distilling of whisky.

basis of an important soap industry, whilst the crushed stones are fed
to cattle.

Closely adapted to the Mediterranean climate regime, the olive
flourishes best in regions of abundant winter rain; yet a long, dry
summer is essential to a full development, and it is remarkable how
even a small summer rainfall will reduce the oil content of the fruit.
Moderate winter warmth is also necessary, though the olive can stand
up to 15° F. of frost for a short time. In spite of its predilection for
regions of moderate rainfall, the olive is tolerant of aridity, and can
grow, with irrigation, on the borders of the desert. This explains its
wide distribution outside the purely Mediterranean areas of the Middle
East: as an oasis plant it extends as far east as Iran. Irrigation becomes
necessary in regions of less than 8 inches of rainfall, but care must be
taken not to apply an excessive amount of water, in order to avoid
reducing oil content of the fruit. Certain districts of the Middle East
stand out as regions of intensive olive culture: the two most important
are (1) the valleys of south-west Anatolia, centring on the Büyük
Menderes (Meander), and (2) the lower Orontes, centring on Antakya
(Antioch), and extending as far inland as Idlib. Other districts are the
Seyhan plain of Turkey, and the environs of Latakia, Tartus, Tripoli
(Lebanon), Damascus, Beirut, and Tripoli (Libya).

The vine is second in importance to the olive. Production has varied
at different periods, the Islamic ban on alcoholic beverages having had
a restrictive effect. At the present time, some wine is made, chiefly, but
not exclusively, by Christians and Jews – Cyprus, the Lebanon, Israel,
and to a lesser extent, Turkey, Iran, and the Alexandria region of Egypt
being the chief wine-producing areas. A large proportion of grapes are
eaten as dessert, and a sweetish confection resembling molasses is also
prepared. In western Asia Minor, most of the grapes are dried and
exported as sultanas.

The vine is much less tolerant of great heat, and is also liable to
contract disease in the damp summer atmosphere of the coastal lowlands. Hilly country, therefore, suits the plant best; and the foothills of
Cyprus, the Lebanon, Israel, almost the whole of the lower hill slopes
of Asia Minor, and many parts of northern and western Iran, are the
home of vine cultivation. In all parts of this zone, extending from the
well-watered hills of Cyprus, western Anatolia and the Levant, to the
high valleys of Armenia and Azerbaijan, and to the oases of central Iran,
vines form an important adjunct to cereal cultivation. Phylloxera, said
to have been introduced into Turkey by the construction of the Orient

Express route in the 1880's, has now necessitated the introduction of American vine stocks (which are more resistant to the disease) in districts of intensive production.

Another plant showing considerable adaptation to Mediterranean conditions is the fig, which has been cultivated in the Middle East from earliest times. Like the olive, the fig needs a long hot summer, but is otherwise able to stand either aridity or abundant moisture, and is therefore of frequent occurrence on the Mediterranean coast, and as far inland as the desert border. Associated with the olive, vine, and fig, but of lesser importance, are the other fruit trees; apricot, peach, and pomegranate. Mention must also be made of the many nut trees – chiefly almond, pistachio, and walnut – which are characteristic of the 'continental' inner zone of the Middle East from south-west Anatolia to Persia; and of the hazels that are more characteristic of northern Asia Minor. A cold winter is essential to the growth of many of the crops.

Another fruit crop of greatly increased importance is the apple – difficult to grow except on the higher hill slopes. Apples are much in demand among the oilfield workers – they keep well, and are often less easily contaminated than the soft fruits. In the Lebanon 'apple land' – above 4,000 feet altitude – now commands higher rentals than warmer terrain nearer sea level.

So far, little has been said of the southern portion of the Middle East. In this zone generally higher temperatures, with only a few short cold spells in winter, together with lower rainfall, give rise to a vegetation complex essentially different from that of the cooler and more humid north. Most typical of the south is the date palm, and the northern limit of its occurrence may be taken as a frontier separating the Middle East into two contrasting provinces. The significance of this division is greater than that of mere vegetation zones. To the north of the boundary lies the more specifically 'Mediterranean' area, with a characteristic social development related to the cultivation of wheat, olives, and vines, and tending to look in some aspects of its political and cultural orientation towards the west and north. South of the boundary is a region showing some affinities to the tropics and to the monsoon lands. Here the date is a staple, and rice, maize, and sugar cane tend in some measures to replace wheat and olives as principal crops. With this alteration go changes in agricultural practices and ways of life: irrigation becomes the basis of cultivation; and contacts with the south and east assume importance.

Damascus and Baghdad, both approximately on the same line of latitude, but on different sides of the boundary, might be taken as typifying conditions in the two zones. The first, an outpost of Mediterranean civilisation, is linked to the west both commercially, and as a part of Christian tradition: Baghdad has fewer contacts with the west, and might be said to appear, in western eyes, as a more remote, exotic, and truly 'Oriental' capital. In Damascus are associations with St Paul and the Omeyyad dynasty, with its offshoots in Spain and North Africa; to Baghdad belong the Abbasids – Haroun al Raschid, and the Arabian Nights.

Date palms require prolonged hot and dry summers for successful growth of fruit. If temperatures fall below 64° F. for any considerable period during the year, fruit will not ripen, although the tree itself may develop normally; and summer rain prevents fertilisation of the flowers. Pre-eminently a tree of the hot deserts, date palms can exist on a minimum of water, and produce fruit even when partially buried in drifting sand. The palms can also stand considerable amounts of water, and heaviest yields of dates are obtained when irrigation is applied to roots (Dowson) so that date palms are also characteristic of most riverine areas in the south of the Middle East. In order to obtain a large crop, the female flower must be fertilised by hand with pollen obtained from a male flower, since natural pollination is somewhat slow and unreliable. A date grove will therefore include two or three male palms per hundred of females, and some trade in pollen dust is carried on from southern Iraq, where date palms are most numerous. The banks of the Shatt el Arab are the region of greatest cultivation, and a large surplus is available for export after local needs have been met. The date is also a principal item of diet in southern Iran, the Arabian peninsula, parts of the Nile valley, and in Libya. Its high sugar content, relative resistance to contamination by the bacteria of human disease, and long-keeping qualities make it ideal as a food for nomadic and semi-nomadic peoples.

Vegetables are becoming increasingly important. Hitherto, the summer drought has been an unfavourable factor; but with recent development of irrigation schemes this difficulty is being overcome; and a further stimulus has been provided by the growth of cheap motor transport. Market gardening is therefore becoming a feature especially in the neighbourhood of large towns; but as Middle Eastern vegetables (onions excepted) often tend to be somewhat coarse and insipid, production is dependent on home demand, and a large export trade is unlikely to develop unless quality improves. The chief native plants are onions, cucumbers, pumpkins, marrow, squashes, beans, and garlic; and to these have been added tomatoes and potatoes. Tomatoes are fairly widespread in the Middle East, but potatoes tend to be restricted to the cooler and damper north, where they form an increasingly important crop.

(c) *Commercial Crops*. In certain more favoured regions of the Middle East, where natural conditions permit, and where the development of communications has led to an abandonment of subsistence agriculture, a number of cash crops are grown, chief of which are cotton, fruit, tobacco, mulberries, and narcotics.

Cotton is a summer crop. The absence of late spring frosts and a long dry summer followed by a distinctly cooler autumn are markedly favourable factors; and where abundant water supplies are available (usually only in irrigated areas) the plant does well. Unfavourable factors are soil salinity, which has a marked deleterious effect, and liability to insect pests. Lower Egypt is the principal area of production, and the famous long-stapled cotton of the region has a world-wide market; a much smaller production in Iraq is mostly exported chiefly to Japan, and a limited quantity of Cypriot cotton again finds its way to southern and central Europe. In Turkey, the Lebanon, Syria, Persia, and Israel production has greatly increased, especially round Adana (Turkey), Aleppo, Latakia, and the Homs-Hama regions of Syria and Isfahan (Persia).

Tobacco is also a summer crop, and is best grown on hill slopes in regions of moderate rainfall. Despite official Moslem disapproval of smoking, tobacco is widely grown throughout the Middle East for local consumption only, but in most areas quality is poor. In western Asia Minor, and in the Latakia district of Syria, more careful methods of cultivation result in a better product, and an important export trade has grown up. Of recent years, the 'Turkish' tobaccos of Anatolia have lost much ground to the Virginian variety,[1] but Latakia tobacco, which is used mainly as a blending ingredient in pipe tobaccos, has maintained its position.

Mulberry plantations for the rearing of silkworms have been a feature of certain parts of the Middle East ever since the cocoons were first smuggled from China in early Byzantine times. Within the last

---

[1] It is interesting to note the change in smoking habits in Britain since 1900. At that time Turkish cigarettes were fashionable, and it was felt necessary to apologise when offering a stronger Virginian 'gasper'.

century, the extent of mulberry plantations has undergone considerable fluctuation: under the Ottomans, a heavy tax restricted development, and outbreaks of disease were frequent, necessitating the import of new plant stocks from America. More recently, the competition of foreign silk from Italy, France, and Japan, and the use of artificial silk brought about a crisis in the Middle Eastern industry, and many mulberry plantations were re-sown with cereals. Famine during the war of 1914–18 also led to change-over to cereals. During the war of 1939, however, the Middle East became one of the few sources of raw silk in Allied hands, and a rapid expansion of production took place, especially in the Lebanon. Now, a renewed phase of competition and decline seems to have taken place, though Bursa and a few other western Anatolian towns still maintain some activity.

The opium poppy and a form of hemp (*hashish*) are grown in the Middle East for medicinal purposes, as a source of morphine and its derivatives. Although production is very small, the high value of the drugs renders the plants extremely useful as cash crops, and there is considerable temptation in the way of the peasant cultivator to produce small quantities above the legal amount allowed. These ultimately find their way to the illicit drug markets of the world. In Turkey, where slightly less than half of the world's controlled supply of morphine is produced, strict governmental supervision is maintained; but elsewhere in the Middle East, although governmental prohibition exists, ineffective supervision leads to the growth of an uncontrolled and illegal market. Opium poppies need a dry and moderately warm spring, with absence of frost. Towards the end of the summer, incisions are made in the capsule of the flowers, and a juice containing opium flows for some 24 to 60 hours, later coagulating into a sticky mass. Rainfall during this period and just before will result in loss of the opium both by washing away the exudation, and also by reducing the alkaloid content. Opium poppies are grown in Persia, where numbers of the people are addicts; and in view of an active smuggling trade into Egypt, there must be some production of hashish in the Levant states. It has even been said that hashish forms the principal export commodity of the Lebanon in some years.

Pests and Diseases affecting Plants. Agricultural production is greatly reduced by losses due to pests and diseases. The locust is probably the greatest single menace to crops, since one-half to three-quarters of the entire yield of a holding may be eaten during one visitation. Locusts originate in the deserts of Arabia and the Sahara, later moving northwards in immense swarms towards the cultivated areas.[1] As the locust is relatively large, measuring some two to five inches in length of body, a considerable quantity of greenstuff is eaten, and whole districts can be stripped bare within a few hours. The Sahara locust, which feeds for preference on grain and fruit, is regarded as more destructive than the Arabian variety, which prefers the leaves of trees. Because of their rapid migration by flight, locusts are an international problem; and a joint committee[2] has been established by a number of Middle Eastern states to develop methods of control. These include crushing the female locusts by heavy rollers, ploughing the eggs into the ground before they can hatch, and the use of flame throwers, and also insecticides such as sodium arsenite, against the adult locust.[3] Another method is to sweep the young locusts into specially dug trenches before their wings are properly developed.

Another pest is the *sunn* or *sunna* insect, which attacks the ears of cereals, just as they are ripening. The sunna seems to be most wide-spread in the damper, cooler parts of the Middle East; and, like the locust, the insect passes the first part of its life cycle outside cultivated areas, migrating into these regions only when fully developed. This habit offers the possibility of control by man, since if crops can be harvested before the arrival of the insect, much loss is averted. Hence quick-growing cereals are favoured in regions infested by the sunna; and barley, which ripens earlier than wheat, is less likely to be attacked.[4] Another form of control is to root out and burn the affected plant, thus destroying the insect, which, being very small, remains inside the ear. Losses from sunna infestation are only slightly less great than those from the locusts: up to 60 per cent. of the crops may be affected. The sunna

[1] An interesting relation between climate and the occurrence of locust swarms has been described by Dr Uvarov. Between periods of invasion by locust swarms, small numbers of locusts have been found to exist as individuals, quite dissociated from any swarm, and harmless to crops. Such 'solitary' locusts approximate closely in appearance and behaviour to ordinary grasshoppers. If, however, the progeny of solitary locusts are reared under crowded conditions (e.g. in a cage) physical changes occur, so that the solitary grasshopper type of locust becomes transformed into a true swarming locust. These changes, demonstrated under laboratory conditions, have also been observed to take place in grassland areas, when, following a season of drought, locusts are forced to congregate in a few relatively low-lying and damper spots. Hence locusts of the swarming type would seem to develop during cycles of slightly increased aridity, and it would thus appear that the factors producing an invasion by locusts are largely climatic.

[2] The *Office International des Renseignements sur les Sauterelles de Damas*.

[3] Spraying from aircraft has proved markedly successful. Another advance has been the discovery of gammexane, an insecticide that, unlike arsenical preparations, is harmless to vertebrate animals, and may therefore be used in grazing areas.

[4] This is one reason why barley, and not wheat, is the chief crop of Iraq.

does not migrate in large numbers over long distances, so that control measures on an international scale are not attempted.

The production of dates suffers from the activities of certain species of spiders, which cover the ripening fruit with thick, close webs. In the dusty atmosphere of date-growing regions, the webs collect sand particles, with the result that sunlight no longer reaches the fruit, and development is arrested. Other insect pests attack both citrus and soft fruit trees. Aphis and the saw-fly do much damage each year, though losses can be reduced by the use of insecticides. On the whole, however, in spite of the great need, preventative spraying is little practised in most fruit-growing regions of the Middle East, growers feeling that the high cost is not justified. The citrus groves of Israel and, to a lesser extent, the vineyards of western Anatolia, are the only districts in the Middle East where insecticides are used on any considerable scale.

Citrus fruit is liable to develop small black ·or red scales, which, although of little harm to the fruit itself, render the crop unsightly and difficult to sell. Hydrogen cyanide spraying is effective in reducing the incidence of scale, but there are obvious drawbacks to its extensive use. Phylloxera is another widespread disease affecting vines, and replacement of the plant stocks is the only effective cure. Rust, a kind of mildew, is also liable to develop on ripening grain; and unfortunately, native species of Middle Eastern cereals seem particularly liable to such attacks.

II. HUMAN DISEASE

The extent to which human activity, and therefore economic life, are affected by the incidence of disease, is so considerable that an outline of the main problems involved can justifiably be discussed as an aspect of the social geography of the region. The wide variation of climatic conditions within the Middle East, with generally high temperatures; its position between large centres of population to east, west, and south; and the flow of pilgrims of various races towards the shrines of Arabia and Palestine, are all in part responsible for a high rate of disease. Further factors must be sought in the mode of life of the people. Overcrowded, insanitary conditions in many areas are responsible for much disease; and these in turn are related to certain geographical factors: a general deficiency of water, lack of material resources in food and building materials, and social and political conditions such as methods of land tenure, or frequent foreign invasion.

Some of the more widespread diseases originate directly from environmental conditions. Malaria, yellow fever, kala-azar, and various other fevers are all spread by insects, the distribution of which is controlled in large part by climate. Other diseases such as bilharzia, dysentery, trachoma, typhus, and infestation by parasitic worms, are caused mainly by insanitary conditions, and are therefore a more specifically human problem. A third group of diseases, chief of which is pellagra, are due entirely to malnutrition, and are thus related to economic productivity.

Few complete statistics of the incidence of disease are available. We may, however, quote Cleland's view that up to 75 per cent. of the total population of Egypt is affected by at least one, if not two, major diseases; surveys during 1942-5 revealed occasional villages in Palestine and Syria where between 50 per cent. and 90 per cent. of the people examined were suffering from chronic malaria; and we need only recall that during the war of 1914-18 in the Middle Eastern theatre, more troops died of disease than by enemy action.[1]

Because of its effects on human activity and therefore on economic production, malaria is still probably the most important disease of the Middle East.[2] Most areas outside the higher mountain regions and unirrigated deserts are affected. The disease, caused by a parasite in the blood, is spread by the female mosquito, which sucks the blood of an infected person, and transmits a minute quantity of infected blood to the second person that it attacks.[3] As the mosquito spends much of its life in, or near, water, any stagnant or slow-moving water in streams, pools, irrigation canals, or even in empty cans and hollows near houses, is a breeding ground, and therefore a potential source of malaria. Although most frequent on warm, marshy lowlands, certain species of mosquitoes can live in moderately hilly country; and many parts of Asia Minor and the Levant are affected up to a height of 4,000 feet.[4] In addition to these regions, malaria occurs on a large scale in Iraq, particularly in the district of the Shatt el Arab; in Egypt; and in Iran where 100 per cent. of the people are affected in certain districts of the

[1] One could also recall the early death of Alexander the Great, and the destruction of the army of Sennacherib, both of which were due to disease.

[2] In *Middle East Science*, which gives an admirable outline of the chief problems involved, Dr Worthington quotes a statement of the Malaria Board of Cyprus: 'Malaria is the fundamental reason for the backwardness of many village areas . . . the people, owing to general debilitation caused by malaria and conditions arising therefrom, are physically and morally incapable of taking advantage of such social services and opportunities for advancement as are provided.'

[3] The female mosquito is impelled to suck blood as part of its reproductive cycle.

[4] Cyprus, once heavily malarial, was cleared of mosquitoes during 1945-50.

Caspian (Neligan). Arabia and Libya are relatively, but by no means entirely, free from the disease.

Malaria can occur in an 'acute' or 'chronic' form. The first has a rapid course, during which the affected person feels very ill, and must retire to bed. Chronic malaria, as the result of which the sufferer feels weak and 'out of sorts', but not sufficiently ill to lie in bed, may persist for many years without any alteration. The latter form of malaria is endemic amongst the native population of the Middle East, and children are affected at an early age, thus perpetuating the disease for generations. Because of its mode of propagation malaria is closely related to agriculture, especially in regions where irrigation is employed; and one serious feature, the liability for malaria to increase when new schemes of irrigation are developed, has already been touched on (p. 75). Rice growing, with its flooded paddy fields, is particularly liable to give rise to malaria; and in Iraq and Egypt, where rice cultivation is an important feature, government decrees restrict the areas which can be devoted to the crop, and also lay down rules for preventing the stagnation of irrigation water.

Control of malaria can best be achieved by attacking the breeding of mosquitoes. Care in disposal of water, attention to drainage, clearing of streams and canals, and the use of insecticides all give good results, but these are usually expensive, and therefore not always within the reach of local populations. A cheaper and simpler method of control, which is likely to be more widely used, is the stocking of streams and cisterns by small fish, which feed on the larvae of the mosquito. Striking results were achieved in parts of Palestine and Egypt by introducing an American minnow.

Yellow fever is in some respects a more dangerous disease, because of its rapid onset, and often fatal termination. It is fortunately not widespread in the Middle East; but an endemic area occurs in Central Africa, and this is probably extending at the present time into the Sudan. Yellow-fever-carrying mosquitoes can be introduced into a non-infested zone by aircraft, and the recent increase in air communication in the Sudan has led to stringent control measures designed to prevent a spread of yellow-fever into the Middle East.

Bilharzia is probably second in importance to malaria; and even more than the latter, is a disease of irrigated lands. The spread of the disease is related to the occurrence of a species of water-snail, which acts as a first host to the bilharzia parasite. After developing in the body of the snail, the parasite later enters the human body, and produces severe debility, which, as in the case of malaria, can continue as a chronic condition for many years. Bilharzia has thus the same effects as malaria upon the energy and initiative of the population.

Egypt is by far the most seriously affected region of the Middle East, and about one-half of the entire population is said to be suffering

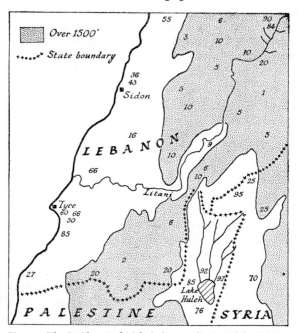

Fig. 33. The Incidence of Malaria in one district of the Levant. Figures show percentage of total child population affected by chronic malaria, 1943

from the disease:[1] one estimate even suggests that over 50 million people in the Middle East may be affected. The lower Tigris and Euphrates, with their tributaries the Karun and Karkeh, is also affected, and small outbreaks have been noted in Syria and Cyprus. Control of bilharzia can be achieved by destroying the water-snail by means of a solution of copper sulphate, and by the eradication of insanitary habits amongst the population. The wearing of shoes is also a safeguard, as the parasite enters the body through the feet.[2]

[1] Worthington quotes the district of Kom Ombo (Upper Egypt) which, a desert in 1900, has recently been irrigated, and now supports a population of 50,000. Of this population 84 per cent. suffers from bilharzia, and 24 per cent. from hookworm.
[2] This is a practice beyond the reach of many fellahin, since the price of shoes ranges

H

Another widespread parasite disease, ankylostomiasis or hookworm, is more directly related to insanitary conditions of life. Egypt, where 40 per cent. of the entire rural population may be affected (Worthington), is the chief centre of the disease, but Iraq, Jordan, Persia, and Turkey are also endemic areas.

Typhus, carried by lice and rat-fleas, is another disease of insanitary conditions, and one more likely to affect urban populations. Severe epidemics can occur from time to time, although with better conditions in the towns, and the greater number of medical men as compared with the country, urban epidemics are becoming less frequent. The stronghold of typhus is Persia; but other parts of the Middle East are affected, particularly in the neighbourhood of ports. Dysentery is also caused by lack of cleanliness, and in a mild form is almost ubiquitous, so that the native inhabitants seem to have developed a very limited degree of 'conditioning' to the disease – the worst sufferers can often be new arrivals.

Trachoma, a severe affection of the eye that often leads to blindness, is specially characteristic of the Middle East. Lack of cleanliness is an important contributing factor. Once again, Egypt is the main endemic area, and it has been suggested that the rate of incidence even exceeds that of bilharzia. Trachoma is widespread among nomads (who may not often wash) and is widespread in southern Libya.

Finally, the two diseases of pellagra and beri-beri are caused by a deficiency of vitamins in diet. It has been shown that pellagra is most frequent amongst communities using maize as a staple cereal; and a similar correlation exists between the eating of polished rice and beri-beri. Pellagra is recognised as an important factor in the backward condition of negro and poor white cultivators in the southern states of the U.S.A.; but so far the disease has occurred only on a small scale in the Middle East. With the extension of maize cultivation in the Middle East, there is a danger that pellagra may also increase; and an unfortunate feature is that greatest development in maize production is occurring in Egypt, which, as we have seen, has an already low standard of public health. In the colder upland regions where people live in closely confined, shut-in conditions for a part of the year, tuberculosis is widespread – especially in Asia Minor, where one investigator recently suggested that there were over a million active cases.

---

between 10s. and £5 ($2 to $15), and his total weekly income averages 5s. to £1 ($1 to $3). The average 'consumption' of shoes for the entire population of Iraq is still estimated (1962) at 0·2 pairs per head per annum – i.e. one pair every five years.

CHAPTER X

General Economic Life (2)

I. PASTORALISM

The pastoral industries of the Middle East lend themselves least to statistical survey, since most pastoralists are nomads, with strong prejudice against any form of census or enumeration, either of themselves or of their animals. Nevertheless, within the last few years a number of estimates of animal populations have been made. These, though useful, should however best be regarded as approximations.

LIVESTOCK 1960

	Saudi Arabia	Egypt	Syria	Iraq
Horses	30,000	42,000	103,000	300,000
Donkeys	22,000	930,000	250,000	1,000,000
Camels	215,000	162,000	100,000	200,000
Cattle	56,000	1,366,000	570,000	540,000
Sheep	3,572,000	1,277,000	4,700,000	7,500,000
Goats	2,000,000	750,000	2,000,000	2,200,000
Buffaloes	—	1,330,000	5,000	280,000

For the most part, agriculture and animal husbandry tend to be separate occupations. The 'mixed' type of farming characteristic of many parts of the world is practised only on a small scale, and many villages maintain one or more shepherds to look after all animals in common, whilst the great majority of owners devote themselves entirely to cultivation. In some parts, there is even antagonism between herders and agriculturalists of the same district.[1] The only areas in which mixed farming may be said to be strongly developed are the farm areas and settlements of Israel, where deliberate emphasis has been placed on a balanced economy of herding and cultivation.[2] In this separation, however, we may trace the operation of a geographical control – herding tends to be restricted to less favourable regions, usually mountain or desert, where water or good soil are lacking. Because of pressure of population, all lands capable of cultivation are

[1] See p. 128. [2] p. 416.

given over to cereal growing, which produces a greater quantity of foodstuff per unit of area than land under pasture.

Because of restriction to a generally unfavourable environment, the quality of animals is poor, and yields of food and other products are low. The size of individual animals is markedly less than in many other parts of the world. This is particularly noticeable in the case of sheep and cattle, many of the former being scarcely larger than European dogs.[1] Hence the yield of meat and milk is small, and wool and hides are of indifferent quality. Middle Eastern wool is in fact extremely hard and 'hairy', so that it cannot be used in the making of certain fine textiles, but instead finds its greatest use in the making of carpets. One compensation for the leanness of Middle Eastern sheep is afforded by the growth of a mass of fat in the tail, which may weigh up to 10 lb. or even 20 lb. This fat is eaten as a delicacy by the Arabs.

The enormous preponderance of sheep will be noted – this holds for most areas. Besides providing a small convenient carcass of excellent meat which can be eaten by a single family group in a short time – a factor of importance in view of the hot climate – the sheep provides milk and wool; and because of its ability to travel considerable distances between pastures it is better adapted than are cattle to existence under semi-arid climatic conditions. Goats are also kept in large numbers, both in steppe and mountain areas. These animals are more agile than sheep, and can find sustenance on less abundant vegetation, though, as we have seen, their voracious cropping of all green plant life makes them a menace in certain parts of the Middle East. Goats are kept for their meat, milk, and for their hair, which can be woven into a thick, smooth cloth that will resist soaking by rain, and is hence favoured for the making of tents and Badawin cloaks. The finer hair from Angora goats (mohair) produced in small quantities – chiefly from Asia Minor – is almost all exported.

Cattle are far less numerous, and tend to be kept in cultivated areas rather than on the steppes. Except in Egypt, fodder crops are rarely grown specially for these animals, which have to find a bare subsistence on stubble pasture after cereals are harvested, or on the weeds that are found on arable and fallow land. Only in a few areas is there any attempt to develop a dairying industry distinct from cereal farming. Chief of these are Israel, the regions of Baghdad, Beirut, Cairo, and Damascus, together with parts of Turkey; and in all cases the presence

---

[1] Sheep are sometimes kept as household pets, particularly by Moslem families, who regard the dog as unclean.

of a large urban population has been the reason for the growth of dairying. Milk cattle are often kept within large cities, and stall-fed on the vegetable refuse – stalks, leaves, etc. – from neighbouring market gardens. Conditions are only too often the extreme reverse of hygienic, and frequently milk becomes the carrier of disease (Himadeh). Beef is not greatly eaten, mutton being preferred, so cattle are usually extremely lean and small.

Because of Jewish and Islamic religious prohibition, pigs are kept mainly by Christians, though there has been some development in pig-keeping in Turkey since 1923. The Lebanon is the chief area, but because of the warm climate, numbers are not large. Water-buffalo are important in the marshes of lower Iraq, in the Nile delta, in the Caspian provinces of Iran, and in the alluvial coastlands of Asia Minor, where in addition to providing milk, they are used for ploughing rice-paddy fields.

Donkeys are the principal draught animals of the Middle East. Hardy, sure-footed on broken ground, and tolerant of indifferent pasture, or poor fodder, these animals are used both for ploughing and for transport of people and goods. The usual ploughing team is a cow yoked with a donkey; and most camel caravans are led by one or more guides mounted on donkeys. To ride a horse is a sign of affluence, and most ordinary people are content to travel on the humbler donkey, though motor transport is reducing the number of animals used in this way.

In certain parts, notably Cyprus and Asia Minor, mules are bred in large numbers, and camels are also found in all countries of the Middle East, though they tend to occur most in the more arid south. Breeds have been developed to resist the winter cold of Turkey and Iran, so camels must not be thought of as purely warm desert animals. They are especially important in Iran, where most of the country is arid; and also, of course, in Arabia.

Horses are the least important of the draught animals of the Middle East, since their natural habitat is the cooler steppe of Central Asia, and they have been introduced only with difficulty into the Middle East. Pasture is usually too rank or poor for much grazing, and keeping a horse is a matter of considerable expense. Hence horses are not much used for ploughing or carrying merchandise, but they fulfil a function exactly similar to that of an expensive motor-car in Europe or America.

II. MINING AND INDUSTRIES

Mining. Apart from oil resources, which will be discussed separately, the mineral deposits of the Middle East, with only a few exceptions, are of restricted importance. Though widely scattered throughout the region, minerals occur only in relatively small amounts; and in many instances, the size of the ore body hardly justifies the establishment of large-scale plant for extraction and treatment. A second disadvantage is the remoteness and inaccessibility of many deposits; because of their association with the folded zone of the Middle East, a number of the most productive veins must be sought at high altitudes, in regions that are difficult both topographically and climatically. After ore is mined, there is a long and expensive haul to centres where it can either be treated locally or shipped abroad. Communications, which are frequently indifferent even in the non-mountainous regions, are extremely poor in many mineralised zones, so that cost of production of Middle Eastern minerals is high, and production occupies a marginal place in world markets, exploitation occurring only when prices are high. Even in Israel, high cost of transport over the 80 miles to the Mediterranean has an adverse effect on the output of minerals from the Dead Sea; and in Asia Minor and Iran, where ores must move several hundred miles to the coast, this drawback is much more pronounced. Railways and roads are few in number; hence special arrangements are necessary, and in some cases special railway lines to mines have been constructed at a high cost. Aerial ropeways for carrying ore are also a feature in Cyprus and Asia Minor.

Another disadvantage is lack of coal, which apart from the general effect on economic life, has a directly restrictive influence on the production of other minerals, since ores cannot be treated or even concentrated at the mines, and must usually move outside the Middle East for refining. Coal of good quality is found only in the north-west of Turkey, in the Eregli-Zonguldak basin; and output is barely sufficient even for the limited needs of Turkey herself.

A fourth obstacle to mineral production is lack of labour. Most mining centres are well away from centres of dense population, and there is little inducement, in the scale of development of mining industries, to attract a large mining population to the hilly zones where minerals could be exploited. The severe winter of the north makes it impossible to continue mining throughout the year in many parts of Anatolia; and most peasants prefer, if at all possible, to combine with mining some part-time cultivation or herding. Even workers in the Turkish coal mines return to the fields for a short time during the harvest season, and, in an effort to maintain production, the Turkish government has been forced to experiment, not altogether successfully, with convict labour.[1]

A further adverse factor, though of minor importance, is the fact that exploitation of metals in the Middle East has been in progress, at least in a sporadic way, since the dawn of history. The gold of Lydia (Asia Minor) where coins were first issued; the copper of Cyprus, and the iron of Anatolia and Phoenicia have all been partly exhausted of their richest ores: and although these considerations obviously do not apply to minerals like asbestos or chromium, certain areas formerly renowned as centres of mineral production have no modern activity. On the other hand, new discoveries have been made on old sites, and improved technique in extraction allows exploitation of ores that were rejected in ancient times as being of too low grade.

It is not proposed at this stage to outline the detailed distribution of the mineral resources of the Middle East: for the present it is sufficient to note that the general picture of mineral production is one of rather sporadic development over a fairly wide area, with a variety of methods of exploitation. These range from haphazard collection of ore from surface outcrops, with no attempt at actual mining, by peasants whose chief livelihood is in agriculture or forestry, to intensive exploitation on a large scale involving the use of modern machinery. As an example of the former method, we may note the chromium deposits of the Amanus Range of south-east Turkey, and also the umber veins of Cyprus, which are both exploited mainly by foresters and cultivators, who merely collect masses of ore lying on the surface of the ground. Modern methods using solar heat are employed at the Dead Sea extraction plants, and it is possible that this source of energy may soon become more utilisable. Another source of fuel is natural gas from oilfields, now in process of development in Iran, Israel, and Saudi Arabia.

III. INDUSTRY

Industrial development in the Middle East is as yet only on a small scale. Probably less than 15 per cent. of the population of the region derives a livelihood from industry; and of this total, a considerable

---

[1] In cases where convicts could not be used, recourse has been had to students in secondary schools and universities. It would not, however, appear that service in the mines was in any way related to previous performance in examinations.

proportion is still engaged in hand craftsmanship or 'cottage' industry, and remains unaffected by modern large-scale methods. Lack of fuel, chiefly coal, is a principal cause of this restricted development; but scarcity of raw materials and poor communications are other serious adverse factors.

We have seen that the coal deposits of the Middle East are few in number; and it is only in recent years that the oil resources of the region, now recognised as extremely abundant, have been developed to any considerable degree. At the present time oil fuel is used only to a limited extent in industry, partly because the bulk of Middle Eastern oil, being handled by foreigners, moves outside the Middle East, and serves relatively few consumers within the region[1] (e.g. less than 1 per cent. of Saudi Arabian output is retained in the country; and Iraq is currently hoping to sell most of its allocation of 12 per cent. of Iraqi oil production to West Africa), and partly because large-scale industrial plant, having been imported from Europe or America, is designed to use coal or electricity as prime fuels.[2] This situation has now begun to alter, with the announcements of plans for 'gas grids' (Chapter XI). So far, no more than 10 per cent. of local oil serves internal consumption.

Before discussing modern industrial production, it is necessary to note the existence of a wide variety of handicrafts and 'cottage' trades. Of these, small-scale working of metals has continued since earliest times. First copper and bronze, then iron smelting were developed from the widespread but rather scanty ore deposits of the north and centre of the Middle East; and this irregular distribution of metals, together with chronic lack of fuel in many parts, has tended to give metal-working in the region the character of a craft industry, with the value of the finished product lying in workmanship rather than in the raw material itself.[3] Highly tempered steel for weapons and harness, ornamental domestic utensils with elaborate chasing and inlay work, and gold and silver ornaments are the chief products of Middle Eastern handicrafts in metal. During the Middle Ages, Damascene steel and inlay work had a world reputation, and something of the ancient tradition still lingers in the modern workshops of the district. Silver-work from Amara (Iraq) and Persia has today more than a local renown.

A second product of small-scale craftsmanship are textiles of various

---

[1] Chiefly for automobiles, and for domestic use in cooking stoves.

[2] Hydro-generation is however developing particularly in Asia Minor, Egypt, and Persia, in association with irrigation barrages.

[3] Cf. the industries of Switzerland, where a similar principle holds good.

sorts. Raw materials are abundant: cotton, flax, silk, and wool are all produced within the area, and as well, camel- and goat-hair are available in steppe regions. The natives of the Middle East use cotton and silk for much of their clothing, and cloaks of finely woven camel-hair serve as an impermeable outer garment for the majority of the Badawin. Although traditional 'Arab' dress is retreating before European styles,[1] it is still worn exclusively by nomads, and by a minority of townsfolk; and a large proportion of the textiles used in this way are of local production.

In addition to the production of textiles for everyday articles of clothing, the Middle East, particularly Syria and Persia, specialises in luxury brocades, which consist of metallic threads of gold or silver interwoven with a base of silk, or silk and cotton. Mohair, woven from the fine hair of angora goats, is produced on a very small scale, chiefly in Asia Minor; and there is some production of linen, mainly from Cyprus.

Wool produced in the Middle East is, as we have seen, often too coarse and too hairy for use in high-quality textiles. Instead, it is used in the manufacture of carpets and rugs, for which parts of Persia and Turkey are world famous. This activity is *par excellence* a small-scale craft: the finest Persian carpets have as many as 400 tufts per square inch, and take years to complete. The wool is tinted by hand, using special processes that are sometimes family secrets handed down through generations; and designs peculiar to each locality make it possible for the connoisseur to recognise from which district the finished carpet has come. Latterly, the competition of cheaper machine-made carpets, and the introduction of aniline dyes have struck a blow at the carpet industry of the Middle East; and competition from India and China, together with changes in fashion, have led to some decline in the European demand for Turkey carpets especially, particularly in Britain. The chief markets are now America, Germany, and the Middle East itself. In the latter region carpets are an essential and much-prized article of furnishing, not merely for the Badawin,[2] but also in the houses of townspeople, where, in addition to their normal function, carpets are used for wall decoration, and as coverings for divans.

[1] Less than a century ago, for example, it was unsafe to appear in the streets of Damascus wearing European dress. Today, about two-thirds of the inhabitants have adopted the newer style.

[2] Carpets, almost the sole furnishing of Badawin tents, are a sign of affluence and social importance – i.e. a considerable 'status-symbol'. An invitation to make use of the carpet of a tribal chief confers 'social standing'.

Another aspect of textile craftsmanship is the needlework and embroidery carried on by women in some districts as a supplement to other occupations. Embroidery, lace-making, and drawn-thread work on silk, linen, and cotton reach a high standard, and testify to a long-continued and skilful tradition. This luxury trade is, however, developed mainly in association with the tourist traffic of the Levant; the product being sold chiefly to travellers and pilgrims. Lace from Nazareth, Beirut, and Aleppo, linen work from Cyprus, and embroidery from the Lebanon, Syria, and Turkey provide a livelihood in areas where population pressure is great, and means of subsistence restricted.[1]

Other small-scale but widespread local industries are the preparation of foodstuffs (olive oil, food pastes, dried fruits, etc.), and soap-boiling. The latter, although of frequent occurrence in olive-growing areas, is still inadequate to supply the real needs of the population.

The craft industries of the Middle East are, with few exceptions, carried on in, or near, the towns; communications being too poor to allow an extensive and purely rural 'cottage' industry similar to that of eighteenth-century Lancashire or Yorkshire. Small workshops maintained by a single owner with the assistance of his family, or at most, five or six paid assistants, are most characteristic; and shops of a similar trade are often grouped together in a single street, e.g. Street of the Coppersmiths. Equipment is scanty and very simple – hand charcoal braziers, hand looms, or primitive oil presses of stone – and often the workshop is little more than an alcove hollowed out in the thick wall of another building.

Within the last quarter-century, native crafts of the Middle East have declined in the face of competition from cheaper, mass-produced foreign imports, and from the products of large-scale mechanised local industry, which in many Middle Eastern countries – though not all – is now developing on a significant scale. This decline was first apparent in the textile industries but has since spread to almost all trades. Under pressure of competition hand craftsmanship has to some extent deteriorated in quality: the finest Persian and Turkish carpets are no longer made, and cheaper imitations of machine-made foreign goods are appearing. At the same time, labour conditions are worsening – as in the first stages of the Industrial Revolution in Europe and America, craft or 'home' industry is degenerating into sweated labour, with 10, 12, or even 13 hours of work per day not uncommon. Seasonal em-

[1] Numbers of Armenian refugees in Syria and the Lebanon have found a living in this way.

ployment is also a recurring feature. Such developments are having a repercussion on social life in the region; there is a marked drift of population to the larger towns, with the growth of a restless under-privileged proletariat often living under conditions of extreme squalor in shanty towns or *bidonvilles*.

Modern Trends. Since 1918, a number of Middle Eastern states have embarked on a policy of industrialisation, with the object of attaining self-sufficiency in certain manufactured goods. This has led to the adoption of modern, large-scale methods, in order to allow newly developed industries to compete effectively in the home market against goods produced in America, Britain, France, Germany, Italy, and further Asia. In Persia and Turkey, a form of state capitalism has been adopted as the best means of stimulating industrial development; in Cyprus, Egypt, Iraq, the Lebanon, and Syria expansion has been con-ducted under private enterprise, with certain concessions, usually a tariff wall against foreign imports, from the state.[1] The Israeli govern-ment has adopted an intermediate system relying partly on private enterprise, and partly on controlled development subsidised by the Jewish state.

In view of the limited resources both in fuel and raw materials, there seems little possibility of Middle Eastern industry entering world mar-kets as a serious competitor. It is even doubtful whether the more modest aim of national self-sufficiency will be fully achieved: lack of iron ore in many regions makes it more than likely that a large pro-portion of machinery and capital goods will continue to come from abroad. As regards textiles, the position is somewhat different, and some further expansion may be expected, in view of the unusually wide variety of textile fibres produced within the Middle Eastern region.

So far, modern industrial development has been concerned with (*a*) textiles, (*b*) chemical production, (*c*) light engineering, (*d*) the pro-cessing of foodstuffs, and (*e*) cement manufacturing. As regards textiles, greatest attention has been paid to cotton. Large-scale spinning and weaving plants are in operation in Egypt, Persia, Israel, the Lebanon, Iraq, and Turkey; and certain of these countries are approaching self-sufficiency in certain types of cotton goods. Silk reeling by modern machinery has also started; and in Turkey a number of woollen mills have been constructed. Engineering in Egypt, Persia, and Turkey has

[1] In Iraq, under the Encouragement of Industries Law of 1929, new industrial enter-prises are exempt from income tax for a period of six years; their raw materials, if imported, are exempt from customs duty; and tariff protection amounting to 25 per cent. or 50 per cent. may be given.

been developed partly with the idea of producing light armaments: and it is significant that the largest single industrial plant in Persia, after the oil installations, is probably the State Arsenal. A similar trend is also apparent in the chemical industries of Iran and Turkey; but even so, armaments produced locally within the Middle East consist chiefly of rifles and ammunition. Aircraft, tanks, and heavy armaments are still obtained, at need, from more evolved nations in Europe and America. Other chemical industries have been developed in Israel-Jordan, where the deposits of the Dead Sea provide potash and bromide; and in Egypt, where local demands are now almost met by home production.

Light engineering has become a feature in Israel, Turkey, and Egypt. In the first country, Jewish capital and technical skill have led to much development in the regions of Tel Aviv and Haifa; and entirely new small-scale industries have also been introduced from Europe.

Processing of foodstuffs is a traditional Middle Eastern occupation. Of late, several canning factories for fish, fruit, and olive oil have been started; and, in view of the climate and indifferent communications of the region, this activity would seem to have future potentialities. Lastly, production of cement has very greatly increased over the last fifteen years. Fuel is the main limiting factor; large outcrops of calcareous strata provide ample raw material; and social conditions, which give emphasis to building construction as one of the few secure outlets for capital investment, are likely to maintain a brisk demand for the finished product.

Development of modern industry to some extent on a nationalistic basis has led to the erection of tariff barriers. In some cases, a cheaper and better foreign product has been excluded in favour of a dearer and inferior home-produced article; and though local manufacturing has in many instances been stimulated, this has occurred at the price of a higher cost to the consumer, and also of a slight deterioration in political relations with neighbour states. For example, a number of Palestinian products, both agricultural and manufactured, were for some years excluded by tariff from Egypt which is in some respects economically complementary to Palestine; and retaliatory discrimination in tariff policy has tended on occasion to assume prominence in several other states.

Another outcome of economic nationalism has been a shift of commercial balance within the Middle East. Under the Ottomans most of the region (excluding Persia) was a single economic unit, and the craft manufactures of Constantinople, the grain markets of Aleppo, and the textile industry of Syria, to name only the chief activities, supplied a wide area. With the resettlement of 1918, markets were restricted in extent; and although the new policy of self-sufficiency has allowed a wider variety of manufactures within individual states, outlets for a number of commodities have been restricted, with a consequent loss of certain of the economies of large-scale organisation. This loss has fallen unequally on certain districts of the Middle East – European Turkey (particularly Istanbul), Syria, and the Lebanon having been the chief sufferers. Israel, Jordan, and much of Anatolia have been unaffected.

Some reference has been made to conditions of labour in the handicraft industries. Unfortunately, with, however, certain conspicuous exceptions, a low standard also prevails amongst workers in modern industry. Labour legislation, restricting hours of work and the employment of women and children, has been enacted in many states of the Middle East but is sometimes allowed to become a dead letter because of lack of inspection and governmental control. Children of 10 or less are to be found at work, sometimes under hard or dangerous conditions; and the large surplus of unskilled labour, due to high birth-rates and to the gradual extinction of handicraft industries, has meant that the collective bargaining power of the artisan has remained low. Trades unions have in fact been looked on with suspicion by a number of governments, and labour organisation is therefore in a rudimentary stage. Another unfortunate feature has been the fact that although prices have risen considerably since 1939,[1] it is doubtful whether there has been an equivalent rise in real wages amongst the lower classes. Moreover, speculation and hoarding by wealthier members of the community have tended to prevent the benefits of a war-time increase in commercial and industrial activity from reaching the poorer classes. These remarks do not apply to Israel, which has strongly developed and active trade unions. Here the position of labour is very different, and European standards prevail.

[1] Changes in the cost of living can be estimated from the following table:

Wholesale Prices Index (Outline)

	1935–8	1945	1952
Egypt	100	330	340
Iran	100	1,200	540
Iraq	100	600	510
Palestine	100	340	420 (Israel only)
Syria and Lebanon	100	1,100	950
Turkey	100	500	450

During the war of 1939, the Middle East was largely cut off from imports of manufactured goods, and hence forced to rely on her own production. Local industry was greatly stimulated, not merely by an increased home demand, but also by large orders for consumption goods placed by Allied military authorities. The presence of numerous Allied troops with a purchasing power much above that of the average native population was a further stimulus. As a result, rapid expansion took place: in particular, the silk trade, which in some regions had been facing extinction in 1939, took on great importance as one of the few silk industries left in Allied hands. Palestine probably derived greatest benefit from war-time expansion, but the effects were felt in many other states, especially Egypt.

In summarising industrial development in the Middle East, it is important to maintain a correct perspective. Although attention has been devoted to recent developments in industry, it is essential to recall that agricultural and pastoral pursuits retain greatest importance, since they occupy an overwhelming proportion of the population. Modern textile industries in Persia and Turkey, cited as examples of active development, do not compare in overall scale with textile production in western Europe, America, or even China and India. Statistics show that despite the undoubted advances of the last few years, a large proportion of manufactured goods must still be imported: the transformation of agricultural products (e.g. brewing, food preparing, fruit packing, milling, refining, and soap-boiling) ranks as the principal industrial activity of the Middle East, followed by textiles, engineering, chemical production, and cement making.

Lack of statistics makes impossible any full or detailed comparisons: one cannot even arrive at an estimate of the exact industrial population in each country, or determine the proportion of workers in craft or 'cottage' industry. All that can be said with certainty is that in the Middle East industry is at present undergoing a transformation comparable with that in Europe during the first stages of the Industrial Revolution. Home industry, carried on in towns and adjacent country districts, is gradually being concentrated and transformed into mechanised operation on a larger scale. The extent of Middle Eastern resources does not, however, warrant the assumption that industry will reach the scale attained in Europe or America: although expanding in certain directions and increasingly favoured by availability of oil fuel, it will most probably remain an activity subordinate to agriculture.

IV. FISHING

In view of the low standard of agricultural productivity, it might be expected that the Middle East, with its long coastline, would have developed an important fishing industry. This is not so; comparatively little sea fishing takes place, and of the meagre quantities of fish produced, slightly less than one-half is obtained from inland waters. There are several reasons for the lack of attention to fishing, and most of these have a geographical basis; but one is mainly psychological – the prejudice of Moslem peoples, and of Shi'a Moslems in particular, against eating certain species of fish.

A second factor is the straight, harbourless, and often sheer coastline, which offers little inducement to seafaring on a small scale. Even in regions where harbours are more numerous, local populations have in a few cases turned their back on the sea, and settled at some distance from the coast, because of the liability to piratical raids in the not-too-remote past. This is especially true of Cyprus, where one might expect fishing to be an important occupation. Other natural factors influencing sea fishing depend on local conditions; and these will now be examined in turn.

Black Sea. Below about 250 feet, the waters of the Black Sea are heavily charged with sulphuretted hydrogen. Fish are therefore restricted to the upper levels; and in winter, storms and ice produce a large-scale migration of fish towards the calmer Aegean and Mediterranean, with a return movement in spring. Much fishing is, therefore, possible in the Bosphorus, Sea of Marmara, and the Dardanelles – one factor, incidentally, in the importance of Istanbul – and large quantities are caught in spring and autumn, at the times of migration, about three-quarters of the total being marketed at Istanbul. In the Black Sea itself, fishing is also a seasonal occupation, and a surprising variety of fish are caught: anchovy, mackerel, sardine, turbot, and tunny being the chief. A proportion of the catch is canned at various ports along the Black Sea, and at Istanbul. Turkish production of fish is higher than in many other Middle Eastern countries; but even so, further development could easily take place, especially in centres at some distance from Istanbul.

Mediterranean. The Mediterranean is far less rich in fish than is the Black Sea, owing to a lack of nutriment for the fish themselves. This lack arises from a deficiency of calcium salts, which in other sea areas are produced by the entry of fresh water from rivers and by interchange of deep and shallow waters under the influence of tides, currents, and atmospheric turbulence. In the eastern Mediterranean, all these factors are of small effect; the Nile is the only large river, and where it enters the sea there occurs the one important fishing ground of the eastern Mediterranean. In late summer and autumn, when the river is in flood, large shoals of sardine move towards the Nile delta to feed upon the nutriment in the fresh water; and heavy catches are obtained during the short season of Nile flood.

Along the coast of the Levant, sardine, mackerel, and mullet are caught; but the number of boats engaged is small. Some development has occurred in Israel, but a limiting factor is the scarcity of fish away from sea areas influenced by Nile water. The eastern Mediterranean is, however, an important area for sponges, and a high-quality product is obtained in most areas, the best coming from the Egyptian coast immediately to the west of the Nile delta. The sponge industry is closely controlled by various governments concerned, since over-fishing can easily occur. Chief areas of production are the Dodecanese Islands, Cyprus, the island of Ruad (off the coast of Syria), Egypt, and Cyrenaica.

Red Sea. Fishing can hardly be said to have yet begun on any scale. During the war of 1939, interest centred on the Gulf of Akaba as a source of extra food for Palestine and Transjordan; but lack of labour and difficulties of communication between Aqaba and its hinterland were serious handicaps. Moreover, it is not thought that the waters of the Gulf are particularly rich in fish. Further to the south, a scanty population along the shores, together with difficulties of communication inland, are almost insuperable obstacles; and activity is limited to a small production of shark, trochus shell (mother-of-pearl), and beche-de-mer, the latter being sold in China. Most of the fishing trade of the Red Sea has been developed from the African shore, chiefly from Port Sudan and Massawa.

Indian Ocean. In contrast to conditions in the Red Sea, fishing on the coasts of southern Arabia is probably the principal activity of the people. In the words of Worthington, the sea is equally as, or more productive than the land. During summer, shark are caught; and in winter, immense shoals of sardine approach the shore, followed by numerous tunny, which prey on the sardines. The native Arabs live for the most part on fish, fresh and dried, which in inland regions is also fed to transport camels; and even forms the chief fodder for cattle in regions east of the Aden Protectorate. It is not surprising to note that the inhabitants of south-east Arabia were known to the ancient Greeks and Romans as the Ichthyophagi (fish eaters).

Persian Gulf. So far, only a small development of fishing has occurred in this area. On general grounds it might be expected that relatively large quantities of fish would occur, especially in view of the richness of the waters of the Indian Ocean off the coast of Arabia, and also because of the entry of fresh water from the Euphrates and Tigris. Some fishing on a limited scale takes place in the lower Persian Gulf and Gulf of Oman; and one canning factory has recently been established by the Iranian government at Bandar Abbas, but output is very small, even below the full capacity of the installation.

At the head of the Persian Gulf, more extensive fishing is carried on to supply local needs in the marshlands of lower Mesopotamia. The Anglo-Iranian Oil Company had before 1950 organised a scheme by which part of the catch was transported to the Abadan region for consumption by the employees of the Company, who at that time numbered some 100,000 natives and Europeans.

Caspian Sea. Fishing in the Caspian is primarily concerned with the production of caviar from the roes of the sturgeon; and this industry, even in Iranian territory, is almost entirely controlled by Russians. Iran receives only the revenues from the caviar industry, with caviar itself and the flesh of the sturgeon being exported to Russia. Apart from this large-scale fishing for sturgeon, local fishing by Iranians produces a small catch which serves the needs of the Caspian provinces, but does not reach the interior of Iran. Fishing in the Caspian has only limited possibilities, since although present production is relatively high, the sea is rapidly shrinking in size, and restriction will be necessary in the future in order to conserve supplies of fish. Production has already fallen by more than 50 per cent. within the last fifteen years.

Inland Fishing. This is, relatively speaking, of considerable importance. One reason is the concentration of population in many riverine areas, as the result of which markets for the catch and a supply of labour are both easily available. In Egypt, areas of inland water (including the four lakes of the Nile delta) amount to one-fifth of the area of cultivated land, and the catch from inland fishing is several times greater than that from the sea. Chief areas of inland fishing are the four delta lakes, Menzaleh, Brullos, Idku, and Mariut, together with Lake Qarun in the Fayyum basin. The latter lake is stocked with fry from time to time, and its fisheries now employ over 2,000 men. The catch provides a most valuable supplement to diet in the Fayyum and Cairo districts.

In the view of Dr Ball, the fisheries of Lake Qarun will decrease in importance because of increasing salinity of the water, which will reduce the number of fish. One remedy, that of raising the water level by allowing inflow from the river Nile, is unlikely to be adopted, because of the loss of agricultural land that would result.

Fishing is also important along the middle Euphrates and Tigris; and, in addition to satisfying a local demand, quantities of fish were at one time sent to Palestine. The fact that fish could profitably be transported some 600 miles across the Syrian desert to places like Tel Aviv, which is itself on the sea coast, gives an interesting side-light on the difficulties

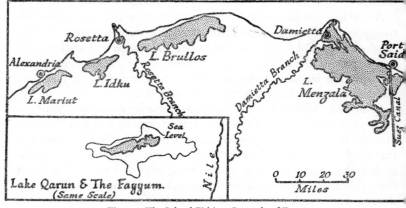

Fig. 34. The Inland Fishing Grounds of Egypt

of fishing in the Mediterranean, and is also an indication of the productivity of Iraqi rivers.

A third area of inland fishing is the Jordan rift, and its continuation northwards. The Dead Sea and lower Jordan are too salt for fish, but the Sea of Galilee (and Lake Huleh before its drainage), and the swamps of Lake Homs and the Ghab on the Orontes are all productive. Output is smaller per unit area than in the case of Egypt, because of certain natural drawbacks (e.g. the presence of hot mineral springs), and because of less efficient methods of fishing and of breeding control. Before 1948 the Jewish Agency for Palestine devoted attention to the breeding of carp for the stocking of inland waters (partly to increase food production, and partly to reduce the incidence of mosquitoes); and since the establishment of the state of Israel this policy has been continued, so that more than 60 per cent. of Israel's supply of fish now comes from breeding ponds – over 6,000 tons annually. Israel also purchased a num-

ber of British trawlers, and trained Jewish crews in the North Sea.
Some North Sea and Atlantic catches are even transported to Israel.

Foreign Aid. In closing this general discussion of Middle Eastern economy some reference may be made to the assistance now proffered by
outside agencies, governments, and individuals to various Middle
Eastern countries. Aid may be direct, in the form of outright payments;
as loans on commercial terms; in the form of purchases of Middle
Eastern products on advantageous conditions; as technical subsidies,
either in cash or by the provision of materials and personnel; in the
form of scholarships, training grants or other educational subsidies to
Middle Eastern nationals; by payments for the use of Middle Eastern
facilities – e.g. military bases; or finally as 'military aid'. The stage has
almost been reached of direct competition between the Western bloc
and Russia to offer aid to Middle Eastern countries – e.g. when America
withdrew offers regarding the financing of the Aswan High Dam,
Russia almost immediately made more acceptable proposals. The following fragmentary table will give an indication of the direction and
scale of foreign aid in the Middle East for sample years.

FOREIGN AID (IN U.S. DOLLARS)
(exclusive of aid from Soviet bloc countries)

	Official Donations and Loans 1956		International Aid 1954-7		Military Aid 1954-7
	Total	$ per head	Total	$ per head	in million $
Turkey	134 m.	5	—	—	230
Israel	184 m.	102	73 m.	24	—
Lebanon	12 m.	8	5 m.	3	—
Jordan	47 m.	32	14 m.	9	20
Iraq	—	—	2 m.	0·5	—
Syria	6 m.	2	1 m.	—	—
U.A.R. (Egypt)	64 m.	3	18 m.	1	—
Libya	24 m.	22	23 m.	21	13 (rent of bases)

Between 1949 and 1962 Turkey received from the U.S.A. $1,200 million as economic
aid, and a further $1,850 million as military aid.

In 1961–2 the following were announced:

O.E.C.D. Grant to Turkey to cover anticipated financial deficit: $45 m.
Credit from the U.S.A., West Germany, Italy, and the International Monetary Fund
to Syria: $40 m.
U.S. Development Fund Loans (1961–2):

To Egypt:	$42 m.	To Jordan:	$39.5 m.
To Iran:	$32 m.	To Israel:	$10 m.

CHAPTER XI

Oil Resources of the Middle East

I. THEORIES OF ORIGIN OF OIL

The process by which the petroleum deposits of the world have been formed is not as yet entirely certain. It was at first thought that mineral oil was of inorganic origin,[1] but more recent opinion is that oil derives from organic matter, and earlier inorganic theories are now largely discarded.

Petroleum would seem to have been formed by the decomposition of various types of marine life – chiefly plankton, but also algae and lowly animal organisms. As the remains of these organisms collected on the floors of seas and estuaries, they were gradually covered by deposits of thick, fine sediment that excluded air and light. Under such conditions, the normal process of decay did not operate: instead partial decomposition, produced by certain bacteria that exist in anaerobic conditions,[2] seem to have transformed the original organic material into globules of petroleum. It is also possible that chemical reactions involving mineral salts contained in the surrounding water and silt played some further part in the process of decomposition.[3]

As sedimentation continued, compression of the mass of silt led to its consolidation into rock measures of various kinds. The recently formed oil globules, at first widely dispersed throughout the entire mass of silt, and intermingled with water-drops, were hence squeezed out of their original parent rock, and forced to migrate, together with water and natural gas (also a product of organic decomposition), to any nearby rock measures such as limestone or sandstone. There, a

---

[1] One theory, due to Mendeleeff, postulated a reaction between chemically charged subterranean water, and metallic carbides in the rocks; a second opinion, due to Bertholot, ascribed the origin of oil to reaction between metallic sodium and ground water containing CO_2.   [2] i.e. without air.

[3] It is interesting to note that the same process of sedimentation and organic decomposition appears to be in process at the present time on the bed of the Black Sea. Similar conditions would also seem to be present in the Gulf of Oman. Black, strongly smelling mud with a high organic content is being deposited, and the waters of the Black Sea below 250 feet are heavily charged with sulphuretted hydrogen (see p. 225).

slow process of separation began, by which oil, as a lighter fluid, floated on top of the denser water, and gradually collected, under the influence of gravity, into large pools. Above the oil, and sometimes partly dissolved in it, occurred a quantity of natural gas; below was always to be found an accumulation of saline water.

In order for concentration of scattered oil globules to take place, some slight disturbance or irregularity of the rock measures would seem to have been necessary. Without the presence of some kind of trap or basin in which liquid could accumulate, the globules of oil would remain dispersed throughout a considerable thickness of rock, in a way that would preclude all possibility of commercial exploitation. Much of the oil might seep gradually away, and be lost. The occurrence of oilfields is therefore closely linked with geological structure; a limited amount of folding and dislocation is essential to allow the accumulation of petroleum in reservoirs, but excessive disturbance may break up the basin-like retaining structures and allow escape of the oil. Petroleum deposits are therefore associated with the outer margins of large fold structures, where disturbance of the rock measures, although present, is greatly restricted in extent.

A further condition for concentration of petroleum in large quantities is the presence of an impermeable rock layer, which acts as a seal immediately above the porous oil-bearing rock. Without this seal, or cap-rock, oil would not be retained in amounts sufficient to allow commercial extraction. Oil accumulation hence depends upon a conjunction of factors: (a) original richness of oil-forming material, (b) the occurrence of porous strata, (c) tilting of the rock measures to allow separation of oil from water, and its concentration in workable quantities, and (d) impermeable cover-rocks to prevent leakage of oil to the surface. The main types of geological structure favourable to oil concentration are shown in Fig. 35, and of these, the first, or anticlinal type, is by far the most widespread.

Conditions in the Middle East are favourable to a remarkable degree for the occurrence of oil. Reasons for this are: (a) long-continued sedimentation in the geosyncline of the Tethys, as the result of which oil was formed in rocks of many different ages and character, (b) the fact that the Tethys was a warm-water sea, and consequently rich in animal life, (c) the further fact that although extensive fold movements took place, these were reduced in intensity over wide areas by the presence of an underlying crystalline platform (the similarity between Fig. 35, which is an idealised diagram, and actual conditions in the

Middle East will be noted),[1] (d) the frequent occurrence of strata that are porous either because of their structure, or because of later fissuring, and (e) a similar abundance of impervious, and sometimes highly plastic rock series near or at the surface: e.g. the occurrence of impermeable beds of sandstone, shale, gypsum, anhydrite, and rock-salt. As a result, even though geological exploration is by no means complete, it is now known that the petroleum deposits of the Middle East

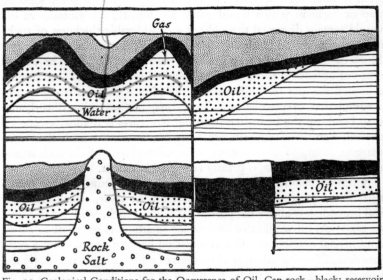

Fig. 35. Geological Conditions for the Occurrence of Oil. Cap-rock – black; reservoir rock – stippled

are on a vast scale, and are indisputably one of the principal assets of the region. Despite the fact that exploitation was delayed, and in some instances is still only in the early stages, it is definite that at present, on a basis of proved reserves, the Middle East is by far the greatest single potential source of petroleum in the world.

A special technique of geological surveying, known as the Seismic Refraction Arc Method, has been developed as a means of locating the oil deposits of Iran, which are for the greater part associated with limestone series. It has been discovered that vibrations from an explosion travel much more quickly through limestones of a certain

[1] In Persia, folds are steeper than in other oil-bearing areas of the Middle East. This is probably because the later series became detached from the crystalline basement as the result of shearing along the Cambrian salt-beds.

type than through other, non-limestone formations. Hence a charge of explosive (usually one to two tons) is detonated underground, and the results recorded at a number of seismometers spaced along the arc of a circle, the centre of which is at the source of the explosion, or shot-point. The seismometers are 10 to 15 miles away from the shot-point, so as to give time for differences in speed of travel of the vibrations to become clearly apparent; and, after allowance has been made for variations in altitude, the readings of each seismometer are compared. Because vibrations travel most rapidly through limestone, the seismometer placed at a point where an underlying bed of limestone approaches nearest to the surface will be among the first to record the explosion. In this way, by taking a number of arcs, buried anticlines and synclines in limestone formations can be mapped, even though these may lie unconformably with the surface strata. When the general trend of folding has been established, more precise observation of the exact crest of an anticline is made by grouping the seismometers in a straight line passing over the shot-point. By this means, using the same theoretical principle, not merely the position of the crest, but also its exact depth can be ascertained. Elsewhere in the Middle East, the more usual method of prospecting by reflection is followed.

II. OIL-PRODUCING AREAS

The productive oilfields[1] of the Middle East can be grouped regionally as follows:

(1) The Khuzistan fields of south-west Persia.
(2) The fields of north Iraq–north-west Persia.
(3) The fields of central Persia.
(4) The fields of south Iraq.
(5) Saudi Arabian and Persian Gulf Coast fields.
(6) The fields of south-east Turkey–north-east Syria.
(7) The fields of southern Israel.
(8) The fields of north-east Egypt.
(9) The fields of Libya.

Khuzistan Fields. These lie on the western flanks of the Zagros Mountains, in the region between Bushire and a mountain range known as the Pusht-i-Kuh. The western Zagros is composed of a series of large

[1] The term 'oilfield' is used in a general sense, to denote an area in which a number of oil pools lie.

anticlinal ridges, all aligned in a north-west–south-east direction, but of unequal longitudinal extent. One such ridge, the Pusht-i-Kuh, forms part of the extreme western edge of the Zagros in the latitude of Baghdad. The range is only some 200 miles long, and where it dies out, both to the north-west and the south-east owing to downward plunging of the fold structures, it is not immediately succeeded by other ranges. Hence the western edge of the Zagros approaches nearer to the river Tigris, and descent to the plain of Mesopotamia is abrupt; but further to the north-west and to the south-east, there are wide lowland embayments within the highland region, where the plain rises more gradually, by a series of foothills, to the main ridges of the Zagros. It is in these two areas of foothills that the major oilfields of Persia and Iraq lie. The southern embayment, drained by the Karun river, contains the Khuzistan fields; in the northern embayment occur the second group of fields – those of north Iraq and north-west Persia – with the Pusht-i-Kuh range as a zone of separation between. Only in the two enclaves, where the transition from plain to mountain is less sudden, and where, as a result, folding is less intense, are oil domes found. In the region of the Pusht-i-Kuh rock series plunge steeply below the sediments of the Mesopotamian plain, and so far have not yielded oil in any quantity.

The valley floors of the foothill region lie at an altitude of 500–800 feet above sea level. Between them run anticlinal ridges, often dissected and terraced, and giving the impression of small plateaus. Towards the west, ridges and plateaus reach a height of about 1,000 feet above the valleys, but further east, topographical features are more strongly marked, with ridges attaining 3,000 feet. On one such ridge, the Kuh-i-Seh Qaleitun, is situated the main production unit of the Gach Saran field, from which oil flows by gravity to tide water on the Persian Gulf.

The oilfields of Khuzistan are related to the occurrence of a bed of limestone, some thousand feet in thickness, which acts as a reservoir for petroleum. This rock, known as Asmari limestone, and of Oligocene-Miocene age, is not, however, in itself especially porous, and were it not for numerous fissures, which have been developed in it as the result of folding movements, oil would not flow in quantities large enough for exploitation. Wells must therefore reach a fissure in the Asmari series before they become productive, but when this is achieved, flow of oil in a single well has sometimes attained one million gallons per day. Because of the presence in the lowest levels of the Asmari beds of a quantity of water, which can be traced downwards without break through several thousand feet, it is inferred that oil has migrated into the limestone from a considerable number of other rocks of differing character.

In the foothill region, the Asmari beds are folded in a number of simple anticlines. Further to the south-west, however, they dip sharply under the sediments of the Mesopotamian plain, sometimes at an angle of 70°, while towards the north-east they outcrop at the surface among the main Zagros folds well to the east of the foothill region. Above the Asmari series is a complex of shale, salt, and anhydrite beds of Miocene age, known collectively as the lower Fars series. These beds act as an impermeable cap-rock, except where a number of faults allow some seepage of oil and gas to the surface. Because of the plastic nature of the salt beds, folding in the lower (Asmari) series did not conform exactly with that in the upper (Fars) series so

Fig. 36. The Oilfields of Iran and Iraq, as developed in 1948. Compare with Fig. 38. Land over 5,000 ft. – stippled. 1. Lali. 2. Masjid-i-Suleiman. 3. Naft Safid. 4. Haft Kel. 5. Agha Jari. 6. Gach Saran

that in the oilfield regions, a number of synclines in the lower Fars strata are underlain directly by anticlines in the Asmari measures. Until this disharmony was discovered, much difficulty was experienced by oil prospectors, since the surface features offered no clue to the nature of underground structures.

The oil occurs in dome-like anticlines, which, each measuring 12 to 20 miles in length, rank amongst the largest oil structures in the world. There is free connexion within the limestone reservoir rock of each dome, so that only a small number of wells are necessary to tap the entire reserve of an individual field.[1] Wells are spaced at intervals of one to two miles on the sides of the anticlines; and, as oil is withdrawn, a uniform pressure fall is apparent at all wells in the same field.[2] Because of the outcropping of the porous reservoir beds at some distance to the north-east, in the relatively wetter uplands of the main Zagros ranges, part of the Asmari series is saturated with water, and there is considerable hydrostatic pressure in the oilfield regions; pressures of 1,000 to 2,500 lb. per sq. inch being recorded. Pumping of crude oil is therefore at present unnecessary – a factor which, with the limited number of borings required, allows an unusually low cost of production. Another favourable circumstance arises from the fact that as crude oil is withdrawn from a well, natural gas held in solution under very high pressure leaves the oil and fills the upper part of the reservoir, greatly restricting the rise of water at lower levels. Normally, as oil is tapped, salt water rises within the oil dome to fill the space left, and ultimately water mingles with and contaminates the last portion of the crude petroleum deposit. Quantities of oil may also be cut off and trapped by rising water, so that they cannot be withdrawn. In the Iranian fields, however, pressure of natural gas greatly restricts the rise of salt water, so that losses by contamination and trapping are much reduced.

Oil was first produced in 1908, from the Masjid-i-Suleiman field. After 1918, output steadily increased; and in 1928, the Haft Kel field was developed. The remaining fields came into production during or after the Second World War. The crude oil is not, however, of particularly high quality, as there is a substantial sulphur and asphalt content, so that an elaborate technique of refining is necessary to obtain aviation spirit. At present, production is from three main areas – Agha Jari,

[1] Cf. conditions in east Texas, where there are 24,000 oil wells.
[2] The small number of wells in Khuzistan as compared with other oilfields of the world led to a charge of deliberate restriction of production being made against the operating company by the Iranian government, which was anxious that production should be maintained at the highest possible level.

Gach Saran and Haft Kel, with the second of these thought to have largest reserves. A number of once-important fields are now declining, and Pazanan has only natural gas.

In 1910–13 a pipeline, 150 miles long, was constructed from Masjid-i-Suleiman to Abadan, then a small port on the Shatt el Arab. Here a refinery was erected, to treat the oil which flows from Masjid-i-Suleiman (3,000 feet above sea level) under the influence of gravity. Port and refinery have since been considerably extended, and the plant has a present capacity of 500,000 barrels per day. Some 100,000 workers are normally employed at the refinery, which is now the largest single installation in the world. Numerous tanker and cargo berths for ocean-going steamers have been constructed at Abadan, and at Khosrowabad, a short distance downstream, but only cargo produced by or consigned to the oil company is handled at either port, so that both towns play a highly specialised role in the economic life of Iran. A pipeline has recently been constructed from Gach Saran to Kharg, a small island in the Persian Gulf. From here, it is expected, will come the bulk of future production, as Gach Saran has greatest future potentialities.

Fields of north Iraq–north-west Iran. These fields lie in the more northerly of the two embayments previously described. Many of the structural features of Khuzistan are repeated in the north: there is the same foot-hill topography some 50–80 miles broad, flanking the main Zagros ranges that lie further to the east; and folding follows a similar pattern of broad anticlines in the foothill zone, with sharper dips to the south-west. The reservoir rock of Eocene-Miocene limestone (termed Main Limestone) is also closely comparable with the Asmari series of Khuzistan, but of rather greater thickness. Four oilfields have been developed, at Kirkuk, Naft Khaneh and Ain Zaleh in Iraq, and at Naft-i-Shah in Iran, the latter lying very close to Naft Khaneh of which it is really a part, but on the opposite side of the Irano-Iraqi frontier.

At Kirkuk there is a single narrow anticline between 50 and 60 miles long – an immense size for an oil dome – and, as in the Khuzistan fields, open connexion within the reservoir rock allows free flow of crude oil, so that 38 wells are sufficient to tap the whole length of the anticline.[1] First developed in 1927, the Kirkuk field now produces between 500,000 and 600,000 barrels daily, from three centres; and this oil moves by pipeline across the Syrian desert to the Mediterranean. Until 1950 Kirkuk was linked by two 12-inch pipes, one routed via

[1] A gas and oil seepage from the crest of this anticline, at Baba Gurgur, is traditionally associated with the 'fiery furnace' of Nebuchadnezzar. (G. M. Lees.)

Haditha on the Euphrates and then through the states of Jordan and Israel to Haifa, where a refinery was built by British (Shell) interests. The other pipeline runs parallel to the first as far as Haditha, and then via Palmyra (Syria) to Tripoli in the Lebanon, where another, at first

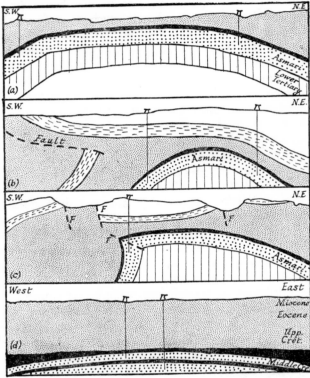

Fig. 37. Structure of Arabian and Iranian Oil Domes. Cap-rock – black; reservoir – dotted. Note that reservoir rock in Iran is Asmari limestone (Tertiary); but Middle Cretaceous sandstone in Kuwait. (a) Masjid-i-Suleiman, (b) Agha Jari, (c) Lali, (d) Kuwait (Burgan)

smaller, refinery is operated by French interests. At intervals along the pipelines west of Haditha are pumping stations, each numbered according to the branch on which it is situated (e.g. T 1 is the easternmost station on the Tripoli branch, and H 5 the westernmost station on the Haifa branch).[1] In 1948, as the result of Arab-Jewish differences, opera-

---

[1] Since their construction, these stations have in some instances taken on added importance as meteorological stations, as halting places for trans-desert traffic, and as strategic points in the policing of the region.

tion of the line to Haifa ceased; and work on a new 16-inch pipeline almost near completion also came to an end. Another 16-inch pipe from Kirkuk to Tripoli was opened in 1949, giving a total capacity of 7·7 million tons of oil per annum. Early in 1952 a 30/32-inch pipeline was completed from Kirkuk to Banias on the Syrian coast north of Tripoli, with a capacity of 14 million tons per annum.

Another oil region occurs further to the south-east, at Naft Khaneh. Here production is much smaller, hardly comparable with that at Kirkuk. Crude oil is refined at Alwand, near Khanaqin, 30 miles away, and the entire output serves the needs of the consumers within Iraq, none being exported. Close by, at Naft-i-Shah, oil is produced for the local market of northern Persia. Crude oil from Naft-i-Shah is conveyed by pipeline to a small refinery at Kermanshah (Persia) which has a capacity of 100,000 tons per annum.

In 1956 significant discoveries of oil were made by an Italian-Persian company in the central plateau area round Qum; but so far there has been no production, pending the building of pipelines.

In 1939 oil was discovered at Ain Zaleh, north of Mosul, but invasion threats in 1941 led to a suspension of activities, and production did not start until 1952. The oil is held in a layer of Cretaceous limestone (i.e. distinctly older than the 'Main Limestone' of Kirkuk). With a daily production of nearly 30,000 barrels (1960) from only eight wells, Ain Zaleh and a smaller site, Butmah, rank as the third most important field in Iraq, and this region is connected by pipeline to Kirkuk. Another later but larger field (second to Kirkuk) has very recently been developed at Zubair and Rumaila near Basra. Here the reservoir rock is of Cretaceous sandstone, and geological conditions are closely similar to those described below for Kuwait and Saudi Arabia. Two pipelines with a total capacity of 8·5 million tons per annum connect Zubair with a loading terminal at Fao on the Persian Gulf.

Other regions of Iraq have been surveyed for petroleum resources, but disappointment has resulted. Large quantities of oil were found at Qaiyara on the Tigris, and in the region between Hit and Ramadi on the Euphrates, but in both cases the crude oil was of very high gravity, so that it was impossible to pump the oil from the ground; and there was in addition a sulphur content of 5 to 10 per cent. (cf. sulphur content of crude oil at Kirkuk, 2 per cent.; at Masjid-i-Suleiman, 1 to 2 per cent.). Oil of a similar heavy type has been found in other districts of the Iraq lowlands, but again little can be done, at

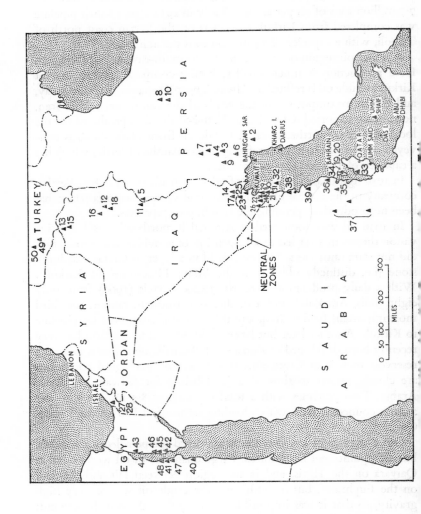

the present stage of technological development, to exploit these resources. Possibly in the future some method will be discovered by which these heavy low-grade oils can profitably be used.

Saudi Arabian and Gulf Coast Fields. Conditions in Arabia and on the southern shores of the Persian Gulf are in marked contrast to those of Iran and Iraq. Folding of the sedimentary measures has been greatly restricted because of the presence of the ancient continental platform of Gondwanaland; hence oil structures are very broad, open anticlines. In some localities, anticlinal structures are visible at the surface; in others, surface topography offers no guide to the presence of oil-domes. The oil reservoir rocks of Arabia range from Jurassic to Cretaceous in age, and are thus considerably older than those of Iran and Iraq. Another point of difference is that in parts of Arabia petroleum is held in porous sandstones, not limestone.

A sandstone reservoir rock occurs in the Burgan district some 30 miles south of Kuwait, where oil was discovered in 1937-9. War conditions hindered development, and only after 1945 was it realised that this field formed one of the largest reservoirs of petroleum in the world. Currently the Burgan field (with two smaller adjacent centres of production at Ahmadi and Magwa, and three new centres at Minagish, Raudhatain, and Sabriya) has the largest number of wells of any oilfield in the Middle East, and produces the greatest quantity of oil – though it is likely in the future to be surpassed in output by the even larger Ghawar field of Saudi Arabia. The Burgan oil is of good quality, but slightly heavier than that of Iran and Saudi Arabia, and sulphur content is 2.5 per cent. The crude oil moves to a refinery at Mena on the Persian Gulf.

A second major oilfield is located in the province of Hasa on the Saudi Arabian shores of the Persian Gulf. Production is from a number of regions, of which Abqaiq and Ghawar are at present the most important. The first field consists of a very shallow dome, some 4 miles long; and the reservoir rocks (lying some 7,000 feet below the surface) consist of Jurassic limestone, with a bed of anhydrite as the cap-rock. Very similar conditions would seem to occur elsewhere in the Saudi Arabian oilfield region, with, however, the Jurassic reservoir rock found at greater depths – in some instances as much as 10,000 feet.

In 1954 it was realised that four producing centres hitherto regarded as separate structures formed one single oil-pool of enormous dimensions. The first 'strike' of oil was in 1948 at Ain Dar, and six months later a second at Haradh. Following discoveries in 1951 and after at

Uthmaniya and Shedgum it became clear that this pool, or field, now known as 'Ghawar', extended for 130 miles from north to south, and 15–20 miles from east to west. Exploration has now spread into the Rub al Khali area of the south, and in 1961 new discoveries in Saudi Arabia exceeded total annual production by 2.1 million barrels. The Ghawar structure alone has a reserve greater than that of the entire United States of America.

During 1951 a new field was discovered three miles off the shores of Saudi Arabia in a district known as Safaniya. The oil, held in a sandstone reservoir rock, is heavier than that obtained from most of the Saudi Arabian fields, but of usable quality; and large-scale production began during 1955. In 1953 yet another field was located at Wafra in the neutral territory between Saudi Arabia and Kuwait; with four producing centres: 'Eocene', Burgan II, Ratawi, and Khafji.

One remarkable feature in the Saudi Arabian oilfields is the occurrence of artesian water supplies (see Chapter XVIII) in porous rock measures above the oil-bearing layers. Because of the great importance of this water in the district, which is extremely arid, special precautions are taken when drilling oil-wells to avoid contamination of the water by crude oil. Another somewhat unusual point is that, in order to maintain reservoir pressure, gas is artificially injected into the oil structure under great pressure.

The oil produced is passed by pipeline to three centres, refineries at Ras Tanura and Bahrein on the Persian Gulf, and to Saida (Sidon) on the Mediterranean. Construction of the well-known 'Tapline' (Trans-Arabian Pipeline) of 30/32-inch diameter over a distance of 1,100 miles was achieved in 1950 after many delays (some of which were political, and some due to world shortages of materials). Refining is carried out at Saida where there is a possible capacity of 25 million tons annually. Ras Tanura handles 11 million tons, and Bahrein a slightly smaller amount.

More than 20 million tons of oil have so far been produced on the island of Bahrein, but reserves are thought to be relatively small, and much less than those of the Arabian mainland. Present annual production of oil from Bahrein averages $1\frac{1}{2}$ million tons per annum, and it would seem that this yield is not likely to increase. As in Saudi Arabia, gas injection is employed in order to maintain reservoir pressure. A refinery at Bahrein city handles both local crude oil, and also a part of the Saudi Arabian output (see above), being linked to the mainland by a system of pipelines. Thus, although the actual resources of Bahrein

Island are limited, the refinery itself will probably gain enhanced importance as an outlet for Saudi Arabian oil; and during the closure of Abadan between 1951 and 1954 it ranked with Ras Tanura as one of the two largest refining centres in the Eastern Hemisphere.

Finally, oil was also discovered at Jebel Dukhan in the Qatar Peninsula during 1939, but for various reasons war conditions brought about a complete cessation of activity, which was not resumed until 1947. Oil was first marketed in 1949, and total production now exceeds 50 million tons of oil. The petroleum occurs at a depth of 6,000 feet in Jurassic limestone; and two pipelines (14-inch and 24-inch diameter) carry the crude oil south-eastwards some 70 miles from the wells at Dukhan to a loading terminal at Umm Said on the eastern side of the Qatar Peninsula.

Turkish Field. In 1940 considerable hopes were raised by the discovery of oil at Ramandagh some 60 miles east of Diyarbekir. By 1944, however, flow from the wells had ceased: but in 1948 new drilling gave better results, and a reserve of 10–15 million tons is believed to exist. The reservoir rock is Cretaceous limestone, and lies at a depth of 4,000–5,000 feet; whilst the oil itself is heavy and distinctly sulphurous. Further discoveries of higher quality oil were made nearby at Garzan (1950) and at Germik (1958). Lack of refining plant is a major obstacle, and some crude oil is used untreated as fuel on the Turkish railways.

Egyptian Fields. On both sides of the Red Sea and Gulf of Suez, geological structure is exceedingly complex, with a wide variation of rock-types that range from pre-Cambrian to Recent. Strong faulting movements at the time of formation of the Red Sea rift have produced severe dislocation, hence structures favourable to the large-scale accumulation of oil are infrequent, and of smaller size than those of Iran, Iraq, and Saudi Arabia. Nevertheless, there are many surface indications of the presence of oil in the Suez region and this has led to much exploitation, the greater part of which, however, was for long unsuccessful.

An oilfield was discovered in 1913 at Hurghada, but has since proved to be of only small size, and output is now declining. The crude oil is heavy, though not so heavy as that of the Tigris–Euphrates region, and there is a relatively high sulphur content. From Hurghada crude oil is shipped to Suez for refining. One refinery is operated by the Anglo-Egyptian Oilfields Company (owners of the Hurghada concession); the other, Egyptian state-owned, and smaller, handles a portion of the oil which, by terms of the concession, is passed over as a royalty to the

I

Egyptian government. In 1938 a second field was quickly developed at Ras Gharib, to the north of Hurghada, with the oil also sent for refining to Suez.

PRODUCTION OF OIL IN THE MIDDLE EAST

Field		No. of wells 1961 (flowing)	Depth (000's ft)	Daily average production 1961 (barrels)	Cumulative production to mid-1961 (mill. bhl)
Iran					
1. Masjid-i-Suleiman	1908	4	2·5	34,000	962
2. Gach Saran	1928	13	7·0	243,000	281
3. Haft Kel	1928	18	3·5	116,000	1,281
4. Naft Safid	1935	14	5·0	33,000	124
5. Naft-i-Shah	1935	4	2·5	7,500	41
6. Agha Jari	1937	32	6·5	707,000	1,630
7. Lali	1938	4	6–8	5,000	43
8. Alborz (Qum)	1956	—	8·5	(not yet producing)	
9. Ahwaz	1958	1	9·0	6,500	3
10. Sarajeh	1955	—	8·3	(not yet producing)	
Iraq					
11. Naft Khaneh	1923	2	3·0	3,500	63
12. Kirkuk	1927	45	2·8	689,000	2,062
13. Ain Zaleh	1939	6	5·8	19,000	60
14. Zubair	1949	28	11·0	78,000	281
15. Butmah	1952	3	5·1	6,500	15
16. Bai Hassan	1953	7	4·8	46,000	17
17. Rumaila	1953	3	10·8	113,000	275
18. Jambur	1954	2	5·7	16,000	11
Bahrein					
19. Bahrein Zone	1932	145	2·2	—	—
20. Fourth Pay	1936	4	4·5	45,000	255
Kuwait					
21. Burgan	1938	263	3·5–4·8	} 1,667,000	4,549
22. Magwa–Ahmadi	1952	80	2·5–4·8		
23. Raudhatain	1955	25	7·8–10·0		
24. Bahrah	1956	1	7·6		
25. Sabriya	1957	1	7·5–8·2		
26. Minagish	1959	4	9·0–10·0		
Israel					
27. Heletz	1955	25*	5·0	2,800	3·5
28. Negba	1960	1*	5·2	(not yet producing)	
Neutral Zone					
29. Burgan	1953	38	3·7	30,500	88
30. Eocene	1954	116	1·2–2·2	81,000	64

31. Ratawi	1955	27	7·1	46,000	47
32. Khafji	1960	15	5·5	10,500	2

Qatar
33. Dukhan	1940	33	6·6	177,000	483

Saudi Arabia
34. Dammam	1936	26	4·9	34,000	413
35. Abqaiq	1941	60	6·8	372,000	1,697
36. Qatif	1945	9	7·3	21,000	114
37. Ghawar	1948	92	7·1	746,000	2,116
38. Safaniya	1951	24	5·6	220,000	168
39. Khursaniya	1956	5	6·9	14,000	3

Egypt
40. Hurghada	1913	22*	0·7–2·5	635	40
41. Ras Gharib	1938	123*	1·2–2·5	16,700	174
42. Belayim	1945	54*	8–9	36,000	43
43. Sudr	1946	14*	3·0	3,000	34
44. Ras Matarma	1948	2*	2–3	291	1
45. Feiran	1949	2	8–9	—	1
Asl	1948	7	2·8–3·8	2,900	30
46. Abu Rudeis	1956	7*	8·5	5,300	9
47. Kreim	1958	22*	2·3	625	40
48. Ras Bakr	1958	36	2·8	3,000	2

Turkey
49. Ramandagh	1945	25*	4·4	3,600	10
50. Garzan	1950	35*	4·7	3,500	4
51. Germik	1958	5*	6·3	500	0·2
52. Bulgardagh	1960		(not yet producing)		

Libya
53. Zelten	1959	31	5·6–7·6	60,000	——

(began production October 1961)

Other fields at Bahi (2 wells), Bir Tlacsin (2), Beda (6), Block 59 (11), Dahra (67), El Amal (2), Em Gayet (7), Mobruk (7), Raguba (11), Hofra (3), Tahara and at Atsham,

* Some wells pumping

Exploration was intensified after 1945, and led to important discoveries on both sides of the Gulf of Suez. As a result, Egypt is approximately self-sufficient in petroleum. But the reservoir rocks (Eocene and Miocene limestone) are highly faulted and disturbed, with rapidly rising water in some parts. Already some fields have been abandoned, and reserves are relatively small.

Israel. After many disappointments, some due to war and disturbed political conditions, petroleum was discovered in commercial quantities

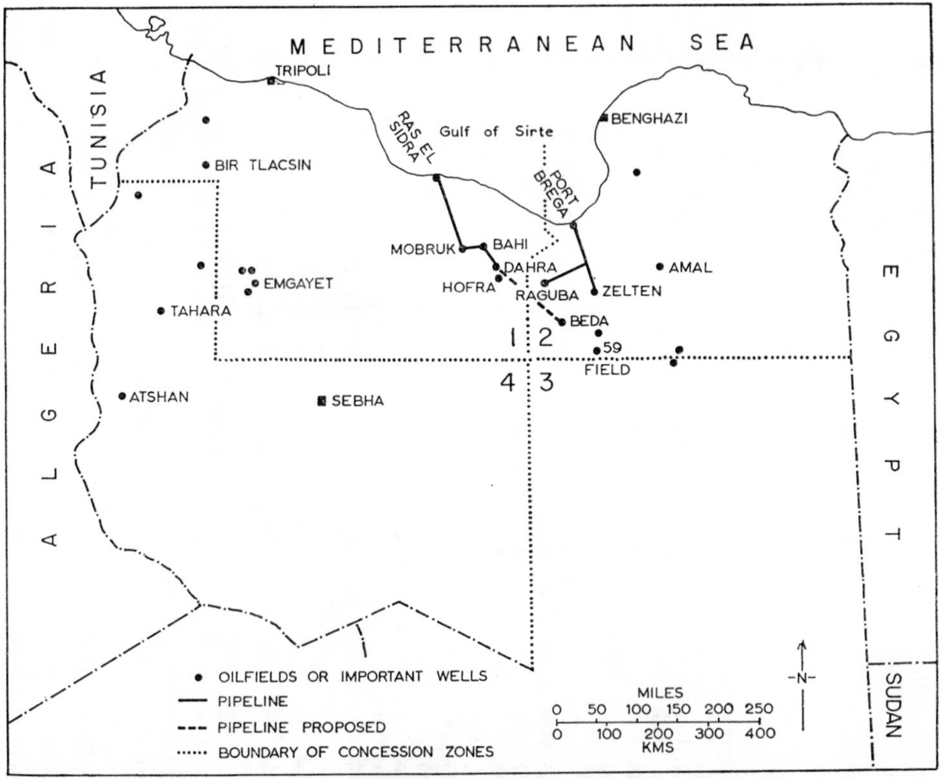

Fig. 22. Oil Development in Libya, 1962

at Heletz and Negba, 4 miles away. Quantities of natural gas are also available; and though production is small, the importance of both deposits to the Israeli economy is very great.

Libya. With the discoveries of oil in the French Sahara, intense exploration began in Libya after 1956, and highly important discoveries were made in widely separated localities:

(*i*) in western Cyrenaica southwards of the Gulf of Sirte, (*ii*) in the Jebel Akhdar of northern Cyrenaica, which is a shallow fold-structure mainly of Eocene limestone, (*iii*) along the western frontier of Libya, towards Tunisia and Algeria, and (*iv*) due south of Tobruk in east-central Cyrenaica. Conditions of occurrence of the oil vary widely: the wells at El Amal (Cyrenaica) would seem to be among the deepest in the Middle East, while elsewhere 5,000–7,000 feet is more normal. Production from Zelten began late in 1961; and it is expected that Libya (and especially Cyrenaica) will ultimately become a highly significant producer, ranking with the largest units, and far ahead of Egypt, Israel, and Syria. Construction of new outlets and harbours is in hand at Sidra and Mersa Brega (Fig. 39).

III. REGIONS OF POSSIBLE FUTURE DEVELOPMENT

Egypt. As noted above, the oil seepages observed in many parts of the Suez region led to much prospecting in the region between the Nile and the Red Sea–Suez Canal, and in the Sinai Peninsula. Two small and very short-lived fields were discovered, at Abu Durba and at Gemsa, but both are now exhausted. Interest continues in the Sinai and towards the frontier with Israel (one reason for the importance of the 'Gaza strip') and there has been much activity in the Western Desert, so far unsuccessful.

Iran. There are grounds for supposing that the Elburz Range of north Iran has close affinities to the Caucasus system of Russia; and in view of the wide extent of oil deposits in the latter region, it would seem that there are prospects for oil development in northern Iran. So far, however, despite the presence of known oil seepage in the Elburz, no exploitation has taken place.

Palestine–Israel. The Dead Sea was known in Classical times as *Lacus Asphaltites* since from time to time large masses of asphalt form on the bed of the lake and later rise to the surface. Another indication of the possible presence of oil is the existence of a large hill of salt, the Jebel Usdum (the Arab name for Sodom) at the southern end of the Dead Sea.[1] (For the significance of this structure, see Fig. 35.)

Syria and the Lebanon. The numerous yet open fold structures of Syria and the Lebanon, particularly those of the eastern part of the region, where folding continues directly into the foothills of Iraq, would seem to offer considerable possibilities for the occurrence of oil. Exploration has taken place, notably in the desert zone east and west of Palmyra, in the Jezireh east and north of the Euphrates, in the Jebel Terbol area east of Tripoli, and in the southern Bekaa. Until 1958, results were however negligible, but strikes were made at Karatchok (1958) and Souedie (1960) in the extreme north-east of Syria. This field would appear to be continuous with and hence structurally a part, of the Ain Zaleh oilfield of Iraq.

Prospection Areas. Other parts of the Middle East where oil prospection is in progress are (*a*) the north and centre of Persia, where Italian, Japanese, and other companies are interested, (*b*) shores of the Persian Gulf, (*c*) the Yemen, where German and American concessions are held, (*d*) the western desert of Egypt, and (*e*) Asia Minor. Oil shows have long been known in the region of the Sea of Marmara, and wells were sunk at Murefta as early as 1914. Similar remarks apply to the Sivas area of central Anatolia, but in both cases results have been negative. More promising may be the Mardin-Diyarbekir area, which includes Ramandagh, where geological structure shows some similarity with that of the Zagros; the plain of Adana; and the Hatay around Iskanderun.

In 1958–9 oil was found off the coast of the Trucial Sheikhdoms, well to the south of previously known deposits; and development is in progress at (*a*) Umm Shaif, in the offshore waters belonging to the Sheikhdom of Abu Dhabi. The oil here is of very good quality, with a relatively low specific gravity, and production (which began in mid-1962) is organised from Das Island, some 80 miles north of the Trucial Coast and 100 miles east-south-east of Umm Said; (*b*) at Murban on the mainland. Here is another reason for the crisis at Buraimi over delimitation of frontiers and spheres of influence.

Ownership of Oil Concessions. In 1872 Baron Julius de Reuter (founder of the well-known news agency) obtained a concession to prospect for oil in Persia, but, following political pressure by Russia upon the Persian government, this concession was soon afterwards withdrawn.

[1] There is a tradition that this salt hill, or pillar, is associated with Lot's wife.

In 1889 a second concession was granted, and an Anglo-German company[1] drilled three wells, all of which, however, proved unsuccessful. In 1901 another concession was obtained by W. K. D'Arcy, an Englishman who had made a fortune in the gold mines of Australia. This concession covered the whole of Iran, except for the extreme north; and after a number of failures, oil was struck at Masjid-i-Suleiman in 1908. Further capital was required to develop the newly discovered field, and a company known as the Anglo-Persian Oil Company came into existence, with the Burmah Oil Company as a substantial shareholder. Six years later, under a threat of imminent war, the First Lord of the Admiralty in Britain, Mr (now Sir) Winston Churchill, was anxious to ensure a fuel supply for the Navy, a part of which had recently been converted to oil-burning; and he arranged that a large interest in the Anglo-Persian Oil Company should be taken over by the British government. Since that time (May 1914), the British government has, therefore, been an important shareholder in the Company.

A few months after the outbreak of the war in 1914, the Ottoman Empire joined the Central Powers, and British supplies of oil from Persia were menaced. A British force was landed in Mesopotamia to protect the oil pipeline which had been constructed from Masjid-i-Suleiman to Abadan; and the Near and Middle Eastern campaigns of 1914–18, both in Mesopotamia and the Levant, had as one objective the safeguarding of oil fuel supplies from Persia.[2]

The concession as negotiated by D'Arcy covered some 480,000 square miles in Persia, excluding only the northern provinces of Azerbaijan, Gilan, Mazanderan, Asterabad, and Khorassan. The terms of the concession, which was to expire in 1961, gave the Persian government 16 per cent. of the net profits of the Company as a royalty; but after 1930, during which time much development had occurred in the oilfields, considerable disagreement arose between the Anglo-Iranian Company and the Persian government, concerning the exact nature of 'net profits', and over other matters. Ultimately, amended terms were negotiated by which the concession was retained until 1993, but reduced in area from 480,000 to 100,000 square miles (in the south-west of Iran), and a greater share of profits given to the Persian government.

An American attempt at prospection about this time in north and east Iran had no success; and somewhat later, during and after the

[1] The Persian Bank Mining Rights Corporation.
[2] Although there were other important objectives (notably the defence of the Suez Canal), the Palestine campaigns of 1916–18 were undertaken partly to relieve Turkish pressure on the Mesopotamian army.

Second World War, American, British, and Russian interests endeavoured to gain other concessions.

In 1951 after a prolonged campaign of agitation and some violence, the Iranian Majlis approved a Bill nationalising all oil concessions and plant, and replacing the A.I.O.C. by a National Iranian Oil Company. Shortly afterwards, British nationals were withdrawn from Iran, and the operation of the oil wells and refining plant at Abadan came almost to a standstill. During succeeding years the Persian government made efforts to obtain crude and refined oil, and to market this, together with stocks already held; but only a trickle of oil was actually disposed of. By 1953 it was apparent that developments in other Middle Eastern fields had made up the loss of Persian oil in world markets, and that there was no longer an assured outlet for any Iranian product. This consideration led to a change in the Persian attitude, and in 1954 negotiations were opened with the A.I.O.C. An agreement was reached in the same year which, whilst making substantial concessions to Persian nationalist feelings, also recognised the fact that by its own resources Iran was incapable of discovering, extracting, refining and marketing its crude petroleum, and must hence rely upon outside technical assistance. Further, the stronger position of the U.S.A. in Middle Eastern affairs was recognised by the allocation of a partial interest in Iranian oil to five leading American oil companies.

The new agreement brought into existence a partnership between a new National Iranian Oil Company (entirely Persian) and a Consortium of foreign interests. Legal ownership of all concessions is vested in the N.I.O.C.; profits from exploitation are divided equally between the two, with the N.I.O.C. responsible for transport, housing, training, and medical care of Persian employees. The N.I.O.C. also operates the Naft-i-Shah wells and the Kermanshah refinery.

The Consortium has a shareholding as follows: the A.I.O.C. 40 per cent., Royal Dutch Shell 14 per cent.,Compagnie Française des Pétroles 6 per cent., and 8 per cent. each to the following five American companies – Gulf, Socony-Vacuum, Standard (New Jersey), Standard (California), and Texas. Operation is through two subsidiaries, one for exploitation and production, the other for refining. Headquarters of the Consortium is in London, with a British servicing company; but the operating subsidiaries are registered in Persia, though incorporated under the commercial laws of Holland. Each operating company has seven Directors, two nominated by the Persian government, the others by the Consortium. Compensation of £25 million from the

Persian government for loss of the concession, and of £215 million from the remaining participants in the Consortium for the loss of 60 per cent. interest in the new arrangement, were paid to the A.I.O.C., which in 1954 changed its name to the 'British Petroleum Oil Company'.

At the present time a joint Persian-Italian company (S.I.R.I.P.) has further concessions in three areas of Persia: north of the 'Consortium area', offshore at the head of the Persian Gulf, and along the northern shore of the Gulf opposite Oman.

Iraq. Developments in Iran during the early years of the twentieth century provoked attention to possibilities in Iraq; and W. K. D'Arcy had begun negotiations with the Turkish authorities even before the deposits at Masjid-i-Suleiman were discovered. D'Arcy was, however, unable to obtain a concession in Iraq; but in 1914 rights were granted to Anglo-German interests, who founded the Turkish Petroleum Company. During the war years, little development took place, but after the settlement in 1918, the newly created state of Iraq confirmed the original grant of oil rights that had been made by the Ottoman government, and the Turkish Petroleum Company was renamed Iraq Petroleum Company. The new company was reconstituted, in order to allow participation by other groups that were greatly interested in Middle Eastern oil; and as a result, the shareholding of the I.P.C. is as follows:

	Per cent.
British Petroleum Co.	23¾
Royal Dutch-Shell Group	23¾
Near East Development Co. (Standard Oil Co. of New Jersey and Standard Vacuum Co. of New York)	23¾
Compagnie Française des Pétroles	23¾
Mr C. S. Gulbenkian (the Armenian intermediary who negotiated the original oil concession)	5

Following later purchases, the I.P.C. and its associates have come to possess rights over the entire area of Iraq exclusive, however, of one small region, the Khanaqin oilfield. Prior to 1914 this formed part of Iran, and hence fell within the region allocated to the A.I.O.C. Control is now entirely by the B.P.O.C.

Egypt. Exploitation of the Hurghada and Ras Gharib fields is carried on by the Anglo-Egyptian Oilfields Ltd, a company in which Shell and B.P.O.C. groups have large holdings. Elsewhere, other companies, chiefly American, hold concessions, and the Egyptian state has a majority ownership in the company that exploits the Belayim and Feiran fields of the south-west Sinai. The Socony-Mobil Oil Company shares equally with Shell the Asl and Sudr rights, and is a minority partner in the Belayim-Feiran area.

The Levant. Until 1948 the principal concession holder was the I.P.C.; but with the establishment of the state of Israel, new licences were granted to Israeli companies and to other individuals, chiefly Jewish and American.

In Cyprus, another I.P.C. subsidiary – Petroleum Development (Cyprus) – held a concession for the whole island, and this, following unfavourable exploration results, was relinquished in 1949. In 1953 Prospectors Ltd., a company of Cypriot ownership, took out a concession near Limassol, but so far has failed to discover oil.

Much the same may be said of Jordan, where until 1956 an I.P.C. subsidiary held a 'blanket' concession. Since that time American and Guatemalan companies have taken up permits covering about one-third of the country.

In Syria and the Lebanon, I.P.C. concessions were relinquished in 1951. Test wells had been dug in many areas, reaching in some cases Palaeozoic strata, but without finding oil. Now, American and German interests have acquired prospection rights, and the Société Libanaise des Pétroles (an association of Lebanese and American groups) holds a concession covering about one-quarter of the Lebanon.

Arabia and the Persian Gulf. The Kuwait Oil Company has developed the Burgan field of Kuwait, and holds rights covering the entire territory of the Sheikhdom. This company, registered in Britain, has a shareholding divided equally between the B.P.O.C. and the Gulf Kuwait Oil Company of U.S.A.

Further south a concession for the island of Bahrein was obtained by a British company, but this was later sold to the Bahrein Petroleum Company, a company registered in Canada, but owned by the Standard Oil Company of California and the Texas Corporation. These two American companies also participate in the Arabian-American Oil Company, which holds sole rights in the Kingdom of Arabia, and is now the largest producing company in the world. The Aramco has a shareholding as follows: Standard Oil (California) 30 per cent., Standard Oil (New Jersey) 30 per cent., Texas Corporation 30 per cent., Socony-Vacuum 10 per cent.

Subsidiaries of the I.P.C. – Petroleum Development (Qatar), (Oman), (Trucial Coast), and Petroleum Concessions Ltd Aden – have

secured oil rights on the mainland of the Arabian peninsula in a territory extending from the Qatar region through the Trucial Coast,
Oman, and the Hadhramaut as far as Aden, whilst Shell Overseas Ltd
also holds an exploration concession in Qatar. In the Yemen, a German
company held a concession for a few years after 1953 on very onerous
terms (75 per cent. of profits to the Yemeni government); but this
company has now withdrawn and another concession has been granted
to American interests. Results are not so far published.

In 1948 a company formed by eleven independent oil producers in
America negotiated with the Sheikh of Kuwait for his half-interest in
the 2,000 square miles of neutral territory lying between Kuwait and
Saudi Arabia, whilst another American company (Getty Oil) holds
the other 50 per cent. share from Saudi Arabia. The financial arrangements were extremely favourable to the Sheikh of Kuwait, who
received a bonus of £7 million, an annual rental of $600,000 until
production actually started, and then a royalty of 33 cents per barrel,
which now brings in $150–200 million annually.

Between the neutral zone and the island of Bahrein, important oilfields lie under the shallow waters of the Persian Gulf. After negotiations between the King of Arabia and two organisations, the Superior
Oil Company of California, and the Central Mining Corporation of
Britain, regarding exploitation of these fields, the concession was
finally acquired by the Caltex Company of America.

As regards concessions in *Turkey*, many mineral resources have been
nationalised since 1923, and a government department, the Maden
Tektik ve Arma Enstitüsü (M.T.A.), is responsible for actual exploitation. Development is co-ordinated under state Five-Year Plans for the
fostering of industry, and funds are made available to the M.T.A.
through a state-controlled bank (the E.T.I. Bank). Between 1950 and
1960, however, a political group far less convinced of the merits of state
ownership of production held power (the Democrat party), and
foreign oil companies were invited to prospect on a large scale once
again in Turkey.

In *Libya* many companies, chiefly American and British, hold concessions. Individual concession areas are relatively small in extent and
it is significant that with the general political changes of the last two
decades, the pattern of concession allotting has also changed – from
the former 'blanket' grants to one company that covered a half or a
whole of one country, to the fragmented pattern now most characteristic of Libya, and adumbrated elsewhere (Fig. 40). This clearly reflects

the changed relations between oil companies and native governments. *Undersea Concessions.* With the possibility of the occurrence of oil below the sea bed, already demonstrated at Safaniya (p. 242), Middle Eastern states have already claimed 'offshore' or 'continental shelf' petroleum rights as part of their national sovereignty. In the Persian Gulf, where rock series dip very gradually below sea level without break, such rights may prove extremely valuable, and underwater drilling is in progress. But in the Red Sea and Mediterranean areas, where coastlines are strongly faulted, prospects are less favourable, though still

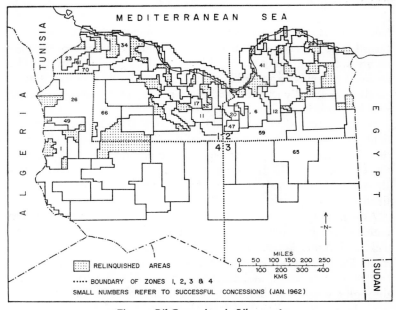

Fig. 40. Oil Concessions in Libya, 1962

none the less claimed. In the Persian Gulf zone various declarations have been made (first with the approval of the U.S.A., later of Britain) that 'continental shelf' rights existed from the shores of the various states to a half-way line between the Persian and Arabian coasts. 'Shelf' rights were then claimed (as mere extensions) by the companies already holding concessions in the landward territories, and this position was successfully maintained by Aramco with regard to the offshore waters of Saudi Arabia. But elsewhere local rulers were in some cases able to establish the opposite principle, and could thus sell new rights to companies different from those already installed on the mainland. Thus the Saudi Arabian offshore rights in the Kuwait–Saudi Arabian neutral zone has been acquired by a Japanese company.

During the Second World War, rapid consumption of petroleum supplies in America gave rise for some concern to the United States government. Proposals were made officially regarding exploitation of American-owned concessions in the Middle East, but these did not find favour with the American oil companies, and came to nothing.

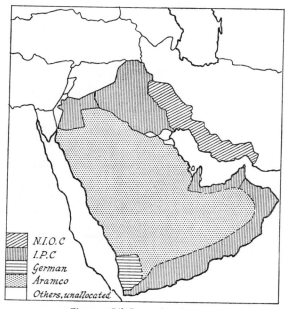

Fig. 41. Oil Concessions in 1954

In contrast with the short-lived attempt at state intervention by the American government, development in British-owned concessions has almost from the start been subjected to governmental influence. As a major shareholder (52·5 per cent.) in the British Petroleum Company, the British government participates to a varying degree in over ten commercial oil organisations. It should, however, be made clear that the British government does not intervene in the affairs of the Companies except at the highest level, and that accordingly day-to-day running is in the hands of the Companies themselves. The B.P.O.C. constructed what is still the largest refinery in the world, at Abadan; and completed another at Aden in 1954. It possesses a tanker fleet of 1½–2 million tons, and in addition owns further refineries in Britain at Llandarcy, Grangemouth, and in Kent.

Other smaller refineries (not in the same ownership) are located at Baghdad, at Mina Abdulla and Mina Saud in the Neutral Zone, and at Zerqa (Jordan).

It remains to mention that the French government has a minority shareholding (35 per cent.) in the Compagnie Française des Pétroles, which participates in the I.P.C.; and that the Italian government participates jointly with the Persian government in the S.I.R.I.P. organisation that is working in various parts of Persia.

B.P.O.C. HOLDINGS IN OIL COMPANIES OF THE MIDDLE EAST

Subsidiaries (complete control)	*Partial Control* (50 per cent. or less of share capital)
Khanaqin Oil Co.	Iraq Petroleum Co.
	Mosul Petroleum Co.
	Basra Petroleum Co.
	Syria Petroleum Co.
	Lebanon Petroleum Co.
	Kuwait Oil Co.
	Petroleum Concessions Ltd
	Anglo-Egyptian Oilfields Ltd
	Consolidated Refineries Ltd

Soc. des Asphaltes et Pétroles de Lattaquie S.A.
Petroleum Development Ltd: (Oman), (Qatar), (Trucial Coast), (Jordan), (Cyprus)

PIPELINES

With the Middle East now supplying most of Europe's needs in petroleum, and the U.S.A. since 1953 an oil-importing country, the bulk of Middle Eastern oil moves westwards – though, however, the markets of eastern Asia, Australasia, and East Africa are increasingly important. Because of the geographical location of the oilfields and the configuration of south-west Asia, sea transport of oil to Europe is a relatively expensive matter, owing to the distance between Abadan, Bahrein, and Ras Tanura to Suez (some 4,000 miles), and also to heavy Suez Canal dues, which are at present 18 cents U.S. per barrel, or $15,000 to $30,000 per cargo. Moreover, tankers must perform the return trip empty, but paying further (though lighter) canal dues.

These considerations have led to the building of pipelines on a large scale direct from the oilfields to the Mediterranean. Besides the five lines from Kirkuk already mentioned, there is the Aramco Tapline, some 1,100 miles in length, and there is at present agreement over a proposed new pipeline from Persia to the Mediterranean seaboard via Turkey – longer in mileage but possibly less subject to political disturbance and economic pressure from interested countries. Broadly speaking, despite high constructional costs (all materials and most skilled labour must be imported) and the necessity of paying wayleave royalties to the states lying *en route*, a saving of up to $5 per ton can be achieved – an annual saving for 'Tapline' alone of the order of $70 millions. A pipeline, unlike a tanker, need never be empty for half its life; and although the Suez Canal Company has shown great sensitivity over diversion of the oil traffic to land routes, and progressively reduced canal dues, the simple geographical advantage of shorter communication by land remains, cutting transport costs by one-half to one-third. A further competitive element is the recent all-Jewish pipeline from Eilat on the Gulf of Aqaba to Haifa.

The terms of transit and wayleave agreements are of interest. In 1952 the Aramco contracted to pay annual royalties of $1,100,000 to Syria, and $1,400,000 to the Lebanon in respect of 'Tapline'; also further payments to local municipalities for pipeline security and maintenance; and agreed to a high loading tax on all oil shipped at Saida, to the employment of Lebanese in the Company, and finally to make available quantities of crude oil for local use at advantageous terms. Since that time, further requests have been made for higher payments to the governments of Syria and the Lebanon.

Two other very interesting possible future developments are (*a*) the transport of crude oil by sea in plastic containers – 'sausages' which, as oil is of lower density, will float and can be towed, (*b*) liquefaction of natural gas for transport by tanker. Much of this is at present wasted, being blown off and ignited. Construction of a 'gas grid' is however under way between Gach Saran and Shiraz, in order to provide fuel for industry in one of Iran's largest towns – with possibilities of other pipelines further north. Another project is an 'Arab gas grid' from Arabia/Kuwait to the Levant and Egypt.

Lastly, suggestions for yet other oil and gas 'grids' in Europe, fed by extensive pipelines from certain European ports (Hamburg, Rotterdam, Marseilles, Genoa, and Venice have been suggested) may alter considerably the pattern of transport for oil even as concerns the Middle East, which is at present the chief supplier of oil to Europe.

CONSEQUENCES OF PETROLEUM EXPLOITATION IN THE MIDDLE EAST

These can only be described, in some respects and for some areas, as revolutionary. In 1938 the Middle East produced 5 per cent. of the total world supply of oil, and 22 per cent. in 1961, from 15 million tons to 275 million. Now the Middle East is already the premier oil-exporting area of the world; and with more than half of all proved reserves in the world (inclusive of the U.S.A., and probably the U.S.S.R.), its position is almost certain to be yet more significant. Moreover, besides the expanded volume of production, the share of profits accruing to Middle Eastern rulers and governments has also greatly risen. The original A.I.O.C. contract allocated 16 per cent. of net profits to the Iranian government: since 1950 the prevailing rate has been 50 per cent., with a 56/44 allocation in one offshore area as between Saudi Arabia and Kuwait on the one hand, and Japanese companies on the other. In terms of actual revenue obtained the figures are striking.

OIL ROYALTIES PAID TO MIDDLE EASTERN GOVERNMENTS
(in millions of dollars)

	Bahrein	Iran	Iraq	Kuwait	Qatar	Saudi Arabia	Libya
1940	1·0	16·0	8·1	nil	nil	1·5	—
1950	3·3	44·7	14·8	12·4	1·0	112·0	—
1958	9·8	246·0	235·0	415·0	57·0	300·9	—
1961	13·0	290·0	265·0	454·0	56·0	406·0	20·0

Total governmental income for the entire state of Saudi Arabia was reckoned in 1930 as barely £150,000, inclusive of the king's privy purse and the total yield of taxes. For 1962 it would appear that royalties of £110–150 million are in prospect, besides other sums to local contractors. In Kuwait before 1945 an even lower budgetary income prevailed; now the Sheikh receives an annual sum equivalent to approximately £300 per head of total population in his state. In several countries royalties from oil now equal or exceed the value of total foreign trade (exports other than oil plus imports), and, at a current average of about £2 per ton, royalty payments to the Middle East have risen from £7·5 million in 1938 to over £550 million in 1962.

The effect of oil exploitation has been in general to create a hierarchy among Middle Eastern countries, ranging from the large actual

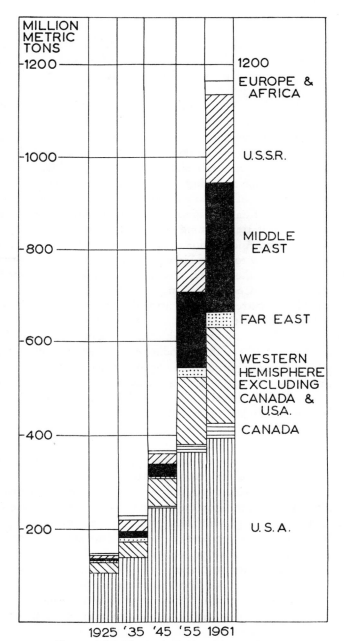

Fig. 42. Oil Production, World and the Middle East

producers (at present, in order, Kuwait, Saudi Arabia, Persia, and Iraq) to such areas as Cyprus and the Yemen, where no oil has so far been found, which are not crossed by pipelines, and have no oil terminals or refineries.

Such sudden accretion of wealth has had far-reaching effects, a very few of which can be sketched here. In certain instances royalties are used to foster schemes of economic development (in Iraq and Persia approximately 70 per cent. of royalties go to a National Development Board). Irrigation projects, road, rail and harbour construction, improved hygiene and sanitation and other amenities have thus been made possible. Also, the effect of regular paid employment on the former semi-nomadic peoples of Saudi Arabia, the Persian Gulf, Iraq, and Persia has been very great, transforming ways of life, outlook, and the actual physique of many. Ancient sites such as Sidon, Palmyra, and Latakia have taken on a new role; and Sidon, until 1945 a drowsy, half-ruined and picturesque market centre, now has its Copacabana, Texas Bar, luxury hotel – and Coca Cola. Similar changes are now developing in Libya, which is currently experiencing the usual 'boom' and inflation that follow oil discoveries.

The changes following new wealth have not proved wholly advantageous. Philby speaks of the corroding effect of sudden affluence and luxury upon the once puritanical Court of Arabia; and a more general difficulty is the widening disparity between various Middle Eastern states, which makes political collaboration difficult. Jordan remains poor and therefore dependent upon a British subsidy; Saudi Arabia, Iraq and Egypt produce oil and can take a more independent and pro-Arab line of policy. There are also differences over political relations. Some Arab countries (not usually those with the largest reserves) feel strongly that Middle Eastern oil is a general asset that should be used for development as a whole within the Arab world – and one obvious use, to some, is as aid to Arab refugees. Though most members of the Arab League appear to accept something of the general argument in public (that is, as regards development), in fact, royalties are still used almost exclusively for national or personal interests, and in some countries even are mortgaged for years ahead.

Internally, too, for certain countries, there are new preoccupations. The rewards of ministerial office can tend to become more valuable when substantial oil royalties pass into the coffers of the state, and the rivalry to obtain or retain high political office is on occasion liable to be intensified. The attitude of a particular Cabinet to oil questions, and its use of royalties can often become the subject of very keen criticism by its political opponents; so that one can to some extent understand, though not necessarily accept, Dr Moussadegh's frequently expressed regret that Middle Eastern oil should ever have been taken out of the ground.

Future Prospects. In 1952 reserves of oil in the Middle East were estimated to comprise 55 per cent. of total world reserves; but since that

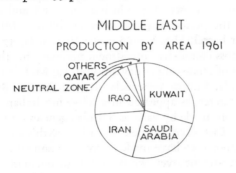

MIDDLE EAST
PRODUCTION BY AREA 1961

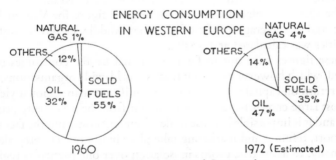

ENERGY CONSUMPTION IN WESTERN EUROPE

Fig. 43. Oil Production and Consumption

time new discoveries have been made in several areas. Longrigg has suggested that within fifteen years some 75 per cent. of the total world reserve of petroleum will be within the Middle East; and already Europe obtains about 80 per cent. of its requirements from Middle Eastern fields. This dependence on oil will undoubtedly increase rapidly with the greater use of motor transport, and the extension of domestic heating by oil. Hence, in brief, future prospects point to an even greater wealth for some Middle Eastern countries, and the further transformation of economic life following the inflow of capital. But with this can be seen three possible dangers: (a) The interest and rivalries of outside powers seeking concessions. As other sources of oil in the world diminish, this may well intensify; (b) The unsettling effect of oil revenues upon Middle Eastern peoples and their leaders; and (c) competition from Saharan oil, which is more closely located to the markets of Western Europe.

At present, the Middle East is exceptionally well placed, as the following figures show: Costs of producing crude oil and expanding production over the period 1948–60 were as follows: Middle East, 16 U.S. cents per barrel; U.S.A., 166 cents; Venezuela, 57 cents; Far East, 87 cents. Gross cumulative investment necessary for the production of one barrel of crude oil per day amounts to: Middle East, $350; U.S.A. and Canada, $4,600; Venezuela, $1,700; Europe, $3,300.

Early in 1963 references appeared in a left-wing Italian weekly to certain investigations made by various outside agencies into the operation of the Middle East oil companies. According to this weekly, the oil interests were supposed to have made an average annual net profit of 66% on their investment over the period 1956–60, with individual rates ranging (by company) from 61% in the case of Aramco to 114% for the Qatar Petroleum Co. The comparable figure for Venezuela is 20%; and the average profit of all other Middle Eastern industrial activities was calculated at 20–25%.

These figures have not so far been denied by the companies concerned, which however point out that as world-wide organisations, the total return on capital invested is more significant than regional yields: in most large enterprises all sections are far from being equally profitable, and it is impossible because of development costs, and the fact that transport, refining and marketing take place in not one country alone, but many, to assess true profits in isolation over one particular region. Further, the figures quoted come from sources some of which have strong economic and political interests in demonstrating a high rate of profit for the oil companies.

Thus, there are many aspects to this matter; but it would, however, seem that costs of oil production in the Middle East are significantly lower than in most other regions of the world.

CHAPTER XII

Demographic Trends in the Middle East

Another aspect of political geography, and one that is now assuming considerably increased importance, is the question of population growth in relation to natural resources. Because of scantiness or imprecision of data, demographic studies in the Middle East cannot be carried very far,[1] but there is ample evidence that at the present time numbers in certain areas are increasing at a rapid rate beyond the limits set by natural resources. As a result, problems of over population, already serious in a few areas, are beginning to affect a growing number of states, and to exert an increasing influence on national policy.

Population Numbers and Trends. Total population of the area treated in this volume could be estimated (1960) at 90-100 million, just about twice as large as that of Great Britain. This figure (as also one of densities on a basis of country) is not very informative, since the chief feature is extreme unevenness in distribution. With so much of the Middle East either mountain or desert, there are large areas almost or totally unpopulated, yet at the same time certain riverine lowlands and oases, and cities with their immediate hinterlands have some of the highest densities occurring in the world. Consequently, a more useful figure is the population density in relation to cultivated area. Thus, while the population density for Syria as a whole is approximately 60 persons per square mile, on a basis of population per area cultivated is 110 per square mile in the Aleppo region, 200 for Latakia, and 540 for the oasis of Damascus. Egypt shows the most striking contrasts, with only

---

[1] Many communities of the Middle East have, in the words of Bonné, 'a mentality which does not always view with favour the exact and numerical approach to reality'. Hence statistics of any sort may be difficult to obtain, but as regards census returns, there are special obstacles. Under the Ottomans, the appearance of official enumerators in a village was the inevitable prelude either to an increase in taxation, or to an approaching military conscription. Thus a number of young men were usually concealed, and a low estimate of numbers given. Moreover, some difficulty attaches to the computation of occupants of harems: as recently as 1937 an over-zealous enumerator failed to return from a visit to a tribal area. On the other hand, certain communities have also discovered that because of the organisation of civil government on a sectarian and communal basis that prevails in a number of states, an exaggerated return of numbers may produce beneficial results in the political field.

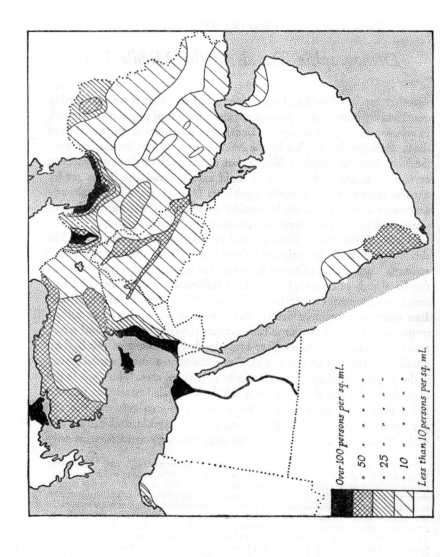

Over 100 persons per sq. ml.
" 50 " " " "
" 25 " " " "
" 10 " " " "
Less than 10 persons per sq. ml.

o·8 per cent. of its population living outside the Nile valley, where the average is 1,550 persons per square mile of territory, reaching over 6,500 persons in a few districts round Cairo.

Principal causes of this remarkable variation in density are clearly geographical – in particular the availability of water: riverine, from direct rainfall, or in relation to underground flow. But water resources alone, or even other factors of physical geography such as terrain, do not provide a complete explanation of population distribution. Certain areas, e.g. the lower Nile valley, the hill-country of the northern Levant, north-west Jordan, the uplands of Syria lying east of the Orontes river with their continuations into south-central Asia Minor, and finally the uplands of Asir and the Yemen – all these have a distinctly greater population density than those of neighbouring areas, in which occur approximately similar water resources, climatic conditions, and even topography. Hence to explain these anomalies it is often necessary to invoke economic, historical, and social factors – an illustration both of the complexity of conditions and also of the interplay of widely differing influences.

POPULATION OF MIDDLE EAST COUNTRIES

	Total Pop. 1960 (est.)	Crude Birth-rate (per 1,000)	Crude Death-rate (per 1,000)	Annual increase (%)
Aden: Colony	145,000	30	12	1·2
Protectorate	700,000	40	20	2·0
Cyprus	570,000	26	6	2·0
Iraq	6,800,000	33	8	2 3
Israel	2,060,000	29	7	2·2
Jordan	1,580,000	38	8	3·0
Lebanon	1,540,000	27	7	2·0
Libya	1,200,000	42	20	2·2
Persia	20,000,000	30	8	2·2
Saudi Arabia	5,500,000	43	25	1·8
Syria	4,330,000	25	5	2·0
Trucial Coast	850,000	45	30	1·5
Turkey	27,700,000	40	10	3·0
U.A.R. Egypt	26,000,000	38	16	2·2
Yemen	4,600,000	40	25	1·5

Birth-rates in the Middle East range from 18 to 60 per thousand of population – figures far in excess of those in Europe and North America (Great Britain 18 per mille, U.S.A. 24 per mille). Figures for the Middle East do not allow much detailed investigation, but it would seem clear that whilst birth-rates are likely to continue high, death-rates are now falling, in some cases quite sharply. Reasons for the high general death-rate are not far to seek: low standards of living, frequency of disease, and low standards of education, medical care, and public health. Death-rates range from under 10 to over 35 per mille, infantile mortality accounting for many of the higher rates. In Egypt, two-thirds of all recorded deaths are of children under 5: and for the Middle East as a whole it is still probable that 35–50 per cent. of all children die before reaching the age of 10. Some observers would even reduce this last figure to 5 years.

With such a situation of high birth-rates and high but now rapidly declining death-rates, there is a swiftly accelerating rate of population growth. In Turkey, birth-rates are thought to average 40 per mille, and death-rates 10–15 per mille, giving a possible overall growth rate of 3 per cent. per annum; and though this is an extreme instance, population in the Middle East as a whole would seem to be increasing by about at least 1·9 per cent. annually – i.e. likely to double itself within another fifty years or less. Comparative figures are: 0·5 per cent. (England and Wales), 0·8 per cent. (France), and 1·3 per cent. (Japan).

The decline in death-rates is due to the operation of two major factors, the first being the ease and rapidity with which a few relatively simple public health techniques can be introduced – water chlorination, eradication of disease vectors by DDT and other insecticides, and the general use of antibiotics. These are often dramatic in effect, and compress into one or two decades improvements in public health which in other countries such as those of western Europe were spread over almost a century. The second factor is improvement in the basic health of a population by raising standards of consumption in food and housing, parallel with improvements in personal medical care, hygiene, and education. As regards the Middle East, much has already been done in the sphere of public health generally with consequent decline in death-rates; but as regards the second factor progress has been very much more limited. Hence as and when this occurs, there is likely to be yet a further fall in deaths – conditions in Turkey indicate what can be achieved.

Yet at the same time, birth-rates are likely to remain fairly high, because (a) social customs, attitudes, and outlook favour large families, e.g. early marriage, and infertility as legal grounds for divorce – to name only a few, and (b) it could well be that with a reduction of child deaths the number of girls surviving to reproductive age will greatly increase and so cancel out any diminution that might occur with possible changes under (a).

Migration. Pressure of numbers has produced a considerable, but very uneven flow of emigrants. Arabia (especially Aden and the Yemen) has a fairly consistent outward movement, not only to adjacent regions of the Middle East (lower Mesopotamia, Jordan, Syria) together with Somalia and Eritrea, but also further afield: to the East Indies, East Africa, Pakistan, and India. It would seem that several millions of Arabs from the Arabian peninsula live outside their homeland either as temporary or permanent residents; and their occupations tend to be commercial, with a minority of soldiers, officials, and labourers. Another region important as a source of emigrants is the Lebanon and Syria. Most migrants are small peasant-proprietors who can sell up their lands to find passage-money; and the chief areas of origin are the hinterland of Beirut as far inland as the Bekaa, the hill country behind Tripoli; the Alawi area; and the uplands north-west and south-west of Damascus. Slightly more Lebanese migrate than Syrians; and the chief receiving countries are: once Egypt, now West Africa, Brazil, the Argentine, and to a limited extent the U.S.A. At least a million Lebanese have emigrated, and it would now seem that as many Lebanese now live outside their country as live within.[1]

Another feature of the last few years has been the movement of educated Arabs to other Arab countries, where they fill professional and technical posts. Many Egyptian teachers staff schools in Libya and in the Persian Gulf states; oil companies recruit all over the Middle East, and Syrian business men are widely scattered especially in Egypt. Overall, however, the scale of migration – merely a few thousands a year at most – can afford little alleviation to the general population problem which in numbers for the Middle East as a whole probably involves an annual increase of $1\frac{1}{2}$ to 2 million people. There is also some ground for considering that internal migration could make a significant contribution to the problem, since as we have noted, distribution of people is still very uneven. But local difficulties – social, political, and financial – have so far inhibited much migration; and even within the United Arab Republic where these factors were for a time less important, there was no major redistribution of population. The Arab refugee situation serves to underline the limited extent to which migration could, in practice, alleviate the general demographic situation.

Population and Subsistence. Between 1960 and 1980 some 30 to 40 million people will, at a conservative estimate, be added to the population

---

[1] Annual totals of emigration are estimated as follows: 1860–1900, 1,000; 1900–29, 5,000; 1929–38, 1,500; 1945–60, 2,500.

of the Middle East – the figure could reach 55 million – and we have noted that during the last few years the rate of increase has tended to grow rather than slacken.

Detailed comparisons are difficult, but it is apparent that the peoples of the Middle East are among the poorest in the world. A survey in Iraq during 1956 gave an average peasant income as £10 ($28) annually per head (just over 6d. per day) and this figure could be paralleled in many other areas. In Egypt, where productivity is higher, it has been reckoned that 5 million people each live on less than £2 per month. During the last decade, annual income per inhabitant (inclusive of all social classes) averaged as follows: Egypt £35, Iraq £28, Libya £44, Israel £131, and Saudi Arabia £15. Thus, although densities of population vary considerably, over-population is now becoming a severe problem (with some few exceptions) for almost every region of the Middle East. In the first edition of this book, the writer was able to distinguish certain extensive areas which could be said to be without population pressure. Now the picture is very different, for within fourteen years since 1948, numbers have increased by a quarter to a third. In Turkey ten years ago few fears were expressed about numbers in relation to production – but now, owing to soil erosion, overcropping and overgrazing, together with a 25 per cent. increase in human numbers, the situation is described as alarming.[1]

Symptomatic of the pressure of numbers is the high rate of underemployment: in Syria there is only one-sixth of the agricultural work available in January as compared with June (though winter crops are grown); and during off-seasons in Iraq work for only one-quarter of the labour force. Agricultural unemployment affects one-quarter of the population in Turkey. As a consequence, the peasant is reckoned to have as little as one-half of the effective income of an industrial worker, or even less – in Israel in 1950 a builder's labourer's wage was four times as much as that of the average farm worker.

Measures to improve conditions are possible. To begin with there are still areas of potentially productive land that are not fully used: estimates range from 27 per cent. of present cultivated area (Egypt) and 60 per cent. (Lebanon) to over 100 per cent. (Syria); and the extreme instance would seem to be Iraq, where only one-fifth of the cultivable land is actually used. Irrigation development is an obvious first phase, but as well, techniques could be improved so as to give heavier crops of better quality – though it must be remembered that

[1] 'A truly heroic programme of land use adjustment is required' – F.A.O. report 1959.

in certain limited instances, particularly for Egypt, yields and quality are already the highest in the world.

Industrialisation is often cited as another extremely important method of supporting an expanding population; and here the example of Israel is significant. But all these possibilities, including a sound, rational plan of interior migration, come up against considerable obstacles – the growing nationalism of the Middle East with its insistence on, and intensification of political frontiers, parallel with the development of autarchic economies; lack of capital and of technical ability; social difficulties – the clear superiority in the minds of most, of town life over rural existence; property regimes which as we have seen involve interlinked religious, social, and technical problems; and finally, the generally low purchasing power and political instability within the region. In the opinion of some, including Dresch, these handicaps are so considerable as to give grounds only for pessimism. It is true that most Middle Eastern governments possess admirable schemes on paper for development and reform; but in many instances these remain on paper in the pigeon-holes of Ministries. Discussion of the concept of over-population in relation to resources can hence, in the prevailing political climate, be largely academic and unreal. On the other hand, it is also fair to say that there has been industrial expansion in some countries of a kind and extent that would have been regarded as totally impracticable even fifteen years ago; especially in Egypt, Turkey, the Levant, and Iran. But, again, these schemes may only at best barely cater in effect for the *excess* population, leaving the basic problem of raising standards generally largely untouched.

Population pressure is greatest in Egypt, where 99·2 per cent. of the population is living on the 4 per cent. of area comprised by the Nile valley. In a few districts near Cairo and Assiut, densities reach 6,500 per square mile; but in the lower delta, because of a proportion of salt marsh and unreclaimed land, the figure falls to 1,000–2,500 persons per square mile. At present, births exceed deaths by some 600,000 annually.

Since 1882, when a census was first taken, the population of Egypt has more than doubled. And as we shall later see, more intensive exploitation of the Nile valley has been rendered possible by a change-over from basin cultivation to perennial irrigation; but at the present time, the limit of expansion may be within sight, and diminishing returns from agriculture are becoming apparent. Already Egypt imports large quantities of fertiliser, since under intensive cropping, Nile floods are no longer entirely sufficient to maintain soil fertility. Moreover, in view of the topography of the country, there are strict limits to the extent of cultivable ground – only land actually on the floor of the Nile valley can be irrigated. In this connexion it has recently been suggested by Cleland that the towns and cities of Egypt, many of which lie within the Nile valley, should be re-sited a short distance away on the desert border, in order to release valuable land which is capable of irrigation. Prospects for further industrialisation are dubious, since raw materials are not very abundant (cotton excepted), there is no coal, and oil resources are, so far, limited. But there is the prospect of hydro-electricity from the new Aswan Dam, and the presence of extensive iron ore deposits nearby is another favourable factor.

At present the population of Turkey is increasing by about 650,000 per year, which suggests that by 1975 the total numbers may attain 40 million. Consumption of animal protein per head is estimated as already close to the minimum necessary for life. Arable land in use has increased from 12·9 million hectares in 1944 to 22·4 million, but it was reckoned by one investigator that only 16·4 million hectares could in fact be ploughed regularly without risk of serious soil erosion. Already, a F.A.O. report states (1959) that slopes are showing deep erosion furrows, and lowlands are partly blanketed in detritus or newly formed marsh. With this extension of cultivated land, which has been brought in from steppe formerly used for grazing, the average feeding area of steppe pasture per animal has decreased by nearly 50 per cent. over the last fifteen years and 'grazing animals are now so seriously underfed that it is surprising that they stay alive' (F.A.O.). Hence immediate schemes of improvement aim at a *reduction* of cereal growing with extension of irrigation, and technical improvements: costly methods but essential if Turkey is ultimately to maintain her projected population.

In the Lebanon, population is also increasing by about 2·0 per cent. per annum, and on a basis of number to area, the country ranks as the most densely peopled in the Middle East. Reasons for this situation are not at first obvious. Much of the country is mountainous, and cultivable land is not widespread – only about one acre per head, as compared with six in Syria – whilst there are no important mineral deposits. However, the country has certain other important geographical assets – a remarkable topographic unity, pleasant climate, and a central geographical position. All of these have been utilised by the energy and ability of the inhabitants, who have a generally higher level of education, versatility, and outward-looking mentality as compared with many Arab neighbours. Remarkable scenic beauty has fostered a tourist activity, a wide variety of fruits are cultivated with markedly improved agricultural techniques, there is a small light industry, the establishment of a free zone has led to much entrepôt trading, and finally, the mercantile sense of many Lebanese has led to the growth of banking and other commercial activities. Numerous educational establishments cater for students from many neighbouring countries; and by no means the least important item is the flow of remittances from Lebanese emigrants. As a result, a deficit in visible trade is converted into a surplus of balance of payment.

Conditions in Israel are more doubtful. There are grounds for expecting that further industrialisation could take place, and the recent discoveries of petroleum, natural gas, and copper are favourable factors. Geographical location in relation to land, sea, and air routes is also advantageous, and experience over the last fifteen years suggests that some Israeli development is soundly based, and can expand. Israel is the only Middle Eastern state in which manufacturing and commerce are more important financially than farming. Unfavourable features are a dearth of raw materials and fuel, and above all, the heavy political atmosphere. Despite all efforts Israel's budget still shows a heavy deficit, and the gap is closed by massive remittances in various forms from abroad. The Israeli pound, at par with sterling in 1947–8, is now (1962) worth only 2s. 4d. (30 cents).

In much of central and eastern Syria (including the Jezireh), irrigation from the major rivers, especially the Euphrates, could be developed to absorb new population. Even more than in Israel and Jordan, space relationships give to Syria the advantage of extensive trading contacts, by which an already dense urban population is supported. Though minerals are not abundant, the discoveries of oil, gas, and copper may be important, and commerce and textile manufacturing might also increase further. Now that political union with Egypt has ended, good relations with neighbours are essential in order to expand markets for grain, and to facilitate capital development.

In Iraq, and to a less extent in Persia, chief problems still arise in some areas from a deficit of population. Although parts of the Mesopotamian valley are now densely settled as the result of the rapid increase in numbers during the last fifty years, other parts of the valley are empty, in contrast to conditions of the Nile valley, which is exploited along almost every mile of its course in Egypt. Wasteful methods, paying little heed to long-term maintenance of fertility, tend to be used, since fresh agricultural sites can be cleared when the first is exhausted. Technically, then, Iraqi agriculture is inferior to that of Egypt; and until the land is more closely occupied it is unlikely that standards will improve.

Conditions in Persia suggest that at one time a considerably larger population found a livelihood. Vast regions have returned to steppe and desert, and part at least of these could be reclaimed. As in Turkey, the presence of minerals is a further advantage; and exploitation of oil is having considerable repercussions on the economic life of the country.

For Libya, withdrawal of most of the Italian colonists, discoveries of oil, the presence of leased military bases, and the availability of foreign aid at present provide reasonably adequate support for the small population, which is no more than 1½ million. Similar remarks may be made regarding parts of the Arabian peninsula, but there are indications of mounting pressure of population in territories such as Aden. The exploitation of oil on a growing scale will soon produce considerable changes in what was until very recently one of the least developed territories in the Middle East.

Differential Growth. Two significant points remain to be discussed: the facts of differential increases firstly as between cultural and national groups, and secondly as between town and country. The generally higher reproductive rate of Moslems as compared with Christians and Jews is in the Lebanon an especially important matter, since this state's *raison d'être* is as a Christian Arab country: already Moslems probably seriously outnumber Christians, but census figures are manipulated to minimise this situation. One factor that drove the Jews to action after 1939 was the realisation that any restriction of immigration could place the Jews at a permanent numerical disadvantage, since Arab net reproduction rates were higher. Similar problems of relative numbers affect minorities such as the Copts of Egypt, and possibly Greek-Turkish relations in Cyprus.

A further matter, which is not always fully appreciated in the West where the demographic situation is different, is that because of (still) relatively high death-rates, the average age of the populations in Middle Eastern countries is low, even under 20. It has been estimated, for example, that more than half of all Turks and Persians are aged 19 or less; and that three-quarters of all Egyptians are less than 30 years old. The implications of this on political life and on the economic position will, fairly obviously, differ from those to which we are accustomed in Western Europe and North America – where, to take one striking example, an ancient Scottish university has as students a minority of Scots.

In most Western countries, urban reproduction rates usually run below those of rural areas; but in the Middle East there is a constant and rapidly growing influx of migrants of young adult age; and public health conditions are often better. Hence towns are now growing at a very rapid rate indeed.

PERCENTAGE RATES OF INCREASE OF RURAL AND URBAN POPULATION

	Total Pop.	Urban	Rural
Turkey	2·0	3·0	1·7
Cyprus	1·7	2·5	1·5
Iraq	2·1	3·8	1·4
U.A.R. (Egypt)	1·5	3·0	1·0

Cairo, with over 3 million population, is by far the largest town in Africa, and comes second only to Rome within the Mediterranean area. Beirut has grown from about 30,000 at the beginning of the present century to about half a million – one-third of the total population of the country – and Baghdad now has over a million inhabitants. The fastest relative growth of all has occurred in Amman, which, a village in 1918, now has something like 150,000 people. Such developments inevitably produce physical and social strains exemplified in the growth of shanty towns (*bidonvilles* or tin-towns) in some districts, and intractable problems of supply, traffic circulation, and government. Many Middle Eastern towns are now involved in a policy of considerable re-building at the centre, or of absorbing new and expensive luxury suburbs, both of which can often divert attention from the tremendous needs of the poorer 'squatter' districts, which grow fastest of all, as the result of migration from rural areas.

PART III

Regional Geography

K

CHAPTER XIII

Persia

As a high plateau ringed on all sides by higher mountain ranges Persia displays a marked physical unity based on separation from its adjoining regions. To the south and west, the contrast between the massive ranges of the Zagros and the lowlands of Mesopotamia is particularly striking; and on the north, there is an equally abrupt descent from the Elburz

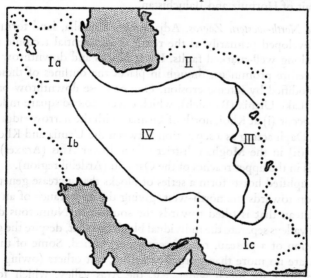

Fig. 45. Natural Regions of Persia

Ranges to the plains of Russian Turkestan and the basin of the Caspian. Elsewhere, however, the mountain ring of Persia continues without much interruption into the highlands of eastern Anatolia, and into the more broken massifs of Baluchistan and Afghanistan.

A summary of the main natural regions of Persia may be made as follows:

(I) The Zagros folds – extending in an arc from Armenia to Baluchistan.

(II) The Northern Highlands – a narrower, but well-defined series of folds that run between the Caucasus Mountains of South Russia, and the Hindu Kush of Afghanistan.

(III) The Eastern Uplands – a more varied, broken, region.

(IV) The Central Plateau.

I. PHYSICAL – THE ZAGROS

This can in turn be sub-divided into three contrasting zones, the north-west, which lies between the 35th and 39th parallels of latitude; the centre, which extends from Lat. 35° N. to about 27° N.; and the south-east portion, termed in its eastern part the Makran, which lies between the Strait of Hormuz and Baluchistan.

(a) *The North-western Zagros.* Adjacent to Anatolia, land forms have been developed primarily as the result of differential tectonic movements along well-marked faults. Horst blocks and downthrow basins are therefore prominent, though in places the outlines of these have been modified by intense erosion. One of these downthrow basins is that of Lake Urmia (Rezaieh), which covers 20,000 square miles; and others occur (i) at Khoi, north of Urmia (with the narrow ridge of the Mashu Dagh acting as a separation between the Urmia and Khoi lowlands); (ii) in the Moghan district of the lower Aras (Araxes) river; and (iii) in the upper reaches of the Qara Su (Ardebil region).

The uplifted horsts form a series of blocks that increase generally in elevation towards the north-west, giving the appearance of an extensive plateau that is tilted towards the south-east. Numerous deeply-incised valleys separate the individual blocks, so that, despite the general impression of a plateau, relief is extremely varied. Some of the river valleys are no more than gorges or defiles; but others (owing to tectonic action) are much wider, e.g. the Aras valley, which forms a corridor some 10 to 40 miles wide, and serves as a frontier between Persia and Russia; and the Safid Rud (named in its lower course the Qizil Uzan), where there is a lowland basin 15 miles in width round the town of Mianeh.

A third important topographical feature in the north-west Zagros is the presence of numerous volcanic cones, formed by the rise of magma along fracture lines. These are often built up on the highest parts of the plateau, producing the imposing peaks of Savalan (14,000 feet), Sahand (12,000 feet), and Kharazana (11,500 feet). Generally

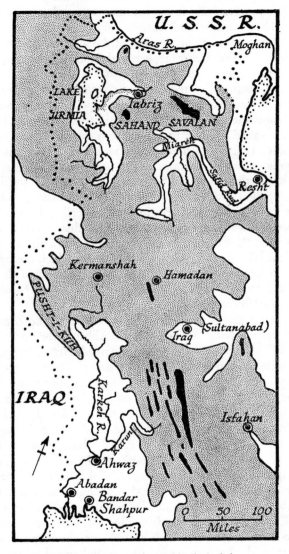

Fig. 46. North-west Persia. Highland stippled; over
8,000 ft. in black

speaking, the plateau uplands, stony and undulating, or covered by masses of recent lava, offer few inducements to settlement. Intolerably hot and arid in summer, and bitterly cold in winter – possibly with the most extreme climate of any part of the world – these regions are sparsely occupied by nomadic shepherds who spend the summer months in searching for pasture, and pass the winter in the valleys. Permanent settlement is restricted to the broader riverine tracts where climatic conditions are less extreme, and where deposits of water-deposited silt allow cultivation. Here population is relatively dense, and a variety of crops are raised – wheat, barley, tobacco, cotton, opium, and fruit.

The most extensive of these settled regions is that situated round Lake Urmia, which is without outlet, and hence extremely saline (though less so than the Dead Sea) with 155 gm of dissolved salts per litre. Unlike the Dead Sea, Urmia is shallow, fluctuating considerably in extent from a maximum area in March–April and a minimum in September, when it leaves an expanse of mud that can reach temperatures of 120° F. Because of this, settlements occur at a distance from the shores of the lake, on the banks of small streams which can be used for irrigation before the water is contaminated by contact with the lake. Tabriz, the second city of Iran, lies on such a stream (the Maiden Chai) 35 miles away from the lake shore.

(b) *The Central Zagros.* The second sub-division of the Zagros comprises the portion lying between Bandar Abbas at the opening of the Persian Gulf, and the sub-region just described. Here folding, and not faulting, is the main feature, hence there occurs a succession of parallel ridges, separated by deep valleys. The ridges are not continuous, but die out at intervals and give place to others, though a single direction of strike is maintained throughout. The series of densely packed folds, aligned in ranks, is most characteristic of the central Zagros, and although the actual size of the folds varies – those in the north being broader and higher, those in the south smaller and finer – they form the principal, almost the only, topographical feature in the region.

On the south-west, towards the Mesopotamian lowlands, the folds are open, and consist of simple anticlines (ridges) and synclines (valleys) – an indication of the recent formation of the entire range – but further to the north-east, towards central Iran, shearing and deformation occur, with the presence of nappes and overthrusting, so that structures are much more complicated. Extensive dissection by rivers has once again led to the development of narrow, steep-sided valleys, some of which are mere slits or defiles, too narrow or too recent in formation even for the smallest alluvium-covered terraces to occur. In certain places the rivers appear to follow a direct path to the Tigris lowlands, and plunge directly through the most massive ridges by a series of enormous clefts or gorges. These gorges, named *tangs*, often cut across the highest parts of the ridges, and it seems unlikely that they can have been entirely formed by river action. Some authorities consider that the tangs were originally great cross-faults, developed at right-angles to the main axis of folding; and that they have since been deepened by water, and in some instances wind action. Certain of the tangs are not indeed occupied by a river.

As the result of the presence of tangs, the drainage of the central Zagros follows an intricate, grid-iron pattern. In some parts, there are no gaps through the ridges, and rivers must flow in longitudinal valleys, weaving a tortuous transverse course from one syncline to the next; in others, there is a shorter, but precipitous descent to the Mesopotamian plain.

Because of the uniformity of the mountain ridges, one finds fewer outstanding single peaks than in north-west Persia; but there is a greater extent of highland, and a considerable number of domes attain an altitude of 13,000 to 15,000 feet. Parts of the Zagros are vegetation-covered, particularly in the north, where rainfall is heavier, but much of the central region consists of bare expanses of rock often startlingly coloured in red, yellow, white, grey, green, or black. Between some ridges lie deep open valleys, the floors of which are 4,000 to 8,000 feet above sea level; and, in contrast, most of these floors are vegetation-covered, with parts even wooded, giving extremely attractive parklike scenery. Where water is available, cultivation is possible on small fields or terraces cut in the sides of hills; but to a far greater extent the region supports a pastoral population. The grassy valley bottoms are used at various seasons of the year, and a well-organised transhumance, reminiscent of that in the Alps, is a prominent feature. Conditions in Persia are, however, somewhat sterner than in Switzerland – ones does not often hear of a Swiss shepherd kicking footholds in the snow for his animals by means of his bare feet, a not uncommon occurrence during spring in the Zagros.

Minor, but striking topographical features of the southern portion of the central Zagros, are numerous salt hills, or plugs, some of which rise to a height of 5,000 feet. It is thought that these plugs have been formed as the result of isostatic pressure on a deep-seated and plastic layer of rock salt, that is considered by G. M. Lees to be of Cambrian age. As later sediments accumulated above the salt, this relatively plastic layer was pressed upwards through younger series in the form of giant eruptions. Some of these plugs are in active upward motion at the present time, forcing their way through overlying strata, and raising impressive glistening sugar-loaf cones above the surrounding country: others have been eroded after eruption to the surface, and the covering rocks have collapsed into the resulting crater as a bewildering jumble of strata.

Another minor feature of the central Zagros is the occurrence of small lowland basins where the north-easternmost of the Zagros folds have impinged upon the buckled edge of the central plateau. Some of these basins, e.g. those of Shiraz and Niriz, are enclosed, with aretic drainage, and hence have salt marshes or lakes in the lowest part; in others a stream has broken through the surrounding highland rim, and there is a normal drainage outwards towards the south-west. It is interesting to note that certain of these basins, intensively cultivated in the non-saline stretches away from the lowest parts, have been the centres of important cultural movements. Niriz was the homeland of the early Persians, who established a continent-wide empire: Shiraz was later renowned as the cradle of Persian poetry, the home of Hafiz and Saadi.

(c) *The South-east Zagros* (*Makran*). Immediately east of Bandar Abbas, the trend of the Zagros ridges alters abruptly. For a distance of 150 miles between Bandar Abbas and Jask, the direction of folding is north-south; then, eastwards of Jask, there is a second change, with, first of all, a trend from west-north-west to east-south-east, and later, from west to east.

In striking contrast to the massive, elongated, and regularly aligned ridges of the central Zagros, topography in the south-east is much more irregular and broken, and on a far less imposing scale. A narrow coastal plain bordering the Gulf of Oman and the Indian Ocean is succeeded inland by a zone of plateau country of an average elevation of 2,000 to 3,000 feet, and this plateau is crossed in places by lines of hills that occasionally reach 6,000 to 7,000 feet. Between these hills lie numerous river basins, noteworthy in that they run directly to the sea, with a more directly consequent alignment than the valleys of the central Zagros, which, as we have seen, tend more to follow a rectangular plan.

Northwards, the plateau zone gives way to an extensive trough, the Jaz Murian basin, which consists of a depression with its lowest point at an altitude of 1,000 feet. This basin is partly filled by a thick layer of silt and wind-blown material deposited in dunes. There is no drainage from the basin, and the centre is occupied by a salt lake fed by two streams, the Rud Halil and the Rud Bampur. Other streams from the surrounding high ground fail to reach the lake, and soon disappear beneath the drift cover. The Jaz Murian basin is defined on the north by a single narrow line of highland, which acts as a divide between the Jaz Murian depression and the interior plateau of central Iran. The average height of the ridge is about 4,000 feet, but a single peak of 11,000 feet occurs in the east, at Kuh-i-Baznan.

Most of the south-eastern Zagros region presents a vista of rugged desolate landscapes, either bare rock or sand dunes, with occasional patches of cultivation – chiefly date-groves – in the few favoured spots where water is available. Dates are a staple, supplemented by small amounts of cereals, by dried fish brought from the coast, and by meat and milk from the few animals that find pasture on the scanty grasses of the lower mountain slopes. Even the Jaz Murian plain is largely uninhabited, or only occupied for a short time by nomads.

THE NORTHERN HIGHLANDS

The northern highlands of Persia consist of two distinct groups: the Elburz Range in the west with its outlier, the Talish Hills, and the more extensive chains of the north-east – chief among which are the Kopet Dagh and the Ala Dagh. Between the two masses lies a trough, part of which is occupied by the Atrek river.

The Elburz consists of a relatively narrow series of folds disposed in a shallow crescent along the southern border of the Caspian Sea. Although narrow, the fold ridges are extremely steep, and a number of summits reach an altitude of over 10,000 feet within a distance of 30 miles from the Caspian shore, which is nearly 100 feet below sea level. Erosion has been very active on the northern slopes of the Elburz – annual rainfall exceeds 100 inches – and this region is hence broken by deep gorges, at the bottom of which great torrents flow directly northwards towards the Caspian. Further to the south, when the northernmost crests are passed, there is a development of longitudinal or strike valleys, recalling on a smaller scale those of the central Zagros, in which flow a number of longer and better developed rivers, e.g. the Shah Rud and the Nur. Although only 60 miles wide in its broadest part, the Elburz region exhibits marked climatic variation, and its southern flanks, where rainfall is moderate or even scanty, are much less dissected by streams, so that here the east–west trend of the folds is more apparent than on the north. As in the north-western Zagros, volcanic cones are a feature, the best known of which, Mount Demavend north of Teheran, reaches 18,000 feet, and carries a permanent snow-cap, while there are small glaciers at Alam Kuh (60 miles north-west of Teheran).

The northern slopes of the Elburz are well wooded up to a height of 7,000 to 8,000 feet, but further south a sharp change occurs, and vegetation soon becomes less luxuriant, passing ultimately, in the extreme south, into scattered patches of scrub, with most of the hillsides entirely bare. When water is available, many parts of the southern Elburz are extremely fertile, especially the alluvial cones and river terraces, where there is a thick deposit of rich soil. In some places, however, the river bed is too deeply incised to allow the deposition of silt, and such valleys are uninhabited.

Bordering the northern edge of the Elburz Range, and its western continuation the Talish Hills, which link the Elburz to the larger massifs of the Caucasus and north-west Zagros, lies the coastal plain of the Southern Caspian. This varies between 10 and 70 miles in width. Close to the Caspian shoreline is a zone of sand dunes, behind which lie salt marshes and lagoons. These are succeeded by slightly higher and firmer ground, most of which is densely covered by the Hyrcanian vegetation to which reference was made in Chapter IV. Some parts of the Hyrcanian forest have been cleared for cultivation, and the coastal plain of the Caspian is now the most closely settled of any part of Persia, containing nearly one-fifth of the total population of the country.

The Caspian plain has been uncovered by a gradual retreat of the Caspian Sea, which once extended as far south as the foothills of the Elburz Range. At the present time, the level of the Caspian is falling by about 8 inches per annum, the precise rate depending on the inflow from various rivers, chiefly the Volga. Despite its steady shrinking, the Caspian is much less salt than most sea water, and is only one-quarter as salt as the Mediterranean. The retreat of the Caspian Sea is having a most unfortunate effect on the economic life of the Persian ports on its shores, which can now only be approached by specially dredged channels resembling canals. A project of long standing, sponsored by the Russians, aims at cutting a canal to link the Caspian and Black Seas, by which the deficiency of water may be made up.

In the extreme east, at about Long. 56° E., the Elburz Range dies down, and is succeeded by a trough or plateau, the lower parts of which are grass-covered, and support a population of pastoral nomads. It is hardly correct to speak of this trough as a lowland, since the average altitude is 5,000 feet, but it serves to divide off the higher Elburz to the west from the more massive and widely spaced ranges to the east. These eastern ranges have a predominantly north-west–south-east trend, in contrast to the due east–west alignment of the Elburz. The most northerly of the ranges, the Kopet Dagh, lies partly in Persia and partly in Russian Turkestan, the frontier following the eastern foothills of this range. The Kopet Dagh (termed Kuh-i-Hajar Masjid in its south-east portion) reaches 10,000 feet in maximum elevation, and is then succeeded by a second chain, named the Kuh-i-Aleh (northern part) and the Kuh-i-Binalud (southern portion). In between the Kopet Dagh and Kuh-i-Aleh lies a well-defined valley, occupied by two rivers: the Atrek flowing north-west to the Caspian; and the Kashuf flowing south-east towards Afghanistan. A third upland range (the Kuh-i-Surkh) occurs at some distance to the south-west, separated once again from its neighbour the Kuh-i-Binalud, by a broader longitudinal trough.

Main interest centres in the lowlands occupied by the Atrek and Kashuf, which provide a natural corridor between the Caspian region and the Turcoman steppes of the district of Merv. Most of the highland is barren and empty, serving only as grazing ground for occasional nomadic tribes; but the riverine lowlands are relatively densely peopled, with numerous cultivated areas. The richest part is the upper Kashuf valley round Meshed, from which comes a substantial proportion of the wheat and barley of Iran. From the abundance of ruins of many ages scattered in this district, it would seem that there was once a very dense population. Present backwardness is probably due, in the main, to tribal wars and invasion, with liability to earthquakes as a further contributing factor. Situated at the principal natural gateway into eastern Persia, the Meshed region bore the first brunt of Mongol and Turcoman raids; but with stronger rule during the present century, there has within the past thirty years been a distinct revival of activity in the region.

THE EASTERN UPLANDS

This term can be applied to the broken and irregular highland region lying between the region just described, and the south-east portion of

Fig. 47. South and East Persia, and the Helmand Basin

the Zagros. There is little geographical unity: the highland massifs are irregular in trend and disposition, and give place in many localities to wide lowland basins. Generally speaking, the entire eastern region is markedly barren and unproductive, for besides the difficulties of irregular topography, with much loose scree, jagged peaks, and drifting sand, there are considerable climatic drawbacks – extremes of heat and cold, great aridity, and a special feature, a persistent and violent wind which blows with great regularity throughout the summer season, and sometimes reaches a velocity of 80 m.p.h. In winter, blizzards of 120 m.p.h. are not unknown. As a result great quantities of sand are lifted, giving rise to a kind of natural sand-blast. In time, the lower courses of buildings may even be etched away by the wind, and fall in ruins.

On the higher ground, permanent settlements are very few indeed, and occur only in sheltered gullies. In the lowlands near hill-slopes outwash fans of pebbles, and scree of jagged material eroded by exfoliation alike offer little inducement to cultivation. In the neighbourhood of the few rivers that exist, some agriculture is however possible. Most important of such areas is the lower basin of the Helmand river, termed Seistan. Water from streams rising in Afghanistan reaches Seistan, and cultivation by irrigation is carried on. Unfortunately, however, the Helmand river terminates in a shallow lake, which varies considerably in size, and causes floods, sometimes covering hundreds of square miles after heavy rains in Afghanistan. A further misfortune is the prevalence of braided streams which are liable to change their course without warning, and overwhelm adjacent districts. Settled occupation on any large scale in these regions is thus extremely difficult.

Despite its natural handicaps, Seistan, like the Meshed region, once supported a larger population; but the present inhabitants are far fewer in number even than those round Meshed, and only one primitive irrigation channel is now in operation. Besides a small number of farmers engaged in growing dates and cereals, the lake supports a few fishermen.

THE CENTRAL PLATEAU

The inner part of Persia, amounting to about one-half of the total area of the country, is occupied by a series of closed basins from which there is no outward drainage of any sort. In the main, the lowest parts of these basins lie at an elevation of 2,000 to 3,000 feet, though they are 1,000 feet lower in the south-east; and the mountain ring, which almost completely encircles the inner plateau, falls little below a general level of 8,000 feet.

At an earlier period – probably late Tertiary and Quaternary – the basins were occupied by lakes, which have left thick deposits of alluvial material. The central plateau is now almost rainless, and so for the most part the region is one of unrelieved desert. There are, however, certain unusual features. The lowest parts of the basins have a deep deposit of black mud, and evaporation at the surface has resulted in the formation of a salt crust. The salt is precipitated in the form of angular blocks or plates, about one inch thick, and several square feet in area. As evaporation proceeds, the crusts increase in size, and are forced one against the other, so that in time, they become arched upwards, and their rough, sharp edges protrude above the surface, giving an appearance rather similar to that of a glacier or ice floe. Beneath the salt crust lies a sticky mass of salt marsh or mud, with drainage channels at intervals that are filled with watery ooze or slime. It is something of a mystery how such an arid area still retains extensive swamps; but possibly the water is a remnant of the old lakes, supplemented at the present by soakage from the mountain crests. The presence in the swamps of magnesium chloride, a strongly hygroscopic substance, may also attract a certain amount of moisture from the subsoil and from the atmosphere.

The salt marshes are extremely dangerous to travellers, since the sharp edges of the salt crust can cause serious injury to men and animals. Graver still, the layer of salt is often insufficient to bear the weight of a man, and the scattered drainage channels, which occur underneath, and of which there is no indication on the surface, are deep enough to overwhelm anyone caught in their sluggish waters. Movement in the region is rendered even more hazardous by frequent winter fogs. As a result, widespread areas of the marshes are uninhabited and even unexplored. A number of attempts have recently been made to survey the region, but only the fringe has so far been mapped.

The name *kavir* is given to the salt marshes of inner Persia, which cover about one-quarter of the total area of the region. Elsewhere, firm sandy or stony stretches occur, giving a more 'normal' desert topography similar to that of Arabia or the Sahara. The term *dasht* is applied to this firm desert, in which sand dunes (*rig*) may occur. Another expression, *lut*, refers to the arid region as a whole, and is hence a generic term, denoting a region in which both *dasht* and *kavir* may occur.

Settlement within the central basin of Persia is almost entirely confined to the flanks of the surrounding mountain chains – e.g. Teheran, on the southern slopes of the Elburz, Qum, Yezd, and Kirman on the eastern foothills of the Zagros – and important routes follow a circumferential path, avoiding the centre of the Lut. Only a few minor tracks attempt a direct crossing.

II. CLIMATE

The main features of the climate of Persia are:

(a) Marked continentality, with extremely high summer temperatures, and an unusually cold winter – much colder, in general, than the average for the latitude.

(b) Great contrasts in rainfall, the extreme north and west receiving considerable amounts, and the remainder of the country little or none.

(c) The frequency of high winds, which intensify the effects of extreme temperatures.

These conditions, sufficiently unusual to be distinguished by de Martonne as a separate climatic regime,[1] arise chiefly as the result of the mountainous nature of the region, and its situation as part of the heartland of Asia. In summer the dried-out monsoonal air stream from north-west India and Baluchistan extends westward over Persia, and gives temperatures comparable with those of the Thar Desert, whilst in winter the country can easily fall under the influence of the Siberian anticyclone, with few topographical barriers to prevent the south-westward spread of intensely dry, cold air. On the other hand, maritime influences are excluded by the high mountain wall, most fully developed on the west and south, so that milder, damper air from the Mediterranean and Caspian Seas, and Persian Gulf, affects only the outer regions of Persia.

Altitude is partly responsible for the unusually cold winters (Teheran and Isfahan mean Jan. temp. 35° F., cf. Aleppo and Beirut, in the same latitude, 42° F. and 56° F.; or Seville, 52° F.) and, although altitude does not much mitigate the intense heat of the day in summer, it does produce a rapid fall of temperature at night (Teheran, alt. 4,000 feet, mean day max. July 99° F., mean night min. July 71° F.; Meshed, alt. 3,000 feet, mean day max. 92° F., mean night min. 63° F.; Kirman, alt. 6,000 feet, mean day max. 101° F., mean night min. 62° F.). Annual range of temperature on the central plateau varies from 35° to 45° F.,

[1] The 'Iranian' type.

with an average January temperature of 35° in the northern and western districts, and 45° F. in the south and east. Frost is, therefore, common in most parts of the central plateau during late autumn, winter, and early spring; and in the higher parts of the surrounding mountains, temperatures are lower still, so that snow may lie for many months (mean Jan. temp. at Tabriz, 17° F.). Temperatures well below freezing have even been recorded on the Shatt el Arab, at sea level, where occasionally ice formation has been seen. The only regions of Persia where frost does not occur are the coastal plains of the Makran. The north-west is the coldest part of Persia, and temperatures below 0° F. are by no means unusual.

During summer, most of inner Persia is intolerably hot, and it has been suggested that the highest temperatures in the world may occur in the Southern Lut region of the interior plateau. As no recording stations exist in this area, the claim cannot be justified or disproved. The mountains experience slightly cooler conditions, and a number of hill stations have been established in the Elburz and Zagros foothills as a refuge from the heat of the cities, where temperatures may exceed 110° F. The mean in parts of Seistan is over 120° F., and in the region of the Persian Gulf 125° has frequently been recorded. Under such conditions human activity comes to a temporary standstill. Shops and offices close, travel and business activity is deferred till the evening, and during one or two hot spells in 1941–5, it was recorded that fires were drawn on a number of locomotives, and trains came to a halt, because of intolerable conditions for the driving crews.

A special feature of summer previously referred to is the persistent northerly wind that occurs in south-east Persia. This is in all probability due to circulation round the main low-pressure centre of the monsoonal system, and because of the very low pressures that prevail, wind strength is correspondingly great. Speeds of 70 m.p.h. for days on end are common throughout the season of onset, which lasts from May until September. A local name for the phenomenon is 'Wind of 120 days'.

Practically all of the rainfall of Persia comes from eastward-moving depressions that originate over or near the Mediterranean Sea. Outflowing air from the Siberian anticyclone is dry and gives no precipitation, and the same is true of the monsoonal air masses of summer, which have lost their moisture on arrival in Persia. Hence the summer is completely arid (except in the extreme north along the shores of the Caspian), and rainfall at other seasons depends on the arrival of maritime air masses from the west. Depressions in this maritime air stream are, however, greatly weakened, as most of their moisture is deposited on the highlands of Asia Minor and the Levant; and the remaining moisture is precipitated during the crossing of the Zagros Ranges, so that little or none falls in the central plateau.

When the track of a Mediterranean depression has lain over land, the quantity of rainfall occurring in Persia is very small, but when a sea track has been followed, the amount of moisture is greater, i.e. depressions moving towards Persia via the Aegean and Black Seas give the heaviest rainfall, whilst those moving due east across Syria and Iraq are almost dried out.[1]

Thus, as might be expected, north-west Persia experiences by far the heaviest rainfall, and the distribution of rainfall in general is closely related to topography. Isohyets tend to follow contour lines, and the north-west Zagros and Elburz regions, lying close to sea areas, receive by far the heaviest rainfall. The amount decreases towards the south-east, markedly so in the lower central plateau, more slowly in the mountain zones. Hence the Kopet Dagh and Ala Dagh of the east, and the south-east Zagros have annual totals of under 10 inches, whilst on the plateau a rain shadow area occurs in which rainfall is under 5 inches.

The season of greatest rainfall varies somewhat over the country. In the north (Caspian provinces excepted) the maximum occurs in spring with March as the wettest month; but in the south, the maximum falls earlier (December at Ahwaz and Khorramshahr, January at Jask). Again, as is usual under Middle Eastern conditions, rainfall is capricious, varying greatly in amount from year to year, and in onset – even in regions where annual rainfall is below 10 inches, falls of 2 inches in 24 hours are known, and in others, years may pass without any precipitation.

Great contrasts exist in humidity. Over most of Persia the air is dry – as would be expected, in view of a deficient rainfall – and figures for Teheran and Meshed, showing a winter maximum, may be considered as typical. On the Caspian coast, however, humidity is high throughout the year, though still with a winter maximum; but in the Persian Gulf humidity is highest in summer, giving rise, in combination with the very high air temperature, to extremely oppressive conditions. Where sea breezes carry in moisture from sea to land, as at Jask, summer humidity is high. At Abadan, the opposite occurs, and with the

[1] It has been suggested that a partial regeneration of these exhausted depressions may occur over the swamps of lower Iraq and the Persian Gulf.

prevailing wind from the north-west (i.e. from the land) humidity is low. This difference in humidity is all the more striking in view of the complete absence of summer rainfall at both places.

PERCENTAGE RELATIVE HUMIDITY

	J	F	M	A	M	J	J	A	S	O	N	D
Teheran	76	64	44	46	51	50	47	49	50	54	66	77
Meshed	83	83	77	68	59	48	45	46	49	62	76	79
Abadan	77	75	59	45	33	25	25	29	33	39	60	75
Jask	63	71	65	65	64	67	68	72	64	64	62	62
Lenkoran (Russian Caspian provinces)	86	87	87	84	81	75	73	76	82	88	89	89

Cloudiness is in general extremely low. The Caspian region, with an average cloud-cover of $\frac{7}{10}$, stands out as unduly cloudy; but the general lack of cloudiness is an important factor in the wide range of temperature, both seasonal and diurnal. During the days of summer, the sun blazes down on an uncovered land surface: at night, and in winter, much terrestrial heat is given out unchecked to the atmosphere.

CLOUDINESS (in tenths of sky covered)

	J	F	M	A	M	J	J	A	S	O	N	D	Mean
Teheran	4	5	4	4	4	1	1	1	1	2	4	4	3
Meshed	5	4	5	5	3	1	1	0	1	2	4	5	3
Seistan	3	3	2	1	1	0	0	0	0	0	0	2	1
Lenkoran	7	7	8	7	7	5	5	4	6	6	8	8	6
Bushire	4	4	4	3	2	0	1	1	1	1	3	5	2

It remains to discuss the special climatic regime of the Caspian region. Here, as the result of the presence of the Elburz Range, and proximity to two expanses of sea, which form a 'storm track' for depressions, rainfall is very much higher. Moreover, the low altitude of the coastal plain gives winter temperatures more in keeping with the latitude. In summer rainfall occurs, though on a reduced scale, and the resulting cloud-cover helps to reduce insolation, so that the high temperatures characteristic of the rest of Persia are not found – it is very unusual for the thermometer to reach 100° F., and the July mean is only 79° F. A hot, but not torrid summer, and a winter milder than in the adjacent areas of Persia, together with abundant rainfall well distributed throughout the year (maximum in early autumn), indicate that climatically, the Caspian provinces stand apart from the rest of the country. Conditions are those of a hothouse, in which vegetation thrives luxuriantly, but in which lassitude and enervation are also found among the people. Although very productive, the Caspian lowlands are a breeding ground for disease, and in some districts chronic malaria affects 80 to 100 per cent. of the total population.

CLIMATIC DATA

REPRESENTATIVE STATIONS IN PERSIA

Temperatures (°F.), and Rainfall (inches)

	J	F	M	A	M	J	J	A	S	O	N	D	Total
Teheran													
Temp.	35	41	49	60	70	80	85	84	77	64	53	42	
Rainfall	1·7	1·0	1·9	1·1	0·4	0·1	0·2	0	0·1	0·3	1·1	1·3	9·2
Rainy days	4	3	6	3	2	1	1	0	1	1	3	4	27★
Meshed													
Temp.	34	38	46	56	67	74	77	74	67	57	47	39	
Rainfall	0·8	1·0	2·2	1·8	1·2	0·3	0·1	0	0	0·4	0·6	0·7	9·1
Rainy days	2	2	5	5	3	1	1	0	0	1	2	2	23
Abadan													
Temp.	53	59	65	76	87	93	97	97	90	81	69	58	
Rainfall	1·5	1·7	0·7	0·8	0·1	0	0	0	0	0·1	1·0	1·8	7·6
Rainy days	1	1	1	1	1	0	0	0	0	1	1	1	5
Seistan													
Temp.	48	51	59	70	81	87	90	89	79	69	57	47	
Rainfall	0·4	0·4	0·5	0·1	0	0	0	0	0	0	0	0·3	1·7
Rainy days	1	1	2	1	0	0	0	0	0	0	0	1	6
Jask													
Temp.	67	69	74	80	85	90	91	89	87	83	76	71	
Rainfall	1·2	0·9	0·6	0·2	0	0·1	0·1	0	0	0·2	0·3	1·2	4·7
Rainy days	2	2	1	1	0	1	1	0	0	1	1	2	9
Lenkoran†													
Temp.	38	41	46	54	65	74	79	78	71	62	51	43	
Rainfall	3·1	3·2	3·7	1·9	1·2	1·1	0·6	2·4	6·6	9·3	6·5	4·6	44·2
Rainy days	11	11	12	10	9	5	3	5	11	13	13	12	115

★ This total may not exactly agree with the monthly total of rainy days, because in the latter, a total of 1 may indicate a fall of rain only once in several years, and should appear as a fraction of unity.

† Russian territory, but the only station in the region with a run of climatic data for more than 10 years.

III. AGRICULTURE

The amount of cultivated land in Persia probably amounts to between 5 and 10 per cent. of the total area; and of this, about one-third is irrigated, with the rest depending upon direct watering by rainfall. Figures of actual production are extremely difficult to obtain, but from observation, it is clear that large areas lie fallow for months – sometimes even years – and that shifting cultivation is fairly widely practised. The physical and social limitations to efficient production that were discussed in Chapter IX apply with considerable force in Persia: besides the handicaps of a low rainfall and a difficult topography, methods of exploitation are primitive, improvements and initiative are discouraged by the system of land tenure – métayage is the most widespread form of tenancy – and bad communications and vast distances hinder a change-over from a mediaeval level of self-sufficiency to specialisation in cash crops.

In the main, the cultivated land of Persia occurs as small patches of oases surrounded by vast tracts of unexploited desert or mountain slopes, and the true picture of conditions is one of a mosaic, with scattered plots and tiny fields alternating with larger arid and barren intervals.

Crops. Wheat is the chief crop, and is grown over most of Persia. The regions of greatest production are: (*a*) the Meshed region of Khorassan province, (*b*) the valleys of the north-west and central Zagros, particularly the districts of Lake Urmia, Hamadan, Kermanshah, Isfahan, Shiraz, and Niriz, and (*c*) the better watered parts of Khuzistan. In most instances, wheat is grown as a winter crop, but in the high valleys of the Zagros and Elburz, sowing is in the spring, so that the harvest takes place in July and August. Barley is second in importance to wheat, and is grown in the same districts as wheat. Barley ripens three to four weeks earlier, however, and hence escapes to some extent the ravages of the sunna insect, which appears in late summer, and causes very considerable losses in Persia – losses which are in general higher than in the rest of the Middle East. Much barley is eaten by the people, and the remainder used as feeding stuffs for animals.

Rice flourishes in the Caspian provinces of Mazanderan and Gilan, with the Resht district (lower valley of the Safid Rud) as the region of most intensive production. Small quantities of rice are also grown in other parts of the country where abundant irrigation water is available, e.g. in Khuzistan, Kermanshah, and the Shiraz basin. Rice cultivation demands much labour, as several ploughings are necessary – the first to break up the land, and again when the paddy fields have been covered in water, and the surface must be broken down to the consistency of mud. For this purpose mountaineers from the Elburz (and to a lesser extent the Zagros) are employed as seasonal workers. The fields are broken up in late winter, then the fields are flooded to a depth of over a foot in April, and sowing takes place in May. Later, the crop is thinned out, either by transplantation, or by trampling down unwanted shoots by foot. Harvesting takes place in August or September. Until the introduction of rice in the tenth century A.D., the Caspian provinces were much less productive, because the climate, with cloudy summers and a very rainy early autumn (i.e. closer to monsoon conditions), does not altogether favour the cultivation of wheat and barley.

Two minor crops, planted chiefly in spring, are millet and maize. Production of the latter is still on a small scale though its cultivation is increasing, especially in Khuzistan, and round Teheran.

Fruit-growing is of considerable importance, since fruit forms an important part of the everyday diet of most Persians. The main regions are situated in the north-west of the country, but small orchards occur in most districts. Persia is famous for its apricots, said to be the finest in the world; and the wide extent of hilly country favours the cultivation of the vine. Many varieties of the latter occur: some are dried as sultanas and raisins, others are used in wine-making,[1] whilst large quantities are eaten fresh. Grapes from the Shiraz district, reputed to be the finest in the Middle East, are exported as far as Iraq and India. The vine is found at altitudes up to 4,500 feet in most parts of the country, and many of the lower hillsides are terraced as vineyards. Other fruit crops are figs, peaches, lemons, melons, and oranges. Some oranges grow to a size of 9 inches in diameter, and melons are also of enormous size. In the north-east, towards Russian Turkestan, the latter attain a weight of over 100 lb.

Citrus fruit-growing is generally confined to the Caspian coastlands, and to the outer foothills of the central Zagros. The wide extent of upland massifs allows a well-marked gradation of cultivation of fruit crops: at the lowest levels oranges, peaches, pomegranates, and melons are found, succeeded at heights of 1,000 or 2,000 feet by apricots, nectarines, and the vine. In the cooler zones about 4,000 feet there is a variety of temperate fruits – plums, cherries, pears, apples, and strawberries. Olives are much less important, and cultivation is mainly limited to the Elburz Range, with the Manzil region of the middle Safid Rud as the chief centre. Scattered olive groves are, however, also found on the eastern side of the Zagros range, towards the inner plateau of Persia.

In the south of Persia, date-growing assumes very high importance,

[1] Despite Moslem disapproval, wine-making has long been carried on in Iran, as the poetry of Omar Khayyám shows.

and in the south-east Zagros and Makran districts, dates form a staple of diet. The country can thus be divided into two distinctive regions, with the northern limit of the date palm as the boundary (see Fig. 32), (*a*) a southern region, hot and arid, with little or no winter frost, where cultivation of any sort is difficult, and where dates provide a large part of the food; and (*b*) the cooler and damper north, where cereals and a wide variety of 'Mediterranean' fruits are grown. The date flourishes most on the coastal plains of the Persian Gulf and Gulf of Oman. About half of the date palms of Persia (total, approx. 10 million) are found round Minab on the Strait of Hormuz, and most of the remainder in Khuzistan, near the banks of the Shatt el Arab.

ESTIMATES OF PRINCIPAL CROP PRODUCTION IN PERSIA
(tons)

	1934–8	1949–51	1956–7	1960
Wheat	1,869,000	2,024,000	3,015,000	2,613,000
Barley	793,000	822,000	1,087,000	904,000
Rice	423,000	430,000	543,000	530,000
Cotton	103,000	64,000	80,000	85,000

COMMERCIAL CROPS

Cotton ranks as the chief cash crop of Persia, since besides supplying a home demand, there is some export – though of recent years the level of production has fluctuated greatly.[1] Irrigation is essential, and growing is, therefore, restricted to the north and west of the country. A moderately long stapled variety of cotton known as *Filestani* is grown in the Azerbaijan, Kermanshah, Fars, and Khuzistan provinces, and accounts for about 50 per cent. of the total of cotton grown. A shorter stapled American variety is found mainly in the Caspian district, whilst a third kind, a native short staple of inferior quality though hardy in growth, is restricted to marginal (i.e. dry or hilly) areas. The cotton plant is also grown extensively for its seed, which yields an edible oil that replaces olive oil as food in many areas. Over 100,000 tons of vegetable oil are produced annually, and of this 90 per cent. is cottonseed oil, the rest coming from sesame, linseed, the castor oil plant, and the opium poppy.

[1] Besides providing raw material for the home textile industry, raw cotton is extensively used as wadding in the quilted material that is widely employed as bedding and as garments for protection against the winter cold. The wadding is prepared by means of a stringed implement resembling an archer's bow, and this operation is a common sight in the bazaars of Iranian towns.

Silk is a traditional product of Persia, but production declined greatly during the nineteenth century as the result of disease amongst the silk-worms. New strains have, however, been introduced from Turkey, and production has lately increased. Mulberry-growing is widespread over most of the north and west, but is particularly a feature of the eastern Caspian plain (Mazanderan province). The silkworms are usually hired out by landlords to the peasants who grow mulberry leaves; and when the cocoons have been spun, two-thirds of the cocoons are given to the landlord, the peasant retaining the remainder.

The growing of opium poppies increased considerably during the nineteenth century, as an alternative to the declining silk industry; and although production was restricted by governmental decree, there is a large illicit crop, since the profits are high, and the temptation in the way of an abjectly poor farmer is very great.[1] Extension of the growing of opium has unfortunately led to addiction amongst many of the population, and opium smoking is now reckoned as one of the chief social problems of the present Persian state.[2] Opium poppies are grown chiefly in the districts of Yezd and Kirman, the former town being possibly the original home of the plant, and also in the lowland basins of the central Zagros (Isfahan, Shiraz, Niriz, Kirmanshah, and Hamadan), and in Khorassan. Production of the drug depends upon complete aridity during the summer season, as a single shower will wash away sap containing opium as it exudes from the stem. Because of this, the Caspian provinces are not suited to opium-growing. In 1955 the growing of poppies for opium (as distinct from oil seed) was totally prohibited, and subsidies were voted to farmers who were affected by the ban.

Other Crops. Sugar beet was introduced by Riza Shah, and its production was greatly fostered by the Persian government as a means of reducing the country's dependence on imports. Because of rather inefficient methods of cultivation, and an environment that is in the main too warm and dry for really intensive cultivation – the beet is more at home in cool temperate latitudes – there is only a low sugar content. The beet crop is dependent upon irrigation, which, however, must be very carefully applied, in order to avoid damage to the plants.[3]

[1] In December 1948, the International Narcotics Committee made severe public criticisms of conditions in Persia.
[2] One estimate suggests that 10 to 15 per cent. of the inhabitants of Persian towns are opium addicts.
[3] Because of the high temperatures of the surface soil, beets can be 'scalded' when watering takes place.

Cultivation is confined to the regions of Teheran, Tabriz, Kermanshah, Shiraz, and Meshed. Successful production of beet sugar in Iran depends upon the existence of refineries close to the beet-growing regions, and under the regime of Riza Shah these were in process of building in various parts of the country. Since his downfall, however, little further building has taken place, and in parts where refineries are lacking, potato-growing has recently tended to replace the cultivation of beet. Cane sugar, widely grown in Persia during the early Muhammadan era, is now restricted to the Caspian provinces (Gilan and Mazanderan) and to Khuzistan. Planting takes place in March or April, and the cane is cut in November.

Tea is another minor crop that owes its extension to the efforts of Riza Shah. Chinese experts were introduced to develop cultivation on the northern foothills of the Elburz and Talish Hills, overlooking the Caspian plain, where climatic conditions somewhat resemble those of the lower Himalaya. Abundant moisture is necessary, so the crop tends to be restricted to the western portion of the Elburz, where rainfall exceeds 35 inches per annum. The eastern province of Mazanderan is used for jute-growing, but production of this latter crop is very small.

Tobacco is grown in most districts for local use, but the more important areas are the north-west and south-east Zagros, and the Caspian provinces. Quality is not high, so that there is little or no export. Finally, a number of dye-plants are important in the carpet-making industry. Production is mainly from the central Zagros region, and the adjoining province of Kirman in the central plateau; the chief crops being indigo, henna, madder, saffron, and oak-gall. Output has greatly declined since the introduction of aniline dyes during the last forty years.

IV. IRRIGATION

Despite the low rainfall of much of Persia, and the fact that irrigated areas give much larger yields than those dependent on rainfall, irrigation methods in Persia are primitive and undeveloped. Cultivators are content to rely on wells, qanats, or on small, crudely formed canals leading from rivers. It is also revealing to note that whereas Riza Shah devoted much attention to the growing of certain crops such as sugar beet, tea, and cotton, little was done for irrigation, and it was not until 1943 – two years after his abdication – that a governmental Irrigation Institute was created. This is all the more surprising in view of the extensive irrigation schemes developed at earlier historic periods – e.g. at Susa, in Khuzistan, and in Khorassan. A survey by the Institute showed that $2\frac{1}{2}$ million acres were capable of irrigation, i.e. the extent of cultivated land could be tripled. About one-half of this total lies in the province of Khuzistan. Because of high costs, and the poverty of the state, and certain social difficulties (i.e. conversion of pastoral nomads to a life of cultivation in newly irrigated areas) it is unlikely that the full potentialities of irrigation projects will be realised for some considerable time. As an interim practical measure, it is, however, proposed to bring about half a million acres under irrigation by means of small relatively inexpensive barrages, chief of which are located on the Karkeh river.

Chief regions involved in this modified scheme are: Khuzistan, Kirman and Seistan, Fars, Isfahan, and Teheran; and already new dams have been built along the Karkeh and Shair rivers to increase the water supply round Ahwaz. Further to the south-east, near Behbehan, some 20,000 acres have been irrigated from river water, and there is some development round Teheran. Unfortunately though, the effect on soil chemistry of increasing water supplies was not sufficiently taken into account, and in parts of Khuzistan, after a short time under irrigation, the soil became markedly saline, so that cultivation declined in certain areas. The valley of the Karun river is particularly remarkable for its tendency to develop soil salinity, and in some districts the land is now completely unusable. Despite these drawbacks, plans are now in hand to construct a high dam on the Dez river, and thus extend considerably the cultivable area of Khuzistan. Other somewhat smaller barrages are in construction at Karaj near Teheran (now in process of filling), and at Bampur. Many of these developments are financed from oil royalties: up to 1957 60 per cent. of royalties were assigned to the National Development Board, and after this, 80 per cent.

V. PASTORALISM

The policy of converting pastoralists to cultivators has nowhere in the Middle East been followed so actively as in Persia. Many tribesmen of nomadic or semi-nomadic habit were compelled by Riza Shah to abandon pastoralism and attempt to take up cultivation. As a result, the number of animals kept has declined considerably, though pastoralism still remains important in many parts of the hill regions. In addition to the social upheaval and human distress, the policy followed by Riza

Shah has brought about much economic loss to Persia, not only in foodstuffs – milk and meat – but also in the carpet industry (which is dependent on local wool); and as affecting a small, but significant export market for raw wool. However, over the last few years pastoralism has again revived, with larger numbers of animals kept, and some corresponding increase in pastoral nomadism.

Sheep are most numerous, with a probable total of 23–25 million, and these animals are kept either in semi-arid or mountainous areas, where they form the main wealth of nomadic tribes, or else close to partly settled agricultural regions. In the latter areas a village herdsman usually takes care of a single large flock, and is repaid in kind by the owners. Shearing takes place in May and September, and the wool is used locally for clothing and blankets, or else sent to market centres to be sold.

Goats are next in importance, numbering about 10 million. Besides providing milk and meat, their hair is woven into cloaks and tent-cloth. Cattle are much less numerous – about 4 millions – most being employed in agriculture for ploughing and irrigation. Dairying is little practised except near a few larger towns. Buffaloes are also found especially in the Caspian provinces. Donkeys are much used as beasts of burden, and by farmers, and there is an important mule-breeding industry carried on in the districts of Fars, Luristan, and Kurdistan. Camels are employed in large numbers as pack animals in the south and east of Persia, and a special breed has been developed in Khorassan by crossing the Arabian and Bactrian[1] species. The Khorassan camel is much stronger than the Arabian variety, being able to carry twice the load, and is better adapted to the climate of Persia, since besides its tolerance of great heat and aridity, it can also support the cold of winter. A significant feature of the last few years has been the expansion of poultry keeping. This has been fostered by the Development Board.

VI. MINERALS

Persia is known to have a number of useful minerals, but complete exploration of the mineral resources has not so far been carried out. Although minerals seem to exist in fair variety, the size of individual deposits is small, and this fact, together with difficulties of access, has greatly restricted exploitation. Apart from oil, the only minerals pro-

---

[1] The Bactrian camel, a native of south-west Turkestan, is adapted to a colder climate. It also has two humps, instead of the one characteristic of Arabian camels.

duced for export are lead, chrome, manganese, red oxide, and turquoise, though many others are exploited to supply home needs. With
few exceptions, mining methods are primitive, since the small extent
of deposits does not often justify the introduction of foreign mining
machinery.

Coal deposits occur in the region of Teheran, and also in eastern
Mazanderan. Production in the first region is from three centres (Shim-
shak and Lashkerak, 30 miles north of Teheran, and a smaller centre
55 miles west-north-west of the same city); and in Mazanderan, from
Zirab and Gulendi Rud near the eastern frontier of the province. The
coal is not of high quality (the best coming from Zirab), and total
annual production has fluctuated between 100,000 and 150,000 tons.
Iron ore is known to exist in four localities – Kirman, Samnan (in
the extreme south-east of the Elburz), at Isfahan, and at Anarak (region
of the Great Kavir, between Teheran and Yezd). Reserves at Kirman
have been estimated at 15 million tons, and plans are in hand to develop
a smelting plant that will ultimately have an annual capacity of 200,000
tons.

The Anarak-Lakhan districts of the north produce the bulk of Persian output in lead; some antimony and nickel (the latter mined with
lead); and small amounts of copper. Copper is also exploited at Abbassabad (south-east Elburz) and at Zenjan, where a modern refining
plant has been installed.[1] Chromium (in demand for tanning of leather)
occurs sporadically in the Elburz Range; and other minerals produced
on a very small scale are alum, arsenic, calcium borate, fuller's earth,
manganese, rock salt, and sulphur. Red oxide is exploited to a somewhat larger extent on the island of Hormuz (Persian Gulf); and other
deposits occur on the adjacent mainland, in association with the salt-
plugs of the central Zagros. Annual production averages 20,000 tons.
Turquoise, once regarded as the finest in the world, is exploited near
Nishapur, but output has declined because of the competition of
American and synthetic stones. Emeralds, formerly a well-known product of Persia, are now little produced, and there is no systematic
prospecting at the present.

It will be seen that mineral occurrence tends to be restricted to a few
districts, and of these south-east Elburz is easily the most important. In
addition to the coal basins near Teheran, other minerals occur to the
north and east, at Samnan and Shahrud. Second in order is probably

---

[1] This plant was installed by Riza Shah, in order to supply materials for the State
Arsenal.

the Bandar Abbas region, where, besides the red oxide deposits, sulphur
and rock salt are also worked. Though transport difficulties will be a
handicap, the vast kavirs of the interior may offer considerable potentialities at a future date, and there may be development similar to that
on the shores of the Dead Sea. Sodium and magnesium sulphate are
known to occur in considerable quantities, and it is probable that
nitrates are also present.

VII. INDUSTRY

Apart from the installations of the A.I.O.C., no modern industry of
any kind could be said to exist before 1934 in Persia, and although
Persia produced a moderate volume of manufactured goods, these
were made entirely by hand, or with the use of primitive machinery.
Efforts were, however, made by Riza Shah during 1930–41 to introduce modern plant as a means of reducing Persian dependence on
manufactured imports; and within the last 15 years over 200 industrial
establishments have been brought into existence. The state has played
a leading part in this development, so that a number of the more important factories are state-owned. In cases where private ownership is
allowed, the government supervises all development and operation.

The location of the new industries has been carefully planned with
the objects (i) of spreading the factories as fairly as possible over the
whole country, whilst at the same time (ii) placing particular industries
in regions where raw materials and labour were available, and communications best developed. This has meant that most provincial
capitals and route-centres have obtained one or more new industries,
and development has in general been widely dispersed. Geographical
advantages in a few regions (e.g. the existence of minerals near Teheran,
and the availability of cotton and wool at Isfahan) have, however, prevented an even spread over the whole of Persia. State activity since 1934
has mainly affected the textile and food industries, and a third, yet
minor, feature has been the creation of a small metallurgical and
chemical industry closely related to supplying light armaments for the
Iranian army and police.

Textiles. About one-half of the cotton production of Persia comes from
the Isfahan district, which is a market and collecting centre for the
cotton-growing districts of the south-west. There are eleven spinning
and weaving mills in the city, the largest being state-owned, and of
recent construction. Minor cotton manufacturing centres are Shahi

(Mazanderan), and Behshahr (Gurgan), with two large mills each; and Kasvin, Kirman, Meshed, and Yezd, where there are smaller units and many handlooms. Woollen goods are produced in ten large factories and many smaller ones. Isfahan is again the chief centre, being placed conveniently in relation to the great pastoral areas of the central Zagros; but Tabriz, another regional capital in the north-west Zagros, and also Kasvin, have a significant production. Jute is woven to a small extent at Resht and Shahi, whilst silk, another product of the Caspian provinces, is woven at Chalus (Mazanderan).

The carpet industry, for which Persia has long been famous, has shown itself to be much less susceptible of concentration and mechanisation under modern conditions, and remains entirely a bazaar craft carried on by hand. The introduction of aniline dyes has lowered the quality of many Persian carpets, since the old colours derived from vegetable dyes are not exactly reproduced by the modern products, and the peculiar coloration of a valuable carpet seems to depend upon a blending obtainable only from vegetable colours. Hence the use of aniline dyes has been prohibited in Iran since 1900, but the effect has been to raise the cost of Persian carpets in the world markets, because other types of carpet can employ aniline colours to much greater effect, and at a cheaper price.

Wool is the chief material used, but cotton is often employed as a foundation or 'warp', because it allows finer work. Silk is sometimes used also. The finest (i.e. closest) work can be done on a cotton or silk warp, and up to 300 knots per square inch can be achieved with woollen tufts, and 400 with pure silk tufts. When woollen warp is used, the carpet is heavier, and of a deeper pile, though less fine. It is possible from pattern and colour to distinguish Persian carpets according to their region of origin. As compared with Turkish and Caucasian products, Persian carpets have a more flowing, curvilinear design, and employ brighter and more varied colours – Turkish carpets in particular show a strong influence of geometric patterns based on straight lines, and colouring is cruder and simpler.

Each district of Persia has its own distinctive designs and colours – e.g. Tabriz specimens employ pastel tints, whilst Sultanabad carpets are more vivid; and the lighter, finer rugs, made on cotton or silk warps, come from Kirman, Tabriz, and Teheran. Heavier carpets in wool are associated with the uplands of the Zagros – Shiraz, Hamadan, and Khurrumabad. Kirman and Tabriz are leading centres for carpet-making; and individual carpets are often made by a 'team' of one adult (man or woman) with one or two children, who may be as young as six or seven years. Other producing towns, besides those already mentioned, are Bijar, Senna (Sanandaj), and Kashan. The finished carpets are sold chiefly in America, to wealthier Middle Easterners, and to Germany and France, where demand has distinctly increased over the last ten years. Nomad and village families also often make carpets for sale as a 'home' craft.

Food Processing. This employs the majority of workers described as 'industrial', and is hence an index of the low industrial level of the Persian state. Ten state-owned sugar refineries have been built, three at Teheran, and the remainder in the north-west provinces. Flour milling is carried on in many places, with the larger mills again in the north-west where the bulk of the cereals are grown. Teheran has most of the remaining factories, which carry out food canning, distillation of spirits (arak) and industrial alcohol, soap-boiling, and the processing of tobacco. The remaining industries of Iran comprise the manufacture of bricks and ceramics, chemicals, glass, paper, and light consumer goods, with developing iron and steel working. Production by modern methods is mainly restricted to Teheran, where an industrial quarter, dominated by several score tall factory chimneys, has grown up over the past 10 years. Sulphuric acid, arsenic insecticides, and caustic soda are produced from local materials, using Elburz coal, and now gas and petroleum. For long the state arsenal was the largest industrial plant at Teheran, but with the building 'boom' brick and cement making and light iron and steel products (from Samnan and Kirman ores) are now more important.

The Second Seven Year Development Plan (1955–62) envisages spending a total of £37 million on industrial expansion, with the aim of developing sugar refining, cement making, food processing, the provision of more electricity and the growth of light engineering – this last in order to reduce the country's almost complete dependence on imports of manufactured consumer goods. Some progress has been achieved, and it is apparent that the relative prosperity offered by developing industry is attracting rural populations to the towns. But even so, manufacturing activities remain on a relatively small scale even for the Middle East: over 80 per cent. of the population is rural, and the number of industrial workers does not much exceed 400,000.

VIII. PEOPLE

The first census of Persia was undertaken in 1956, and showed 18,945,000 people exclusive of nomads. Fig. 48 gives an extremely generalised picture of the position; but details are not possible, since even the areas of provinces are only approximately known. In order to relate the generalised distribution, as shown on the map, to actual

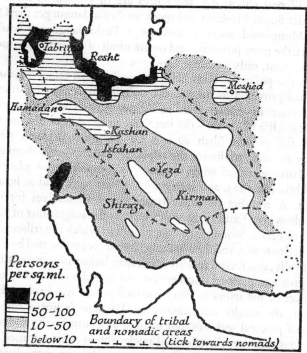

Fig. 48. Sketch of Population Distribution in Persia. Data very unreliable

conditions, it should also be borne in mind that except in the province of Gilan, where the population is evenly distributed over the whole area, extreme irregularity is the main characteristic. For the most part, people are closely crowded into the few fertile spots, with a wide extent of surrounding empty land.

An important feature of the Persian population is the extent of tribal groups. The chief tribal areas are shown on Fig. 48, from which it will be seen that, as might be expected, tribal life is closely related to nomadism. The tribe exists to undertake the complicated routine of seasonal migration from winter to summer pastures, and as natural resources are limited, the size of tribes is relatively small. The broken nature of the Zagros has prevented large-scale amalgamation of tribal units; hence intertribal warfare and raiding, with resulting internal disorder, have long been characteristic of the tribal areas. Disunity has been further emphasised in Persia by the varying racial and cultural affinities of the different tribes; e.g. the Kurds are of Armenoid racial stock, fairly strict Sunni Moslems and speak an Aryan language; the Qashqai are of Mongoloid ancestry and use a Turki language; whilst the Bakhtiari, the most powerful and outstanding of Persian tribesmen, are, to say the least, only nominal Moslems.

It was the policy of Riza Shah to break down tribal organisation, which had proved a menace to the stability of the Persian monarchy (the Bakhtiari have intervened at various periods with great effect in the political life of Persia – the last time, somewhat oddly, in 1953 to support the present Shah against Dr Moussadegh) and strenuous efforts were made to disarm the tribesmen, and to settle them as cultivators. Force was used when necessary: a campaign took place against the Bakhtiari in 1925, and many tribal chiefs were held as hostages at Teheran. A number of entire tribes found themselves forcibly resettled elsewhere,[1] and there was a ban on the migrations of Kurds in and out of Persia. Stone houses were built, in which the tribesmen were compelled to reside, and their grazing lands were confiscated by the Shah.

Politically, this forced re-settlement may have had some justification; the Zagros was pacified, local unrest and disorder came to an end, and the power of the tribes to sway national policy was broken. Socially, however, the results were disastrous. Hygiene is not a conspicuous feature of pastoral societies, but so long as a community moves regularly to another site, the effects of uncleanliness are minimised. When, however, a family is compelled to remain in one spot, disease soon develops, and large numbers of Persian tribesmen were wiped out by virulent epidemics. Equally seriously, pastoralism is the only possible way of life in many districts of Persia where rainfall is inadequate for crop-growing; and the attempt to introduce an occupation unsuited to geographical conditions was bound to fail. Persia was deprived of a number of useful commodities – milk, meat, wool, hides, and draught animals – whilst the pastoralists themselves, unaccustomed to a life as cultivators, and living in a difficult semi-arid region, were unable

---

[1] A traditional policy in the Middle East. Cf. Nebuchadnezzar and the Jews.

to feed themselves. Thus between the two evils of disease and lack of food, virtually whole tribes were decimated between 1920 and 1940, and the economy of the hill regions greatly disturbed.

Since the abdication of Riza Shah, a reaction has set in; and with the weaker authority of the present Persian government, tribal power is to some extent reviving. Pastoralism is again on the increase: certain grazing lands have been reclaimed, and the rule of the chiefs is somewhat stronger. Other influences, though slower and more indirect, may also prove to be of importance in modifying the traditional tribal organisation in western Persia. These are (i) the employment offered to tribesmen by the oil companies, whose activities mainly take place within tribal territory. A secure cash wage and regular employment is having great effect on the habits and even the physique of former nomads;[1] and (ii) conscription, both for the army, and for schools,[2] which has brought many young tribesmen into towns, and given them a taste for urban life.

IX. COMMUNICATIONS AND TOWNS

Persia has long been a centre of routeways linking east and west, but as a result of invasion and misrule in the later Middle Ages, and the change in space-relationships which diverted commerce from China and India to the sea, the road system of Iran decayed, and is at the present time an important contributing factor to the economic backwardness of the country. Despite a certain activity under Riza Shah, there are not much more than 10,000 miles of motorable roads and many are not passable at all seasons. The smallness of this total will be apparent when account is taken of the great size of the country – it is 800 miles from the Caspian to the head of the Persian Gulf, and 1,500 miles from Tabriz in the north-west to Zahidan in the extreme south-east.

Railway building, too, has been sporadic, and up to 1927 the only lines existing were a small extension from the Indian rail system (5′ 6″) across the south-east frontier to Zahidan, and a Russian-owned broad-gauge link from Tabriz to Julfa in the Soviet Union. In 1927, however, a trans-Persian railway was planned between Bandar Shah on the Caspian, to Teheran, and Bandar Shahpur on the Persian Gulf. Eleven

[1] This has been commented on by Twitchell in the case of the nomads of Saudi Arabia, who, markedly small in stature when living as pastoralists, seem to develop considerably when they enjoy cash wages as oilfield workers, and can afford to buy imported foods.

[2] As part of Riza Shah's policy of de-tribalisation, all tribes were compelled to send 10 per cent. of their children to the towns, where they were educated in special boarding schools, and hence lost some of their desire for a life of nomadism.

L

years later, the line was complete. Further lines from Teheran to Tabriz and Meshed were for long under consideration and equally long under construction. Both have very recently been completed, and an extension from Qum through Yezd to Kirman is almost finished. This will ultimately be joined to Zahidan. During 1941–5 operation of the Persian railways was taken over by the Russians and the British, the

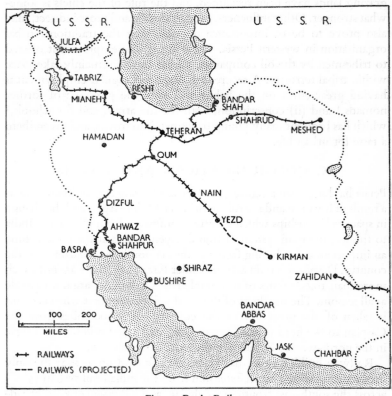

Fig. 49. Persia, Railways

latter being replaced by Americans. New lines were laid to connect the trans-Persian line to Khorramshahr and Basra, thus making Ahwaz a rail junction. All existing lines are single-track, with infrequent passing loops. Now, as part of CENTO plans for development, a through rail link from Turkey to Pakistan is planned, extending existing lines from Muş to Tatvan on the shores of Lake Van, and onwards to connect to the Persian system at Sharif Khaneh, west of Tabriz.

From Zahidan another link will run westwards to Bam, Kirman, and Yezd.

It has been said that railway operation in Persia is the most difficult in the world. Besides the irregular terrain, which results in very high constructional costs, water supplies are few, and the water, even when available, is at times quite unfit for use in boilers because of salinity. Cuttings and gorges on the routes become so hot and humid that traffic through them has to cease at certain times of the day, and heavy gradients necessitate a special sand car in front of the locomotive, since normal methods of sanding the track are ineffective. This explains some of the delay in developing subsidiary lines – but on the other hand there are strong strategic, political, and social motives (as well as purely economic considerations) that favour railway construction in Persia.

The current Iranian Development Plan envisages much trunk road improvement, e.g. a macadam surface on most of the highway between Teheran and Shiraz (now in process of realisation). As well, CENTO has plans for roads linking Teheran and Tabriz direct to central Turkey, and Pakistan to Yezd. Special attention is given to improving communications to Bandar Abbas, which is to be developed as a port for the south-east.

Towns. Despite their predominance in the life of the country, Persian towns are not large, and only four exceed 200,000 in population. The exceptional size and importance of Teheran (est. pop. 2,300,000) arises partly from its position on the Veramin plain – the largest of a number of tongues of fertile land that extend southwards from the flanks of the Elburz Range into the central desert – and partly from its command of routes. Owing to the presence of a 'dead heart' in Iran, the choice of a capital has not been easy – any town was bound to have an ex-central position, and relations with the rest of the country would be of necessity rather difficult. Teheran is, however, situated astride the important east–west route that follows the southern slopes of the Elburz, at a point where the route divides, one branch continuing west-north-westwards towards Azerbaijan and Asia Minor, the other turning south-westwards to the central Zagros, Baghdad, and the Persian Gulf. From Teheran northwards, three separate passes, from east to west the Gudar Guduk (7,000 feet), the Imamzadeh (9,000 feet), and the upper Chalus (11,000 feet), give access to the densely populated Caspian lowlands.

The supremacy of Teheran dates only from 1788, when it was chosen as capital. Previously, a number of other cities mainly in the south-west

had fulfilled the function of metropolis, and one can see in this shift of
influence the operation of several factors: firstly, the difficulty of finding an adequate central site for a capital; secondly, the enhanced

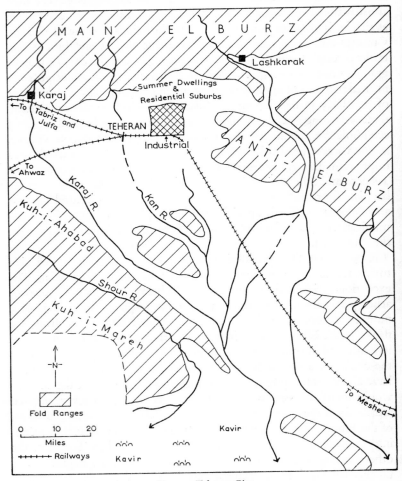

Fig. 50. Teheran City

economic importance of the northern provinces within the last two
centuries; and thirdly, the change in political influence as reflected in
the northward movement of the capital. Throughout earlier history,
Persian interests had centred on the west and south, and the ancient

capitals were near the Zagros region; but with the modern rise of Russia, the political centre of Persia has gravitated northwards.

As the result of extensive building by Riza Shah, Teheran has a modern air, and in addition to the occupations usually associated with a capital city – printing, administration, catering, etc. – the district has become the principal industrial centre of Persia, with light engineering (armaments and light consumer goods), chemicals, textile, tobacco, building, and food processing industries, amounting to about 30 per cent. of the entire modern plant in Persia. Important factors in the rise of Teheran have been the growth of road and rail communications during the last 30 years, and the development of nearby coal resources, with other minerals within moderately easy reach (copper from Anarak and Abbassabad; lead, antimony, nickel, and sulphur from Samnan).

Tabriz (pop. 590,000) is situated in the upper part of one of the largest valleys that drain into the Urmia basin, in a district where there are numerous small alluvial fans formed by erosion of soft lava. The soil is hence extremely fertile, and this, together with the presence of non-saline water, makes Tabriz a rich agricultural area. Moreover, the site of the city, close to the Turkish and Russian frontiers, gives it an importance as a centre of communications. There is considerable exchange of products between the farmers of the lowlands round Tabriz and the pastoralists of the more distant uplands; and a large market is one of the features of the city. Industries based on the agricultural and pastoral products of the two regions (tanning, fruit-drying, soap-boiling, distilling, and textile manufacturing) are carried on, partly by means of modern plant introduced by Riza Shah. Carpet-making is on an extensive scale, and there is also a certain amount of trade with Turkey and Russia, particularly through Ezerum.

As the largest town of the north-west, and a former capital of Persia, Tabriz is the chief city of Azerbaijan, and has played an important role in political affairs, mainly as the centre of Kurdish and Azerbaijani dissident movements against the central government. Russian influence is strong, and likely to increase. Political instability is also accompanied by physical disturbance – the city, lying on a tectonic fracture line, is liable to earthquakes, and few buildings are higher than a single storey.

Isfahan (pop. 680,000) lies on the eastern margins of the Zagros, in the centre of a lowland basin occupied by the Zaindeh Rud. Like Tabriz, the city lies in the middle course of a stream which lower down

terminates in a salt marsh. Abundance of water supplies, and a rich
alluvial soil, make Isfahan a very productive agricultural region, and
there is in addition the special function of serving as an outlet for the
animal products of the pastoral Bakhtiari country of the central Zagros.
With supplies of raw cotton, silk, and wool produced in the immediate
district, Isfahan has become the largest textile centre of Iran, and the
industry is carried on both in modern mills and as a bazaar craft.

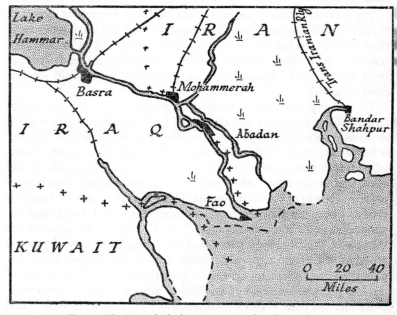

Fig. 51. The Port of Abadan. Frontiers and Railways shown

Clothing, carpets, and luxury brocade are the chief products, but there
is a considerable output of dried fruit, foodstuffs, and light metal-work.
The open nature of the country to the east, and a command of mountain passes leading westward through the Zagros to the Tigris lowlands,
makes the city another important route centre of Persia. Again like
Tabriz, Isfahan is one of the ancient capitals of Persia. A special feature
is the famous Maidan, an enormous open square, in which the game of
polo is said to have originated – an indication of the importance of
horse-breeding in the district. Tourism is also a thriving industry due
to its collection of mosques and ancient buildings, unrivalled in Iran.

Meshed (pop. 550,000) is the chief town of the north-east and functions as a market centre for the productive agricultural regions of Khorassan, with some importance as a route centre into Central Asia. As well, there is much pilgrimage to the local Shi'a shrines – from Afghanistan and Central Asia as well as Iran. Textile and carpet manufacturing are carried on, and there is an extensive bazaar trade, with samovars more in evidence than elsewhere in Iran. Turquoise is a local product. Meshed has a reputation for clericalism and conservatism amounting at times to fanaticism, and has in the past been a centre of opposition to the Teheran government.

The remaining Persian towns fulfil on a smaller scale the functions of route-centre, local market, and manufacturing site. Conveniently placed for centralising the economic activity of a small district, they facilitate exchange of agricultural and pastoral produce, and have small-scale manufacturing trades based on locally produced raw materials. Some degree of specialisation exists: carpet-making at Kirman, metal-working at Kashan, fruit-drying at Kazvin, sugar and oil refining on a limited scale at Kermanshah, metal-work and the export of fresh grapes from Shiraz, and the production of oil seeds and henna from Yezd. Resht has jute, tea, silk, and flour mills, and handles most of the trade between Caspian Iran and Russia. The chief commodities of this trade are caviar, isinglass, salt fish, and tea.

One other function of certain Persian towns is that of receiving pilgrims and theological students (usually Shi'a Moslems). About one-sixth of the population of Qum is directly dependent on this traffic, whilst Meshed is another famous centre of Shi'a pilgrimage, with a famous Moslem seminary.

Ports. Only one port in Persia is of large size. This is Abadan (pop. 257,000), built and developed entirely by the A.I.O.C. since 1910, and now the largest oil port in the world. The docks can handle ships up to 20 or 30 feet in draught, the limiting factor being the depth of water in the Shatt el Arab. The town has been laid out on Western lines, and is growing rapidly in size, a feature which, in view of the great potentialities of Persian oilfields, is likely to continue. One drawback is the land communications of the port, which is rather isolated by the presence of braided river channels, and so far, there is no rail communication with the interior. Apart from oil and stores for the refinery, Abadan handles no general traffic, so that the principal outlet for Persian commodities is at Khorramshahr, better known as Mohammerah, which lies at the confluence of the Shatt el Arab and the Karun river, some 11 miles above Abadan. A small quantity of oil is also normally handled. The small size of the port (population is under 50,000) is an indication of the restricted overseas trade from Persia, and greatest activity was during 1941–5, when harbour works were undertaken and Khorramshahr became an important base for the supplying of Russia.

The remaining ports of the country are small, ill-equipped, and often mere roadsteads without shelter for ships. Cargo must usually be trans-shipped into lighters, and this is the case at Bushire, on the Persian Gulf. Enzeli (recently re-named Pahlevi) is the chief Persian port of the Caspian, with some fishing trade as well. Bandar Shah, chosen by Riza Shah as the northern terminus of the Trans-Persian railway, was extremely badly sited, and has been greatly affected by the shrinkage of the Caspian. Within one year of the opening of the railway, the harbour was silted up, and although there was a temporary re-opening by the Russians during 1942–5, the port is now abandoned.

Ahwaz is a trans-shipment point on the Karun, Persia's only navigable river. A stretch of rapids above the town makes further ascent impossible, and the importance of Ahwaz has greatly increased since the opening up of south-west Persia and Khuzistan by oil interests.

Bandar Shahpur, the southern terminus of the Trans-Persian railway, has not developed as was originally hoped, and is unimportant.

A recent development of the last few years has been an interest in Bandar Abbas as a possible outlet for the south-east of Persia, and even for west Pakistan. Until now, this region has remained isolated and little developed; but the extension of the oilfields partly towards the south-east, the space-relations of the site (giving tidewater access closer in to the centre of Iran) and general strategic considerations have provoked attention to development possibilities (1962). In some respects Bandar Abbas might provide a more direct route from the Indian Ocean to the Caspian.

CHAPTER XIV

Asia Minor

I. PHYSICAL

Like Iran, Asia Minor consists essentially of an inner plateau ringed by
mountain ranges that for the greater part fall away steeply on their
outer margins, either to the sea, or to lowland areas. Only in the extreme east of Asia Minor are the mountain ranges continued without

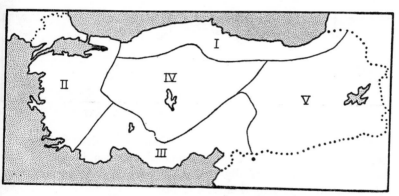

Fig. 52. Natural Regions of Asia Minor

break; and there the confused highland topography of eastern Anatolia merges on the north-east into the Caucasus, and on the south-east
into the Zagros. Within Asia Minor, geographical sub-regions can be
distinguished as follows:

- (I) The Black Sea coastlands, extending from the Caucasus of
  Russia as far west as the region of the Bosphorus.
- (II) The Aegean coastlands, with which may be grouped the region
  of the Straits, and European Turkey.
- (III) The Mediterranean coastlands.
- (IV) The Central Plateau.
- (V) The Eastern Highlands.

The Black Sea Coastlands. Present features have come into existence as the result of the foundering of the Black Sea region in Pliocene times. An extensive series of east–west trending fracture lines was developed on the northern side of the main plateau of Asia Minor; and differential movement along these fracture lines, with downthrow mainly towards the north, has produced the present abrupt and harbourless coastline. Fracturing did not, however, take place in a simple pattern: faults are arranged in arcs rather than in a single straight line, so that between Eregli (Heraclea) and Sinop there is a northward bulge of the coastline which is sharply defined by a small number of bold fracture lines; whilst further east, between Sinop and Samsun, smaller interlocking faults have given rise to an embayment with a somewhat more irregular and indented coast. In the extreme east, beyond Samsun, there is a return to a simpler pattern of a few large faults comparable with those

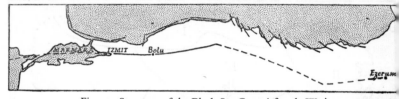

Fig. 53. Structure of the Black Sea Coast (after de Wet)

in the west; but extensive lava flows along the fault-lines have obscured the fault-planes, and again produced a broken, irregular coastline that contrasts markedly with conditions in the extreme west, although fundamentally there is a similarity in origin (Fig. 53).

The steep and rocky coast of the western Black Sea region, which is only occasionally broken down into bays and estuaries by the erosive action of rivers, is succeeded inland by an irregular line of highlands that rise to 6,000 to 7,000 feet within 15 or 20 miles from the sea. For the most part there is hardly any intervening coastal plain, a feature which is characteristic of the entire northern coast of Asia Minor. Eastwards of Sinop, mountains front the coast on an even more imposing scale. Behind Trabzon (Trebizond) and Rize the maximum heights attained are 10,000 to 12,000 feet, and the ranges are distinguished by special names. At Trabzon the coastal ranges are known as the Çakirgol Dagh, and further east, near the Caucasus, as the Tatus Dagh. The entire coastal uplands are really a series of horst blocks, some relatively undisturbed, others tilted; and the higher elevation of summits in the east is due to outpouring of lava, giving a series of volcanic cones superimposed upon the general plateau level.

Further inland still, towards the south, the coastal ranges give way to a series of lowland troughs that are defined once again by east–west running tectonic lines. Cross-faulting on a minor scale has also occurred, so that the inland lowland region cannot be said to consist of a single rift valley but is better regarded structurally as an irregular series of downthrow basins sometimes opening one from another, sometimes separated by low divides. Later erosion by rivers has reduced the height of these divides, so that an interior lowland valley system, broad and open in the west, but increasingly narrow in the east, is now a feature of the Black Sea coastal region, and can be traced from the Gulf of Izmit in the north-east of the Sea of Marmara as far as the Russian frontier.

The rivers of the Black Sea coastlands consist chiefly of short torrents cascading from the coastal ranges towards the sea. Here and there, however, valleys have been cut back far enough to reach the inner lowland trough, where an east–west (longitudinal) drainage pattern has developed. The larger rivers, therefore, consist of two distinct portions, a long upper reach, with a generally east–west trend, and a shorter lower stretch aligned from south to north, in which the river breaks through intervening ridges – often by a gorge or rapids to reach the Black Sea. Examples of such rivers are the Çoruh, Celkit, Kizil Irmak, and Yenice.

The steep and rocky nature of the coast, absence of harbours, and difficulties in the way of penetrating inland, have all restricted human activities in this region. On the west, the absence of harbours is particularly noticeable; further east, where the coastline is more indented, the mountain barrier is higher. Another disadvantage is that because of the cascades and gorges on the lower courses of the rivers, very few river valleys provide easy routes inland – it is significant that none of the rivers mentioned in the previous paragraph have any settlement at their mouth, and all important towns stand away from the larger streams. Instead, the inner lowland region has come to serve as a line of communications, which, therefore, tends to run from west to east from the Aegean region, rather than southwards from the Black Sea coast itself. In the western half of the trough access from one lowland basin to another is relatively easy, and rail and road construction have been facilitated. A considerable handicap throughout the whole region is, however, a liability to devastating earthquakes, since earth movement

along tectonic lines has not yet ceased. Generally speaking, therefore, the Black Sea coastlands are not thickly populated, and development is confined to a small number of districts where there is either a
special geographical advantage – e.g. the presence of coal at Eregli
and Zonguldak – or where access with the interior is facilitated, as at
Trabzon.

The Aegean Coastlands. There is no distinctive break between the Black
Sea coastlands just described, and the Aegean region. The great fault-
lines that define the coast of the eastern Black Sea continue without
interruption as far as southern Bulgaria, and the foundered trough
zone of the interior can be traced from the lake-studded lowlands at
the head of the Gulf of Izmit into the Gulf itself, and finally into the
northern basin of the Sea of Marmara. Thus east–west trending tectonic lines are again outstanding in the Aegean area, not merely in the
extreme north near the Black Sea, but also as far south as the island of
Rhodes. The broad valleys of the Gediz and Büyük Menderes are
east–west running rifts enlarged by later erosion.

Besides the existence of east–west fracture lines, two other features
must be noted. These are (*a*) extensive cross-faulting with a north–
south trend, and (*b*) foundering of the central portion of the Aegean,
with consequent invasion by the sea. Occurrence of cross-faulting and
foundering in the Dardanelles and Bosphorus justifies the inclusion of
the Straits district in the Aegean sub-region, rather than in the Black
Sea coastal zone, to which it might at first sight seem more properly
to belong. Cross-faulting and later drowning has led to the development of a highly intricate, broken coastline, with many irregularly
shaped islands and long, twisting estuaries. The islands are small horsts
standing above the sea floor; and on the mainland of Asia Minor the
same conditions are repeated, with irregular upland horsts serving to
separate broad and shallow rift valleys.

Involved cross-faulting with later erosion and drowning have been
responsible for the formation of the Bosphorus and Dardanelles. In
the extreme north along the Black Sea, an extensive mass of resistant
granite and gneiss has been fractured by the east–west trending faults,
leaving a narrow neck of upland joining Europe and Asia, with the
Black Sea to the north, and the Sea of Marmara to the south.[1] This
neck, or long narrow horst, broadens out westwards to form the

---

[1] The scale of this fault system can be gauged from the extent of downthrow in the
Sea of Marmara, which reaches 4,000 feet in depth, with parts of the nearby coastlands
1,500 feet above sea level. During 1934–41 the Istanbul region experienced 580 earth
tremors, 180 of which were strong.

Istranca highlands of European Turkey, and is tilted towards the south, so that there is a scarp-face towards the north, down which a number of small torrents fall steeply to the Black Sea. On the southern (Marmara) side there is a much gentler dip slope, and a more extensive drainage system has developed. In many instances lines of weakness due to small north-north-east–south-south-west trending faults have been eroded into narrow valleys, and a number of small synclines have also been occupied. Thus erosion along one such north-north-east running fault gradually pushed back the head of a small stream flowing to the Sea of Marmara, until the highland ridge was cut through, and a channel opened between the Black Sea and the Sea of Marmara. A tributary of this stream that flowed partly in a synclinal valley also entered the Bosphorus on the western side; and subsequent drowning of this tributary has given rise to the Golden Horn (see Fig. 61). The Bosphorus is 16 miles in length, and on average 1 mile wide; but it narrows in places to less than 700 yards. Both banks, Asiatic and European, rise steeply from the water, and form a succession of cliffs, coves, and landlocked bays. Most of the shores are densely wooded, and are occupied by numerous towns and villages.

The Dardanelles Strait has been formed in a similar manner – by erosion along fracture lines, and later drowning; but the rock series of this latter region are much softer, being composed of limestones and sandstones, hence erosion has been much more extensive, and land forms are gentler. The Dardanelles is 25 miles long, and increases in width towards the south, from 2½ miles at the northern extremity to 4½ miles in the south. Another contrast is in vegetation – the shores of the Dardanelles are only sparsely covered by trees, the chief vegetation type being a low garrigue. Again unlike the Bosphorus, the Dardanelles has few settlements of any kind along its shores; the whole region being generally empty and desolate, and given over to rough grazing. Because of intense evaporation in the eastern Mediterranean, together with considerable supplies of river water in the Black Sea, there is a continuous flow of markedly cold water southwards from the Black Sea, producing a strong current in the Bosphorus and Dardanelles. This current averages 3 m.p.h. at Istanbul, and 1½ to 2 m.p.h. in the Dardanelles.

Further south, the immediate hinterland of the Aegean Sea is made up of a complex of east–west trending fault valleys, broken at frequent intervals by rather less strongly developed north–south running fractures. This development has imposed a markedly rectangular pattern of detached horsts and somewhat fjord-like valleys. An excellent example is the valley of the Büyük Menderes, with its numerous sharp elbows and tributary valleys set at right angles to the main stream.

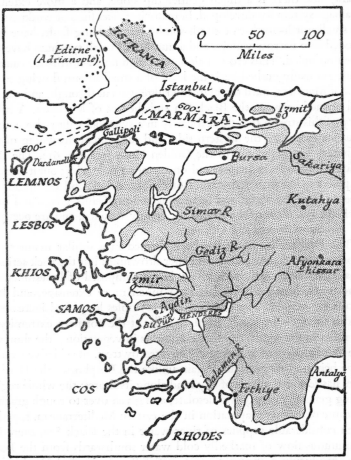

Fig. 54. The Straits and Aegean Coastlands. Mainland above 600 ft. stippled

Other similar, but less extensive valleys are (from north to south) the Sakariya, which runs mainly in a north–south trending rift, and hence reaches the Black Sea, though passing within a short distance of the Gulf of Izmit; the Simav, which enters the Sea of Marmara; and the Gediz and Dalaman, both of which reach the Aegean. Generally speaking, all valleys are broad, flat-bottomed, and with relatively steep sides. The floors are covered by rich alluvium deposited in great quantities in the lower reaches, and, as a result, an extensive flood-plain has been built up, upon which the river develops a classic 'meander' pattern. To find well-developed meanders in a region of broken plateaus and highland massifs may seem unusual, until it is remembered that the lower valleys of most rivers have been formed entirely by tectonic action, and not by fluvial erosion. Large quantities of silt are carried down towards the coast, and the lower ends of the valleys are being steadily filled up, so that the mouths of the rivers are advancing westwards towards the Aegean Sea. The Büyük Menderes mouth is now, for example, some 25 miles further west than it was in Roman times.

When drained and cultivated, the valleys are extremely productive, and the Aegean coastlands are the most prosperous and advanced part of Turkey. One disadvantage is, however, liability to malaria. A number of larger valleys are also important as routeways to the interior of Asia Minor, since they rise gently inland, and form corridors leading directly to the inner plateau region. In some cases, though (e.g. the Simav and Dalaman), the valleys end abruptly at a cross-fault, being hence shut in by mountain massifs, and useless for communications.

The Mediterranean Coastlands. Here there is a sharp contrast with the last region described, since fold ranges, not rift valleys and horst blocks, are the chief structural feature. Along the southern edge of the Anatolian plateau, a series of folded arcs has been developed; but because of the complexity of the inner plateau region, around which the arcs have been folded, the fold structures themselves are highly irregular, with sudden changes in trend. Structural features consist in some parts of parallel ranks of folds, in others of single anticlines, and again in others of overthrusts and nappes.

This westernmost arc can be traced from the district of Fethiye north-eastwards towards Afyonkarahissar, then south-eastwards towards Silifke. This series of folds, known as the Western Taurus, is not disposed entirely symmetrically, since the western limb of the arc is shorter and more irregular than the eastern limb. In the north, the Western Taurus folds are closely packed against the plateau of Anatolia; and because of recent formation, rivers occupying synclinal valleys have not always been sufficiently long in existence to have cut valleys leading outwards to the sea. Numerous lakes – most of which are saline – are therefore characteristic of the northern part of the

Western Taurus; and a second feature is the completeness of the mountain wall, which acts as a barrier to movement. Roads are few; no rail communication exists with the rest of Turkey, and the whole of the region is in marked isolation from its neighbours.

To the south, fronting the Mediterranean, small streams reach the sea, and have built up a lowland plain that is spoken of as the Plain of Antalya. Here the soil is fertile, although marshy in some places; but the prevalence of malaria and difficulties of communication with the remainder of Turkey have greatly hindered development. The coast is straight and shelving because of the rapidity of deposition of sediment from the rivers; and harbours are thus poor and infrequent. As a

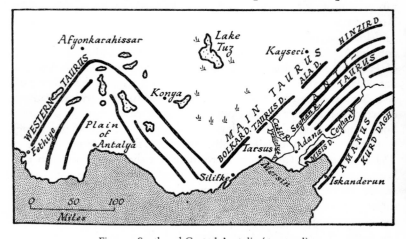

Fig. 55. South and Central Anatolia (structural)

result, the Antalya plain is sparsely populated, despite good soil and a favourable climate.

East of Silifke, the Western Taurus gives way to a second arc, with an abrupt change of trend. This second fold range, the main Taurus, runs north-eastwards from Silifke as a single narrow fold as far as Hinzir (between Kayseri and Sivas), and has been cut into four separate massifs by river action. From south-west to north-east these massifs are: the Bolkar Dagh, the Taurus Dagh (hence the general name Taurus), the Ala Dagh, and the Hinzir Dagh, the last massif being a smaller range detached from the main chain, and lying at some distance to the north-east (Fig. 55).

Though distinctly narrower than the Western Taurus, the main

Taurus is much higher, reaching 12,000 feet in the Ala Dagh region. Owing, however, to its restricted width, erosion has been more active, and, as we have seen, a number of narrow and precipitous river valleys have been cut right through the entire chain at certain points. These gorges offer practicable routes through the mountain barrier, and one such defile, that of the Yeziloluk, a tributary of the Tarsus river, forms the well-known Cilician Gates – a relatively easy, but rather indirect route between central Anatolia and the Mediterranean coast: another valley, that of the Çakit river, offers a more direct but steeper passage, and is now used by the railway from Ankara to Aleppo.

East and south-east of the Ala and Hinzir Dagh, a further series of fold ranges runs parallel to the main Taurus system. These are known in a general way as the Anti-Taurus Range, but the name is loosely applied, and two smaller ranges, structurally an undoubted part of the Anti-Taurus, and of a similar trend, are separately distinguished as the Amanus Range and the Kurd Dagh. The latter can be termed the last member of the Anatolian mountain system: further to the east and south-east the land drops to form the low plateau and plain of northern Syria; whilst to the south-west the Amanus and Kurd Dagh can be traced respectively into the Karpass and Troödos ranges of Cyprus.

Little can be said of the Anti-Taurus region, since some parts of it are unexplored, and the northern portion is largely buried under sheets of lava. Between the upfolds lie valleys, sometimes mere gorges, but at times, especially towards the east, broader alluvium-covered lowlands that support a relatively dense population. Chief of these lowland areas are the Elbistan plain, and the upper Ceyhan valley centring on the town of Maras. Five main ranges can be discerned within the Anti-Taurus system, four of which die away 40 miles to the north-east of Adana and give rise to a lowland basin, the Seyhan–Ceyhan plain. The fifth range continues further to the south-west as the Misis Dagh, and forms the western side of the Gulf of Iskanderun. The Gulf lies between two fold ranges, the Amanus and the Misis Dagh, and owes its continued existence as a deep-water gulf to the absence of any large river entering it from the north-east. A short distance to the west, what would appear to have been a similar gulf between fold ridges has been filled up by silt brought down by the Seyhan river, and now forms a plain, with a low-lying, lagoon type of coastline.

The Seyhan plain is in many respects similar to the Antalya plain of the western Mediterranean coastlands: there are the same features of low relief, a rich alluvial soil, a straight shelving coastline, and considerable prevalence of malarial infestation. The Seyhan plain is, however, much less isolated by its surrounding mountain chains, as a number of cols give access to central Anatolia, eastern Asia Minor, and north-western Syria. Hence the Seyhan region carries a markedly denser population than its western counterpart, particularly in the slightly higher parts where drainage is easier; and certain districts are now in process of development as important crop-growing centres.

The Central Plateau. This region consists essentially of an extensive and irregular plateau ringed on all sides by higher mountain ranges. In the north, east, and south the mountain ring is well defined, being 2,000 to 4,000 feet higher than the plateau it surrounds; but on the west, towards the Aegean coastlands, the hills are fewer, and less imposing. The plateau itself consists of a rolling upland diversified by numerous sunken basins, or *ova*, that are occupied by marshes and mud flats; and also by small highland massifs that consist either of volcanic cones or horst blocks. The floors of the *ova* stand at about 3,000 feet above sea level, that of the largest *ova* (Lake Tuz) being 3,200 feet in altitude. The general level of the plateau surface may be taken as between 3,000 to 5,000 feet, whilst the upland masses reach 6,000 to 8,000 feet above sea level. Because of its *ova* morphology, Lake Tuz is shallow, and varies enormously in area according to recent rainfall – from little more than a salt-marsh to many hundreds of square miles in extent.

Towards the east, the plateau is about 1,000 feet higher, and in contrast to the confused structures of the western plateau, uplands tend to occur more often in the form of definite ridges with a well-marked trend. Volcanic cones on a large scale are also a feature, some reaching 10,000 or 12,000 feet in height.

At one time the entire plateau region of Anatolia probably consisted of a series of small basins of inland drainage, with no outlet to the sea, i.e. conditions closely approximated to those of present-day Iran. Differential earth movements – downthrow on the northern (Black Sea) side, and uplift on the southern (Taurus) side – seem, however, to have increased the erosive power of streams on the northern flanks of the plateau, so that these have cut back through the mountain ring, and now drain wide areas of the plateau itself. The basins of the Sakariya, Kizil Irmak, and Yesil Irmak cover more than half the plateau, leaving only the south-west as a region of aretic drainage. The rivers themselves are often deeply entrenched below the level of the plateau; and their valleys, consisting in places of a series of captured *ovas* linked by gorges, are irregular and discontinuous. The whole surface of the northern plateau is deeply eroded, with, in many districts, precipitous valley walls, and sheer, rugged hillsides.

The enclosed basins of the south-west are disposed in a rough crescent between Afyonkarahissar (west), Konya (south), and Kayseri (east). In the absence of drainage, there are no deep valleys, and the whole region is open and undulating, a feature which has favoured the growth of road and rail communications. It will be recalled that Konya was the starting point of the old Baghdad Railway.

Because of its enclosed nature, much of the central plateau of Asia Minor is arid, and supports little plant or animal life. Wooded areas are confined to the extreme north-west and north-east; and cultivation is restricted to the neighbourhood of rivers, in parts where the valleys are sufficiently wide to allow terracing, or where an *ova* structure provides a stretch of level ground. For the greater part, the central plateau is bare and monotonous country given over to grazing.

Eastern Turkey. There is little physical unity in eastern Turkey, since the region consists of a series of mountain ranges, extensive and continuous in the north, but falling away on the south first into a broken plateau country, and finally into an undulating plain which continues through north Syria and Iraq. Further disunity arises from the presence of several large river-basins – those of the Aras (Araxes), Euphrates, and Tigris; from the existence of a number of downthrow basins (*ova*), some with outward, some with aretic drainage; and from the occurrence of vast outpourings of recent lava, which have buried whole valleys, and created a wide expanse of fairly level but inhospitable plateau. One such eruption from the cone of Nemrut has blocked a river valley and impounded the water to form Lake Van.

The mountain ranges have a confused trend. On the north, the folds bordering the Black Sea coast run at first in an east–west direction, but later, as in the Gavur Dagh near Ezerum, the trend alters to south-west–north-east, turning once again to the original direction on approach to the Caucasus system. Further south, in the region of Erzincan–El Aziz, the line of the Anti-Taurus is continued by a series of folds that later swing round in a great arc towards the south-east, where they form first the Kurdish Taurus (south-west of Lake Van), and finally merge with the Zagros Range. In the hollow part of the arc lies an expanse of plateau country (region of Diyarbekir, Mardin, and Urfa) which can be regarded as the northernmost extension of the Syrian steppe.

The northern and eastern parts of eastern Turkey form the ancient country of Armenia. Here, because of the extremely recent volcanic outpourings, soil cover is often very thin or entirely absent. The rivers have cut immense gorges in the soft lava, and often lie several thousand feet below the level of the surrounding plateau. Their upper reaches are too narrow for settlement; but lower down expanses of alluvium have been deposited, and these, when cultivated, are extremely fertile. The region of Lake Van once supported a moderately dense population, though because of the brackish nature of the lake water, cultivation was

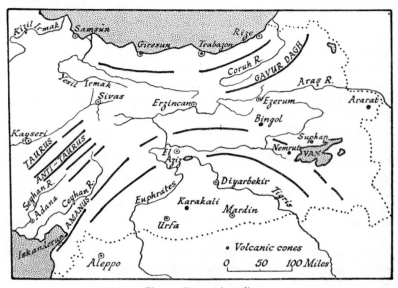

Fig. 56. Eastern Anatolia

limited to the middle levels of the lake basin, as is the case round Lake Urmia.[1]

Because of their altitude (7,000 feet) and barren surface, the lava uplands are for the most part uninhabited. Here and there immense volcanic cones rise several thousand feet higher (the largest, Ararat, reaches 17,000 feet above sea level), and the heavier rainfall near such peaks allows a scanty Alpine flora that provides seasonal grazing for Kurdish shepherds. The population was greatly depleted by the massacres of 1916–18, and at the present time the Turkish government is attempting to settle immigrants from the west in the empty valleys of Armenia.

[1] The waters of Lake Van are less saline than those of Lake Urmia, but contain a high proportion of sodium carbonate.

Further south, round Diyarbekir and Urfa, topography is much less rugged, though the rivers are deeply slotted into the plateau surface, and the extent of cultivable land is greatly restricted. Certain districts, where water can be more easily raised to the fields, support a number of agricultural communities, but in large measure pastoralism is the predominant way of life. Lower elevation, though facilitating movement, condemns the southern part of eastern Turkey to semi-aridity.

II. CLIMATE

General. The climate of Turkey, like that of Persia, is one of extremes. Parts of the western coastlands never experience frost, yet in Armenia snow lies even in the valleys for a third of the year; and in respect of rainfall much of the entire country has a deficient water supply, whilst the north-east has an excess. Season of onset of rainfall also varies, from winter in the south and west, spring in the central plateau, summer in the northern coastlands, and autumn in the extreme north-east. The reasons for such contrasts are to be found in (*a*) relief, (*b*) the position of Asia Minor on the margin of the 'Mediterranean' and interior Asiatic climatic zones, and (*c*) the extent of sea, which has a modifying influence on the western part of the country. It should be noted that the Anatolian plateau is considerably higher on average than the interior of Iran, although the surrounding mountain chains are less developed. This gives rise to lower winter temperatures, and hence to the frequent occurrence of a separate and distinctive high-pressure system over Asia Minor during the months between November and April. The effect is to divert rain-bearing depressions as they move along the eastern Mediterranean either to the north or the south of Asia Minor, so that relatively few can penetrate into the interior of the plateau. It is thus possible to appreciate why a winter maximum of rainfall is by no means universal in Turkey.

During the summer and autumn, on the other hand, the north of Asia Minor lies in the outer margins of the current of monsoonal air that moves westwards from India and Iran in a circuitous passage round the Cyprus low-pressure area. Intermixture with an easterly moving air stream from western Europe (the 'westerly' circulation) can thus easily give rise to the development of cyclonic rain in the Black Sea regions; and the effects of such mixing are enhanced by the contrasts of relief along the northern coast of Turkey.

As in Persia, the high encircling ranges receive a disproportionate share of precipitation, and the interior lies in a rain shadow area. Aridity is, however, much less complete than in Iran, since the eastern portion of the plateau stands at an elevation of 5,000 to 7,000 feet, and so receives more rain than the lower-lying interior basins of western Anatolia.

It is convenient to discuss the climate of Asia Minor on a basis of the natural regions already distinguished. In the *Black Sea Coastlands* winters are mild, summers moderately hot, and little difference is apparent between east and west. Rize, on the extreme east, shows an average January temperature of 43° F., Samsun one of 44° F., and Trabzon one of 45° F. Highest temperatures occur in August, and corresponding means are Rize 71° F., Samsun 68° F., Trabzon 74° F. Inland, the moderating influence of the sea is much less felt – Merzifon, a short distance south of Samsun, in the interior lowland trough, has a January mean of 30° F., and a July mean of 68° F. A special feature of the eastern Black Sea coastlands is the prevalence of Föhn winds in winter. These occur when heavy stagnant air from the plateau moves towards the coastlands. As much as 30° to 40° F. of warming may take place during the 7,000 to 10,000 feet of descent from the interior, hence, although the air may be initially below freezing-point, temperatures of 60° F. or even 85° F. may be attained at sea level. Thus instead of a beneficent wind that tempers the rigours of winter, an unduly warm blast may actually wither growing vegetation, and is responsible for the barren condition of many of the foothills of the region, which would normally be thickly forested. It is significant that at Rize and Samsun, temperatures of 70° F. have been recorded in January and February, and over 80° F. in March.

Rainfall is almost everywhere abundant in the Black Sea coastlands, and ranges from 25 inches in the west to over 100 inches in the east. At Izmit (extreme west) February is the wettest, and August the driest month, though no month is without rainfall. Rize (annual rainfall 96 inches), with a maximum in November, and a minimum in late spring, has a rainfall that is well distributed throughout the year.

The Aegean Coastlands. Temperature conditions in this region have some similarity to those of the Black Sea region, though local variation is somewhat more prominent, and there is a marked rise in temperature towards the south. In winter there is a January minimum of 41° to 46° F. on the coast, and 35° to 40° F. inland; whilst in summer, July and August show little difference in temperature, each having figures that range from 74° F. at Istanbul to 81° F. at Izmir. Despite the presence of the sea, diurnal variation of temperature is very pronounced during the summer months, and much more prominent than in the Black Sea region: day temperatures frequently exceed 90° F. during July (and also in the south during August), with correspondingly cooler nights – indications that the Aegean comes more definitely within the Mediterranean regime. Even Istanbul has a mean July maximum of 91° F.

Rainfall is fairly evenly distributed over the entire Aegean coastlands, with amounts ranging from 20 to 30 inches per annum near the coast, and 15 to 20 inches in the extreme east, on the borders of western Anatolia. December is everywhere the wettest month, and it may be noted that although many areas have a fall of under 1 inch during each of the three months, June, July, and August, there are few instances of an entire absence of rain during the summer. One feature of the west is the steady northerly winds (termed Etesians, or Meltemi) which blow throughout the summer, and, except in the sheltered lowlands, temper the heat of the day. In the deeper valleys, which are often shut in by hilly massifs, moisture can be brought in by sea breezes, and humidity is high – too high, often, for comfort and sustained human activity.

The Mediterranean Coastlands have slightly hotter summers than the Aegean region (mean 83° F., mean daily max. 91° to 95° F.), with August usually the warmest month on the coast, and July further inland. This clearer difference between July and August temperatures as compared with conditions in the Aegean may arise as the result of the straighter coastline – maritime influences are restricted to a narrower coastal belt, and are not carried inland by long estuaries or broken fretted shorelines. Winters are considerably warmer, at least, on the coastal lowlands, January temperatures ranging from 48° F. at Adana to 52° F. at Iskanderun. Rainfall is moderate in amount, but considerable local variation occurs, depending on aspect and altitude. In general, the south-facing ranges of the Taurus systems receive more than 30 inches per annum, whilst the seaward-facing plains at the foot of the mountains receive between 20 and 30 inches, though in a few districts that are especially open to the sea (e.g. Antalya and Fethiye), rainfall is slightly above 30 inches.

December or January are the wettest months; July and August the driest. In summer a very slight rainfall is recorded, usually less than half an inch in the two months together, but towards the east, in the regions of the Seyhan plain and the Hatay, the total fall is higher.[1] Summers are therefore not entirely arid, like those of the Syrian, Lebanese, and Israeli coasts.

Humidity is again high during summer, and maxima for the year tend to occur during June, July, or August – a feature common to the eastern Mediterranean and Red Seas. Iskanderun, with a relative humidity of 59 per cent. in January, and of 74 per cent. in August, is a typical example, though it should be remembered that the Hatay and adjacent Seyhan lowlands, ringed by mountain chains and open to the prevailing south-west winds, are a little damper than the Antalya region further west.

The Central Plateau is characterised by a wider range of temperature and by greater aridity. Winters are cold – January temperatures averaging 30° F. over most of the plateau; and all districts have more than 100 days of frost during each year (cf. Izmir 13, Adana 16). Summers are warm, with high day temperatures and cool nights, though the mean for July (the hottest month), as the result of distinctly colder nights, lies between 68° and 73° F. At Ankara and Konya, day temperatures during July rise to 86° F., but fall at night to 54° F. Diurnal variation is also pronounced in winter, day maxima in January averaging 38° F., and night minima 17° to 22° F.

Between 10 and 17 inches of rainfall are received annually, the precise amount depending largely upon altitude. Konya and Ankara, at approximately similar elevation, have 11·5 and 10·0 inches respectively, whilst Sivas, situated 1,000 feet higher, has 17 inches. It is somewhat remarkable that May is in general the wettest month, and July and August, only a few weeks later, are the driest. This curious regime is probably due to the occurrence of a high-pressure system in winter – on its collapse in late spring rain-bearing winds can more easily penetrate into the interior. As is common in regions of deficient rainfall, irregularity of onset is a prominent feature, and most areas record whole months without any precipitation: at Ankara, for example, absolute drought can occur on seven out of the twelve months of the year.

Eastern Turkey is a region of great extremes, with a climate that is one of the most varied and severe in the world. Summers are hot and arid, particularly towards the south and east, where, as the steppes of Syria are approached, maximum temperatures exceed 100° F., and in the deep calm valleys figures of 110° to 120° F. are reached. Summer temperatures are a little lower in the north-east, but 90° F. during the

[1] Cf. the extent of cloudiness during July and August. Antalya 0·9 and 0·6 tenths of sky covered; Adana 1·0 and 1·80; Iskanderun 1·8 and 1·1.

day is common, although marked diurnal variation, with a cold night, brings the daily average to 65° to 70° F.[1]

Winters are cold, even in the extreme south, where Diyarbekir has a mean January temperature of 31° F. Further north, cold becomes intense; and Kars, in the extreme north-east of the region, has a *mean* January temperature of 9° F., with a night minimum of − 5° F. Absolute minima of less than − 30° F. have been recorded; and on the higher plateaus, figures of − 40° F. are not unknown. Thus it is not surprising that snow lies for over 120 days each year in the north-east but only for 7 to 10 days at Diyarbekir.

CLIMATIC DATA FOR REPRESENTATIVE STATIONS
ASIA MINOR (in ° F., and inches)

	J	F	M	A	M	J	J	A	S	O	N	D	Total
1. Black Sea													
Trabzon													
Temp.	45	44	47	51	61	68	73	74	69	64	55	49	
Rainfall	2·5	2·6	2·5	2·4	1·6	2·2	1·6	2·2	3·8	3·4	4·5	4·1	33·4
2. Aegean													
Izmir													
Temp.	46	47	53	59	68	76	81	80	73	66	57	50	
Rainfall	4·2	4·6	3·0	1·6	1·4	0·4	0·2	0·1	0·8	1·7	3·1	4·9	26·5
Rainy days	10	9	8	6	5	2	1	1	2	4	9	10	68
3. Mediterranean													
Adana													
Temp.	48	50	56	63	71	78	82	83	78	71	60	51	
Rainfall	3·2	3·2	2·6	1·9	2·0	0·9	0·3	0·3	0·6	1·3	3·0	4·5	23·8
Rainy days	6	8	7	5	5	3	1	1	1	4	6	8	53
4. Central Plateau													
Konya													
Temp.	30	34	42	52	60	68	74	74	65	56	45	35	
Rainfall	0·9	1·0	0·9	1·0	1·9	1·3	0·2	0	0·5	0·8	0·9	1·9	11·5
Rainy days	9	10	9	8	7	5	1	0	2	4	6	8	68
5. Eastern Turkey													
El Aziz													
Temp.	19	28	40	52	61	69	77	77	68	59	44	31	
Rainfall	1·4	2·1	2·0	2·4	2·7	0·9	0·1	0	0·3	1·3	2·3	1·9	17·4
Rainy days	9	12	12	13	15	7	1	0	4	8	13	12	106

Because of greater altitude, eastern Turkey is better watered than the central plateau, this despite an inland position; and the total rainfall varies between 17 and 24 inches. The months of heaviest rain tend to

---

[1] A diurnal variation of the order of 50° or 60° F. can bring the night minimum below freezing-point, even in summer.

be February and March, but towards the north-east there is some approach to conditions of the Black Sea region (i.e. a maximum in summer or autumn), so that at Ezerum, May is the wettest month, and at Kars, July.

The climate of eastern Turkey stands out as one of the most difficult and inhospitable in the world. Summers are hot, arid, and markedly dusty; winters are bitterly cold, and spring and autumn are both subject to sudden hot or cold spells – the former due to Föhn winds, and to southerly (Khamsin) winds from the Arabian desert, the latter to outbursts of cold air from inner Asia, which may give snowfalls as late as the month of May.

III. AGRICULTURE

Though by no means all of the cultivable land of Asia Minor is actually exploited, Turkey stands out among Middle Eastern states as having one of the most successful and developed agricultural economies. Whilst in many neighbouring regions the problem of feeding local populations is a principal concern, and food must be imported to augment a deficient home production – a feature in Egypt, Israel, the Lebanon, and Jordan – Turkey supplies a considerable proportion of her own needs, with certain agricultural commodities for export. Under the Ottomans, little attention was paid to agriculture: but since the revolution of 1923, serious attempts have been made to increase production by instructing the peasants in better methods of cultivation, and by improving communications. As a result, production has more than trebled since 1923, with further remarkable increases since 1950. Yet certain of the wasteful practices described in an earlier chapter are still characteristic of Turkish agriculture, and though much progress has been made, amounting to what some observers call a 'revolution', the situation is not without its disquieting aspects, and further technical improvements are both necessary and possible.

Greatest importance is given to the growing of cereals, which account for 80 per cent. of the total crop acreage of the country. Wheat is by far the most important, occupying just over one-half of the land given over to cereals, or about 45 per cent. of the total cultivated area. The western part of Asia Minor is the main growing region, and the steppe zones flanking the inner plateau of Anatolia are particularly important. Here there is a wide extent of fairly flat territory, and rainfall is a little heavier than in the centre of the plateau. Another important wheat-growing region is the northern Aegean region, inclusive of European Turkey. Until 1930, Turkey was far from self-sufficient in wheat supplies and therefore imported extensively, but now in good years (e.g. 1953) there is an export surplus. Yet still in bad years imports are necessary. The problems of soil erosion produced by Turkish efforts to extend the area under cereals have been touched upon in Chapter XII; and a solution would seem to lie in improving yields from a reduced arable area – easy to enunciate, but supremely difficult to achieve in practice.

Barley is the second cereal crop, occupying about 35 per cent. of the acreage of wheat; though because of its tolerance of heat and aridity, yields per unit cultivated are often higher. Its main use is as a fodder crop, and it has a wide distribution, notably on the steppe zones flanking the inner plateau of Anatolia (districts of Ankara, Konya, and Çorum especially), also the inner coastlands of the Aegean, with Konya by far the most important region. In all of these regions it is often grown on the drier parts, where annual rainfall is from 15 to 18 inches. In the northern Aegean, barley is grown as an export crop, primarily for malting purposes, and there is an annual export of over 120,000 tons, chiefly to Britain. The inferior variety of wheat known as spelt is often grown mixed with, or alongside barley, but only when fodder is required. Over most of Asia Minor all the three cereals wheat, barley, and spelt are sown as winter crops (i.e. in autumn); but in the extreme east, winters are too cold, and sowing takes place in spring with the harvest delayed until late summer.

Next in importance after wheat and barley is maize, which flourishes in the warm and humid Black Sea coastlands, especially round Samsun, and, with irrigation, in the Aegean coastlands. Rye is also important as a cereal of marginal lands, where conditions are too dry or too cold for wheat or barley. Eastern Turkey and the inner parts of the central plateau, away from the salt steppe region, are the main districts of production. In places where the soil is poor but climatic conditions a little more favourable, a mixture of wheat and rye, termed *maslin*, is often grown.

On the low, humid plains of the Mediterranean coast, rice is an important crop, with the districts of Adana and European Turkey as chief producing centres. Rice-growing is also found as far east as Maraş and Diyarbekir, with more restricted and patchy distribution in the marshy Aegean valleys and also in the region of Trabzon. Yet another crop of Turkey is oats, which flourishes on the central plateau, and in the cooler north and north-west Aegean districts. The fact that production of oats is five or six times greater than that of rice is a reminder of Turkey's position as the most northerly of Middle Eastern countries; outside Asia Minor oats grow only with some difficulty on the higher upland regions, and have small importance as a crop. Millet is grown

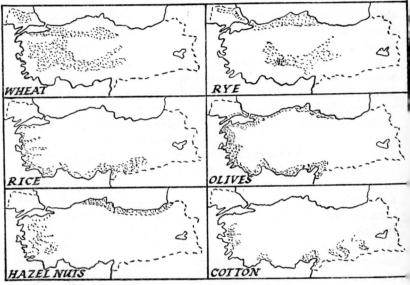

Fig. 57. Distribution of Crops in Asia Minor

on a small scale as a rotation summer crop in southerly districts, principally the Hatay, chiefly for use as a cattle and poultry food, and as an adulterant for bread. There is also a very restricted export, chiefly, again, to the United Kingdom.

CEREAL CROPS IN TURKEY (tons)

	Average 1934-8	Annual Production Average 1950-2	1954-5	1960
Wheat	3,412,000	4,700,000	4,900,000	8,450,000
Barley	1,954,000	2,340,000	2,400,000	3,700,000
Maize	557,000	738,000	914,000	1,000,000
Rye	336,000	521,000	440,000	700,000
Oats	223,000	334,000	325,000	500,000
Rice	64,000	70,000	110,000	97,000
Millet	44,000	55,000	50,000	53,000

Potatoes are increasing rapidly in importance, and production has trebled since 1930. Here again a colder climate is an advantage, since only the sweet potato (yam) will grow in many parts of the southern Middle East. Iran, Cyprus, and the Lebanon are the only other countries which rival Turkey in the growing of potatoes, and at present, production in Asia Minor is in excess of the individual output from all the other countries. Potato-growing tends naturally to be restricted to the north, and to the higher parts of the central plateau; and the plant is now of increasing value in the extreme east, where it plays a considerable part in the resettlement programme of the Turkish government.

Fruit Crops. These are extremely important in most districts of Asia Minor, and the wide extent of fruit-growing arises from (*a*) a generally favourable climate, with, in the west and south, mild winters, and long sunny summers, (*b*) a rich volcanic soil in many areas, which is particularly advantageous for vine-growing, and (*c*) varied topography, which allows a wide range of species, from sub-tropical to temperate fruits, on the same hill slopes.

Olives are probably the main crop, though by far the greater proportion are for local consumption, and are hence never marketed, so that statistics of production show only a moderate yield. The olive flourishes best on sloping ground, and away from the coast its productivity falls off considerably – 60 to 75 miles inland is usually regarded as the limit for intensive cultivation. Thus the foothills of mountain ranges close to the sea are usually given over to olive-growing, and groves are found all round the coasts of Asia Minor, with the western and southern districts as areas of most intensive cultivation – i.e. the region of Izmir and the lower slopes of the Taurus and Amanus Ranges backing the Seyhan plain, and the Hatay (Mersin, Iskanderun, Antakya). Izmir is a centre for processing the oil, and for export; though export was stopped for a time in 1944–5.[1] It will be recalled that too much moisture lowers the oil content of the fruit: similarly a rich soil produces large luxuriant trees, but a small fruit crop. For these reasons, the best olive groves are on dry stony ridges, and the highest yield is often from gnarled, stunted trees. These facts explain the popularity of the olive in many regions of Turkey.

Vines are the second most important fruit crop of Turkey, and, in contrast to olives, tend to be grown mainly for export. In normal times dried sultanas rank as one of the most valuable exports of the country, but during the war period, there was a marked decline in sales abroad.

[1] The chief buyer is Germany.

Within the last twenty years great improvements have taken place, and imported stocks of American and French vines have been distributed by the government in order to enhance quality; and now in some years Turkey is the principal world exporter of sultanas. Vines are grown on flat or slightly undulating land; and although fairly widespread over most of the country, even as far east as the valleys of Armenia, large-scale production for export is restricted to the Aegean area (vilayets of Izmir and Manisa). The best grapes grow in a small region situated between the Gediz and Büyük Menderes valleys; and from these grapes are made the famous *sultanas*, which after drying for one week in the sun on sheets of paper spread on the ground, are then cleaned, bleached, and packed for export.[1] North of the Gediz valley slightly cooler and damper sea-breezes have a markedly deleterious effect – the yield per plant falls to one-fifth of that in the favoured central Aegean region. Raisins are also produced from muscat grapes, which are darker in colour; and the inferior grades of grapes are used for wine-making, particularly a spirit flavoured with aniseed, and known as *raki*. The total production of wine and spirits during an average year is over 3 million gallons.

Figs are also grown on a considerable scale for export, and once again the Büyük Menderes–Gediz region is the chief centre of production. Turkish figs have a special flavour that is said to be due to the presence in the fruit of numerous seeds, which are fertilised by certain species of insects that occur only under the special climatic conditions of the Aegean coastlands. The figs ripen in August, when the hot dry Meltemi winds are fully developed. For some weeks previously, during the late spring, westerlies have prevailed, and the succession first of mild damp maritime air swells the fruit, and then later the hot modified monsoonal air of the Meltemi completes the ripening stage. After drying in the sun, packing of the figs takes place at Izmir. Considerable quantities – even as much as 40 to 50 per cent. of the total crop – may be lost during the drying period, when a single slight shower can spoil large numbers; and as few figs are actually picked (most are allowed to drop off the trees), many are over-ripe. The rejected fruit is used in the manufacture of industrial alcohol.

In the valleys of the Aegean coastlands, there is a well-marked sequence of cultivated plants according to altitude. On the lowest parts of all, which are liable to flooding, small fields of rice are found, and

---

[1] During the last war quality greatly deteriorated, because paper to cover the soil could not be imported into Turkey.

lsewhere on the valley bottoms, vines and cereals grow. On the owest slopes of the valley sides, figs are planted; then, at slightly higher evels, olives replace figs. Sometimes cereals are also grown among live plantations. Above this, at slightly varying heights (1,500 feet n the north, 1,800 to 2,000 feet in the south), scrub forest and nut trees ccur.

Besides olives, vines, and figs, large quantities of other Mediterranean ruit are grown chiefly for home consumption. Apricots and peaches ake the place of figs in the eastern and central provinces; cherries are bundant on the Black Sea coastlands – Giresun (Cerasus) is the original ome of the cherry – and plums are grown in the northern Aegean (both in European and Asiatic Turkey), and on the damper parts of he central plateau. Some of these plums are dried – prunes from the Edirne (Adrianople) district of European Turkey having a high repu-ation – and quantities are exported. The cultivation of citrus fruit is greatly increasing – five- to ten-fold over 1950 levels – with tangerines n the Black Sea coast, and 'jaffas' on the Aegean; and some bananas re now produced in the hot and steamy valleys of the Mediterranean coastlands. Temperate fruits, especially apples, are a feature in Anatolia, and in the east, apple trees outnumber other species of fruit.

Another important export is that of hazel-nuts, of which half the world's marketed supply comes from Turkey. The nuts yield an oil that is of value as a lubricant for aeroplanes (in air-screws), and in the making of varnish. Quantities of nut are also used in confectionery and chocolate-making, and as dessert. About 65,000 tons of hazels are gathered annually, and of this total, about two-thirds is exported, the bulk going at present to Switzerland and the U.S.A. Chief areas of production are the 'Pontic' forests that clothe the ridges of the Black Sea coastlands; and the nuts are shipped from Giresun, Trabzon, and Samsun. The Aegean region also produces important quantities of both hazel-nuts and walnuts. Almonds and pistachios are grown in the south-east, round Maraş and Diyarbekir, and also in the central plateau.

Commercial Crops. Besides cereals and fruit, Turkey produces a number of commercial crops, chief of which are (in order of importance) cot-ton, sugar beet, tobacco, valonea, liquorice, oilseeds (sunflower and sesame), and opium. Cotton is grown chiefly on the Seyhan plain between Adana and Mersin, and in the Izmir region, with a total acreage of 1,500,000, chiefly in the former area. Small quantities are also produced in south-eastern Turkey, round El Aziz and Diyarbekir.

Production has increased considerably over the last twenty-five years, and has doubled since 1949 – the rise in world price having proved a considerable stimulus. Just before this, during the Second War, production had fallen, since the chief markets (Germany and eastern Europe) could no longer be supplied; and chief emphasis was then laid on the production of oilseed, which has taken on great importance as a feeding-stuff for cattle. Recently, however, exports of raw cotton have been resumed, and now rank in some years as the principal Turkish export commodity.

Two varieties of the plant are grown, one native and the other American. Irrigation is necessary in many areas, and the expansion of cotton-growing has been related to irrigation projects, notably round Adana and in the Büyük Menderes valley.

Sugar beet is a recent introduction, and as in Persia, its development was greatly stimulated by the government as a means of reducing the country's dependence upon imported cane sugar. By 1941 this objective was achieved, and there is an export of about 10,000 tons of sugar out of a total production of 200,000 tons. The contrast with Iran, where sugar beet has not been introduced with complete success, arises from the difference in elevation, and hence in temperature – the crop is precarious in the warmer uplands of Iran, but well established in Asia Minor. Chief regions of production are on the western and north-western fringes of the central plateau, in the districts of Eskeşehir, Afyonkarahissar, and Birejik. There is also some production in European Turkey; and in both areas the districts selected for beet-growing are carefully placed along railway lines so that there is easy transport to refineries. Cane sugar is also grown on a small scale in the plain of Adana, but as yet accounts for only a small proportion of Turkish output of sugar.

Tobacco is a traditional Turkish crop, and because of its high value ranks as a principal export commodity. At one time tobacco was widely grown all over Turkey, but in an effort to improve quality, the government has restricted cultivation during the last twenty or so years to two main regions, the Aegean coastlands (chief centres Izmir, and Bursa, near the Sea of Marmara), and the Black Sea coast with centres at Samsun and Trabzon (the latter producing the strongest Turkish tobacco). Tobacco is an exhausting crop, hence rich soils with a varied mineral content and an adequate water supply are necessary. Heaviest yields are obtained in the Izmir region, but highest quality occurs round Samsun and Bursa. The crop is controlled as a government monopoly, and normally about one-half of the total production is retained for home use, and the rest exported. There has been much fluctuation during the last ten years: up to 1941 the principal customer for Turkish tobacco was Germany; now America takes the largest proportion, mainly for use in blending with Virginian pipe-tobaccos. Poland, Czechoslovakia, and Egypt are other important buyers. Since the post-1945 dollar shortage in Europe, there has been some increase in shipments to Britain, and total production, which averaged 60,000 tons annually up to 1942, is now 110,000–120,000 tons.

The valonia oak grows only in the borderlands between the Aegean and western Anatolia, and is for the most part restricted to altitudes exceeding 3,000 feet. From the cup which holds the acorn an extract useful in tanning, and known as valonea, is obtained. The main regions of growth of the valonia oak are the uplands at the head of the Büyük Menderes, Gediz, and Simav rivers; and the inner slopes of the Western Taurus and main Taurus. Acorns and cups are picked during the period August to October, then dried in the sun for several weeks, following which some acorns are exported, and some treated at Izmir to obtain the extract. About 50,000 tons of acorns are produced, and of these about two-thirds are exported, the principal buyers being France, Great Britain, and the U.S.A. Liquorice grows wild over much of Asia Minor, but occurs mostly in the drier parts of the south and east, towards the Syrian steppe. No actual cultivation takes place, but some 30,000 tons are gathered annually, and most of this is sent either as dried root or in a concentrated extract to the United States, where it is used chiefly for flavouring tobacco, and also as a sweetmeat.

Sesame is grown for oil in the lowlands of Antalya and Adana, whilst sunflowers are cultivated on an increasing scale in many parts, especially round the Sea of Marmara. In addition, smaller quantities of poppy-seed, colza, hemp, and linseed are also produced, chiefly from the Aegean region. Attention has recently been given to increasing the cultivation of flax, both for fibre and for seed, particularly in the newly irrigated areas round Adana, and the production of linseed oil has greatly expanded.

Once again, however, owing to extensive home use of these crops, statistics are hardly more than estimates.

Opium is also grown on the volcanic soils of the western plateau, especially round Afyonkarahisar (*afyon* = opium), and Konya. Like tobacco, opium production is a state monopoly, and Turkey produces 225 tons, half of the world's legal supply. Though only 70,000 acres

M

PRODUCTION OF OILSEEDS IN TURKEY (tons)

	Annual Average 1940–60	Production 1950–60
Cotton	120,000	250,000
Sesame	26,000	32,000
Sunflower	25,000	105,000
Poppy	12,000	10,000
Linseed	10,000	25,000

are planted with the opium poppy, the value of the crop is very high, and occasionally, if other crops have failed, farmers may obtain permission to grow a small amount as recompense for other losses. An increase in the cultivation of mulberry trees for silkworms has recently taken place; the activity being located in the west and south. Another advance has been the introduction during 1933–5 of tea-growing in the Rize area, where conditions are in certain respects comparable with those of Assam. Because of lower temperatures, however, yields of tea are smaller in quantity, though quality is moderate or good, and Turkey is now practically self-sufficient in tea supplies. Other less important agricultural products of Turkey are gum tragacanth, aniseed, hemp, attar of roses, and madder (for dyeing of rugs and carpets). Mention must also be made of the increasing cultivation of vegetables of all kinds.

IV. IRRIGATION

The irrigation problems of Turkey differ in certain respects from those of most other Middle Eastern countries. In the first place, with slightly higher rainfall, river water is actually more abundant; but in the interior, the extremely deeply entrenched river courses make it difficult to raise water to the surrounding agricultural land; whilst closer to the coast, broad alluvium-filled tectonic troughs are most often subjected to floods, and become filled with marsh and swamp. Irrigation in Asia Minor is thus often combined with river control and draining of marshes – particularly in the north and west of the country – and existing works are on a relatively modest scale, hardly comparable with those of the Nile, Euphrates, or Tigris.

The largest irrigated area at present is found in the Seyhan plain, where a barrage just north of the town of Adana allows the watering of 30,000 acres. The output of cotton from this district has doubled since water supplies were increased, and maize- and rice-growing are expanding. A little further west, extensive swamps are in process of reclamation near Tarsus; and the whole area of the Seyhan lowlands is expected to become one of the most productive agricultural regions of the country.

Irrigation canals and flood-control works are in construction in many parts of the Aegean coastlands, notably the valleys of the Great and Little Menderes, Gediz, and Simav rivers; and the aggregate acreage of land involved is expected ultimately to exceed that of the Adana irrigation scheme. Improvements are also taking place along the course of the Yesil Irmak, (i) around its headwaters in the central plateau of Anatolia, (ii) in the region of Amasya, and (iii) close to the mouth, just east of Samsun. Marsh reclamation in this latter area will allow increased cultivation of tobacco, cereals, and fruit. Other important dams are on the Sakariya river, and at Hirfanli on the Kizil Irmak – the latter being one of the largest barrages in the country.

Irrigation from the Euphrates in the region of Malatya is extending the fruit-growing activities of the region; here the river is less deeply slotted into the plateau, and small-scale canals are being constructed with the aim of bringing 250,000 acres into use. Lastly, mention must be made of developments in the central plateau. A large barrage has been built near Ankara (the third largest in Turkey), partly to secure a good domestic water-supply for the city, and also to allow increased cultivation of cereals and vegetables. Round Eskeşehir, some 10,000 to 20,000 acres have recently been made available for sugar-beet growing.

After several decades of experience, it is now recognised that irrigation has not proved wholly successful, or even popular. Some reasons for this situation are (a) lack of knowledge by farmers of suitable techniques – necessary changes in crop rotation, choice of seeds, etc., and the use of fertilisers and insecticides, (b) the relationships of drainage to soil salinity, and (c) soil erosion and reservoir silting. Because of the special geographical nature of Turkish rivers an unusually high proportion of silt is carried – on the Kizil Irmak (Red River) flood-waters may carry as much as 80 gm. of sediment per litre. Thus, rapid silting of irrigation works can often be expected, and, depending upon the precise load carried, an effective life may be calculated. In some instances, this life amounts to less than fifty years; and for small barrages on the periphery of the Anatolian plateau as little as 20–25 years – an extremely important factor in the cost of operation of irrigation schemes.

V. PASTORALISM

The large extent of mountain and semi-arid steppe, too dry or too cold for agriculture, has led to the development of stock rearing on a considerable scale. In many areas considerable seasonal movement from winter to summer pastures takes place, amounting in certain districts of the east and south to semi or full nomadism; whilst in agricultural regions a kind of mixed farming prevails, with stock keeping as an important supplement to cultivation. The importance of animal rearing in Turkish economy is shown by the fact that Turkey comes second only to Great Britain as a European producer of wool, and surpasses all other Mediterranean countries.

Sheep are most numerous, and, though widespread over practically the whole country, greatest concentration occurs in the western districts of the central plateau (centres: Eskeşehir, Afyonkarahissar, and Kayseri); in the provinces bordering Syria and Iraq; and in European Turkey. Milk, wool, and meat are obtained, and there is a considerable trade in live animals with neighbouring countries. Normally some 250,000 sheep are exported, mainly to adjacent countries. Turkish wool is, unfortunately, rather coarse, and cannot be used in the making of good quality cloth; but within recent years, the government has attempted to improve the yield by introducing merino sheep.

Goats are often kept with sheep, since both animals thrive on the limited vegetation of the central plateau. Angora goats are especially valuable as yielding mohair, a soft, fine fibre about 6 inches in length, which is woven into a durable, silky cloth. As the name suggests the Ankara region is the main home of these goats; and elsewhere, the ordinary black goat is most common.

LIVESTOCK (in ooo's)

Sheep	33,614	Horses	1,200
Goats (black)	19,000	Water-buffaloes	1,130
Goats (angora)	5,800	Mules	140
Cattle	12,000	Pigs	121
Donkeys	1,800	Camels	45

Cattle are less important than either sheep or goats, since these animals are much less tolerant of semi-arid conditions, and cannot travel long distances in search of fresh pasture. The main regions of cattle rearing tend, therefore, to occur in the damper coastlands of the

north and west; and relatively few are kept in the centre and south-east
of Asia Minor. Breeds are poor, and the yield of meat and milk low;

LAND UTILISATION IN TURKEY
(Official Estimates)

	Area in Hectares		Percentage of Total	
	1934	1957	1935	1957
Land under cultivation	10,556,000	22,161,000	13·7	28·2
Crops				
Cereals			7·6	18·8
Commercial crops			0·6	2·1
Vegetables			0·6	1·8
Fallow			4·8	5·5
Grazing Land	44,329,000	29,748,000	57·3	37·8
Market Gardens and Orchards	1,121,000	1,915,000	1·4	2·5
Market gardens			0·2	1·0
Fruit orchards			0·4	1·3
Vineyards			0·5	0·5
Olive groves			0·5	0·5
Rose gardens			0·01	0·01
Forests	9,170,000	10,418,000	11·8	13·6
Unproductive	12,058,000	13,462,000	15·6	17·2

but as in the case of sheep, the government has made efforts to improve
methods and stock by the establishment of model farms, research and
breeding institutes, and by the introduction of foreign breeds. Along
the Black Sea coast, water-buffaloes are important both as a source of
milk, and also for transport and ploughing. Elsewhere in Turkey,
donkeys, horses, camels, and mules are used for transport, and many
mules are imported from Cyprus. Camels, once numerous in the south-
west, are now steadily declining, as more and more of the caravan
traffic is carried in motor lorries.

VI. MINERALS

Asia Minor has long been renowned as a centre of mineral production.
The first coins ever to be issued were those of Croesus, king of Lydia,
and these were fixed quantities of gold, the purity of which was
guaranteed by the personal seal of the monarch. Gold was also an
ancient product of the north-east; and in the home of the legendary
Golden Fleece, alluvial gold is still obtained from rivers by washing silt
against an oily fleece, to which particles of gold adhere. Iron was first

developed by the Hittites of Anatolia *c.* 1250 B.C., and copper was
exploited at a much earlier date.

Owing to various handicaps – low-grade or limited reserves, scattered distribution, and difficulties of access – Turkey was to some extent
a marginal producer, and at times output has been very small indeed.
But with world rises in prices since 1940, Turkey has greatly increased
the scale of exploitation, both as a source of raw material for her own
industry, and as an export trade. This general increase has been most
conspicuous since 1950.

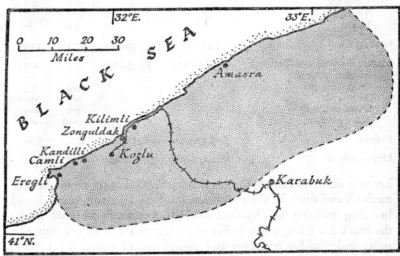

Fig. 58. The Coal Basin of Eregli–Zonguldak. Stippling indicates the possible extent
of coal measures

The largest mineral deposits of Turkey are the coal beds of the Eregli
(Heraclea)–Zonguldak–Amasra region. The coal, interbedded with
Carboniferous sandstones, is of very high grade, fully comparable in
quality to the best British or German coal. Seams extend for about
100 miles along the Black Sea coast, and are much affected by fracturing, so that individual seams tend to be discontinuous, and difficult to
mine. At the present, coal is not worked below a depth of 150 feet,
hence there is a possibility of considerable reserves at greater depths.

Production takes place from five centres: Kilimli, Zonguldak, Kozlu,
Kandilli, and Camli (Fig. 58); and annual production averages about
6½ million tons, of which about 65 per cent. comes from the Kilimli–
Zonguldak area. Production in the eastern part of the coalfield is

declining. The whole coal region has been worked in a sporadic way since 1828, and immediately prior to 1918, was operated by Italian interests, production being less than 500,000 tons each year. The coal is used by the metallurgical and chemical plants at Karabuk, for generation of electricity (35-40 per cent. of total power produced is from coal), for the railways, and by industry. There is a small export chiefly to shipping and to nearby countries.

There are three considerable disadvantages in the Eregli coal basin: lack of labour, poor communications, and fragility of the coal itself. Reference to the first factor has previously been made; as regards the second, the broken, forested nature of the coastal uplands hinders land transport of the coal, which for the most part moves by sea. Aerial ropeways have been constructed to carry coal to the coast, but on the coast itself, as we have noted, harbours are few and poor, so that ships must lie off the shore, and cannot load coal in bad weather (this occurs on average for 150 days each year). Fragility of the coal leads to considerable loss in washing and handling – on average, 35-40 per cent., so that of 6-7 million tons raised over 2 million are lost. As a result, the price of coal is high, and the mines have operated since 1939 at a loss, which has at times amounted to £5 st. per ton sold. Now, the effects of technical improvements are showing, and production has recently risen markedly.

Lignite occurs in several localities, chiefly on the western plateau of Anatolia. About 25-30 separate districts produce in aggregate some 500,000 tons per annum; and the largest output is from the Kutahya field west of Ankara, where a reserve of 1,000 million tons exists. About 45 per cent. of electricity generated thermally is from lignite as fuel.

Iron is produced at Divrik (Divrigi), 300 miles east of Ankara, and at Çamdag, close to the head of the Gulf of Izmit. Other deposits, not fully investigated, are believed to occur at Torbali, Hasancelebi, and Elbistan in the eastern plateau region. At Divrik the iron occurs in a mountain range that lies some 5,000 feet above sea level; and the first ore was of a very high quality (60-65 per cent. iron content). Latterly, quality has declined, and as reserves are not thought to be great, there has been some attention to Çamdag where a better ore was discovered some years ago. The greatest obstacle to iron exploitation is lack of coal close at hand. Divrik is over 600 miles from coal deposits, and Çamdag some 200. Blast furnaces, so far the only ones in Turkey, were built at Karabuk so as to be near the Zonguldak coalfield, yet out of range of naval bombardment; and these were planned before either of the existing iron ore deposits had been discovered. Despite these handicaps, which result in a high cost of production for Turkish iron and steel, annual production of iron ore is just under 1 million tons.

Chrome has for long been produced in Turkey, which was at one time the chief world producer; but Russia now holds first place, with Turkey second. The mineral occurs as lodes or lenses in association with serpentine, and is usually quarried, mined by adit, or even collected from the surface. At Güleman (west of Lake Van) workings developed in 1925 produce 20–30 per cent. of total Turkish output, the remainder coming from a number of smaller mines in the districts of Bursa and Eskişehir (N.W. Anatolia), Fethiye and Antalya – the last two zones being worked by private companies. Production from Güleman is partly from surface outcrops, and the ore moves by lorry to railhead, then 400 miles to Mersin and Iskanderun. Production is interrupted by cold weather for about ten weeks each winter. A ferro-chrome concentrator was recently built – the first in Turkey.

Copper is mined at two places, Ergani Madeni (about 60 miles north-west of Diyarbekir), and Hopa, on the Black Sea close to the Russian frontier. At Ergani, a high-grade deposit estimated to amount to 3 million tons is worked by open-cast methods, and fair progress has been made since the opening of the railway to Mersin, though the haul is over 350 miles. The Hopa region began production in 1948. Most of the copper produced in Turkey is used within the country chiefly in the manufacture of armaments and electrical equipment. Until 1939 there was some copper mining from the Artavan district in north-east Turkey, but deposits are now worked out.

Lead and zinc, with small quantities of gold and silver, are sometimes found together, or with copper (as at Ergani Madeni), and when all minerals can be extracted, profitable working is possible. Exploitation is, however, on a restricted scale. Balya Madeni and Keban Madeni are the chief centres for lead and zinc blende, and as both of these are ancient mining sites, much of the present remaining ore is low grade. Output from Keban Madeni moves to Mersin, which is well placed for handling the minerals of the south and east of Turkey, and can offer transport rates by sea which are lower than those direct to the north-west by rail.

Other minerals exploited on a very small scale, yet collectively important, are alum (Black Sea region), antimony (Black Sea), arsenic (Izmir), asbestos (Kars), boracite for borax (Bandirma), manganese

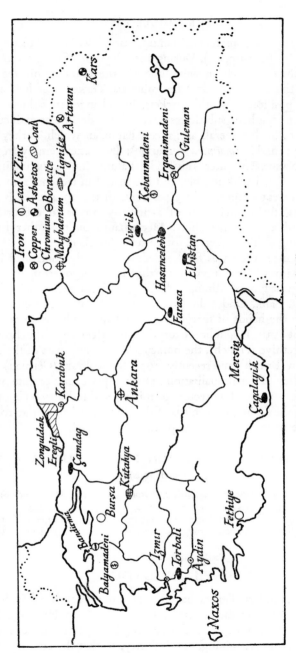

Fig. 59. Mineral Distribution in Asia Minor

(various regions), mercury (Izmir), molybdenum (Ankara), and sulphur (Kecibolu-Isparta). During 1954 deposits of tungsten containing quantities of wolfram were found in the Uludagh hill region of Bursa. In the case of certain other minerals, Turkey once held a commanding position in world markets, but changes in fashion or the invention of synthetic substitutes have led to a decline or extinction of production. Such minerals are: meerschaum, in which Turkey had a monopoly; marble (*marmara* = marble); and natural emery from the island of Naxos. The latter is an oxide of aluminium occurring in small masses associated with marble, and is dug out in trenches rather than mined. Current output, only 3 per cent. of the 1914 level, is under 5,000 tons, the competition of artificially produced carborundum having had a restrictive effect. Meerschaum on the other hand is experiencing a minor revival, for costume jewellery.

Mining in Turkey was for long almost entirely controlled by the state, with immediate supervision in the hands of a government Department, the Institute of Mining (M.T.A.), with finance supplied by the state E.T.I. Bank. Under the Ottomans, exploitation had come to be entirely in the hands of foreign concessionaires, who were nearly all bought out by the Republic – exceptions being certain of the chromium mines at Fethiye (French), the boracite (American), part of the emery production (British), and recently (1958) the wolfram (German). Since 1950 a policy of denationalisation has taken place, and private ownership is a feature in a few sectors of mining and industry – about one-quarter of the lignite, two-thirds of the chrome, a half of the iron ore, and all the manganese are now privately produced.

PRODUCTION OF MINERALS IN TURKEY
(metric tons)

	Coal	Lignite	Chromium	Iron	Copper	Manganese	Sulphur
1939	1,600,000	150,000	183,000	—	6,000	1,000	—
1953	5,600,000	1,310,000	520,000	342,000	24,000	12,000	10,000
1959	6,515,000	3,680,000	397,800	872,900	25,000	36,100	13,300

VII. INDUSTRY

Like Persia, modern Turkey has attempted to approach self-sufficiency in manufactures by direct state intervention. Two Five-year Plans, launched in 1934 and 1936, had the aims (1) of fostering closer integration of agriculture, mining, and industry, so that the country would be less dependent on imports, and (2) of bringing about a degree of industrial development in central and eastern Anatolia, where geographical conditions are less favourable for agriculture than in the west. This latter aim was also conditioned by strategic and political considerations: it was felt that the manufacturing centres of Istanbul and Izmir were somewhat accessible to possible attack; and also that difficulties might arise in maintaining political balance between a relatively prosperous and developed west, with both agriculture and manufacturing, and the poorer semi-nomadic, and sparsely peopled centre and east. It was thus held as desirable that any future development of Turkish industry should take place in Anatolia, leaving the Aegean region for intensive agriculture, for which, of all regions of Asia Minor, it is the most suited.

Most of Turkish industry before 1953 was financed internally, since experience of 'Capitulations' made the government reluctant to employ foreign capital, or allow foreign ownership. With political changes after 1950, however, the inflow of foreign capital was made easier, and in addition, private enterprise (both Turkish and foreign) has benefited by the de-nationalisation of certain state enterprises. As a result both of this and of governmental action (which may, however, have led to over-capitalisation of Turkish industry) there have been marked advances: industry produces about 17 per cent. of the gross national income, employing over 1 million workers; and the number of industrial establishments approximately doubled between 1950 and 1955.

The first Five-year Plan[1] gave chief attention to stimulation of the textile industry, with mineral exploitation and chemical industries (producing artificial silk, paper, glass, pottery, and fertilisers) as secondary adjuncts. Much machinery was imported, mainly from Russia, Britain, and Germany, and rapid developments occurred. With considerable internal production of textile fibres (wool, cotton, silk, and mohair), Turkey is relatively well placed for textile manufacturing, though the scale of the industry cannot be compared with that of western Europe or the U.S.A. There are now over a million spindles and 25,000 cotton looms, together with three modern silk mills and a much larger number of smaller and older factories making silk cloth and carpets. The privately owned cotton mills are well placed near cotton-growing areas (at Izmir, Adana, Tarsus, Mersin, and Istanbul), whilst the state mills are further inland, on the plateau (at Kayseri,

[1] Directed by the state Sumer Bank.

Nazilli, Eregli, Malatya, and Bakirköy). Bursa, Istanbul, and Izmir are the chief woollen-manufacturing towns. Carpet-making has been carried on for centuries as a bazaar trade in many towns, especially those on the steppes of Anatolia. As in Iran, there are traditional patterns and colours associated with particular districts. Bursa is also a centre of mohair and silk weaving (both natural and artificial silk), and smaller factories exist at Istanbul and Izmir.

A recent development has been the creation of an iron and steel industry at Karabuk, the equipment used being British. Coking plant has been built at Zonguldak, and the Karabuk installations include blast furnaces, open hearth furnaces, and a foundry, from which rails and steel plate are produced. It has been noted earlier that strategic considerations led to the siting of the plant over the first crests of the longitudinal mountain chains, at the cost of the economic advantages of nearness to fuel supplies and to sea transport. Plans are in hand for reorganisation of the plant so as to improve its efficiency, and light engineering is also developing. Current production is now 400,000 tons compared with under 100,000 tons per annum up to 1950. Within the last few years a number of assembly plants for cars and domestic equipment have grown up, using imported parts. These, together with a few repair-shops, make up the rest of engineering activities in Turkey.

A noteworthy feature of Turkish economy has been the development of 'agricultural' industries: flour milling, sugar refining, packing and canning of fruit and meat, soap-boiling, and distilling. Here the distribution of factories is very wide, and individual establishments are small in size. Six sugar refineries are located in the north-west; fruit canning is carried on at Istanbul, Bursa, Malatya, and Adana. Izmir is the centre of the wine trade. In order to develop the north and east, food-packing factories (meat, fish, and cheese) have been established at Kars, Samsun, and Trabzon; and the two latter handle an increasing lumber trade that is based on the rich Pontic forests of the coastal ranges. Attar of roses is distilled at Istanbul and Isparta. Though the output is only about 250 lb. of attar annually, over 400 tons of rose petals are needed for this.

Other industries are chemical production (chiefly associated with the coking plant at Zonguldak); cement manufacturing, which, in common with conditions elsewhere in the Middle East, has greatly extended. In terms of tonnage, cement is now Turkey's most important industrial product. A deposit of good glass-sand occurs near Istanbul, and Kutahya is the centre, with Konya, of a long-standing pottery trade.

When the scale of industrial achievement during the last 15 to 20 years is set alongside the previous low stage of development, it will be apparent that considerable progress has been achieved. Turkey is now some way towards attaining balanced exploitation of the unusually varied resources of the country; and this following so soon after the collapse of 1918 is a measure both of the resource-richness of Asia Minor, and of the strength, social and economic, of the Republic. Further advances are to be expected both in agriculture and in industry, with some set-backs from time to time that indicate the need for careful planning and approach. Nevertheless, it is necessary to preserve a perspective. Among the 'European' states of the northern Mediterranean, Turkey still ranks as possibly the most retarded, with low standards of consumption and development. Though much effort has undoubtedly gone into industrial expansion, methods have not always been wise, and this activity still remains a minor one. Nearly four-fifths of the Turkish people are still concerned with agriculture and herding.

VIII. COMMUNICATIONS

For long the great size and difficult topography of Asia Minor, together with thinly spread population and limited natural resources, proved very considerable obstacles to the construction of communications. Isolation and remoteness were in turn regarded as important contributory causes to the slowness of economic development. As late as 1950 it was possible to say that despite efforts by the Republic since 1923, Turkey had only 12,000 miles of all-weather roads, and that many regions especially in the south and east (including several sizeable towns) were accessible only by mule-tracks. There was 1 mile of road to 1,640 people in Turkey, as compared to 1 : 256 in Britain. With the enhanced strategic status as a member of NATO, outside aid, and the improvements undertaken by the Turks themselves, it has recently been possible to develop road and rail links both within Turkey itself and with neighbouring countries. A culmination in one sense of the communications programme is the construction of a Bosphorus suspension bridge, expected to be completed in the early 1960's.

Railways. At the fall of the Empire in 1918 there was only a skeleton railway system consisting of disconnected lines operated by various non-Turkish companies, and suffering greatly from war damage. These lines had been laid without any general overall plan in districts where the prospect of immediate financial return seemed greatest, and in some

cases there was an onerous monetary guarantee from the state to
the operating company.[1] The most important of these pre-1923
lines were (1) the Eastern Railway (Austrian-owned) that linked
Istanbul to the main European system, (2) the Anatolian Railway
(German) from Haydarpaşa on the Asiatic shore opposite Istanbul to
Konya, with a branch to Ankara, (3) the Baghdad Railway (German)
from Konya to Nisibin, on the Syrian frontier, with branch to Aleppo
and Damascus, (4) shorter lines (one British, one French) running
inland from Izmir via the valleys of the Büyük Menderes and lower
Gediz, and (5) a line built by the Russians during the war of 1914, and

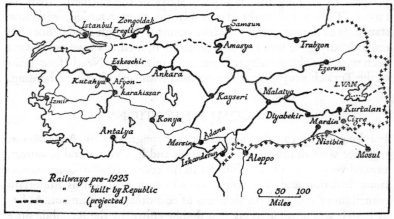

Fig. 60. Railway Construction in Asia Minor

of narrow gauge from Ezerum eastwards to within 100 miles of the
Russian frontier, then of Russian broad gauge as far as the frontier.
The Baghdad line played an important part in the campaigns of 1916–
18, and was completed as far as Nisibin by British prisoners of war.

It was the policy of the new Turkish Republic (i) to repair existing
railway lines which were badly damaged, (ii) to secure national
ownership by buying out foreign concessionaires – a process that was
virtually completed by 1940, (iii) to develop a network of new lines
that would link the older isolated sections, and also open up new
districts hitherto untouched by rail transport, and (iv) following the
shift of political influence from Istanbul to Ankara, to bring northern
Anatolia more fully into the rail network of Turkey.

---

[1] i.e. either a guarantee of dividends up to 5 or 10 per cent., or a payment per length
of line laid.

Since 1950 there have been plans (now in process of realisation) to link the Turkish and Persian rail systems by a line from Muş via Tatvan and Lake Van; for an extension from Kurtalan via Cizre to Mosul, giving a more direct access from Ankara to the Persian Gulf (this was considered as an alternative to the Berlin–Baghdad route via Adana in 1902); and a direct link between Amasya and the Gulf of Izmit via Bolu, using the longitudinal valleys of the Black Sea coastlands. As well, suburban electrification has begun round Istanbul, and extensive replacement of rolling stock is taking place.

Shipping. With a coastline some 4,000 miles long, and difficult relief inland, it is not surprising that communications by sea play an important part in the life of Turkey. Under the Ottomans, sea traffic was mostly in the hands of the Greeks, though Turkish-manned craft were found in the Black Sea; but since 1923 a Turkish merchant marine has been built up, and Turkey now has an important share in the trade of the Aegean and Mediterranean ports. Since 1940 more than half the tonnage using all Turkish ports has been of Turkish nationality. With an export trade now reaching 2 million tons annually there has been acute need for port development; and within the last few years improvements have been undertaken: works at Iskanderun and Mersin including facilities for handling chrome and other ores; improvements at Giresun, Izmir, and Samsun, now increasingly active as outlets for the tobacco crop; reconstruction at Haydarpaşa, the Asiatic road and rail terminal facing Istanbul across the Bosphorus; and the building of a totally new port at Salipazari. Handling over 60 per cent. of the total trade of the country, Istanbul is by far the leading port of Turkey (about one-half is foreign trade). Izmir stands next, with about 20 per cent., followed by Samsun, Iskanderun, Trabzon, and Mersin.

IX. TOWNS

As elsewhere in the Middle East, a feature of the present-day Turkey is the rapid growth of cities; and of these Istanbul (former name, Constantinople) is still by far the largest. The city was founded in 658 B.C. by Greek colonists, who established a settlement on the low plateau formed by the promontory lying between the Sea of Marmara and the drowned valley of the Golden Horn. This site, dropping steeply to the water, was easily defensible by the construction of fortifications on the western (landward) side; and in the centre of the promontory there grew up a succession of fortresses, one of which, the headquarters of the Ottoman rule, came to be known as the Sublime Porte.[1]

From this ancient nucleus, the city gradually developed; but it was not until the Middle Ages that the opposite (northern) bank of the Golden Horn was occupied and made part of the city. This district, called Galata, is now the modern business quarter, with the residential district of Pera occupying a ridge well above the city on the north.

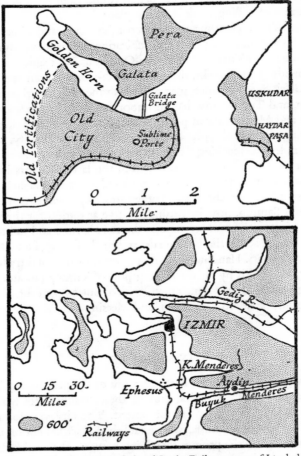

Fig. 61. The Sites of Istanbul and Izmir. Built-up areas of Istanbul stippled

---

[1] Hence the use of the term to denote the Ottoman Caliphs.

Uskudar, on the eastern (Asiatic) side of the Bosphorus, was the ferry-point facing Istanbul, and thus the terminal for routes leading eastwards into Asia Minor and the Levant (Uskudar = courier); but in the last two centuries its importance has greatly declined in favour of nearby Haydarpaşa, which, with a better harbour, has now become the port of entry into Asia Minor, and the terminus of the Anatolian railway system.

The importance of Istanbul derives from a number of factors. Firstly, the Golden Horn is the only good harbour in the entire region of the southern Black Sea, the coastline of which is, as we have seen, straight, sheer, and abrupt, and devoid of shelter during the bad weather that is frequently a feature. Secondly, Istanbul has an important natural resource in the good fishing of the Straits, which is due to the seasonal migration of fish from and into the Black Sea.[1] Thirdly, easy communications by land and sea make it the natural outlet for the relatively fertile Marmara region and its hinterland: though European Turkey is not outstandingly rich, regional differences in land utilisation give rise to a variety of products, mainly foodstuffs and animal produce, which are marketed at Istanbul. In addition, however, to this local traffic there were for long two major routes that intersected in the region of the Straits: one by sea from Russia and the Black Sea towards the Mediterranean, the other the land route from south-east Europe to Asia Minor. Whereas the importance of the latter route has declined since the Middle Ages, the sea route is likely to develop further with the rise of Russia, hence Istanbul will remain a port of call for shipping using the Black Sea.

Central position in relation to Ottoman territories made Istanbul a natural choice for a capital, and it may be noted that as compared with the bleak uplands of south-east Europe and the arid, 'continental' steppes of Asia Minor, the city has an extremely agreeable climate. Its function as capital attracted many secondary activities – military and naval construction, and administration, so that, like Vienna, Istanbul took on importance as a cultural and economic centre that transcended the limits of a single geographical region. In 1914, Istanbul had over 1 million inhabitants, but after the decision to transfer the capital of Turkey to Ankara, population fell for a time by a quarter; being now about 1,400,00. It is the one remaining town in Turkey with large Greek and Armenian minorities, who work as artisans: these were allowed to remain in the country because of their importance to the

[1] The name 'Golden' Horn is supposed to refer to the abundance of fish in its waters.

national economy. At the present time Istanbul is a market centre for exchange of local produce; a manufacturing centre (textiles, metals, light engineering, glassware, brewing, and leather); a fishing and commercial port, and something of a growing tourist centre.

Izmir, until 1950 the second city of Turkey (pop. 390,000), also has a fine natural harbour, formed by the head of a drowned estuary. A right-angled bend in the lower part of the estuary (due to cross-faulting) provides complete shelter for shipping; but in order to avoid rapid silting up of the port, a feature very common in the Aegean region, the river has been diverted to a new channel away from the town. Izmir is the natural centre for the Aegean coastlands, which are the richest part of Asia Minor; and its position midway between the two largest valleys of the region – those of the Gediz and Büyük Menderes – gives it special advantages from the point of view of communications with the interior. There is a choice of easy routes inland as far as the plateau of western Anatolia.

Chief activity is the export of fruit and vegetable products: raisins, figs, olives, tobacco, wheat, barley, opium, and vegetable oils are the most important. In addition to these cultivated products of the lowlands, liquorice, valonia acorns, gum tragacanth, and nuts are collected from the forested uplands, and Izmir is also the outlet for the pastoral districts of the central plateau. Wool, hides, meat, carpets, and woollen cloth are exported, with a return traffic of machinery and cotton goods. There is some fishing and boatbuilding – a speciality is sponges, which are exported in some quantity. A fourth activity is the shipping of untreated minerals that are produced in small quantities from the immediate hinterland: chrome, iron, manganese, sulphur, emery, and salt. Local manufacturing of soap, spirits, and textiles is carried on; and the importance of the city is likely to increase with the greater development of the Aegean coastlands, potentially far the richest of all the agricultural regions of Turkey. With the current improvements in port facilities, and expansion in demand for Turkish agricultural produce – also its tourist attractions both in its own right and as a centre for the considerable Classical remains of the district – it is well placed for further growth. One minor adverse factor is liability to moderately severe earthquakes – an indication of the site of the city in a region of tectonic disturbance.

Ankara was for long the chief regional capital of the northern half of the central plateau, a district formerly known as Galatia. The town had some importance as a Hittite capital; but until 1923 was surpassed in influence by Konya, which, as the centre of the richer southern plateau region, could rightly be termed the metropolis of the entire Anatolian plateau.[1] When, however, the founders of modern Turkey wished to develop Turkish nationalism, and break away from the 'pernicious' cosmopolitan atmosphere of Istanbul, Ankara, because of its Hittite associations which have been made much of as the basis of modern

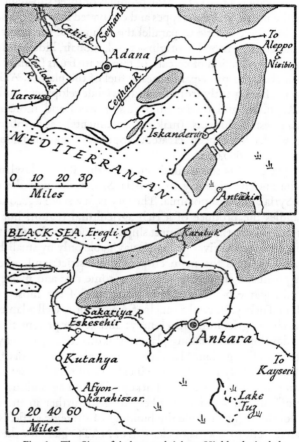

Fig. 62. The Sites of Ankara and Adana. Highland stippled

---

[1] This is shown by the choice of Konya as the terminus of the Baghdad Railway – Ankara was merely a station connected by branch line to the main trunk route. Another indication of the importance of Konya was the strong religious associations of the city, which became the centre of the Dervish order, and still has some of the finest mosques in Turkey.

nationalist feeling, was chosen as the new capital. The city lies at the confluence of a number of streams which are deeply incised into the plateau surface, and the centre portion of the town is placed on a residual ridge surrounded by steep slopes. The surrounding country is open, and relatively easy of access, so that it lies on the ancient routeway from east to west that follows the northern rim of the inner plateau of Anatolia. Ankara is a market for the products of three sub-regions – the forests of the north, and the steppes and cultivated lands of the southern interior – but there is little to parallel the richness of the Izmir region. Chief products are pastoral in origin – wool, mohair, hides, and carpets; there is some production of cereals, of temperate fruits (mainly apples), and of charcoal, the principal domestic fuel of the plateau. Ankara has of course profited greatly from the industrial development undertaken by the Republic, and textile mills (using wool and mohair), light engineering establishments (making armaments), and tobacco and printing works have been created. Population has increased from 50,000 in 1923 to 660,000.

Adana (240,000) is the natural centre of the Seyhan lowlands, and lies on the ancient highway from Asia Minor through the Cilician Gates to Syria and Mesopotamia. The city is in a sense a second Izmir, for it handles the produce of a rich agricultural region; but Adana, lying 25 miles from the coast, must ship her products through the port of Mersin, because the river Seyhan is navigable only by small boats up to Adana. Cotton is the main crop of the district; and other commodities produced are cereals (including some rice and maize), citrus fruits, and sugar cane. The Adana plain, one of the most extensive lowlands in Turkey, is, unlike much of Asia Minor, well adapted to the use of modern agricultural machinery; and at the present time, considerable development is taking place in this direction, parallel with the improvement of irrigation. Malaria is a handicap, but control of streams for irrigation is likely to reduce the incidence of this disease; and with the opening up of south-eastern Turkey – both to agriculture and as a supplier of minerals – Adana is likely to gain further in importance. Recent developments include the building of strategic airfields (under American direction) as a major element of NATO plans for the defence of the Middle East. Next in importance are Bursa and Eskeşehir.

In site and function, Bursa (160,000) could be regarded as a smaller replica of Izmir. With a good harbour site, it centralises the trade of the northern Aegean coastlands of Asia Minor, and has its own activities of silk and other textile production. The fig and olive are here less

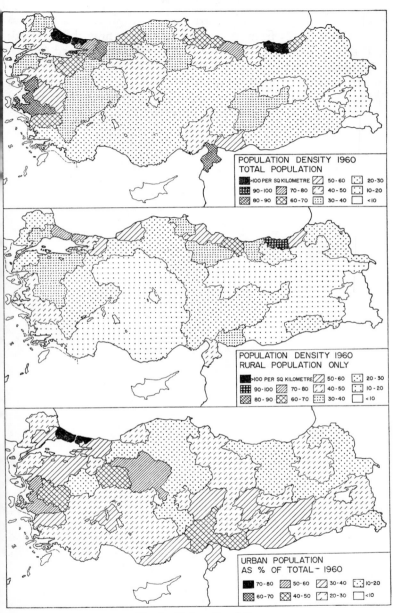

Fig. 63. Turkey: Population

productive – mulberries and nut-trees take their place. As well, Bursa has gained generally from its situation on what is now the main axis of Turkish economic activity – the zone between Istanbul and Ankara.

Eskeşehir (150,000) is traditionally a route-centre and market for the extreme west of the inner Anatolian plateau; but the exploitation of lignite, and increased currents of activity within Anatolia, have led to its emergence in recent years as an important town.

CHAPTER XV

The Tigris–Euphrates Lowlands

In the regions so far considered, political boundaries coincide to a large degree with natural geographical limits. Further to the south and west, however, this concordance is much less a feature, and there arises the problem of deciding on what basis to proceed to a discussion of the geography of the area. Two possibilities present themselves: (i) an

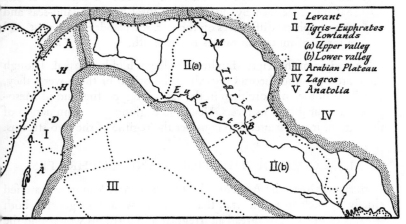

Fig. 64. Natural Physical Units

examination, country by country, as is most usual in geographical literature, and thus taking political frontiers as a criterion of division; or (ii) discussion on a basis of natural physical units, ignoring political boundaries. Of the two alternatives, it has been thought preferable to adopt the second, since, as we have seen, certain national frontiers in the Middle East are of very recent creation, and also in some respects artificial – therefore, liable to change. The solution proposed is not ideal, particularly as concerning economic matters, since trade statistics are grouped by countries; but in using purely geographical limits it is nevertheless felt that a clearer and more reasoned picture can be presented.

The following major natural regions have been recognised:

(a) The valleys of the Tigris and the Euphrates between the plateau of Asia Minor and the Persian Gulf – i.e. chiefly the state of Iraq, but also including parts of northern and eastern Syria.

(b) The Levant coastlands – western Syria, the Lebanon, Israel, western Jordan, and Cyprus.

(c) The plateau of Arabia, comprising the whole of the peninsula, together with the interior desert regions of Syria, Jordan, and Iraq.

(d) Egypt, which from many points of view has marked physical unity, as consisting of the Nile trench and its associated desert regions.

(e) Libya, which though in some ways merely a segment of the Sahara, is defined by significant natural barriers: sand-seas and topographical differences on the east, scarplands on the west, and a series of mountain ranges in the south.

The origin of the Tigris–Euphrates valley is highly unusual. Though there are opposing theories regarding the origin of the lower valley, equally if not even more than in the case of Egypt, the land of Mesopotamia is the gift of its rivers. Hence, in beginning an examination of the region, it is first useful to consider the regime of the two streams.

I. REGIME OF THE TIGRIS AND EUPHRATES

Both rivers rise in the Armenian highlands of Asia Minor, and are fed chiefly by melt from snowfall that occurs in winter. In general, both streams can be said to thread an irregular and tortuous way round the east–west running folds of the Anatolian system, following a course towards the south-east. At times, however, quite large folds are directly cut across by deep gorges, suggesting that in some parts, at least, the rivers existed before the mountain ranges were uplifted to their present height, and that drainage is therefore antecedent. Another interesting feature has been the blocking of parts of the Euphrates and Tigris by lava flows, with consequent deviation of the rivers. This is well shown south-east of Malatya, where the Euphrates makes a sudden bend south-westwards, because of the presence of lava erupted from the Karacali volcano.

Leaving behind the tangled ridges of Asia Minor, both rivers emerge on to the lower plateau uplands of northern Syria and Kurdistan, and make their way directly south-eastwards to the Persian Gulf. During its crossing of the north Syrian steppe, the Euphrates receives two important left-bank tributaries – the Balikh and the Khabour, both of which also rise amongst the hills of Asia Minor. No tributaries of any size are received from the Syrian and Arabian deserts (the last right-bank tributary joining the main stream at Carchemish in Turkey) but a number of large empty wadis indicate that in earlier times there was substantial right-bank entry of tributaries. The Khabour is the last tributary of any kind to enter the Euphrates, and so for the rest of its course across the hot plains of Iraq, there is considerable evaporation, which reduces the volume of water in the river. In this respect, a parallel with the Nile will be noticed.

The Tigris, on the other hand, lies much closer to the Zagros Ranges, and along the whole length of its course from Asia Minor to the Persian Gulf, receives many affluents, some quite large, like the Great and Little Zab, the Diyala, and the Karun; others small, though collectively important in the aggregate volume of water that they supply. The entry of tributaries has important consequences, since the Euphrates, being dependent on rainfall that occurs in a single and relatively restricted catchment area, does not fluctuate rapidly in volume in its middle and lower courses; whereas the Tigris draws its waters from a much wider catchment zone extending from south-east Anatolia to the northern coast of the Persian Gulf, and local rain in one district can soon affect the height of the river. Sudden floods are, therefore, a feature. Much of the water of the Euphrates comes from slow percolation of melt-water or rainfall through porous rock strata – i.e. temperature conditions in Asia Minor exert considerable control – but a large part, though not all, of the Tigris effluent is due to direct surface run-off from mountain torrents. A local rainstorm in the Zagros can thus produce marked changes in river level within a few hours, and a rise of 8 to 12 feet during 24 hours is not unusual.

For streams of such large size, the slope of both river beds towards the sea is distinctly steep. This is the result of oscillation of the land surface during Tertiary and Quaternary times. Most of the fall occurs in the portion between Anatolia and the Baghdad region: the Euphrates drops 800 feet between Jerablus and Ramadi (1 in 3,000), and hence its current is swift, precluding upstream navigation to all but highly powered boats. The gradient of the Tigris is even sharper, the river falling nearly 1,000 feet between the Turkish frontier and Baghdad (1 in 1,750); and though the width of the Tigris is less than that of the

Euphrates, the volume of water carried is far greater. The speed of the current in both rivers means also that their erosive action is considerable, hence much sediment is carried at all seasons; and all the year round, the Tigris and Euphrates appear as turbid, rapidly moving streams, in strong contrast to the Nile, which for seven or eight months of the year is clear and placid.

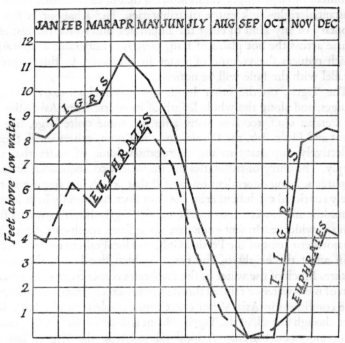

Fig. 65. The Regimes of the Tigris and Euphrates (data by Ionides). The datum for low water on the Euphrates is given by the lowest level at Ramadi (151 ft. above m.s.l.); and for the Tigris by lowest level at Baghdad (95 ft. above m.s.l.)

Because of the swift current, sudden fluctuation, and great volume of the Tigris, this river is especially subject to devastating floods. An exceptional rise in level may sweep away existing channels, and inundate many hundreds of square miles of territory, with the river ultimately carving for itself an entirely new course. Several old channels, still occupied by distributaries, or else used as irrigation canals, are still to be seen: one for example at Hilla, on the Euphrates, and another east of Baghdad, between Samarra and Ctesiphon.

Annual Regime. Both rivers are at their lowest in September and
October. Decreased evaporation as the result of a fall in temperature
during autumn causes a slight but perceptible rise in the Euphrates
during November (a feature that does not occur in the Tigris); but the
effects of the first onset of winter rainfall, which are clearly to be seen
in the Tigris, are almost entirely masked in the Euphrates owing to
percolation of rain into the porous subsoil. From December onwards,
both rivers begin to rise considerably, because of heavier rainfall over
the whole region; yet differences once again become apparent in later
spring.

The maximum flood of the Tigris takes place during April, but
owing to slower melting, and the effect of percolation, high water in
the Euphrates does not occur until May. It is also interesting to compare
the volume of the two rivers. At Hit, the Euphrates discharges an
average of 8,800 cubic feet of water per second in September, and
54,300 cubic feet per second in May, with a flood level 11 feet above
low water. At Baghdad the Tigris discharges a minimum of 11,900
cubic feet per second in September, and a maximum of 106,650 cubic
feet in April, with a rise in level of 18 feet – this though the Tigris at
Baghdad is narrower than the Euphrates at Hit. A further point of
importance is that at Baghdad both rivers contain 30–33 parts per
100,000 of salt: in the lower courses this figure reaches 90. The Haigh
Commission of 1949 estimated that 60 per cent. of all irrigated land in
Iraq had become salinated to some extent, that 20–30 per cent. of
irrigated land had been abandoned since 1935 (i.e. 1 per cent. of area
per annum), and that crop yields declined by 20 per cent. in most areas,
and by as much as 50 per cent. in some districts.

II. THEORIES OF ORIGIN OF THE
LOWER MESOPOTAMIAN VALLEY

According to de Morgan both the Tigris and the Euphrates at one time
(c. 10,000–5,000 B.C.) followed entirely separate courses, and entered
the Persian Gulf by distinct mouths. At this period the shoreline of the
Gulf was situated much further to the north-west, and lay only a few
miles below Baghdad. The two rivers built up separate deltas, which
gradually extended towards the south-east, into the waters of the Gulf.
Besides the Euphrates and the Tigris, other rivers also emptied into the
Persian Gulf; and two of these, the Karun and the Karkeh, rose in the
relatively humid uplands of the Zagros where evaporation was less than

on the plain. By reason of their rapid descent from the hills, both these latter streams had enormous erosive power.

Large quantities of silt brought down by the Karun and Karkeh were deposited as deltas along the northern shore of the Persian Gulf, and these latter deltas grew in size more quickly than those of the Tigris and Euphrates further to the north-west. Hence a platform of alluvial material was pushed southwards across the head of the Persian Gulf,

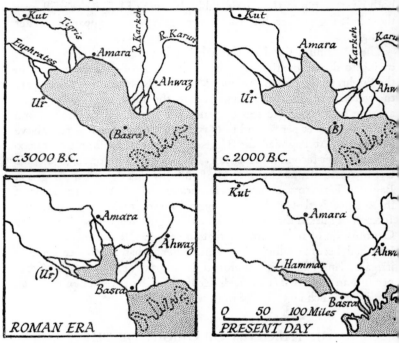

Fig. 66. Stages in the Recession of the Persian Gulf (after de Morgan)

ultimately forming a barrier behind which the waters of the Tigris and Euphrates were ponded back in a series of enormous lagoons and swamps. By the commencement of the Christian era the Karun and Karkeh deltas had joined together and reached the Arabian shore on the southern side of the Gulf, thus partially cutting off the Tigris and Euphrates from the sea. This meant that the latter rivers were slowed down, and their burden of silt, which would normally have been carried away by sea currents, was deposited inland. Vast mud swamps intersected by drainage channels have hence come to be characteristic of much of Mesopotamia south of Baghdad, and the whole region may be considered as a low platform of alluvium built up by the coalescence of a number of river deltas. The higher parts are now dry and firm, but the intervening stretches are still water- or marsh-covered, with a great number of distributary channels of varying width that are constantly shifting. From the latitude of Baghdad southwards the braided channels of the Euphrates and Tigris have altered considerably within historic time; and at the present day, the south-eastward advance of the head of the Persian Gulf, which has proceeded during several millennia at the rate of one mile per fifty years, is still in progress. As the coastline advances, due to the continuing deposition of sediment, the land behind it slowly dries out in certain places, though by no means everywhere. As a result, marshland and braided river drainage, which are found only in the last 100 miles of the course of the Nile, occupy approximately one-third to one-half of the lowlands of Mesopotamia, and cover several hundred thousands of square miles.

It is hence possible to subdivide the lowlands of the Euphrates–Tigris into two contrasting regions: (*a*) the southern, or lower valley, which has only recently emerged from the sea, and where land forms associated with fluviatile deposition – marshland, braided channels, and embanked river-courses (levees) – are the chief features; and (*b*) the upper Mesopotamian region, a somewhat more complex area, where features due to erosion predominate. In this latter area there are the two distinct river basins (with smaller tributary valleys) separated by a broad stretch of upland and plateau, where several closed drainage basins occur. The line of division between the upper and lower regions of the Euphrates–Tigris lowlands can be taken at what was termed by de Morgan the prehistoric coastline of the Persian Gulf. This feature is a low ridge or shelf some 250 feet above the flood-plain, running eastwards from Ramadi to a point a little to the south of Baghdad. De Morgan's views of the origin of the Mesopotamian lowlands are still regarded by many as authoritative and well-founded; but a radically different explanation has been put forward more recently by Lees and Falcon. A summary of these later views is given in Appendix III.

III. GEOGRAPHICAL SUB-REGIONS

Lower Valley. Topographically, this region consists of an alternation of marshland and low mud plain, diversified by sluggish drainage channels. The whole area is extremely flat, with a fall of only 1 inch per mile over the last 100 miles of the Euphrates, and about 2 inches

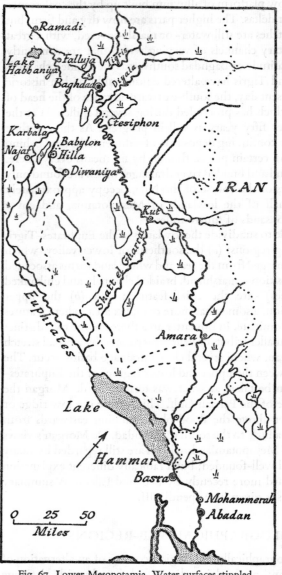

per mile along the Tigris. This means that over a stretch extending for 100 miles north-west of Qurna, which lies at the head of the Shatt el Arab, the Euphrates drops only 8 feet in base-level, so that annual flooding, which may be of the order of 5 to 10 feet, regularly inundates immense areas of country (highest flood-level recorded was 29 feet – on the Tigris – in 1954). As a result, much of the region is undisturbed swamp, and parts are still entirely uninhabited and unsurveyed. The Shatt el Arab, formed by confluence of the Tigris and Euphrates, is a broad navigable waterway, fringed by a belt of palms

Fig. 67. Lower Mesopotamia. Water surfaces stippled

for a depth of 1 to 2 miles, behind which occur masses of tall reeds

ometimes more than 20 feet in height. The Euphrates joins the Tigris
hrough an outflow from a large sheet of water, Lake Hammar, which
s an old lagoon or swamp now fed by the Euphrates. Here the fringe of
>alm trees gives place to reeds and aquatic vegetation that form a
:anopy over sluggish creeks and sand- or mud-spits. In spring, the
:eason of flood, virtually all the country in the triangle Basra–Amara–
Vasirjya is one expanse of continuous marshland.

The inhabitants of these districts follow a mode of life different from
hat of their countrymen further north. Dwellings are built of bundles
>f reeds fastened by ropes made of the same plant, and are set either on
hick bundles of brushwood as a foundation, or else on the few sand-
,pits that stand above the water. Rice is a staple, and diet is varied by
:ish, salted or dried, and by a species of edible rush known as *ageyl*.
Water-buffalo are almost the only animals kept, and these provide
:urds, butter, and cheese, together with dung which is the only fuel
1vailable.

Further north, the zone of marshland decreases in extent, though
:emaining a ubiquitous feature. Numerous old drainage channels occur,
1nd whilst a good many of these are occupied by swamps or lakes (e.g.
Lakes Habbaniya and Aqaquf), others are dry. An important feature is
the variation in level between the main streams of the Tigris and
Euphrates. From Baghdad as far as Qurna, the bed of the Tigris lies at
1 slightly higher altitude than that of the Euphrates, allowing the easy
construction of free-flow irrigation channels. In the region of Baghdad,
the position is reversed, with the Euphrates lying higher than the Tigris.
This circumstance has for centuries been utilised with much effect by
irrigation engineers.

Upper Valley. Above the latitude of Ramadi, both the Tigris and
Euphrates flow in well-defined valleys comparable in certain respects
with that of the Nile. In parts, the rivers meander over extensive
flood-plains; at others, they have cut deeply into soft, horizontally
bedded rock measures, and lie in a trench or shallow gorge. Here and
there, though less frequently than on the Nile, outcrops of harder rock
have resisted erosion, and stretches of rapids or 'narrows' occur. A
special feature of the Tigris (and not the Euphrates) is that because of
the meandering course of the river, and the presence of natural levees,
tributaries enter only with difficulty. This is the case on the eastern bank
of the Tigris between Baghdad and Mosul, where numerous small
streams descend from the Zagros Ranges. At their junctions with the
Tigris there is sometimes an area of poorly drained marshland.

Relief in parts of the Euphrates and Tigris valleys strongly suggests that the regime of both rivers was at one time markedly different than that occurring now. Much of the river bed even in the plains area is deeply incised, with the river flowing in a notch well below the level of the surrounding plain, and bounded by cliffs sometimes 200 to 300 feet in height. Incised meanders are a common feature on the middle Euphrates, recalling on a larger scale the land forms of the Seine valley below Paris. River rejuvenation at no very distant date would seem to be the causative factor, and this would appear to have taken place as the result of one or more of the following: (i) the possible sinking of the floor of the Persian Gulf, due to the accumulation of masses of sediment, (ii) the rise of the fold ranges of Anatolia. It is also possible that a temporary climatic phase of increased humidity in Tertiary or early Quaternary times, could have produced a greatly increased volume of water in the rivers.

At the present time, this slotted drainage in upper Mesopotamia has certain disadvantages. Irrigation is difficult in regions where the river is well below the level of the surrounding plain; and miniature gorges and rapids hinder navigation. Thus in some parts the banks of both rivers are entirely isolated from the streams themselves, and wide stretches remain uninhabited.

Between the upper Tigris and Euphrates lies the region known as the Jezireh (Arabic – island), which is bounded on two sides by the rivers, and on the north by the fold ranges of Asia Minor. For the most part, the Jezireh consists of an undulating plain or low plateau, lying at an altitude of 500 to 1,000 feet above sea level, with a number of small closed basins from which there is no drainage outlet. The largest of these basins is a long, narrow trench cut deeply into the plateau and known as the Wadi Tharthar. Streams enter the Wadi from the north, but terminate towards the southern end in a salt marsh. The Wadi may be a tectonic feature, or even an old river valley now dried out; and it is now used as an immense storage basin for flood-waters (see p. 383).

To the north-west of the Wadi Tharthar lies the Jebel Sinjar, a prolongation of the Syrian fold structures. As the highest parts reach 3,000 feet, there is a heavier rainfall on the upper slopes, and some settled cultivation is therefore possible. The Yezidi, who inhabit the Jebel, practise mixed arable and pastoral farming. Another important feature of the Jezireh is the Khabour valley, the ancient region of Mitanni, where irrigation was formerly developed on an extensive scale, and a relatively dense population maintained. Though nowadays

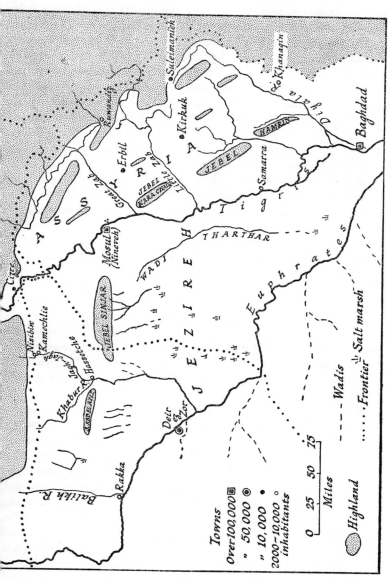

Fig. 68. The Upper Valley Region

the river is malarial, and its waters charged with sulphur, improvement is once more taking place. Modern pumps for irrigation are being installed, and colonies of immigrants – chiefly Armenians, Assyrians, and Arabs – are slowly being absorbed into new agricultural settlements.

The region on the eastern bank of the Tigris is known as Assyria. Here the land rises in steps from the Tigris towards the north-east, each step being marked by increasingly prominent ridges that are aligned generally from north-west to south-east. The first of these ranges is the Jebel Hamrin (max. height 1,600 feet), which fronts the Tigris along a part of its course. Numerous tributaries of the Tigris have broken through the ridges, forming gaps or gorges, so that the whole region of Assyria has been dissected, giving on the south-west a fairly broad open plain with occasional higher ridges. This passes towards the north-east into an increasingly broken and mountainous country with scattered lowland basins shut in by hills. Ultimately, the main Zagros Ranges are reached on the east, and the Anatolian arcs on the north. Both of these higher upland regions are occupied by Kurds, hence the name Iraqi Kurdistan is sometimes applied to the parts of the mountain massifs that lie within the Iraqi state.

IV. CLIMATE

The lowland region has two marked seasons – a dry and intensely hot summer, lasting from May to October; and a relatively cold, damp winter from December to March, with spring and autumn as short transition periods between the two.

With the development of summer monsoonal low pressure conditions over the Persian Gulf and north-west India, air is drawn towards the south-west, giving remarkably regular and constant north-westerly winds over the whole of Iraq. These are known as *Shamal*, and blow without interruption during the summer. The air is dry; no cloud forms, and the sun beats down uninterruptedly over the lowland, giving rise to shade temperatures that exceed 95° F. on most days, and not infrequently reach 120° F. Some relief is obtained during the night, as diurnal variation of temperature is marked: and near the rivers and marshes, intense evaporation may lower the day temperature by a few degrees. Lacking the possibility of moving to nearby hill regions, most Iraqis are driven to constructing underground shelters (*sirdab*) in which to pass the hottest part of the day. A further unpleasant feature is blowing dust, raised by the strong *Shamal,* which reaches a climax in late afternoon, and drops at night.

With the wind blowing towards the Persian Gulf during the summer season, there is little mitigating effect from the presence of the sea – temperatures for Basra, Baghdad, and Mosul show a remarkable uniformity, though it may be noted that nights are cooler inland, and the length of the summer is somewhat shorter in the north. It is also noteworthy that over much of the Mesopotamian lowlands, the maximum of temperature tends to occur in August – an unusual feature for an inland region, but possibly due to the development of the monsoonal circulation which takes some time to become established.

In winter, temperatures generally lower than might be expected can be explained by the presence of snow-covered mountains to the east and north. Differences are apparent between the north or upper basin, and the south; the former region experiencing something approaching a continental regime, the latter a milder climate, due to latitude and the influence of the sea. A comparison between Mosul and Basra shows that for the coldest month (January) there is 9° F. difference of temperature.

Another significant fact is that the absolute maximum of temperature recorded at Shaiba in January is 81° F., and at Mosul 66° F. – i.e. 'hot' spells can occur during the winter in the south, but not in the north. Diurnal variation is again of great importance, and somewhat remarkably, this is smaller in the north during winter than elsewhere (e.g. Mosul 16° F., as compared with 20° F. for the rest of the region). Despite its low altitude, the whole of the riverine lowlands may experience spells of frost of some severity (absolute minimum temps. at Deir ez Zor 16° F., Mosul 12° F., Baghdad 19° F., Basra 30° F.), though the worst effects naturally occur in the north.[1] Cold weather usually occurs when the Siberian anticyclone extends beyond the south-west of central Asia, and cold, stagnant Polar Continental air covers Persia and adjacent regions.

Because of the predominating off-shore wind, the high air humidities characteristic of the Persian Gulf do not occur on such a wide scale in the Euphrates–Tigris region. Nevertheless, as we have seen, evaporation close to rivers and lakes is high, and the air over a short distance becomes very humid – on the actual banks of rivers, wet-bulb temperatures of over 80° F. are common, though a mile or two away, there is a sharp drop. This fact, which does not always appear in climatological records, is responsible for a difficult 'physiological' climate, in which

[1] Cf. the contrast with coastal Syria, at a similar latitude, but where frost is unknown.

heat stroke and exhaustion can easily occur; and this goes far to explain the notorious reputation of southern Iraq – a reputation which does not at first sight seem justified until one takes into account the local variation of humidity.

Rainfall occurs only during winter, and is almost entirely due to the

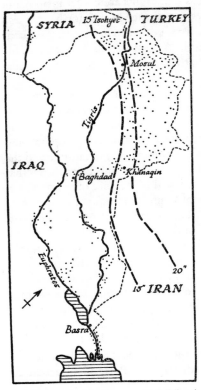

Fig. 69. The Relation between Rainfall and Settlement in Iraq. (Settled villages shown as dots.) Rainfall increases eastwards towards the Zagros Range

arrival of moist maritime air from the Mediterranean, in the form of shallow and somewhat degenerate depressions. The damp air has previously passed over the mountainous country of Anatolia or the Levant, there depositing much of its moisture, so that on arrival in the Tigris–Euphrates basin, only a reduced rainfall occurs, with annual totals ranging in the lowlands from 1 to 20 inches. On uplift over the Zagros ranges, however, considerable precipitation, exceeding 40 inches, occurs – a figure rather higher than at one time believed – and, in order to explain this apparent anomaly of abundant rainfall from weakened and dried-out depressions, it is necessary to recall that all rainfall in Iraq is of the instability type (Chapter III), and is therefore intensified by a mountainous topography. There may also be a further factor: rejuvenation of the depressions by absorption of water vapour from the vast tracts of swamp and lake in lower Mesopotamia, or, more distantly, from the waters of the Persian Gulf. A strong south-easterly air current, cold and relatively damp, and known as a *Sharki*, usually develops in front of an advancing depression, and this may bring moisture northward from the Gulf.

Because of the regularity of land forms, the distribution of rainfall follows a simple pattern. Late January or early February is the wettest period, and normally no rain falls between the end of May and the end of September. Over most of the country annual falls do not exceed 5 inches, but towards the mountains on the east and north there is a rapid increase. The foothills of the Zagros stand out as relatively well-watered, and the Assyrian region receives over 15 inches, an amount sufficient to allow cultivation without irrigation. The 15-inch isohyet is of extreme importance in Iraq and northern Syria, since it marks the effective limit between desert and cultivated land[1] (Fig. 69). With less than 15 inches annual rainfall agriculture is dependent on irrigation, and settlement is confined to the neighbourhood of rivers – away from water supplies, the population is nomadic.

	J	F	M	A	M	J	J	A	S	O	N	D	Total	Rainy Days
Temperatures (° F.)														
Deir ez Zor	45	48	52	66	77	85	92	89	83	71	59	48		
Mosul	41	48	55	63	75	84	95	95	82	72	59	47		
Baghdad (Hinaidi)	48	52	61	71	82	90	94	94	87	76	63	52		
Basra (Shaiba)	52	57	65	75	86	91	96	97	90	80	68	55		
Rainfall (in.)														
Deir ez Zor	1·6	1·0	0·3	0·6	0·1	0	0	0	0	0·2	1·5	1·0	6·3	29
Mosul	2·6	3·8	1·6	1·8	0·5	0	0	0	0	0·2	1·8	2·5	14·8	60
Baghdad (Hinaidi)	1·2	1·1	0·3	0·4	0·4	0	0	0	0	0·1	1·0	1·0	5·5	28
Basra (Shaiba)	1·3	1·2	0·4	0·5	0·1	0	0	0	0	0·1	1·1	1·0	5·7	21

V. OCCUPATIONS

(a) *Agriculture.* This is overwhelmingly the most important occupation of the people, since industry could scarcely be said to exist on an important scale before 1950, and is still only in the first phases of development. Nevertheless, only about one-sixth of the land suited to cultivation is actually used, and of this a large part lies fallow for one or more years, particularly in regions dependent on irrigation, where increasing salinity of the soil, due to over-watering, is an ever-present danger. Generally speaking, despite the extent of fertile alluvium,

---

[1] Ten inches of rainfall is normally regarded as the boundary between arid and moist regions, but in the Middle East, because of high temperatures, the 15-inch isohyet is a better criterion.

agricultural yields in this area are lower than in many other parts of the Middle East, and the reasons are to be found in a blend of natural, social, and economic factors. Besides the difficulties of climate, and the river system with its shifting banks, marshland, and rapid floods, insect pests occur on a considerable scale. Archaic methods of land tenure and exploitation are a further obstacle.[1] Yet another difficulty – uncommon in the Middle East – is a lack of manpower, as the result of which potentially fertile regions are left unexploited. Even in 1951-3 the average income for an Iraqi *fellah* and his family was calculated at only £14 ($40) per annum.

The division into two climatic provinces – a wetter (rain-watered) region and an arid (irrigated) region, with the 15-inch isohyet as boundary – has very great significance not only in relation to settlement, but also in relation to the crops grown, because it coincides roughly with another important line of demarcation, that of the northern limit of the date palm. Thus to the south, barley, rice, and dates are staples, all being grown under irrigation; whilst in the north barley, wheat, and Mediterranean fruits are the chief crops.

Barley is the most widely grown, since it thrives best of all cereals under Mesopotamian conditions, being more tolerant than wheat of aridity and of soil salinity, and also growing in a shorter time, a feature which reduces loss by the sunna insect pest. As a result, the yield per acre of barley is double that of wheat. Most barley is of native varieties, which are of poor quality; but within the last 20 years better strains have been introduced from Morocco and California. The main regions of production are the plains of Assyria (Mosul, Erbil, and Kirkuk districts), the lower Tigris valley (districts of Kut and the Shatt el Gharraf, an old drainage channel), and the middle Euphrates (Nasiriya district). Besides being consumed in the country, partly in bread, and partly as fodder, there is an export of the better varieties in normal times. Barley from the Tigris–Euphrates lowlands is, however, of indifferent quality, and suffers from the competition of American and Russian products in the world markets. There is much fluctuation in demand, and during the 1930's, when world prices were low, exports from Iraq greatly diminished. The opposite occurred during the Second World War, but now there is again a period of fluctuating prices, and highly variable export levels.

Wheat, like barley, is grown as a winter crop, but its occurrence

---

[1] Most Iraqi fellahin are métayers who receive less than 40 per cent. of the crops they cultivate. (See p. 196.)

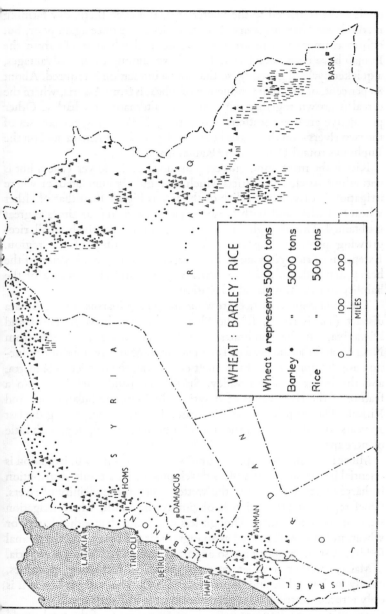

Fig. 70. Cereal Crops

tends to be restricted to the wetter area, and even there, dry farming methods are often necessary. Native varieties are once again poor, but efforts at improvement are being made, and wheat stocks from the Punjab have been introduced. These have, amongst other advantages, a quicker cycle of growing, so that sunna infestation is reduced. About 80 per cent. of the Iraqi production of wheat is from Assyria, where the cereal is grown together with, or as an alternative to, barley. Other productive areas are scattered along the middle and upper courses of the two rivers – on the Tigris between Baghdad and Amara, and on the Euphrates round Deir ez Zor, Ramadi, and Hilla.

Rice is the most important crop in much of the lower valley, but is naturally restricted to districts which are regularly inundated, or where irrigation is easy. The quality of the rice is higher than that of either wheat or barley, and with heavy irrigation, a yield four times as great is obtained. Thus though the area of cultivation is relatively small, rice-growing plays an important part in the economy of the region. Extension of rice-growing is, however, limited by law, because of the heavy demands on available water supplies, and also because of the liability to extend malarial infestation.

The chief regions of rice-growing are (1) the marshes of the Amara district (Tigris river), (2) the Shamiya district, between Najaf and Diwaniya, on the Euphrates, and (3) the lower Euphrates from Nasiriya as far as the head of Lake Hammar. Minor regions of production are the upper part of the Shatt el Gharraf, the district of Samarra, and the lower Khabour valley. Small-scale paddy fields are also a feature of the river banks of Assyria – chiefly round Sulaimanieh and Kirkuk. The crop has greatly increased in importance during the last 15 years, and almost all of the rice is for home consumption, with little or no export.

Millet is a summer crop, and thus wherever it is grown, irrigation is essential in the later stages of its development. As a result, distribution is sharply restricted, even in the wetter zone, to the vicinity of rivers. Chief region of production is obviously the south, where irrigation water is more abundant. Though less important than either barley or wheat, millet is widely used as an ingredient for bread, and for animal fodder. A small quantity is also exported, mainly to Turkey and Syria.

Maize, another summer crop, is grown in increasing quantities, chiefly in the middle and upper parts of both river valleys; but as it is only a recent introduction, present output is still very small.

Commercial Crops. Iraq produces about 80 per cent. of the total world supply of dates – that is, of the proportion of dates that form an article of commerce, because most dates are eaten directly by the growers, or else bartered. The general conditions under which date palms thrive have already been touched upon, and it is sufficient to recall that the palms can flourish in dry, saline, sandy, loamy, or even waterlogged soils, although the maximum yield of fruit is obtained when abundant water is available.

The region of the Shatt el Arab is pre-eminently suited to date-production, and both banks are lined with date groves extending inland for about a mile and a half. Some 25 to 30 million palms are cultivated throughout the region, and of these, one-half are found close to the Shatt el Arab, the rest occurring along the river banks as far north as Latitude 33° N. A curious feature is the rise of the river under the influence of the incoming tide. Fresh water is ponded back in the Shatt el Arab, and floods the banks to a depth of as much as 3 feet to provide natural and regular irrigation of the groves – a phenomenon that from the point of view of the native farmer is wholly estimable.

In order to ensure a good crop, the land is dug over once every four years; and because of the frequent presence of creeks and water-courses, this must be done by hand. Artificial pollination is, as we have already seen, highly necessary; and though most groves include 3 per cent. of male palms, the district of Fao has developed a special trade in male pollen dust, from which other date-growing regions are supplied.

About 130 varieties of date are known, but three are most widely grown. The *Halawi* palm produces the finest fruit, but gives only a moderate yield (44 lb. per tree) (Dowson), whilst the *Sayir* produces slightly less, but is more tolerant of inferior growing conditions, and is probably the most widely grown. The *Zahidi* does not give a fruit of high quality, but the yield is over 120 lb. per tree, and this compensates for the low price obtained. Fertilisation of the female palm takes place in April, and picking begins in August, when large numbers of nomadic tribesmen move into the date-growing areas to work as seasonal harvesters.

Besides forming an extremely important part of local diet, dates are used in the distilling of *arak* – the chief fermented beverage outside the vine-growing areas, and one thought to have value as a prophylactic against malaria. The crushed stones are fed to cattle, and both leaves and trunk of the palm are used in light constructional work (houses, boats, even bridges), and also in the manufacture of paper. About one-half of the average annual production of 350,000 tons is retained for home consumption, the rest exported.[1]

Cotton is the second commercial crop of the riverine lowlands, but in strong contrast to the successful development of date-growing, cotton has experienced many vicissitudes. Some cotton has for long been grown to meet the needs of local craft industry; but large-scale production for export began after 1920. Iraq had no modern textile machinery before 1940. There are a number of handicaps, chief of which are insect pests and soil salinity (the latter being especially prevalent on irrigated land). Periodic invasions by locusts from the Nejd cause damage, and the price of cotton fell because of the world slump of 1929–31. Some improvement then occurred, and a market was found in Japan, which absorbed most Iraqi production between 1937 and 1940. With the war of 1939 this trade eventually disappeared, and most of the land was replanted with food crops. Dollar shortages in Europe, and high world prices have more than restored the situation. There is now a regular home demand from the textile mills installed since 1940, and over the last ten years, exports have averaged more than £1 million annually, with Japan, Hong Kong, and central Europe the principal customers.

Minor Crops. Tobacco is widely grown in the foothills of the north-east, particularly in Kurdistan, but the product is consumed only within the country. Though some improvement has recently taken place following the introduction of new stocks from the Balkans and Turkey, the crop is still of indifferent quality, and unlikely to compete in outside markets. Vines are also an important feature in the north-eastern foothills, and in some districts of Kurdistan may be said to be a principal crop. Numerous varieties of other fruit and vegetables are also grown, more especially in the wetter zone of the north, though Baghdad is increasingly important for figs and vegetables. As elsewhere in the Middle East, market gardening associated with growing urban centres is a recent development of increasing significance.

An ancient silk industry still survives on a small scale, with mulberry trees grown chiefly in gardens or small enclosures in the Baghdad district. Output is not large – insufficient even for local demand – and

[1] It should be noted that dates are one of the few products of the Middle East which hold a commanding position in world markets. The situation of the date groves adjacent to tide water allows an unusually low cost of transport, so that competitors in North Africa – especially in Biskra, which has slow and difficult land communications with the Mediterranean – are at a disadvantage. The chief drawbacks to Iraqi dates are: poor packing methods, and variation in quality of the fruit, due to lack of grading and breeding control. Of recent years, some improvements have occurred.

there is strong competition from foreign-produced and artificial silks. Other reasons for the backwardness of this industry are a lack of modern machinery, and the absence of a skilled artisan population. Attempts have recently been made to introduce sugar, jute, citrus fruit, vegetables, and nut-trees.

Besides the cultivated plants mentioned above, three others grow wild, and have a place in the economy of the region. Liquorice is found along the banks of both rivers as far south as the Shatt el Arab. The root is dug up and then dried for a period of 12 to 18 months, after which it is ready for use. Some is retained locally, but most is exported to the U.S.A. and to Great Britain. Another product is gum tragacanth, which is collected from bushes that are natives of the semi-arid steppe or desert. Most of the world's supply comes from the Tigris–Euphrates lowlands and from Iran, and is used in the manufacture of pharmaceutical products, and sauces and pickles. In the north-west the valonia oak is important. Clumps of these trees grow on the higher, damper patches of the Zagros and Anatolian Ranges, and from these districts leather industries located in Aleppo, Mosul, and Baghdad are supplied. Small quantities of the gall-nut are also exported.

VI. IRRIGATION

Control of river waters for irrigation presents an unusual problem: because of the occurrence of floods in spring, at a time when all crops except rice are partly grown, cultivated areas cannot simply be inundated, as in Egypt; and water must be impounded as far as possible within the banks of the rivers themselves. This is achieved by the construction of large artificial embankments or levees; but at times when the river is dangerously high, breaches are deliberately made in the levees to allow flooding to take place in areas where damage will be least.

Another problem is to drain off stagnant flood-water, which, if left on the land, is very prone to induce soil salinity. In ancient times a simple but effective system of canals was created with the dual functions of watering arid areas and draining waterlogged zones, and to achieve this, skilful use was made of the variation in relative level between the Tigris and the Euphrates. A large number of canals were constructed on both sides of the Tigris from Tikrit southwards, and five major channels also led water from the Euphrates to the Tigris in the region of Baghdad and Babylon. Irrigation reached its highest development in

the early Abbasid period (*c.* A.D. 850–1000); and from that time onwards there was a prolonged decline. Since about 1880, however, a
major revival has occurred. Old channels have been cleared and
repaired, and a system of new barrages and canals built.

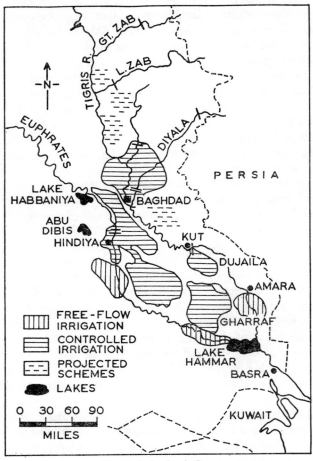

Fig. 71. Irrigation in Iraq

There are two separate problems involved: control of floods in order
to prevent destruction on a large scale (much of Baghdad was badly
damaged by floods in 1954), and utilisation of river water for irrigation
and de-salination. Flood control on the Euphrates involves two basins,

at Habbaniya and Abu Dibbis. A barrage across the river at Ramadi (containing a fish-ladder and a navigation lock for river craft) raises river level to allow diversion into the Habbaniya depression. Water stored in this basin can then be led back into the Euphrates in the dry season by an outlet canal at Dhibban. In addition, another channel leads to the Abu Dibbis depression, which is at present used only to receive excessive flood-water from Lake Habbaniya in an emergency. So far, water from Lake Habbaniya is not stored at Abu Dibbis for irrigation purposes, since the latter has extensive saline deposits which contaminate the water.

Because of greater volume, the largest flood control scheme of Iraq is located on the Tigris, in the Wadi Tharthar. This is another aretic drainage basin, with its lowest point 10 feet below sea level, and there could hence be produced a lake over 60 miles long, comparable in size to the Dead Sea. A barrage has been built at Samarra to deflect in river water through a canal 40 miles long, and the fall of level gives considerable potentialities for the generation of hydro-electric power. The Wadi Tharthar scheme was inaugurated in 1956, but it will take ten years for the basin to fill completely; and it is not yet certain whether seepage through porous rock-strata and possible salinity will allow the stored water ever to be used for irrigation. As a prevention of flooding, however, the scheme is already highly successful.

Another regulator dam is almost finished on the Lesser Zab river, at the Dokhan gorge some 40 miles north-west of Sulaimaniya. This is a high dam (350 feet), and besides its primary purpose of storing water for irrigation, it will be an important flood control measure, and a potential source of hydro-electric power. Further extensions of the Dokhan scheme are in progress at Batma and at Udhaim; and another multi-purpose dam is under construction at Darband-i-Khan. Proposals have also been made for other dams (a) at the Bekhme gorge on the Greater Zab river, and (b) on the Tigris just north of Mosul.

A number of older barrages and weirs serve to raise the river level for irrigation. The oldest barrage is at Hindiya, on the Euphrates, and was constructed in 1913, with additions in 1922. Its functions are (i) to divert water from the Euphrates into a canal that was one old channel of the Euphrates, and which runs parallel to the modern river through Hilla; and (ii) to raise the general level of the Euphrates and thus allow irrigation in the region of Karbala (on the right bank of the river opposite Hilla), and also upstream on the left bank as far as Ramadi. Another irrigation canal, dependent on a barrage at Daghgara, has become silted-up, and is now of little use. Altogether, some 3 million acres of land are irrigated, and a recent survey suggested that by further expansion of canals and de-silting, a further 19 million acres of unused land could be made productive.

Smaller schemes on the Euphrates include (i) the Greater Musayyib project (1956) which has brought under irrigation nearly 300,000 acres; (ii) regulators on the lowest part of the Euphrates just before it enters Lake Hammar – these would allow more extensive rice cultivation; (iii) similar regulators at Shamiyah in order to maintain river level in the dry season.

A barrage at Kut, on the Tigris, was completed in 1943. Some 2,100 feet in length (over three times the size of the Hindiya dam), it will eventually bring under cultivation two extensive areas that lie south and south-east of Kut; respectively the region of the Shatt el Gharraf, and the region of the Shatt el Dujaila, both of which are braided distributaries of the Tigris, but have no outlet at their lower end. Water is not available all the year round in these areas: it can only be supplied during the winter, since the summer flow is required for rice cultivation downstream at Amara.

The Diyala weir feeds six canals which irrigate an extensive area north and north-east of Baghdad. Altogether, about 330,000 acres are watered, as compared with 925,000 acres in the Hilla region of the Euphrates, 380,000 acres (Ramadi region), and a potential estimate of 750,000 acres round the Shatt el Gharraf and 230,000 acres round the Shatt el Dujaila. In the Kirkuk plain, a canal has recently been constructed to tap the waters of the Little Zab, and 125,000 acres are irrigated. Further developments of irrigation and drainage are in progress along the Greater Zab; at Ishaqi on the Tigris below the Tharthar barrage; around Basra, the Shatt el Arab and Lake Hammar; and on a much smaller scale in the north – at Mosul, Erbil, Kirkuk, and Sulaimaniya.

Within the last ten years, separate drainage projects have also been developed. These involve the construction of large outfalls, which lower the water-table in the subsoil by leading off groundwater either into rivers or natural depressions. Sometimes, gravity flow is possible, but in most cases pumping is required; and because of the prevalence of dust- and silt-laden winds, artificial dredging and wind-breaks are also necessary. So far some £30 million has been allocated for the construction of field drains.

In the south of the Tigris–Euphrates valley, the river has raised its bed in places above the level of the surrounding land, and here there is sometimes no need to build barrages, since river water can be led off directly to the fields. Areas of such 'uncontrolled' irrigation are found along the lower Euphrates from the region of Najaf as far as the head of Lake Hammar, and along the Tigris south of Amara. About 300,000 acres are watered in this way; but the system tends to be precarious, as any slight change in the water level of the rivers – produced by the formation of a new distributary, or by artificial control of waters upstream – may result in a cessation of flow. There is, too, the possibility, during the flood season, of receiving far more water than is really required.

Finally, reference must be made to the extensive lifting of water by mechanical means – by modern pumps with diesel engines, and also by more primitive norias, sakiyas, and shadufs. About one-half of the irrigated land of Iraq is still watered by lift, and one-half of the total number of pumps is found on the banks of the Tigris round Baghdad and Kut, with about one-quarter on the middle and upper Euphrates, and the rest (just under one-quarter) along the Shatt el Arab. The inhabitants of the region consider that irrigation by lift produces more valuable and better cultivated land, as compared with irrigation by flow, since amounts of water can be adjusted closely to crop needs, and the chances of inducing soil salinity are less.

VII. STOCK REARING

This forms a considerable supplement to agriculture in most of the Tigris–Euphrates lowlands, and predominates in the Jezireh and parts of Kurdistan, so that on balance stock rearing is more widespread than in many other countries of the Middle East. The reason would seem to be the close proximity of semi-arid or unirrigable land to cultivable stretches; and even in the lower riverine zones one may come across small expanses of higher ground perhaps only half a mile from a water-course, yet too elevated for irrigation, and hence fit only for grazing. In Egypt there is a single sharply defined boundary between desert and sown, and in Syria there are broad zones of steppe, but in Mesopotamia the intermingling and close alternation of marsh, alluvial tract, and upland ridge provides special inducement to the keeping of animals alongside cultivated areas.

Sheep predominate, being most numerous in the Jezireh and on the right (southern) bank of the Euphrates. Other pastoral regions are the southern margins of the Assyrian plains, between the Jebel Hamrin and the first foothills of the Zagros, and the Gharraf region between Kut and Hilla-Daghgara. Generally speaking, the sheep are bred for wool, which, though coarse, is exported in considerable quantities. Some is retained at home for the weaving of carpets and cloaks; most of the remainder goes to Britain, where it is regarded as equal in quality to the coarser Australian wools.

Goats tend to be more restricted to the north and east of the region since they prefer a hillier habitat, and a 1962 estimate gave a total for Iraq of about 2–3 million goats, as compared with 7 million to 8 million sheep. Milk is the most important product, forming a large part of the diet of tribesmen; some meat is also eaten, and goat hair is used in the making of tents.

In contrast to goats, which are associated with nomadism, cattle are kept mainly by settled and semi-settled cultivators living near rivers and marshes, where green fodder is available throughout the year. Cattle are valuable in two ways: as draught animals (for ploughing, for transport, and for the operation of irrigation wheels), and as producers of milk. Little meat is eaten.

There is some export of live sheep and cattle from the region, mainly to Syria and Jordan. This trade is of long standing: up to 20 years ago the main route followed was via the steppelands of the Fertile Crescent, and the animals were driven on foot towards the markets of the west by way of Rakka and Aleppo. One handicap was the variable rainfall of the region, which might result in a dearth of pasture along the route, and hence restrict or prevent the movement of animals. Construction of a railway between Iraq, Turkey, and Syria altered the position, and Aleppo and Rayak are now the principal terminals for the unloading of Iraqi cattle. An even more recent innovation is motor transport for sheep: it has been found that these latter animals can be moved most economically by road, whilst the larger beasts are best moved by rail. Small numbers of cattle are kept by the marsh Arabs of the south, though water-buffaloes are by far the more important. Over 80 per cent. of the total for the riverine areas are found in the four southern provinces of Amara, Diwaniya, Muntafiq, and Basra.

Camels are bred in large numbers in the deserts of the south-west, but in many parts of the alluvial lowlands, terrain is too soft and swampy, so that these animals are few outside the steppes. In recent years, with the growth of motor transport across the desert, camels for transport purposes have been much less in demand, and more and more are now bred for sale in the towns as food. In riverine regions the donkey is the chief beast of burden; horses, as is usual in the Middle East, being an exotic and costly rarity. Mule breeding is carried on by the Kurds.

The importance of stock-raising in the economy of the Tigris–Euphrates lowlands is shown by the fact that in some years exports of pastoral produce can approach or even (1948) exceed exports of agricultural products.[1] The scale of animal exports could be further increased were better methods of breeding practised and more attention given to feeding and maintaining the animals themselves – as it is, current methods are backward and unenlightened. The importance of stock rearing also serves to emphasise the fact that a prosperous pastoral industry might contribute considerably to raising the standard of living of the farmer; and many authorities believe that the answer to economic problems in much of the region lies in an extension of mixed farming. Too often the legend of an agricultural prosperity in past ages had caused modern governments to develop irrigation and cultivation, without regard for the potentialities offered by a thriving pastoral industry.

VIII. MINERALS AND MANUFACTURES

Apart from oil, the mineral wealth of the Tigris–Euphrates lowlands is extremely scanty. A small deposit of lignite is worked at Kifri (on the edge of the Zagros foothills, south-east of Kirkuk), but production is now sporadic, and was rarely above 2,000 tons annually. Salt and gypsum are the only other minerals produced in any significant quantity.

Industry is on an equally restricted scale. There are small craft industries chiefly concerned with textiles, building, food processing, metalwork, and tanning, but most products are of indifferent quality, and none but home markets are supplied. Textile products include rugs, carpets, and materials for Arab style of dress, using wool, cotton, silk, and a little mohair; and it is significant that the better-quality carpets sold in Iraq are imported from Persia and Turkey.

A few modern factories and manufacturing plants have come into existence over the past 25 years; and more recently impetus has been given by state participation in oil refining, asphalt, sugar, tobacco, and cement production, and small-scale shipbuilding and repairing. Textiles

[1] Respectively £7 m. and £4 m. 1948 was, however, a very bad year because of drought.

are the most important industrial activity (chiefly cotton and rayon), followed by brickmaking and building. A report by A. D. Little in 1956 advised the creation of a small chemical industry with by-products (plastics, fertilisers, etc.), an industry built upon the date (syrup and animal feeding-stuff), a steel rolling mill, and further expansion of existing activities. Some but not all of these suggestions are in process of development.

About 90 per cent. of Iraqi industry (craft and modern) is located in Baghdad, and the only other 'industrial' centres are Mosul and Basra. These three cities together consume about 90 per cent. of all electricity generated in Iraq – with the exception of Kirkuk, where almost all local current is used in the oil refinery. It will thus be clearly apparent that industry plays an exceedingly small part in the general life of the region – smaller, on average, than in most Middle Eastern countries, and considerably smaller than in the neighbouring region of the Levant.

IX. COMMUNICATIONS

Unlike Iran, where mountain ranges and deserts have proved severe obstacles to movement, the riverine lowlands stand out as a region of easy access. On either side of the two rivers the undulating plains are not entirely without water and vegetation, and have for many centuries furnished a variety of easy routes from the Indian Ocean to the Mediterranean. Though in the lower valley routes must avoid the lakes and marshland, keeping to the steppes on either side, the rivers themselves are navigable for hundreds of miles, even though with some difficulty at certain seasons of the year. Here is a considerable contrast with Iran, where a short stretch of the Karun river below Ahwaz is the only navigable waterway in the country.

In the upper parts of both the Euphrates and Tigris and their larger tributaries, a special form of water transport has for long been a feature. This is by *kelek* – a raft made of brushwood and small pieces of timber, supported by inflated animal skins. The usual number of skins in one raft is 50 to 100, but keleks of 250 skins are known, and these can carry loads of 50 tons. These rafts are almost unsinkable, and carry timber, hides, and charcoal from the forests of Asia Minor to the practically treeless lowland region. Because of the numerous rapids and gorges on the headstreams of the rivers, transport by any other craft is impossible. An extra hazard to a journey by kelek is the possibility of attack by

Kurds, who for centuries have been accustomed to take toll of river traffic by wrecking occasional keleks and appropriating the cargo.

Because of the swiftness of the current, upstream navigation is not possible, and on arrival at their downstream terminus the kelek is broken up; the brushwood sold, and the timber framework and deflated skins carried by pack animal back to the starting point, where they are used again to construct another kelek.

Further downstream where the waters are quieter, numerous types of boat are found, ranging from *mashufs* – small canoes for use in the marshes – to sailing craft large enough to carry 40 to 70 tons of cargo. Below Baghdad there are river steamers that tow barges between the capital and Basra; but these are small, since the Tigris has no more than 4 feet of water in winter, and only 3 feet in summer. Navigation on the Euphrates is less easy, since the average depth of water in the regions of Hindiya and Lake Hammar is only 2 feet 6 inches, and motor launches or small sailing craft replace the steamers of the Tigris.

The waterways until recently carried the greatest volume of traffic; but of late years, partly owing to increased use of the rivers for irrigation, their importance for communication has greatly declined, and they are now supplanted by the railways. The first railway to be laid was a short section between Baghdad and Samarra, built by German engineers as part of the projected Berlin–Baghdad system. This was of standard gauge. During the war of 1914, the British laid a number of lines, of metre and 2 feet 6 inches gauge, using material and stock from India. The disposition of the lines was governed by immediate strategic and economic considerations, so considerable alteration became necessary when the war ended. The 2 feet 6 inches lines were relaid to a metre gauge, but there are still two gauges in use – standard and metre, with the break at Baghdad. Metre gauge lines connect Baghdad and Basra via Hilla, Samarra, Nasiriya, and the Euphrates valley; and another branch runs from Baghdad to Kirkuk and Khanaqin. The former line was routed via the Euphrates partly because of the denser population and greater productivity of the lower Euphrates, and partly because of the restricted possibility of river navigation on this river as compared with the Tigris.

A line of standard gauge links Baghdad and Mosul, with an extension to Tel Kotchek on the Syrian frontier, whence direct communication exists with Aleppo, Ankara, and the Bosphorus. Construction of the northern part of this line was much delayed by political difficulties in the vilayet of Mosul, and was not completed until 1940.

During the war of 1939–45, further development occurred as the result of increased demand for oil, the enhanced strategic importance of the region, and the necessity to furnish military supplies to Russia. Much of this activity has proved ephemeral, but two permanent improvements may be cited; the provision of numerous passing loops on the railway system (most of which is single track) and the building of a rail link across the Shatt el Arab, giving direct access to the Persian railway system. In 1949 a line was completed from Baghdad through Kirkuk to Erbil in the extreme north-east; and in 1956 another standard gauge line was begun to link Baghdad–Kut–Nasiriya–Basra, thus providing unbroken standard gauge connexion from north to south.

Roads. There are still less than 1,000 miles of good roads in the whole region, and most of these occur in the immediate vicinity of large towns, or in the mountainous parts, where stone is available. In the plains, road metal is absent, but a surface capable of bearing light traffic is made by levelling large quantities of moist alluvium and allowing it to dry. In the wet season, these tracks degenerate into mud, especially near the rivers, where inundation occurs, and so road communications in many parts of lower Iraq are poor or non-existent. This explains the importance of rail and river traffic. However, with the achievement of flood control in 1956 there is now much more scope for permanent construction, and an extensive road-building programme is planned, which, when complete, will radically alter the situation.

In the north, conditions are better. The hardness and flatness of the surface allows light traffic, and motors can be driven at surprisingly high speeds over many parts of the steppe. Routes are indicated by beacons, and there is no attempt to use a single track – in fact, tracks are often rutted, and it is better to drive on the empty land on either side. Both rivers are followed by roads starting from Basra, neither of which is yet fully bitumenised for its entire length. The Euphrates road makes a wide detour to the south of the Hammar lake, then continues through Abu Kemal to Deir ez Zor and Aleppo. Both roads used to be impassable for a period of weeks during the rainy season. A third road – better termed a track, since only a part of it is maintained – crosses the desert, and is used by a motor service from Damascus to Baghdad.

Population. A 1962 estimate of the population of the Tigris–Euphrates lowlands amounts to 8½ million, of which just over 7 million live in the state of Iraq. Distribution is extremely unequal, with large numbers crowded into a few – but not all – of the riverine areas, and most of the steppe inhabited only by nomads, who are said officially to number only 5 per cent. of the population – probably an under-estimate. An important exception to this occurs in the north-east, where, because of higher rainfall, the population is much more evenly scattered over the entire lowlands, and concentration near rivers is much less a feature. In broad aspect, two fairly extensive regions of relatively dense population can be discerned: (a) the riverine district centred on Baghdad, and bounded roughly by the towns of Ramadi, Diwaniya, Kut, and Samarra. Here the extent of cultivable land is large, extending to considerable distances away from the actual river channels. Further south, the alluvial stretches are increasingly interspersed with arid ridges that carry only a sparse population. (b) The wetter zone of the north which may be said to include the provinces of Erbil, Kirkuk, and Sulaimanieh together with the northern half of the province of Mosul.

It is customary to regard the Tigris–Euphrates lowlands as closely similar in physiography to Egypt, and, therefore, it has come to be thought that the population situation in both countries must be again somewhat similar. This is far from being the case. In the first place, there is little correspondence in physical features or in river regime; and whereas the cultivable parts of the Nile valley are sharply limited to the floor of the valley, which for most of its length is no more than 6 miles wide, we have seen that potentially cultivable land extends for many miles on both sides of the Tigris and Euphrates. The feature of close concentration of population on actual river banks that is so marked in Egypt, is much less a feature in Iraq; and the only instances are regions where the rivers are deeply entrenched, e.g. on the Euphrates above Hit, and on the Tigris near Samarra. Moreover, the enormous densities in Egypt, amounting to 1,500 or 6,000 persons per square mile, are not found in Iraq, where, a few urban centres excepted, the highest density is 850 persons per square mile. In the light of this, one may recall the statement in an earlier chapter, that much of the Tigris–Euphrates region is under-populated, and in need of increased manpower to develop natural resources. As Sir W. Willcocks put it 'The Nile is a gentleman' – this goes far to explain the inequalities of population distribution.

We may next consider the urban population of the region. A few years ago, it was possible to say that urban life was little developed in Iraq: but within the last two decades there has been heavy migration from the countryside to towns, which have become correspondingly more important. The Iraq *Times* stated that by 1956 no less than 85 per cent. of the farming population in some areas had migrated to the towns. Baghdad has grown by 50,000 persons each year over the last ten years, and now has well over a million inhabitants, while Mosul is approaching the million mark. The effects of this hurried mass movement are to be seen in the 'shanty-towns' – in Iraq, huts of reeds, tin cans, mud, or odd strips of cloth. A survey made in 1956 suggested that about 80 per cent. of all habitations in Iraq were of this type, though by no means all of this number represent recent 'shanty' accretions to large towns. Four cities, Baghdad, Mosul, Basra, and Kirkuk stand out as the main urban centres. *Baghdad* (est. pop. 1962, 1,300,000) lies on the Tigris at the head of navigation of the river, and in the 'waist' of the lowlands, where the Tigris and Euphrates approach closely to each other, and hence give the best possibility of constructing irrigation canals. This narrow inter-riverine zone also provides a convenient crossing-place, since the marshland is reduced in extent and the firmer platform of steppeland provides a useful east–west route between the Mediterranean and Iran. The region of Baghdad thus has an important nodal position at the junction of routes from east and west across the desert, and from north, north-east, and south along the river valleys. It should be noted that all the factors mentioned above apply to a region and not to an actual site.

It is easy to see why a town should have grown up within the district of Baghdad, but the extra smaller scale features that usually fix the site of a town in one particular spot are less in evidence. Local changes in topography due to the shifting of drainage channels have led to the growth of three separate cities at various periods, and so within the Baghdad region there has arisen first Babylon, the ancient capital that lay closer to the Euphrates, some 60 miles to the south of modern Baghdad. Babylon was in turn succeeded by Ctesiphon, only a few miles from Baghdad, and this city remained the nodal centre until superseded by Baghdad in the early Muhammadan era. Baghdad itself dates only from the 8th century A.D., and a 'golden age' occurred when its Abbasid rulers supplanted the Omeyyads of Damascus and made it the capital of the Moslem world. Baghdad suffered greatly from Mongol invasion, and most of the older buildings have disappeared. The modern city is sprawling and undistinguished – in fact, an extreme disappointment to visitors who may wish to evoke the 'Arabian Nights'. As we have noted, many houses are of mud or tin cans, and until 1957 flooding was a frequent feature (Fig. 72).

Baghdad is the undisputed commercial centre of Iraq, with numerous, but usually small factories, workshops and distributing houses.

Industry is still partly confined to bazaar crafts, and is concerned with textiles, metals, foodstuffs and derivatives, pottery, and building materials. Commerce is often in the hands of Europeans, Jews (some

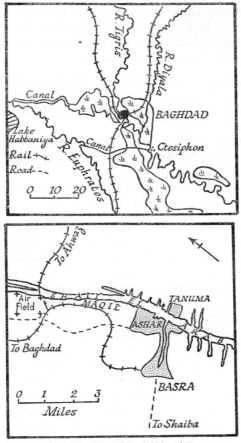

Fig. 72. The Sites of Baghdad and Basra

10,000 still remain in Iraq), and Armenians, with Iraqi Christians as clerks, supervisors, and foremen. An upper class – mainly Sunni Moslems – carries on the administration of the country; and a third element in the life of the city is a large group of absentee landlords.

Mosul (est. pop. 1962, 900,000), like Baghdad, dates only from the early Muhammadan era, though on the opposite bank of the river

Tigris the ruins of Nineveh go back to the second millennium B.C. Like many other sites in the Middle East, the fallen clay walls of the ancient city form an enormous *tell* or mound. Here, again, is an example of regional factors outweighing local influences in determining the growth of a city. The importance of the city arises from its position in the centre of the upper basin of the Tigris, at the junction of four contrasting geographical regions for which it acts as commercial outlet and exchange centre. These regions are:

(a) The plains of northern Assyria, where there is a dense agricultural population.
(b) The hills of Kurdistan, occupied by shepherds practising transhumance.
(c) The steppes of the Jezireh, where there is a mixed population of true nomads rearing sheep, cattle, and draught animals; and sedentary farmers.
(d) The uplands of the Jebel Sinjar, where pastoralism and agriculture are carried on by the Yezidi.

As a result, there is extreme heterogeneity of peoples within the city. Arabs are in the majority, with smaller groups of Kurds, Christians, Jews, and Yezidi, most of whom speak their own languages. An important mediaeval textile industry (note the word *muslin*) has now disappeared, though coarser textiles using wool as a raw material are still produced in the bazaars, and a recent feature has been the introduction of artificial silk weaving. Mosul is also important for leather working – a reflexion of its position on the edge of the steppe. Manufacturing is, however, less important than trade: grain, timber, hides, and manufactured goods are exchanged, and there are long-distance communications with Baghdad and south-east Turkey. Some produce from Turkey still comes by kelek (p. 388).

Basra (est. pop. 1962, 600,000) is an agglomeration of small sites grouped along the western bank of the Shatt el Arab some 70 miles upstream from the Persian Gulf. Basra proper is situated on a small creek 2 miles distant from the Shatt el Arab, and the principal port is at Ashar, on the main river. Modern docks have also been constructed at Maqil, 4 miles upstream from Ashar, and since 1939, further development has taken place at Tanuma on the eastern bank of the Shatt el Arab, opposite Ashar. Because of the recession of the head of the Persian Gulf, the growth of the port is relatively recent, and dredging on a considerable scale is necessary to prevent silting of the channel. Basra handles the greater proportion of the foreign trade of Iraq, and is the centre of the date-growing region, being itself surrounded by date-groves. Dates form the chief item in its export trade. Second in importance amongst exports is grain, with wool, liquorice root, and hides as subsidiaries. Imports consist chiefly of manufactured goods (cement, cotton and woollen textiles, machinery), tea, and sugar. Basra can be reached by large ocean-going ships, but about 10 per cent. of its commerce is still carried on in small native craft.

Kirkuk (est. pop. 1962, 500,000), though now overwhelmingly an 'oil' town, also has importance as a regional and route centre, and as the largest town in the Kurdish area of Iraq: a close neighbour, Sulaimaniya, is however sometimes spoken of as the 'capital' of Iraqi Kurdistan.

CHAPTER XVI

The Coastlands of the Levant

The region lying between the Mediterranean Sea and the deserts of Syria and Arabia, sometimes spoken of – particularly by the French – as the Levant, has a strong geographical unity. Structurally, it is a zone of junction, where sediments laid down into the Tethys are folded on to the buckled and broken edge of the Arabian platform; climatically, there is a striking 'Mediterranean' rhythm of abundant winter rainfall and absolute summer drought; one can observe a special economy based on intensive 'garden' cultivation, with commerce and craft industries as important adjuncts; and finally, in the sphere of human relations, the concept of a boundary zone occurs once more, since the Levant has in a unique way acted throughout historic time as an intermediary between east and west. This fundamental unity both from the physical and human standpoints, has to a certain extent been obscured by political developments since 1919; but it will be recalled that for centuries before the Versailles settlement the name 'Syria' was held to apply to the whole of the coastal region between Asia Minor and the Sinai desert – and, moreover, as an indication of the essential unity of the Levant, we may recall that only when the region was organised as a single unit did periods of greatest advance and prosperity occur. There is hence abundant justification for discussing the Levant as a single grouping, with boundaries that transcend existing political divisions which over the past forty years have showed themselves to be fluid and liable to alteration.

Structural Features. As has been stated, the main feature is the junction of ancient and recent rocks. In the east and south, younger sediments lie thinly, sometimes discontinuously, upon the mass of the Archaean basement, which is exposed in a few places; but towards the north and west, the basement rocks can no longer be traced, and the sedimentary rocks are thicker and more varied. Thus in Israel and Jordan, Archaean strata lie close to the surface, providing a core to the hills of Judaea and western trans-Jordan, but in northern Syria, the oldest series occurring is of Jurassic age. From this a number of significant features arise: in the south, rock types are fewer, and, because of the rigidity of the underlying mass, less disturbed, whilst in the north, strata are more varied, and folding is a conspicuous feature.

Fracturing along a generally north–south direction, with minor cross-faults at intervals, has given rise to a series of detached upland masses separated from each other by small lowland areas arranged in a roughly rectangular pattern. We can thus recognise a considerable number of separate sub-regions, each somewhat distinct from its neighbours; and writers on the geography of the region have suggested various schemes of division, ranging from a simple outline of coastal plain, mountain ranges, and interior lowlands, to a more elaborate classification recognising some

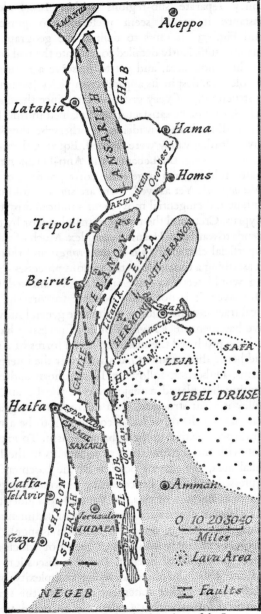

Fig. 73. The Geographical Sub-regions of the Levant

thirty separate sub-regions within Israel alone. In the present instance it would seem preferable to pursue a middle course, and Fig. 73 attempts to delimit the geographical sub-regions in a manner sufficiently detailed to indicate the real complexity and variety of the whole area, and yet to preserve a measure of simplicity. The whole area, despite its apparent simplicity (which is perhaps deceptive), is structurally of very great interest, since there are numerous features which cannot be satisfactorily explained in full. Faulting is prominent – it is difficult to consider how otherwise the Red Sea and even the lower Jordan valley were formed. Equally, the massive nature of some structures – e.g. the Lebanon and Anti-Lebanon ranges – suggest deep-seated folding on a large scale, corresponding to what Argand termed 'plis de fond'. Yet as well, there are signs of folding produced by more distant and tangential movement – indicated by the 'garland' effects in Cyprus, Crete and the northern mainland, or by the 'bunching' of fold trends towards the Hermon complex. Much of this folding is of a more superficial character (plis de couverture): and there is further difficulty in ascribing a timetable to the various processes – since in the east, folding would seem to have significantly affected Quaternary deposits. Moreover, it is not easily possible to correlate the development of local fractures and folding with more general movements of the primitive basement nuclei which must of necessity have occurred in order to have produced the massive plateau forms of Asia Minor and Persia; and hence disagreement has arisen over the interpretation of structural forms. Dubertret, following Blankenhorn and others, considers that faulting has played a major role in the Levant, and that the Bekaa valley is a rift structure, with downthrow in places of 8,000 feet. De Vaumas, on the other hand, considers it to be a syncline that has been upwarped relative to the Lebanon massif. To explain this, he suggests that with the accumulation of sediments in the Iraqi–Persian geosynclinal area, the eastern portion of the basement of Arabia has been depressed and tilted, hence raising its western edge which has become unstable. Because of this, de Vaumas concludes that there has finally developed a downward movement of sedimentary layers in the extreme west (i.e. in the main Lebanon Range). The whole question involves extremely wide issues, many of which are possibly of little direct geographical interest. But this discussion may have served to indicate a little of the underlying complexity of conditions, and to reinforce the earlier statement regarding the surprising variation in structural forms within a relatively restricted area. In the succeeding section, the views of Blankenhorn and Dubertret form the basis of the exposition.

I. GEOGRAPHICAL SUB-REGIONS

Beginning in the north-west, we may first discuss the Jebel Ansarieh, which consists of a broad, gently folded anticline, with Jurassic lime-stone rock as the core, and later series (chiefly limestone and sandstone) on the flanks. The average height of the Ansarieh crest is just over 4,000 feet, and the highest peak, Nebi Yuness, reaches 5,200 feet. In the north, where the range is folded against the Amanus, fracturing has taken place, so that the anticlinal structure is somewhat broken up, and fault-valleys alternate with irregular horsts of higher ground. The most important fault structure is the Ghab, a lowland rift 50 miles long by 10 miles wide, that is now occupied by the middle Orontes river. The valley floor lies 3,000 feet below the summits of the Jebel Ansarieh, with a steep, almost precipitous western boundary. In winter, the floor is covered by flood-waters from the Orontes, and in summer, by a malarial swamp.

On the western (Mediterranean) side of the Ansarieh range, oscilla-tion of sea level has given rise to a number of broad wave-cut terraces covered by marine deposits that tend to be less porous than the lime-stone substratum. Thus these western slopes of the Ansarieh offer greater possibilities of cultivation, and are the most densely peopled part of the region. Elsewhere, extreme permeability of the limestone reduces surface water to a minimum, and although annual rainfall exceeds 30 inches, many parts are karstic, with vegetation restricted to a stunted garrigue. Only in the extreme north (Slenfeh district) are trees at all numerous; and much of the south and east is thinly populated.

East of the Ghab, the land rises gradually to form an irregular plateau, of which the highest parts are the Jebel Zaouieh between Idlib and Hama, and the heights just east of Hama, where there is a maxi-mum elevation of 1,500 to 2,000 feet. Much of this plateau is open, fertile, and easily cultivable, giving the impression of a plain rather than an upland; but, because of its altitude, streams are entrenched in narrow, steep-sided valleys, and the raising of irrigation water to the fields is a matter of difficulty.

Adjacent to the Ansarieh range in the south is the lowland corridor sometimes spoken of as the Tripoli–Homs gap, and sometimes as two separate districts, the Plain of Akkar (Tripoli region) and the Bukeia (Homs region). The gap is occupied by a small river, the Nahr el

Kebir, which has laid down rich alluvium derived from the varied sedimentary rocks and numerous basalt intrusions of the district. As a result, parts of the gap are closely settled by a farming population, but the full agricultural potentialities are not developed, because of the prevalence of malaria, which is especially prevalent in the north of the plain of Akkar.

The Lebanon Range. This is the highest of the mountain massifs of the Levant. The culminating peak, Qornet es Sauda (lying east-south-east of Tripoli), is just over 10,000 feet, whilst Mount Sannin (east-north-east of Beirut) is only a thousand feet lower. The entire range consists of a single upfold, open in the north, more arched and constricted in the south, and intersected by numerous faults, along some of which there have been intrusions by basalt. A feature of great importance, peculiar to the Lebanon, is the occurrence of a complex of impermeable rocks of Cretaceous age, consisting of sandstone, marl, and lignite. These rocks are exposed only on the western slopes of the range, where they overlie massive Jurassic limestone. Above the impermeable Cretaceous strata comes a cap-rock of porous Cretaceous limestone that forms the highest parts of the mountains. At the line of junction of the two differing series there occur many springs of water, where rainfall that has been absorbed in the porous rocks is forced to the surface. The occurrence of these springs at the unusual altitude of 3,000 to 5,000 feet above sea level is one of the curiosities of the Middle East, and as many of the springs are large – sometimes rivers rather than streams – extensive districts can be irrigated from them (Fig. 74).

Because of the occurrence of abundant water supplies, and a varied, fertile soil derived from different rock outcrops, the middle slopes of the Lebanon Range are intensely cultivated, and provide much of the wealth of the Lebanese state. Another interesting feature of human occupation related to the occurrence of these impermeable beds has been the refuge offered to persecuted religious minorities. The soft underlying Jurassic series has weathered into deep ravines, with forbidding cliffs often several thousand feet in height – a considerable obstacle to penetration inland from the coastal plain. At higher levels, where the more resistant Mesozoic strata are reached, erosion has been less active, and there is a piedmont zone that is at once more fertile, and less difficult topographically. Here refugees have been able to settle in comparative safety, and gain a living by agriculture. At the present time, the region is occupied by small tourist centres, and by monasteries and schools, which are especially numerous in the Lebanon.

As in the Jebel Ansarieh, the eastern limit of the Lebanon massif is marked by a great fault-line, with a downthrow to the east of 3,000 to 5,000 feet. This is a single fault rather than a true rift, though superficially at least the presence of the valley of the Bekaa, lying between

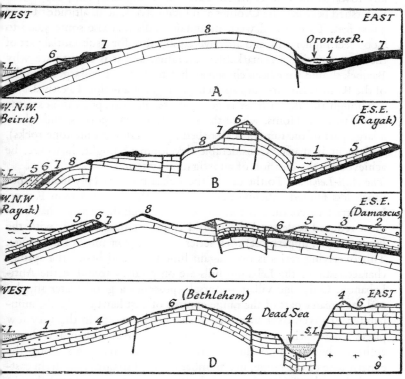

Fig. 74. Sections, Ansarieh, Lebanon, Anti-Lebanon, and Judaean Ranges. A – Jebel Ansarieh; B – Lebanon; C – Anti-Lebanon; D – Judaean hills. Key to Geological Strata: 1. Recent alluvium; 2. Miocene and later; 3. Eocene (permeable); 4. Upper Cretaceous (calcareous marl); 5. Upper Cretaceous (impermeable); 6. Upper Cretaceous (permeable); 7. Middle and Lower Cretaceous (impermeable); 8. Jurassic (permeable); 9. Pre-Cambrian base-rocks. Contrast conditions in Judaea and the Lebanon

the Lebanon and Anti-Lebanon Ranges, suggests that the Jordan trough is continued northwards. This is not entirely the case: the Bekaa fault is distinct from the two Jordan faults, the westernmost of which can be traced north from the Sea of Galilee as far as Beirut, where it would seem to have played some part in the formation of the headland

and bay on which the city stands. The Bekaa fault has a different trend, and is quite separate from the Jordan system.[1]

Much of the Bekaa valley has been filled by recent (Quaternary) sedimentation, and there is a gently sloping floor that rises very gradually towards the centre, where Baalbek, its highest point, lies on the watershed between the Orontes and Litani rivers, at an altitude of over 3,000 feet. To east and west, mountain walls that rise some 5,000 to 7,000 feet higher still, and are covered in snow for a substantial part of the year, provide a remarkable panorama; and it is easy to see why Baalbek should have been chosen as the site of one of the largest temples of the Roman Empire, and again nowadays for a national Festival.

Though the Bekaa floor is generally fertile (except in the extreme north, towards Homs, where the soil is stony and porous, and where a large part of the rainfall is absorbed by underlying limestone rocks), settlement is sparse. Considerable development might, however, be achieved by the creation of an irrigation system.

The Anti-Lebanon. To the east of the Bekaa rises a steeply inclined but much less faulted anticline that comprises the Anti-Lebanon Range. In contrast to conditions further west, tectonic disturbance has been on a reduced scale, and the upfold is almost undisturbed, with the youngest (i.e. uppermost) rock series exposed over most of the range. This overlying series is once again limestone, and hence the springs characteristic of the Lebanon hills are only rarely found in the Anti-Lebanon. Only one village – Aarsal – possesses a good water supply, and the greater part of the range consists of vast karstic uplands, uninhabited or given over to nomadic shepherds, except in the very few places where springs occur. The rainfall of the Anti-Lebanon is almost entirely absorbed into the ground, but water reappears along the eastern base of the range, in a number of small streams that drain eastwards into the Syrian desert, and ultimately terminate in salt basins. Of this kind are the Maraba, Awaj, and Barada (Abana) rivers.

The Hermon Range (Jebel esh Sheikh) is a continuation of the Anti-Lebanon, but there are slight differences of structure (e.g. a slightly greater degree of folding in the Hermon uplands); and a cross-fault enlarged by water action into a narrow defile, and occupied by the

[1] This is indicated by the existence of a broken mass of high ground at the head of the Jordan trough, north of Lake Huleh. The high ground was for long a barrier to communications, and a through road from the Bekaa to the Jordan was not opened until 1943. Further evidence is furnished by seismological records made at Ksara, in the Bekaa, from which it would seem that earth movements along the Jordan faults are not directly transmitted to the Bekaa region.

Barada river, separates the two massifs. Mount Hermon reaches 9,200 feet, 2,000 feet more than the highest peak of the Anti-Lebanon, and like its northern neighbour, is composed chiefly of limestone. All but the lowest slopes are uninhabited, save by wild bears and hyenas.

The Anti-Lebanon system may be taken as a prototype of most of the other fold ranges of central Syria, which consist essentially of a simple anticlinal structure, trending from south-west to north-east and dying out towards the Euphrates. Such are the Jebel Kalamun, north of Damascus, the Jebel esh Sharki, the Jebel et Tar, and Jebel Bishri of Palmyra. The upper slopes of these ranges are bare of soil and vegetation, the lower slopes carry grass for a few weeks each year, and nomadism is the predominant way of life. Permanent settlement is limited to a few oases such as Nebek, Qariatein, and Palmyra, where springs occur in association with faults.

The Hauran, Jebel Druse, and Leja. South of Damascus, topography is dominated by lava flows formed by very recent upwelling in the fractured edge of the Arabian platform. It has been noted that small-scale intrusions are common in north and west Syria (the largest being in the neighbourhood of Homs, where the marshy course of the Orontes is the last stage in the drainage of a lake impounded by a basalt sill), but in south-west Syria and northern trans-Jordan much wider areas are entirely buried under igneous material. The whole region as far as central trans-Jordan forms an irregular plateau, lying at an altitude of 1,000 to 2,000 feet. In the west, towards the Jordan valley, the landscape is open and rolling, with level stretches and broad valleys interspersed with occasional basaltic ridges or volcanic cones, some of which reach 3,000 feet in height. This open region, termed the Hauran, can, with a good water supply, be extremely productive, since the soil, being derived from lava, is very fertile. In Roman times the Hauran was one of the main granaries of the Empire, but at the present, cultivation is on a very much smaller scale.

Further east, the plateau becomes higher and more rugged. Vast numbers of boulders scattered over the surface become an increasing obstacle to cultivation, and the highest part of the plateau is reached in the Jebel Druse, an irregular dome of basalt, capped by low volcanic cones, the largest of which, Tel Guineh, is just under 5,000 feet above sea level. Adjacent to the Jebel Druse on the north-west and north-east lie two barren and desolate expanses of lava, El Leja and Es Safa. El Leja is probably the more forbidding of the two: here the lava crust has hardened quickly, and then been cracked and broken up by later

o

upwelling from below, giving the impression of rough chaotic vaulting. The lava flows are too recent for much soil to have formed; hence there are few inhabitants apart from a number of outlaws and bandits who live in the caves formed in the lava-sheet.[1]

The Uplands of Galilee and Judaea. Towards the south, the Lebanon Range becomes less imposing, and ultimately passes without break into the plateau of Galilee, the average height of which is 1,000 to 2,000 feet, although several minor peaks top 3,000 feet. The precipitous cliffs, deep ravines, and rocky slopes of the Lebanon proper are replaced by low rounded hills, smooth outlines, and grass-covered uplands, reminiscent in a few places of parts of the English Pennines. The whole upland system, which may be termed the Lebano–Galilean massif, comes to a somewhat abrupt end at the Plain of Esdraelon, which is a tectonic trough formed by subsidence along west-north-west–east-south-east running fault-lines. The northern fault-line is irregular, and consists of a number of steps, with a detached part of the Galilean massif, Mount Tabor, interrupting the continuity of the plain on the south-east. The southern edge, formed by the ridge of Mount Carmel, is much more clearly defined, with a steep rise along a single fault-line.

Because of the irregular nature of its northern boundary, the Plain of Esdraelon varies in width; where it reaches the sea, at Acre, there is a wide bay some 20 miles across; but further inland the plain shrinks to a mere corridor only 1 or 2 miles wide, ultimately widening once again towards the Jordan to an expanse of 5 to 10 miles. The floor of the plain is flat, and formed of a rich, deep black soil weathered from the limestone and basalt dykes of the Galilee plateau. A small river, the Kishon, drains the western part of the plain, reaching the Mediterranean just north of Haifa. Like the Plain of Akkar, much of this lowland was until recently highly malarial.

South of the Plain of Esdraelon lies the upland block of Judaea, which may be subdivided into three component areas: Samaria, the Judaean plateau, and the Sephalah. Samaria is a deeply dissected upland region, slightly lower in average altitude than Galilee, and with only one peak of 3,000 feet. The Carmel ridge, which forms part of Samaria, appears imposing, since it rises from a low coastal plain, but its maximum height is only 1,800 feet. Active weathering has hollowed out many valleys, some of which are narrow and gorge-like, others broad and fertile, and in the latter cultivation is usually possible. As

---

[1] Even in the days of the French Mandate, travellers or government officials found it advisable to take with them an armed guard when visiting these districts.

compared, however, with Galilee, Samaria is definitely less favoured in natural resources. Limestone and chalky marl are practically the only rock types exposed, and basalt dykes are fewer, so that the soil is poorer, and springs far less numerous. Settlement is largely confined to the bigger valleys, with the uplands given over to pastoralism.

Samaria merges gradually into the plateau proper of Judaea, which can be said to commence south of Nablus (i.e. about the latitude of Tel Aviv). Much of Judaea lies between 1,500 and 3,000 feet above sea level, and, because of diminished rainfall, erosion has been far less active, so that the deep valleys and irregular topography of Samaria are much less a feature. Judaea remains an unbroken upland plateau, with few diversifying elements. The general impression is one of a karst country: limestone and chalky marl are still the predominant rock series, and these outcrop frequently at the surface without any soil cover. Wide expanses of bare rock, numerous scattered boulders and scree, and occasional small valleys etched in the hill slopes, often dry and waterless, with caves and underground drainage, are characteristic of the Judaean landscape. Vegetation is rarely more than patches of scrub and thorns. In regions where marl predominates, a different, but equally inhospitable type of scenery is found – a series of greyish white or yellow hillocks, unrelieved by touches of green or brown vegetation. This is the Wilderness of Judaea, a bare, dusty, and repelling region. Cultivation in Judaea is limited to occasional patches of alluvium occurring in the deeper valleys where water is obtainable; and only five settlements of importance are found in this region: Jerusalem, Bethlehem (4 miles away), Ramallah, Hebron, and Beersheba.

South of Hebron there is yet another east–west running fault, which serves to differentiate the main Judaean plateau from the Negeb, an irregular upland region only slightly lower than Judaea, and which from the structural aspect is closer to the Arabian foreland than any region of the Levant yet considered. The covering of sedimentary rocks is generally thin, and often absent towards the east and south, where Archaean basement rocks are exposed. For the greater part, the Negeb consists of a tableland lying between 1,000 and 2,000 feet above sea level; but occasional wrinkling of the sedimentary cover in the centre and east has given rise to scattered fold ranges some thousand feet higher than the surrounding plateau. Wide areas of the northern and central Negeb are buried under a deep mantle of potentially fertile loess, and of late much interest has centred in schemes of development sponsored chiefly by Zionist organisations. The limiting factor is, however, water supplies, and as practically no rainfall occurs, artesian wells or large-scale irrigation canals to bring water from the north, are an essential to development. Great efforts have been made to develop irrigation by water brought from the north, and by using springs and local catchment methods, but there are many areas still unoccupied or given over to nomadism. Here occur many of the 'pioneer' settlements of Jewish immigrants.

The Sephalah is really an intermediate zone between the uplands of Samaria and Judaea and the Mediterranean coastal plain, and its origin is due to faulting, which has produced a series of downthrow basins or terraces on the western slopes of the Judaean hills. Towards the Mediterranean there is an upland ridge 700 to 1,000 feet above sea level that serves to divide off the Sephalah from the coastal plain. The chief rock series exposed is the same chalky marl as was described in the section on the Judaean Wilderness, but because of the wetter climate of the Sephalah, there has been considerably more erosion, with the formation of gently sloping hills and broad shallow valleys, covered by a moderately deep layer of rich soil. Hence the Sephalah, though an upland region, lends itself to cultivation, and in contrast to the higher plateaus of which it is an outlier, carries a dense population.

Coastal Plain of the Mediterranean. This is narrow and discontinuous in the north, but increasingly wide and extensive towards the south. In north-west Syria, fronting the Jebel Ansarieh, the plain consists merely of a series of enclaves interrupted at frequent intervals by mountain spurs that reach the sea. Something of the same aspect persists in the Lebanon, where the coastal plain, at its maximum near Beirut, is only 4 miles wide. At such places as Shekkah and Ras en Nakura, foothills again rise directly out of the sea. Road and railway must tunnel through the spurs, or cling precariously to ledges cut in the cliff-face.

At Haifa a terrace only 200 yards wide between the sea and Mount Carmel is sufficient to carry the road and railway southwards; but a short distance to the south the plain then widens to 10 to 15 miles in extent, and is here known as the Plain of Sharon. Further south still the coastal lowlands are even more extensive, with a width of 20 miles. This section, with Gaza as its centre, is the ancient region of Philistia.

The Plain of Sharon is formed of alluvium brought down from the hills of Samaria and Judaea – hence, where water is available, the land is extremely fertile. Close to the coast sand dunes occur and these some-times block the lower courses of streams that cross the plain, giving rise to swamps and marshland at a short distance inland from the sea. The varied nature of the soils allows specialist cultivation: citrus fruit on the sandy soils close to the coast, other fruit trees and vegetables on the heavier, damper alluvium further inland, then, as the ground rises towards the Sephalah, and soils are drier, cereals and fodder crops, with olives and nut-trees (almond, etc.) on the ridges that define the western limit of the Sephalah. In the region of Gaza, dunes become increasingly prominent, and the coastal lowlands of the extreme south are far less productive than the Plain of Sharon, because of the prevalence of blown sand. A slow battle, which man cannot as yet be said certainly to be winning, has for centuries been waged against encroaching dunes in this region.

The Jordan Trough. From the 1,000-foot contour (just north of the Israeli–Lebanon frontier), which may be taken as the effective northern limit of the trough, the Jordan Rift extends for 250 miles to the head of the Gulf of Akaba. The floor of the depression is not uniform, and the lowest part occurs in the region of the northern Dead Sea, where the lake bottom is 2,598 feet below sea level. Southwards of this point the floor rises, and reaches sea level some 80 miles to the south of the Dead Sea. The name El Ghor is sometimes applied to the whole depression, but the term is more usually held to apply only to the part from Lake Tiberias to the Dead Sea – a region lying entirely below sea level. The rift varies in width from 2 to 15 miles, and almost throughout its entire length it is bounded by the steep-sided, faulted edges of the Arabian platform to the east, and the massifs of Galilee, Samaria, and Judaea to the west. As the Judaean and trans-Jordanian plateaus rise some 3,000 feet above sea level, there is a precipitous descent to the Jordan floor, which lies 1,300 feet below sea level at the Dead Sea shore. A number of small streams plunge down the valley sides, and have carved deep notches in the plateau-edge, a few of which are used by roads. In many places, however, the descent is too steep, and direct communication, even by track, is impossible.

In the north, basalt flows across the valley at two points resulted in the formation of lakes. The smaller and northernmost was Lake Huleh (now largely drained), once extremely shallow and overgrown by papyrus swamps that were a breeding ground for mosquitoes.[1] Further south, a second barrier is responsible for the existence of Lake Tiberias.

[1] Until recently, some villages near Lake Huleh had a malarial incidence of 98 per cent.

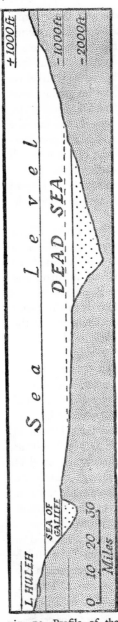

Fig. 75. Profile of the Jordan Depression

This lake is 13 miles long, and 5 to 8 miles wide, with the surface of the water 686 feet below sea level, and deepest part 700 feet lower still. The waters of the Jordan emerge through a narrow channel cut in the basalt dam, and are used for the generation of electricity. Below Tiberias, the Jordan meanders extensively across the floor of the Ghor, in which it has incised its bed some 150 feet, giving rise to shallow bluffs. A dense jungle of willow trees, tamarisk, and aquatic plants covers the banks of the river, which after winter floods carry an unpleasant mass of rank, decaying vegetation. Lower still in its course, the river becomes strongly saline, and intense evaporation leads to the formation of slimy colloidal compounds near the river, and to extensive multi-coloured mineral deposits at some distance away, giving the impression of a chemical slag-heap in an industrial area. The whole of the lower Jordan, whether jungle or saline 'bad-lands', is extremely uninviting. Tracks are difficult to construct because of the rapidly shifting meanders, sticky slimy soil, or dense vegetation, and few settlements exist. The shore of the Dead Sea itself consists of salt marsh interspersed with areas of salt-encrusted steppe.

The fault-lines of the Levant are of such recent origin (Oligocene) that adjustment along them has not completely ceased. From time to time minor displacements occur, giving small-scale earth tremors. These are not on a scale comparable with the earthquakes of the great east–west tectonic zone of northern Asia Minor, though the effects are seen, for example, in the minor earthquake of 1929, which destroyed buildings in Jerusalem, in the shock of 1758 which wrecked the pagan temple at Baalbek, and in the cracking of the floor of the Cave of the Nativity at Bethlehem.[1]

II. DRAINAGE

Little need be added to the survey given in Chapter II. The largest river in the Levant is the Orontes, which rises in the northern Bekaa, and is fed by springs from both the Lebanon and Anti-Lebanon Ranges. Over much of its course, the Orontes is shallow and marshy, being ponded back by basalt dykes; but in northern Syria it has cut deep meanders in the soft rocks, and lies well below the level of the surrounding plains. A special type of irrigation machine has been evolved to lift the river water to the level of the plain. This is the *noria*, a large wooden wheel some 20 to 70 feet in diameter, with paddles and buckets round the circumference. The wheel is turned by the force of the current only, like a water mill[2] and thus, unlike most irrigation machines, requires no motive power.

Close to the headstreams of the Orontes is the source of the Litani river (classical Leontes), which flows southwards through the Bekaa towards the upper Jordan valley. A downward warping on the coast of the Lebanon strengthened a short consequent torrent flowing to the Mediterranean, and this torrent was able to cut back through the main Lebanon ranges, finally capturing the lower waters of the Litani, which now make a sharp bend westwards and plunge through the mountains in a deep gorge. Because of this, the river was not used for irrigation until very recently (a dam was first built in 1952), and its valley does not even furnish an easy route to the interior.

A number of streams feed the upper and middle Jordan. Most of these rise in trans-Jordan, where rainfall is appreciably heavier than on the eastern side of the Judaean plateau. Torrents in winter, and trickles in summer, these tributaries lie for the most part in narrow gorges, with frequent cascades and rapids. Two somewhat larger streams, the Yarmuk and the Zerka, have cut large valleys, the former being used by the railway from Haifa to Damascus via Deraa, the latter by the main road from Jerusalem to Amman. The waters of the Yarmuk are also developed for hydro-electric power.

The remaining rivers of the Levant consist either of streams that

---

[1] Also, in certain of the events at the time of the Crucifixion ('And the veil of the temple was rent in twain, and the earth did quake, and the rocks rent, and the graves were opened', Matt. 27, li).

[2] Many *norias* are of considerable age, and show great skill in their construction. As they turn on wooden axles, the noise of a *noria* in operation can be almost deafening.

drain into closed, salt basins, or of small consequent torrents flowing directly from the coastal ranges to the sea. Towards the south, these short streams cease to be perennial, and the Yarkon (Auja), which enters the Mediterranean just north of Tel Aviv, is the most southerly of the rivers that flow all the year round.

III. CLIMATE

The outstanding feature in the climate of the Levant is the rapidity with which conditions alter away from the coast. This is due to the presence of well-developed mountain massifs running parallel to the coastline, which has the effect of restricting maritime influences to a narrow littoral zone. Continental influences hence approach closely to the Mediterranean, and, in addition, because of the height and continuity of the coastal ranges, there is a special 'mountain' regime characterised by lower temperature and a higher rainfall.

Besides this well-marked gradation from west to east, climatic differences are also apparent as between north and south. For all seasons of the year, the dominant prevailing wind is from west-south-west: hence in the north, winds are moister than in the south, since they have a long sea 'fetch'. In the south, air is drier, because winds blow from the land mass of north Africa and the Sinai. This is shown by the fact that the extreme north-west of Syria and the Hatay of Turkey have rain all the year round, with a slight, but perceptible fall in July and August. In the Lebanon and Israel, on the other hand, there is no summer rainfall, and aridity increases southward until, beyond Gaza, true desert conditions are reached.

Coastal Zone. In this region, winters are mild and summers only moderately hot, and rainfall is relatively abundant. Frost is almost unknown, though slight falls of snow may occur at long intervals – once in 10 or 20 years being the normal for Haifa and Beirut. The coldest period of the year is late January and February, when temperatures average 54° to 57° F. There is a fairly pronounced diurnal variation of temperature, with bright sunshine on about half the days of winter, giving a daily maximum temperature of 63° to 65° F., and a night minimum of 50° F. (Jan.). In March, a rapid change to warmer conditions begins. A feature of spring – and, indeed, winter – is the occurence of *shlouq* (khamsin) conditions, shown by figures of absolute temperature: Beirut has recorded a temperature of 79° F. in January, and Gaza one of 84° F.

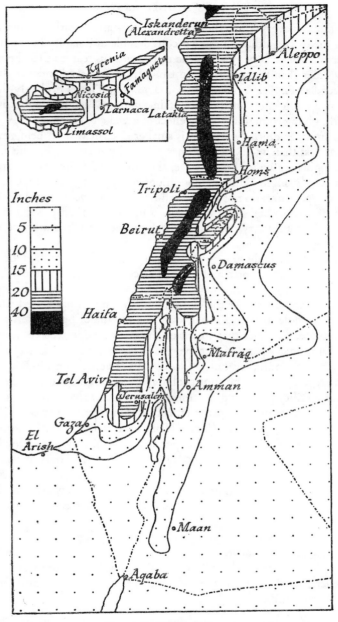

Fig. 76. Rainfall in the Levant

August is everywhere the hottest month – an indication of maritime influence – and although there is considerable uniformity in conditions over the whole zone, there is the rather curious feature that the north is warmer than the south (August monthly means: Iskanderun 82° F., Beirut 84° F., Tel Aviv 81° F., Gaza 78° F.). This is probably due to the sheltering effect of the mountain ranges, which are higher in the north, giving something of the effect of a walled garden.

In summer diurnal variation is smaller than in winter, being everywhere less than 15° F., and in many parts less than 10° F. This means that nights are unduly oppressive, though actual temperatures are not particularly high. Summer conditions are prolonged until October, and temperatures do not usually fall much below 70° F. until the latter part of November. December too is usually markedly warmer than January or February, and open-air festivities at Christmas are often possible.

Rainfall is for the most part adequate, though great differences are apparent between north and south. The coast of Syria and the Lebanon receives over 30 inches, and Gaza only 14 inches. January is the wettest month, and, except for the extreme north, rainfall has ceased entirely by the middle of June, so that, until the middle of September, aridity is absolute. The fact that much of the coastal zone receives as much rainfall as many parts of Europe, yet in far fewer rainy days (January, the rainiest month, has only 11 to 14 days of actual rain), indicates that falls are very heavy, but not prolonged.[1] An unpleasant feature is the high humidity prevailing in summer, which, as we have seen, is actually at a maximum in some parts: cf. Iskanderun max. 74 per cent. (July), Beirut max. 73 per cent. (June), Haifa max. 73 per cent. (June), Gaza max. 77 per cent. (Jan.), and 72 per cent. (July). Dew is as a result extremely heavy, and in the words of C. Combier, 'Roofs in the early morning stream with moisture as though there had been a downpour of rain during the night.' It has been calculated that dew accounts for as much as 25 per cent. of the total precipitation recorded in certain districts.

High summer humidity, together with only slight diurnal variation of temperatures, makes the summer season more unpleasant than figures of climate would appear to indicate, and large numbers of town dwellers, particularly in the Lebanon, migrate into the hills for the summer months.

[1] For example, Beirut has an annual rainfall greater than that of Manchester, England, and this falls during 73 rainy days, as compared with 194 in Manchester.

Mountain Zone. A remarkable change is found, even in 5 miles, as one leaves the coastal plain for the mountains. Winters are cold, and snow is of regular occurrence each winter. In the Lebanon Range, snow may lie for 2 to 4 months, and the three peaks, Qornet es Sauda, Sannin, and Hermon are white for at least half the year.[1] Jerusalem, at 3,000 feet, has short falls in most winters. Climatic statistics are fewer for this upland region, but it would seem that average January temperatures are some 10° to 15° lower in the north than on the adjoining coastal plain, and 8° to 10° lower in the south (El Kareya – Lebanon – 41° F., Nazareth 49° F., Jerusalem 47° F.). Summer temperatures are again rather lower (by 10° in the north, and 5° to 10° in the south), but a special feature is wide diurnal variation in summer, so that the daytime is moderately hot, and the night cool. During summer there is thus a most pleasant change at night; and although afternoon temperatures may be very little different from those of the plain, the nights are more restful. This is well shown at Aley, a summer resort only 5 miles from Beirut, but 2,500 feet above sea level.

TEMPERATURES IN AUGUST

	Beirut	Aley
Mean daily maximum	87	85
Mean daily minimum	73	64

Considerable diurnal variation of temperature during the summer months is one of the underlying factors in the development of summer stations and holiday resorts in the Lebanon.

As would be expected, rainfall, which is of the instability type, is abundant, even heavy. On the Ansarieh and Lebanon mountains, there are annual falls of 40 to 50 inches, though the figure drops to under 30 inches in Galilee, and to 15 to 25 inches in Samaria and Judaea. The number of rainy days, however, remains low, despite increased precipitation, averaging 80 to 85 per annum in Syria and the Lebanon, and 40 to 60 in Israel; i.e. only 5 to 10 more than in the corresponding coastal areas, so that rainfall can be termed really intense. This has important effects on the soil cover, which, unless held by a retaining wall, can be soon swept away and lost. Hence terracing on a considerable scale is a feature of all parts of the mountain zone; and in certain districts it is possible to observe hillsides terraced continuously at intervals of 3 or 4 feet over 2,000 to 3,000 feet of altitude.

[1] The name Lebanon is said to be derived from the Aramaic *Leben* (whiteness) in reference to the vista of snow-clad peaks seen from December to June.

Steppe Zone. Immediately east of the crest of the coastal ranges, rainfall diminishes sharply in amount, though the season of onset remains the same. This affords striking indication of the control of rainfall by relief, and D. Ashbel has gone so far as to construct a rainfall map of the Levant in which isohyets are directly related to contours. Whether or not one is willing to accept this rather extreme correspondence, there can be no doubt that the relationship is much closer than is usually the case in cool temperate regions.

Under such circumstances, the lowland troughs of the Ghab, Bekaa, and Ghor display a climatic regime markedly different from that of the highlands to the east and west. Though none of the troughs greatly exceeds 10 miles in width – being often much less – we can distinguish a separate regime approximating to steppe conditions. De Martonne has given the name 'Syrian' to this type of climate, which is characterised by moderate or somewhat deficient rainfall, with a fairly cold winter and a hot summer. Ksara, on the floor of the Bekaa, is one example: coldest month (Jan.) 41° F., hottest (Aug.) 81° F.; diurnal variation 17° in winter, 20° in summer, annual rainfall 25 inches.

The great depth of the Jordan Rift, and its openness to the direct rays of the sun, give rise to higher temperatures and to a greatly diminished rainfall (Jericho – coldest month (Jan.) 57° F., hottest (July) 88° F., diurnal variation 18° in winter, 28° in summer, annual rainfall 5 inches). Evaporation from the lakes is high, especially from the Dead Sea, where it attains half an inch daily,[1] and heavy mists are of frequent occurrence in the lower Jordan and, to a slightly less extent, further north. Dew is, therefore, again an important feature, and at Homs, it is estimated that at least one-quarter of the precipitation recorded is from this source.

Eastward, there is a heavier rainfall on the uplands of the Anti-Lebanon and the north-west of trans-Jordan, but further inland still, a rapid diminution once more occurs, and we arrive again in the steppe regime. Temperatures are more extreme, both in annual and diurnal range (Aleppo: coldest month 42° F., warmest month 89° F.; diurnal range 17° in winter, and 30° in summer), and annual rainfall is less, varying from 10 to 17 inches.

In this steppe zone, no more than a narrow strip between the western mountains and inner deserts of Arabia, lie a large number of towns and villages, in which life continues only by the ingenious utilisation

---

[1] Total evaporation from the surface of the Dead Sea during one year has been estimated at 159 inches (Piche method).

of a limited water supply. Qanats of up to 10 miles in length, water channels hacked out of abrupt hillsides, and water lifts of many kinds ranging from small hand machines to petrol-driven *sakias*, are all methods by which man has adapted to his occupation an increasingly hostile environment. It may also be noted that south of a line joining Gaza, Hebron, Beisan, and Maan, where the Levant lies within the 'rainshadow' of north-east Africa and the Sinai peninsula, conditions pass into true desert, and Arabian influences reach the coast of the Mediterranean, interrupting the north–south alignment of the climatic zones of the Levant.

At Aleppo, frost and snow are common in winter, but summer temperatures regularly exceed 100° F. on most days in July and August. Because, however, of much lower relative humidity in the interior, these higher summer temperatures are much more tolerable than the sultry heat of the littoral, and the traveller finds it difficult to credit that the interior is some 10° to 15° F. warmer than the coast.

CLIMATIC DATA
REPRESENTATIVE STATIONS IN THE LEVANT
Temperatures (° F.), and Rainfall (inches)

	J	F	M	A	M	J	J	A	S	O	N	D	Total
1. Coast (Beirut)													
Temp.	51	58	61	66	72	78	82	84	81	76	68	61	
Rainfall	7·8	8·3	3·7	2·1	0·6	0·2	0	0	0·4	2·0	5·1	7·7	37·9
Rainy days	15	14	11	6	3	1	0	0	1	4	9	13	77
2. Mountain (El Kareya)													
Temp.	41	45	48	56	65	68	71	72	67	63	53	46	
Rainfall	11·1	13·7	7·7	3·7	1·4	0·3	0	0	0·3	2·0	6·5	10·0	56·7
Rainy days	15	12	14	7	5	2	0	0	1	6	10	12	84
3. Steppe (Aleppo)													
Temp.	42	45	51	61	70	78	88	89	77	67	51	49	
Rainfall	2·9	3·0	1·3	1·3	0·4	tr	0	0	tr	0·9	1·6	3·1	14·6
Rainy days	10	10	8	5	2	1	0	0	1	4	5	9	54

PERCENTAGE RELATIVE HUMIDITY

	J	F	M	A	M	J	J	A	S	O	N	D
1. Beirut	70	71	71	72	71	70	70	72	68	67	69	69
Haifa	72	71	69	69	70	72	71	68	67	66	69	72
Gaza	77	75	69	65	63	67	72	72	71	70	69	73
2. Ksara	78	75	63	55	49	46	45	46	49	54	65	76
3. Jericho	70	68	56	48	43	44	45	46	52	54	59	66
Aleppo	82	78	70	61	48	42	45	52	60	65	70	80

IV. AGRICULTURE

Because of the varied environment, with rapid topographical and climatic changes, agriculture in the Levant can best be viewed as a mosaic, in which intensively cultivated patches alternate with barren or neglected areas, and where one crop quickly gives place to another, as environmental conditions alter. Over most of the area there is, however, the normal pattern of self-subsistence, with wheat and barley as the chief crops, fruit and vegetables as important adjuncts, and occasional specialisation in cash crops. In Israel only is there considerable deviation from this scheme: here farming methods, already advanced by 1947, have undergone profound transformation. Capital was made available for drainage, the improvement of communications and public health, and the construction of entirely new settlements. Scientific investigation together with practical experimentation have allowed improved use of existing land, betterment of plant and animal strains, and the incorporation of inferior land; and rural credit and technical assistance are available far more easily than in most other parts of the Middle East. Israel has invested over £300 million in agriculture since 1947; the number of rural settlements has more than doubled, more fertiliser is used per head of population than in any other country of the Middle East, and agricultural productivity has increased at an annual rate of 15–17 per cent. Since 1947 the total cultivated area (according to F.A.O. reports) has expanded by nearly 150 per cent., and the irrigated area by about 300 per cent. This is emphatically not to imply that no progress has been made elsewhere in the Levant: but there has not been the sustained and massive overall improvement that characterises Israeli agriculture, where mixed farming with emphasis on dairying, poultry raising, cereal and fodder crops, and market gardening is the principal feature.

Wheat predominates, as a winter crop, everywhere except in Israel. Native varieties (i.e. emmer) are chiefly grown, but the French introduced softer species of north-western European bread wheats, and other varieties adapted to warm and semi-arid conditions have been introduced mostly by Jewish colonists. Wheat is grown up to an altitude of 5,000 feet, and it is difficult to distinguish any regions of especially heavy production, since it is a staple in most districts. An interesting feature is, however, that whilst Syria is now wholly self-sufficient in wheat supplies, with a substantial surplus available for export in most years, this is not the case in Jordan, the Lebanon, and

Israel, all three of which must import substantial quantities – in some years the largest single item in each country's list of imports.

Except in Israel, barley ranks second in importance; and, being more tolerant of heat and aridity, is favoured in regions bordering the steppe. Acreage amounts to 30 to 50 per cent. of the area under wheat. Since 1948 barley has become the chief cereal crop in Israel, with wheat and maize more or less second equal in importance. Maize is increasingly grown on the coastal plain of Israel, in the upper Jordan valley, and also in the Lebanon; but elsewhere in the Levant cultivation is still restricted to the oasis of Damascus and the Tripoli–Homs lowland. Another summer crop is sorghum, the cultivation of which has greatly developed in Israel and Jordan, but hardly exists in Syria and the Lebanon. Oats are grown in a few highland areas where especially cool and damp conditions obtain, but output is very small. Rice is greatly esteemed as a delicacy, but most is imported, small quantities being produced chiefly round Damascus, Homs and Aleppo.

PALESTINE (ISRAEL): TOTAL YIELDS
(in metric tons)

	Wheat	Barley	Vegetables
1937	127,000	75,000	120,000
1941	90,000	69,000	190,000
1960 (Israel only)	35,000	65,000	260,000

Vegetables are increasing in importance as communications develop, and a growing urban population stimulates demand. Large market gardening areas have come into existence on the coastal plains, near big inland towns, and also in the middle Orontes region between Homs, Hama, and Idlib. A very wide range of plants is grown, but squashes (gourds), pumpkin, marrows, tomatoes, cucumbers, and aubergines are the chief favourites. The emphasis on 'succulent' vegetables will be noted. Potatoes are also greatly increasing in quantity, but tend to be somewhat restricted, like oats, to higher, damper regions. The Bekaa is a large producer, and the Galilee uplands supply Israel, whilst increasing amounts are grown in the Ansarieh region. In warmer, drier regions, the sweet potato sometimes replaces the ordinary variety, but the importance of the latter is much less. It may be noted that agricultural statistics, even though fragmentary and incomplete, suggest that vegetable-growing is in some parts the principal agricultural activity. Although the extent of land given over to vegetables is very small, the high yields obtained per acre as compared with cereals make market gardening an increasingly attractive proposition. On a basis of actual

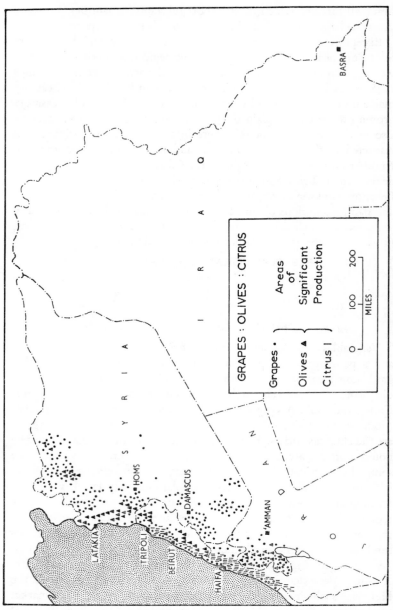

Fig. 77. Fruit Crops

production by weight, the yield of vegetables in Israel has come to exceed the total production of all cereals.

Fruit-growing is another very important activity. The olive is probably the most widespread, since it occurs in all parts of the west from the dry uplands of Judaea to the alluvial lowlands of the lower Orontes. Three regions of especially intensive production can be distinguished: (1) the lower Orontes valley and its borderlands, stretching between Latakia, Idlib, and Antioch, (2) the coastal plain immediately south of Beirut, including the villages of Shweifat and Damur, (3) the oasis of Damascus. About 80 per cent. of the olives produced are for local consumption, and by far the greater part is pressed for oil, though many fresh olives are eaten. Production methods are not of the best: the olive trees are sometimes left without much fertilisation, and the boughs are beaten with sticks to cause ripe fruit to fall. Oil presses, too, are primitive, hence much Syrian oil was until 1940 exported to Italy, where it was refined and then re-sold as Italian produce.

In the coastal plain, oranges are grown, with a now considerable production in the Lebanon – tangerines from Saida, oranges from Beirut and Tripoli. But the Plain of Sharon and Acre district are the outstanding regions. Oranges have been grown in Palestine for over 200 years, but great expansion took place following the immigration of Jewish settlers after 1880. During the 1930's oranges were one of the most important productions of Palestine, accounting for 70 to 80 per cent. of total exports. In 1938 citrus fruit groves occupied 75,000 acres[1] (as compared with 10,000 acres in the Lebanon) but serious signs of over-production had developed, and competition from South Africa, California, and Brazil led to a reduction by 5,000 acres during the next two years. In 1940 the principal outlet – the British market – was entirely closed, because of the impossibility of sending cargo ships through the Mediterranean. This was a catastrophe for Palestine, where fruit rotted on the trees and accumulated in piles on the streets.

EXPORTS OF CITRUS FRUIT FROM PALESTINE/ISRAEL

(cases)

1937–8	1938–9	1939–40	1940–1	1941–2	1959–60
11,500,000	15,300,000	7,600,000	100,000	nil	10,175,000

For a time subsidies and tax remissions were granted to orange growers, both Arab and Jew, but acreage fell at one time to half the

[1] Approximately 55 per cent. of this area was owned by Arabs.

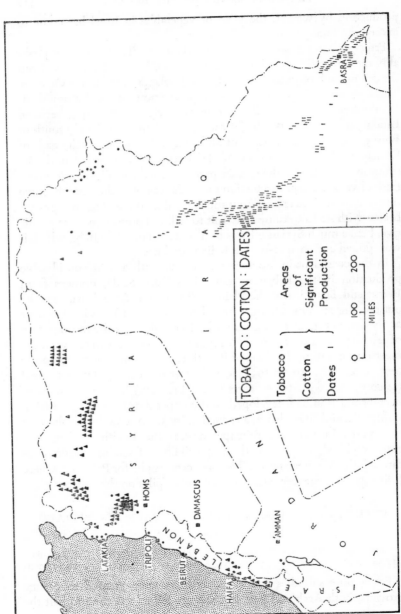

Fig. 78. Commercial Crops

pre-war figure with, since 1955, something of a recovery, owing to Israel's need of export commodities. Many growers turned in large measure to mixed farming, i.e. the growing of fodder crops for dairy cattle, together with ceral production.

Oranges thrive in the fairly light sandy areas, whilst grapefruit and lemons prefer rather heavier soils. The Shamuti (jaffa) orange is native to the region, but some Valencia oranges are also grown. Proportions are broadly as follows:

CITRUS CROP

(per cent.)

Oranges (Shamuti)	Oranges (Valencia)	Grapefruit	Lemons	Limes
70	8	13	4	5

A third fruit is the vine, which is cultivated on the lower foothills up to 3,000 feet. Most grapes are eaten fresh, or else made into varieties of local wine, often with a flavouring of aniseed. In certain parts, however, a large-scale wine industry has developed, the chief centres being the central Bekaa (Ksara and Zahleh) and the Lydda district of Israel (Rishon le Zion and Latrun). There is a restricted local market for wine chiefly among Christians and Jews, and increasingly, among Moslems, who are somewhat less strict than formerly. The wines are generally not of a quality comparable with those of western Mediterranean countries, and a large export trade is unlikely to develop.

Other fruits grown in the Levant are apricots, bananas, figs, peaches, and pomegranates. Bananas thrive best in the Lebanon, where they are grown on small alluvial terraces on the floors of deep river gorges. Here the air is hot, steamy, and calm, being sheltered by the high cliffs. Abundant water is available, though it must be led to the plantations in irrigation channels. Conditions in Israel are less suitable, though there is a significant and expanding production. Banana-growing (main centres, Beirut, Antelias, Damur) has greatly increased in the Lebanon, particularly since oranges have been affected by scale disease; and bananas and citrus fruit now rank, with apples, as a most important export commodity in the Lebanon. Here it is possible to observe a zonal arrangement of crops. On the flat coastal plain, wheat, vegetables and citrus fruits are grown, with bananas in the sheltered river gorges. On the lowest slopes of the hills, olives, figs, and cereals occur, then, at 1,000 to 3,000 feet, vines. Apricots, peaches, and plums occupy the middle slopes (2,000 to 4,000 feet), with potatoes, apples, and pears on the highest parts above 3,000 feet. Apple-growing, in common with market gardening generally in the Lebanon, has greatly expanded of recent years because of improved living standards and owing to demands from the oilfields of the Persian Gulf.

A number of cash crops are grown to a relatively small degree. Mulberry-growing is a feature of the north and central Lebanon (Qartaba, Ehden, and Bsharreh) and the Ansarieh uplands; and at one time silk production was the principal occupation of Tripoli and Latakia. The industry has undergone many vicissitudes, the latest phase (1962) being one of severe decline following war-time expansion. The silkworms are reared on large wicker trays in special huts, and fed on mulberry leaves for about six weeks, during which a cocoon is spun. The cocoon is then dried and sent to a reeling mill, where is is unravelled, nearly 3,000 feet of silk thread being obtained from a single cocoon.

Cotton-growing was widespread in Syria during the Middle Ages, but up to 1950 was largely restricted to the irrigated districts of Homs, Hama, Idlib-Aleppo, and Latakia. Over the last ten years, production has greatly increased, particularly in the eastern sectors of the 'Fertile Crescent', and in the Jezireh tributary valleys of the Euphrates (Balikh and Jagh-Jagh rivers) where production began only in 1948. Cotton is now the principal export commodity of Syria. Some 10,000 tons of raw cotton are now also produced annually in Israel – this supplies fully the internal demand.

Tobacco is produced in most areas, mainly for local consumption, but quality is not high, except in the region round Latakia where there is a small but important export.

It will be seen from the foregoing that the degree of land utilisation varies considerably throughout the Levant. Only the western coastal plain can be said to be considerably in use, and even there stretches of unreclaimed marsh, dunes, and mountain spurs are to be found. Further eastwards, cultivation becomes distinctly more sporadic, because of increasingly unfavourable topography and climate. In the extreme north-east, the Aleppo region (centred on the middle Qweiq basin) is separated from the fertile lower Orontes (Idlib region) by an interval of salt marsh; further south, the districts of Hama and Homs are ringed by expanses of arid steppe and upland; and the Bekaa, hemmed between the sterile Anti-Lebanon and the precipitous eastern slopes of the Lebanon range, is very productive, but only where water is available. Parts are still largely empty and unused. In the east, there are certain favoured localities, outstanding among which is the Ghuta (Plain of Damascus) where, over an area some 15 to 20 miles square, the presence of the Barada river and its six tributaries allows extensive irrigation. For the greater part, however, the countryside is given over to pastoralism – by no means all of the shores of Lake Tiberias are cultivated – and agriculture takes on the characteristics of oasis occupation or of a 'pioneer fringe' in an increasingly difficult environment.

In these areas the 15-inch isohyet may be said to mark the effective

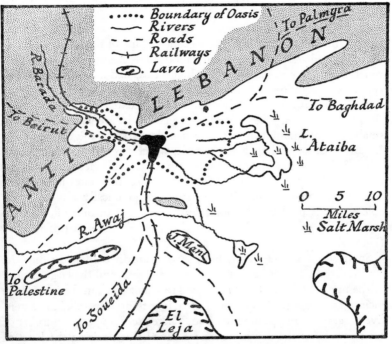

Fig. 79. The Oasis of Damascus

limit of normal (non-irrigated) cultivation, and the 8-inch isohyet the absolute margin even of dry farming, with the population living on the lowest subsistence level. This means that cultivable land in trans-Jordan is restricted to the extreme north-west, to the area lying between the western frontier and the railway line from Damascus to Amman. Between Amman and Petra the semi-arid steppe is reached, and so over most of the country nomadic pastoralism becomes the principal activity.

Within the last fifteen years, however, there have been far-reaching developments over much of the Levant. In Israel, afforestation, fodder-growing, dairy farming and the propagation of orchards even in semi-arid areas like the Negeb have greatly altered the pattern of land use. In Syria, development of riverine stretches in the Jezireh and Euphrates zones, and extension of irrigation round Aleppo, Homs, and Hama using motor pumps, artesian wells, and free-flow canals have pushed back the edge of the steppe and desert zones many miles further east.

Irrigation. In view of the foregoing, it will be appreciated that irrigation plays a most important part in the economic life of the Levant, even in the north and west, where rainfall is moderately heavy. In ancient times, much of Syria, especially the north and east, had a highly developed system of irrigation, but most of this has decayed through war and misrule, so that now the only region with an extensive canal system is the Damascus area, where about 400 square miles are watered from the small streams draining into the Syrian desert from the eastern Anti-Lebanon. Chief of these is the Barada, which has also been harnessed, where it leaves the uplands for the plain, to provide electric power for the city. The irrigation canals of Damascus are small but of very great age – some pre-Roman – and in summer practically all the avail-able water is used up. At other seasons a small quantity flows east-wards to the salt basin of the Bahr el Ataiba, 10 miles east of the city (Fig. 79).

Small-scale canal systems, using *norias*, are in existence along the banks of the Orontes between Homs and Hama, and the large springs of the upper Lebanon Range are used to water fields in the immediate vicinity; but, generally speaking, there is nothing to parallel the exten-sive schemes of Egypt, or even Iraq. There are, however, a number of recent projects: the damming of the Litani river, raising the level of the Lake of Homs by building an artificial barrier above the natural basalt dam, and the use of the waters of Lake Yammouneh to irrigate the Baalbek district. Moreover, it is planned ultimately to utilise water from the Euphrates to irrigate some 300,000 hectares; and already the high returns from cotton-growing round Aleppo have allowed the boring of deep artesian wells run by motor pumps. Even so, it is reckoned that the irrigated area of Syria could be tripled from its present extent.

The Lebanon has a better water supply than any of its neighbours, but even here, irrigation could at least improve crop yields greatly, and bring under cultivation further areas which are only partially used –

e.g. the Bekaa, and parts of the coastal plain between Saida and Tyre, and round Tripoli. Streams flowing east from the main Lebanon range are utilised notably at Lake Yammouneh, a depression on the eastern flank of the hills above Baalbek; and in addition to the one dam already completed on the Litani, others are planned. Some water schemes are mainly for hydro-electricity, with irrigation a subsidiary element; whilst others can be described as partly political – in that they envisage changing the courses of the headstreams of the Jordan river as a means of putting pressure upon Israel.

In 1953 the Syrians agreed to a joint project with Jordan whereby the waters of the Yarmuk river would be used jointly for irrigation on the lowlands immediately east of the Jordan and Sea of Galilee.

Conditions in the south are more complex. Rainfall is markedly lower, rivers deeply entrenched, and the greater extent of porous limestone outcrops – more extensive even than in the Lebanon – results in much loss of surface water. It has been stated by the former Water Commission of Palestine that the total rainfall over the whole of Palestine could be taken as 7,500 million cubic metres per annum, of which one-third falls on the eastern (Jordan) side of the hills. Of the proportion received on the east (2,500 mill. cu. metres), 69 per cent. is returned to the atmosphere by evaporation from the surface, and transpiration by plants; and a further 7 per cent. is storm water, which drains rapidly to the Dead Sea and cannot be used for irrigation. The remaining 24 per cent. goes to feed rivers, springs, etc., but is in part lost through percolation into porous rock, or by contamination with saline strata, so that only 16 per cent. is estimated to remain for effective use. Of this 16 per cent. between one-quarter and one-half (i.e. 4 to 8 per cent. of the total rainfall) is already in use, leaving only a very limited possibility of future expansion.

For the precipitation received on the western slopes, the corresponding figures are:

	Per cent.
Loss by evaporation and transpiration	70
Storm water	6
Underground penetration	16
Available at surface	8

Because of the high degree of underground penetration, a Royal Commission stated that 'Irrigation from wells is, and is likely always to remain, the chief source of irrigation water in Palestine.' Dams to retain surface water have been constructed, but experiences at Beersheba illustrate the difficulties in the way of successful development. It was found that only 7 per cent. of the rainfall of the catchment area reached the reservoir, the remaining 93 per cent. percolating into the soil, or undergoing evaporation. Of this 7 per cent., only one-fourteenth part (i.e. 0·5 per cent. of the total rainfall) remained in the reservoir at the end of a few weeks, the rest undergoing evaporation or absorption into the porous substrata. Another difficulty in the west of Israel is that unless a 'head' of fresh water is maintained in the porous underground rocks, salt water from the Mediterranean percolates inland. Near Haifa and Tel Aviv, over-pumping from wells has lowered the water-table below the level of the sea, and a number of wells are now invaded by salt water. Early in 1960 some apprehension was voiced regarding the steady fall of underground water level in the centre and south of Israel, and the rise of salinated water in the north.

There have been a number of proposals for large-scale irrigation schemes in Israel. Probably the best known is that of Lowdermilk, who suggested using the upper Jordan for irrigation purposes in northern Israel, and replacing the loss of water to the Dead Sea by introducing sea water by means of a canal from the Mediterranean. A drop in level of some 1,200 feet between the Mediterranean and the Dead Sea would allow generation of hydro-electric power. A second plan, due to Savage and Hays, also of America, envisages even more elaborate developments, to take place in stages. The first stage would be the damming of certain headstreams of the Jordan – the Hasbani, within the present Lebanese state, and the Yarmuk, within the state of Jordan; part of the latter being used for irrigation, and part diverted directly into Lake Tiberias. Existing hydro-electric stations on the Yarmuk would become redundant, and would have to be replaced by other stations using water introduced from the Mediterranean as in the Lowdermilk scheme. Later, a high-level irrigation canal would be constructed from the Lebanese frontier through western Galilee and Samaria to Gaza and the Negeb. Water for this canal would be drawn from the Litani river of the Lebanon, and from small catchment dams in the wadis of the Judaean plateau. A somewhat modified and reduced Jordan–Negeb canal is now in process of construction. These schemes have been criticised notably by E. C. Willatts and by M. G. Ionides on the following grounds: (1) Physical difficulties have been largely ignored – e.g. (a) the building of dams in a region of porous limestone outcrops, (b) the possibility of tectonic disturbances, which might damage the canals, or allow seepage along fault-lines, and (*c*) the difficulty of carrying canals across a deeply dissected countryside.

(2) High cost of the projects. Total expenditure would be at least £50 million ($200 million), in order to irrigate 625,000 acres, giving a minimum cost of £80 per acre. This, as Willatts pointed out, is about forty times the cost of the Aswan and Punjab schemes, and six times that of the Godavari scheme.

(3) There may not be sufficient water actually within Israel to allow

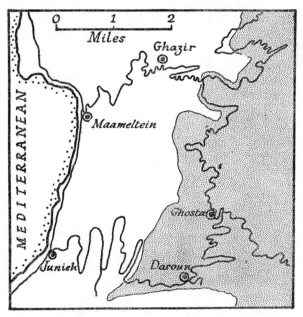

Fig. 80. Mountain Roads in the Levant (about 10 miles N. of Beirut). All roads shown are motorable. Land over 2,000 ft. stippled

the development of extensive irrigation schemes. Besides a highly variable annual rainfall, which can fall 60 per cent. below average in a given year, there is another point to consider. Much of the present irrigation development is from wells sunk in artesian basins which have been tapped only on a large scale during the past 20 years, and previously lay unused. The fact that in some parts the water-table has sunk 10 or 15 feet during 20 years of exploitation suggests that like the woodlands of the region, water supplies represent an earlier, expendable accumulation which, once used up, will not be easily replaced. During past centuries, when agriculture relied on surface water only, a reserve accumulated underground, and it may be that this is now being tapped at a rate which exceeds replenishment by percolation from the surface.

Most irrigation development in Israel (using chiefly wells and motor pumps) has taken place round Tel-Aviv; in the upper Jordan valley, where the shallow Huleh basin has been entirely drained; along the Kishon river; and in parts of the Negeb. Cost has sometimes been a minor factor only; the inflow of immigrants making essential the expansion of agriculture; and now there are about $\frac{1}{3}$ of a million acres of irrigated land in the Negeb.

The overall situation is heavily shadowed by political conditions. In an area where irrigation water is available yet not fully or efficiently used, an overall plan of water development could best be devised treating the region as a single unit. But realisation of such a plan is inhibited by the alignment of frontiers, and so long as present attitudes continue, there will be recurring counter-proposals, friction, and strife.

Pastoralism. This activity is as yet not very great, since it tends in many places to be restricted to the more arid and hillier parts. A conspicuous exception is the recent extensive development of mixed farming amongst the Jewish colonies of Israel, where fodder crops, like vegetables, far outweigh the production of cereals, and attention is given to stock breeding and selection, with some import of foreign pedigree animals.

In the north, goats predominate – an indication of the difficult terrain of many areas. Sheep are next in importance, especially in the Lebanon, and there is much transhumance between summer and winter pastures, involving journeys of up to 30 miles. The central and northern Bekaa, and the valleys of the Anti-Lebanon are also much used as winter pastures by nomadic Badawin from the Syrian desert. The Jebel Ansarieh and south-west Syria stand out as cattle areas, the number of cattle being three or four times as great as those in the Lebanon. Pig keeping is also of some importance in the cooler Lebanon – this is also related to the numerical importance of Christians – but few pigs are found elsewhere. The chief draught animal is the donkey, with horses second in importance. Mules and camels are also reared in most regions, even the hillier and damper Lebanon.

Though dairy cattle predominate in the lowlands of Israel, conditions in the Judaean hills much resemble those of Syria and the Lebanon, with goats and sheep as the main animals kept. Transhumance is less developed; but the lower Jordan valley, like the Bekaa, is used during winter by nomads from the east.

Jewish Colonisation in Palestine/Israel. The first Jewish colonists purchased their own land and equipment, and were free to exploit it as they pleased. Funds for purchase, etc., were, however, in most cases advanced by the Palestine Jewish Colonial Association through one of several Jewish colonising agencies. Part of the sum advanced was treated as a loan, with repayment over 50 years at low interest; the rest as a gift. This system resulted in the settling of about 50,000–60,000 colonists on an area of about 150,000 acres, in villages known as *mochavim*.

The Jewish Agency, which later became the national body, organised several forms of directly communal settlement, with strict social organisation. Colonists were expected to work for a unitary wage, without salary differentials, personal property or personal advantage, on tasks that were allotted by an elected committee. Social services – medical, educational, child care, etc., were provided for all members; and these communal settlements, named *Kibbutzim*, were carefully planned, with large-scale methods of land exploitation. They were expected to be financially viable as a unit, i.e. though in certain ways 'communistic' in detailed organisation they were expected to function as a state capitalist enterprise – an interesting mixture. Size of each Kibbutz was normally between 250 and 300 inhabitants, though occasional settlements were three or four times this number; and in all, there were some 200 of them – with a total population of about 75,000. The Kibbutzim functioned much more definitely as pioneer settlements – in difficult territory geographically, new settlements in Arab areas, and as military posts. With the establishment of the state of Israel, the Kibbutzim have become less important, and their numbers have declined.

Intermediate between the strict communal life of the Kibbutzim and the freer 'capitalist' settlements are the *mochavim shitoufim* and *mochavim ovdim*, the former close to the Kibbutzim in economic organisation, but allowing a family life for the workers; the latter more in the nature of a peasant co-operative with some private ownership of land, and some communal working. Ovdim settlements are most numerous: and they include a variety of occupants – former Kibbutz members, private owners, and colonists supported by national funds. Finally, a temporary kind of settlement has been provided by the *maabarot*, which are transit work–camps to absorb new arrivals. Main tasks, undertaken by direction, are the clearing of new sites for settlement, improvement of irrigation and communications, and re-afforestation. These camps have been necessary, as many Jewish immigrants (especially since 1947) have been destitute and without experience; but they have been criticised within Israel by 'right-wing' Jewish politicians as being too close to Fascist labour camps.

V. MINERALS

The mineral wealth of the Levant is somewhat more important than was at one time supposed. Within the last few decades oil, natural gas, copper, and phosphates have been discovered and exploited in commercial quantities. Small deposits of lignite have also long been known to occur in the Lebanon, and sporadic mining occurs at Bsharreh (east-south-east of Tripoli) and at Bikfeia (north-east of Beirut). The latter mines were first worked by Muhammad Ali a century ago, and are practically exhausted.

Oil prospecting as we have seen has on the whole had rather disappointing results, though search is still in progress. One productive field is at Heletz-Negba (Negeb); and a pipeline carries natural gas from Rosh Zohar to the Dead Sea chemical works at Sdom (Sodom). Other deposits of natural gas have recently been proved at one locality in the Syrian Jezireh. Asphalt and bitumen occur in a few parts of the Lebanon, Anti-Lebanon, and Ansarieh ranges, and as lumps that form on the bed of the Sead Sea and later rise to the surface. There is little attempt at development of any of these deposits. The Dead Sea is, however, important for its mineral salts, and ranks as the chief source of mineral products in the Levant. Analysis shows that at the surface, each litre of Dead Sea water contains 227 to 275 grams of dissolved salts. At a depth of 360 feet, the water is chemically saturated, and the corresponding figure is 327 grams.

CHEMICAL CONTENT OF DEAD SEA WATER
(in grams per litre)

	Surface	360-ft. depth
KCl	10·0 to 11·8	15·7
$NaCl$	71·0 to 82·4	87·4
$MgCl_2$	109·5 to 142·4	169·0
$CaCl_2$	31·0 to 33·0	46·7
$CaSO_4$	1·3	0·6
$MgBr_2$	3·9 to 4·5	7·3

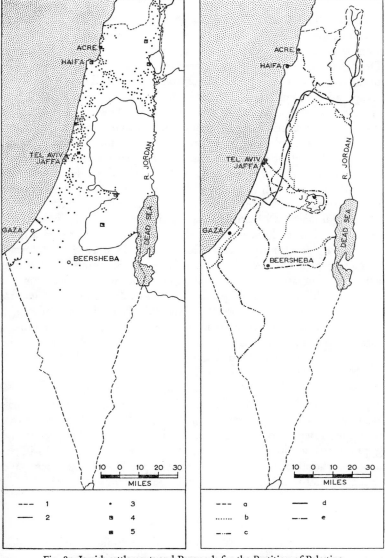

Fig. 81. Jewish settlement; and Proposals for the Partition of Palestine

1 Frontiers of Palestine
2 Frontiers of Israel (where different)
3 Jewish settlement, 1947
4 Towns – mixed Arab and Jewish pop.
5 Predominantly Jewish towns

a Palestine (Mandate)
b Present frontiers of Israel (where different from a)
c Proposed by U.N. Partition resolution
d   ,,   ,, Royal Commission, 1937
e   ,,   ,,   ,,   ,,
         (Jerusalem International Zone)

In 1930 the Palestine Potash Corporation began extraction of mineral salts, using a simple process of solar evaporation, which, as we have seen, is particularly active in the region of the lower Jordan. Pans of Dead Sea water are allowed to evaporate, and after 40 to 50 days, most of the unwanted common salt has crystallised out, and can be removed. Evaporation is continued, and a mixture of potassium and magnesium chlorides, known as carnallite, is next obtained. This can be purified by re-crystallisation (still using solar heat) to give a salt consisting of 20 per cent. potassium chloride, 70 to 80 per cent. of magnesium chloride, and a small content of sodium chloride. Further fractional crystallisation gives a much purer magnesium chloride, and finally, magnesium bromide, from which bromine itself is extracted. The potash salts are used principally as fertilisers, whilst bromine is increasingly valuable in the manufacture of armaments (explosives and lethal gases), and in the blending of high octane fuels. War conditions proved a great stimulus to development, and after destruction during 1948 certain extraction plants are now rebuilt. Israel produces about 150,000 tons annually of potash, and 2,000 tons of bromine, with smaller amounts by Jordan. Though cost of production is low (solar heat and natural gas being employed) the cost of transport to the coast is a handicap.

Phosphate rock occurs in quantity at Ar Rusayfa, north of Amman. Other deposits are known at Hasa further south, elsewhere east of the Dead Sea, in southern Syria, and in Israel, at Oron and Ein Yahat in the Negeb. Annual production averages 200,000 tons.

Manganese has been proved, but is not so far worked. Iron was first exploited by the Phoenicians, and is now exhausted, whilst small amounts of gold, copper, chromium, lead, and magnesium are known to occur. A deposit of sulphur is worked near Gaza, and limestone and gypsum provide local building material. Along the coast, and in the neighbourhood of the salt basins of Aleppo, Homs, Damascus, and Jerusalem, salt refining is carried on, often by primitive methods.

VI. INDUSTRY

Under Ottoman rule, Syria was probably the most industrialised region of the Middle East, with a fairly extensive textile industry in Aleppo, Damascus, Homs, Hama, Beirut, and Tripoli that supplied most of the needs of the whole empire. Palestine was largely agricultural, without any industries of importance. In the twentieth century, however, Syrian trade had begun to decline considerably because of competition from foreign machine-made goods, and this decline was further emphasised after 1918, when the Syrian market was reduced to Syria herself. During the last 30 years, therefore, Syrian industry has been subjected to two influences: an overall decline in the face of foreign competition and shrinking markets, and the beginnings of modern organisation and mechanisation, which has led to concentration of industry in the towns.

In Israel, on the other hand, great expansion has occurred as the result of Jewish immigration, and it is clear that since about 1940-5 the degree of industrialisation has definitely come to exceed that in the north. In this connexion it is important to recall that nearly 80 per cent. of the Jewish population of Palestine now lives in towns and not in rural (country) areas, and Jewish industry has approximately doubled in extent since 1950, though it still produces only about one-quarter of the national income, and employs 20-25 per cent. of all workers.

The textile industries of Syria and the Lebanon use cotton, silk, rayon, and wool as raw materials, and part of these (silk excepted) are imported, though cotton is increasingly grown. Aleppo and Damascus specialise in luxury cloths – brocade and *crêpe de chine* – which are bought mainly by tourists;[1] but there is also considerable production of cheaper cloths (poplin, muslin, marocain, and coarser cottons), together with some camel-hair cloth worn by richer Badawin. Homs and Hama produce a cotton and silk mixture cloth for everyday use as clothing; but it is significant that most of the home-produced cloth is used in Arab style of dress, and 'European' suits, worn increasingly by younger people, are imported. A modern cotton mill at Tripoli produces medium quality cloth; and the silk industry of the Lebanon, with reeling and weaving centres in and near Beirut, developed considerably during 1941-5. This has recently declined.

In Israel new cotton and woollen textile industries have been established at Haifa and Tel Aviv, together with many small workshops or home industries on Jewish agricultural settlements. Raw materials other than cotton, must often be imported. A small Arab textile industry was located at Majdal and Gaza – no 'mill' had more than 50 looms – and home production also occurs in many parts of the Judaean uplands. Bethlehem and Nazareth have a small lace industry that in normal times caters for the tourist-pilgrim market.

Statistics indicate that textiles now occupy the most workers of any

[1] Some of this production is exported to other tourist centres of the Middle East – e.g. Egypt. During the war of 1939 there were many purchases by Allied troops.

single industry in Israel; and though detailed figures for Syria and the Lebanon are lacking, it is probable that the same situation holds true there. Metal-working now ranks second in importance in both countries, considerable development having occurred in Israel since 1939. The main Jewish centre is Haifa, where light engineering products (spare parts, electric batteries, and household implements) are made, and there is a railway repair shop. Further north, metal-working is carried on almost entirely as a craft industry without the use of modern machinery, in old-fashioned workshops at Beirut, Tripoli, Damascus, and Aleppo. Damascus has long had a tradition of metal-working, but is now equalled in number of workshops by Beirut.

Preparation of foodstuffs, etc., ranks close to metal-working as an industrial activity – again an indication of the small extent of true industrialisation in the Levant. Because of the abundance of olives, soap-boiling is carried on in many areas, Beirut, Nablus, and Jaffa being the chief centres, and the extraction of oil, cigarette making and distilling of arak and brandy are features of most towns. A recent development has been the growth of new 'industries' in Israel – diamond cutting at Nathaniya and Tel Aviv, and the manufacture of artificial teeth at Tel Aviv – both of which require only small amounts of imported raw material. Other developments are the assembly of motor-cars, tractors, and domestic appliances, using imported parts. Cement making is growing in importance, and in Israel light industries producing glass, paper, fertilisers, chemicals, rubber, and plastics have also developed. State enterprises account for just over one-half the total industrial activity in Israel; and there is a substantial and growing export of manufactured goods – one of the few countries of the Middle East of which this is true.

In view of this industrial progress, by which the number of Jewish industrial workers rose from 5,000 (1925) to 160,000 (1963), it is of interest to examine the factors underlying development. We have already noted the unfavourable features of a lack of home-produced raw materials, and high cost of transport. Favourable factors are:

(1) Availability of cheap sources of power – hydro-electricity, already developed in the middle Jordan, crude oil, natural gas, and, exceptionally, the solar heat of the lower Jordan.

(2) Rapid growth of population, both Jewish and (until 1948) Arab, which provided a source of cheap labour, and also an expanding market for finished products.

(3) The marked increase of technical skill, due to Jewish immigra-

tion from Europe. Many refugees also brought machinery with them rather than money, especially those coming from Hitlerite Germany, from which the export of currency was forbidden.

(4) A large import of capital during the last forty years – on a *per capita* basis the highest of any nation in the world, including the United States (Kohn). This amounted in some years to a total of £10 ($40) per head of population, and has tended within the last fifteen years to increase faster than the flow of immigrants. Funds have hence been available to start new projects even when the strict economic return seemed dubious.

(5) The demand for goods by the Allied forces during 1941–5. Willatts estimates that industry trebled in size during these years.

The best possibilities for continued advance involve amicable and extensive foreign relations, especially, but not entirely, with neighbouring countries, by which commercial markets can be expanded. The Israeli government is well aware of this, and has been concerned to develop trading relations, for example with

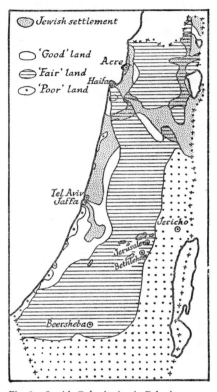

Fig. 82. Jewish Colonisation in Palestine, 1944

the newly independent states of Asia and West Africa – e.g. India and Ghana.

VII. COMMERCE AND TRADE

The countries of the Levant derive important advantages from a transit traffic with the interior of south-west Asia. The ancient long-distance trade with India and the Far East has now been diverted to the sea; but

P

parts of eastern Turkey, north-west Iran, and northern Iraq are most easily reached from the Levant coastlands, and not from their own seaports. Although camel caravans are increasingly giving way to motor traffic, there is still an important trans-desert trade with the east and north-east that adds to the prosperity of the Mediterranean ports, and, to a less extent, of the inland towns on the edge of the desert.

The countries of the Levant are unequally placed for this trade. Jordan derives little benefit from it, as she is isolated on the west by the difficult Ghor depression. Israel, too, with a straight shelving coastline, has only one good harbour – at Haifa, where an extension of the Carmel ridge forms a bay sheltered from the prevailing south-west winds. Haifa currently handles over 80 per cent. of Israel's shipping movements. Jaffa–Tel Aviv have no real harbours: a new port is under construction at Elath on the Gulf of Akaba to serve the Negeb, and also possibly to provide an alternative to the Suez route particularly for oil. The low productivity of the Negeb and control of the Gulf of Akaba by Egypt are adverse factors. Syria has had only one small port, Latakia, since Iskanderun (Alexandretta) was ceded to Turkey in 1939. Latakia until 1952 possessed only a poor harbour, and is shut off eastwards by the mass of the Jebel Ansarieh; hence until 1952 there was no rail communication, and traffic from north Syria tended to move to Beirut and Tripoli, where (especially at Beirut) port sites were better. With both these harbours, the Lebanon handles much of the trade of Syria and Jordan, though competition from the new port of Latakia (constructed 1952) – and in normal times from Haifa – is likely to increase. The chief items of transit trade are (1) fruit, grain, cotton, silk, carpets, and hides (outward), and (2) textiles, vehicles, and machinery (inwards to the Middle East). Over the last few years transit traffic has accounted for some 70 per cent. of the total trade of the Lebanon.

The economy of the Levant countries presents some very unusual features. Though predominantly agricultural, only Syria approaches self-sufficiency in foodstuffs, and a large range of these must be imported. Israel and Jordan both depend in large measure on cash subsidies from abroad – chiefly the U.S.A. and Britain, whilst the Lebanon has no major export commodity, but depends upon an aggregate of items – fruit, olive oil, and pastoral products – to assist in maintaining a trade balance. Large quantities of manufactured goods and fuel (machinery, vehicles, textiles, and oil) must be imported; and in Israel, Jordan, and the Lebanon there is often a considerable deficit of exports as compared with imports.[1] Since 1948 Syria has usually had an export surplus based on cotton and grain.

One highly useful source of revenue is, however, the tourist-pilgrim traffic, which brings large numbers of visitors from other countries. Though the individual sums expended may be small, the total amount is great, and much of the commercial activity of Jerusalem is derived from catering for pilgrims, Christian, Jewish, and Moslem, in hotels, hospices, and monasteries. Moreover, many convents and religious houses are financially supported from abroad, but consume local produce. Pilgrims are also buyers of souvenirs and relics – in olive-wood, mother-of-pearl, and lace-work, the manufacture of which is an important activity in Jerusalem, Tel Aviv, Bethlehem, and Nazareth. Further north, there are fewer pilgrims, but the scenery and amenities of the Lebanon attract a growing number of summer and winter visitors, mostly from Egypt and Iraq. The number of such tourists is normally 20,000–30,000, of whom under 1,000 are winter sports visitors.

VIII. RAILWAYS

The first lines to be constructed were from Jerusalem to Jaffa (1890), of standard gauge, and from Beirut to Damascus via Rayak-Zahleh (1895). Because of the difficulties of the latter route, involving an ascent of 5,000 feet above sea level, a gauge of 1·05 metres was adopted, and a quarter of the whole line used a cog-rail. In 1904–6 the 'Pilgrim Railway' from Damascus to Maan (Jordan state) was opened. This was also of narrow gauge, and a branch from Deraa reached the port of Haifa, with other less important extensions to Suweida and Bosra, the Suweida branch being of a different gauge. Shortly afterwards a standard gauge line was laid from Rayak to Homs, Hama, and Aleppo, with a branch from Homs to the coast at Tripoli. From Aleppo there was connexion to the Anatolia–Baghdad railway, which, incomplete in 1914, was carried to Baghdad and Basra in 1934–40.

Further development in Palestine occurred during 1917, when invading British forces laid a light railway (standard gauge) across the Sinai desert into the Plain of Sharon, as far as Haifa, to meet the Deraa branch. This British line became, after improvement, the main railway

[1] In 1953 exports from Israel amounted to 20 per cent. of the value of imports, in 1958 34 per cent. and in 1960 44 per cent., with citrus fruit by far the largest export item.

of Palestine. At Lydda there is a junction with Jaffa–Tel Aviv and Jerusalem. In 1942, during a second war, British forces continued the standard gauge line northwards along the coast to Beirut and Tripoli, thus providing (at least in theory) direct rail communication between Britain and Cairo. A swing bridge takes the line over the Suez Canal at Kantara to join the main Egyptian system. Since 1948 the line from Beirut to Haifa has been closed.

It may be noted that all these railway lines are single track, and in a number of places speed is restricted to 15 k.p.h. (11 m.p.h.). Any considerable development of a rail network is doubtful, since road transport is probably better adapted to Middle Eastern needs, and the poverty of many areas does not justify the heavy capital expenditure necessary for railway construction. Improvement of roads is likely to be the way in which future development will take place; and one of the conspicuous results of the mandatory regime has been a great improvement in road communications. Greatest achievement was probably in the Lebanon, where an exceptionally difficult terrain was the chief obstacle, and in places it was necessary to build 10 miles of road to reach a spot only 2 miles distant as the crow flies (Fig. 80). A recent report on the economy of Syria noted that most of the traffic on the Beirut–Damascus line was in transit to Jordan, and reported that despite a great decline in passenger traffic, the line still fulfilled a useful function in relieving heavily overcrowded roads. In 1956 a link was completed from the main Israeli system through Beersheba to Elath.

IX. TOWNS

Until very recently, the largest urban centre of the Levant was Aleppo (est. pop. 1962, 480,000). Many geographical factors have contributed to this supremacy, which is of long standing, for after the decline of Abbasid Baghdad, Aleppo ranked as the second city of the Ottoman Empire. Chief of these factors is the location of the city on the borders of four strikingly dissimilar geographic regions. To the north lies the difficult hill country of Asia Minor, to which relatively easy access is given by the pass of the 'Cilician Gates', and by the upper valleys of the Euphrates, Khabour, and Tigris; to the south-west lie the agricultural 'oases' of Hama, Homs, and Damascus, with at a greater distance the more intensely exploited Lebanon, backed by the Mediterranean ports of Iskanderun, Latakia, Tripoli, and Beirut, for all of which Aleppo acts as distributor and collector of produce. South-eastwards lies the pastoral Syrian desert; and eastwards the steppes of the Fertile Crescent, providing an easier, though longer, route to Iraq and Iran. Hence there is an important market for wool, livestock, and hides from the steppes; cereals and fruit from the oases, manufactured articles from the ports and inland towns, and wood, charcoal, and metals from Asia Minor.

Aleppo has controlled much of the inter-continental trade of the Levant, and, offering a choice of two routes across the desert, both less

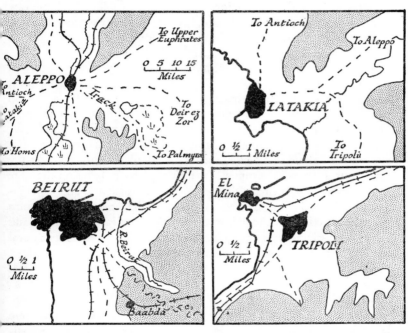

Fig. 83. The Sites of Aleppo, Latakia, Tripoli, and Beirut. Railways and main roads shown

arduous and less dangerous than those from Damascus and Petra, the city held an advantage over its rivals. In caravan days the supremacy of Aleppo was not challenged, and the continued importance of the city as a focus of modern routes is shown by its present importance as a rail junction, with, by Middle Eastern standards, a considerable net-work. Besides its commercial relations, Aleppo has, as we have seen, many local industries, the most extensive of any in Syria. Though now overshadowed politically by Damascus, it still retains much trading and industrial activity, and is less affected by westernisation than most other parts of the Levant. As a city it retains many of its ancient monuments, and hence, to westerners, appears more truly 'Oriental' than many other towns of the Levant.

Damascus (est. pop. 490,000), like Aleppo, owes its rise to trade and industry. Its position as a 'desert port' gave it early importance, and with Aleppo it claims the title of oldest continuously inhabited city in the world – a matter by no means certain. Local advantages are the presence of abundant irrigation water, the availability of local raw materials (cotton, silk, wool, wood, etc.), and an excellent location at the eastern end of a series of gorges and lowland gaps that offer the best east–west route through the Anti-Lebanon range.

Modern Damascus owes most to its agricultural productivity, based on intensive exploitation of the Ghuta, so, even more than Aleppo, it has become a market for exchange of produce between Badawin and cultivators. Textile manufacturing continues, and more than Aleppo, Damascus is in contact with a tourist traffic that provides an outlet for the sale of trinkets, small inlaid furniture in walnut, luxury silks, rugs, and carpets (a kind of Middle Eastern 'Birmingham ware'). Under the Ottomans, Damascus occupied a marginal position, lying on the edge of the Imperial domain, with Aleppo in a more central and advantageous position. Today, the situation is reversed: Damascus is the centre of the new Syrian state, with a developed communication network, and Aleppo is distinctly more in isolation, cut off from much of its natural hinterland and sea outlet by the newly-drawn frontier with Turkey, though intended port development at Tartus should improve this situation.

The rapid rise of Beirut, now the largest town in the Levant (est. pop. 1962, 600,000), has been a feature of the last fifty years. This has come about because of the natural advantage of the Bay of St George, sheltered, like Haifa, from south-west winds by a westward jutting promontory. Once the disadvantage of difficult access to the interior had been overcome in the late nineteenth century by the building of a road and railway across the Col du Beidar (5,000 feet above sea level), Beirut soon rose to be the chief port of the northern Levant, and since 1948 became the chief commercial outlet for the state of Jordan. Textile manufacturing, food processing, and light engineering are also important. Since Byzantine days Beirut has also had a reputation as an educational centre, and the presence of three Universities (American Presbyterian, French Catholic, and Lebanese National), U.N.E.S.C.O.,

ınd numerous institutions and boarding schools (native and foreign)
ıas brought economic benefits.

A further advantage has been the highly developed commercial
sense of its inhabitants, who handle a significant share of the international trade in gold bullion and certain other commodities. Thus Beirut
has now grown from its original nucleus (dating to Roman and earlier
times) along a northward-facing fault-scarp fronting St George's Bay.
In the extreme west of the promontory, Ras Beirut is a fashionable

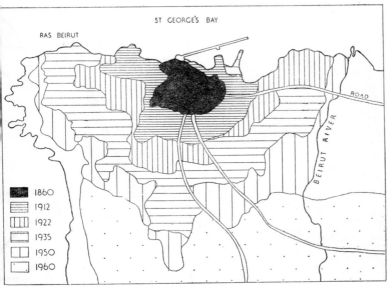

Fig. 84. The Growth of Beirut City

well-built suburb reminiscent of Rome or San Francisco: towards the
east, once-malarial lowlands of the small Beirut river were thirty years
ago a 'squatter' area, inhabited chiefly by Armenian refugees – now
there are improved dwellings and light industries.

Tripoli, though lacking a first-class harbour, has the advantages of
easy communications inland, and the availability of raw material from
the cotton-growing region round Homs. As a result, it has become a
natural outlet of north and west Syria, to the detriment of Latakia; and
the oil pipeline from Kirkuk was first brought to Tripoli by way of
the Bukeia-Akkar lowlands, rather than across the Lebanon ridges to

Beirut. There is a small but long-standing cotton industry, now in process of changing to modern methods; and oil refining is important. Tripoli is predominantly a Moslem town, though its hinterland in the Lebanon is mainly Christian.

Three centres dispute urban leadership in Israel. Haifa (population *c.* 250,000) is as we have noted the leading seaport, and like Tripoli

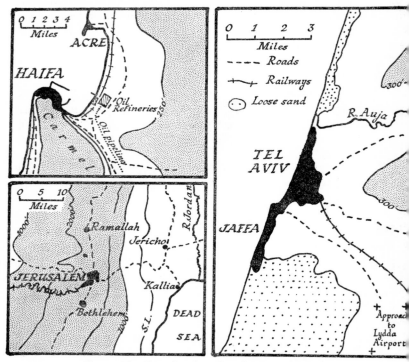

Fig. 85. The Sites of Haifa, Jaffa–Tel Aviv, and Jerusalem

controls an easy lowland route to the interior which is also followed by an oil pipeline (closed since 1948). Crude petroleum is now imported from the Caribbean area. Hence a local industry based on oil fuel and related to transport needs (railway and motor repairs, etc.) has developed on a relatively impressive scale; and the once malarial river flats of the Bay of Acre are now being covered by industrial installations, chief of which is the oil refinery of the Iraq Petroleum Co. Haifa does not, however, occupy a central position within Israel, and her immediate hinterland, the rocky spurs of Mount Carmel, and the indifferently fertile country of Samaria, is not particularly productive.

Tel Aviv (population 400,000), once a suburb of Jaffa, is better placed as an outlet for the richer Plain of Sharon, from which come the bulk of the citrus exports. The city is much more centrally placed within Israel, hence its choice in 1948 as the provisional capital of the state of Israel. Jaffa, the older town (population 1948, 102,000), is now continuous with Tel Aviv. Once the chief port of Palestine, its importance has declined considerably due to port developments in Haifa and Tel Aviv, and to the flight of many of its inhabitants (almost all of which were Arab) during 1948. Haifa currently handles five times the volume of port traffic as compared with Jaffa–Tel Aviv together.

Jerusalem (population of the Old City – Arab – c. 120,000; of the New City – Jewish – 170,000) has few geographical advantages of any kind. Difficult of access, remote from trade routes, and lying in an arid, unproductive region, its water supplies were for long sufficient to maintain only a small settlement, and many inhabitants were dependent on open cisterns cut in the rock. Today, water must be pumped from the lowlands to the north and west. There was however one advantage – strength as a defensive site, and this probably gave Jerusalem an original importance in early times as a tribal settlement. Since then, religious association and tradition have gradually fostered its growth as a centre of Jewish, Christian, and Moslem pilgrimage; and as in Mecca, the circulation of pilgrims can be said to provide the principal means of livelihood for its inhabitants. Catering, printing, local commerce, and the tourist-pilgrim traffic are in normal times the chief activities, and the presence of a seat of government has further stimulated development. The city is now partitioned between the states of Israel and Jordan; and it has been a deliberate policy to settle the 'Jerusalem corridor' as thickly as possible with Jewish immigrants. 'New Jerusalem' (Jewish) comprises the outer suburbs: the Old City, still with its boundary wall and four gates, contains most Christian shrines, as well as the Mosque of Omar, and is in the state of Jordan.

CHAPTER XVII

The Coastlands of the Levant (continued)

I. CYPRUS

It is dubious whether Cyprus can best be considered a part of the Levant or of Asia Minor. Structurally, there is little doubt that the island is part of a fold garland that can be traced into the Amanus ranges of Asia Minor; and, curiously, the topography of Cyprus partly repeats on a small scale the pattern of an interior basin shut off from the

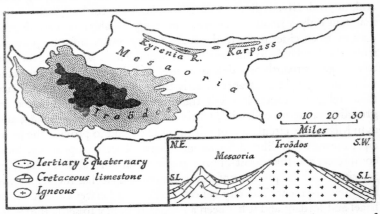

Fig. 86. Cyprus: Orography and Structure. Land over 1,000 ft. stippled; over 3,000 ft. in black

sea by encircling fold ranges which is characteristic of Asia Minor as a whole. In the sphere of human and economic geography, however, connexion with the Levant and Egypt is much more apparent, and commercial intercourse is today almost entirely towards the east and south, rather than towards the north.

The remarkable shape of the island – sometimes compared to that of a lion's skin pegged out to dry – has been determined by two almost parallel and slightly curved fold ranges. The northern arc, known in its western portion as the Kyrenia Range, and as the Karpass in the

444

extreme north-east, is a simple narrow anticline rising from the sea to a maximum height of 3,000 feet just over 4 miles inland. The southern arc is larger, but has been shattered by great upwellings of magma in the core of the folds, so that the central part of the arc now consists of an enormous boss of plutonic material surrounded by broken fold structures. This boss forms the Troödos Range, the highest part of the island, with a maximum height of 6,400 feet. Between the two arcs lies a lowland plain some 12 to 15 miles wide, known as the Mesaoria. The plain, below 500 feet in height, and slightly undulating, is open to the sea on the east and west.

The rock series of Cyprus are all of comparatively recent formation, the oldest being of late Cretaceous age. The Kyrenia mountains are formed of a massive flexure of this Cretaceous limestone, which passes locally into dolomite and marble. The presence of limestone is again a marked feature in Cyprus, since in addition to the Cretaceous series, which is the thickest and best developed of any in the island, there are younger limestones of Miocene and Pliocene, and Pleistocene age. Chalk and chalky marl outcrops are also numerous.

II. CLIMATE

The climate of Cyprus conforms to the usual eastern Mediterranean type. Frost is practically unknown on the coast, but may occur occasionally in lowland areas inland, and frequently on the hills, though the average winter temperature is 40° on the hills, and 55° F. on the lowlands. Despite the surrounding sea, rainfall is limited to 9 months of the year, the summer being completely dry. Control of rainfall by topography is very marked, with annual rainfall varying from 18 inches on parts of the plain to over 40 inches in the higher parts of the Troödos Range.

Reference has previously been made to the frequency with which low-pressure systems develop over the island. This gives a degree of changeability in weather greater than for most other parts of the Middle East, shown particularly in the greater length of spring and autumn. Because of this, plant life in certain parts is more varied, and a wide range of crops is possible. Another special feature is the high summer temperature of the interior plain. Once again, in view of the presence of the Mediterranean, it could be expected that a modification of summer heat might occur, but in fact, temperatures of 95° to 105° F. are common on the Mesaoria. This may be due to the effect of the

coastal ranges, which, besides excluding maritime influences, may produce a concentration of heat in the basin-like interior. The prevalence
of dazzling white calcareous rock series may also be another, very
minor, factor. Whatever the cause, however, the effects of summer
heating are seen in the dusty, baked, and barren appearance of the
Mesaoria, which, surprisingly, recalls parts of inner Arabia or Asia
Minor rather than the verdant slopes and orchards of the Mediterranean
coastlands.[1]

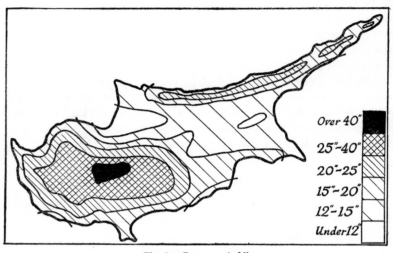

Fig. 87. Cyprus: rainfall

REPRESENTATIVE CLIMATIC CONDITIONS
(° F. and inches of rainfall)

	J	F	M	A	M	J	J	A	S	O	N	D	Total
Kyrenia (coast)													
Temp.	53	55	58	64	71	78	83	84	79	73	63	57	
Rainfall	4·6	3·2	2·4	0·8	1·0	0·2	0	0	0·2	1·3	3·8	4·9	22·4
Rainy days	11	9	8	3	3	1	0	0	1	3	8	10	57
Nicosia (Mesaoria)													
Temp.	50	54	57	66	73	84	90	87	82	74	66	58	
Rainfall	4·3	3·1	2·0	0·7	0·9	0·1	0	0	0·1	1·1	3·0	4·7	19·0
Rainy days	11	8	6	2	2	1	0	0	1	3	7	9	50

[1] Another indication of the fierce summer heat of the Mesaoria is the frequency of
convectional air currents, which make the Nicosia airfield notoriously one of the most
'bumpy' of the Middle East.

	J	F	M	A	M	J	J	A	S	O	N	D	Total
Troödos (mountain)													
Temp.	44	48	51	57	60	66	70	69	65	59	52	46	
Rainfall	6·4	5·1	4·4	3·1	2·4	1·0	0	0	0·5	4·3	6·7	8·5	41·4
Rainy days	13	10	8	5	4	2	0	0	2	8	14	16	82

III. AGRICULTURE

The soils of Cyprus are in general very fertile. On the flanks of the Troödos Range material derived from a mixture of igneous and sedimentary rocks gives a rich soil particularly adapted to the growing of vines; and on the Mesaoria itself there is a layer of light loam, 15 to 20 feet in depth, which has been formed of material eroded from nearby hill slopes. The chief limiting factor in cultivation is, however, water supply. Few perennial streams exist, because of percolation into porous rock measures; and the heavy, intermittent character of precipitation leads to much soil erosion. Hence though at first sight an average annual rainfall of 20 to 40 inches would seem adequate for agriculture, there is, in fact, a considerable water problem. Because of rapid run-off and evaporation, areas of good soil have become saline, and irrigation projects must overcome the difficulties of a porous bedrock and an irregular topography, which, as in Israel, make the construction of barrages difficult. Another adverse circumstance is the system of land and water rights, which continue as under the Ottomans, with the familiar names of mulk, miri, and waqf. Unrestricted grazing by goats is another problem.[1] Malaria was once widespread, especially in the Mesaoria, but since 1945 the anopheles mosquito has been eradicated from the island.

Nevertheless, Cyprus ranks as the most highly cultivated territory of the Middle East, and, with a proportion of over 50 per cent. of the total area under cultivation, is much further advanced than any other country.

Barley is now the chief crop, occupying over 40 per cent. of the cereal area, but wheat though grown on a smaller area produces heavier yields. Barley is partly but by no means wholly a crop of the drier or hillier areas. Besides providing fodder and an adulterant for wheaten flour, there is some export of barley for malting and distilling purposes.

[1] Special laws have been enacted to reduce this menace. Damages may be claimed against the owner of goats that graze in cultivated land; and, if the owner cannot be traced, a communal fine may be inflicted on the entire animal-owning community. A village may vote to exclude all goats from its area, and special districts may be reserved for tree planting in which grazing is forbidden. Finally, shepherds and goatherds must be licensed, and the numbers of their flocks are controlled.

Production of wheat is, on the other hand, sufficient for only about half total consumption, and quantities are imported. A speciality of Cyprus is the carob – a moderately large, spreading tree that produces a long, sweet-tasting pod somewhat resembling a large broad bean in appearance. Carobs are eaten as food by poorer people, and also widely used as animal fodder. The taste of the carob makes it acceptable as a sweetmeat in many parts of the world (it was at one time sold in Great Britain under the name of 'locust bean'), and carobs are therefore used in the making of chocolate and confectionery. The pod takes 11 months to form after the flower has appeared, so that it is essential to preserve the ripening pod throughout the winter. Though an unusually 'long term' crop, even for the Middle East, carobs are of the greatest importance in the economy of Cyprus, and rank first among agricultural exports.

Potatoes thrive particularly on the sandy plains of the south-east (Famagusta region), and are exported in large numbers. Attention has recently been given to flax-growing, and new plant strains have been introduced from New Zealand and Britain. Some of the flax is retained in the island as the basis of a home lace industry that provides occupation for women and girls, and the remainder is exported, chiefly to Britain. Tobacco is another crop which has increased in importance following an improvement in methods of cultivation. The Latakia variety is widely grown, chiefly for home consumption, though small quantities are sold abroad, some to Britain, as an ingredient in the blending of pipe tobaccos, the rest as cigarettes to Egypt. A small cigarette-making industry has developed in the town of Nicosia.

All the crops mentioned above are grown on the lowlands and lowest hill slopes below 1,000 feet. Most productive are the lowlands immediately adjacent to the hill ranges, since in these parts rainfall is heavier, streams are more numerous, and the soil richer and deeper. Towards the centre of the Mesaoria lack of water imposes an increasing control, and the inner parts of the plain are often left uncultivated. It is significant that Nicosia, the capital, and centre of a rich agricultural region, is located close to the southern slopes of the Kyrenia Range, and not, as might be expected from the topography, in the centre of the Mesaoria.

The coastal plain, narrow in many places, is highly cultivated, though exploitation is sharply limited by rapidly rising fold ranges. Terracing exists, but is less a feature than in the Lebanon, where the presence of high-level mountain springs is a special inducement to develop the hill slopes. For the most part the higher parts of the Kyrenia and Troödos Ranges are given over to grazing. Because of differences in geological structure, however, there are considerable contrasts between the utilisation of the two ranges. The Kyrenia–Karpass folds, being composed of porous limestone, are karstic in many places, and vegetation often consists merely of a thin garrigue, giving scanty grazing for a few goats. The Troödos, on the other hand, is less rugged, though much higher, and has a heavier rainfall and lower temperatures. As the component rocks are impermeable, there is thus more surface water. Woodland (pine and oak) is a feature in many places, though until recently the area of forest was steadily being reduced by un-restricted grazing and cutting of timber for fuel. Now a scheme of afforestation has begun with control of grazing, and it is hoped to preserve and extend this valuable natural resource.

On the middle slopes of both the Kyrenia and Troödos mountains, vine-growing is important. The most productive area lies near the south-east of the Troödos boss, where there is a very rich, semi-volcanic soil. Cyprus has for long been the principal wine producer of the Middle East, and wines and spirits rank high in her list of exports. Cyprus wine does not compare in quality with the best products of France and Spain, but there is a moderately extensive market within the Middle East, and up to 1939, quantities were shipped to France for mixing with French wines. A special product of the island is 'Commandaria', a heavy sweet wine somewhat resembling port, the manufacture of which is said to have been introduced into the island by the Knights Templar. A 'sherry' type of wine is also produced in considerable quantities, and brandy is distilled at Nicosia and Limassol. Famagusta and Limassol, both close to the major wine region, handle the bulk of Cypriot exports of wine, some of which goes to Britain.

Besides their use for wine, grapes are dried and exported as raisins. The importance of raisins in the export trade of Cyprus is a reminder of the geographical relationship with Asia Minor, where raisins form a chief export. Oranges are also grown on an increasing scale, especially on the sandy soils of the coastal plains; and nut-trees (almond, and to a less extent pistachio, walnut, and hazel) are also abundant.

The acreage under cotton has quadrupled since 1900. The cotton plant cannot tolerate a saline soil, but does well under a long, arid summer, so development has tended to occur on the inner regions of the Mesaoria in parts where water can be made available. Towards the west a number of salt lakes and springs are found, and cotton cannot be grown. The best qualities of cotton are obtained when irrigation is applied, and in these irrigated areas American plants have been introduced, whilst native varieties are still grown in non-irrigated regions. Some raw cotton is used in the island for home weaving and embroidery, but an increasing market has been found in Europe, with France, Germany, and Greece as chief buyers. Other, very minor crops are: sesame, hemp, cumin, and aniseed.

IV. PASTORALISM

This is still important, though of recent years the herding of goats and sheep has been increasingly restricted. Now, with more than half the total area of the island under cultivation, herding on a large scale is a feature only of the more arid and mountainous districts. A traditional occupation in Cyprus is mule breeding, and, as mules are infertile, both horses and asses must also be kept. Mules proper (i.e. with an ass as sire) are chiefly used as harness animals – for ploughing and riding, whilst jennets (i.e. with a horse as sire) are smaller but surer-footed, and hence find employment as pack animals. Mules rank as a minor but significant export item, though during the war years the demand was very much greater.

LIVESTOCK IN CYPRUS

	Sheep	Goats	Asses	Cattle	Pigs	Horses and Mules
1938	301,000	184,000	54,000	40,000	28,000	16,000
1958	390,000	120,000	40,000	30,000	35,000	10,000

V. IRRIGATION

Until recently, the development of irrigation in Cyprus was very slow, and on a small scale. Sir Ronald Storrs, a former Governor of the island, suggests that one reason for this may be found in the conservative outlook of the peasants, and the deadening effect of long years of subsistence cropping by traditional methods. Other factors are geographical – deriving from structure and topography, since the problems discussed for Israel recur in Cyprus. There is no large river that might be impounded; many of the rocks are porous, so that a large proportion of the rainfall is lost to the surface, and any barrage built must be 'waterproofed' on the floor and sides before it will retain water. Another adverse factor, this time related to high summer temperatures and rapid evaporation, is the frequent occurrence of saline deposits, which sometimes render irrigation water, when it has been collected and stored, brackish and unfit for use.

Small-scale irrigation channels have for centuries been used to lead water from the lower mountain ranges to the edges of the Mesaoria. Within the last two decades, larger schemes have been undertaken, involving the damming of small river valleys near their head, and the irrigation of patches up to several hundred acres in extent. Most of these developments have been round the Troödos massif, and in the majority of cases works are on a small scale: no comparison is possible with developments in Egypt or Iraq, though by existing standards in Cyprus, the advance has been considerable. Parallel with the development of irrigation schemes, re-afforestation has proceeded, with an attempt to find a livelihood for former goatherds and shepherds as forest watchers and fire guards. In this way the extent of cultivated land has increased, and the more wasteful aspects of pastoralism have been reduced. Moreover, with a stronger forest cover, soil erosion, which has come to be an urgent problem in some areas, is slowly being checked.

VI. INDUSTRIES

Mining. The name Cyprus is said to be derived from *cyprium* (copper), which has been exploited in the island since Bronze Age times. Many veins of copper and other minerals still exist, though most are small, and widely scattered. As would be expected, the Troödos area is naturally the most favoured region for the occurrence of minerals, but there are a few deposits associated with the igneous intrusions of the Kyrenia Range. Iron and copper pyrites (sometimes mined together) are the most important minerals, but within the last two decades there has been considerable fluctuation in output. In 1962, iron pyrites easily headed the list of mineral exports in terms of tonnage (though copper was the more valuable item). The chief centres of mining are Mandios, from which the ore is carried to Limassol and Larnaca for shipment, and Skouriotissa, from which a light railway gives access to Pendayia, on the Bay of Morphou (north-west Cyprus). Because of lack of fuel, treatment of the ore is carried out in Britain and the U.S.A.

Copper is mined at Mavravouni (with treatment and concentration at Xeros), and there is also a smaller production from Kalavassos. There is also sporadic working at another centre, Limni, which is an ancient site re-opened in 1929 with open-cast workings for treatment of ore formerly rejected as being too low-grade. An interesting feature has been recent prospecting by aerial survey for copper and other mineral deposits; this has centred on Mathiaki and Apliki, which are again in the Troödos area. Other centres are Sha, Agrokopia, and Kinousa.

Deposits of asbestos occur on the sides of Mount Troödos itself, but these were not at first regarded as valuable, since the fibres are short in length, and could not be used. Modern technique has latterly found a means of handling the short fibres – by using them in packing material, and in the manufacture of 'asbestos board' – so that the Troödos deposits are now exploited, and form the third most valuable mineral export. Amiandos is the chief centre, and the asbestos is shipped through Limassol, the nearest port.

The presence of small igneous dykes has led to metamorphism in surrounding sedimentary rocks, and certain of these metamorphic aureoles contain deposits of coloured earths, two of which, ochre and umber, are exploited on a commercial scale. Both earths are derived from grey Miocene marl, altered by intense heating to a yellowish or brown colour, and are mined in quantity at Mavravouni, north-west of Limassol. Italy and the United States are chief buyers of these pigments. A third coloured earth, known as *Terra Verte*, consisting of silicates of iron and potassium, is a product of the weathering of basalt. At one time the production of Terra Verte was considerable, but its importance has now declined. Chromium also occurs on the slopes of the Troödos Ranges, but individual deposits are very small, and there is no real mining – instead, lumps of chromite are collected by peasants. It has been suggested that the conditions of occurrence of this chromium are closely similar to those of the Ural Mountains of Russia, and hence other minerals – platinum and nickel – may also exist. So far, however, these hopes have not been realised.

Another product of metamorphism is marble, which is found in many parts of the Kyrenian Range, and is used for building. There is no export. Gypsum of a high degree of purity is frequently found in the Tertiary series of the Mesaoria, and because of ease of working and proximity to the sea, there is an important export to the Levant states. Gypsum from Cyprus can undersell locally produced gypsum in the Levant states, hence it has been much used in the considerable building programmes now under way. Salt lagoons are found at Larnaca and Limassol, where it would seem that sea water penetrates inland through porous rock strata, emerging later at the surface to form lagoons, which dry out in summer, leaving a naturally formed salt deposit. There is some exploitation for home use, and also for export.

EXPORT OF MINERALS FROM CYPRUS, 1959 (value in £000's)

Copper	Iron Pyrites	Asbestos	Chrome	Gypsum	Umber
5,900	2,000	910	125	64	49

It is of interest to note the wide variety of mineral production from such a small region, and also the varying methods used in exploitation. Iron, copper, and asbestos are developed by large-scale companies using modern machinery, whilst part of the umber is produced by systematic methods of exploitation in open trenches. The remaining minerals are often gathered from the surface, and brought to merchants in Nicosia and Larnaca by farmers or foresters who are not directly engaged in mining.

Industries. The industries of Cyprus are small in extent, and almost all related to agriculture. Fruit drying and packing, wine- and cigarette-making, olive oil pressing, and soap-boiling are some of the chief activities. There is in addition a small textile industry carried on with native raw materials – cotton, flax, and wool – which is located in Nicosia and Famagusta. More important than this is, however, an extensive craft industry carried on in the home, the precise extent of which it is difficult to ascertain, since much of it is part-time work carried on by women and by agricultural workers. Large numbers of buttons are made, this item ranking fifth in the list of exports. The buttons are made from vegetable ivory (the dom nut) which is entirely imported from the Sudan. It is interesting to note that imports of the dom nut are only one-quarter as valuable as exports of the finished buttons – an example on a small scale of the value of craftsmanship applied to a small amount of raw material. Mention was made earlier of the lace-making and embroidery, which, using cotton, linen, and silk, reach a very high level of artistry. Both activities are *par excellence* a home occupation, and the villages of Lefkara and Lefkoniko are renowned as production centres, from which finished articles are sent to Nicosia for sale. Tourists provide the chief market for the lacework.

Though the Mesaoria is unattractive, the pine woods of the Troödos, and to a less extent the northern and south-western coasts, provide ideal summer stations, and Cyprus may claim to rank second to the Lebanon in natural scenic beauty. Sea communications with the mainland are not very good, but a regular air service with the Levant and Egypt brings a growing number of summer visitors from both regions. Troödos and Kyrenia are the main resorts. With settled political conditions, and an increased standard of living in the Middle East, there is some prospect of an increase in the tourist traffic of the island.

Fishing is not well developed, partly for historical reasons, and the activities of the ports are mainly in trading. There is, however, some sponge-fishing for five months of the year. Famagusta, on the east coast, is best placed for traffic with the Levant and Egypt, and also has easiest and most direct communications with Nicosia, the capital. As a result, Famagusta handles the bulk of the general trade of Cyprus, with the greatest share of imports, and most of the exports of the three commodities, carobs, fruit, and buttons. Limassol is next in importance,

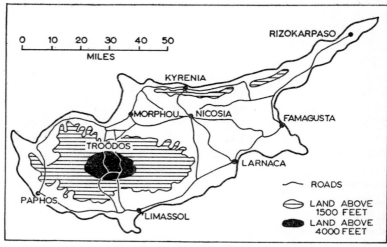

Fig. 88. Towns and Roads in Cyprus

and its situation close to the Troödos Range gives it an advantage as an outlet for the minerals and produce of the Troödos vineyards. Asbestos and wine are the chief exports. Larnaca shares some of this trade also, and handles most of the exports of umber and common salt. Nicosia, (population 81,000), is the natural centre of the island, and acts as a collecting centre for the agricultural produce of the Mesaoria. The town is a focus of routes: one leading northwards through a gap in the hills to Kyrenia and the northern coastlands, another south-westwards to the Troödos, and a third south-eastwards to Famagusta and Larnaca. There are a number of small industries: textiles, fruit packing, cigarette- and wine-making, and, in addition, arising from its function as an administrative centre, some activity in printing, building construction, and light engineering. One feature indicative of the importance of Nicosia as a route centre is an elaborate system of fortifications, designed by the sixteenth-century Venetian rulers, which still dominates the lay-out and appearance of the town.

Since 1946 there have been two development schemes for Cyprus – the first, a Ten Year plan during which £6 million was spent on agriculture, housing, education, and the improvement of communications; and the second, begun in 1956, and completed in 1961, with an allotment of £38 million. In relation to population numbers, these grants are remarkable by Middle Eastern standards.

As a sombre background to this pattern of economic advance, political events have often reduced the public acceptance and utility of the material improvements, and even with the settlement of 1960 there remain considerable possible difficulties: to what extent will Cyprus continue to find markets for her agricultural produce outside the area of Commonwealth Preference: how far did the British military bases provide employment for local labour – directly and indirectly; and what will be the relationships of the 96,000 Turkish-speaking inhabitants with the 425,000 Greek-speaking majority?

CHAPTER XVIII

The Arabian Peninsula

From the environs of Palmyra as far as the Indian Ocean, and from the Red Sea to the shores of the Persian Gulf, there extends the vast platform of Arabia – a single block of ancient crystalline rocks that forms the largest unit of the Middle Eastern region. Complementing structural unity is a climatic unity: the whole of Arabia, with very small and local exceptions, has an annual rainfall of less than 10 inches, while at the same time temperatures are among the highest recorded in the world. Such physical unity has had an effect on the human geography of the region. From Arabia has arisen the special way of life spoken of as 'Arab'; and though as a desert Arabia may appear unattractive and sparsely peopled, yet human activities in neighbouring lands have been closely conditioned by occurrences in the peninsula, and both from the physical and cultural aspects, Arabia emerges as the core, or heartland, of the entire Middle East.

PHYSICAL UNITS

Except in the north where it passes gradually into the Syrian steppes, and in a few parts of the north-east, where there is a continuity with the shorelands of the Persian Gulf, the Arabian platform is defined on all sides by a well-developed series of faults which can be traced southwards from Jordan state along the whole length of the Red Sea littoral as far as Aden, then eastwards as far as Oman, northwards in parts of the Persian Gulf, and finally on a smaller scale along the western margins of the Euphrates valley as far as central Iraq. Because of this remarkable trend of faulting, the Arabian peninsula can be considered a single gigantic horst, with drowned lowland basins to south, east, and west; and a part of the ancient geosyncline of the Tethys to the north.

The block itself is covered in many places by sheets of later sediments, which consist for the most part of calcareous series, or of sandstones. In the west, lava flows are also a feature. Though information is incomplete, it would seem that large-scale dislocation is absent: and important evidence of the simplicity of structure over most of central Arabia is furnished by the existence of copious springs of water on the shores of the Persian Gulf, particularly near and on the island of Bahrein. Flow of water from these springs greatly exceeds the total rainfall of the district, and it is thought that the source of the water must be the highlands of the Nejd, many hundreds of miles to the west – an indication that permeable rock series must extend without great disturbance for considerable distances. Further, it has been noted that the oilfields of the Persian Gulf consist of extremely flat domes, with a minimum of crustal disturbance. One exception to this general rule occurs, however. In the region of Oman, fold movements have uplifted a mountain chain to a height of 10,000 feet, but, as we have seen, this region is properly a part of the Zagros Range.

Almost all of the west and centre of Arabia lies at an altitude of at least 2,000 to 3,000 feet, with many ridges that reach considerably higher; but the plateau has been tilted so that the western edge stands much higher than the eastern side; and to the east of a straight line drawn from Abu Kemal on the Euphrates to the Kuria Muria Islands, the surface of Arabia is everywhere (Oman excepted) below 1,000 feet in altitude. Rise of magma along fracture lines in the west has further raised the level of the surface by producing extensive basaltic plateaus, with frequent volcanic cones that exceed 8,000 or 10,000 feet. The presence of igneous rocks is a prominent feature along the entire western side of Arabia, from south-west Syria as far as Aden. Further inland, basaltic eruptions become more of a minor occurrence, and are almost absent in the east.

Although no perennial rivers now exist, the whole Arabian plateau has been heavily dissected by fluvial action, as is shown by the presence of numerous deep wadis, many of which are still covered by thick layers of clay. The best developed wadis are those that follow the dip slope of the plateau in the east and north-east, and hence open towards the Persian Gulf and Euphrates valley. It would, however, appear that certain wadis have not been entirely formed by river erosion, but are tectonic features subsequently enlarged by water action. One of the largest of these latter is the Wadi Batin, which can be traced from the region between Basra and Kuwait, where it is a steep-sided depression 4 miles wide, as far to the south-west as central Nejd. Another slightly smaller valley, but of similar origin, is the Wadi Sirhan, which runs south-east from the neighbourhood of Amman (Jordan) as far as Al

Jauf. Parts of both wadis are now filled by deposits of blown sand, and the original outline obscured.

We may subdivide the Arabian peninsula as follows:

  (I) The Western Highlands, extending from the Gulf of Akaba to the hinterland of the Straits of Bab el Mandeb.

 (II) The Southern Coastlands, from Bab el Mandeb to Oman.

(III) The Oman region.

(IV) The Eastern Coastlands.

 (V) The Interior Deserts.

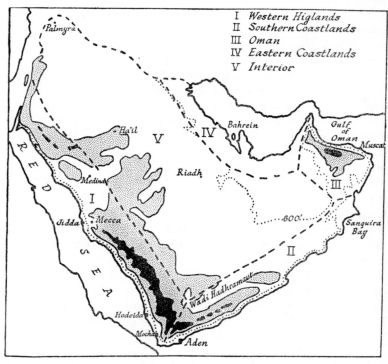

Fig. 89. Natural Regions of Arabia. Land above 3,000 ft. stippled, above 10,000 ft., black

I. THE WESTERN HIGHLANDS

The territory extending from the head of the Gulf of Akaba as far south as latitude 20° N., is spoken of as the Hedjaz. In terms of topography and structure, however, it is feasible to regard much of the west as made up of roughly parallel zones aligned parallel to the Red Sea. The westernmost of these zones is the Tihama, or coastal plain. This is very narrow indeed in the north-west, but opens towards the south, and is further characterised by heat, aridity, and high atmospheric humidity. Fronting the Tihama along a series of well-developed fault-scarps is the highland zone, formed by uptilting and buckling of the plateau-edge, and composed of pre-Cambrian crystalline rocks (granite, schist, porphyry) with numerous lava flows (*harra*). This upland which reaches 9,000 feet in places is known in the Hedjaz as the Madian, and further south (in Asir) as the Serah. Many wadis have been deeply incised into the westward-facing scarps, and these are now occupied once in several years by torrents of a few days' duration, following a rare but heavy downpour of rain. Though short-lived, the torrents have considerable erosive power, and their course is often marked by ungraded deposits of silt, scree, and boulders.

On the eastern (dip) slope of the Hedjaz uplands, relief is distinctly less broken, though topography is by no means uniform. Shallow folds and synclinal depressions, with isolated massifs, are typical, and this inner zone thus lends itself more to settlement, and to the development of communications. Even though rainfall is sparse (being for the most part less than 5 inches per annum), and, as we have seen, extremely capricious in onset, water can be somewhat more easily retained and stored in the shallower, broader valleys of the eastern side of the mountains. A limited degree of oasis cultivation is therefore possible. The upland basins of the east also contain fairly extensive deposits of clayey alluvium, in the lower layers of which rainfall collects and is shielded from the effects of the sun, thus allowing a little irrigation from wells. On the seaward (western) side of the Madian, the effects of rain-fall are soon dissipated by rapid run-off; and as a consequence towns and routeways are not found, even on the coastal plain. A further draw-back to life on the coastal plain is the excessive atmospheric humidity produced by damp on-shore breezes that bring in much moisture from the Red Sea.

Development has taken place only in the interior of the north-west Hedjaz. The extreme west, with its bare, rugged landscapes of jagged black and red rocks, is desolate; but at some distance inland, on the eastern flanks of the mountain ranges, there is a line of oases – Mudaw-wara, Tebuk, El Ala, and Medina – where garden cultivation is carried on to a small extent, and trade routes have been developed with the far north and south of the Arabian peninsula.

South of latitude 24° N. the mountain fringe decreases considerably in height, with a maximum elevation in many places of only 3,000 feet. The coastal plain is wider, and because of the lowness of the upland barrier, access to the interior is facilitated. Here the Tihama is at its maximum extent, providing a 'gateway' to central Arabia, not merely by reason of its general lower altitude, but also, to a minor degree, because it lies in the 'waist' of Arabia, giving the shortest distance between the Persian Gulf and the Red Sea. Though rainfall is no more abundant than in the Madian, there is a greater concentration of population, due in the first instance to the development of long-distance trade, with the people of the Tihama acting as middlemen, and afterwards, as the result of historical accident, to the growth of pilgrimage to the cities of Mecca and Medina.

Over the greater part of the entire Hedjaz, vegetation is limited to a very few stunted bushes, and agriculture or even nomadic pastoralism are both virtually impossible except in a few inland wadis, where as we have noted the occurrence of clay soil retains a little water that elsewhere is soon evaporated. In such relatively favoured spots there is a little cultivation of dates, millet, wheat, barley, and Mediterranean fruits, with stock rearing on the drier outskirts of the settlement. The towns of the Hedjaz were for long mere trading posts precariously self-sufficient in foodstuffs, and dependent for much of their existence on long-distance caravans, by which they could offer services, and hence obtain the means of importing extra food. Since the Muhammadan era the pilgrim traffic has been the chief economic activity of the district, and now that the former overland traffic in incense and coffee is carried by sea, such centres as Mecca, Medina, and Jidda would hardly exist at all, certainly not as towns of their present size.

Mecca itself, with a population of about 80,000, is situated on an alluvial-filled wadi, and the produce of its oasis can support less than one-fifth of its present inhabitants. Up to 1952 there was a heavy tax on all pilgrims (£28 per head), which was the financial mainstay of the Saudi Arabian state; but with oil royalties the tax was abolished. About 500,000 pilgrims (five times the 1951 level) now visit Mecca from all parts of North Africa, the Middle East, Pakistan, the East Indies, Central Africa, and even China – 20,000 now by air and 120,000 by sea. From these pilgrims most of the population of Mecca and Jidda is recruited, and extreme cosmopolitanism is a feature, the vast majority of merchants and *entrepreneurs* being non-Arab in origin. Medina was once rather more important than Mecca, as it has a slightly larger oasis and easier communications; but although it caters for a certain number of pilgrims,[1] it is now overshadowed by its southern neighbour. Jidda handles imports of manufactured goods for the state of Saudi Arabia – a traffic that has greatly increased over the last decade – but many of its activities are still connected with pilgrimage. There are now motor-coach pilgrimages from North Africa, and some arrivals use the new railway from the Persian Gulf via Hofuf. The old Pilgrims' Railway from Damascus for long remained unrepaired after the ravages of 1914–18, but there are now plans to reopen it.

South of Lat. 20° N. lies Asir, where the Tihama is once again narrow, there occur the extensive Serah uplands. The general effect is still unmistakably that of a tilted and dissected tableland, with abrupt westward-facing faultscarps; but most of Asir lies above 5,000 feet, with the highest points just under 10,000 feet above sea level. By reason of their elevation, slightly greater than those of the northern Hedjaz, the uplands of Asir have a moderate precipitation, partly in the form of summer rains, and part from fog and dew. As a result, there are a number of short but fast-flowing streams for several months of the year, though none of these reach the sea, except during exceptionally heavy floods.

In their upper courses, the streams are deeply entrenched in steep valleys, which carry a dense 'jungle' vegetation of evergreen bushes, thorns, and moderately sized palms. At some distance away from the valley bottoms, this vegetation changes to thick grassland, with clumps of taller trees. The higher slopes of the valleys have been cleared and terraced for the cultivation of millet, wheat, bananas, dates, coffee, yams, and vines. In the west, at the junction of the uplands and a narrow coastal plain, the streams lose themselves in the sand, but here occur fields of millet, and groves of a special kind of palm (the Daum), which produces a hard fruit that is eaten by the Badawin of the region. As Philby has suggested, the entire region of Asir might be a part of Africa. The savanna-like aspect of the upper valleys, a climatic regime of summer rainfall, strongly African fauna, clusters of beehive-shaped huts made of straw and clay, elaborate basket-work implements, and the predominant crops of sorghum, bulrush millet, bananas, and coffee – all these recall East Africa or the Sudan rather than the mainland of Arabia.

One unusual feature, described by Thesiger, is the shifting cultivation practised in Asir. When rains fail, as they may, in one particular valley,

---

[1] Medina ranks as the second holy city of Islam, with Jerusalem the third.

the whole population migrates to another district where precipitation
has been more abundant. Here they help in the routine of cultivation,
and later return home with a share of the crops that they have had a
hand in growing, also with the knowledge that when rains fail in other
parts, they too may be called upon to receive destitute neighbours.

As the land drops towards the Red Sea, it becomes increasingly arid
and sandy. On the fringes of the piedmont zone, there are a number of
communities of pastoral nomads who rear goats; but close to the coast
there is insufficient vegetation even for grazing, and most of the plain
is devoid of inhabitants.

The Yemen. South of Asir lies the state of the Yemen, independent since
the withdrawal of the Turks in 1918. The country extends for about
300 miles between L. 18° and 12° N.; and, with a territory half the size
of Great Britain, has a population estimated at 4–5 million. For long it
was a closed region into which foreigners were not encouraged to
enter; but although this is still the case, within the last few years
German, American, and Japanese oil prospectors have gained access,
and the country has declared itself part of the United Arab Republic,
though this would not appear to mean much in practice. Nevertheless
occasional journeys by travellers are still the main source of information
on geographical conditions.

As regards topography and structure, the Yemen is closely similar
to Asir, except that conditions are on a slightly larger scale in the south.
The structure of a tilted plateau continues, but is more imposing, with
wide areas lying between 7,000 and 10,000 feet; and the highest summit in the whole of Arabia (Bani Shaib, 30 miles west of Sa'ana) is
estimated to reach 14,000 feet above sea level. The plateau surface is
deeply eroded by water-courses, but there are also extensive level areas,
many of which are highly cultivated. On the Red Sea side, the plateau
falls steeply to a coastal plain that is a continuation of the Tihama of
Asir, but again on a larger pattern; and there is the same feature of
streams rising in the uplands but failing to cross the coastal plain to
reach the sea. Lava flows are prominent on the plateau, and frequently
weather to a rich fertile soil.

Because of the differences in altitude in the Yemen, there is wide
variation in climatic conditions. On the plateau, winter temperatures
fall below 40° F., and frost and snow are of regular occurrence on the
higher ridges, though actual snowfall is less a feature than in the
Hedjaz further north. Sheepskins are, however, worn by most
Yemenites during the winter. In summer, because of nearness to the

Equator, temperatures are high, but by no means as high as in the rest of Arabia, partly because of greater elevation, and partly owing to the fact that there is a well-marked rainy season which gives a cloud cover during the months of July, August, and September. Little can be said with precision concerning the climate of the Yemen; but it is, however, definite that rainfall exceeds 20 inches per annum over most of the plateau, and may reach 40 inches on the highest parts. Most rain seems to fall in heavy, intermittent showers, often during the night; and there are two seasons of onset – a major rainy period from July to September, which is obviously related to the monsoonal conditions that affect Abyssinia and India; and a minor rainy season in March, which may be a remnant of the Mediterranean regime that is typical of the rest of the Middle East. It is to be emphasised that these wetter conditions obtain only in the higher parts of the Yemen: the coastal plain adjoining the Red Sea has a very scanty rainfall, with a maximum discernible in winter.

Because of rapid transition from plain to interior plateau, there is a succession of climatic zones (and hence of patterns of human occupation) that recall in a very limited way conditions in the Lebanon. The flat or gently undulating coastal plain, up to 50 miles wide, is desolate, and occupied only by a very small and mixed population chiefly of African origin (Danakils, Somalis, and Abyssinians). Near the coast of the Red Sea are swamps and lagoons; further inland, dry torrent beds full of pebbles and scree alternate with loose sand that is frequently raised in dense clouds by the strong wind. Two small ports, Hodeida and Mocha (Mocca), are outlets for trade from the interior highlands, and have little contact with their immediate hinterland, the barren coastal region. Without the plateau, neither port could exist.

The lowest slopes of the plateau are deeply weathered into ravines and rocky spurs, and access to the interior is a matter of considerable difficulty – an important element in the physical and political isolation of the state of the Yemen. At first, on the borders of the plain, vegetation is scanty, consisting of cactus, tamarisk, acacias, and dates, which support a small semi-pastoral population. Above 3,000 feet, Mediterranean plants appear: carobs, figs, and walnut trees. At 4,500 feet begins the most productive zone of the Yemen. Cereals (wheat, millet, and barley) are found wherever there is sufficient soil, or wherever terraces can be cut; and one finds a considerable variety of fruit trees and vegetables: apricots, citrus fruit, vines, pomegranates, onions, tomatoes, carrots; and also lucerne. Two plants merit special mention: the coffee shrub, which grows between altitudes of 4,000 and 5,000 feet; and the qat plant. Coffee is not now cultivated on a large scale, and tends to be restricted to the damper western side of the plateau, in the district of Manakha, which lies behind the once important and now declining port of Mocha, where one kind of coffee gained its name.

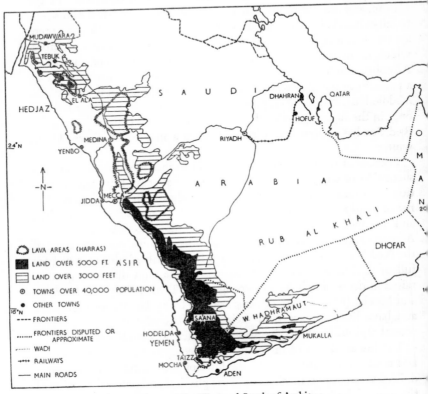

Fig. 90. The West and South of Arabia

The qat (*Catha edulis*) is a shrub somewhat like the tea plant, that grows to a height of about 10 feet, and its leaves, when chewed or infused, have a strongly narcotic effect like that of alcohol – a sense of well-being is induced, though a state resembling intoxication may be brought on by considerable indulgence. Qat eating is widely practised by all sections of the population, and extensive areas in the Yemen are given over to its cultivation, with the state deriving much revenue from taxation of qat plantations. The plant itself is restricted, like coffee, to high altitudes, actually 5,000 to 9,000 feet; and fairly abundant moisture is necessary in the later stages of growth. Whilst it is cultivated all over the Yemen, the main centre of production occurs in the extreme south-west, round Ta'izz; and there is a growing export to neighbouring regions, especially Aden, where, because of lower relief, the plant will not grow. Opinion regarding the use of qat is sharply divided. Some consider it a grave social evil, in that menfolk become addicted, spend a large part of their income on it, and become physically debilitated through lack of food and sleep. Family life is also greatly undermined. On the other hand, certain other observers refuse to regard qat as a real narcotic, and point to beneficial effects following limited use. What is perfectly certain is that the commodity is an important item of trade – Aden Colony imported nearly 4 million lb. at a cost of just under £2 million until the plant was banned in 1957 (of which half a million lb. were from the Yemen and the rest from Ethiopia). Such is the liking for qat that the ban was removed as unenforceable in 1958 and, in the words of Clarke Brooke, 'it is reasonable to assume that the market for qat will now continue to increase' – in part because of the new factor of air transport – and 'in spite of the social problems corollary to its use' the qat is bound to have continuing commercial importance in the Middle East.

Sa'ana, the capital of the Yemen (50,000 inhabitants), lies at an altitude of about 7,500 feet, in the centre of a fertile district given over to the cultivation of cereals, fruit, and vegetables, with irrigation from wells and cisterns. Dates do not ripen at this altitude, but there is a wide range of Mediterranean fruits; and sheep, cattle, and camels are kept. Besides the Zaidi (Shi'a) majority (p. 119) there are smaller groups of Sunni Moslems, and until 1950 a fairly considerable community of Oriental Jews, who had been settled in south-west Arabia since the Dispersal. Many Jews were artisans in stone, glass, and metal, and in textiles: and Jewish quarters were a feature not merely of Sa'ana, but also of many towns in western Arabia. Since 1949 most Jews have emigrated to Israel.

Little can be said of the external economic relations of the Yemen. Small quantities of coffee are still exported, now chiefly from Hodeida rather than Mocha; and qat is carried into the interior by camel, but as it must be used within a week of picking, the volume of this traffic is distinctly limited. Otherwise the Yemenites live a self-sufficient life, and contacts with the rest of the world are deliberately kept to a minimum.

A strict social order, with autocratic control by a few notables, makes this possible, though now (1963) there are some changes.

II. THE SOUTHERN COASTLANDS

The main feature is a gradual drop in elevation from west to east. In the extreme west, there is a plateau only slightly lower than that of the adjacent Yemen, but towards the east average altitude is under 3,000 feet in the region of Saihut (Long. 51° E.), and less than 600 feet at Sanquira Bay (Long. 57° E.). A special topographical element peculiar to the south-west of Arabia is the presence of a broad, well-defined valley, the Wadi Hadhramaut, which runs parallel to the coast some 120 miles inland, and extends for a distance of 200 miles before making a sharp turn south-eastwards, and cutting through the coastal ranges to reach the Indian Ocean near Saihut. One curious point about this wadi, which is a faulted synclinal structure, is that the upper part is much broader than the lower end. The present form of the valley would seem to be due in part to intricate river capture, with a small stream working back through the southern coastal uplands and diverting to the Indian Ocean a larger river that had followed a west–east course along the dip slope of the Arabian plateau to enter the Gulf of Oman.

In structure, southern Arabia closely resembles the western region previously described. There is the same underlying pre-Cambrian basement of granitic and metamorphosed series, overlain by sedimentary limestones and sands, with massive basaltic intrusions and occasional volcanic cones. Near the coast, fracturing and disturbance are outstanding features, so that folding and step-faulting occur; but further inland, the rocks lie almost horizontally. In the west, a narrow coastal plain 5 to 10 miles wide gives way to a tableland some 4,000 to 7,000 feet above sea level that is heavily dissected into dry wadis. These wadis are often quite devoid of vegetation. North of the tableland lies the trough of the Wadi Hadhramaut, with, still further north, a much lower but fairly level plateau 1,000 to 2,000 feet in height, which continues into inner Arabia.

Rainfall is distinctly less than in the Yemen. A few of the higher parts of the Hadhramaut and Dhofar may receive as much as 25 or 30 inches annually; the rainy season occurring in summer; but over most of the south of Arabia the annual average falls below 7 inches, and the rainy season is late winter, summer being quite dry. Because of higher relief, the west is somewhat wetter than the east, and Aden has 5 inches of rain annually, whilst towards Oman, rain may fall only once in 5 or 10 years. By reason of reduced elevation as compared with the Yemen, temperatures are high; and so for the most part the southern margin of Arabia is barren, with agriculture confined to a very few and scattered districts – such as the alluvial terraces and flat beds of wadis where winter flood-water is retained in the clayey subsoil; or near hills where seasonal streams can be led into tanks and cisterns.

The cultivated plants of southern Arabia differ markedly from those of the remainder of the Middle East. Being isolated towards the north by deserts, the inhabitants tend to look more to the east and south-west, and the crops grown have therefore some resemblance to those of India and East Africa. Millet is the chief cereal, with barley and wheat as subsidiaries, and such trees as the date palm, sago palm, mango, paw-paw, banana, and guava are found, together with some cotton, castor oil, indigo, and tobacco. The oases in which cultivation takes place are naturally more numerous in the west, the largest being at Lahej (Aden Protectorate), and at Meifa and Sha'il (north-west and north-east of Mukalla). The presence of subterranean water in the Wadi Hadhramaut suggests that some considerable development of agriculture might be possible in this latter region, provided an irrigation scheme based on wells could be created. At present, cultivation in the Wadi is limited to the middle portion, where the river actually flows for a part of the year, and where the side-valleys are dammed to provide irrigation water. Use of animal and fish manure allows a marked variety of crops – some 'African', some 'Asiatic', together with the staples of millet and dates. Lower down the slopes, towards the sea, water is much scarcer and agriculture far less a feature.

Two products of southern Arabia are frankincense and myrrh. The former is hardened sap, obtained by cutting gashes in the trunk; myrrh is a gum-like exudation, both from trees that grow on the slightly wetter hill slopes above 3,000 feet. Collection is in late spring and early summer, before the onset of the rains, mainly by migrant Somalis and other Africans. At one time there was a considerable trade in these products with the north, and tradition speaks of an 'Incense Route' somewhere in south-west Arabia, along which caravans moved north-wards to Medina and the Levant. Nowadays the output of frankincense and myrrh is very much smaller, most coming from the uplands of Dhofar.

Towards the east, as relief declines and rainfall diminishes, cultivation becomes more and more precarious, and fishing is the main occupation.

Q

Large quantities of shark, tunny, and sardines are caught (Chapter X), most of which are dried as food both for humans and for camels. In addition, an oil is prepared from the fish for use in woodworking. Mukalla and Shihr are the chief fishing centres, and in these towns rows of fish drying in the sun for food, and rotting in heaps to produce oil, are prominent, and according to some visitors, unforgettable, features.

With a barren hinterland, many activities in southern Arabia centre on the sea; and, in addition to fishing, trading by dhow is important. The Arabs of the south are the Greeks of the Indian Ocean, and cargoes are carried between East Africa, Arabia, the Persian Gulf, and India – even, at times, the East Indies. From their sea-trading, the natives of Aden and the Hadhramaut derive a livelihood that allows the import of foodstuffs into the country – as it is, local production of food is quite insufficient to maintain the existing population, and part must come from the outside. A cosmopolitan outlook, and wide commercial contacts, strongly contrasting with conditions in the Yemen, are strikingly indicated by the architectural styles in southern Arabia, which are very greatly influenced by East Indian models. Many storied, semi-fortified houses, with elaborate woodwork and carving, are most characteristic. After a life of trading, perhaps with many years spent away from his country, the southern Arab often returns to Aden or the Hadhramaut with a small fortune that will keep him in comfort for the rest of his life.

Aden is the principal town of the region, and its harbour, the only good one along the entire coast, from Bab el Mandeb to Muscat, is formed by a deep bay partially enclosed by two volcanic necks. The town, of c. 200,000 inhabitants, owes its development to British influence, as a coaling station and garrison; and with its settled political conditions which are in contrast to the turbulence and unrest of the remainder of southern Arabia, Aden has come to be a collecting centre and market for the products of the entire region, though its own immediate hinterland is not especially productive. Coffee is brought in native boats from both sides of the Gulf of Aden, frankincense comes from Dhofar and the Hadhramaut, cereals and other foodstuffs from India, and timber for houses and boatbuilding from the East Indieas and Burma. An oil refinery has recently been constructed to handle crude oil from the Persian Gulf.

Politically, most of the southern coastlands of Arabia are under British influence. Aden itself is a Crown Colony, whilst its immediate hinterland is a British protectorate; and further east, in the Hadhramaut, there is a rather vaguer British suzerainty over Arab rulers. The low-lands of Shihr adjoining the Hadhramaut are now part of the state of Oman. In many instances, however, the frontiers between various spheres of influence are not fully delimited, and on some maps the boundaries of the Yemen, Saudi Arabia, Oman, and the British-protected territories appear only as approximations.

III. OMAN

In the extreme south-east of the Arabian peninsula lies the region of Oman, distinct structurally from the rest of Arabia, and isolated on the landward side by the desert of the Rub al Khali, or El Dahna – Philby's Empty Quarter. Because of this isolation, Oman has few contacts with the interior; and in its culture and economic life looks more towards Persia and India, rather than towards the Arab lands of the north and west. This explains the long-standing political independence of Oman.

Oman consists of an enormous upfold of rock series of many ages, with disturbed pre-Cambrian rocks as the core, and later sedimentaries (chiefly limestone), resting upon this core in irregular masses. Faulting has occurred on a considerable scale; and extensive dislocation in the north, in the region of the Musandum peninsula, has given rise to a varied topography of tectonic valleys and upland horsts. Subsequent drowning by the sea has produced a fjord type of coastline, with long, deep inlets shut in by steep-walled cliffs. The largest of these drowned troughs is Elphinstone Inlet at the head of the Musandum Peninsula, which is 10 miles long, and surrounded on all sides by cliffs 3,000 to 4,000 feet in height. These deep-water estuaries make excellent harbours, but are greatly handicapped by lack of access to the shore – as there are no rivers, most inlets come to an abrupt end in a sheer wall. This is the case at Muscat, which has a moderately good harbour, but is extremely difficult to approach from the land. Another serious draw-back is the extreme heat and humidity of the inlets, which, surrounded by high cliffs, are calm, and intolerably steamy. Climatic conditions in these creeks have been described as consistently the worst in the world for sustained human activity. The few inhabitants spend only a part of the year in Oman, where there is a little winter fishing, and migrate for the summer months to Iraq, where they find employment as date harvesters.

The interior of Oman is for the most part a high tableland of about 4,000 feet in elevation, with a central ridge, the Jebel Akhdar (lying west-south-west of Muscat), that rises to 9,000 or 10,000 feet above sea level. Numerous deep and steep-sided wadis are a prominent feature, most being aligned in a south-west–north-east direction. Rainfall is thought to be less abundant than in the Yemen (statistics are lacking) but there is certainly a fall of more than 10 inches, since numerous springs occur, many of them impregnated with mineral salts. From these springs, as also from direct rainfall stored in tanks, many oases are irrigated. The higher parts of the plateau (region of the Jebel Akhdar) have a steppe vegetation, with occasional patches of small trees. Lower down, on the northern rim of the plateau, overlooking the Gulf of Oman, water is led from wadis that are deeply incised into the scarp

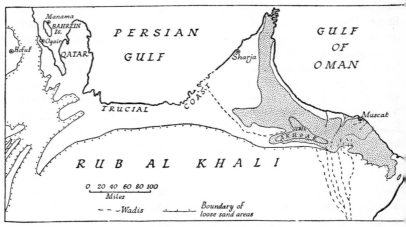

Fig. 91. Oman and Eastern Arabia

edge to numerous terraced plots; and here millet, wheat, barley, apricots, figs, vines, and coffee trees are cultivated. On the south-western side of the plateau, overlooking the Arabian desert, water supplies are fewer, and cultivation is therefore restricted to a narrow zone along the foot of the hills, where a line of springs is found.

On the lower slopes of the northern plateau-edge, date-growing becomes increasingly important. Irrigation is necessary, and this is maintained by a system of qanats (known locally as *feledj*), which tap the waters of thermal springs. On the lowlands close to the coast of the Gulf of Oman, known locally as the Batina, some oasis cultivation of dates also occurs, especially towards the east; but owing to lower relief and higher temperatures, the coastal zone is far less productive than the interior.

As in southern Arabia, many of the coastal dwellers turn to the sea for a living; and fishing, fish curing, and long-distance trading by dhow are the principal activities of this region. The deserts of the interior are generally too extensive to cross, and practically all communications, even with the west, are by sea. Trade from Oman itself is, however, on a small scale. Quantities of dates and dried fish are exported in return for cereals (chiefly rice), teak for boatbuilding, and for small manufactured goods such as rifles, ammunition, and knives.

Like that of its south-western neighbour, the population of Oman is of very mixed racial origin; and besides indigenous Arabs, there are many African negroes (some still slaves),[1] and a number of tribesmen from the northern shore of the Gulf of Oman. Structurally an outlier of Iran, Oman displays a curious cultural link with its larger neighbour: in religion the Shi'a faith is dominant; and observers have commented on the fact that ways of life seem closer to Persian habits than to normal Arab practice. In fact, both as regards physical and human geography, Muscat and its neighbour Matra are in a sense outliers of Persia and India.

Muscat, the chief town and port of the region, has great strategic importance through its command of the southern entrance to the gulf of Oman. As a centre of trade, however, it is handicapped by the low productivity of its immediate hinterland, and its difficult landward communications. In one sense, it can be regarded as a mirror-image of Aden on the east side of the Arabian peninsula, since main emphasis is on sea traffic and control of a sea-gulf. Like Aden too, Muscat turns its back upon the land, and depends for its existence on relations by sea.

IV. THE EASTERN COASTLANDS

From the peninsula of Musandum as far as the Shatt el Arab, the coastal region is everywhere below 600 feet, and consists for the greater part of an undulating plain, diversified very occasionally by low hills. In the north-west, towards the head of the Persian Gulf, the plain is either sandy or covered by stones and scree, the product of exfoliation; and on its seaward side there is a wide zone of lagoons and mangrove swamps. Because of rapid deposition of sediment from the Shatt el Arab, the coastline is being built up from the sea, hence numerous small islands, reefs, and shifting sandbanks are characteristic of the southern Gulf coast.

[1] Oman was for long the base for Arab slave-raiding in the African continent.

Reference was made earlier in the chapter to the remarkable phenomenon of springs of water occurring in many parts of Hasa, and
especially on the island of Bahrein. There are even springs of water
issuing from the sea bed, giving freshets of drinkable water in the open
sea. Careful investigation has established that the source of supply must
lie in the western highlands of Arabia; and it would seem to be definitely
not a question of supply from a local artesian basin of restricted extent,
as is the case in Israel and the London Basin. There is, however, one
limiting factor – the amount of spring water is related to the amount
of rain falling in the west, and so the total supply is not inexhaustible.
Within the last few years, owing to excessive sinking of wells, the flow
of water has been reduced.

As annual rainfall is less than 4 inches, cultivation is possible only
where springs occur, or where artesian basins can be tapped. The largest
of these better-watered spots occurs round the periphery of the island
of Bahrein, and others found near Qatif, on the mainland opposite
Bahrein island. Another artesian area extends for about 10 miles in the
district of Sharja. Dates are the chief crop, and millet and wheat may be
grown in addition if sufficient water is available.

The fact that the coast from Ras Musandum to the base of the Qatar
Peninsula was known as the Pirate Coast indicates the low productivity
of the region; and now that piracy has been brought to an end as an
economic activity, the western stretch of coastline from Abu Dhabi to
the Qatar peninsula is largely uninhabited.[1] The Qatar region is a small
upfold of limestone that reaches a height of 250 feet above sea level, and
the entire inland zone consists of empty karstic upland. Round the
coast, where artesian water occurs, there are a number of oases with
date palms, and tiny ports – some of which are expanding because of
oil exploitation.

Though small, the island of Bahrein is one of the most productive
regions of the Persian Gulf. The island itself, one of an archipelago,
consists of a shallow limestone dome, the centre of which has been
eroded to form a series of lowland basins or *poljes*. The periphery of the
island, especially on the northern side, is irrigated from the springs
previously mentioned, and much of the north is covered by date groves
with smaller patches of citrus fruit, cereals, and fodder crops. Until the
discovery of oil, the interior was uninhabited, but now considerable
development has taken place in the district of the Jebel Dukhan, and

[1] A British expedition in 1819 ended the power of the pirates, and the region is now
termed the Trucial Coast.

drinking water is imported both into the interior, and also into the chief port, Manama, as local supplies are hardly sufficient. Manama is the capital of Bahrein, and besides handling the exports of the islands – oil, pearls, mother-of-pearl, hides, dates, and cereals – is also the centre of a fishing trade. Fish are caught and dried in large numbers, mainly for

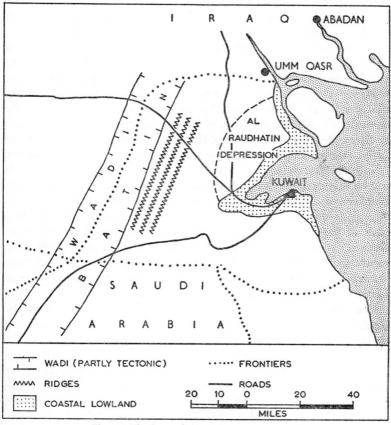

Fig. 92. The State of Kuwait: Natural Regions

human consumption, but to some extent as cattle fodder. The population of Manama is about 50,000.

North of Qatif as far as Kuwait and the delta of the Tigris–Euphrates the coastal plain of Hasa is barren and almost uninhabited. Extensive coral reefs fringe the shore, and inland there are wide expanses of lagoon and salt marsh, which reach their greatest extent towards the north-west, in the neutral zone between Kuwait and Saudi Arabia. One very small port, Oqair, with a poor harbour, handles a tiny traffic for the interior of Arabia via Hofuf and Riadh.

In sharp contrast to the difficult coast of Hasa, where ships of any size cannot approach nearer than 20 miles to the land, there is one good harbour in the north, with a deep-water inlet. This is at Kuwait, which has a long, landlocked bay that provides the only sheltered anchorage on the southern side of the Persian Gulf. A number of springs occur, and some cultivation is carried on – chiefly of dates, vegetables, and cereals; but water supplies are now inadequate for the town of Kuwait, which has grown considerably since the development of its oil resources. Drinking water is therefore imported from the Shatt el Arab, nearly a hundred miles away. Kuwait (population *c.* 100,000) is the natural outlet for the north-east of Arabia, and in some respects is a rival to Basra. Because of the rather difficult land communications of Basra (due to the extent of marsh), Kuwait has a small trade with the interior of south-west Iraq and Arabia in livestock and hides, since live animals can be driven on the hoof to Kuwait along the narrow zone of steppe that fringes the lowlands of Mesopotamia. An important activity in Kuwait is shipbuilding, and many of the larger dhows and pearling craft of the Persian Gulf are built there, from teak imported from Burma. Owing to its good harbour, it has also come to be a collecting centre and transhipment point for commodities moving to and from the smaller Gulf ports, which, as we have seen, are not accessible to larger vessels. Most of the trade is with India.

Pearl fishing is an important occupation from many ports of the Persian Gulf, though the last 20 years has witnessed a considerable decline, partly because of a change in fashion, and partly owing to the competition of artificial pearls. Fishing is a seasonal activity, being limited to the four months between May and September. The chief centre is Bahrein, and it is estimated that about 250 boats take part each year, as compared with 170 from Kuwait. Most of the pearls are sold at Bahrein; the pearl shell also being an important article of commerce.

Life in Kuwait has been enormously changed by oil exploitation. Much of the town has been physically rebuilt since 1950, and ways of life and outlook have been suddenly transformed by contact with the material civilisation of the west.

In addition to the exploitation of oil resources which as we have seen is having enormous repercussion on the general life and economy of the Persian Gulf generally, mention must also be made of a second recent development. This is the growth of long-distance air transport between Europe, America, and Asia. Because of the flat, open nature of the east coast of Arabia, and its accessibility in certain parts by sea, a number of large air bases have recently come into existence, and the Gulf region, 50 years ago a torrid backwater isolated from commercial activity, has now regained importance owing to its situation on the main route to India and the east. Air bases exist at Sharja (100 miles south-west of the Musandum peninsula), at Khor Khaliya (near Manama on Bahrein Island), and at Kuwait.

V. THE INTERIOR DESERTS

Though generally referred to under the single term of 'desert', the interior of Arabia is by no means of uniform character. North of a line drawn roughly from the Gulf of Akaba to Jauf and Kuwait, lies the Badiet esh Sham, 'steppes of the north' – a level, open region, which is partly true desert, and partly steppe. Further south, between Jauf and Ha'il, is the Great Nefud, a region of loose sand and bare rock. The Nefud is continuous on the south-east with a much larger expanse of sandy desert, which sweeps south-eastwards in a great arc between Hofuf and Riadh, and then expands southwards to occupy most of inner Arabia between Oman, the Hadhramaut, Yemen, and Asir. This is the Rub al Khali (Abode of Emptiness) or Dahna, the largest and most forbidding of all hot deserts in the world. On the west, between the Nefud and the Rub al Khali and defined summarily by a triangle, the points of which might be taken as Riadh, Medina, and Mecca, there lies the Nejd – a somewhat less barren region, which is the homeland of the Wah'habi confederation.

The Badiet esh Sham is in the main an upland region. From the region of Jauf, which lies at about 2,000 feet, altitude gradually increases towards the north, reaching its maximum of 3,000 feet between Rutba and Damascus; after which it again declines gently north of Palmyra towards the lowlands of the Euphrates. The crystalline basement is completely buried under thick layers of Mesozoic and Tertiary rocks; hence the north gives an impression of a vast plain interrupted only by shallow wadis that trend generally towards the north-east, and are partially filled by alluvial and aeolian deposits. These wadis often retain small quantities of water after the scanty winter rains, and are thus the focal points of activity for the nomadic Badawin of the region. Two prominent lines of wells have led to the establishment of routeways from east to west across the desert. One line can be traced north-westwards from Jauf along the Wadi Sirhan as far as the Hauran of south-west Syria; the other runs south-west from Karbala as far as Ha'il.

Fig. 93. The Interior of Arabia

As the result of a rainfall that varies between 2 and 6 inches per annum, the northern desert carries a vegetation cover for part of the year: grass in late spring and early summer, and in the autumn after the first onset of rain succulent plants like the *hashish* family, and a number of bushes that provide camel fodder. Hence in the Badiet esh Sham pastoralism finds its fullest development, and the uniformity of the land surface, lacking depressions like those of Siwa or Kufra (in which cultivation based on irrigation from artesian basins might develop), precludes any way of life other than strict nomadism. Largely self-sufficient, the Badawin cover enormous areas in their annual movements, and the small quantity of agricultural produce that they consume is still in certain measure obtained from reluctant cultivators on the desert margins. By reason of its openness in topography, and relatively narrow extent, the northern desert has from earliest times been a channel of routeways and transport. Palmyra, one of the few oases of the region, where a warm and strongly sulphurous spring allows date-growing, was once a centre of trade; but is now merely a pumping station on the oil pipeline to Tripoli, and a garrison from which to police the north-west. Interest has shifted to Rutba, near the junction of the Haifa and Tripoli branches of the pipeline, which has now come to be a halting place on the motor route between the Levant and Baghdad.

Immediately southwards, the Great Nefud consists of rocky outcrops, principally of hard sandstones, which have been more disturbed. Tilting has produced a series of upstanding ridges that have been worn down by water action, and later still, eroded by wind action into grotesquely shaped pinnacles and crags. Between the ridges lie lowland basins that are mostly covered in loose sand, sometimes in the form of dunes several hundred feet in height. Rainfall is extremely rare, occurring only once or twice per annum, or even once in several years; and the enclosed nature of the basins produces wide range in temperature. In summer a diurnal range of 40° F. is not unusual, with day temperatures reaching 115° or 120° F.; and in winter, frost is common. A specially unpleasant feature of the Nefud is its violent winds, which spring up and die down with equal rapidity. Owing to the local character of these winds sand dunes are aligned in many directions, in a manner quite different from the regular succession that is typical of the eastern Sahara.

In certain of the lowland depressions, water is retained by an impermeable sub-stratum, and oasis cultivation of dates and barley can be carried on. The largest of these oases are in the west, where some of the heavier rainfall in the mountains of the Hedjaz finds its way eastwards into artesian basins. One well, at Teima, is 65 feet deep, and measures 120 feet in diameter. The presence of such oases, some of which have a population of up to 15,000 people, is in marked contrast to conditions in the Badiet esh Sham.

The Rub al Khali, covering approximately 400,000 square miles, long remained unknown; the first European to cross it was Bertram Thomas (1930). But latterly it has become the object of intensive oil prospection, and hence much of its mystery has now gone. Consisting mainly of a plateau dropping towards the east and south-east, there are a number of wadi formations often partly or wholly buried in sand. Loose sand formations are widespread and also on a large scale, equal to if not larger than those of the central Sahara. Regularity of the underlying sedimentary rock measures has allowed some percolation of water, probably from the better-watered highlands of Asir and the Yemen; and these can be tapped as artesian wells. A very few oases have grown up on the shallower springs, but apart from oil prospectors, there are very few inhabitants. The extreme isolation of the whole area is shown by slowness with which cultural features have penetrated: for example, on the fringes towards central Arabia, groups of hunters and collectors still survive; and, until their conversion during 1923–5, several tribes on the east practised paganism – this in the country adjacent to Mecca.

The remaining area, Nejd, is somewhat complex in its structure. A certain amount of dislocation of the basement of Arabia would seem to have taken place, for we can trace a zone of weakness that runs east-north-east from the Tihama of the southern Hedjaz (where, as was noted, the mountain barrier is distinctly lower) through Riadh and Hofuf as far as the coastal plain of Hasa. Further evidence to this effect is given by the occurrence of fault-lines, along which upwelling of magma has occurred, with the formation of desolate lava-fields like those of the Jebel Druse of Syria. In a number of localities, the granitic basement is exposed at the surface, as a series of highland massifs, sometimes 4,000 and 5,000 feet in height; and a further feature of the Nejd is a series of north–south running scarps that have been formed by successive exposures of sedimentary rocks, once horizontally bedded, but now dipping towards the east.

The oldest sedimentaries – chiefly of Jurassic age – are exposed in the west, and later rocks, up to the later Tertiary measures of the Persian Gulf coast, appear in an alternation of ridges and valleys. The most prominent scarp is the Jebel Tuwaiq, formed of Jurassic limestone, and rising 1,000 feet above the surrounding plateau.

The drainage pattern originally developed on these scarplands was complicated, though now all valleys are entirely dry, and partly obliterated by sand. There were a number of consequent main-streams that flowed eastwards to the Persian Gulf, and in so doing, broke through the north–south aligned scarps, in a way somewhat similar to the Thames as it cut through the ridges of the Clay Vale and the Chilterns. The presence of lowland valleys set at right-angles to the main line of drainage also favoured the growth of numerous transverse rivers. Hence at the present time there are considerable differences in topography between the Nejd, which is a diverse region of uplands, small plateaus, scarps, broad valleys, and dry river gaps, and the surrounding dune-covered wastes of the Nefud and Rub al Khali.

Rainfall is very small on the lowlands, but heavier showers occur on the higher mountains, and a certain amount of this precipitation ultimately finds its way into the lowlands, or else is retained above the occasional impermeable layers that exist in the uplands. Owing to this, oasis cultivation is possible in certain areas of the lowlands, and, to a less degree, in the higher regions. Dates are the staple crop, with barley wheat, millet, and lucerne as adjuncts; and a variety of fruits – walnuts, figs, apricots, and vines – are also produced. The largest of the oases are Riadh (now the capital of Saudi Arabia), Bureida, Ha'il, Jabrin, Anaiza, and, on the extreme east, Hofuf.

In addition to cultivation, nomadic pastoralism plays a significant though now declining part. Because of varied terrain, with far fewer of the open stretches characteristic of Syria, nomadism involves distinctly less movement annually, and there are hence many gradations from semi-settled cultivation to full nomadism. The camel is the basis of pastoral life, but each nomad group possesses one or more permanent strongholds together with a few tributary agricultural villages. This somewhat complex social group – chieftains and noble class, warriors and herders, semi- or fully sedentary cultivators, and slave-peasants of the oases make up a tribal unit. Until very recently the King of Arabia himself moved with his retinue from place to place seasonally – indicating the importance of the nomadic tradition and way of life.

Within the central triangular zone of better terrain with its varied rock type and alternation of ridge and valley – in a very broad sense a kind of Weald, or Paris Basin – has grown up the Wahhabi state. Though until recently there was little internal or external trade and few natural resources, the Nejd stood out as an island of relative fertility in an expanse of often waterless desert and barren upland ridges. Now the royalties from oil allow the import of manufactured goods; and a road-system with petrol points is under development.

As in the Persian Gulf area, development of oil resources is provoking fundamental changes at enormous speed in the Saudi Arabian economy.

Whilst this process advances, Saudi Arabia is experiencing considerable social and other stresses that arise as former Badawin living on the extreme margin of subsistence find regular paid work in the oilfields, and can afford to supplement their diet by imported food – with results that show both in a better physique and in a desire for an enhanced standard of living. Here is an appetite that increases as modes of living improve, and one that sooner or later involves political considerations. The present social evolution in Saudi Arabia carries considerable dangers, and during the next few years, as the country takes its place as one of the leading oil producers of the world, a special responsibility rests upon its leaders and counsellors, both Arab and foreign.

CHAPTER XIX

The Lower Nile Valley

I. PHYSICAL

The extreme north-east of the African continent shows topographical and structural transition from the accidented and disturbed conditions of the Levant to the relatively simple and uniform conditions of the interior plateau. The region comprises the irregular edge of the Gond-wana foreland, and crystalline basement rocks underlie most of the area, occasionally outcropping in certain districts. Within Egypt, which forms a convenient territorial delimitation, four major sub-regions can be distinguished.

(I) The Sinai peninsula.
(II) The Eastern Highlands of Egypt.
(III) The Nile valley.
(IV) The western desert of Egypt.

and of these, the Nile valley is of overwhelming importance, since it contains over 95 per cent. of the total population of the region.

THE SINAI PENINSULA

This consists for the most part of an irregular tableland or plateau, which is tilted upwards towards the south. The southern half lies between altitudes of 2,500 and 5,000 feet, and occasional peaks rise some 3,000 feet higher, the largest being the Jebel Catherina (8,750 feet). On the south-western side of the peninsula, along the Gulf of Suez, the plateau drops to sea level by a number of step-faults, the lowest of which forms the coastal plain of El Qaa, which is from 3 to 8 miles wide. In the south-east, along the Gulf of Akaba, dislocation is restricted to a much narrower zone, so that instead of a series of steps, the highlands approach closely to the sea, and there is a bold, rocky coastline which is for the most part devoid of any coastal plain. To-wards the Mediterranean Sea the level of the plateau decreases, and gradually gives way to a broad coastal plain below 600 feet in altitude, which extends from the Suez region through El Arish, and passes without break into the lowlands of western Israel. Thus on the north there is a low sandy coastline, diversified by lagoons and sandspits; and this region has provided a convenient corridor for movement between the Nile valley and the Levant.

Though now extremely arid, with an annual rainfall of 6 inches in the north and 2 or 3 inches only in the south, the entire Sinai region is deeply dissected by river valleys eroded at earlier geological periods. In the north, where gradients are small, the valleys are broad and open,

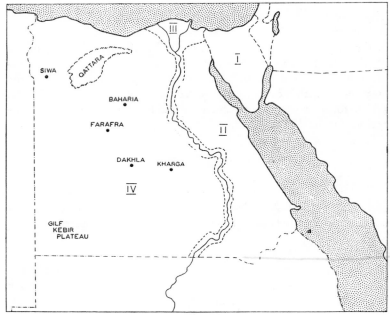

Fig. 94. Natural Regions of Egypt

the largest being the Wadi el Arish, which can be traced inland from the Mediterranean to a point south of Nekhl. In the south, the wadis are much more deeply incised into the plateau, and often consist of gorges and ravines several thousand feet in depth, which break the surface of the plateau into a series of detached massifs. None of these wadis contains perennial streams, but after a rare rainy spell they can fill for a few days, and can overwhelm passing travellers, or even whole villages.[1]

[1] Four British servicemen travelling by car were drowned near El Arish in 1944.

Many parts in the north are covered by deposits of loose, shifting sand that frequently form dunes. There is difficulty in maintaining settlements and communications, since any projecting object may provoke the formation of a dune several feet in height. Houses, and even railways and roads, can thus become partly buried, and much effort is needed to clear constantly encroaching sand. In a few regions, however, cultivation is possible, because rainfall quickly sinks through the sand, and is retained in hollows in the underlying basement rocks. Wells sunk into such hollows allow small-scale irrigation, and there is an oasis cultivation of dates and cereals, the chief of such centres being El Arish, El Auja, Nekhl, and Themed. Further south, settlement is entirely restricted to the plain of El Qaa, and nomadism is the principal way of life over most of the Sinai; though there is increasing exploitation of minerals, chiefly petroleum and manganese, on the western side of the plateau.

THE EASTERN HIGHLANDS

This region, a broken upland lying between the Nile valley and the Red Sea, has been formed by dislocation and uptilting of the crystalline basement rocks. In its northern part (i.e. between the latitudes of Cairo and Assiut), there is a covering of later sedimentary series – Nubian sandstone, Jurassic and Cretaceous limestones and sands – but south of Lat. 26° N. pre-Cambrian series are exposed on a considerable scale. Though somewhat larger in area than the Sinai, the Eastern Highlands of Egypt are lower in altitude; the general level is between 1,000 and 2,500 feet, with the highest peak (Jebel Shayeb) reaching 7,175 feet. Like the Sinai, the highlands are heavily dissected by wadis running westwards and southwards to the Nile, and eastwards to the Red Sea. Many of these wadis are narrow, but extremely deep, so that again, as in the Sinai, there is a complicated relief pattern with a series of detached upland masses.

On its western side, the Highland region is bounded by the Nile trough; and because of the numerous wadis that enter the river from the east, the adjacent edge of the trough is rather less clearly defined than the opposite (western) side, where, owing to the virtual absence of wadis, there is a strongly marked cliff. On the east, the abrupt change from desert plateau to riverine lowland is slightly less a feature.

Parts of the Eastern Highlands – more especially the deeper wadi floors, which are sheltered from the sun's rays – carry a light vegetation. Water is retained in hollows in the harder rocks, or beneath alluvial deposits in a stream bed; and there are occasional springs at the junction of certain pervious sedimentary rocks and the crystalline basement. Water resources are, however, on a very small scale, partly because of

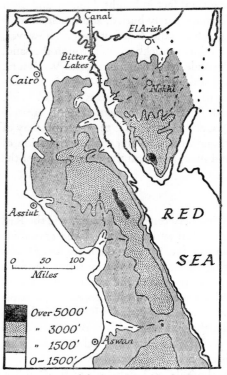

a rainfall lower even than that of the Sinai (everywhere below 4 inches per annum), and partly because of the disturbed geological succession, which inhibits the development of large artesian basins. Cultivation is as a result almost impossible, and the few inhabitants live for the most part as nomadic shepherds. Owing to the difficulty and isolation of the region (there are no trade routes as in the Sinai, and all traffic follows the Nile valley) there is no incentive even to oasis cultivation, and no permanent settlements exist, apart from a few villages and small towns on the Red Sea coast.

Fig. 95. Sinai and the Eastern Highlands of Egypt

There are, however, a number of mineral resources. Petroleum is worked in the sedimentary cover of the north-eastern flanks of the uplands at Hurghada and at Ras Gharib; and also near the Red Sea coast are located deposits of phosphate, which are developed commercially in two districts (Qoseir and Safaga). Production is, however, as yet on a small scale. Iron and manganese occur, and an extremely large deposit of the former near Aswan is now worked at the rate of 400,000 tons annually.

THE WESTERN DESERT

This region presents a number of contrasts to the region just described. To the west of the Nile, geographical features are on a vaster plan, and the geological disturbances caused by the formation of the Red Sea rift are absent. As a result, there is an uninterrupted expanse of basement rocks covered by extensive but fairly shallow layers of horizontally bedded sediments, giving an expanse of plain or low plateau, with

	Loose sand	
	1500'	
	600' Below Sea Level	

Fig. 96. The Oases and Depressions of the Western Desert

gentle gradients and wide vistas, that are relieved only occasionally by slight ridges or scarps where one rock series gives place to another. Thus about one-half of the western desert of Egypt lies below 600 feet in altitude, and few parts exceed 1,000 feet. The most conspicuous scarps lie in the north-west, along the Mediterranean coast near the boundary with Cyrenaica.

There are, however, a number of deep basins, with fairly steep scarped edges, formed by erosion of softer strata either through aeolian action or by solution of soluble rock measures. The largest and deepest of these basins is the depression of Qattara, which covers an area of several thousand square miles in the region to the south-west of Alexandria. Here the floor lies some 400 feet below sea level. Other basins are those of Dakhla, Kharga, Behariya, Siwa, and the Fayyum (Egypt); Jarabub, Jalo, and Kufra (Cyrenaica). Wide stretches of pervious rock overlying impervious basement series have given rise to numerous artesian basins, and it may in fact be stated that most of the western desert consists of one vast artesian basin. Hence on the floors of the depressions, considerable quantities of water are sometimes available. In certain instances (e.g. the Qattara depression) artesian water seeps to the surface naturally, and is evaporated, producing a salt marsh; and in the Fayyum there is, as we have noted, a lake, which at one time actually drained to the Nile. For the most part, however, wells must be dug to tap the water, and then cultivation is possible. The Qattara depression, with its badlands and marshes, has few inhabitants, but the others have populations ranging from 1,000 (Farafra) to over 20,000 (Dakhla) and over 700,000 (Fayyum), which is supplied by a canal from the Nile.

Outside the basins, the desert surface consists of an alternation of bare rocky outcrops, stony wastes, or loose sand. The latter formation is increasingly prominent in the interior, producing dunes, some of which are fixed, and some mobile. In the far south-west, towards the central Sahara, sand covers the entire surface, producing the 'Sand Sea' of Calanshio (southern Cyrenaica). This is a major obstacle to communications, and served effectively to isolate Egypt and its neighbour Libya. Until the Second World War only one track through it was known – but a few others were discovered during the various campaigns.

THE NILE VALLEY

The course of the Nile presents many points of interest, with certain anomalies, chief of which is the actual slope of the river bed. In the extreme south, the region of the East African lakes, slope averages 1 in 1,200, but further north, from Juba as far as Malakal, there is a fall of only 1 in 139,000. This is the Sudd region (*Sudd* = blockage) – an alluvial plain extending some 250 miles from east to west, and covered by papyrus, reeds, and other swamp vegetation. Here is the flattest portion of the Nile's course, not, as is normal, near the mouth (cf. the Tigris and Euphrates), but 2,000 miles upstream. Below Malakal the thalweg is still extremely flat, falling only 25 feet in 500 miles (i.e. 1 in 101,000); but although deep alluvial soils occur, swamps are no longer found. Between Khartoum and Aswan lies the Cataract zone – a hilly and almost rainless region through which the river has cut a deep trench. In several localities exposures of hard crystalline rock have proved more resistant to erosion than the surrounding Nubian sandstone; hence rapids and cascades are a feature, and river navigation is interrupted. With an average fall of 1 in 6,440, the cataract zone of the Nile is remarkable as the only stretch of the river outside of East Africa and Abyssinia in which active erosion is still proceeding. Here, a Pharaonic monument known to be at river level in 1900 B.C. is now 25 feet above the banks, indicating that the river bed is being lowered at the rate of about 1 foot per 160 years – whereas elsewhere in the lower Nile valley deposition of silt is occurring, and the bed of the river is actually rising.

From Aswan northwards, the Nile flows in a well-developed notch out into the plateau surface, with cliffs forming the boundary of the valley. Two points are of importance here: there are Pliocene marine sediments at high levels along the valley sides; the valley itself cuts diagonally across a number of Miocene and Pliocene folds and fault-scarps, suggesting an antecedent or possibly super-imposed pattern of drainage.

Until it broadens into the Delta below Cairo, the river valley is about 6 miles wide, and the river itself about half a mile wide. For the most part, the Nile flows closer to the eastern valley wall: thus the greater part of the cultivated area lies west of the Nile, though there are many loops and meanders in the river. At Cairo the delta region begins, with two main distributaries, the Rosetta branch (east) and the Damietta branch (west – and 14 miles longer), together with an infinity of smaller streams. About one-half of the Delta is still occupied by lakes and swamps, with four larger sheets of water, Lakes Brullos, Idku, Mariut, and Menzala covering between them 845 square miles of territory.

The remarkable pattern of geomorphological units which make up the Nile basin has provoked several theories of origin. One such theory postulates that the Nile originally flowed much further west through the oasis belt (Kharga to Qattara); another suggests that the Sudd area was once a large lake basin without river outlet, which was later breached and drained in Pleistocene times through the cutting back southwards of the headstream of a shorter proto-Nile. This 'Lake Sudd' theory involves major changes in East Africa – the existence of river-flow southwards from Lake Victoria to the Indian Ocean, this flow being then diverted northwards about 20,000–25,000 years ago to swell the pre-existing Lake Sudd. There is further the question of whether the White Nile was 'captured' by stronger streams from the Blue Nile, or whether junction came about by a normal shift of course in a very flat terrain. It is perhaps most feasible to regard the Nile as having developed in early Tertiary times, with later changes that have arisen from (a) later earth movements (folding and faulting), (b) downwarping and transgression by the Mediterranean, followed by re-emergence of the land in Pliocene times, (c) rejuvenation of the river in humid climatic periods producing downcutting that was interrupted by (d) arid cycles during which erosion gave place to deposition of silt on the valley-floor.

REGIME OF THE NILE

The regular annual flooding of the Nile is due to spring and summer rainfall occurring over the highlands of East Africa. This rainfall usually begins as early as April in some areas. The Nile within Egypt is a combination of three principal streams: the White Nile, Blue Nile, and Atbara, each of which has different peculiarities. The White Nile is the most regular of the three, providing just over 80 per cent. of the total flow (measured at Aswan) during the dry season, but only 10 per cent. in the flood period – i.e. its regime corresponds closest to that of a river in temperate latitudes. This is because it passes through a number of lakes, which reduce fluctuation and slow it down, and because of the long course through the Sudd area, which evaporates quantities of water (especially in summer), thus further reducing its flow. Despite all this, however, involving a journey of 28–43 days through the Sudd (Malakal to Aswan), its flood-waters are the first to reach Aswan. Owing to the slow movement, much of the material in suspension has settled out, and its waters remain relatively clear, though with a high proportion of dissolved solids.

The Blue Nile contributes only 17 per cent. of the low-water flow; but it rises very rapidly and flows more swiftly, until at high-water season it is contributing 68 per cent. of the total water passing Aswan. As its current becomes established, it partially ponds back the slower-flowing White Nile. Coming from the extensive lava regions of Abyssinia its waters are highly turbid, due to erosion of the basaltic 'harras'.

The Atbara contributes very little water at low-water season, but rises rapidly after June, bringing 22 per cent. of the total high-water flow; and its waters are also highly charged with brown sediment. The Blue Nile and Atbara are thus more characteristically Middle Eastern rivers, and superimpose an enormous flood upon the more regularly flowing White Nile.

FLOW AT ASWAN (in millions of cubic metres per day) (Hurst)

	White Nile	Blue Nile	Atbara
Low water	37	7	almost nil
High water	70	485	157

Minimum water level in Egypt is reached during May and early June; and the beginning of the flood period is indicated normally about the third or fourth week of June by the arrival of 'green water' from the White Nile, which contains algae brought down from the Sudd region by the first floods. Later, with the arrival of Blue Nile and Atbara floods, and yet more water from minor tributaries, the main river water turns reddish-brown. Persistence into this period of decaying algae (dull red in colour) may on occasion thicken Nile water and give it an offensive odour: hence the 'turning to blood' of the Bible. Maximum flood level is reached in mid-September, and at this period river water takes only six days to reach the Delta from Aswan, as compared with twelve in low-water season. Flow at this latter season averages 500 million cubic metres per second (Aswan) and 8,000 million cubic metres at flood time, but there is wide fluctuation. In 1913 less than half the normal flow occurred, and in 1878-9, 50 per cent. more than usual, with a flow of 13,500 million cubic metres. Height of flood-water at Aswan can thus vary from 21 to 33 feet above low water; and if the maximum flood occurs early (i.e. in or near August) even with copious water supplies, low water will also take place earlier in April instead of May-June, thus producing crop famine. It will consequently appear that despite the general regularity of onset, the actual height, periodicity, and hence economic value of Nile floods is distinctly variable (cf. the story of Joseph); and some observers have suggested a cyclical pattern of flood level, related to rainfall cycles and hence to sunspots. More investigation is however necessary.

A further matter is the loss of river water during its passage northwards. Losses by evaporation between Aswan and Cairo alone are estimated at 15 per cent. of the total flow in the cool season, and

27 per cent. in summer; and a further 15 per cent. at least may seep into bedrock through porous outcrops.

About 110 million tons of sediment are carried annually past Wadi Halfa, and as most is derived from the erosion of volcanic rocks in Abyssinia and East Africa, this silt is extremely rich in mineral substances. Of the total burden of silt, it is estimated that 15 per cent. is spread on the land by pumps, 33 per cent. subsides to the river bottom, and so serves to build up the river bed, and the remainder, 52 per cent., reaches Cairo. Here, over 55 million tons of silt is carried by the floodwaters of summer, and the remainder, about 1½ million tons, during the rest of the year. Besides suspended solids, considerable quantities of matter are fully dissolved in the river water, and these amount to 7½ million tons at Cairo, all but 14,000 tons being carried at the flood season. The principal substances in solution are calcium and magnesium carbonates, and sodium chloride. From this will be seen the enormous importance of the Nile floods – not merely for the water itself, but also for the fertilising mud laid down annually. The rate of deposition of Nile mud is as follows:

Upper Egypt (basin-irrigated lands)	4·1 in. per 100 years
Lower Egypt (basin-irrigated lands)	1·2 in. per 100 years
Lower Egypt (perennially-irrigated lands)	0·2 in. per 100 years

When first laid down, Nile mud is soft and sticky, but it soon hardens to a tough, hard earth that can be used for embankments and canals, or, when sun-dried, as bricks. Because of its high chemical content, there is, however, a tendency for salinity to develop, particularly under intensive irrigation. This is most noticeable in the northern part of the Delta, where soils approaching a solonchak type are occasionally found. Because of the emphasis on cotton-growing in Egypt – cotton plants being especially sensitive to soil salinity – care is necessary in developing irrigation schemes. This is one reason why parts of the Delta are still unreclaimed swamp.

II. CLIMATE

Before discussing irrigation developments in Egypt, a short summary of climatic features may be given. Because of low relief, and a landlocked position, conditions are remarkably uniform over the whole country of Egypt. Summers are hot, with day maxima reaching 100° F. in most places, though nights are distinctly cooler. Over most of the country July is the hottest month; exceptions occurring in the extreme south, where, with an approach to intertropical conditions, the maximum occurs in June; and in the extreme north, near the Mediterranean, where the maximum is postponed until August. The Mediterranean coast is distinctly cooler in summer because of the tempering effect of the sea; and in Alexandria, which is the summer capital of Egypt, day temperatures are some 10° to 15° F. below those of Cairo. The prevailing onshore wind from the north-west is an important factor in reducing summer heat.

Winters are mild, allowing continuous plant growth, and though severe frost is unknown in the Nile valley itself,[1] occasional short-lived cold spells occur, and slight snow showers may spread as far south as Aswan. A factor more harmful to crops than frost is the prevalence of Khamsin conditions, when hot dry winds from the desert may scorch the tenuous strip of cultivated land along the river banks. The table below (for Burg el Arab, a few miles west of Alexandria) gives an indication of conditions in average, and in bad years.

FREQUENCY OF MODERATE AND SEVERE DUST STORMS
(Oliver)

	J	F	M	A	M	J	J	A	S	O	N	D	Total
1940	1	1	1	3	2	0	0	0	0	0	0	0	8
1944	3	4	4	1	3	1	2	2	0	1	0	0	21

The whole of Egypt has a rainfall of 8 inches or less. The Mediterranean coast receives 4 to 8 inches, with Alexandria the wettest part of the country; and south of Cairo, the annual average falls to less than 2 inches. This is in some respects a fictitious figure, since a fairly heavy onset of rain may take place only once in two or three years; and the fact that a half of the 2 million inhabitants of Cairo live in houses made of dried mud bricks indicates the scantiness and unreliability of rainfall. Without the Nile, Egypt would be no more than a collection of oases like those of Siwa or Dakhla.

III. IRRIGATION

There are at present two methods of irrigation in Egypt. The first, known as basin irrigation, has been in vogue since the Nile mud was first cultivated several thousand years ago, and this method consists of

[1] Harder frost may, however, occur in the uplands of eastern Egypt, and in the Sinai. The absolute minimum of temperature recorded in Lower Egypt is 25° F.

dividing off the fields into shallow basins by a series of earthen embankments some 4 to 8 feet in height. Flood-water from the river fills the basins, depositing a layer of silt, and as the river level declines later in the season, water is retained on the fields for a few weeks, until the soil is saturated. This system of irrigation allows one crop per year, and because planting of seeds must necessarily take place in the autumn, as the river subsides, only those crops that can grow in relatively cool winter conditions (i.e. wheat, barley, and fodder) can be grown on a large scale. Rice, millet, and cotton, all of them summer crops, are not very suited to basin irrigation, which has hence been superseded in many parts of Egypt by the second type, known as perennial irrigation. Basin cultivation is, however, still predominant in most of Upper Egypt.

Perennial irrigation involves the construction of large-scale barrages to control and distribute the waters of the Nile. It should, however, be noted that not all of the dams on the Nile fulfil the same function. Two especially large barrages, at Aswan and at Jebel Awliya in the Sudan, impound flood-waters for several months, thus extending the season of Nile floods beyond the normal, and increasing the amount of water available in early summer. The great dam at Aswan, $1\frac{1}{4}$ miles in length, was built in 1903 at a spot where an igneous dyke traverses the valley to form the First Cataract. Successive heightenings of the dam in 1908–12, and 1933–4, have now made it possible to store 5,300 million cubic metres of water, and the river level has been permanently raised by 121 feet, thus drowning many parts of the upper valley. In 1959 an even more ambitious scheme was begun to raise the level further. After much delay, Sudanese agreement was secured for a proposal that will result in the flooding of the valley beyond Wadi Halfa, which will be covered as far as the Third Cataract. The High Dam project, undertaken with Russian aid, will, it is hoped, even out floods from year to year, and provide important quantities of hydro-electricity.

During the season of flood, when ample water is available throughout the Nile valley, all sluices are opened; but in autumn, they are partially – though not completely – closed.[1] This reduces the volume of water below Aswan during the months of November, December, and January, but the deficit is made up in the succeeding 6 months. River level at this period (February to June) is 23 inches higher than it was before construction of the barrage.

[1] This is to avoid silting up of the barrage, which would quickly take place if the sluices were fully closed.

Besides the two regulator dams, there are minor barrages whose function is to raise the local level of the water, thus improving basin irrigation, and bringing new regions within reach of feeder canals. These barrages are (1) at Zifta, on the Damietta branch of the Nile, about half-way between Cairo and the Mediterranean (constructed 1901). Here the water level of canals irrigating the eastern part of the Delta has been raised by about 10 feet, (2) immediately north of Cairo, where the Mohammed Ali Barrage (built 1861, re-sited 1939) raises the water level by nearly 13 feet, and supplies the southern Delta region, (3) at Assiut, 200 miles above Cairo, where the largest of the minor dams, built in 1902, and 900 yards long, raises local water level by 13 feet, and has permitted considerable agricultural development in districts previously too high for irrigation, (4) at Nag Hammadi, 160 miles south of Assiut, where a slightly smaller barrage (built 1930) fulfils a similar function for the province of Girga. Other barrages have been built at Edfina and Faraskour, respectively on the Rosetta and Damietta distributaries of the Nile. Besides allowing local irrigation, these also prevent the incursion of brackish Mediterranean water. During the low-water season they are often entirely closed, so that no water reaches the sea, and the Faraskour dam is temporary, being removed and rebuilt each year.

Besides these smaller barrages, large pumping stations have been installed in the Delta, where, because of low relief, barrages are difficult to construct, and pumping is an easier method of distributing water. These stations are at Abil Menaga, Balama, Fua, and Atf. Lastly, the barrage at Esna (1909) has recently been extended to allow local irrigation and also storage of extra flood-water from one season to another.

As a result of these developments, irrigation is now possible all the year round, and two or three – even occasionally four – crops can be raised annually, as compared with the single crop of basin-irrigated lands. Summer crops (*seifi*), cotton, rice, millet and maize, have now become Egypt's staple commodities, and together occupy over 40 per cent. of the total area under cultivation. Both crops are dependent upon perennial irrigation, and their extension in Egypt has closely kept pace with the construction of river barrages. Already the actual cropped area exceeds the cultivable area by about 50 per cent., and some 83 per cent. of this is now under perennial irrigation.

The advantages which perennial irrigation has brought to Egypt – specialist cultivation of high-quality cash crops, and doubling or trebling of the food supply, leading to an unparalleled growth in population

– are considerable, but these have not been achieved without certain disadvantages. In the first place, the increase in soil water due to perennial irrigation has led to a marked increase in soil salinity, because

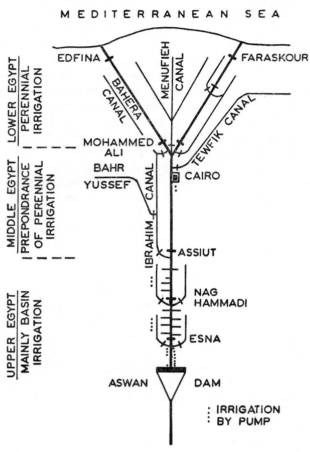

Fig. 97. Irrigation Works on the Nile (data partly from H. E. Hurst)

of more extensive evaporation from the soil. In some areas, particularly those given over to cotton-growing, salinity has become a menace; and Issawi states that drainage of the soil, rather than its irrigation, has now come to be regarded as the more acute problem facing Egypt. As might be expected, the Delta is the most seriously affected by this new danger;

but with the turnover from basin watering to perennial irrigation in the upper Nile, the same tendency is likely to develop in other parts of the Nile valley.

Secondly, with the greatly increased frequency of cropping on irrigated land, soil exhaustion is now beginning to be apparent in Egypt for the first time in its history. Deposition of the silt contained in the river water has hitherto been more than enough to counteract the effects of one cropping per annum; but with two or three crops from the same field there is gradually increasing debilitation of the soil, especially as the water held in large barrages has had time to settle, and deposit some of its alluvial burden *before* it reaches the fields. It will be recalled that the rate of deposition of silt on perennially-irrigated lands is less than that on basin lands (p. 490). Hence artificial fertilisers must now be applied in an increasing scale; and superphosphates and nitrates, first used in about 1900, are now applied to the extent of some 700,000 tons annually, giving an annual consumption of 160 lb. per acre of crop as against 84 lb. (Holland), 33 lb. (Denmark), and 18 lb. (France). The dependence of the Egyptian farmer on fertilisers was clearly demonstrated during 1940–6, when, because of war, the annual import of fertilisers was reduced to 300,000 tons. The effects on crop yields are indicated by the table below, and even now, 1938 standards have not been fully regained.

YIELDS OF CEREAL CROPS IN EGYPT
(in ardebs per feddan*)

	Wheat	Maize	Millet
1938	5·99	7·3	9·8
1946	4·89	6·45	7·65
1958	6·6	6·4	9·2

* 1 ardeb = 5·4 bushels. 1 feddan = 1·04 acres.

Thirdly, the utilisation of water resources within Egypt would seem to be reaching its maximum possible limit. Already, alteration of water level at one particular point can be felt at all districts downstream; and further improvements on a large scale depend on control schemes in the higher reaches of the Nile – in East Africa, Abyssinia, and the Sudan. Hence the considerable interest of Egypt in the political future of the Sudan, where a general increase in irrigation facilities might have the effect of reducing the volume of water available in Egypt; but where also the enormous losses by evaporation in the Sudd area could be reduced by engineering projects.[1] The Jebel Awliya scheme, completed

[1] i.e. by straightening the courses of rivers in the Sudd area, and by raising the level of Lakes Albert and Tsana, which would increase the flow of water in the main Nile.

in 1937, is on a relatively small scale, the total amount of river water retained being less than half of that impounded by the existing Aswan barrage. Egypt has also contributed financially to the Owen Falls project affecting Lake Victoria.

Despite these drawbacks listed above, production from irrigated lands is extremely high. With an average yield of 17 cwt. of wheat per acre, Egypt approaches the average for north-west Europe, where the heaviest crops of the world are produced per unit area; her yield of maize (1 ton per acre) is the highest in the world; and in cotton with 600 lb. per acre, she is well ahead of the Soviet Union (368 lb.), the U.S.A. (238 lb.), and India (112 lb.).

IV. AGRICULTURE

The main feature of Egyptian agriculture is the important place occupied by cotton-growing – far greater than for any other part of the Middle East. Up to 1938, cotton was the principal crop of the country and accounted for 21 per cent. of the cultivated area; but since that time, as the result of war, production has fluctuated. In 1944, it was less than one-half of the 1938 figure, but by 1952 had more than regained the pre-war figure. In this year the Egyptian government regulated the cotton acreage – to be at a maximum no more than one-third of the total cultivated land.

At times, a two-year cycle of crops is maintained. In November of the first year, wheat, clover, or beans are sown, with the harvest in May. After two months of fallow, maize is planted, and reaped in November. The land again lies fallow for two months, then cotton is sown in February, and picked in August–September. This rotation can be very exhausting to the soil, particularly at the beginning of the period, when planting of cereals takes place immediately following the growing of cotton. As a result, a three-year cycle with longer fallow periods is followed by some farmers, so as to allow recovery of the land.

Cotton is still the mainstay of Egyptian agriculture, and, as raw cotton accounts for 70–85 per cent. of Egyptian exports, it may also be said to be the mainstay of Egyptian commerce and business life. The reasons for the importance of the plant in Egyptian economy are:

(1) Suitability of soil and climate. Besides the unique fertility of the

soil, the long, arid summer, frost-free autumn, and 'controllability' of water supplies from canals, are specially favourable factors. The effect of all these is seen in the extraordinarily heavy yield obtained.

(2) Under present trends of prices in world markets, cash profits from growing cotton are 50 to 100 per cent. higher than from growing cereals. Egyptian cotton is of first-class quality; Egyptian cereals are much less valuable.

(3) Cotton-growing is admirably suited to prevailing methods of land tenure in Egypt, i.e. exploitation by absentee landlords. The peasant is under no temptation to consume the crop himself, as is the case with foodstuffs, and is the more dependent upon his landlord in marketing his share of the crop. Because of its long-keeping qualities, raw cotton is also a good form of outlet for capital investment – a point of importance in a land where such outlets are few. Mortgages can easily be raised on a cotton crop not yet grown.

Many varieties of raw cotton have been introduced, but quality has for the most part tended to fall off after a few years, generally because of hybridisation (mixing) with other species, as the result of which the specially advantageous qualities of a particular species are lost. In a few instances degeneration has also been due to attack by insect pests. This was the case with the well-known Sakellarides and Giza 7 varieties, which at one time occupied over 80 per cent. of the total area under cotton. Now, the most widespread varieties are: Menufi (long staple, over $1\frac{3}{8}$ inches), Ashmouni, of medium staple ($1\frac{1}{8}$ to $1\frac{3}{8}$ inches), Dendera (long), and Karnak (long).

Until about 1925 the quantity and quality of cotton produced by an individual plant showed a steady decline, with a fall in yield of 5·8 cantars per feddan[1] (1900), to 3·4 cantars (1921). Energetic governmental action resulted in the formation of a Cotton Research Board, which has developed new species, controlled hybridisation and the incidence of pests, and popularised improved methods of cultivation. As a result, the yield improved for a time to 5·0 cantars, but since 1951 has again declined to 4·0 cantars per feddan.

Five varieties of cotton are grown on a large scale, three being long staple (over $1\frac{3}{8}$ inches), and two short. The long-staple varieties are Karnak, Dendera, and Menufi; the others Ashmouni and Zagira. Giza

[1] 1 cantar = 99 lb.

30, evolved by the Cotton Research Board, has now declined in importance.

Though cotton is so important, large-scale cultivation would seem to be restricted mainly to wealthier owners and farmers; and the vast majority of poorer fellahin produce food crops – a view that accords with the general character of Middle East agriculture as being one of subsistence – and it would appear true to say that cotton-growing is far more popular with landlords than with tenants.

Though the acreage devoted to cotton in Egypt is only about 15 per cent. of the cotton lands of the United States, superior quality gives Egyptian cotton a commanding position. Some 60 to 70 per cent. of the world's production of long-staple, and 30 per cent. of its short-staple cotton is supplied by Egypt, and there are certain manufacturing processes in which Egyptian cotton is exclusively used, e.g. in the making of aeroplane tyres, windproof clothing, and sewing thread. The entire cotton crop is sold in August, and is not usually completed till the end of September. Much of the crop moves to Alexandria for export, only a small though increasing proportion being retained at home.

Cereals. Maize is in some years the most important cereal crop, and since 1939 it has generally occupied the greatest extent of land under cultivation, though in value it still stands second to cotton. Being a summer crop, maize needs copious watering; and as it thrives best on a heavy clayey soil, the Delta is the chief region of production, though the plant is found all over the Nile valley. In recent years, strains of maize have been greatly improved by governmental control and research, and the yield per feddan has increased by 12 to 15 per cent. Now maize forms the principal article of diet of the people, being mixed with wheat flour to make bread.

Wheat is a winter crop, since it thrives in cooler conditions; and though it is again grown in all parts of the Nile valley, heaviest yields are obtained in Upper Egypt, where the warmer winters and a lighter soil are special advantages. Conspicuous improvements in yield have been achieved over the last 20 years (amounting to 20 to 25 per cent. increases); but some of this progress was lost during 1940–50. Until the Second World War, Egypt was in a position to export small quantities of wheat, and may be said to have been self-sufficient in bread supplies; but since 1941 the increase in population and lower yields of cereals have necessitated imports of wheat on an increasing scale (average 1950–61, 400,000 tons). Improvements in methods of cultivation are thus imperative, and we may note yet another country of the Middle East which, although overhwelmingly agricultural, is forced to depend on imports of wheat. Rice is in some years the second cereal crop of Egypt, the area having quadrupled since 1930. This plant is tolerant of waterlogged and saline soils, so that it is a favourite crop in the northern Delta region, where salt marsh is in process of reclamation, and where also over-watering is tending to increase soil salinity. Because of its heavy demands on water, the area that can be devoted to rice-growing is limited each year by government decree, in accordance with the height of Nile floods. There is now a considerable export, mainly to India and Ceylon; and during war years, the surplus of rice balanced the deficit of wheat.

Millet is an alternative summer crop, and flourishes best in Upper Egypt, where temperatures are higher than in the Delta. Since 1937 production has more than doubled, but the yield per unit of area has tended to fall. Nevertheless, the importance of millet in Egypt is steadily increasing – an indication that the country is after all a part of Africa, and lies closer to intertropical regions than many other parts of the Middle East.

With the rise of millet and rice production, barley is slowly declining in importance. In general, the plant is now grown as an alternative to wheat; and, because of its tolerance of drier conditions, it was once frequently grown on the outer parts of the Nile valley, where irrigation is difficult. Now, with the development of perennial irrigation, emphasis can be given to summer crops, which produce a greater cash return or a heavier quantity of food per unit area, and there is less interest in barley as a substitute for wheat. The main area of barley cultivation is Upper Egypt; so that, as regards cereal production over the whole country, we may distinguish two contrasting zones: (i) Lower Egypt, where maize and rice predominate, and (ii) Upper Egypt, where wheat, millet, and barley are the chief crops.

PRODUCTION OF THE CHIEF CROPS GROWN IN EGYPT
(in 000's of metric tons)

1934–8	Cotton	Maize	Wheat	Rice	Millet	Barley	Sugar	Beans
Production	400	1,616	1,184	609	426	225	146	296
Percentage of total area	21	18	17	6	5	4	0·5	5
1953–60								
Production	250	1,650	1,520	680	605	98	270	233
Percentage of total area	23	22	20	7	7	2	3	5

R

Other Crops. Berseem, or Egyptian clover, increases the nitrogen content of the soil, and is hence widely grown as a soil regenerator, in rotation with cotton and cereals. The clover is used as animal fodder, both green (in winter), and dried (in summer). Broad beans, which also have the same properties of soil regeneration, are grown to a rather small extent partly for summer fodder, and partly for human consumption. One or other of these crops is grown by most cultivators, and the area under berseem at times exceeds that of any other crop, amounting to 20 to 23 per cent. of the total.

Sugar cane is grown to an increasing extent, chiefly round Aswan, and in Qena and Sohag provinces where longer, warmer summers are an advantage. It is largely a landlord's crop. Yield of sugar is low compared with that in other countries (60 per cent. only of the average in Java, 45 per cent. of that in Hawaii), but the cane ripens in a shorter time than in either of these countries, and can successfully compete with foreign sugar in the home market. The cultivation of flax, castor oil seeds, and groundnuts is also developing, mainly because of world shortages in edible oils; and vegetables are increasingly important. The chief vegetable grown in Egypt is the onion; and, besides supplying a considerable home demand, there is some export. Egypt is also the world's largest exporter of lentils, which are grown mainly in Upper Egypt.

Fruit-growing is not extensive, the low purchasing power of the peasant restricting development – emphasis must be laid on cereals and oil seeds, because of their greater food value. Natural geographical conditions are also less favourable in Egypt than in many other parts of the Middle East. Dates are, however, grown all along the Nile valley, and especially in the south; oranges are produced in the Delta; and in the extreme north, on the cooler Mediterranean coast, vine-growing is extending. There are small wine-making industries based on the vineyards of Gianaclis and Mariut, close to Alexandria.

WATER REQUIRED PER CROP
(in cubic metres per feddan)

Crop	Lower Egypt	Upper Egypt
Wheat	1,140	1,510
Barley	1,030	1,575
Maize	2,670	3,400
Millet	2,670	2,510
Rice	10,000–16,000	—
Cotton	3,740	4,640
Berseem	2,630	3,560

Figures from M. Macdonald, *Nile Control*, Vol. I, 1920

V. PASTORALISM

Because of intense population pressure, most attention in Egypt is given to arable farming; but the increasing necessity of maintaining a crop rotation that includes such nitrogen-fixing plants as berseem and alfalfa is leading to a marked development of stock-raising. Within the last 20 years there has been a sharp, almost spectacular rise in the number of animals kept; but the increase in human food supply has been proportionately much less, as most animals are used for draught purposes on farms, and meat yields are low. As a result Egypt imports quantities of dairy produce, and there are considerable seasonal movements of cattle into the Nile valley from the desert areas of Egypt, and also from Libya and the Sinai.

Sheep, estimated at about $1\frac{3}{4}$ million, are the most numerous, and can be seen in most villages, where they are kept either on fallow land, or on the edge of the desert. Cattle number about $1\frac{3}{4}$ million, but their use for ploughing reduces milk yields, and they supply only one-quarter of the total of milk consumed in Egypt. Water-buffaloes are almost as numerous as cattle, a fact that is hardly surprising in view of geographical conditions, and these animals supply 70 per cent. of the dairy produce of Egypt. Goats have now declined, and number under 1 million. Donkeys are also very numberous; but camel breeding tends to be confined to the nomadic Arabs of the deserts. Most milk produced in Egypt is made into butter, curd, or cheese. Poultry keeping has some importance, though quality and size of both birds and eggs is not great; and in normal times there is a substantial export of eggs. Pigeons are kept in many villages, and many owe some of their popularity to the fact that they do not always restrict their eating to the food supplied by their owners.

In the opinion of some experts, there is room for further expansion and improvement of the animal husbandry in Egypt. At present, little attention is given to breeding and to improving stocks; but with the extension of crop-growing during the summer, which is the main season of difficulty to animal herders, increased supplies of fodder are now available throughout the year. As regards arable farming, the position of diminishing returns may have been reached in a few areas – a fact underlined by the increasing dependence on artificial fertilisers – and there is great need for a diversification in production. Yields from wheat and barley are relatively low; there is danger in expanding maize and rice production for human food;[1] cotton production is somewhat hazardous with Egypt (because of the smallness of her production), occupying a marginal position, and dependent on price levels in America.[2] Hence many things point to improvement through an increase in mixed farming with greater emphasis on stock rearing and the development of intensive market gardening in vegetables, for which conditions in Egypt are exceptionally favourable.[3]

VI. MINERALS

Output of oil has greatly increased since 1938 (the date of discovery of the Ras Gharib field), and all home requirements for motor spirit are met, together with about 45 per cent. of the requirements of crude oil, and 15 per cent. of the consumption of paraffin, the latter being the chief domestic fuel. Oil easily ranks first in the list of Egyptian mineral production: second place being taken by phosphate rock, which is mined at various places along the north-eastern coast of the Red Sea (mainly at Tor and Qoseir). Working is in the hands of two companies, one British, the other Italian (now temporarily controlled by the Egyptian government); but of recent years the level of output has fluctuated, and in 1960 was only two-thirds of the 1938 total. Most of the phosphate is exported, mainly to Australia, and South Africa, since Egypt itself is in need of nitrates rather than phosphatic fertilisers.

Next in importance come various sodium salts, which are produced by evaporation of salt pans in the artesian basins of the Western Desert. By far the most important centre is the Wadi Natrun (Natrum = nitre), a long, narrow depression running north-west–south-eastwards between Cairo and Alexandria. Here a variety of salts have been obtained for centuries, but today sodium carbonate and sulphate hold chief place. There is a rather sporadic production of manganese ore from low-grade deposits at Abu Zeneima, on the Red Sea coast. Production was interrupted for a time after the Second World War, but has now resumed. One important factor is the level of dues in the Suez Canal, which can render exploitation of the ore uneconomic. Gold is obtained in small but significant quantities, recent rises in price having had a stimulating effect. Other minerals produced on a small

[1] See Chapter IX.
[2] e.g. the price of raw cotton fell by 25 per cent. during the month of May 1949.
[3] A further difficult point is the variation in gross profit obtainable from different crops. In 1952 this profit averaged (per feddan) cotton £78; onions £63; wheat £11; maize £5.

scale, sometimes, as in Cyprus, by collection rather than systematic exploitation, are talc, ochre, pumice stone, asbestos, diatomaceous earth, and common salt. Quarrying of building stones (limestone, sandstone, granite, and basalt) is on a scale somewhat larger than in most Middle Eastern countries.

PRODUCTION OF MINERALS IN EGYPT
(metric tons)

	Petroleum	Phosphates	Manganese	Common Salt	Nitre	Sodium Sulphate and Carbonate
1938	226,000	458,000	115,000	145,000	8,000	5,000
1961	3,755,000	620,000	313,000	560,000	5,000	4,000

	Talc	Sulphur	Asbestos	Kaolin	Gold (oz.)	Iron Ore
1938	1,000	—	—	—	2,000	—
1961	2,000	40,000	1,500	25,000	—	420,000

In 1937 a large deposit of high-grade iron ore, estimated at 1,000 million tons (cf. total reserves in France, 4,500 million tons), was discovered 30 miles east of Aswan. The ore lies close to the surface, and is now exploited, using hydro-electric power from the Dam. In 1960 it was announced that a further deposit of iron ore had been discovered on the Red Sea coast, 35 miles south of Qoseir. Reserves were estimated at 35 million tons, and another large discovery was made in 1961 in the Behariya Oasis.

VII. INDUSTRY

The last 40 years have seen the rise of a number of industries in Egypt. Initial impetus was given by civilian shortages and military needs during 1914–18, when a number of local activities were started, chiefly concerned with textiles, foodstuffs, and chemicals. After 1918, certain of these industries proved uneconomic, and disappeared; but some survived, and further development took place when Egypt ended Capitulations in 1930, and was henceforward free to erect tariff barriers to protect her home markets against foreign imports. In contrast with Iran and Turkey, industrial development in Egypt has been carried out entirely by private capitalist enterprise, with no state control.

During the Second War, an even larger trade 'boom' occurred, with almost all Egyptian manufacturing plant working at full capacity. Since 1945 there has been some falling off in local production, with a number of uneconomic marginal companies forced to cease production;

but in general it may definitely be said that the level of industrialisation has increased since 1939. It is significant that those activities that have managed to hold their own or develop further are those which draw their raw materials from Egypt herself, e.g. cotton textiles, sugar refining, cement-making, and chemical production.

Textiles are by far the most important industry in Egypt, and there are now between 35 and 45 large companies engaged in production. Cotton spinning and weaving predominate, and Egypt is now self-sufficient in the making of cotton piece goods, though substantial quantities of yarn and thread are still imported. The present volume of imports of manufactured cotton is, however, little more than 25 per cent. of the 1938 figure; and greatly expanded imports of cotton-spinning machinery indicate that a greater degree of home production of textiles may shortly be expected, with a corresponding decline in foreign purchases.

Woollen goods are also manufactured on a fairly considerable scale, but the lower quality of Egyptian wool as compared with Egyptian cotton places the woollen industry under a handicap; and better quality woollens are still imported. The volume of imports of woollens has risen since 1944, indicating that Egyptian industry cannot compete with entire success against outside manufacturers, even though native output has increased. Silk, rayon, and linen are also manufactured, but to a much smaller extent; and it is doubtful whether the silk industry will ever be very extensive, as all raw material must be imported. Prospects for linen are better, as flax is grown within the country. Rayon has recently become more important – wood pulp is now imported as a raw material.

Cement manufacturing has increased by some 600 per cent. since 1939, but a limiting factor is the availability of fuel. Despite this, Egypt is self-sufficient in supplies of cement, and there is a small export to surrounding countries, limited by home demand.

Processing of agricultural products – sugar refining, preparation of alcohol from molasses, brewing, canning and preserving, cigarette-making, and the pressing of cotton seed for edible oil – is in the aggregate relatively extensive, as would be expected from the economy of the country. A large number of companies and of workers are engaged, though individual output is generally small, and machinery primitive.

Leather working has tended to increase with the recent development in stock-raising, and current output is 25 to 50 per cent. above 1938 levels. This is especially a local craft industry scattered throughout most towns and villages. Other small industries are the production of chemicals, in which Egypt now supplies all her own needs; soap-boiling, which, because of the absence of olive groves in the country, is forced to depend on imported oils; and light engineering, e.g. the manufacture of electric light bulbs, paper, and glassware, with assembly plants for cars and electrical machinery. There is also a new blast-furnace at Helwan, using Aswan ore.

A recent departure has been the growth of a small Arab film in-dustry. Egypt now shares with India the world market for Arabic-speaking films, which have a circulation throughout most of the Arab lands from Morocco to China, and also in the U.S.A. and the Argen-tine. This activity has grown up as a complement to the film industries of America and Europe, the products of which are not always to Arab taste.[1] The climate of Egypt is a considerable advantage, and further development in film-making may take place.

The expansion of Egyptian industry is, however, held back by a number of adverse factors, chief of which is lack of fuel. No coal of any kind is found in Egypt; local oilfields are not large; and with the exception of Aswan, the slight gradients of the Nile valley do not favour the large-scale generation of hydro-electric power. Hence the amount of electricity produced (mainly from thermal plants using oil and imported coal) is small in comparison with other countries. Coal is still imported, though on a smaller scale than formerly, mainly for motive power in industry.[2] Shortage of fuel has led to a concentration of industry in the cities of Cairo and Alexandria, and, to a far less extent, Port Said, where fuel supplies are most easily available. The smaller towns of the Delta are chiefly agricultural markets, and Upper Egypt has no industry whatever.[3]

A second handicap is the low purchasing power of most Egyptians, which greatly restricts the scope and efficiency of home manufacturers. This is very apparent in the cotton trade, where locally grown cotton, which is of the highest quality, must be made into the lowest quality goods. So long as food prices remain high, and wages low, the *fellah* will be unable to buy manufactured goods; hence, lacking markets

---

[1] In particular 'psychological' dramas and the emancipated status of women are not greatly liked. Amatory scenes and prolonged osculation are also at times regarded as indelicate by Arab audiences.

[2] Until 1939 the bulk of Egypt's coal came from Britain, with Germany and Poland as minor suppliers. Now one-half comes from India and South Africa.

[3] In an attempt to improve the energy supplies of Egypt, the project has been discussed of generating hydro-electricity by admitting the waters of the Mediterranean to the Qattara depression.

outside of Egypt, the extent of industrial activity within the country is likely to remain circumscribed.[1] Under present conditions, Egypt can hardly rank even as a moderately industrialised country. Over half her workshops are one-man concerns, and the numbers employed in industry amount to only $3\frac{1}{2}$ per cent. of the total population, a figure lower than those for Israel, the Lebanon, and Syria. Issawi gives a striking index for the cotton industry, Egypt's principal manufacturing activity: in Egypt there is 1 mechanical spindle per 64 inhabitants; in India, 1 per 36 inhabitants; in Brazil, 1 per 15; and in the U.S.A., 1 per 5. *Future Prospects.* Developments in the oilfields of the Sinai, and the discoveries of iron are encouraging signs for the future; but against this must be set the general lack of raw materials. Only a moderate expansion may be envisaged, and Egypt is likely to remain overwhelmingly an agricultural country. Issawi suggests that future industrialisation should be restricted to a few branches in which abundant supplies of locally produced raw materials are available: cotton textiles, leather, chemicals, and foodstuffs. Much greater emphasis could be placed on purely agricultural industries – canning, preserving, and food processing, as well as on fertiliser and certain chemical products.

VIII. COMMUNICATIONS AND TOWNS

Railways. The railway network of Egypt is remarkably complete, and on a basis of length of line per inhabited area, Egypt is as well supplied as France, with over 14 km. per 1,000 square kilometres. It should, however, be recalled that less than 10 per cent. of Egypt is inhabited. Railways were built in the nineteenth century, and added to during 1914–18 and again in the 1930's, so that all parts of the Nile valley are linked by a standard-gauge system. The main lines are state-owned, and there were until recently nearly 900 miles of light railways (privately owned), which served the Fayyum and parts of the Delta not touched by main lines. In recent years a change-over has occurred from steam to diesel locomotives, and most of the light railways are disappearing. *River Transport.* From the geography of the country, there would seem to be much scope for this; but water transport is less developed than might be expected, because (*a*) main importance is given to irrigation, and river level is often low, with many small weirs and irrigation works

---

[1] Egyptian products are of moderate or inferior quality, and unlikely to compete in outside markets.

that impede traffic, and (b) low bridges are numerous, because of the slight relief of the region. Nevertheless, an increasing amount of traffic is passing from the railways to river barges, and nearly 80 per cent. of the raw cotton of Upper Egypt, and 10 per cent. of the cotton of Lower Egypt moves by water to Alexandria. The ratio of water-borne to rail traffic has altered from 1 : 4 in 1925–30 to 1 : 3 in 1945–60. Most of the crops of Lower Egypt – particularly vegetables such as onions – are carried by rail, but as the years pass a larger proportion is now diverted to the river.

Most commercial and industrial activity is located in Cairo and Alexandria, the former having about 35 per cent. and the latter about 25 per cent. of important enterprises. Cairo is situated

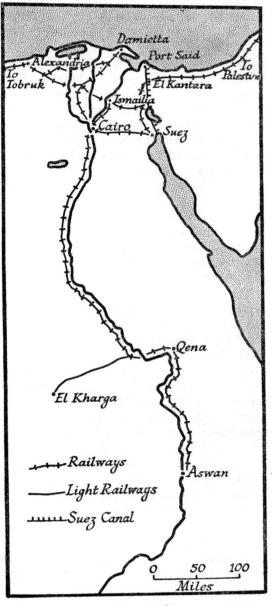

Fig. 98. Egypt: Railways

at the head of the Delta, where the Nile waters divide, at a spot where a large island provides a convenient crossing place; and this central site, on the borders of Upper and Lower Egypt, and fairly close to the productive oasis of the Fayyum, makes Cairo a distribution and market centre for the whole of Egypt. As compared with Alexandria, which does not lie in a particularly productive region, and is to some extent isolated by large brackish lakes, Cairo is far better placed for internal exchange; and most of the foodstuffs of the Delta are marketed there. Rail communication with Alexandria, Port Said, and Port Tewfik (with a branch at Kantara across the Suez Canal to the Sinai and Gaza) has allowed the import of fuel and raw materials, so that although there is no outstanding richness in natural resources, Cairo has developed a diversity of industries, chiefly concerned with processing of agricultural materials: textiles,[1] cement-making, food packing, brewing (with imported hops), oil pressing, printing, and the making of light consumption goods, metal furniture, and railway wagons. Cutting of the Suez Canal and the growth of air transport have been a considerable stimulus to expansion; and, with a population of over 3 million, Cairo far exceeds any other city in the Middle East.

The centre of Cairo is well built and laid out, and, with its opulent department stores, would challenge comparison with Rome, Paris, or San Francisco; but away from the centre, mud brick soon replaces stone and ferro-concrete, and electricity is no longer the main illuminant. There are however now some new and opulent outer boulevards.

Alexandria is the chief port of Egypt, and handles almost all of the cotton and rice crops. There are numerous cotton ginneries, which for the half of the year following the harvest provide occupation for 40,000 people; and rice-husking is another activity, though this is also spread amongst the smaller towns of the northern Delta – Damietta, Mansura, and Rosetta. The city lies close to a small promontory of land that runs north to join a small island: in this way there is a kind of natural quay, and a double sea frontage, with an eastern and a western harbour. One disadvantage is that landward communications are rather difficult – road and rail must pass on a causeway between two large sheets of water, Lakes Mariut and Idku, now being partially drained and reclaimed.

The situation of Alexandria, on the extreme north-west of the Delta – so as to be removed from the danger of silting by Nile waters – has

[1] The largest textile centre in Egypt is, however, a small town of the Delta, Mehalla el Kubra.

tended to produce a certain isolation from the main currents of Egyptian communications, which, especially since the construction of the Suez Canal, are stronger in the east of the country. As a result, the city ceased to be the main capital in 1863. Because, however, of communications by sea, Alexandria has one advantage over Cairo in the matter of imported fuels, coal and oil; hence a number of large cotton spinning

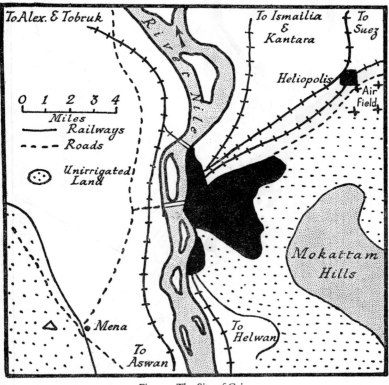

Fig. 99. The Site of Cairo

and weaving mills have been started, and cigarette-making is important. There is now a Ford assembly plant using imported parts. The cool summer has made Alexandria a favourite summer resort, and under the monarchy it functioned as the summer capital. Population (1962) was 1.6 million.

Port Said, with approximately 250,000 inhabitants, is mainly a port of call for passenger steamers, and in terms of shipping movements

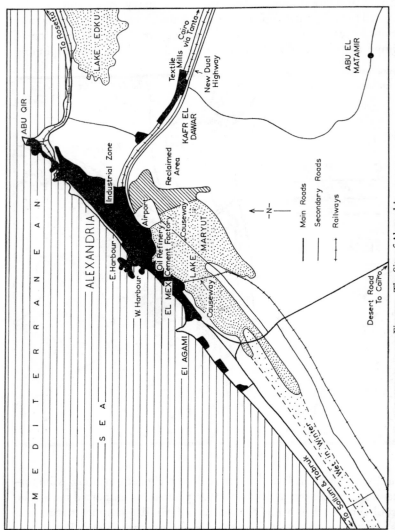

Fig. 100 The Site of Alexandria

now surpasses London and New York. Despite this, the share of Port Said in the export trade of Egypt amounts to less than 10 per cent., and the chief activity (apart from handling ships in transit) is exporting minerals, chiefly salt.

Suez, now possessing three oil refineries, and fertiliser and chemical works, is a growing industrial centre.

CHAPTER XX

Libya

Both physically and from the human aspect, Libya shows greater geographical affinities to the north-east of Africa, rather than to the north-west. In structure, it repeats many, though not all, of the basic patterns characteristic of Egypt – a tabular plateau-formation influenced by faulting, warping, and differential erosion – rather than showing the intense folding characteristic of Morocco and Algeria. Climatically also, there is much resemblance to Egypt, with however occasional and restricted zones of distinctly heavier rainfall; whilst ethnically it derives in greatest part from Arabia, and forms a stronghold of orthodox Muslim culture. Yet Libya also has an individuality of its own. It is far from being a mere prolongation or continuation of Egypt; and whilst it lacks the clear unity deriving from a single large river valley, a more limited and tenuous social cohesion is conferred by the existence of almost impassable 'sand seas' to the east on the frontiers with Egypt; by the Tibesti uplands in the south; and by irregular and partly sand-covered terrain in the west. Within this loosely containing physical frame have developed distinctive human responses – ranging from the unusual style of dress to the separate sectarian outlook of the Senussi movement – which are in process of consolidation towards a national state.

I. PHYSICAL

Like Egypt, Libya may be regarded as in large measure a part of the Gondwana plateau. This complex of ancient metamorphosed series outcrops to form much of the Tibesti and associated ranges in the far south, and underlies much of the centre and south of the country. Oscillation of this plateau surface at various geological periods has led to the accumulation of aeolian and marine sediments in layers of varying thickness. These are for the most part horizontal or only slightly tilted and deformed, the more ancient outcropping generally in the south, and the more recent in the north. Much fracturing has however

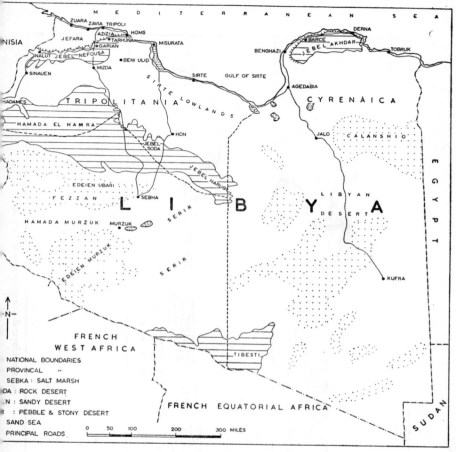

Fig. 101. Libya

taken place, with associated vulcanicity (mainly but not wholly of the sheet type), so that extensive *harras* occur, especially in the north-west.

The whole of the pre-Cambrian basement has been generally down-warped towards the geosynclinal of the Mediterranean zone, and dis-location becomes more prominent in the coastal areas fronting the Mediterranean. Here, faulting with downthrow to the north is the most important feature: extensive fault-scarps lie actually at the coast in Cyrenaica, but in Tripolitania these strike inland from the coast

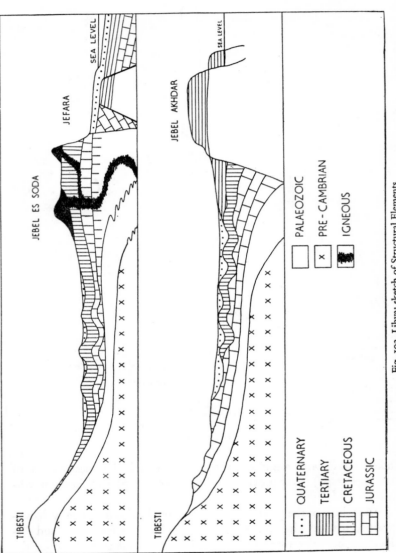

Fig. 102. Libya: sketch of Structural Elements

TIBESTI

JEBEL ES SODA

JEFARA

SEA LEVEL

TIBESTI

JEBEL AKHDAR

SEA LEVEL

QUATERNARY

TERTIARY

CRETACEOUS

JURASSIC

PALAEOZOIC

PRE-CAMBRIAN

IGNEOUS

at Homs–Misurata, giving rise to a plateau-edge that is increasingly set back from the sea coast.

In addition, there has been a limited but significant degree of buckling of the sedimentary rock layers, producing shallow anticlines and synclines. As in Arabia, these sedimentary layers above the basement complex extend uninterruptedly over many miles, with important results: because of the northward dip, water and petroleum have accumulated at shallow depths chiefly along the northern margins. There are hence broad physical and structural similarities between Libya and the Arabian peninsula. If the former could be regarded as re-oriented through 90°, thus making the Tibesti range run from north to south instead of its true direction east–west, then one might equate the Tibesti with the western uplands of Asir and the Hedjaz in Arabia. There is the same narrow upland zone, dropping gradually to a varied plateau surface which shows extensive cuesta formation, and is covered extensively, though by no means entirely, by loose sand. Lava areas occur, diversified by ridges of cones; and there is even a certain, limited parallel to the detached and folded outlier of the Jebel Akhdar of Oman in the Jebel Akhdar of Cyrenaica – though in the latter the intensity of folding is much less.

TRIPOLITANIA

The most northerly feature is the Jefara, which is a triangularly shaped coastal plain some 200–250 miles in east–west extent, and about 100 miles at its broadest portion in the extreme north-west. The Jefara is a zone formed by a subsided shallow anticline of sedimentary rocks, defined on the south by the imposing fault-scarps of the inner plateau, which as stated above run inland from the Mediterranean at Homs, ultimately reaching Tunisia.

The surface of the Jefara rises very gently from sea level at about 1 : 350 and the surface is composed in large part of Quaternary aeolian sands, gravels, conglomerates, and desertic crusts underlain by Tertiary and Secondary rock series (especially Miocene and Triassic) which in places are exposed at the surface. Topography of the Jefara is by no means uniform: near the coast in some places are extensive dunes; and again inland, especially in the centre and west, loose sand areas occur and build up into ridges and furrows.

The southern escarpment is really the eastern limb of a large crescent that runs first west-south-westwards from the Homs area, and then swings northwards into Tunisia as far as Gabès. The Tripolitanian portion of the arc is by no means regular: in the extreme east near Homs it tends to be fairly sharply defined by straight fault-scarps, but its maximum elevation is not much more than 1,000 feet. In the centre (i.e. between Garian and Jefren), it reaches over 2,500 feet, and its

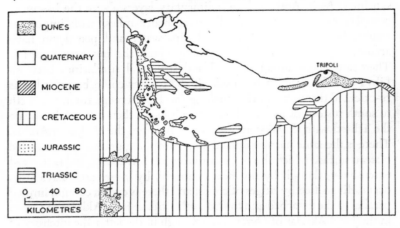

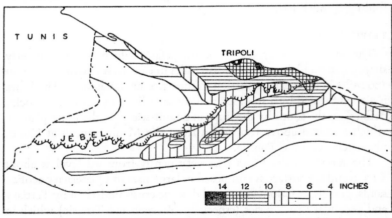

Fig. 103. The Jefara of Tripolitania: Geology and Rainfall

original cliff-like formation has been broken down by many wadis, so that there is a more irregular edge, with numerous projecting tongues of upland. Further west, relief is again more subdued, with a general maximum height of about 2,000 feet. Parts of the escarpment are fissured, and intersected by lava flows which have locally raised summits by 500–1,000 feet, so that an occasional peak of over 2,500 feet can occur. This is particularly true of the Garian region, where vulcanicity is very prominent. Heavier dissection by several larger northward-running wadis has split the entire escarpment into a series of somewhat distinct massifs, each of which has a local name – successively westward from Homs the Jebels Misurata, Tarhuna, Garian, and Nefusa, all of which are however usually referred to collectively as 'the Jebel'.

East of Homs as far as Misurata there is a zone of somewhat broken country where the fault-scarps reach the sea; and further east still the land rises gradually and without much break from a low-lying coastal plain. This is the Sirtica area – of low relief; land forms being produced by aeolian deposition and the occurrence of marine terraces here and there on a small scale.

South of the Jebel area occurs an extensive plateau – *hamad* or stony desert, composed of exfoliated materials upon a partly sandstone and partly karstic surface. In places, also, particularly towards the south-east, there are extensive basaltic exposures, with, here and there, lava cones singly or in groups. These latter may form definite ridges that sometimes reach 1,000 feet above the general plateau level, which is 1,500–1,700 feet above sea level. Local names indicate the differences in structure and geology: *hamada el homra* (red stony desert), *Jebel es Soda* (Black Hills), etc.

THE FEZZAN

Further south still, the general level falls, and passes into a series of extensive basins and depressions, some irregular in shape, others oval and aligned in something approaching an east-north-east–west-south-west direction, and enclosed by rocky ridges, with loose sand in the lower parts. This is the Fezzan, really a series of artesian basins where oasis cultivation is possible, and which form 'islands' in the surrounding sandy and stony desert. Sebha and Murzuq are most important of these basins, which lie in a rough arc from north-east to south-west. Many other water-bearing zones also occur, the most distant being that of Gat, in the extreme south-west corner of Libya near the frontier with Algeria. One should not be carried away, so to speak, by the intrinsic physical and human interest of the Fezzan: despite its large territorial area (greater than that of Tripolitania) it has no more than about 60,000 inhabitants, all but 10,000 or so being oasis cultivators. A significant point is that the precise administrative boundary between the Fezzan and Tripolitania still remains undefined: there are in fact five widely differing variants.

CYRENAICA

Westward of Egypt the Archaean platform is thickly covered by later sedimentary and aeolian series, principally Miocene and Eocene limestones, with Quaternary sands. As in Tripolitania, marked faulting has occurred, but here this is actually at the coast, with a more intricate development of minor cross-faults that have produced bays and inlets. Consequently, northern Cyrenaica stands like a promontory into the Mediterranean, partly isolated on the west by the Gulf of Sirte, and to a smaller degree by the Gulf of Bomba and Gulf of Sollum, with its northern side dropping by a series of steep fault-scarps to the Mediterranean. Although by trend and disposition the northern uplands might on the topographical map suggest a connexion with Asia Minor or Sicily, folding is in fact largely absent, and existing land forms are due to differential movement along fault-planes. A number of small subregions may be discerned within Cyrenaica – four occurring on the northern flanks of the massif, and three on the southern edge.

(a) *The North.* Here the edge of the uplands has been broken into several steps, giving a series of scarps that face north and west. The lowest step, spoken of as El Sahel, is a narrow and often discontinuous coastal plain which runs from the Gulf of Sirte to the Gulf of Bomba. In places only a few hundred yards wide, it reaches its maximum extent (12 miles) near Benghazi. Because of its broken nature, routes cannot follow the coast, but must keep inland, particularly towards the northeast and east. In the neighbourhood of Benghazi and Tocra numerous salt-pans occur, fed (as in Cyprus) by seepage from the Mediterranean. Brackish lakes or marshes during winter, the pans dry out in summer, hence the plain is much less exploited than one might expect, and cultivation is limited to a very few patches.

The second step (El Arqab) appears as a series of ridges in the east, and as a flatter and more open terrace (the plain of Barce) on the southwest. In the east, consequent drainage from the interior uplands has heavily dissected the ridges, producing a tangled country of deep wadis and isolated hills. Though scattered patches of alluvium may be found on some wadi floors, most wadis are in general too bare of soil for extensive human occupation, and are covered by maquis or scrub.

The third step comprises a moderately high plateau, broad and rolling in the west (inland from Benghazi) but narrower in the east, where it rises to just under 2,000 feet above sea level, and forms in its extreme eastern portion the small dissected ridge of El Hamrin, which is the highest part of Cyrenaica. By reason of its green

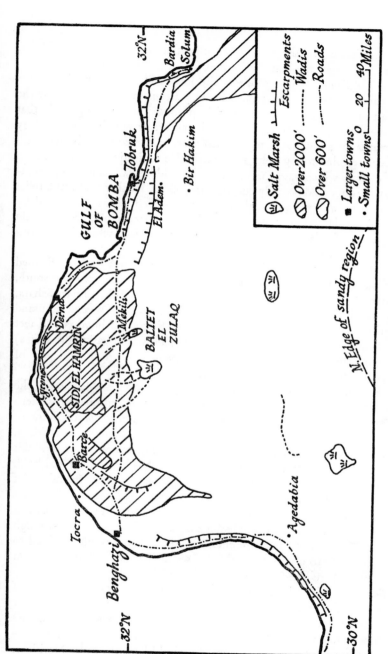

Fig. 104. Cyrenaica: Physical

vegetation cover, the entire plateau is often termed the Jebel Akhdar, and here occur the best possibilities for settled occupation.

(b) *The South.* To the south of the Jebel Akhdar, the surface slopes gradually down to the main Saharan plateau. Immediately below the crest of the Jebel lie a number of deep, southward-running wadis that were developed at an earlier period, and are now either occupied by streams for a few days only in each year, or else completely dry. This deeply eroded topography is a remarkable indication of the variation of climate which has supervened in the Middle East, since no present-day stream could possibly cut such deep clefts. Further south still, relief is gentler, and playas – shallow, alluvium-filled basins – separated by low irregular ridges, with, now and again, a larger hill, are the main features. The largest playa is the Baltet el Zulaq, which has several wadis and streams draining into it.

Finally, the playa region gives way to true desert – at first formed of masses of stones with a thin layer of sand. In the extreme south, however, sand predominates, until, in the heart of the eastern Sahara, we reach the Sand Sea of Calanshio. This consists of several thousand square miles of mobile sand, with dunes that reach hundreds of feet in height. Very occasionally, there occurs a lowland basin (e.g. Kufra) where artesian water is available, and where a very limited degree of human settlement is therefore possible.

East of the Gulf of Bomba, in the region known as Marmarica, the variety in topography which is characteristic of central and western Cyrenaica does not occur. Instead, there is a simpler *cuesta* succession of north-facing scarps rising in a series of shallow steps, or low ridges. Beyond Mersa Matruh, the coast is low-lying; but westwards of this point, the first step occurs at the coast, which is hence high and bold, with an occasional cove, e.g. as at Sollum and Tobruk. Inland, relief is distinctly lower than in western Cyrenaica, since none of the ridges attain a height greater than 1,500 feet. Owing to this, Marmarica is much more arid; but artesian basins exist in certain districts even though their water may be rather saline. Settlement is as a result confined to the coast, or to a very few inland oases such as Jarabub and Siwa (in Egypt), where good artesian water is available.

Climate. Topography exerts a highly significant effect on the climate of Libya. In the first place, because of its relatively open nature, with few extensive upland ranges, air masses of very different origin and qualities can penetrate very easily, giving a marked variety – even abruptness – in weather conditions, as Saharan, Tropical Maritime, Polar Maritime,

Polar Continental, and even Arctic air interact over the region. Secondly, position in relation to north-west Africa and the Mediterranean Sea (it should be noted that the coast of Libya is far from straight), together with a moderately varied relief, produce certain regional differences. The extreme north-west of Tripolitania lies in a definite 'rain-shadow' relative to the moisture-bearing north-westerlies, whilst the promontory of northern Cyrenaica, partly surrounded by sea, is much better watered, with its highest points receiving as much as 15–20 inches of rain annually.

CLIMATIC DATA – REPRESENTATIVE STATIONS

	J	F	M	A	M	J	J	A	S	O	N	D	Total
Benghazi													
Temp. ° F.	57	59	63	66	71	76	78	80	79	74	76	77	
Rainfall (in.)	2·6	1·5	0·7	0·2	0·1	0	0	0	0·1	0·6	1·9	2·4	10·1
Tripoli													
Temp. ° F.	54	55	60	65	68	74	78	79	78	73	65	54	
Rainfall (in.)	3·0	1·7	0·9	0·3	0·2	0	0	0	0·4	1·4	2·6	2·7	14·2
Azizia													
Temp. ° F.	53	55	61	69	73	81	84	85	83	75	65	55	
Rainfall (in.)	1·9	1·3	0·8	0·4	0·2	0	0	0	0·2	0·6	1·1	2·0	8·5
Garian													
Temp. ° F.	47	50	55	63	69	76	80	81	75	69	60	50	
Rainfall (in.)	2·9	2·0	1·6	0·6	0·5	0	0	0·3	0·4	0·9	1·6	2·1	12·9
Nalut													
Temp. ° F.	46	49	56	63	70	79	82	81	77	69	59	49	
Rainfall (in.)	0·8	1·0	0·9	0·5	0·3	0	0	0	0·2	0·4	0·7	0·7	5·5

Chief feature is, of course, aridity; but along the coast there is a zone of distinctly higher rainfall, brought by depressions that pass along or near the seaboard; and these, as we have noted earlier (Chapter III), can deepen appreciably in the Gulf of Sirte. But these depressions are not always well established, and because of the outward-jutting mass of Tunisia may pass well to the north in a particular season, resulting in drought for the whole of Libya. As well, extremely hot continental air can flow northwards from the central Sahara, and its normally high temperatures and low humidity are intensified by adiabatic heating on descent from the high interior to the coast. Variable temperature and rainfall conditions – distinctly more so than in Egypt – are hence a feature of the north in Libya. About twice every ten years, and sometimes in successive seasons, there is a pronounced failure of the rains.

Tripolitania is on the whole rather hotter and more arid, and there is greater liability to disastrous sand winds (*ghibli*). These occur on average 7 times per annum on the coast, and 12–14 times at some distance inland on the Jefara. As well, the Tripolitanian Jebel has a locally more severe winter: several feet of snow have fallen in certain years.

Bolder relief in northern Cyrenaica reduces temperatures: in winter sleet is common, and for periods of an hour or two each winter the higher hills may carry a snow cover. In winter too there are distinctly lower temperatures in the Cyrenaican Jebel – at sea level conditions much resemble those of Alexandria. Inland, temperatures may often reach 100° F., particularly in Tripolitania and the Fezzan. A feature on the northern coastlands, especially in the east, is the formation of dew and early morning fog. The former occurs mainly throughout the summer months, but occasionally in winter – atmospheric humidity is highest in summer near the coast – and this is generally of distinct importance to agriculture, especially on the Jefara of Tripolitania.

Hydrology. There are no perennial surface streams in Libya, but human settlement is rendered much more possible by the existence of underground water. In the limestone areas of the Cyrenaican Jebel, caverns with underground streams occur; one of these being an underground pool large enough to float a rowing-boat – and there are a few flowing springs and even one waterfall (at Derna). Elsewhere in several parts of the country there are both water-tables at varying depths, and flows of water which either emerge themselves at the surface, or can be tapped by wells.

The inland oases of Libya (and also Egypt) have water features which are of considerable interest. Many of these are large irregular basins, of natural as opposed to man-made formation, with water flows of varying kinds. At Qattara water seeps slowly from the sides and lower parts, producing an extensive salt marsh: at Siwa and Jarabub it rises as a large natural fountain of great force and volume, and at Aujila and Jalo it must be tapped by shallow wells. Further, the water itself varies considerably in chemical content. It may be fresh and cold, or highly brackish, so that it is unusable for humans or for agriculture, and warm, or even hot, as at Zuara. There may be a considerable gaseous content – of free nitrogen at Siwa, and of carbon dioxide in a few other localities.

In the Jefara of Tripolitania three separate water-bearing layers are distinguished. The first (phreatic) layer occurs near the coast at 15–50 feet depth, but at 100 feet or more inland; a second aquifer related to lower Quaternary or possibly Pliocene strata is found at 100–200 feet; and finally there is an artesian layer at 800–1,500 feet.

Several theories have been put forward to explain the occurrence of this relatively abundant groundwater in Libya: these range from suggestions that there is a kind of siphoning effect from the Lake Chad basin over the Tibesti, that there is percolation westwards from the Nile, and that there is heavy rainfall over the Tibesti itself (one difficulty here being the absence of any observations of such heavy rainfall) to more solidly based views (a) that the present water supplies are due to gradual seepage northwards in tilted and porous strata of rainfall that occurred in Quaternary and prehistoric times, and (b) that the water is maintained by extremely rapid absorption of present-day rainfall into an exceptionally porous subsoil – i.e. rainfall seeps into the ground before it can evaporate, and thus much of the sporadic but temporarily heavy rainfall is preserved underground. In this connexion it may be noted that according to one observer some 15 million cubic metres of flood-water pass annually down the Wadi Megenin at Tripoli city.

The implications of the two theories are obviously extremely important. If the first is the real explanation, then most of the ground water of Libya is a kind of fossil, mineral resource that once used can never be replaced. The second view holds out more prospect for long-term development. Space forbids a discussion of the whole problem, which is of extreme interest and, of course, great relevance; but it is sufficient to repeat that both views are strongly maintained at the present time.[1]

Soils and Vegetation. Most of the soils of Libya have been produced by physical rather than chemical weathering, and frequently approach the skeletal, detrital type. Oasis cultivation is often in what many observers would call desert sand; but in the Tripolitanian Jefara a wider range of soil types is found. A few patches of alluvial soils occur on the lower-lying parts, brought from the uplands by temporary streams; and dune sands occur both near the coast and in the interior. Soils of seirozem type also occur in certain localities, particularly the centre of the

[1] For example, certain of the natural seepage basins are below present sea level. They must have been eroded out by aeolian action, or by hydrostatic pressure acting upwards from the aquifer – any erosion by water is largely ruled out. Other problems are (i) the variation of water levels, which in some places is seasonal and at other places not; and (ii) a suggestion, now discounted, that the extensive lowland area running east-north-eastwards from the Gulf of Sirte through Aujila, Jarabub, and Siwa and now occupied by numerous salt marshes with marine flora and fauna, was once an arm of the sea. The marine forms are thought not to be indigenous, but to have been carried by migrant birds.

Jefara, as fine grey-brown structures, mainly sandy but with a small fraction of clay and loam. Elsewhere solonchak soils and desert crust are widespread.

As a result of distinctly higher rainfall, parts of north-western Cyrenaica have a soil of true *Terra Rossa* type, but south of the Jebel Akhdar, this quickly gives way to seirozems of various kinds, in which extensive crustal deposits occur. Hard pan is especially noticeable in Marmarica, from the region of Sollum as far west as Tobruk, Bir Hakim, and even Derna. Then, as the Sahara proper is approached, white solonchak soils are increasingly prominent, until, beyond the playa zone, full desert conditions are reached.

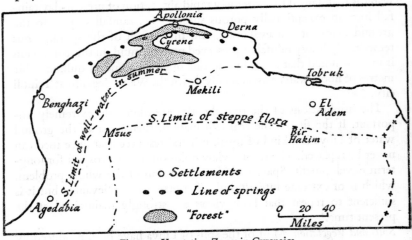

Fig. 105. Vegetation Zones in Cyrenaica

In Tripolitania, natural vegetation consists mainly of scrub or semi-desert types. Extensive date groves and stands of Australian eucalypts of recent introduction have however greatly modified the vegetation in a few places. Over northern Cyrenaica, the various soil types tend to carry a characteristic vegetation cover. Garrigue is most widespread on the coastal plain, with scattered clumps of cultivated fruit trees (including the date palm) in better watered areas. The presence of salt marsh reduces the growth of typical Mediterranean flora, hence tamarisk often takes the place of evergreens. On the second of the plateau-steps (El Arqab) extensive woodland is a feature. This is a low, but fairly dense growth of juniper and lentisk trees, with occa-sional olives, Mediterranean pines, and evergreens; and this vegetation has a surprising extension over northern Cyrenaica. The importance of this 'forest' (or better, shrubbery, since few trees exceed 8 feet in height) is very great, since it provides grazing for animals in poor seasons; and remarkably enough, it seems able to resist even damage by goats. Evans-Pritchard writes, 'There is no evidence that the forest has anywhere been destroyed by goats, or even severely damaged by them'; and it would appear that the goat actually thrives best in wooded areas. Even cattle can be kept there permanently, provided that there are occasional open clearings where grass grows.

The woodland ceases below the crest of the Jebel Akhdar, giving way to more open expanses of garrigue, and scattered grass-covered stretches. South of the crest, steppe vegetation is increasingly a feature, with the lotus in the deeper and damper valleys, and juniper on the uplands. Ultimately again, vegetation becomes extremely sparse, and of true desert type.

II. ECONOMIC AND HUMAN

Agriculture. Three distinctive patterns can be distinguished, each related to the physical conditions of the locality: (*a*) oasis cultivation, (*b*) the agriculture of the Jefara and adjacent regions of the Tripolitanian Jebel, and (*c*) the pattern of mixed exploitation characteristic of northern Cyrenaica.

Oasis cultivation is based on two staples, dates and millet. The Fezzan oases consist chiefly of extensive date groves undercultivated with cereals and vegetables. Altogether, there may be as many as fifty million date palms in Libya; and in the oases, human consumption of dates has been calculated at well over one pound per head per day with little else to eat at certain seasons. Unfortunately, quality is not high – nowhere near that of Biskra, so there is no trade outside the oases. Millet (the bulrush type *dukhn*) suits the climatic conditions better than either barley or wheat, though a little of both these last two may also be grown. As well, a wide range of squashes, peppers, tomatoes, and other Mediterranean vegetables are grown, together with a little fruit. Apart from exchanges with nomads, and occasional markets for early tomatoes, production is for local use only.

The Jefara is by far the most productive area of Libya, and is furthest developed, largely, but by no means entirely, because of Italian activities since 1930. Barley is the main crop, owing to its tolerance of drier, hotter conditions, with wheat one-third or one-quarter as important, both being winter crops. A little maize is produced as a

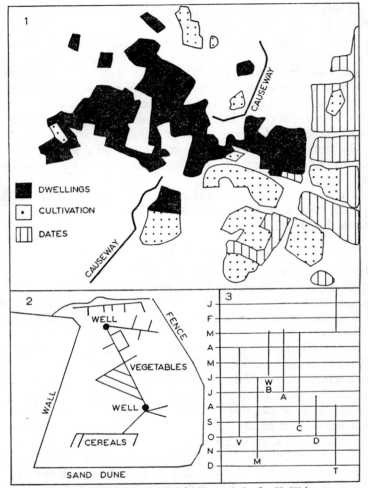

Fig. 106. Oasis Cultivation in Jalo (Cyrenaica), after K. Walton

1. Pattern of settlement. The log causeway provides an entry for wheeled traffic through loose sand.
2. A single holding, showing irrigation pattern and crops.
3. Seasonal rhythm of cultivation for vegetables, millet, wheat and barley, alfalfa, capsicums (peppers), date ripening and harvesting, and tomatoes.

summer crop where abundant irrigation water is available, and some farms also grow lucerne for a very small number of stall-fed cattle. Groundnuts have recently been introduced with some success, and another significant crop is broad beans.

Tree crops are widespread: olives, almonds, vines, and citrus fruit. Olives are a traditional crop, second only after barley, though possibly less cultivated now than formerly. Of the 19 lb. of edible fats and oils consumed per head of population in Libya during 1958, nearly 15 lb. comprised olive oil. The Italians introduced their own stocks alongside Arab varieties, but although they produce more fruit and a better oil, they are less tolerant of poor soil and aridity, hence they have by no means ousted Libyan varieties. There is some export both of oil and the raw fruit. Vines are grown extensively, but much less than in Italian colonial times, since with Arab rule the market for wine has contracted, and there is no export, as quality is not high. Almonds were planted in large numbers during the later phases of Italian rule, and are now coming to maturity. Present world demand for these nuts is brisk, and so they form a significant export item. Citrus cultivation is developing more slowly, and again quality does not compare with Israeli oranges, though local consumption is increasing. Vegetables, especially potatoes, aubergines, artichokes, and tomatoes, are important as is also tobacco for home use; the growth of Tripoli city and presence of foreigners (military personnel, 'aid' agents, film actors and technicians, and oil prospectors) having a stimulating effect on market gardening.

Conditions in Cyrenaica show more of a gradation between herding and cultivation. Pastoralism is the principal activity, but most of the Badawin plough, even if to a limited extent. The life of a majority of Cyrenaicans could be described as mixed farming, with animal husbandry the major element, and cultivation (except in a few areas) a minor feature. Barley is again the chief crop, being sown in the lowlands as soon as the first autumnal rains have fallen; but on the plateau lower temperatures often retard planting until January, and the harvest (which takes place on the coast in May) is correspondingly later (often August). By sowing two separate plots, one on the lowlands and the other at higher altitudes, it is possible to spread the work of cultivation over a longer period, and to some extent mitigate the effects of capricious rainfall. As barley will grow wild in Cyrenaica it can thrive on a minimum of attention, and the farmer may move off with his animals, and leave his fields unattended till the harvest.

Wheat is again much less grown, and barley predominates in all regions. Some millet is found, and maize has recently been introduced, but it is confined to areas where irrigation water is available.

Fruit and vegetables are grown in small gardens along the coastal plain, but such cultivation is at least partially dependent on irrigation, with the distribution of gardens controlled by the occurrence of springs. On the north coast, conditions are really too damp and cool for dates, but grapes do well, especially at Derna, which lies on a narrow shelf by the sea, and is sheltered to landward by a high escarpment from which emerges a curiosity of Libya – a waterfall. Because of this shelter and abundant water, Derna is the only place in Libya where bananas are grown in quantity. Other Mediterranean fruits and nuts are cultivated on a small scale.

The differences between Tripolitania and Cyrenaica are summed by the following figures, which however are mere approximations:

LAND UTILISATION (millions of acres)

	Tripolitania	Cyrenaica
Total of Productive Land (i.e. as distinct from desert)	25	5
Of which: Rough grazing for animals	20	3
Shifting agriculture	4 ⎫	0·86
Sedentary agriculture	1·0 ⎭	
Irrigated land	0·12	0·003
Forested	0·03	0·9

The total area of Libya is approximately 435 million acres

Pastoralism. In Cyrenaica, many Badawin move south with their animals into the steppe region during December, after barley sowing; and they return to the northern plateaus in late spring when pasture in the south is exhausted, but still growing on the cooler, damper slopes of the Jebel. Furthest south reached by most pastoralists is the line Bir Hakim–Agedabia; and by the month of August, most herders have returned to the plateau, though a few may stay in the region of deep wadis and playas where scanty pasture can last all year. The majority of Arabs living in the north move only a few miles between the coastal terraces and the higher ridges of the Jebel Akhdar. One factor in this restricted movement is the occurrence over much of the north of a plant, drias (*Thapsia gargantica*), which, when dried for fodder, is poisonous to cattle that have not previously grazed on it earlier in the same year. This means that animals must stay in the one region during spring and summer, and cannot be moved in from winter pastures in the south. The extreme north of Cyrenaica tends to be given over to goats and cattle, which as we have noted can thrive in the woodland and scrub of the upland terraces. In the south, sheep and camels are the most numerous, and these animals can exist without drinking for one to four days: sheep even can be accustomed to go entirely without

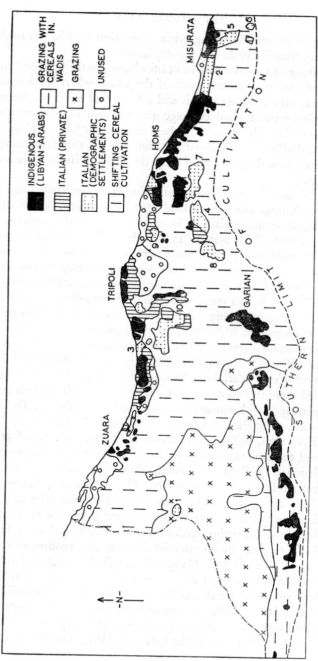

Fig. 107. Land Use in Northern Tripolitania (in part, after A. R. Taylor)

INDIGENOUS
(LIBYAN-ARABS)

GRAZING WITH
CEREALS IN.

WADIS

ITALIAN (PRIVATE)

GRAZING

ITALIAN (DEMOGRAPHIC
SETTLEMENTS)

UNUSED

SHIFTING CEREAL
CULTIVATION

ZUARA

TRIPOLI

HOMS

MISURATA

GARIAN

SOUTHERN LIMIT OF CULTIVATION

watering in winter and spring when vegetation is rich, and to drink only every fourth day during the dry season.

Something of a similar pattern of life obtains on the Jebel of Tripolitania, and also on adjoining parts of the Jefara, where semi-nomadic pastoralists may cultivate cereals and a few other crops on the wadi-floors. Government plans envisage an extension of tree cultivation (olives and almonds) in parts of the Tripolitanian Jebel, and this will involve a decline in nomadism: but there are still significant numbers of pastoralists on the Jefara itself – e.g. the Siaan, in the extreme southwest angle.

Italian Colonies. After the conquests of 1924 (Tripolitania) and 1932 (Cyrenaica), large amounts of land were expropriated (either openly or by legalistic manipulation) in order to allow the settlement of Italian colonists. Two systems prevailed: private concessions, where owners bought fairly large tracts which they would then exploit, partly with local Arab labour – i.e. somewhat like tropical plantations; and the so-called demographic settlements, maintained financially and directed by the Italian state, with tenant peasant-farmers who could look forward to becoming owners after a period of 20–30 years. The kind of crops grown, and marketing of the produce, were in the hands of governmental agencies. About 200,000 acres were taken over in this way within Cyrenaica, but ultimately entirely abandoned during the Second World War. Arabs have now re-occupied the holdings and continued them in various ways, sometimes living themselves in tents in the gardens, and keeping their beasts in the farmhouse. The Barce area is still one of the most productive areas of Cyrenaica.

In Tripolitania, individual concessions occupied a total of 317,000 acres, and the demographic colonies a further 240,000 acres – in all, more than half of all the cultivated land in Tripolitania, and most of it being relatively of the best quality. The concessions, having been established on land carefully chosen for its economic value as a commercial proposition, were best equipped and efficiently handled; and they still furnish the major part of the agricultural produce of Tripolitania. In short, they are an essential element, as a productive unit, in the economic life of Libya. Many Italians left after 1940, but a significant number still remain; and among the many problems of the present governments are those of ensuring that the former Italian concessions, whether still Italian-run or now in process of returning to Arab hands, will remain as efficient producers. Differing answers can be given regarding the future of the Italians in Libya, but there can be no doubt as to the necessity for maintaining the concession lands as the best farmed areas of the country.[1]

The demographic colonies had not begun to show such definite progress. Being on more marginal land, and financed on long-term bases (e.g. 20–30 year repayments for stock and capital) with heavy subsidies, they were only a few years old when overtaken by the events of 1939–45. As a significant part of their activity concerned the growing of vines and tobacco, they are somewhat less significant to the economy of Libya, though very far from negligible. Moreover, there was a political basis to their foundation; hence many, though by no means all, have reverted to Arab exploitation. Once again, it is possible to have strongly differing views about the future of these 'colonies' – but, lacking the subventions of Fascist times it is likely that they will become entirely Arab, with lower standards of living.

Human Geography. So far, pending development of oil resources, there are relatively few activities in Libya other than agriculture and pastoralism. Esparto grass grows wild, particularly on the scarps of the Tripolitanian Jebel; and this has a market abroad in the making of high-grade paper. Just after the Second World War over-collection led to near-exhaustion of the plant, and production is now more strictly controlled at a low level. Another sort of post-war collection was that of scrap metal (especially in Cyrenaica) from the battlefields; and in some years scrap metal has been the principal export item of Libya – this is now almost ended.

In Italian times some manufacturing took place mainly in Tripolitania, but also to a very limited extent in Cyrenaica: processing of oil seeds, tobacco, wheat pastes (macaroni, etc.), canning of sardines and tunny, soap-boiling, wine-making, distilling, and working in leather and crude textiles. Hardly any of these survive in Cyrenaica, but some continue in Tripoli and Misurata. Almost all modern manufactured goods and machinery must be imported.

Of the total of 1,092,000 inhabitants (1954 census) some 55,000 live in the Fezzan (10,000–12,000 being nomads); and 291,000 in Cyrenaica, a majority of whom are still nomadic or semi-nomadic with something at least of a tribal social organisation. About 25 per cent. of Libyans

---

[1] One indication of the methods and problems involved is given by a figure of use of water on one area of the Jefara. It is easier and cheaper to dig shallow wells to tap only the first (phreatic) water-table, but yields of irrigation water are poorer. Of 70 Italian and 70 Arab farms in the area, use was as follows: 174 Arab and 26 Italian wells use the first layer, no Arab and 129 Italian wells tapped the second aquifer; and 2 Italian wells the third (deepest) aquifer.

S

are now town-dwellers, this relatively high proportion being due to the Italian campaigns against the Senussi and southern nomads, which greatly reduced livestock in the steppe zones. A feature of some interest are the troglodyte dwellings in some areas, especially around Garian (Tripolitania). There are relatively elaborate caverns hollowed out of the softer rock measures, and esteemed locally as offering greater protection against summer heat and winter cold. Underground habitations are tending to increase in some parts, even on the outskirts of towns. By far the largest town in Libya is Tripoli (c. 250,000), which

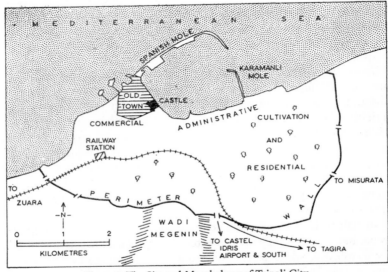

Fig. 108. The Site and Morphology of Tripoli City

has one of the few reasonably good harbours in an otherwise almost harbourless coastline. It was for long a pirate stronghold; and besides controlling the important coastal route east–west was a point of departure for the trans-Saharan caravans. Its walled Old City is still a tightly built maze of craft-booths, light manufacturing in tinplate, covered suqs, mosques, and dwellings. Alongside it is the modern town, of basically Italian construction – an administrative centre now active as the focus of oil prospection and development aid schemes, and other foreign agencies. A large fraction of the inhabitants of this new town are foreign officials, technicians, and servicemen with their families.

Benghazi (c. 100,000) lies on the widest part of the coastal plain west

of the Jebel Akhdar, much though by no means all of which is cultivated. A gradually rising hinterland provides fairly easy access to the
plateau for the east–west route that can no longer follow the coast, and
is anyway more direct. A small harbour, unfortunately open to the
north-west winds that prevail in winter, has a small trade in animals and
animal products, sponges, and stores for Cyrenaica. Benghazi is the

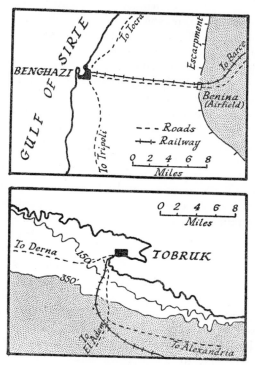

Fig. 109. The Sites of Benghazi and Tobruk (high ground stippled)

main outlet and market centre for the more prosperous west and north
of Cyrenaica.

Other towns are basically local centres of greater agricultural fertility
that also possess some nodality and can thus function as regional
markets. Homs and Misurata had a little manufacturing in Italian days.
Derna has a poor, now silted harbour, but a very productive though
small oasis; Agedabia is an administrative centre and market for the
infertile Sirte region; and Tobruk lies on a small creek, functioning as

the outlet for the scanty pastoral products of Marmarica, and as a
centre for the east of Cyrenaica. Proximity to El Adem (19 miles
south), which has taken on some importance as a staging-post in the
East African and Far East air routes, is another favourable factor.

Many other once-famous centres, Leptis Magna, Sabratha, and the
Pentapolis (with Benghazi) of Tocra, Tolmeita, Apollonia, and
Cyrene, are now villages or hamlets. Some have considerable tourist
attraction by reason of their extensive Classical remains, many of which
were re-furbished in Italian times, as a matter of Fascist policy. Though
the technical methods used are criticised by some archaeologists, the
resulting effect is often very striking.

Problems of Present-day Libya. The Federal nature of the Libyan state
reflects certain real differences in geographical environment. Tripolitania with its agricultural basis, and increasing emphasis on irrigation
from deep wells which allows the production of cash crops for export,
is steadily gaining predominance. Already the three Jefaran items of
olive oil, groundnuts, and castor seed account for one-half of all Libyan
exports, and Tripoli city is increasingly the centre of activity for the
whole country (although it shares the function of capital alternately
with Benghazi) with a cosmopolitan, 'advanced' population display-
ing a 'Mediterranean' outlook. Cf. its population, two-thirds of that
of the whole of Cyrenaica, and nearly four times that of the Fezzan.

Cyrenaica, somewhat wetter, more pastoral, and more deeply
affected by the religious appeal of Senussi teaching, has fewer general
contacts, and is more affected by the proximity of the Egyptian market
for its chief export product – cattle. Already an Egyptian company
has financed large-scale agricultural development on the Jebel Akhdar
(by purchasing and improving over 1,000 farms); and Cyrenaica tends
at times to look eastward with its trade towards a more powerful and
fascinating territory, to which economically, culturally, and geographically it is close.

The Fezzan is poor and isolated. For a time Murzuq and then Sebha
were included as Federal capital in the Tripoli–Benghazi cycle, but
political expediency has latterly yielded to geographical realities.

With such a limited degree of productivity, Libya has great difficulty
in paying for the modest volume of manufactured imports that are
felt necessary. Schemes of economic development are financed from
abroad: the Italians spent £40–50 million between 1913 and 1942;
and since 1951 for example there has been made available over £6
million, of which over 75 per cent. was contributed by the U.S.A.,

12 per cent. by the U.K., and smaller amounts by Egypt, United Nations, France, Italy, and Turkey. In addition, subsidies are paid directly to the Libyan government for the use of military bases: on average over the last few years £4 million, and half a million have been paid respectively each year by Britain and the U.S.A., as compared with the total of £2 million raised by national taxation.

Despite the political unity gained in 1951, Libya does not yet possess economic independence. Hitherto there has been the asset of strategic value to outsiders, which may now be declining, as the result of changes in overall military strategy within the Mediterranean basin. Many hopes are now of course turned to development of oil reserves, which are undoubtedly very rich – as was stated earlier, commercial production actually began late in 1961. Whilst the effect of this exploitation is undoubtedly going to be very great indeed, there will be several concomitant problems – first, the social effects of new wealth in what has hitherto been a distinctly poor territory. Second, it has been agreed that revenues from oil shall be retained in the province from which the crude oil is derived; and as so far most discoveries have been in Cyrenaica the economic disparity with Tripolitania (sketched above) may hence be reversed within a short time – bringing further considerable social and political changes. Lastly, despite the now clearly rich deposits of petroleum, the precise significance of oil to the Libyan economy will remain somewhat uncertain: with the existence of Saharan oil, annually increasing production from the Persian Gulf, and the recent (1962) entry of Russia as a major exporter, a pattern of development as in Kuwait may be retarded or less fully attained. Hence there remains a need to improve the basic economic position; and the aims of many of the survey development groups now working in Libya are directed to resource evaluation: the types of crop best suited to local conditions; the role of irrigation as a subsidiary, or fundamental; and the place of animal husbandry. Libya represents a considerable challenge – not the least to the geographer.

Outline of the Geological History of the Middle East

In pre-Cambrian times, the greater part of the Middle East area consisted of a complex of igneous and metamorphic rocks, forming a widespread land area. This ancient Archaean continent extended over the greater part of Africa, and continued unbroken through Arabia, Iraq, Iran, Armenia, and much of Turkey. In the extreme north-east of the Middle East region a mountain range may have come into existence in late Archaean or early Cambrian times, as the result of fold movements. Further to the east, much of northern India was covered by sea, with a coastline approximately in the area of the present north-west Provinces; and a less extensive sea or gulf would also appear to have existed over north-west Arabia, in the region of the Wadi Araba. Later, in the Cambrian age, certain outlying portions of the Archaean platform underwent subsidence; and well-developed Cambrian series of limestone, shale, rock-salt, and anhydrite can be traced in a number of regions of the Middle East, particularly in the north and east, along the zone of the present Zagros mountains, with continuations into Armenia, central Iran, and Israel-Jordan.

Quiet conditions seem to have prevailed throughout much of the remaining lower Palaeozoic epoch, so that deposits are generally scanty, uneven in thickness, and local in extent. The Devonian age saw considerable flooding by sea of many parts of the northern region, with a corresponding deposition of sediments in much of western Turkey, in a narrow zone along the Black Sea coast, in Armenia, and also in parts of Iran.

During the succeeding Carboniferous age the emergence of a landmass took place in central and eastern Europe, accompanied by warping movements in the region of Asia Minor. The northern part was uplifted, and a large area round the Black Sea emerged as low-lying land bordering a shallow sea. In this basin, which was one of a series extending westwards through central Europe as far as the British Isles, extensive but discontinuous coal deposits were laid down. The greater portion of the Carboniferous structures of the Black Sea area, one of the major coal basins of the world, are preserved in the Donbas region of Russia; but a much smaller coal basin also occurs in the Eregli-Zonguldak area of north-western Turkey. Further south, a down-warping led to the transgression of the sea over north-west Syria and the north of central Arabia, with probably temporary marine transgressions as far as western Iran. Deposits in Oman province indicate that the sea may have formed a gulf extending as far as south-east Arabia.

During the Permian age, further flooding occurred, so that most of the northern and eastern parts of south-west Asia became submerged beneath a great sea, to which the name Tethys has been given. This sea probably extended from southern Asia, leaving a narrow strip of unsubmerged land in the extreme north of Turkey. Punjabian limestone of middle Permian age, found in the region of the Iranian Zagros, and the Araxes valley of Turkestan indicates the great extension of the Tethys.

In late Permian times, fold movements due to compression occurred in Anatolia. These were probably influenced in the north by the structure lines of the Carboniferous basin, and hence the folds themselves run east–west for some distance to the south of Zonguldak. Folds of similar age, but with a generally north–south trend, occur in the Maraş district of southern Anatolia; and contemporaneous folding on a small scale may also have taken place in central Iran. Elsewhere, the main features were (a) the extensive sea area covering Syria, Iraq, and western Iran, with (b) the stable block of north Africa and Arabia forming a shoreline at some distance to the south and west.

In Turkey, regional uplift followed by considerable denudation gave rise to a number of small, but relatively stable and resistant, land masses, surrounded by more yielding and pliable sediments. The nucleus of a few of these resistant blocks can be considered as fragments broken off the Archaean platform underlying the south-west of the Middle East region; but this is by no means the whole story, since several of the blocks appear to have no Archaean foundation, and instead, show signs of intensive folding of Palaeozoic age – the indication being that they themselves have been sufficiently rigid to offer resistance to later fold movements. Trends are, however, so confused with one direction frequently giving place to another over a short distance, that no definite plan of folding can be distinguished. The westernmost of these blocks occurs in the Rhodope massif of the Balkans; and others have been delimited by Salomon-Calvi and Tromp in the Cyclades region of the southern Aegean; in the area transversed by the Büyük Menderes of south-west Turkey; and in the Konya region of the central plateau.

The early Mesozoic period was one of wide submergence. Considerable masses of Jurassic limestone were laid down in western Syria, Armenia, and Iran; and other marine sediments of this epoch show that the Tethys extended from Spain to Northern India. From the opening of the Mesozoic period until middle Cretaceous times, the permanence of the geosyncline of the Tethys was the main feature in the northern, central, and western parts of the Middle East region. The deepest part of the geosyncline lay most probably along an axis running from north-west to south-east, on the extreme eastern limits of the present-day Zagros, since in this region Triassic and Cretaceous radiolorian chert series, formed from deep-water organisms, are a widespread feature.

In middle Cretaceous times a series of fold movements affected Turkey and the north-eastern margin of the geosyncline. The resistant blocks of the former region were brought closer together, with a consequent compression of the later sediments surrounding them. A series of asymmetrical folds thus developed in southern Turkey, with a trend closely influenced by the disposition of the harder blocks; but rapid erosion after elevation soon reduced the folds to mere stumps. In Iran, intensive folding occurred in the region of the north-western Zagros, between Niriz and Kirman, with the result that the site of the deeper part of the Tethys was displaced towards the south-west.

Further south, somewhat similar earth movements (chiefly during upper Cretaceous times) have been shown to have had great influence on the structure of the lower Persian Gulf. For a distance of some 600 miles from Ras Musandum, at the head of the peninsula separating the Persian Gulf and the Gulf of Oman, to Ras Madraka on the Arabian coast of the Indian Ocean, a strongly developed series of folds, with a complex of overthrusts and nappes, together with widespread vulcanicity, form the main structural feature. The trend of folding is generally north and south, and in the north there are signs that the mountain range continues into southern Iran at least as far as Niriz. The southward extension is much more difficult to trace, and several alternatives present themselves.[1]

The Tertiary period opened quietly in most areas, with extensive

[1] For a discussion of these alternatives see G. M. Lees, 'Oman', *Geol. Mag.*, Vol. XXX, 1940.

sedimentation in the geosynclinal trough, due to erosion from the recently elevated land masses further to the north and east.[1] The progressive filling up of marine basins is shown by a considerable development of shallow water limestones that can be traced in Asia Minor, and from Cyrenaica across northern Libya and Egypt into parts of Arabia and southern Iran. Deposition continued further in Oligocene times. The geosyncline became even shallower, with the emergence of dry land on the margins. In many areas, particularly southern Turkey and the regions round the Persian Gulf, salt and anhydrite beds of Oligocene age indicate increasing desiccation in land areas and their adjacent shallow seas.

It is suggested that the geosyncline may have been divided laterally by the development of a shallow water platform in the region of the middle Persian Gulf, since at this period the rock series formed in the north-west differ from those formed to the south-east. The division of the geosyncline into two relatively shallow basins would thus advance the precipitation of chemical deposits, which are a conspicuous feature of the early and middle Tertiary periods. The formation of these deposits was also aided by slight oscillation, which produced two periods of uplift each followed by marine transgression.

In the Miocene period, considerable folding took place. The effects were greatest in the north, where younger and less resistant sedimentary measures of Asia Minor were compressed against the still resistant plateau blocks, with a widespread development of fold structures controlled once more by the extent and disposition of the older masses.

The Taurus Mountains became a prominent feature along the southern edges of the Aydin and Anatolian plateau blocks, although of a somewhat lower elevation than now; and more irregularly disposed arcs came into existence to the east and west, i.e. between the Aydin and Cyclades masses; north of the Gulf of Alexandretta; and south of the basins of Van and Urmia. In the last area the arcs are wider in extent.

Further to the south-east, the geosyncline underwent subsistence, with the development of folds on the north-eastern margins. Regression of the sea then followed, with a considerable shrinkage of the geosynclinal area as a whole; yet a further displacement of the site of the deeper portion took place, bringing the axis more towards the south-west, along the borders of Iraq and Iran.

---

[1] There was, however, some disturbance in central Iran, which led to marked volcanic activity during Eocene times.

T

The continuation of orogenic movements during the middle Tertiary led to a second phase of mountain building in the north and north-east of the Middle East region. The composite mass of rock series of varying age proved resistant to further fold movements, but continued compression led to extensive fracturing of the rigid, although relatively brittle, strata. Widespread faulting accompanied by differential movement gave rise to a series of horsts and downthrow basins. In Turkey, this development is particularly well marked: recently formed fold structures and older blocks hitherto resistant to all earth movements were alike extensively fractured. The opening of cracks and fissures in the crust of the earth allowed the rise of magma from the interior, and intrusion by igneous rocks, with a considerable development of volcanic cones and lava flows, is hence characteristic of this period.

The earlier Tertiary folding movements were of greater importance in the north: a final period of activity in Pliocene times had its maximum effect in the east and south-east. The remnant of the Tethys continued to shrink, and to retreat towards the south-east, although subject to minor oscillations, whilst great fold structures began to develop on the north-eastern limb. The Zagros Mountains took their present form: an immense series of folds and nappes, with a remarkable unity of trend from north-west to south-east, continuing unbroken for a thousand miles between Armenia and Bandar Abbas. Further to the south and east, in the Makran, the trend gradually takes on a more easterly direction; and finally, in the extreme east, towards Afghanistan and India, the direction turns south-west to north-east, under the influence of the pre-existing structures of the Suleiman Mountains of north-west India.

Pliocene disturbances also had important results in Turkey. Minor folds were formed along the southern edge of the region. More important, however, was the renewed fracturing of the whole of Asia Minor, followed by uplift on a considerable scale. The interior basins of the west were elevated to an average height of 3,000 feet, and those of the east to 7,500 feet, with fold ranges rising above this height on the margins. This last movement – one of wholesale uplift, not merely in Asia Minor, but also affecting central Iran – would appear to have been episodic, since at least four separate river terraces can be traced in all the major rivers.

Extensive movement along tectonic lines broke down the northern and western edges on the newly-raised land mass of Asia Minor. In the north, downward warping along generally east–west aligned faults gave rise to the present Black Sea coastline – straight, sheer, and harbourless; in the west, more involved cross-faulting produced an extremely broken shoreline bordering a drowned central basin, out of which stand irregular fragments in the form of islands. The Bosphorus was formed by the drowning of a channel opened by north–north-east–south-south-west running minor faults in a land mass defined by east–west tectonics.

Inland, differential movement along fault-lines accentuated the topography of the interior basins, and hence controlled the development of the great lakes – Tuz, Van, Gokce, and Urmia. Finally, a renewed outburst of volcanic activity raised the massive cones of Ararat, Suphan, and Nemrut that now form the highest points in the country. Movement along the numerous tectonic lines in Asia Minor has by no means ceased, even at the present time, so that earthquakes are frequent. A number of districts in Turkey that lie on great fault zones are badly affected.

Tectonic Evolution. Interesting views on the detailed pattern of tectonic evolution within the Middle East have recently been put forward. These, whilst based in general on the existing concept of ancient 'shield' massifs separated by the Tethyan geosynclinal, invoke as a new element, in order to explain certain details of structure and stratigraphy, the idea of gravity sliding on a large scale.

Broadly speaking, it is suggested (e.g. by Klemme) that the ancient pre-Cambrian masses were extended by the welding on to them of Hercynian (and possibly Caledonian) fold structures, in which occurred anticlinals and troughs. During this phase of accretion, tension could be expected to develop between the growing nuclear masses (pre-Cambrian plus accretions) and the adjacent geosynclinal, which would be subjected to infilling by sediments eroded from the nucleus, and hence down-warped. This tension could give rise to a major zone of crustal weakness lying between the centre of the geosyncline and the centre of the nuclear shield; and in this zone of weakness faulting, fissuring, and the uprising of magma would be features. On emergence, the magma would tend to flow or creep towards the lower parts of the trough, which would thus become more rapidly infilled – by magma and associated material, as well as by material eroded from the nucleus.

At this stage, a major upthrust would seem to have occurred; and this, with its associated fold and overthrusting movements, appears to have had the effect of raising by many thousands of feet the former floor of the trough, now partially or wholly infilled. From the newly created highland zones, further gravity 'slides' would develop from basement and later rocks, which break off as blocks and move down the newly formed topographical slopes. With the culmination of epeirogenic uplift a new highland mass of younger rocks will have been formed as an extension of the older nucleus; and the original trough converted to a mountain range (e.g. as in Asia Minor, and in the Zagros Range, where deep-water sediments were raised 10,000–20,000 feet above sea level). A final phase, not to be found everywhere, but highly significant in certain areas (e.g. Iran), could be the foundering along major fault zones of a part of the folded areas, producing a second basin or trough within the boundaries of the ancient nucleus or its extension. Further gravity slides could then take place into this new ('back-deep') trough or basin.

Temperature Distribution in the Atmosphere

If for any reason a quantity of air is compelled to change its position vertically in the atmosphere, heating or cooling takes place according to whether the air sinks or rises. On sinking, the parcel of air moves into a part of the atmosphere where pressure is greater, so that compression occurs, and the parcel shrinks in volume. The heat energy within the air remains unaffected by the change in volume, and thus if no transfer of heat from, or to, external sources takes place, the energy contained in the parcel of air itself now has a reduced air mass upon which to exert its heating action. The temperature of the air rises, because an unaltered quantum of heat is existent in a reduced volume of air.

Conversely, if a parcel of air ascends in the atmosphere, reduced pressure leads to expansion in volume, with a resulting fall in temperature, since the heat energy has now a larger mass upon which to exert its influence.[1] Such changes of temperature in response to changes of pressure are termed *adiabatic*, because they develop within the air mass itself and are quite independent of external temperature conditions. For dry air, the rate of heating or cooling following adiabatic contraction or expansion is $5.4°$ F. per 1,000 feet; and for saturated air (i.e. 100 per cent. humid) $2.7°$ F. The difference arises owing to absorption or liberation of latent heat.[2]

The phenomenon of adiabatic heating or cooling is of great importance in meteorology, since it influences weather conditions in several ways. As regards the Middle East region, adiabatic effects are most marked (*a*) in producing changes in temperature and relative humidity in an air mass as the result of ascent or descent over mountain ranges (i.e. Föhn effects); and (*b*) in leading to the development of stable and unstable conditions.

Influences of Changes in Altitude. Let us suppose that a mass of air, damp but not saturated, is forced to rise. If the initial temperature of the air

[1] Compare the effect of moving an electric radiator from a smaller to a larger room.
[2] An everyday example of adiabatic heating may be noted in a bicycle pump. As air is compressed during the inflation of a tyre, heat is generated and the pump becomes warm. Intense adiabatic cooling takes place when highly compressed gases are allowed to expand quickly. This principle is utilised in certain types of refrigeration plant.

is 50° F., and its dew-point 45°, an ascent of slightly less than 1,000 feet will bring it to its dew-point, i.e. the air will become saturated, and cloud will form.[1] From this point, if ascent is continued, cooling will be at the rate of 2·7° F. per 1,000 feet; but at the same time, the air will remain saturated, and further cooling will be accompanied by the precipitation of water in the form of clouds or rain. Let us assume that the air ascends 3,000 feet above its starting level. Temperature will fall to approximately 39·6° F., and although the air will still be saturated, the total quantity of water-vapour held in it will be diminished, since air at 39·6° cannot hold as much water as air at 45°. The excess water will have formed cloud or rain; and the dew-point will of course also have fallen to 39·6° F.

If the air now descends, adiabatic heating at the saturated rate will begin; and, for a time, so long as water-drops persist in the air, and can be evaporated to keep the air 100 per cent. humid, this will continue. But the quantity of water-drops will be limited, because their presence on the downward slope is due merely to mechanical transfer from the upward slope, and none will be formed from the air itself. Hence when all the water-drops have been evaporated, the air mass will cease to be saturated, and further heating will then take place at the dry adiabatic rate. The dew-point, 39·6° F. at the summit, will rise at the rate of 2·7° so long as the air remains saturated; and, as has been said, allowing for certain persistence of water vapour and water-drops past the summit, could be expected to reach 40° or 41°. Over much of the 3,000 feet of descent, the greater part will, however, be at the rate of 5·4° per 1,000 feet, giving an approximate figure of 13° F. rise in temperature. Thus on completing its descent, the air mass will have reached a temperature of 53° to 54° F. as compared with its original 50°, and it will in addition be considerably drier, having lost a quantity of its vapour during the journey (new dew-point 40° or 41° as compared with the original 45°).

These theoretical considerations must be slightly modified in practice, because a certain amount of heat is lost by conduction to the land surface, and the gain in heat is therefore actually less than would be expected. Nevertheless, an important topographical barrier can produce marked changes in the air passing over it, and such changes become even more striking when air descends without having undergone previous ascent, e.g. from an interior plateau to a coastal plain.

[1] As the air mass is not at first 100 per cent. humid, it will cool at the rate of 5·4° per 1,000 feet of ascent until it reaches its dew-point.

Heating is almost entirely at the dry adiabatic rate, so that abnormally high temperatures result, giving rise to the well-known phenomenon of Föhn winds. These are frequent in many parts of the Middle East, where high interior plateaus are a common feature; and Asia Minor is probably the most outstanding region in this respect.

Atmospheric Stability. The above considerations relating to adiabatic heating and cooling apply only to *air actively in vertical motion.* Obviously this does not hold for the greater part of the atmosphere, which remains either still, or in fluctuating horizontal motion, with only a very slight vertical component.

The atmosphere as a whole takes on a temperature distribution controlled by the presence of various local heating agencies – isolation, the character of the surface, or the presence of solid matter in the air: and adiabatic laws play no direct part in influencing the temperature of the general atmosphere, *so long as vertical motion is not involved.* It therefore follows that the atmosphere can vary considerably in temperature from place to place and from day to day, not merely in a horizontal direction, but also vertically. Being controlled by local weather changes, temperature distribution is subject to no fixed laws. Excessive heating of the ground will affect only the lower layers of the atmosphere; and differential heating of the opposite kind occurs when a warmer air mass over-runs a colder.

The figure of 3° F. drop in temperature per 1,000 feet of ascent, normally quoted in geographical text-books, is merely an approximation based on average conditions, and bears only the most general relationship to existing temperatures. It is usually exceeded in tropical regions, but may not be attained during spells of settled weather in higher latitudes. Variation takes place almost from hour to hour. Determination of the vertical distribution of temperature in the atmosphere (or lapse rate), is employed by meteorologists as the indispensable preliminary of weather forecasting, and to observe the lapse rate, elaborate methods involving radar, and balloon and aeroplane flights are necessary.

It has, however, been shown that air actually rising in the free atmosphere is immediately influenced by adiabatic cooling; and its temperature will therefore change at a definite rate. Let us now consider the behaviour of a small mass of air which, we will assume, is forced to rise

(*a*) within an atmosphere where the lower layers are very warm, and the upper layers unduly cold. Assuming an average decrease in temperature, or lapse rate, of 7° F. per 1,000 feet for this atmosphere, it will be apparent that the longer the small mass continues to rise, the warmer it will become *relative to its surrounding environment*, since the small air mass will cool only at the rate of 5·4° F. so long as it remains dry, and at 2·7° after saturation, in accordance with adiabatic laws. Being relatively warmer than the atmosphere around it, the small mass will have a lighter density, and its vertical motion will thus tend to increase, in the same way as a lighter hydrogen balloon will ascend in denser air, or a bubble of oil rise through water to the surface. The longer ascent continues, the greater the disparity in temperature between the air mass and its surrounding atmosphere, and therefore, the greater the acceleration upward. (See table below.)

(b) If the lapse rate of the atmosphere changes only slowly, i.e. temperature differences between higher and lower layers are small, a rising air mass will cool more rapidly than the atmosphere round it, and will become relatively denser, hence heavier, than its environment. Vertical motion will be retarded, and ultimately damped out completely. (See table below.)

	Air Mass (x) ° F.	Atmosphere (a) ° F.	Atmosphere (c) ° F.
5,000 feet	33·0	25	50
4,000 ,,	38·4	32	52
3,000 ,,	43·8	39	54
2,000 ,,	49·2	46	56
1,000 ,,	54·6	53	58
Surface	60·0	60	60

Column (x) represents actual temperature changes undergone by a mass of air, initial temperature 60° F. during 5,000 feet of ascent under dry adiabatic conditions.

Column (a) gives conditions in an atmosphere with an assumed lapse rate of 7° F. per 1,000 feet. Dry air (col. x) rising in this atmosphere will be 8° warmer than its environment after an ascent of 5,000 feet.

Column (b) gives conditions in an atmosphere with an assumed lapse rate of 2° F. per 1,000 feet. Dry air (col. x) rising in this atmosphere will be 17° colder than its environment after an ascent of 5,000 feet.

Summing up, we may say that under conditions of rapid variation of temperature in the atmosphere (i.e. steep lapse rates) air masses are aided in an upward motion they may acquire, and such motion increases the higher they rise. When the atmosphere cools only slowly with height, air masses within it cannot develop any marked vertical motion.

In order to understand this conception, it is essential to distinguish clearly between the *general atmosphere*, which is not involved in a vertical motion, and is hence free to develop a temperature gradient (lapse rate) of its own, and a *rising air mass*, which cools at a fixed rate determined by the laws of adiabatic change. An atmosphere is said to be *unstable* if it has a great vertical range of temperature, that is, if air masses within it can easily develop vertical motion. A *stable* atmosphere is one with a relatively slow lapse rate, and a restricted range of temperature, in which vertical motion tends to be damped out.

The practical importance of this feature of the atmosphere is very great. Under conditions of instability, small-scale eddies formed near the ground as the wind blows against obstacles such as hills, buildings, or even trees, can develop into large updrafts of air. This in turn gives rise, if moisture is present, to the elaboration of cumuliform cloud, leading to showers, heavy rain, or possibly hail and thunder. Squally winds, blowing violently for short periods, then rapidly changing in direction of onset, are also characteristic of atmospheric instability.

Excessive surface heating leads most easily to the development of unstable atmospheric conditions, and this, as we have seen, is widespread in the Middle East. Weather phenomena associated with instability are therefore highly characteristic of the climatic regimes of the area.

(A) The Origin of the Mesopotamian Plains

An entirely different interpretation of the origin of the Mesopotamian plains has recently been put forward by G. M. Lees and N. L. Falcon ('The Geographical History of the Mesopotamian Plains', *Geographical Journal*, Vol. CXVIII, Part 1, March 1952). The earlier view by de Morgan that the land-growth at the head of the Persian Gulf has been due mainly to ponding-back by the Karun delta of sediment-charged waters from the Euphrates and Tigris is shown to be in some respects untenable; and the opinion is advanced that certain archaeological evidence must be re-interpreted, discounting the idea of a single cataclysmic and widespread flood in early Sumerian times.

In very broad outline, the views of Lees and Falcon are that Lower Mesopotamia and the Persian Gulf are together an area of crustal subsidence; and that the marshlands of lower Iraq represent a delicate balance between the deposition of silt from the Tigris and Euphrates, which by itself would rapidly raise the level of the land, and sinking of the underlying strata presumably under the weight of accumulating deposits from the two rivers. A further complicating factor in this relationship of land and sea is the oscillation in general sea level during and after the Ice Ages.

Lees and Falcon point out as evidence in support of their theory of subsidence as the principal causative factor (*a*) that rivers flowing from the Zagros Range towards the Persian Gulf were much rejuvenated in Pleistocene and Recent geological times, thus greatly increasing the rate of deposition of sediment in Mesopotamia. Detailed observations of the volume of silt carried and then deposited by the Tigris and Euphrates in their lower courses indicate that a minimum average deposit of 0·22 inches per annum could be expected over an area of 1,500 square miles. Hence, bearing in mind that much wind-blown dust and sand can also be 'trapped' by the water of the marshes, there might well be a rate of deposition of the order of 15 to 20 feet per 1,000 years – consequently it would seem that the marshes and lakes of lower Iraq could not survive for more than a few centuries unless there were some kind of subsidence.

(b) Geological deposits of all ages subsequent to the Pliocene are fresh-water in character to the north-west of the present coastline, and marine to the south-east, suggesting that the present coastline dates roughly from Pliocene times.

(c) British Admiralty charts exist for the area from 1851 onwards. In some parts, very little extension of the land area is observable – suggesting that a rapid south-eastward 'creep' of the land is not in fact occurring; but in other parts, sedimentation has undoubtedly taken place on a significant scale. Thus cartographical evidence is inconclusive.

(d) Borings for oil some 20 miles north-west of Basra give a sequence first of 90 feet of alluvial clay and sands, with fresh-water shells at the base, resting on Miocene bedrock – indicating a subsidence of 90 feet by an original inland lake, not a former portion of the sea bed gradually invaded by silt.

Altogether, Lees and Falcon advanced the opinion that conditions must be viewed as a complex pattern of advance and retreat by the sea, with subsidence in the main predominating. This would give rise to sudden local floods, possibly catastrophic over a small area, but not widespread. Then probably at times there may have been periods of relative stability during which deposition by the two rivers raised land level. The balance between subsidence and sedimentation would seem to have been in the past and still at the present extremely finely poised; and rather than building forward a normal delta, the Tigris, Euphrates, and Karun, as Lees and Falcon see matters, are discharging into a slowly and irregularly downwarping tectonic trough.

(B) The Origin of the Nile Valley

Doubt has recently been thrown upon the 'Lake Sudd' theory of origin of the Nile valley (as outlined on p. 481) following the discovery by Mr W. J. Arkell of what would seem to be a human-shaped artefact in the region of the central Sudan. If, as is suggested, the artefact dates from some 60,000 years B.C., then it would seem highly unlikely that the region of the central Sudan could have been a lake as late as 21,000 B.C., since the artefact might well indicate human settlement in this area; and thus the idea of a Lake Sudd is more difficult to sustain. (Private communication to the author.)

The Racial and Cultural Affinities of the People of Israel

Following the flight of between 750,000 and one million Arabs from Palestine in 1948, and the subsequent immigration of numbers of Jews from all parts of the world, the state of Israel is now over 90 per cent. Jewish, with small minorities (totalling in all about 175,000) of Sunni Moslems, Druses, Samaritans, Christians, and others.

A problem of growing magnitude has been the assimilation of Jewish immigrants through the development of a common culture and language. Hebrew, current in Biblical days, underwent considerable decline after the Diaspora; and by the twentieth century A.D. most European Jews spoke (besides the language of the country in which they lived) either Yiddish or Ladino. The former is a Hebrew-Germanic dialect current in eastern and central Europe: the latter a form of Spanish. Hence even by 1931 over 60 languages were used within Palestine; and to these major differences in speech were added important variation in Jewish ritual, beliefs, and ways of life, as between the Ashkenazim (from eastern and central Europe) and the Sephardim (from southern and western Europe).[1] A third but far from homogeneous group was that of the Oriental Jews, many of whom had become at least in racial character and outlook partly assimilated to various Oriental peoples – Arabs, Persians, Abyssinians, etc.

One solution to the problem has been found in the revival of Hebrew as a common language for general everyday use; and this revival has been a potent influence in the unifying of the Israeli-Jewish people. At the present, divergence between Ashkenazim and Sephardim is declining; and main problems now arise firstly from the increased volume of immigration of Oriental Jews since 1949, whose outlook and way of life can be very different from that of European Jews: secondly from the clash between those Jews who wish to see religion as a fundamental

---

[1] It is a distortion, but perhaps not wholly inapposite, to recall that Benjamin Disraeli was of Sephardim origin, and Karl Marx of Ashkenazim stock.

and prominent element in daily life, and those who follow a more 'modernist' view. In 1952 the latter issue came to a head over the question of religious teaching in schools, and resulted in the fall of the Israeli Cabinet.

DISTRIBUTION OF JEWISH IMMIGRANTS IN ISRAEL BY REGION OF BIRTH, 1949 and 1951

(Percentage of Total)

From:	1949	1951
(1) Middle Eastern Countries	30	58
of which Turkey	11	17
Iraq	1	53
Persia	1	5
the Yemen	15	1
(2) Africa	17	12
of which Libya	6	5
(3) Eastern Europe	22	2
of which Poland	20	2
(4) Balkan Europe	16	24
of which Rumania	6	23
(5) Rest of Europe	14	2
of which Czechoslovakia	7	0
Hungary	13	1
(6) America	1	1

Glossary of Geographical Terms

Unless otherwise shown as Greek, Persian, or Turkish
all words used are of Arabic origin.

Abu	father of (tribal)	Jebel	hill
Ain	spring	Kara (T)	black
Akhbar	greater	Kasr, Qasr	castle, barracks
Akhdar	green	Kebir	great
Ala (T)	very high	Kefr	village
Asir	isolated	Khan	night stopping place
Aya (Ayos) (G)	saint		for caravans
Bab	gate, strait	Khor	open water, salt
Bahr	sea, lake		steppe
Balkan (T)	wooded hill	Maaden (T)	mine
Beit	house	Maidan (P)	open expanse, small
Bekaa	fertile plain		plain
Bir	well	Mar	saint
Birkeh, Birket	pool, tank	Mawsil	confluence
Büyük (T)	great	Merj, Marj	plain
Col (T)	desert	Meskin	poor
Dagh (T)	mountains	Nahr	river
Dar	dwelling	Nakle	palm tree
Deir	monastery	Ova (T)	plain, basin
El (al, em, en,		Qanat (P)	canal
er, esh, et)	the	Ramle(h)	sand
Gezira, Jezireh	island	Ras	cape, headland
Ghab	forest	Rud (P)	river
Ghor	hollow	Sabkha	salt marsh
Göl (T)	lake	Sahel	plain
Hamad	barren	Sidi	tomb of holy man
Harra	lava field	Sü (T)	river
Hedjaz	boundary	Sur (P)	fortress
Hosn, Husn	fortress	Tel, Tell (plural	
Ibn	son of	Tulul)	small hill
Irmak (T)	river	Tuz (T)	salt

Bibliography

(Titles without an indicated place of publication have appeared in London)

GENERAL

P. BIROT and J. DRESCH, *La Méditerranée et le Moyen Orient*, 2 vols., Paris, 1956

R. BLANCHARD, *Asie Occidentale*, Géographie Universelle, Vol. VIII, Paris, 1929

R. BULLARD, *Britain and the Middle East*, 1952

G. B. CRESSEY, *Crossroads: Land and Life in Southwest Asia*, Chicago, 1960

R. ETTINGHAUSEN, *Books and Periodicals in Western Languages dealing with the Near and Middle East*, Washington, 1952

H. A. R. GIBB, 'Middle East Perplexities', *International Affairs*, Vol. 20, 1944

D. G. HOGARTH, *The Nearer East*, 1905

C. HOLLINGWORTH, *The Arabs and the West*, 1952

B. A. KEEN, *The Agricultural Development of the Middle East*, 1946

T. E. LAWRENCE, *Seven Pillars of Wisdom*, 1935

G. LENCZOWSKI, *The Middle East in World Affairs*, Ithaca, N.Y., 1952

G. LESTRANGE, *Lands of the Eastern Caliphate*, 1905

ROYAL INSTITUTE OF INTERNATIONAL AFFAIRS, *The Middle East, a Political and Economic Survey*, 2nd ed. 1954

E. C. SEMPLE, *The Geography of the Mediterranean Region*, 1932

G. A. SMITH, *Historical Geography of the Holy Land*, 1895

E. B. WORTHINGTON, *Middle East Science*, 1946

Journal of the Middle East Institute, Washington (quarterly)

CHAPTER I

K. A. H. MURRAY, 'Some Regional Economic Problems of the Middle East', *International Affairs*, Vol. 23, 1947

554   BIBLIOGRAPHY

CHAPTER II

E. ARGAND, *La Tectonique de l'Asie*, Brussels, 1924

K. W. BUTZER, *Quaternary Stratigraphy and Climate in the Near East*, Bonn, 1958.

F. G. CLAPP, *The Geology of Eastern Iran, Bulletin of the Geol. Soc. of America*, Vol. 51, 1940

L. DUBERTRET and J. WEULERSSE, *Manuel de Géographie de la Syrie et du Proche Orient*, Beirut, 1940

R. FURON, 'La Géologie du Plateau Iranien', *Mém. Musée Nat. d'Hist. Naturelle*, Vol. 7, Paris, 1941

J. W. GREGORY, 'The Geology of Cyrenaica', *Journ. Geol. Soc.*, Vol. 67, 1911
    The Structure of Asia, 1929
    The Geology of Mesopotamia, 1918

E. KRENKEL, *Geologie Afrikas*, Band II, Hamburg, 1925

G. M. LEES and F. D. S. RICHARDSON, 'The Geology of the Oilfield Belt of S.W. Iran', *Geol. Mag.*, Vol. 77, 1940

E. SUESS, *The Face of the Earth*, Vols. I and III, 1902

CHAPTER III

C. COMBIER, 'La Climatologie de la Syrie et du Liban', *Rév. de Géogr. Phys. et de Géol. Dynam*, Vol. VI, Paris, 1933

CHAPTER IV

G. E. POST, *The Flora of Syria, Palestine, and Sinai*, Beirut, 1933

A. REIFENBERG, *The Soils of Palestine*, 1938

CHAPTER V

T. ARNOLD, *The Caliphate*, 1930

D. BUXTON, *The Peoples of Asia*, 1925

C. S. COON, *Caravan*, New York, 1951

H. FIELD, *The Anthropology of Iraq*, 4 vols., Chicago, 1940–52

A. C. HADDON, *The Races of Man*, 1929

P. HITTI, *History of the Arabs*, 1937

A. KAPPERS, *Introduction to the Anthropology of the Near East*, Amsterdam, 1934

B. J. KIDD, *The Churches of Eastern Christendom*, 1927

CHAPTER VI

J. W. CROWFOOT, 'The Arabs To-day', *Geog. Jour.*, Vol. XCIX, 1942

H. R. P. DICKSON, *The Arab of the Desert*, 1949
H. A. R. GIBB, *Modern Trends in Islam*, Chicago, 1949
　　　Mohammedanism, 1949
A. H. HOURANI, *Minorities in the Arab World*, 1952
B. LEWIS, *The Arabs in History*, 1950
J. THOUMIN, *Géographie Humaine de la Syrie Centrale*, Paris, 1936
J. WEULERSSE, *Le Pays des Alouites*, Tours, 1940

CHAPTER VII

C. BROCKELMAN, *A History of the Islamic Peoples*, New York, 1947
Cambridge Ancient History, 1932–6
Cambridge Mediæval History, Vol. II
H. R. H. HALL, *The Ancient History of the Near East*, 1927
G. KIRK, *A Short History of the Middle East*, 1948
H. J. E. PEAKE and H. J. FLEURE, *The Corridors of Time*, 1927–33
M. ROSTOVTZEFF, *Caravan Cities*, 1932

CHAPTER VIII

A. ANTONIUS, *The Arab Awakening*, 1935
I. BOWMAN, *The New World*, 1922
J. HOPE SIMPSON, *Refugees*, 1936
W. L. WESTERMANN, 'The Kurds', *Foreign Affairs*, New York, July 1946
W. A. WIGRAM, *The Assyrians*, 1928
W. YALE, *The Near East*, Ann Arbor, U.S.A., 1958

CHAPTER IX

A. BONNÉ, *The Economic Development of the Middle East*, 1945
S. C. DODD, *A Controlled Experiment in Rural Hygiene*, Beirut, 1934
S. B. HIMADEH, *The Economic Organisation of Syria*, Beirut, 1934
A. K. S. LAMBTON, *Landlord and Peasant in Persia*, 1953
H. J. E. PEAKE, *The Origins of Agriculture*, 1928
G. SAAB, *Motorisation de l'Agriculture et Développement Agricole au Proche Orient*, Paris, 1960
D. WARRINER, *Land and Poverty in the Middle East*, 1947
　　　Land Reform and Development in the Middle East, 1957
J. WEULERSSE, *Paysans de Syrie et du Proche Orient*, Tours, 1946

CHAPTER XI

Bull. of the American Association of Petroleum Geologists (for annual summaries of development)

G. M. LEES, 'Oil in the Middle East', *Journ. R. Central Asian Soc.*, Vol. XXXIII, 1946

S. H. LONGRIGG, *Oil in the Middle East*, 1954

The Science of Petroleum, New York, 1932

CHAPTER XII

A. M. AMMAR, *Demographic Study of an Egyptian Province*, 1948

W. W. CLELAND, *A Population Plan for Egypt*, 22nd Annual Conference Millbank Memorial Fund, New York, 1944

E. JURKAT, *Prospects for Population Growth in the Middle East*, ibid.

C. V. KISER, *The Demographic Position of Egypt*, ibid.

F. W. NOTESTEIN and E. JURKAT, *Population Problems of Palestine*, ibid., 1945

CHAPTER XIII

A. J. ARBERRY (ed.), *The Legacy of Persia*, 1952

L. P. ELWALL-SUTTON, *Iran*, 1941

R. FURON, *L'Iran*, Paris, 1952

W. S. HAAS, *Iran*, New York, 1946

J. DE MORGAN, *Mission Scientifique en Perse*, Paris, 1905

N. S. ROBERTS, *Iran* (Overseas Economic Surveys, H.M. Govt.), 1948

H. H. VREELAND, *Iran*, New Haven, Conn., 1957

CHAPTER XIV

INTERNATIONAL BANK FOR RECONSTRUCTION AND DEVELOPMENT, *The Economy of Turkey*, Washington, 1951

J. JONES, *Turkey* (Overseas Economic Surveys, H.M. Govt.), 1948

K. KRÜGER, *Die Turkei*, Berlin, 1951

H. LUKE, *The Making of Modern Turkey*, 1936

O.E.E.C., *Economic Conditions in Turkey*, Paris, 1959

M. THORNBURG, G. SPRY and G. SOULE, *Turkey: an Economic Appraisal*, New York, 1949

CHAPTER XV

Admiralty Handbook of Mesopotamia, 1916

E. DOWSON, *An Enquiry into Land Tenure (Iraq)*, Baghdad, 1932

V. H. W. DOWSON, *Date Cultivation in Iraq*, 1921

F. H. GAMBLE, *Iraq, Economic and Commercial Conditions*, 1949

H.M.S.O., *Overseas Economic Survey: Iraq*, 1953

INTERNATIONAL BANK MISSION, *The Economy of Iraq*, Baltimore, 1952

S. LONGRIGG and F. STOAKES, *Iraq*, 1959

A. SOUSA, *Iraq Irrigation Handbook*, Baghdad, 1944

W. WILLCOCKS, *The Irrigation of Mesopotamia*, 1917

CHAPTER XVI

Admiralty Handbook of Syria, 1915

ANGLO-AMERICAN COMMITTEE OF INQUIRY, *Report to the United States Government and His Majesty's Government*, Lausanne, 1946

R. FEDDEN, *Syria: An Historical Appreciation*, 1946

G. DE GAURY, *The New State of Israel*, New York, 1952

HACKER, M. J., *Amman*, Geog. Res. Papers No. 3, Durham University, England, 1960

H. HALPERIN, *Changing Patterns in Israeli Agriculture*, 1957

P. K. HITTI, *The Lebanon in History*, 1957

A. H. HOURANI, *Syria and Lebanon*, 1954

INTERNATIONAL BANK MISSION, *The Economic Development of Jordan*, Baltimore, 1957

The Economic Development of Syria, Baltimore, 1955

H. G. IONIDES and G. S. BLAKE, *Report on the Water Resources of Transjordan*, 1940

M. G. IONIDES, 'The Perspective of Water Development in Palestine and Transjordan', *Journ. R. Central Asian Soc.*, Vol. XXXIII, 1946

A. E. KAHN, 'Palestine', *Amer. Econ. Rev.*, Vol. 34, 1944

D. H. KALLNER and E. ROSENAU, 'The Geographical Regions of Palestine', *Geog. Review*, Vol. 29, 1939

W. C. LOWDERMILK, *Palestine, Land of Promise*, 1944

R. R. NATHAN, O. GASS and D. CREAMER, *Palestine: Problem and Promise*, Washington, 1946

A Survey of Palestine (for the information of the Anglo-American Committee of Inquiry), Jerusalem, 1946

B. U. TOUKAN, *A Short History of Transjordan*, 1945

E. C. WILLATTS, 'Some Geographical Factors in the Palestine Problem', *Geog. Journ.*, Vol. CVIII, 1947

CHAPTER XVII

Cyprus (Oxford Survey of the British Empire), 1914

GOVERNMENT OF CYPRUS, *A Ten-Year Programme of Development for Cyprus*, Nicosia, 1947

H. C. LUKE and D. J. JARDINE, *Handbook of Cyprus*, 1930
R. STORRS and B. J. O'BRIEN, *Handbook of Cyprus*, 1935

CHAPTER XVIII

Admiralty Handbook of Arabia, 1920
A. CATON-THOMPSON, 'Climate, Irrigation, and Early Man in the Hadhramaut', *Geog. Journ.*, Vol. XCIII, 1939
C. M. DOUGHTY, *Arabia Deserta*, 1888
G. DE GAURY, *Arabia Phoenix*, 1946
R. HAY, *The Persian Gulf States*, Washington, 1959
W. H. INGRAMS, *Report on the Social, Economic and Political Condition of the Hadhramaut*, 1938
H. ST J. PHILBY, 'The Land of Sheba', *Geog. Journ.*, Vol. XCII, 1938
         The Empty Quarter, 1933
         Arabian Jubilee, 1951
Report on Aden for 1949–50 (Colonial Office), 1951
W. THESIGER, 'A New Journey in Southern Arabia', *Geog. Journ.*, Vol. XVIII, 1947
         Arabian Sands, 1959
K. S. TWITCHELL, *Saudi Arabia*, Princeton, 1947

CHAPTER XIX

H. AWAD, *La Montagne du Sinai Central*, Cairo, 1951
J. BALL, *Contributions to the Geography of Egypt*, Cairo, 1939
A. M. FROOD, 'Some Post-War Economic Developments in Egypt', *The Advancement of Science*, Vol. VI, No. 21, 1949
H. E. HURST, *The Nile*, 1952
H. E. HURST and P. PHILLIPS, *The Nile Basin*, Cairo, 1931
C. ISSAWI, *Egypt at Mid-Century*, 1954
J. K. S. LACOUTURE, *Egypt in Transition*, New York, 1958
F. W. OLIVER, 'Dust Storms in Egypt', *Geog. Journ.*, Vol. CVIII, 1947

CHAPTER XX

E. AHLMANN, *La Libia Settrentrionale*, Rome, 1928
N. BARBOUR, *Survey of N.W. Africa*, London, 1959
J. I. CLARKE and S. G. WILLIMOTT (ed.), *Field Studies in Libya*, Geog. Res. Papers No. 4, Durham Univ., England
E. E. EVANS-PRITCHARD, *The Sanussi of Cyrenaica*, 1945

w. b. fisher, 'Problems of Modern Libya', *Geog. Journ.*, Vol. CXIX, 1953

b. higgins, *The Economic and Social Development of Libya*, New York, 1953

r. w. hill, *A Bibliography of Libya*, Geog. Res. Papers No. 1, Durham Univ., England

international bank mission, *The Economic Development of Libya*, Baltimore, 1960

w. mechelein, *Forschungen in der Zentralen Saharen*, 1960

h. h. thomas, *Economic and Commercial Conditions in Libya*, 1955

h. s. villard, *Libya*, Ithaca, 1956

Index

Abadan, 237, 313
Abana (Barada) river, 402, 424
Abbasids, 146
Abqaiq oilfields, 241, 244
absentee landlords, 196
Acre, 147
Adana, 337, 358
Aden, 177–9, 466–9
Adonis, 106, 109, 120
Aegean Sea, 318, 321, 538–9
Afyonkarahissar, 338
Agha Jari oilfield, 236, 244
agriculture (general), 191–208
Ahmadi oilfield, 240, 244
Ahwaz, 310–11, 314
Ain Dar oilfield, 241, 244
Ain Zahleh oilfield, 239, 244
air masses, 41–9
Akaba (Aqaba), Gulf of, 407, 475
Akhdar, Jebel (Cyrenaica), 24, 515, 518–20
Akhdar, Jebel (Oman), 467, 470
Akkar, plain of, 399
Ala Dagh, 323
Alawi (Alawites), 90, 96, 119
Aleppo, 431–3, 438–40
Alexandretta, see Iskanderun
Alexandria, 508–11
Ali (nephew of Muhammad), 117
'Alpine' race, 91
Amanus Range, 323
Amman, 409
Anatolia, central, 324–25
    eastern, 324–7
    northern, 324
    southern, 321–4
    western, 324
Angaraland, 20
Anglo-Egyptian Oilfields Ltd, 251, 256
Anglo-Iranian Oil Co., 249–51
    see also 'British Petroleum Oil Co.'
Angora, see Ankara
Angora goats, 342
Ankara, 356–8
Ansarieh, Jebel, 391–400
Antakya (Antioch), 131, 202

Antalya, 322
Anti-Lebanon Mts, 19, 402–3
antimony, 301, 346
Anti-Taurus Mts, 323–4
apples, 337, 421–2
apricots, 295, 337, 421, 463, 470
ARABIA, Ch. XVIII, 456–80
    eastern coastlands, 471–5
    interior, 475–80
    modern history, 177–9
    oilfields, 241–3
    physical divisions, 456–8
    southern coastlands, 466–9
    western highlands, 458–66
Arabian American Oil Co., 252
Arabic language, 102, 104–5
Arab League, 187–90
Arabs, 87, 96–8
Aramaic languages, 102–5
Ararat, Mount, 326
Aras (Araxes) river, 278, 325
aretic drainage, 30–1
Armenia, 165–6, 182–4, 325–7
Armenian language, 102–5
'Armenoid' race, 91–2
arsenic, 346
asbestos, 346, 452
Ashkenazim Jews, 110, 550
ASIA MINOR, Ch. XIV, 315–60
    agriculture, 332–40
    climate, 327–32
    communications, 351–3
    industry, 348–51
    irrigation, 340–1
    minerals, 343–8
    modern history, 161–7
    pastoralism, 342–3
    physical geography, 315–27
    towns, 353–60
Asir, 461–2
asphalt, 247, 423, 430
Assassins, 118–19
Assiut barrage, 493
Assyria, 138, 372
Assyrians, 184–5
Aswan barrage, 492–4

Atrek river, 285
attar of roses, 340
Awliya, Jebel, barrage, 492
Azerbaijan, 311

Baalbek, 83
Babylon, 397
Badawin Arabs, 122–9
Badiet esh Sham, 475–7
Baghdad, 392–3
Bahrein Island, 242, 244, 472–3
Bakhtiari tribe, 99
bananas, 337, 421, 461, 467, 528
Bandar Shah, 316
Bandar Shahpur, 314
barley, 198, 200, 294, 333–4, 376, 417,
     447–8, 460, 463, 467, 470, 499,
     525
Basra, 394–5
Beirut, 440–1
Bekaa, 398, 401–2
Benghazi, 522–3
Bethlehem, 405, 437
bilharzia, 210–11
birth-rates, 265
Black Sea, 225–6, 230, 536–7, 541
boracite, 346
Bosphorus (Bosporus), 318–19, 541
buffalo, water-, 342, 386, 501
Bukeia, 397, 399
Burgan oilfield, 241, 244, 252
Bursa, 347, 358–60
Büyük Menderes (Meander) river, 318,
     320–1, 341, 538
Byblos (Jbeil), 136
Byzantine Empire, 144

Cairo, 508–9
Caliphate, 146
Caltex Oil Co., 252
camels, 342, 386–7
'Capitulations', 155–7
caravan-routes, 63–4, 143
carobs, 82, 448, 463
carpets, 219, 303–4
Caspian Sea, 227, 284
cattle, 8, 214, 342, 386–7, 428–9, 501
caviar, 227
cedars of Lebanon, 83
cement, 221, 224
cephalic index, 90
cereals, 198–201
Chaldeans, 112

chemical industries, 221, 224
chemicals, 430–2, 503–5
cherries, 337
Christianity, 110–13
chromium, 301, 346–8, 452
Circassians, 90, 101
citrus fruit, 295, 337, 419–21, 463, 527
CLIMATE, Ch. III, 35–65
     variations in, 60–5
coal measures, 26, 301, 344–5
coffee, 460, 461, 463–4
Constantinople, see Istanbul
copper, 301, 346, 432, 451–2
Copts, 111–13
Coruh river, 317
cost of living, 223
'cottage industries', see crafts
cotton, 205, 296, 302, 337–8, 349, 380,
     422, 449–50, 467, 496–8
crafts, 219–20
Crusades, 147–9
cultivated area, 192
CYPRUS, Ch. XVII, 444–55
     agriculture, 447–50
     climate, 445–7
     industries and minerals, 451–5
     irrigation, 450–1
     pastoralism, 450
     physical, 444–5
Cyrenaica, 518–23, 524, 527, 528, 530,
     531, 532, 533, 534, 535

Daghghara barrage, 383–4
dairying, 214–15, 428–9
Damascus city, 430
     oasis, 417, 419, 423, 424
Dammam oilfield, 245
D'Arcy, W. K., 249
Dardanelles, 318
dates, 204, 295–6, 378–9, 460, 463, 467,
     470, 477, 500
Dead Sea, 26, 407–8, 426–7
death-rates, 265–6
deforestation, 63, 64, 78
demography, 263–73
Derna, 522, 524
dew, 54, 412
disease, human, 208–12
Diyala river, 363, 384
drias, 520
Druse, Jebel, 403
Druses, 90, 96, 118
Dukhan, Jebel (oilfield), 243, 245

Earthquakes, 317–18, 541
EGYPT, Ch. XIX, 481–511
　agriculture, 496–500
　ancient, 135–6
　climate, 490–1
　communications and towns, 506–11
　Eastern Highlands, 483–4
　irrigation, 491–6
　minerals and industry, 502–16
　modern history, 158–61
　Nile valley, 486–90
　oilfields, 243–5
　pastoralism, 501–2
　physical units, 481
　Sinai, 481–3
　Western Desert, 484–6
Elburz Mts, 283–4
emery, 348
emigration, 267, 272
Eregli (Heraclea), 344–5, 537
erosion, soil, 63, 64, 73, 268
Esdraelon, plain of, 404
Eskesehir, 342
Etesian winds, 329
Euphrates river, 31, 361–9, 548–9
Ezerum, 332, 352

Famagusta, 448, 453, 454
faulting, 17
Fayyum, 485, 486
Feisul I, King, 167, 170–1
'Fertile Crescent', 57, 89, 422
fertilisers, 495
Fezzan, 517
figs, 203, 336, 463, 470, 479
film industry, 505
fire worship, 109
fishing, 225–9
flax, 500
foggaras, 32–3, 470
Föhn winds, 328, 332, 543
forests, 82–4, 449
'Former rains', 77
France, interest in Middle East, 155,
　157–9, 162–8, 171–2, 185–7
frankincense, 467

Gach Saran oilfield, 237, 244
Galatia, 356
Galilee (district), 404–6
Galilee, Sea of, see Tiberias
gall-nuts, 298
garrigue, 80

Gediz river, 318
geology, 536–42
Georgia, 171–2
Germany, interest in Middle East, 155,
　175
Ghab, El, 399
Ghor, El, 407–8
Ghuta, El, 422
Gilan, 298
goats, 342, 386, 428
gold, 343, 502–3
Gondwanaland, 13 et seq.
grapefruit, 421
grapes, 295, 336
Greek language, 105
Greek Orthodox Church, 111, 113–15
Greeks, 166
Gulbenkian, C. S., 251
gum tragacanth, 340, 356, 381
Gurzan oilfield, 243–5
gypsum, 452

Habbaniya, Lake, 383
Hadhramaut, Wadi, 466–8
Haditha, 238–9
Haft Kel oilfield, 237, 244
Haifa, 442–3
Hama, 399, 424
Hamadan, 303
Hammar, Lake, 369
Hamrin, Jebel, 372
Hasa, 153, 473–4
hashish, 206
Hatay, 410
Hauran, 403–4
Haydarpasa, 355
hazel-nuts, 203, 337, 356
Health, public, 208–12, 266
Hebrew language, 102, 105, 550–1
Hedjaz, 458–60
Heliopolis (Egypt), 509
　(Lebanon) = Baalbek
Helmand river, 287
Hermon, Mt, 403
Hindiya barrage, 383
history before A.D. 1800, Ch. VII, 135–
　154
　after A.D. 1800, Ch. VIII, 155–90
Hittites, 137, 356
Homs (Lebanon), 417, 424
　(Libya), 517, 533
hook-worm (ankylostomiasis), 212
Hormuz (Ormuz), 152, 174

horse, 215
Huleh, Lake, 407
humidity, relative, 53–4, 412
humus, 68–9
hydro-electric power, 383, 408, 492
hydrography, 26–34
Hyksos, 137

Ibn Saud, King, 120, 178
Idlib, 419
igneous rocks, 25
Imams, 118
Indo-Aryans (Indo-Europeans), 92, 99
industry (general), 217–24
infantile mortality, 266
insecticides, 210, 266
Iran, see Persia
'Iranian' race, 92
IRAQ, Ch. XV, 361–95
  modern history, 170–1
Iraq Petroleum Co., 251–2, 256
iron, 301, 345–6, 451, 503
irrigation, 74–5, 210, 298–9, 340–1, 379, 381–5, 424–8, 450–1, 491–6
Isfahan, 294, 297, 302
Iskanderun, 113, 436
Islam, 115–20
Ismail, Khedive, 159
ISRAEL, Ch. XVI, 396–443
  demography, 265
  modern, 170
  see also Levant
Istanbul, 353–6
Italy, interest in Middle East, 163–5, 179–80, 530–1
Izmir, 356

Jacobites, 112–13
Jaffa, 436, 437, 443
Janissaries, 150–1
Jaz Murian basin, 282–3
'Jebel' of Tripolitania, 516–17
Jefara (Libya), 515, 522, 530
Jerusalem, 437, 443
Jews, 98, 109–10, 168–70, 272, 429–30, 434, 443, 550–1
Jezireh, 370–1
Jidda, 54, 461
Jordan river, 407–8
JORDAN STATE, Ch. XVI, 396–443
  origin, 168–70
Judaea, 404–5

juniper, 82
jute, 198

Kandilli, 344
Kantara, El, 508
Karabuk, 345
Karkeh river, 299, 365–7
Kars, 331
Karun river, 314, 365–7, 548
kavir, 288, 302
kelleks, 388–9, 394
Kemal Pasha, Mustapha, 166
Kermanshah, 239, 294, 297
Khabour river, 29, 363, 370
Khamsin winds, 45–6, 332, 410, 491
Khorassan, 294, 297, 299, 300
Khorramshahr, 313–14
Khuzistan, 294, 296, 299
  oilfields, 233–7, 244
Kirkuk oilfields, 237–9, 244
Kirman, 302
Kishon river, 404
Kizil Irmak river, 31, 341
Konya, 357
Kopet Dagh, 285
Ksara, 414, 421
Kufra, 520
Kurd Dagh, 323
Kurdistan, 182, 362, 372
Kurds, 90, 100, 124, 166, 180–2
Kutahya, 345
Kuwait, 241, 244, 252, 257–60, 473–5

Lali oilfield, 244
land forms, 17, 22–4
land tenancy, 191–8
languages, 101–5
Larnaca, 451, 453, 454
Latakia, 439, 441
Latin (R.C.) Church, 111–13
'Latter rains', 77
lava, 11, 17–19, 25
Lawrence, T. E., 163, 178
lead, 299, 346
leather-working, 504
LEBANON, see Ch. XVI, 396–443
  emigration from, 267
  modern history, 162, 167–8
  population problem, 270–1
  race, 96
Lebanon Mts, 398, 400–2
Leja, El, 403–4
lemons, 421

LEVANT, Ch. XVI, 396–443
  agriculture, 416–30
  climate, 410–15
  industry and commerce, 432–8
  minerals, 430–2
  modern history, 167–70
  pastoralism, 428–9
  railways, 437–8
  sub-regions, 399, 409
  towns, 438–43
LIBYA, Ch. XX, 512–35
  agriculture, 525–8
  climate, 520–2
  human geography, 531–5
  hydrology, 522–3
  Italian colonisation, 530–1
  modern history, 179–80
  pastoralism, 528–30
  physiography, 512–20
  soils, 523
lignite, 28, 345, 387, 430
limes, Roman, 142
limestone, 24
linen, 453
liquorice, 84, 337, 381
Litani river, 22, 409
locusts, 206–7
loess, 69
lucerne, 463, 479
Lusignans, 147
Lut, 288

Magwa oilfield, 241, 244
Mahdi, 118
maize, 333, 378, 417, 496, 498, 525–6
Makran, 282–3
malaria, 209–11, 321, 322, 324, 399, 441, 447
Malatya, 341, 362
Mandaeans, 121
Mandates, 168–70
manganese, 346, 432, 502
maple trees, 83
marble, 348, 452
market gardening, 204
marls, 24
Marmara, Sea of, 318–19
Marmarica, 520, 534
Maronites, 90, 112–13, 162
masha (musha'a), 193
mashuf, 389
Masjid-i-Suleiman oilfield, 236–7, 244
Matarma oilfield, 245

matrukhi, 192–3
Mazanderan province, 294, 297
Mecca, 460–1
Medina, 460
Mediterranean Sea, 14
  fishing, 225–6
'Mediterranean' climate, 35, 39–40
'Mediterranean' race, 91
'Mediterranean' vegetation, 80–1
meerschaum, 348
meltemi, see Etesian winds
mercury, 348
merino sheep, 342
Mersin, 346
Mesaoria, 445–7
Mesopotamia, ancient, 135–9
  origin of plain of, 365–7
  see also Ch. XV, 361–95
metal work, 218, 434
Metwali, 90, 98
migration, 88–9, 267
millet, 200, 295, 334, 378, 460, 461, 463, 467, 470, 479, 499, 525, 527
Millets, 113–15
minerals, 25–6
mining, 216–17
minorities, 180–6
miri, 192
Misurata, 533
mohair, 219, 342
Mohammed, see Muhammad
Mohammerah, see Khorramshahr
molybdenum, 348
'Mongoloid' race, 93
monsoons, 43–4
mosquitoes, 209–10
Mosul, 393–4
mother-of-pearl, 473
Muhammad, 115–17
Mukalla, 467
mulberry, 205–6, 380, 422
mules, 450
mulk, 192
Murzuq, 517, 534
Muscat, 471
myrrh, 467

Naft-i-Shah oilfield, 239, 244
Naft Khaneh oilfield, 239, 244
nationalism, Arab, 153–4, 162–3
  Egyptian, 159–61
  Iranian, 171–7
  Israeli, 169–70

nationalism, Turkish, 154, 161–7
nazzaz, 71
Nefud, Great, 475–7
Negeb (Negev), 405–6
'Negrito' race, 94, 100
Nejd, 475, 478–9
Nestorians, 112–13
Nicosia, 454
Nile delta, 487
  regime, 488–90
  river, formation, 486–90
Nineveh, 394
nomadism, 129–30
'Nordic' race, 92–3
nut-trees, 203, 337, 449

Oak trees, 82–3
oak, valonia, 82, 339, 381
oats, 200, 334, 417
ochre, 452, 503
'offshore rights' (oil), 253–4
OIL DEPOSITS, Ch. XI, 230–62
  deposits, 233–47
  future possibilities, 247–8
  origin, 230–3
  ownership of concessions, 248–56
  pipelines, 256–7
olives, 80, 201–2, 335, 419
Oman, 469–71
onions, 500, 502
opium, 206, 297, 339–40
Oqair, 474
oranges, 295, 337, 419–21, 449, 527
Orontes river, 402, 409
Ottoman Empire, 149–54
Ottoman (Osmanli) Turks, 95, 149–52
ovas, 324

Paganism, 120–1
Palestine, see Ch. XVI
  modern history, 167–70
  see also Israel
Parsees, 109
Parthia, 141
pastoralism, general, 213–15
peaches, 421
pearl-fishing, 474
pellagra, 212
PEOPLES, Ch. V, 87–122
PERSIA, Ch. XIII, 277–314
  agriculture, 293–8
  climate, 289–9
  communications and towns, 307–14

industry, 302–4
irrigation, 298–9
minerals, 300–2
modern history, 171–7
pastoralism, 299–300
peoples, 304–7
physiography, 278–89
population, 265, 305
Persian Gulf, recession of, 365–7, 548–9
pests, insect, 206–8
Philistia, 406
Phoenicians, 138
phosphates, 26, 432, 484, 502
phrygana, 80–1
phylloxera, 202, 208
Pilgrim Railway, 437, 461
pilgrims, 313, 460
pine trees, 83
Pirate Coast, 472
plums, 295, 337, 421
poplar trees, 80
population problems, 267–73
Port Said, 508, 511
potatoes, 335, 421, 448, 527
precipitation, 55–9
'Proto-Nordic' race, 92–3
Pusht-i-Kuh, 233–5

Qaiyara, 239
qanats, see foggaras
Qarmatians, 118
Qarun Lake, 227–8
Qashqai tribe, 99
qat plant, 464–5
Qishm, 174
Qornet es Sauda, 400
quarrying, 503
Qureish tribe, 115

Race, 90–5
raids, tribal, 127–8
railways –
  Egypt, 506–7
  Iraq, 389–90
  Levant, 437–8
  Persia, 307–9
  Turkey, 351–3
rainfall, 55–9
raisins, 336, 449
Ramandagh oilfield, 243, 245
Red Sea, origin of, 14–23
  fishing, 226
religions, 105–22

Resht, 294
Riadh, 478–9
rice, 200, 294–5, 333–4, 378, 417, 499
rift valleys, 14–18
Riza Shah Pahlevi, 175–7, 297, 306
rock salt, 281–2
Roman Catholics, 111–13
Rub al Khali, 475–8
Russia, interest in Middle East, 171–7, 183–4
rye, 333–4

Saadabad, Treaty of, 187
Sa'ana, 465
Safaniya oilfield, 242, 245
saffron, 298
Sahand, Mt, 278
Sahara desert, 486, 520
Saida (Sidon), 242, 259, 419
Sakariya river, 341
salinity, 26, 69–72, 74–5, 365, 426, 490
Samaria, 404–5
Samaritans, 90
Samsun, 338, 353
sandstorms, 46, 491
Sannin, Mt, 400
Sanussi (Senussi), 120, 179–80
sardines, 226, 468
Sassanids, 144
Saudi Arabia, see Arabia
sea breezes, 53
Sebkha, 517
Seistan, 287, 299
Seleucids, 140
Sephalah (Shephalah), 406
Sephardim Jews, 110, 550
sesame, 339
Sèvres, Treaty of, 165–6
Seyhan plain, 323–4, 337
shamal, 372–3
sharki, 374
Sharon, plain of, 407–8
Shatt el Arab, 173, 368, 379
Shatt el Dujaila, 384
Shatt el Gharraf, 384
Shedgum oilfield, 241
sheep, 214, 300, 342, 385–6, 428, 450, 501, 528–30
Shell Oil Co., 251–3
Shi'a Moslems, 117–19
shlouq, 45–6
silk, 206, 297, 387, 422, 433

silver, 346
simoom, 46
Sinai, 481–3
Sinjar, Jebel, 370–2
sirdab, 272
sirocco, see Khamsin
Sirtica, 517
Smyrna, see Izmir
snowfall, 47–8
Socony Oil Co., 252
Soils, Ch. IV, 66–75
sorghum, 417, 461
sponges, 226, 454
stability, atmospheric, 543–7
Standard Oil Co.,
    California, 249–52
    New Jersey, 250–3
    Texas 253
steppes, 81–2
Structure, Ch. II, 12–22
sturgeon, 227
Sudan, 159–61
Sudd, Lake, 488, 549
Sudr oilfield, 245
Suez Canal, 158–9
sugar, beet, 297, 337
    cane, 298, 500
sultanas, 336
sunna insect, 207–8
Sunni Moslems, 117, 119, 121
Sykes-Picot Agreement, 165
Syria, see Ch. XVI
    modern history, 167–8

Tabriz, 311
tamarisk, 82, 408, 463, 524
Tanura, Ras, 243, 256
'Tapline' (pipeline), 257
Taurus Mts, 322–4
taxation, 194
tea, 298, 340
Teheran, 309–11
Tel Aviv, 436–8
Terbol, Jebel, 248
Tethys, Sea of, 13, 231, 537
textiles, 218–20, 302–4, 349–50, 387, 432–3, 453, 504
Tharthar, Wadi, 370
Tiberias, Lake, 407–8
Tigris-Euphrates Lowlands, Ch. XV, 361–95
    agriculture, 375–8
    climate, 372–5

TIGRIS–EUPHRATES (*contd.*)
communications and **population**, 388–93
irrigation, 381–5
minerals and manufactures, 387–8
physical divisions, 367–72
Tigris river, regime, 363–4
tobacco, 205, 298, 338–9, 380, 422, 448, 467, 527
Tobruk, 533
tourism, 356, 437, 453, 534
Trabzon (Trebizond), 350
trachoma, 212
trade routes, ancient, 129–32, 143
transit trade, 435–6
tribes, 123–6
Tripoli (Lebanon), 433–4, 436, 442
Tripoli (Libya), 532, 534
Troodos Mts, 445
Trucial Coast, 472
tunny, 226
Turkey, *see* Asia Minor
'Turki' race, 93–4
turquoise, 301
Tuwaiq, Jebel, 478
Tuz, Lake, 322, 324, 541
typhus, 212

Umm Said, 242
Uniate Churches, 112–13, 185
United Kingdom, interest in Middle East, 158–80, 184–7
United States, interest in Middle East, 169, 183–7
Urmia, Lake, 31, 278, 280, 539, 541
Uthmaniya oilfield, 242, 245

Van Lake, 31, 539, 541
vegetables, 201, 416, 417, 500, 525
vegetation, Ch. IV, 75–84
Veramin Plain, 309
vines, 80, 202–3, 295, 335–6, 380, 421, 449, 461, 500, 527
volcanic cones, 278, 324–6

Wah'habis, 120, 178, 475
walnuts, 80, 337, 463, 479
waqf, 193–4
wheat, 80, 198–201, 294, 332–4, 356, 376–8, 416, 448, 460, 461, 463, 467, 470, 472, 479, 492, 525, 527
winds, 36–41
wine, 202, 295, 336, 421, 449
wool, 214, 219, 300, 342, 358, 386

Yarmuk river, 409, 425
yellow fever, 210
Yemen, 179, 462–6
Yezidi, 90, 100, 120–1
Yezil Irmak river, 341

Zab, Great, river, 363, 383
Zab, Lesser, river, 363, 383
Zagros Mts, 20, 21, 24, 25, 26, 83, 278–83, 538, 542
Zaidis, 119, 465
Zelten oilfield, 245, 246, 247
Zerka river, 409
zinc, 346
Zionism, 168–70, 429–30
Zoroaster, 109
Zubair oilfield, 239, 244